COMMENTARIES

ON

THE EPISTLE OF PAUL THE APOSTLE

TO

THE ROMANS

COMMENTARIES

ON THE

EPISTLE OF PAUL THE APOSTLE

TO

THE ROMANS

BY JOHN CALVIN

TRANSLATED AND EDITED

BY THE REV. JOHN OWEN,
VICAR OF THRUSSINGTON, LEICESTERSHIRE

BAKER BOOK HOUSE
Grand Rapids, Michigan

Wipf and Stock Publishers
199 W 8th Ave, Suite 3
Eugene, OR 97401

Commentaries on the Epistle of Paul the Apostle to the Romans
By Calvin, John and Owen, John
Softcover ISBN-13: 979-8-3852-1645-1
Hardcover ISBN-13: 979-8-3852-1646-8
eBook ISBN-13: 979-8-3852-1647-5
Publication date 2/13/2024
Previously published by Baker Book House, 2005

This edition is a scanned facsimile of the original edition published in 2005.

TRANSLATOR'S PREFACE.

ON no portion of THE NEW TESTAMENT have so many COMMENTARIES been written as on THE EPISTLE TO THE ROMANS. We have indeed no separate Comment extant by any of the Fathers on this Epistle; though it has been explained, together with other parts of Scripture, by *Origen* in the third century; by *Jerome, Chrysostom*, and in part by *Augustine*, in the fourth; by *Theodoret* in the fifth; by *Œcumenius* in the tenth; and by *Theophylact* in the eleventh century. But since the Reformation, many separate Expositions have been published, beside a learned Introduction by *Luther*, and Notes or *Scholia* by *Zuingle* and *Melancthon*.

The first complete COMMENTARY, as it appears, was written by *Bullinger;* the second by *Bucer*, a Professor of Theology at Cambridge for a short time in the reign of Edward the Sixth; and the next in order of time was this Work by CALVIN, composed at Strasburg in the year 1539. The fourth was by Peter *Martyr;* and this was translated into English in the year 1568. Another was afterwards published by Rodolph *Gualter*, Minister at Zurich.

Early in the next century the learned *Pareus*[1] delivered lectures on this Epistle, as Professor of Theology in the University of Heidelberg—a work of great learning and of great merits, though written in a style too scholastic to suit the taste of the present day. His special object was to rebut the arguments and expose the sophistries of Popish writers,

---

[1] His original name was Wangler, but he Grecised it, as *Erasmus* had done, and as others did in that age.

particularly those of *Bellarmine*, the acutest, the subtlest, and the most learned of all the Jesuits of his own age, and perhaps of any in after ages. There is hardly a subject in any measure connected with the contents of this Epistle which *Pareus* does not discuss : at the end of every chapter a number of questions are stated and answered, especially such as refer to the disputes between Papists and Protestants. He also controverts the perversions of Socinianism.

The next work that requires particular notice is that of *Turrettin*, a Professor of Theology in the University of Geneva. It was published about the commencement of the last century; the author died in the year 1737. The doctrine of *Calvin* had somewhat degenerated in his time, though his work on the whole takes the side of orthodoxy. It yet shows a leaning to those views, which commonly issue in sentiments subversive of the essentials of true Christianity.

The first Commentary published in this country, composed in English, was by Elnathan *Parr*, B.D., Rector of Palgrave in Suffolk. He was, as it appears, the personal friend of Sir Nathaniel *Bacon*, an elder brother of Lord *Bacon*. He dedicated his work to Sir Nathaniel, and speaks of him as having been a hearer of what he published when delivered from the pulpit.[1] His style is that of his age, and appears quaint now; but his thoughts are often very striking and truly excellent, and his sentiments are wholly in accordance with those of the Reformers.

Since that time until this century, no work of any note has appeared separately on this Epistle. But within the last thirty years several Commentaries have been published. Besides those of *Flatt* and *Tholuck* in Germany, three at least have appeared in this country, and three in America. The authors in America are Moses *Stuart*, M.A., Professor of Sacred Literature at Andover, in Massachusetts, the Rev. Albert *Barnes*, and Charles *Hodge*, Professor of Biblical Literature at Princeton. Those in this country are the Rev. J. *Fry*, Rector of Desford, Leicestershire, Robert *Haldane*,

---

[1] This work must have been published before the year 1615, for his patron died in that year. The copy seen by the writer is the *third* edition, and was published in 1633.

Esq., and Dr. *Chalmers*. The doctrine held by *Calvin* is essentially maintained in all these works, and in most of them in its fullest extent. Of our American brethren, the most learned and the most versed in criticisms is Professor *Stuart;* the fullest and the minutest expositor is the Rev. A. *Barnes;* and the acutest and the most concise commentator is Professor *Hodge*. The two first seem, in some instances, like *Turrettin*, to deviate somewhat from what may be considered strict orthodoxy, at least in their mode of explaining some subjects: the last is liable to no charge of this kind.

Respecting our own countrymen, there is a more perfect unanimity, though they belonged to different Churches. The Lectures of the Rev. J. *Fry* are those of a strict Predestinarian, and yet replete with remarks, both experimental and practical. The layman, R. *Haldane*, Esq., has displayed very high qualifications as an expositor; he is strictly and even stiffly orthodox, and can brook no deviation from what he regards as the truth. Of Dr. *Chalmers'* Lectures, comprised in four volumes, 12mo, it is difficult to pronounce an opinion. They are the productions of a philosopher, and one of the highest grade, who, at the same time, possessed the heart and the experience of an humble Christian. He expatiates over the whole field of truth with the eye of an eagle, and with the docility of a child, without ever overleaping the boundaries of revelation. He was evidently a man by himself, taller by his shoulders than most men, either in this or in any other age, having a mind as sound as it was vigorous, an imagination as sober as it was creative, and a capacity to illustrate and to amplify quite unequalled.

All these works have their peculiar excellencies, adapted to different tastes and capacities, and no doubt they have their defects. The same must be said of *Calvin's* work. But as a concise and lucid Commentator he certainly excels. He is not so much an expounder of words, as of principles. He carries on an unbroken chain of reasoning throughout, in a brief and clear manner. Having well considered the main drift of a passage, he sets before us what it contains, by a brief statement or by a clear process of reasoning; and often by a single sentence he throws light on a whole passage: and though his mind possessed more vigour of intellect and sound good sense, than what is called imagination; yet there are some fine thoughts occasionally occurring, beautifully expressed, to which that faculty must have given birth. There is also a noble grandeur and dignity in his sentiments, rarely to be found in other writers.

Professor *Stuart* has justly characterized this Work by saying, that it contains " fundamental investigation of the logic and course of thought contained in the Epistle;" and that it embraces " very little verbal criticism. Many a difficulty is solved without any appearance of effort, or any show of learning. *Calvin,*" he adds, " is by far the most distinguished of all the Commentators of his times."

It was mainly to supply the defect named above, the want of verbal criticism, that NOTES have been added in the present Edition. They are also designed to furnish the reader with such expositions as have been suggested by posterior critics and commentators. And as we are generally desirous of knowing the names of authors, they have been for the most part given. Much light is thrown on a passage by conveying the full meaning of the original. This has been done partly by giving such different versions as seemed most entitled to approbation, and partly by referring to other passages where such words occur: so that a common reader, unacquainted with the original, may, to a certain extent, have the advantage of one well versed in the Greek language.

Variety of meanings given to words, and also to passages, has been deemed by some to lessen the certainty of truth, but without any solid reason; for this variety, as found in the works of all sound and judicious critics, seldom or *ever* affects any thing important, either in doctrine, experience, or practice, and tends often to expand the meaning and to render it clearer and more prominent. There has been indeed sometimes a pruriency in this respect, an unholy ambition for novelty, a desire for new discoveries, an indulgence of mere curiosity, which have been very injurious. Much of this sort of mania prevailed among some of the German divines in the last century, as *Wolfius* clearly shows in his works, in which he notices and disproves many vagaries assuming the name of critical expositions; and much of a similar kind of spirit seems to prevail still in that country. It is a mania for criticism, for its own sake, without any concern or solicitude for the truth: and ingenious criticism has often been resorted to by the oppugners of vital Christianity as means for supporting heterodoxical sentiments. But there is a palpable difference between men of this character, the mere gladiators of criticism, and those who embrace the truth, and whose object it is faithfully to explain it in consistency with the general tenor of what is revealed, and who have what is indispensably necessary for such a work, a spiritual experience, which often affords better assistance than any critical acumen that can ever be possessed. The man who has *seen* a thing has a much better idea of it than the man who has only heard it described.

Attempts have been made by various authors to show and prove, that the STYLE OF THE EPISTLES, especially those of PAUL, is consonant with that of classical writers. *Blackwall* laboured much to do this in this country, as well as many German divines, particularly in the last century. In common with some of the Fathers, they thought to recommend in this way the Apostolic Writings to the attention of literary men. But it was a labour not wisely undertaken, as it must have necessarily proved abortive: for though some phrases may be classical, yet the general style is what might have been naturally expected from the writers, brought up, as they had all been, in the Jewish religion, and accustomed, as they had been, to the writings of the Old Testament. Hence their style throughout is Hebraistic; and the meaning of many of the Greek words which they use is not to be sought from the Classics, but from the Greek Translation of the ancient Scriptures, and sometimes from the Hebrew itself, of which that is a translation.[1]

[1] " The writers of the New Testament, or rather (with reverence be it spoken!) the Holy Spirit, whose penmen they were, wisely chose, in ex-

Much evil and no good must result from a claim that cannot be supported: nor is it at all necessary to make such a claim. It has been long ago repudiated, and repudiated by Paul himself. Writers have often ascribed to Paul what he himself distinctly and entirely disclaimed, and never *attempted* to attain or to practise, and that on principle, " Lest the cross of Christ should be made of none effect." It was not by " excellency of speech" that he courted the attention of the classical and refined Grecians, that he recommended the gospel to them ; it was not by the tinsel of mere eloquence that he succeeded in his preaching, nor by the elegance and beauty of his diction ; but by something much higher, much greater, much more powerful and efficient. We ought to follow his example, and stand on his high ground, and not to descend to that which is no better than a quagmire. It is a happy thing, and no doubt so designed by God, that the shell should not be made of fine materials, lest men's minds should be attracted by it and neglect the kernel. God might, if he chose, have easily endued his Apostles with eloquence more than human, and enabled them to write with elegance more than Grecian ; but He did not do so, and Paul expressly gives us the reason, " that our faith should not stand in the wisdom of men, but in the power of God."

It is generally agreed, that the EPISTLE TO THE ROMANS was written at CORINTH, and about the end of the year 57, or at the beginning of the year 58, and that it is the *fifth* Epistle in order of time ; the two Epistles to the *Thessalonians*, the Epistle to the *Galatians*, and the first to the *Corinthians*, having been previously written. Then followed the second Epistle to the *Corinthians*, the Epistles to the

---

pressing evangelical notions, to employ such *Greek* terms as had been long before used for the same purposes by the *Greek* Translators of the New Testament : and thus the *Septuagint* version, however *imperfect* and *faulty* in many particulars, became in this respect, not to the first age of the Church only, but also to all succeeding generations, the connecting link between the languages of the Old and New Testament, and will be regarded in this view as long as sound judgment and real learning shall continue among men."—*Parkhurst*.

Ephesians, Philippians, Colossians, Philemon, and the *Hebrews,* the first to *Timothy,* the Epistle to *Titus,* and the second to *Timothy.* The common date assigned to Paul's conversion is A.D. 35. He wrote his first Epistle, that is, the first to the *Thessalonians,* in 52, seventeen years after his conversion. His second Epistle to *Timothy,* his last, was written from Rome in 65. So that he wrote his fourteen Epistles during these thirteen years. The whole extent of his ministry seems to have been about thirty years; for it is not supposed that he long outlived the date of his second Epistle to *Timothy.* Tradition says, that he was beheaded at Rome, June 29, A.D. 66.

Paul's first coming to ROME was in the spring of the year 61. He continued there as a prisoner for two years.[1] When he was released, most writers are of the opinion, that he returned early in 63 to Judea, in company with Timothy, and left Titus at Crete; that he visited the Churches in Asia Minor, then the Churches in Macedonia; that he wintered at Nicopolis, a city of Epirus, in 64; that afterwards he proceeded to Crete and also to Corinth; and that early in 65 he again visited Rome, was taken prisoner, and beheaded in the following year.[2] This account clearly shows that he did not accomplish his purpose of visiting Spain, as tradition has recorded.

The first introduction of the Gospel into ROME is involved in uncertainty. The probability is, that some of the "strangers of Rome," present at the day of Pentecost, were converted, and at their return promoted the spread of the Gospel. Paul mentions two, "Andronicus and Junia," as having professed the faith before him, and as having been noted among the Apostles. He makes mention, too, of another eminent Christian, "Rufus," whose father, as it is supposed, carried our Saviour's cross, Mark xv. 21. It is not improbable, that these were afterwards assisted by such as

---

[1] It was while a prisoner at this time at Rome that he wrote his Epistles to the *Ephesians, Philippians, Colossians, Philemon,* and the *Hebrews* also, as it is generally supposed.

[2] See *Horne's* Introduction, vol. iv. part ii. ch. iii. sect. 1.

had been converted under the ministry of Paul; for he speaks of some of those whom he salutes at Rome as being "beloved," and as having been his "fellow-workers."

What some of the Fathers have related was in the first instance a tradition, as there was nothing recorded on the subject before the latter part of the second century, except what has been ascribed to *Dionysius* of Corinth, preserved by *Eusebius*. *Irenæus* and *Tertullian* were the first retailers of the tradition, that Peter, in conjunction with Paul, was the founder of the Church at Rome. This tradition increased considerably by the time of *Jerome*, who, in the fourth century, says, that Peter had been bishop of Rome for twenty-five years! But this account is so clearly inconsistent with what we learn from the Acts of the Apostles respecting Peter, that some of the most reasonable of the Papists themselves have given it up as unworthy of credit.[1]

It appears next to a certainty that Peter was not at Rome when Paul wrote his Epistle in 57 or 58, for he sends no salutation to Peter:—And also that he had not been there previous to that time; for it is wholly unreasonable to suppose, that, had he been there, Paul would have made no reference to his labours. It further amounts almost to a certainty, that Peter was not at Rome when Paul was for two years a prisoner there, from 61 to 63; for he makes no mention of him in any way, not even in the four or five Epistles which he wrote during that time: And that Peter was not at Rome during Paul's last imprisonment in 65 and 66, is evident from the second Epistle to Timothy; for he makes no mention of Peter, and what he says of Christians there, that they "all forsook him," would have been highly discreditable to Peter, if he was there. So that we have the

---

[1] The inconsistencies of what the retailers of this tradition say, are quite palpable. *Irenæus* affirms, that "the Church at Rome was founded and constituted (*fundata et constituta*) by the two Apostles, Peter and Paul." *Epiphanius* says, that they were the first "*Bishops*" at Rome, as well as Apostles, while *Irenæus* declares, that they both "delivered the episcopal office into the hands of Linus;" and it is said in what are called the Apostolical Constitutions, that "Linus was ordained bishop by Paul, and Clement after the death of Linus by Peter."—See Dr. *Barrow* on the Pope's Supremacy, pp. 127-129.

strongest reasons to conclude, that Peter had no part in forming and establishing a Church in Rome during Paul's life, whatever share in the work he might have had afterwards.[1] But the first tradition, or the first account, given by *Irenæus* and *Tertullian*, refers only to a co-operation: and yet this co-operation is wholly inconsistent with what has been stated, the force of which no reasonable man can resist.

The learned *Pareus* proceeds in a different way to prove that Peter was never at Rome. He shows from different parts of the Acts of the Apostles and the Epistle to the Galatians, that Peter was in Judea at the time when tradition declares that he was at Rome. Peter was in Judea when Paul was converted, Acts ix.; and *three* years after this—that is, in the year 38, Gal. i. 18. He was in Judea in the year 45, when he was imprisoned by Herod, Acts xii.; and in 49, *fourteen* years after Paul's conversion, Acts xv.; Gal. ii. 1-9. Had he been to Rome during this time, some account of such a journey must surely have been given. After this time we find that he was at Antioch, Gal. ii. 11. If it be asked, where did he afterwards exercise his ministry? Where more likely than among the Jews, as he had hitherto most clearly done; for he was the Apostle of the Circumcision, and among those to whom he sent his Epistles. The dating of the first at "Babylon," has led some to conjecture that it was a figurative term for Rome; but why not for Jerusalem, or for Antioch? for Christians were at that time treated everywhere like captives or aliens, and especially in the land of Judea.

What then are we to say as to this tradition? The same, according to the just remark of *Pareus*, as what we must say of many other traditions of that age, that it is nothing

---

[1] But this cannot be admitted, as the same informant, Tradition, tells us, that Peter and Paul suffered martyrdom at the same time. The only thing which Peter appears to have had to do in forming and founding a Church at Rome, was to have been the instrument in the conversion, at the day of Pentecost, of those who in all probability were the first who introduced the Gospel into Rome: and it is probable that it was this circumstance which occasioned the tradition, that he had been the founder of that Church. Less occasion has often produced tales of this kind.

but a fable, which, like many others, would have passed away, had it not been allied to a growing superstition. With respect to what *Eusebius* says of the testimony of a presbyter, named *Caius*, that about the beginning of the third century he saw the graves of Peter and Paul at Rome, it may be easily accounted for: it was the age of pious fraud, when the relics of saints could be found almost everywhere; and, in the next century, the wood and the nails of the Cross were discovered! Those who can believe these things, may have a credulity large enough to swallow up the testimony of *Caius*.[1]

The most probable account, then, of the commencement of a Christian Church at Rome, is what has been already stated. The condition of that Church, when Paul wrote to it, we may in a great measure learn from the Epistle itself. It had a high character, viewed in a general way; but there were some defects and blemishes. Its faith had been widely reported: there were at the same time some contentions and divisions among its members, arising especially from the prejudices of the Jewish believers. To remove the causes of this dissension, was evidently one of the main objects of Paul in this Epistle.

THE ORDER AND ARRANGEMENT OF THE EPISTLE have been somewhat differently viewed by different authors. *Pareus* includes the whole in this brief summary—" The Jews and

[1] Let it not be supposed, that by discrediting *some* things, we discredit *every* thing said by the Fathers. They ought to be treated as all other historians. What we find on examination to be unfounded, ought to be so viewed: and what we have every reason to believe to be true, ought to be so received. Even such a man as Dr. *Lardner* seemed unwilling to reject this tale, from fear of lessening the credit of history; evidently mistaking the ground on which history has a title to credit. The many authorities adduced respecting Peter being at Rome may be reduced almost to two—*Irenæus* and *Tertullian*. They were the first to stamp as it were a kind of authority on this report, and also on others to which no credit is given even by those who would have the Fathers to have been almost infallible.

The learned Dr. *Copleston*, the present Bishop of Landaff, in his pamphlet on the Errors of Romanism, justly says, " It is even a matter of serious doubt whether St. Peter was ever at Rome. There is no good historical evidence of the fact; and there is much probability against it."
—P. 87.

Gentiles are equally guilty; they are equally justified freely by faith in Christ, without works; they are equally bound to lead a holy life, to be humble, and to love one another." *Stuart* says, that the whole of what the Epistle contains may be expressed in a single brief sentence—" Christ our justification and sanctification."

In giving a more specific view of the contents of this Epistle, the former author divides it into *two* parts—*doctrinal*, i.-xi.; and *hortative*, xii.-xvi.: but the latter divides it into *three* parts—*doctrinal*, i.-viii.; *answers* to objections, ix.-xi.; and *hortatory*, xii.-xvi. The analysis of Professor *Hodge*, who takes the same view with Professor *Stuart*, is the following:—

" The Epistle consists of three parts. The *first*, which includes the first eight chapters, is occupied in the discussion of The Doctrine of Justification and its consequences. The *second*, embracing chapters ix., x., xi., treats of The Calling of the Gentiles, The Rejection and Future Conversion of the Jews. The *third* consists of Practical Exhortations and Salutations to the Christians at Rome."

A more particular ANALYSIS may be thus given:—

I. ADDRESS—A desire to visit Rome—a brief View of The Gospel; i. 1-18.
II. JUSTIFICATION,—
  1. A proof of its necessity—the sin and guilt of both Gentiles and Jews, i., from ver. 18; ii., iii., to ver. 21.
  2. Its Nature and Character—Examples, Abraham and David, iii., from ver. 21, iv.
  3. Its Effects or Fruits—Peace and Fulness of Grace, v.; Death unto Sin and Eternal Life, vi.; Immunity from The Law and The Reigning Power of Sin, vii.; Holiness, The Spirit's help, Patience in Afflictions, Perseverance, viii.
III. GOD'S DEALINGS VINDICATED,—
  1. Election and Reprobation, ix.
  2. Unbelief and Faith, x.
  3. The Rejection of the Jews, The Adoption of the Gentiles, The Restoration of the Jews, xi.

IV. CHRISTIAN DUTIES,—
  1. Devotedness to God, Proper Use of Gifts, Love, Doing Good, xii.
  2. Obedience to Authority, Love to all, Purity, xiii.
  3. Forbearance towards Weak Brethren, xiv.
  4. Help to the Weak, Unanimity, Christ the Saviour of Jews and Gentiles, xv., to ver. 13.
V. CONCLUSION,—
  1. Paul's Labours and Purpose to Visit Rome, xv., from ver. 13.
  2. Salutations, Avoiding Disturbers, Promise of Victory, Praise to God, xvi.

We have set before us in this Epistle especially two things, which it behoves us all rightly to understand—the righteousness of man and the righteousness of God—merit and grace, or salvation by works and salvation by faith. The light in which they are exhibited here is clearer and brighter than what we find in any other portion of Scripture, with the exception, perhaps, of the Epistle to the Galatians. Hence the great value which has in every age been attached to this Epistle by all really enlightened Christians; and hence also the strenuous efforts which have often been made to darken and wrest its meaning by men, though acute and learned, yet destitute of spiritual light. But let not the simple Christian conclude from the contrariety that is often found in the expositions on these two points, that there is no certainty in what is taught respecting them. There are no contrary views given of them by spiritually-minded men. Though on other subjects discussed here, such men have had their differences, yet on these they have ever been found unanimous: that salvation is from first to last by grace, and not by works, has ever been the conviction of really enlightened men in every age, however their opinions may have varied in other respects.

It may seem very strange, when we consider the plain and decisive language, especially of this Epistle, and the clear and conclusive reasoning which it exhibits, that any attempt should ever be made by a reasonable being, acknowledging the authority of Scripture, to pervert what it plainly teaches, and to evade what it clearly proves. But a right view of what human nature is, when unrenewed, as exhibited in God's Word, and as proved by history and made evident by observation, enables us fully to account for what would otherwise remain an enigma. No truth is more fully confirmed by facts (and it ought ever to be remembered) than that " the natural man receiveth not the things of the Spirit of God," and that he " cannot know them, because they are spiritually discerned." This declaration clearly accounts for the fact, that men of great learning have often misunderstood many things in Scripture, and such things as are plain enough even to the unlettered when spiritually enlightened. The learned Scribes and Rabbins were blind leaders of the blind, when even babes understood the mysteries of the kingdom of God : and no better than the Scribes are many learned men, professing Christianity, in our day.

There is indeed a special reason why, on these points, unenlightened men should contrive means to evade the obvious meaning of Scripture ; for they are such things as come in constant contact with a principle, the strongest that belongs to human nature in its fallen state. Other doctrines may be held as speculations, and kept, as it were, at a distance but when we come to merit and grace, to work and faith, man's pride is touched ; and as long as he is under its prevailing influence, he will be certain, in some way or another, direct or evasive, to support merit in opposition to grace, or works in opposition to faith. When the authority of tradition supplanted the authority of Scripture, the doctrine of merit so prevailed, that the preposterous idea, that merits were a saleable and a transferable commodity, gained ground in the world. A notion of this kind is too gross and absurd to be entertained by any who acknowledge God's Word as the only umpire in religion ; and yet what is not essentially different has often been maintained ; for to say that salvation is partly by faith and partly by works, is really the same thing, inasmuch as the principle of merit is thereby admitted. Man naturally cleaves to his own righteousness ; all those who are ignorant are self-righteous, and all the learned who understand not the gospel; and it is wonderful what ingenious evasions and learned subtleties men will have recourse to in order to resist the plain testimony of Scripture. When they cannot maintain their ground as advocates of salvation alone by merits, they will attempt to maintain it as advocates of a system, which allows a part to grace and a part to works—an amalgamation which Paul expressly repudiates, Rom. xi. 6.

But it is remarkable how the innate disposition of man has displayed itself in this respect. Conscious, as it were, in some measure of *moral* imperfections, he has been striving for the most part to merit his salvation by *ceremonial* works. This has been the case in all ages with heathens: their sacrifices, austerities, and mechanical devotions were their merits; they were the works by which they expected to obtain happiness. God favoured the people of Israel with the rituals of religion, which were designed merely as aids and means to attain and preserve true religion; but they converted them to another purpose, and, like the heathens, regarded them as meritorious performances, and expected God's acceptance for the very religious acts which they exercised: and in order to make up, as it were, a sufficient quantity of merit, they made additions to those services which God had appointed, as though to multiply acts of this kind was to render their salvation more certain. The very same evil crept early into the Christian Church, and still continues to exist. The accumulation of ceremonies is of itself a sufficient proof, that salvation by faith was in a great measure lost sight of: we want no other evidence; it is what has been ever done whenever the light of truth has become dim and obscure. We see the same evil in the present day. Outward privileges and outward acts of worship are in effect too often substituted for that grace which changes the heart, and for that living faith which unites us to the Saviour, which works by love and overcomes the world. The very disposition to over-value external privileges and the mere performances of religious duties, is an unequivocal evidence, that salvation by faith is not understood, or very imperfectly understood, and not really embraced.

The only remedy, as means for this evil, is that which we find employed by Paul in this Epistle. He begins by showing what every man, Jew and Gentile, is by nature; he proves by the clearest evidence, that all have sinned and become guilty before God. And having done this, he discloses the way of salvation which God himself has planned and revealed; and he teaches us, that it is altogether by grace and through faith that we can be saved, and not by works. In order cordially to embrace this latter truth, it is necessary to know the first, that we are sinners under condemnation. It is impossible, according to the very constitution of man's mind, that he should really and truly accede to the one, without a real and deep knowledge of the other. The whole need not a physician, but the sick. It is only he who is really convinced of sin and who feels its guilt and its burden intolerable, that ever will, or indeed ever can, really lay hold on that free salvation which God has provided. And when this free salvation is really known, all other things compared with it will be deemed as nothing; and then all outward privileges will be viewed only as means, and all outward acts of religion only as aids and helps; and then also all our works, however great and self-denying, will be regarded in no way meritorious, but imperfect and defective, and acceptable only through the merits of our High Priest at God's right hand.

It has not been deemed necessary to give in this Edition any specimens of title-pages, &c., from former Editions, either in Latin or in English; as they are to be found in the Old Translation already in the hands of the subscribers.

J. O.

THRUSSINGTON, *August* 1849.

COMMENTARIES

ON

THE EPISTLE OF PAUL THE APOSTLE

TO

THE ROMANS.

THE EPISTLE DEDICATORY.

JOHN CALVIN

TO

SIMON GRYNÆUS,[1]

A MAN WORTHY OF ALL HONOUR.

I REMEMBER that when three years ago we had a friendly converse as to the best mode of expounding Scripture, the plan which especially pleased you, seemed also to me the most entitled to approbation: we both thought that the chief excellency of an expounder consists in *lucid brevity*. And, indeed, since it is almost his only work to lay open the mind of the writer whom he undertakes to explain, the degree in which he leads away his readers from it, in that degree he goes astray from his purpose, and in a manner wanders from his own boundaries. Hence we expressed a hope, that from the number of those who strive at this day to advance the interest of theology by this kind of labour, some one would be found, who would study plainness, and endeavour to avoid the evil of tiring his readers with prolixity. I know at the same time that this view is not taken

---

[1] The account given of *Grynœus* by *Watkins* in his Biographical Dictionary, taken from *Moreri*, is the following:—" A learned German, born at Veringen, in Hohenzollern, in 1493. He studied at Vienna, after which he became Rector of the school at Baden, but was thrown into prison for espousing the Lutheran doctrines. However, he recovered his liberty, and went to Heidelberg, afterwards to Basil, and, in 1531, he visited England. In 1536 he returned to Basil, and died there in 1540." It is somewhat singular, that in the same year, 1540, another learned man of the same name, John James *Grynœus*, was born at Berne, and was educated at Basil, and became distinguished for his learning.—*Ed.*

by all, and that those who judge otherwise have their reasons; but still I cannot be drawn away from the love of what is compendious. But as there is such a variety, found in the minds of men, that different things please different persons, let every one in this case follow his own judgment, provided that no one attempts to force others to adopt his own rules. Thus it will be, that we who approve of brevity, will not reject nor despise the labours of those who are more copious and diffused in their explanations of Scripture, and that they also in their turn will bear with us, though they may think us too compressed and concise.

I indeed could not have restrained myself from attempting something to benefit the Church of God in this way. I am, however, by no means confident that I have attained what at that time seemed best to us; nor did I hope to attain it when I began; but I have endeavoured so to regulate my style, that I might appear to aim at that model. How far I have succeeded, as it is not my part to determine, I leave to be decided by you and by such as you are.

That I have dared to make the trial, especially on this Epistle of Paul, I indeed see, will subject me to the condemnation of many: for since men of so much learning have already laboured in the explanation of it, it seems not probable that there is any room for others to produce any thing better. And I confess, that though I promised to myself some fruit from my labour, I was at first deterred by this thought; for I feared, lest I should incur the imputation of presumption by applying my hand to a work which had been executed by so many illustrious workmen. There are extant on this Epistle many Commentaries by the ancients, and many by modern writers: and truly they could have never employed their labours in a better way; for when any one understands this Epistle, he has a passage opened to him to the understanding of the whole Scripture.

Of the ancients who have, by their piety, learning, holiness, and also by their age, gained so much authority, that we ought to despise nothing of what they have adduced, I will say nothing; and with regard to those who live at this day, it is of no benefit to mention them all by name: Of those who have spent most labour in this work, I will express my opinion.

Philipp *Melancthon*, who, by his singular learning and industry, and by that readiness in all kinds of knowledge, in which he excels, has introduced more light than those who had preceded him. But as it seems to have been his object to examine only those things which are mainly worthy of attention, he dwelt at large on these, and designedly passed by many things which common minds find to be difficult. Then follows *Bullinger*, who has justly attained no small praise; for with learning he has connected plainness, for which he has been highly commended. In the last place comes *Bucer*, who, by publishing his works, has given as it were the finishing stroke. For in addition to his recondite learning and enlarged knowledge of things, and to the clearness of his mind, and much reading and many other excellencies, in which he is hardly surpassed by any at this day, equalled by few and excelled by still fewer—he possesses, as you know, this praise as his own—that no one in our age has been with so much labour engaged in the work of expounding Scripture.[1]

As then it would have been, I know, a proof of the most presumptuous rivalry, to wish to contend with such men, such a thing never entered my mind; nor have I a desire to take from them the least portion of their praise. Let that favour and authority, which according to the confession of all good men they have deserved, be continued to them. This, however, I trust, will be allowed—that nothing has been done by men so absolutely perfect, that there is no room left for the industry of those who succeed them, either to polish, or to adorn, or to illustrate. Of myself I venture not to say any thing, except that I thought that my labour

---

[1] There were at least two other Reformers who had written on the Epistle to the Romans: but whether they were published at this time the writer is not able to say. There is by *Luther* an Introduction to it, which has been much praised, and has attained the name of the *golden* preface. Peter *Martyr* wrote a large comment on this Epistle, which was translated into English early in Queen Elizabeth's reign, in the year 1568. It is rather remarkable that there was *no commenter* among our English Reformers, while on the Continent there were a great many commentators. —*Ed.*

would not be useless, and that I have undertaken it for no other reason than to promote the public good of the Church.

I farther hoped, that by adopting a different plan, I should not expose myself to the invidious charge of rivalry, of which I was afraid in the first instance. *Philipp* attained his object by illustrating the principal points: being occupied with these primary things, he passed by many things which deserve attention; and it was not his purpose to prevent others to examine them. *Bucer* is too diffuse for men in business to read, and too profound to be understood by such as are simple and not capable of much application: for whatever be the subject which he handles, so many things are suggested to him through the incredible fecundity of his mind, in which he excels, that he knows not when to stop. Since then the first has not explained every passage, and the other has handled every point more at large than it can be read in a short time, my design has not even the appearance of being an act of rivalship. I, however, hesitated for some time, whether it would be better to gather some gleanings after these and others, by which I might assist humbler minds—or to compose a regular comment, in which I should necessarily have to repeat many things which have been previously said by them all, or at least by some of them. But as they often vary from one another, and thus present a difficulty to simple readers, who hesitate as to what opinion they ought to receive, I thought that it would be no vain labour, if by pointing out the best explanation, I relieved them from the trouble of forming a judgment, who are not able to form a judgment for themselves; and especially as I determined to treat things so briefly, that without much loss of time, readers may peruse in my work what is contained in other writings. In short, I have endeavoured that no one may justly complain, that there are here many things which are superfluous.

Of the usefulness of this work I will say nothing; men, not malignant, will, however, it may be, have reasons to confess, that they have derived from it more benefit than I can with any modesty dare to promise. Now, that I sometimes dissent from others, or somewhat differ from them, it is but right that I should be excused. Such veneration we ought indeed to entertain for the Word of God, that we ought not to pervert it in the least degree by varying expositions; for its majesty is diminished, I know not how much, especially when not expounded with great discretion and with great sobriety. And if it be deemed a great wickedness to contaminate any thing that is dedicated to God, he surely cannot be endured, who, with impure, or even with unprepared hands, will handle that very thing, which of all things is the most sacred on earth. It is therefore an audacity, closely allied to a sacrilege, rashly to turn Scripture in any way we please, and to indulge our fancies as in sport; which has been done by many in former times.

But we ever find, that even those who have not been deficient in their zeal for piety, nor in reverence and sobriety in handling the mysteries of God, have by no means agreed among themselves on every point; for God hath never favoured his servants with so great a benefit, that they were all endued with a full and perfect knowledge in every thing; and, no doubt, for this end—that he might first keep them humble; and secondly, render them disposed to cultivate brotherly intercourse. Since then what would otherwise be very desirable cannot be expected in this life, that is, universal consent among us in the interpretation of all parts of Scripture, we must endeavour, that, when we depart from the sentiments of our predecessors, we may not be stimulated by any humour for novelty, nor impelled by any lust for defaming others, nor instigated by hatred, nor tickled by any ambition, but constrained by necessity alone, and by the motive of seeking to do good: and then, when this is done in interpreting Scripture, less liberty will be taken in the principles of religion, in which God would have the minds of his people to be especially unanimous. Readers will easily perceive that I had both these things in view.

But as it becomes not me to decide or to pronounce any thing respecting myself, I willingly allow you this office; to whose judgment, since almost all in most things defer, I ought in everything to defer, inasmuch as you are intimately known to me by familiar intercourse; which is wont somewhat to diminish the esteem had for others, but does not a little increase yours, as is well known among all the learned. Farewell.

STRASBURGH, 18*th October* 1539.

EPISTLE TO THE ROMANS.

THE ARGUMENT.

WITH regard to the excellency of this Epistle, I know not whether it would be well for me to dwell long on the subject; for I fear, lest through my recommendations falling far short of what they ought to be, I should do nothing but obscure its merits: besides, the Epistle itself, at its very beginning, explains itself in a much better way than can be done by any words which I can use. It will then be better for me to pass on to the Argument, or the contents of the Epistle; and it will hence appear beyond all controversy, that besides other excellencies, and those remarkable, this can with truth be said of it, and it is what can never be sufficiently appreciated—that when any one gains a knowledge of this Epistle, he has an entrance opened to him to all the most hidden treasures of Scripture.

The whole Epistle is so methodical, that even its very beginning is framed according to the rules of art. As contrivance appears in many parts, which shall be noticed as we proceed, so also especially in the way in which the main argument is deduced: for having begun with the proof of his Apostleship, he then comes to the Gospel with the view of recommending it; and as this necessarily draws with it the subject of faith, he glides into that, being led by the chain of words as by the hand: and thus he enters on the main subject of the whole Epistle—justification by faith; in treating which he is engaged to the end of the fifth chapter.

The subject then of these chapters may be stated thus,— that man's only righteousness is through the mercy of God in

Christ, which being offered by the Gospel is apprehended by faith.

But as men are asleep in their sins, and flatter and delude themselves with a false notion about righteousness, so that they think not that they need the righteousness of faith, except they be cast down from all self-confidence,—and further, as they are inebriated with the sweetness of lusts, and sunk in deep self-security, so that they are not easily roused to seek righteousness, except they are struck down by the terror of divine judgment,—the Apostle proceeds to do two things—to convince men of iniquity, and to shake off the torpor of those whom he proves guilty.

He *first* condemns all mankind from the beginning of the world for ingratitude, because they recognised not the workman in his extraordinary work: nay, when they were constrained to acknowledge him, they did not duly honour his majesty, but in their vanity profaned and dishonoured it. Thus all became guilty of impiety, a wickedness more detestable than any thing else. And that he might more clearly show that all had departed from the Lord, he recounts the filthy and horrible crimes of which men everywhere became guilty: and this is a manifest proof, that they had degenerated from God, since these sins are evidences of divine wrath, which appear not except in the ungodly. And as the Jews and some of the Gentiles, while they covered their inward depravity by the veil of outward holiness, seemed to be in no way chargeable with such crimes, and hence thought themselves exempt from the common sentence of condemnation, the Apostle directs his discourse against this fictitious holiness; and as this mask before men cannot be taken away from saintlings, (*sanctulis*—petty saints,) he summons them to the tribunal of God, whose eyes no latent evils can escape. Having afterwards divided his subject, he places apart both the Jews and the Gentiles before the tribunal of God. He cuts off from the Gentiles the excuse which they pleaded from ignorance, because conscience was to them a law, and by this they were abundantly convicted as guilty. He chiefly urges on the Jews that from which they took their defence, even the written law; and as they were proved to have transgressed it, they could not free themselves from the charge of iniquity, and a sentence against them had already been pronounced by the mouth of God himself. He at the same time obviates any objection which might have been made by them—that the covenant of God, which was the symbol of holiness, would have been violated, if they were not to be distinguished from others. Here he first shows, that they excelled not others by the right of the covenant, for they had by their unfaithfulness departed from it: and then, that he might not derogate from the perpetuity of the divine promise, he concedes to them some privilege as arising from the covenant; but it proceeded from the mercy of God, and not from their merits. So that with regard to their own qualifications they were on a level with the Gentiles. He then proves by the authority of Scripture, that both Jews and Gentiles were all sinners; and he also slightly refers to the use of the law.

Having wholly deprived all mankind of their confidence in their own virtue and of their boast of righteousness, and laid them prostrate by the severity of God's judgment, he returns to what he had before laid down as his subject—that we are justified by faith; and he explains what faith is, and how the righteousness of Christ is by it attained by us. To these things he adds at the end of the *third* chapter a remarkable conclusion, with the view of beating down the fierceness of human pride, that it might not dare to raise up itself against the grace of God: and lest the Jews should confine so great a favour of God to their own nation, he also by the way claims it in behalf of the Gentiles.

In the *fourth* chapter he reasons from example; which he adduces as being evident, and hence not liable to be cavilled at; and it is that of Abraham, who, being the father of the faithful, ought to be deemed a pattern and a kind of universal example. Having then proved that he was justified by faith, the Apostle teaches us that we ought to maintain no other way of justification. And here he shows, that it follows from the rule of contraries, that the righteousness of works ceases to exist, since the righteousness of faith is introduced. And he confirms this by the declaration of David, who, by making the blessedness of man to depend on the mercy of God, takes it away from works, as they are incapable of making a man blessed. He then treats more fully what he had before shortly referred to—that the Jews had no reason to raise themselves above the Gentiles, as this felicity is equally common to them both, since Scripture declares that Abraham obtained this righteousness in an uncircumcised state: and here he takes the opportunity of adding some remarks on the use of circumcision. He afterwards subjoins, that the promise of salvation depends on God's goodness alone: for were it to depend on the law, it could not bring peace to consciences, which it ought to confirm, nor could it attain its own fulfilment. Hence, that it may be sure and certain, we must, in embracing it, regard the truth of God alone, and not ourselves, and follow the example of Abraham, who, turning away from himself, had regard only to the power of God. At the end of the chapter, in order to make a more general application of the adduced example, he introduces several comparisons.

In the *fifth* chapter, after having touched on the fruit and effects of the righteousness of faith, he is almost wholly taken up with illustrations, in order to make the point clearer. For, deducing an argument from one greater, he shows how much we, who have been redeemed and reconciled to God, ought to expect from his love; which was so abundantly poured forth towards us, when we were sinners and lost, that he gave for us his only-begotten and beloved Son. He afterwards makes comparisons between sin and free righteousness, between Christ and Adam, between death and life, between the law and grace: it hence appears that our evils, however vast they are, are swallowed up by the infinite mercy of God.

He proceeds in the *sixth* chapter to mention the sanctification which we obtain in Christ. It is indeed natural to our flesh, as soon as it has had some slight knowledge of grace, to indulge quietly in its own vices and lusts, as though it had become free from all danger: but Paul, on the contrary, contends here, that we cannot partake of the righteousness of Christ, except we also lay hold on sanctification. He reasons from baptism, by which we are initiated into a participation of Christ, (*per quem in Christi participationem initiamur;*) and in it we are buried together with Christ, so that being dead in ourselves, we may through his life be raised to a newness of life. It then follows, that without regeneration no one can put on his righteousness. He hence deduces exhortations as to purity and holiness of life, which must necessarily appear in those who have been removed from the kingdom of sin to the kingdom of righteousness, the sinful indulgence of the flesh, which seeks in Christ a greater liberty in sinning, being cast aside. He makes also a brief mention of the law as being abrogated; and in the abrogation of this the New Testament shines forth eminently; for together with the remission of sins, it contains the promise of the Holy Spirit.

In the *seventh* chapter he enters on a full discussion on the use of the law, which he had pointed out before as it were by the finger, while he had another subject in hand: he assigns a reason why we are loosed from the law, and that is, because it serves only for condemnation. Lest, however, he should expose the law to reproach, he clears it in the strongest terms from any imputation of this kind; for he shows that through our fault it is that the law, which was given for life, turns to be an occasion of death. He also explains how sin is by it increased. He then proceeds to describe the contest between the Spirit and the flesh, which the children of God find in themselves, as long as they are surrounded by the prison of a mortal body; for they carry with them the relics of lust, by which they are continually prevented from yielding full obedience to the law.

The *eighth* chapter contains abundance of consolations, in order that the consciences of the faithful, having heard of the disobedience which he had before proved, or rather imperfect obedience, might not be terrified and dejected. But that the ungodly might not hence flatter themselves, he first testifies that this privilege belongs to none but to the regenerated, in whom the Spirit of God lives and prevails. He unfolds then two things—that all who are planted by the Spirit in the Lord Jesus Christ, are beyond the danger or the chance of condemnation, however burdened they may yet be with sins; and, also, that all who remain in the flesh, being without the sanctification of the Spirit, are by no means partakers of this great benefit. He afterwards explains how great is the certainty of our confidence, since the Spirit of God by his own testimony drives away all doubts and fears. He further shows, for the purpose of anticipating objections, that the certainty of eternal life cannot be intercepted or disturbed by present evils, to which we are subject in this life; but that, on the contrary, our salvation is promoted by such trials, and that the value of it, when compared with our present miseries, renders them as nothing. He confirms this by the example of Christ, who, being the first-begotten and holding the highest station in the family of God, is the pattern to which we must all be conformed. And, in the last place, as though all things were made secure, he concludes in a most exulting strain, and boldly triumphs over all the power and artifices of Satan.

But as most were much concerned on seeing the Jews, the first guardians and heirs of the covenant, rejecting Christ, for they hence concluded, that either the covenant was transferred from the posterity of Abraham, who disregarded the fulfilling of the covenant, or that he, who made no better provision for the people of Israel, was not the promised Redeemer—he meets this objection at the beginning of the *ninth* chapter. Having then spoken of his love towards his own nation, that he might not appear to speak from hatred, and having also duly mentioned those privileges by which they excelled others, he gently glides to the point he had in view, that is, to remove the offence, which arose from their own blindness. And he divides the children of Abraham into two classes, that he might show that not all who descended from him according to the flesh, are to be counted for seed and become partakers of the grace of the covenant; but that, on the contrary, aliens become his children, when they possess his faith. He brings forward Jacob and Esau as examples. He then refers us back here to the election of God, on which the whole matter necessarily depends. Besides, as election rests on the mercy of God alone, it is in vain to seek the cause of it in the worthiness of man. There is, on the other hand, rejection (*rejectio*), the justice of which is indubitable, and yet there is no higher cause for it than the will of God. Near the end of the chapter, he sets forth the calling of the Gentiles and the rejection of the Jews as proved by the predictions of the Prophets.

Having again begun, in the *tenth* chapter, by testifying his love towards the Jews, he declares that a vain confidence in their own works was the cause of their ruin; and lest they should pretend the law, he obviates their objection, and says, that we are even by the law itself led as it were by the hand to the righteousness of faith. He adds that this righteousness is through God's bountiful goodness offered indiscriminately to all nations, but that it is only apprehended by those, whom the Lord through special favour illuminates. And he states, that more from the Gentiles than from the Jews would obtain this benefit, as predicted both by Moses and by Isaiah; the one having plainly prophesied of the calling of the Gentiles, and the other of the hardening of the Jews.

The question still remained, " Is there not a difference between the seed of Abraham and other nations according to the covenant of God?" Proceeding to answer this question, he first reminds us, that the work of God is not to be limited to what is seen by our eyes, since the elect often escape our observation; for Elias was formerly mistaken, when he thought that religion had become wholly extinct among the Israelites, when there were still remaining seven thousand; and, further, that we must not be perplexed by the number of unbelievers, who, as we see, hate the gospel. He at length alleges, that the covenant of God continues even to the posterity of Abraham according to the flesh, but to those only whom the Lord by a free election hath predestinated. He then turns to the Gentiles, and speaks to them, lest they should become insolent on account of their adoption, and exult over the Jews as having been rejected, since they excel them in nothing, except in the free favour of the Lord, which ought to make them the more humble; and that this has not wholly departed from the seed of

Abraham, for the Jews were at length to be provoked to emulation by the faith of the Gentiles, so that God would gather all Israel to himself.

The *three* chapters which follow are admonitory, but they are various in their contents. The *twelfth* chapter contains general precepts on Christian life. The *thirteenth*, for the most part, speaks of the authority of magistrates. We may hence undoubtedly gather that there were then some unruly persons, who thought Christian liberty could not exist without overturning the civil power. But that Paul might not appear to impose on the Church any duties but those of love, he declares that this obedience is included in what love requires. He afterwards adds those precepts, which he had before mentioned, for the guidance of our conduct. In the *next* chapter he gives an exhortation, especially necessary in that age: for as there were those who through obstinate superstition insisted on the observance of Mosaic rites, and could not endure the neglect of them without being most grievously offended; so there were others, who, being convinced of their abrogation, and anxious to pull down superstition, designedly showed their contempt of such things. Both parties offended through being too intemperate; for the superstitious condemned the others as being despisers of God's law; and the latter in their turn unreasonably ridiculed the simplicity of the former. Therefore the Apostle recommends to both a befitting moderation, deporting the one from superciliousness and insult, and the other from excessive moroseness: and he also prescribes the best way of exercising Christian liberty, by keeping within the boundaries of love and edification; and he faithfully provides for the weak, while he forbids them to do any thing in opposition to conscience.

The *fifteenth* chapter begins with a repetition of the general argument, as a conclusion of the whole subject—that the strong should use their strength in endeavours to confirm the weak. And as there was a perpetual discord, with regard to the Mosaic ceremonies, between the Jews and the Gentiles, he allays all emulation between them by removing the cause of contention; for he shows, that the salvation of both rested on the mercy of God alone; on which relying, they ought to lay aside all high thoughts of themselves, and being thereby connected together in the hope of the same inheritance, they ought mutually to embrace one another. And being anxious, in the last place, to turn aside for the purpose of commending his own apostleship, which secured no small authority to his doctrine, he takes occasion to defend himself, and to deprecate presumption in having assumed with so much confidence the office of teacher among them. He further gives them some hope of his coming to them, which he had mentioned at the beginning, but had hitherto in vain looked for and tried to effect; and he states the reason which at that time hindered him, and that was, because the churches of Macedonia and Achaia had committed to him the care of conveying to Jerusalem those alms which they had given to relieve the wants of the faithful in that city.

The *last* chapter is almost entirely taken up with salutations, though scattered with some precepts worthy of all attention; and concludes with a remarkable prayer.

COMMENTARIES

ON THE

EPISTLE OF ST. PAUL TO THE ROMANS.

CHAPTER I.

1. Paul, a servant of Jesus Christ, called *to be* an apostle, separated unto the gospel of God,
2. (Which he had promised afore by his prophets in the holy scriptures,)
3. Concerning his Son Jesus Christ our Lord, which was made of the seed of David according to the flesh,
4. And declared *to be* the Son of God with power, according to the spirit of holiness, by the resurrection from the dead:
5. By whom we have received grace and apostleship, for obedience to the faith among all nations for his name;
6. Among whom are ye also the called of Jesus Christ:
7. To all that be in Rome, beloved of God, called *to be* saints: Grace to you, and peace, from God our Father, and the Lord Jesus Christ.

1. Paulus, servus Iesu Christi, vocatus Apostolus, selectus in Evangelium Dei,
2. Quod ante promiserat per Prophetas suos in Scripturis Sanctis,
3. De Filio suo, qui factus est è semine David secundum carnem,
4. Declaratus Filius Dei in potentia, per Spiritum sanctificationis, ex resurrectione mortuorum, Iesu Christo Domino nostro:
5. Per quem accepimus gratiam et Apostolatum, in obedientiam fidei inter omnes gentes, pro nomine ipsius;
6. Inter quas estis etiam vos, vocati Iesu Christi:
7. Omnibus qui Romæ estis, dilectis Deo, vocatis sanctis: gratia vobis, et pax a Deo Patre nostro, et Domino Iesu Christo.

1. *Paul*, &c.[1]—With regard to the word Paul, as it is a subject of no such moment as ought to detain us, and as nothing can be said which has not been mentioned by other

[1] "The inscription of the Pauline Epistles," says *Turrettin*, "is according to the manner of the ancients, both Greeks and Romans. They were wont to prefix their name; and to those to whom they wrote they added their good wishes." We have an example in Acts xxiii. 26.—*Ed.*

expounders, I should say nothing, were it not proper to satisfy some at small expense without being tedious to others; for the subject shall be despatched in a very few words.

They who think that the Apostle attained this name as a trophy for having brought Sergius, the proconsul, to the faith of Christ, are confuted by the testimony of Luke, who shows that he was so called before that time. (Acts xiii. 7, 9.) Nor does it seem probable to me, that it was given him when he was converted to Christ; though this idea so pleased *Augustine*, that he took occasion refinedly to philosophize on the subject; for he says, that from a proud Saul he was made a very little (*parvulum*[1]) disciple of Christ. More probable is the opinion of *Origen*, who thought that he had two names; for it is not unlikely to be true, that his name, Saul, derived from his kindred, was given him by his parents to indicate his religion and his descent; and that his other name, Paul, was added, to show his right to Roman citizenship;[2] they would not have this honour, then highly valued, to be otherwise than made evident; but they did not so much value it as to withhold a proof of his Israelitic descent. But he has commonly taken the name Paul in his Epistles, and it may be for the following reasons: because in the churches to which he wrote, it was more known and more common, more acceptable in the Roman empire, and less known among his own nation. It was indeed his duty to avoid the foolish suspicion and hatred under which the name of a Jew then laboured among the Romans and in their provinces, and to abstain from inflaming the rage of his own countrymen, and to take care of himself.

A servant of Jesus Christ, &c.—He signalizes himself with these distinctions for the purpose of securing more authority to his doctrine; and this he seeks to secure by two things—

---

[1] Thereby expressing the meaning of *Paulus*, which in Latin is little. "Paul," says the quaint Elnathan *Parr*, "signifies little, and indeed not unfitly, for he is reported to have been low in stature, and to have had a very small voice, which is thought to have been objected to him in 2 Cor. x. 10."—*Ed*.

[2] Most writers agree in this view, regarding *Saul* as his Hebrew name, and *Paul* as his Roman name.—*Ed*.

first, by asserting his call to the Apostleship;[1] and secondly, by showing that his call was not unconnected with the Church of Rome: for it was of great importance that he should be deemed an Apostle through God's call, and that he should be known as one destined for the Roman Church. He therefore says, that he was a *servant* of Christ, and called to the office of an Apostle, thereby intimating that he had not presumptuously intruded into that office. He then adds, that he was *chosen*, (*selectum*—selected,[2]) by which he more fully confirms the fact, that he was not one of the people, but a particular Apostle of the Lord. Consistently with this, he had before proceeded from what was general to what was particular, as the Apostleship was an especial service; for all who sustain the office of teaching are to be deemed Christ's servants, but Apostles, in point of honour, far exceed all others. But the *choosing* for the gospel, &c., which he afterwards mentions, expresses the end as well as the use of the Apostleship; for he intended briefly to show for what purpose he was called to that function. By saying then that he was servant of Christ, he declared what he had in common with other teachers; by claiming to himself the

---

[1] " A called Apostle—vocatus apostolus—κλητὸς ἀπόστολος:" our version is, " called *to be* an Apostle." Most consider " called" here in the sense of chosen or elected, " a chosen Apostle." Professor *Stuart* observes, that κλητὸς in the writings of Paul has always the meaning of efficient calling, and signifies not only the invited, but the effectually invited. He refers to 1 Cor. i. 1, 2; i. 24; Rom. i. 6, 7; viii. 28; compared with Gal. i. 15; Jude i. 1; Heb. iii. 1; Rom. xi. 29; Eph. iv. 1.

He was an Apostle by a call, or as *Beza* renders it, " by the call *of God*—ex *Dei* vocatione apostolus." The meaning is the same as what he himself expresses it in Gal. i. 1. *Turrettin* renders it, " Apostolus vocatione divina—an Apostle by divine vocation."

The difference between " a called Apostle" and " called to be an Apostle," is this, that the first conveys the idea that he obeyed the call, and the other does not.—*Ed.*

[2] 'Ἀφωρισμένος, separated, set apart; " segregatus," *Vulgate;* " separatus," *Beza.* " The Pharisees," says *Leigh,* " were termed ἀφωρισμένοι, we may English them *Separatists:* they separated themselves to the study of the law, in which respect they might be called ἀφωρισμένοι εἰς τὸν νόμον, separated to the law. In allusion to this, saith *Drusius,* the Apostle is thought to have styled himself, Rom. i. 1, ἀφωρισμένον εἰς εὐαγγέλιόν, separated unto the Gospel, when he was called from being a Pharisee to be a preacher of the Gospel." *Separated* is the word adopted both by *Doddridge* and *Macknight,* as well as by our own version.—*Ed.*

title of an Apostle, he put himself before others; but as no authority is due to him who wilfully intrudes himself, he reminds us, that he was appointed by God.

Then the meaning is,—that Paul was a servant of Christ, not any kind of servant, but an Apostle, and that by the call of God, and not by presumptuous intrusion: then follows a clearer explanation of the Apostolic office,—it was ordained for the preaching of the Gospel. For I cannot agree with those who refer this call of which he speaks to the eternal election of God; and who understand the separation, either that from his mother's womb, which he mentions in Gal. i. 15, or that which Luke refers to, when Paul was appointed for the Gentiles: but I consider that he simply glories in having God as the author of his call, lest any one should think that he had through his own rashness taken this honour to himself.[1]

We must here observe, that all are not fitted for the ministry of the word; for a special call is necessary: and even those who seem particularly fitted ought to take heed lest they thrust themselves in without a call. But as to the character of the Apostolic and of the Episcopal call, we shall consider it in another place. We must further observe, that the office of an Apostle is the preaching of the gospel. It hence appears what just objects of ridicule are those dumb dogs, who render themselves conspicuous only by their mitre and their crook, and boast themselves to be the successors of the Apostles!

The word, *servant*, imports nothing else but a minister, for it refers to what is official.[2] I mention this to remove the mistake of those who too much refine on this expression, and think that there is here to be understood a contrast between the service of Moses and that of Christ.

---

[1] Some combine the four separations. " Set apart in the eternal counsel of God, and from his mother's womb, Gal. i. 15, and by the special commandment of the Holy Ghost, Acts xiii. 2, confirmed by the constitution of the Church, Acts xiii. 3; Gal. ii. 9."—*Parr.* But the object here seems to have been that stated by *Calvin:* nor is it just or prudent to connect any other idea with the word except that which the context requires; for to do so only tends to create confusion.—*Ed.*

[2] Moses, Joshua, David, Nehemiah, &c., were, in a similar sense, called servants; and also our Saviour. They were officially servants.—*Ed.*

3. *Which he had before promised,* &c.—As the suspicion of being new subtracts much from the authority of a doctrine, he confirms the faith of the gospel by antiquity; as though he said, " Christ came not on the earth unexpectedly, nor did he introduce a doctrine of a new kind and not heard of before, inasmuch as he, and his gospel too, had been promised and expected from the beginning of the world." But as antiquity is often fabulous, he brings witnesses, and those approved, even the Prophets of God, that he might remove every suspicion. He in the third place adds, that their testimonies were duly recorded, that is, in the Holy Scriptures.

We may learn from this passage what the gospel is: he teaches us, not that it was promulgated by the Prophets, but only promised. If then the Prophets promised the gospel, it follows, that it was revealed, when our Lord was at length manifested in the flesh. They are then mistaken, who confound the promises with the gospel, since the gospel is properly the appointed preaching of Christ as manifested, in whom the promises themselves are exhibited.[1]

3. *Concerning his own Son,* &c.—This is a remarkable passage, by which we are taught that the whole gospel is included in Christ, so that if any removes one step from Christ, he withdraws himself from the gospel. For since he is the living and express image of the Father, it is no wonder, that he alone is set before us as one to whom our whole faith is to be directed and in whom it is to centre. It is then a definition of the gospel, by which Paul expresses what is summarily comprehended in it. I have rendered the words which follow, *Jesus Christ our Lord,* in the same case; which seems to me to be most agreeable with the context. We hence learn, that he who has made a due proficiency in the knowledge of Christ, has acquired every thing which can be learned from the gospel; and, on the other

---

[1] The verb is προεπηγγείλατο, only here; it comes from επαγγέλλομαι, which, *Schleusner* says, means in the middle voice, to promise. " Which he had before promised," is then the proper rendering, and not, " Which he formerly published," as proposed by Professor *Stuart*. Both *Doddridge* and *Macknight* have retained our version, with which that of *Beza* agrees.—*Ed.*

hand, that they who seek to be wise without Christ, are not only foolish, but even completely insane.

Who was made, &c.—Two things must be found in Christ, in order that we may obtain salvation in him, even divinity and humanity. His divinity possesses power, righteousness, life, which by his humanity are conveyed to us. Hence the Apostle has expressly mentioned both in the summary he gives of the gospel, that Christ was manifested in the flesh— and that in it he declared himself to be the Son of God. So John says; after having declared that the Word was made flesh, he adds, that in that flesh there was a glory as of the only-begotten Son of God. (John i. 14.) That he specially notices the descent and lineage of Christ from his ancestor David, is not superfluous; for by this he calls back our attention to the promise, that we may not doubt but that he is the very person who had been formerly promised. So well known was the promise made to David, that it appears to have been a common thing among the Jews to call the Messiah the Son of David. This then—that Christ did spring from David—was said for the purpose of confirming our faith.

He adds, *according to the flesh;* and he adds this, that we may understand that he had something more excellent than flesh, which he brought from heaven, and did not take from David, even that which he afterwards mentions, the glory of the divine nature. Paul does further by these words not only declare that Christ had real flesh, but he also clearly distinguishes his human from his divine nature; and thus he refutes the impious raving of *Servetus,* who assigned flesh to Christ, composed of three uncreated elements.

4. *Declared*[1] *the Son of God,* &c.: or, if you prefer, *deter-*

---

[1] "Declaratus," ὁρισθέντος. Some of the ancients, such as *Origen, Chrysostom, Cyril,* and others, have given to this verb the meaning of "proved —διχθέντος;" "demonstrated—ἀποφανθέντος;" "exhibited—ἀποδειχθέντος;" &c. But it is said that the word has not this meaning in the New Testament, and that it means, limited, determined, decreed, constituted. Besides here, it is found only in Luke xxii. 22; Acts ii. 23; x. 42; xi. 29; xvii. 26; Heb. iv. 7. The word, *determined,* or *constituted,* if adopted here, would amount to the same thing, that is, that Christ was visibly determined or constituted the Son of God through the resurrection, or by that event. It was that which fixed, settled, determined, and manifestly

mined (definitus); as though he had said, that the power, by which he was raised from the dead, was something like a decree, by which he was proclaimed the Son of God, according to what is said in Ps. ii. 7, " I have this day begotten thee:" for this begetting refers to what was made known. Though some indeed find here three separate evidences of the divinity of Christ—" power," understanding thereby miracles—then the testimony of the Spirit—and, lastly, the resurrection from the dead—I yet prefer to connect them exhibited him as the Son of God, clothed and adorned with his own power.

Professor *Stuart* has conjured a number of difficulties in connection with this verse, for which there seems to be no solid reason. The phrase, *the Son of God,* is so well known from the usage of Scripture, that there is no difficulty connected with it: the full phrase is the *only-begotten Son.* To say that Christ's resurrection was no evidence of his divine nature, as Lazarus and others had been raised from the dead, appears indeed very strange. Did Lazarus rise through his own power? Did Lazarus rise again for our justification? Was his resurrection an attestation of any thing he had previously declared? The Rev. A. *Barnes* very justly says, that the *circumstances* connected with Christ were those which rendered his resurrection a proof of his divinity.

Professor *Hodge* gives what he conceives to be the import of the two verses in these words, " Jesus Christ was, as to his human nature, the Son of David; but he was clearly demonstrated to be, as to his divine nature, the Son of God, by the resurrection from the dead." This view is taken by many, such as *Pareus, Beza, Turrettin,* &c. But the words, " according to the Spirit of Holiness"—κατὰ πνεῦμα ἁγιωσύνης, are taken differently by others, as meaning the Holy Spirit. As the phrase is nowhere else found, it may be taken in either sense. That the divine nature of Christ is called Spirit, is evident. See 1 Cor. xv. 45; 2 Cor. iii. 17; Heb. ix. 14; 1 Pet. iii. 18. *Doddridge, Scott,* and *Chalmers,* consider the Holy Spirit to be intended. The last gives this paraphrase:—" *De-clared,* or determinately marked out to be the Son of God and with power. The thing was demonstrated by an evidence, the exhibition of which required a putting forth of power, which Paul in another place represents as a very great and strenuous exertion, ' According to the working of his mighty power when he raised him from the dead.'—*The Spirit of Holiness,* or the Holy Spirit. It was through the operation of the Holy Spirit that the divine nature was infused into the human at the birth of Jesus Christ; and the very same agent, it is remarkable, was employed in the work of the resurrection. ' Put to death in the flesh,' says Peter, ' and quickened by the Spirit.' We have only to do with the facts of the case. He was demonstrated to be the Son of God by the power of the Holy Spirit having been put forth in raising him from the dead." As to the genitive case after " resurrection," see a similar instance in Acts xvii. 32.

The idea deduced by *Calvin,* that he is called here " the Spirit of Holiness," on account of the holiness he works in us, seems not well-founded, though advanced by *Theodoret* and *Augustine.—Ed.*

together, and to reduce these three things to one, in this manner—that Christ was declared the Son of God by openly exercising a real celestial power, that is, the power of the Spirit, when he rose from the dead; but that this power is comprehended, when a conviction of it is imprinted on our hearts by the same Spirit. The language of the Apostle well agrees with this view; for he says that he was declared by power, because power, peculiar to God, shone forth in him, and uncontestably proved him to be God; and this was indeed made evident by his resurrection. Paul says the same thing in another place; having stated, that by death the weakness of the flesh appeared, he at the same time extols the power of the Spirit in his resurrection; (2 Cor. xiii. 4.) This glory, however, is not made known to us, until the same Spirit imprints a conviction of it on our hearts. And that Paul includes, together with the wonderful energy of the Spirit, which Christ manifested by rising from the dead, the testimony which all the faithful feel in their hearts, is even evident from this—that he expressly calls it the Spirit of Holiness; as though he had said, that the Spirit, as far as it sanctifies, confirms and ratifies that evidence of its power which it once exhibited. For the Scripture is wont often to ascribe such titles to the Spirit, as tend to illustrate our present subject. Thus He is called by our Lord the Spirit of Truth, on account of the effect which he mentions; (John xiv. 17.)

Besides, a divine power is said to have shone forth in the resurrection of Christ for this reason—because he rose by his own power, as he had often testified: "Destroy this temple, and in three days I will raise it up again," (John ii. 19;) "No man taketh it from me," &c.; (John x. 18.) For he gained victory over death, (to which he yielded with regard to the weakness of the flesh,) not by aid sought from another, but by the celestial operation of his own Spirit.

5. *Through whom we have received*, &c.—Having completed his definition of the gospel, which he introduced for the recommendation of his office, he now returns to speak of his own call; and it was a great point that this should be proved to the Romans. By mentioning grace and apostle-

ship apart, he adopts a form of speech,[1] which must be understood as meaning, gratuitous apostleship or the favour of the apostleship; by which he means, that it was wholly through divine favour, not through his own worthiness, that he had been chosen for so high an office. For though it has hardly any thing connected with it in the estimation of the world, except dangers, labours, hatred, and disgrace; yet before God and his saints, it possesses a dignity of no common or ordinary kind. It is therefore deservedly counted a favour. If you prefer to say, " I have received grace that I should be an Apostle," the sense would be the same.[2]

The expression, *on account of his name*, is rendered by *Ambrose*, " in his name," as though it meant, that the Apostle was appointed in the place of Christ to preach the gospel, according to that passage, " We are ambassadors for Christ," &c. (2 Cor. v. 20.) Their opinion, however, seems better, who take *name* for knowledge; for the gospel is preached for this end—that we may believe on the name of the Son of God. (John iii. 23.) And Paul is said to have been a chosen vessel, to carry the name of Christ among the Gentiles. (Acts ix. 15.) *On account* then *of his name*, which means the same, as though he had said, that I might make known what Christ is.[3]

[1] " Hypallage," a figure in grammar, by which a noun or an adjective is put in a form or in a case different from that in which it ought grammatically to be.—*Ed.*

[2] If this view be taken, the best mode would be to render καὶ, even, " favour, even the apostleship." But, as *Wolfius* says, " both words would perhaps be better rendered separately, and " grace" or favour be referred to the conversion of the Apostle himself, and " apostleship" to his office. See 1 Tim. i. 12-14; and Acts ix. 15; xiii. 2; xxii. 21.—*Ed.*

[3] He has taken this clause before that which follows, contrary to the order of the text, because he viewed it as connected with the receiving of the apostleship.

" *Pro nomine ipsius*,"—ὑπὲρ τοῦ ὀνόματος αὐτοῦ ; " ad nominis ejus gloriam —to the glory of his name," *Turrettin;* " for the purpose of magnifying his name," *Chalmers. Hodge* observes, " Paul was an apostle that all nations might be obedient, to the honour of Jesus Christ; that is, so that his name may be known." Some, as *Tholuck*, connect the words with " obedience to the faith," as they render the phrase, and, in this sense, " that obedience might be rendered to the faith among all nations for the sake of his name." But it is better to connect the words with the receiving of the apostleship: it was received for two purposes—that there might be the obedience of faith, and that the name of Christ might be magnified.—*Ed.*

For the obedience of faith, &c.—That is, we have received a command to preach the gospel among all nations, and this gospel they obey by faith. By stating the design of his calling, he again reminds the Romans of his office, as though he said, " It is indeed my duty to discharge the office committed to me, which is to preach the word; and it is your duty to hear the word and willingly to obey it; you will otherwise make void the vocation which the Lord has bestowed on me."

We hence learn, that they perversely resist the authority of God and upset the whole of what he has ordained, who irreverently and contemptuously reject the preaching of the gospel; the design of which is to constrain us to obey God. We must also notice here what faith is; the name of obedience is given to it, and for this reason— because the Lord calls us by his gospel; we respond to his call by faith; as on the other hand, the chief act of disobedience to God is unbelief, I prefer rendering the sentence, " For the obedience of faith," rather than, " In order that they may obey the faith;" for the last is not strictly correct, except taken figuratively, though it be found once in the Acts, vi. 7. Faith is properly that by which we obey the gospel.[1]

Among all nations, &c. It was not enough for him to have been appointed an Apostle, except his ministry had reference to some who were to be taught: hence he adds, that his apostleship extended to all nations. He afterwards calls himself more distinctly the Apostle of the Romans, when he says, that they were included in the number of the nations, to whom he had been given as a

---

[1] It might be rendered, "that there might be the obedience of faith," or, " in order to produce," or, " promote the obedience of faith." The obedience is faith. The command is, " believe," and the obedience must correspond with it. To obey the faith, as in Acts vi. 7, is a different form of expression: the article is prefixed there, it is *the* faith, meaning the gospel.—See 2 Thess. i. 8. Professor *Stuart,* and *Haldane,* agree in this view. The latter refers to Rom. x. 3, where the Israelites are charged for not *submitting* to God's righteousness; and, in verse 16, it is said, that they had not all *obeyed* the gospel, " for Esaias saith, Lord, who hath *believed* our report?" Then to believe the gospel is in an especial manner to obey it.—*Ed.*

minister. And further, the Apostles had in common the command to preach the gospel to all the world; and they were not, as pastors and bishops, set over certain churches. But Paul, in addition to the general undertaking of the apostolic function, was constituted, by a special appointment, to be a minister to proclaim the gospel among the Gentiles. It is no objection to this, that he was forbidden to pass through Macedonia and to preach the word in Mysia: for this was done, not that there were limits prescribed to him, but that he was for a time to go elsewhere; for the harvest was not as yet ripe there.

Ye are the called of Jesus Christ, &c. He assigns a reason more nearly connected with them—because the Lord had already exhibited in them an evidence by which he had manifested that he had called them to a participation of the gospel. It hence followed, that if they wished their own calling to remain sure, they were not to reject the ministry of Paul, who had been chosen by the same election of God. I therefore take this clause, "the called of Jesus Christ," as explanatory, as though the particle "even" were inserted; for he means, that they were by calling made partakers of Christ. For they who shall be heirs of eternal life, are chosen by the celestial Father to be children in Christ; and when chosen, they are committed to his care and protection as their shepherd.[1]

7. *To all of you who are at Rome,* &c. By this happy arrangement he sets forth what there is in us worthy of commendation; he says, that first the Lord through his own kindness made us the objects of his favour and love; and then that he has called us; and thirdly, that he has called us to holiness: but this high honour only then exists, when we are not wanting to our call.

Here a rich truth presents itself to us, to which I shall briefly refer, and leave it to be meditated upon by each individual: Paul does by no means ascribe the praise of our

---

[1] "The called of Jesus Christ," *i.e.*, the called who belong to Christ. Κλητὸς means, not only those to whom the *external* call of the gospel has been addressed, but those who have been also *internally* called."—*Stuart.* The same author renders the words κλητοῖς ἁγίοις, in the next verse, " chosen saints," or, " saints effectually called."—*Ed.*

salvation to ourselves, but derives it altogether from the fountain of God's free and paternal love towards us; for he makes this the first thing—God loves us: and what is the cause of his love, except his own goodness alone? On this depends our calling, by which in his own time he seals his adoption to those whom he had before freely chosen. We also learn from this passage that none rightly connect themselves with the number of the faithful, except they feel assured that the Lord is gracious, however unworthy and wretched sinners they may be, and except they be stimulated by his goodness and aspire to holiness, for he hath not called us to uncleanness, but to holiness. (1 Thess. iv. 7.) As the Greek can be rendered in the second person, I see no reason for any change.

Grace to you and peace, &c. Nothing is more desirable than to have God propitious to us, and this is signified by *grace;* and then to have prosperity and success in all things flowing from him, and this is intimated by *peace;* for however things may seem to smile on us, if God be angry, even blessing itself is turned to a curse. The very foundation then of our felicity is the favour of God, by which we enjoy true and solid prosperity, and by which also our salvation is promoted even when we are in adversities.[1] And then as he prays to God for peace, we must understand, that whatever good comes to us, it is the fruit of divine benevolence. Nor must we omit to notice, that he prays at the same time to the Lord Jesus Christ for these blessings. Worthily indeed is this honour rendered to him, who is not only the administrator and dispenser of his Father's bounty to us, but also works all things in connection with him. It was, however, the special object of the Apostle to show, that through him all God's blessings come to us.[2]

---

[1] "The ancient Greeks and Romans," says *Turrettin,* "wished to those to whom they wrote, in the inscription of their epistles, health, joy, happiness; but Paul prays for far higher blessings, even the *favour* of God, the fountain of all good things, and *peace,* in which the Hebrews included all blessings."—*Ed.*

[2] "*From God our Father,*—if God, then able; if our Father, then willing to enrich us with his gifts: *and from our Lord Jesus Christ,*—from our Lord, who has purchased them for us; from Jesus, for without

There are those who prefer to regard the word *peace* as signifying quietness of conscience; and that this meaning belongs to it sometimes, I do not deny: but since it is certain that the Apostle wished to give us here a summary of God's blessings, the former meaning, which is adduced by *Bucer*, is much the most suitable. Anxiously wishing then to the godly what makes up real happiness, he betakes himself, as he did before, to the very fountain itself, even the favour of God, which not only alone brings to us eternal felicity, but is also the source of all blessings in this life.

8. First, I thank my God through Jesus Christ for you all, that your faith is spoken of throughout the whole world.
9. For God is my witness, whom I serve with my spirit in the gospel of his Son, that without ceasing I make mention of you always in my prayers;
10. Making request (if by any means now at length I might have a prosperous journey by the will of God) to come unto you.
11. For I long to see you, that I may impart unto you some spiritual gift, to the end ye may be established;
12. That is, that I may be comforted together with you, by the mutual faith both of you and me.

8. Primum quidem gratias ago Deo meo per Iesum Christum super vobis omnibus, quia fides vestra prædicatur in universo mundo.
9. Testis enim mihi Deus, quem colo in spiritu meo in Evangelio Filii ipsius, ut continenter memoriam vestri faciam;
10. Semper in orationibus meis,[1] rogans, si quomodo prosperum iter aliquando mihi, obtingat per voluntatem Dei, veniendi ad vos.
11. Desidero enim videre, vos, ut aliquod impertiar vobis donum spirituale ad vos confirmandos;
12. Hoc est, ad cohortationem mutuo percipiendam in vobis per mutuam fidem, vestram atque meam.

8. *I first*[2] *indeed*, &c. Here the beginning commences, altogether adapted to the occasion, as he seasonably prepares them for receiving instruction by reasons connected with himself as well as with them. What he states respecting them is, the celebrity of their faith; for he intimates that they being honoured with the public approbation of the churches, could not reject an Apostle of the Lord, without disappointing the good opinion entertained of them by all; these we cannot be saved; from Christ, for he is anointed with grace and peace. John. i. 16."—*Parr*.

[1] Margin, "in all my prayers."
[2] "It does not mean here the first in point of importance, but first in the order of time."—*Stuart*. The same author thinks that μεν here has its corresponding δε in verse 13, Οὐ θέλω δὲ ὑμᾶς, &c.—*Ed*.

and such a thing would have been extremely uncourteous and in a manner bordering on perfidy. As then this testimony justly induced the Apostle, by affording him an assurance of their obedience, to undertake, according to his office, to teach and instruct the Romans; so it held them bound not to despise his authority. With regard to himself, he disposes them to a teachable spirit by testifying his love towards them: and there is nothing more effectual in gaining credit to an adviser, than the impression that he is cordially anxious to consult our wellbeing.

The first thing worthy of remark is, that he so commends their faith,[1] that he implies that it had been received from God. We are here taught that faith is God's gift; for thanksgiving is an acknowledgment of a benefit. He who gives thanks to God for faith, confesses that it comes from him. And since we find that the Apostle ever begins his congratulations with thanksgiving, let us know that we are hereby reminded, that all our blessings are God's free gifts. It is also needful to become accustomed to such forms of speaking, that we may be led more fully to rouse ourselves in the duty of acknowledging God as the giver of all our blessings, and to stir up others to join us in the same acknowledgment. If it be right to do this in little things, how much more with regard to faith; which is neither a small nor an indiscriminate (*promiscua*) gift of God. We have here besides an example, that thanks ought to be given *through Christ*, according to the Apostle's command in Heb. xiii. 15; inasmuch as in his name we seek and obtain mercy from the Father.—I observe in the last place, that he calls him *his God*. This is the faithful's special privilege, and on them alone God bestows this honour. There is indeed implied in this a mutual relationship, which is expressed in this promise, "I will be to them a God; they shall be to me a people." (Jer. xxx. 22.) I prefer at the same time to confine this to the character which Paul sus-

---

[1] "*Faith* is put here for the whole religion, and means the same as your piety. Faith is one of the principal things of religion, one of its first requirements, and hence it signifies religion itself."—*Barnes*. It is indeed *the* principal thing, the very basis of religion. Heb. xi. 6.—*Ed.*

tained, as an attestation of his obedience to the end in the work of preaching the gospel. So Hezekiah called God the God of Isaiah, when he desired him to give him the testimony of a true and faithful Prophet. (Is. xxxvii. 4.) So also he is called in an especial manner the God of Daniel. (Dan. vi. 20.)

Through the whole world. The eulogy of faithful men was to Paul equal to that of the whole world, with regard to the faith of the Romans; for the unbelieving, who deemed it detestable, could not have given an impartial or a correct testimony respecting it. We then understood that it was by the mouths of the faithful that the faith of the Romans was proclaimed through the whole world; and that they were alone able to judge rightly of it, and to pronounce a correct opinion. That this small and despised handful of men were unknown as to their character to the ungodly, even at Rome, was a circumstance he regarded as nothing; for Paul made no account of their judgment.

9. *For God is my witness,* &c. He proves his love by its effects; for had he not greatly loved them, he would not have so anxiously commended them to the Lord, and especially he would not have so ardently desired to promote their welfare by his own labours. His anxiety then and his ardent desire were certain evidences of his love; for had they not sprung from it, they would never have existed. And as he knew it to be necessary for establishing confidence in his preaching, that the Romans should be fully persuaded of his sincerity, he added an oath—a needful remedy, whenever a declaration, which ought to be received as true and indubitable, vacillates through uncertainty. For since an oath is nothing else but an appeal to God as to the truth of what we declare, most foolish is it to deny that the Apostle used here an oath. He did not notwithstanding transgress the prohibition of Christ.

It hence appears that it was not Christ's design (as the superstitious Anabaptists dream) to abolish oaths altogether, but on the contrary to call attention to the due observance of the law; and the law, allowing an oath, only condemns perjury and needless swearing. If then we would use an oath aright, let us imitate the seriousness and the reverent manner exhibited by the Apostles ; and that you may understand what it is, know that God is so called as a witness, that he is also appealed to as an avenger, in case we deceive ; which Paul expresses elsewhere in these words, " God is a witness to my soul." (2 Cor. i. 23.)[1]

Whom I serve with my spirit, &c. It is usual with profane men, who trifle with God, to pretend his name, no less boldly than presumptuously ; but the Apostle here speaks of his own piety, in order to gain credit ; and those, in whom the fear of God and reverence for his name prevail, will dread to swear falsely. At the same time, he sets his own spirit in opposition to the outward mask of religion ; for as many falsely pretend to be the worshippers of God, and outwardly appear to be so, he testifies that he, from the heart, served God.[2] It may be also that he alluded to the ancient ceremonies, in which alone the Jews thought the worship of God consisted. He then intimates, that though he retained not observance of these, he was yet a sincere worshipper of God, according to what he says in Phil. iii. 3, " We are the true circumcision, who in spirit serve God, and glory not in the flesh." He then glories that he served God with sincere devotion of heart, which is true religion and approved worship.

But it was expedient, as I have said, in order that his oath might attain more credit, that Paul should declare his piety towards God ; for perjury is a sport to the ungodly, while the pious dread it more than a thousand deaths ; inasmuch as it cannot be, but that where there is a real fear of God, there must be also a reverence for his name. It is then the same thing, as though Paul had said, that he knew how much sacredness and sincerity belonged to an oath, and that

[1] The passage in Matt. v. 33-37, has been often wholly misunderstood. That oaths in common conversation are alone prohibited, is quite evident from what the passage itself contains. In solemn oaths there was no swearing by " heaven," or by " God's throne," or by " the earth," or by " Jerusalem," or by " the head." Such forms were only used in conversation, as similar ones are still used : and these kinds of swearing are alone condemned by our Saviour.—*Ed.*

[2] " *Sincerè et verè*—sincerely and truly," *Wolfius;* " not merely externally, but cordially," *Hodge.*

he did not rashly appeal to God as a witness, as the profane are wont to do. And thus, by his own example, he teaches us, that whenever we swear, we ought to give such evidence of piety, that the name of God, which we use in our declarations, may retain its sacredness. And further, he gives a proof, even by his own ministry, that he worshipped not God feignedly; for it was the fullest evidence, that he was a man devoted to God's glory, when he denied himself, and hesitated not to undergo all the hardships of reproach, poverty, and hatred, and even the peril of death, in advancing the kingdom of God.[1]

Some take this clause, as though Paul intended to recommend that worship which he said he rendered to God, on this account,—because it corresponded with what the gospel prescribes. It is indeed certain that spiritual worship is enjoined on us in the gospel; but the former interpretation is far the most suitable,—that he devoted his service to God in preaching the gospel. He, however, makes at the same time a difference between himself and hypocrites, who have something else in view rather than to serve God; for ambition, or some such thing, influences most men; and it is far from being the case, that all engage cordially and faithfully in this office. The meaning is, that Paul performed sincerely the office of teaching; for what he says of his own devotion he applies to this subject.

But we hence gather a profitable doctrine; for it ought to add no little encouragement to the ministers of the gospel, when they hear that, in preaching the gospel, they render an acceptable and a valuable service to God. What, indeed, is there to prevent them from regarding it an excellent service, when they know that their labour is pleasing to God, and is approved by him? Moreover, he calls it *the gospel of the Son* of God; for Christ is in it made known, who has been appointed by the Father for this end,—that he, being glorified, should also glorify the Father.

---

[1] ’ἐν τῷ εὐαγγελίῳ τοῦ υἱοῦ αὐτοῦ, " by the preaching of the gospel, &c.," *Stuart.* " In predicando evangelio—in preaching the gospel," *Beza.* " I serve God, not in teaching legal rites, but a much more celestial doctrine," *Grotius.*

That continually, &c. He still further sets forth the ardour of his love by his very constancy in praying for them. It was, indeed, a strong evidence, when he poured forth no prayers to the Lord without making mention of them. That the meaning may be clearer, I render παντοτε, " always;" as though it was said, " In all my prayers," or, " whenever I address God in prayer, I join a mention of you."[1] Now he speaks not of every kind of calling on God, but of those prayers to which the saints, being at liberty, and laying aside all cares, apply their whole attention to the work; for he might have often expressed suddenly this or that wish, when the Romans did not come into his mind; but whenever he had previously intended, and, as it were, prepared himself to offer up prayers to God, among others he remembered them. He then speaks peculiarly of those prayers, for which the saints deliberately prepare themselves; as we find to have been the case with our Lord himself, who, for this purpose, sought retirement. He at the same time intimates how frequently, or rather, how unceasingly he was engaged in such prayers, since he says that he prayed continually.

10. *Requesting, if by any means*, &c. As it is not probable that we from the heart study his benefit, whom we are not ready to assist by our labours, he now adds, after having said that he was anxious for their welfare, that he showed by another proof his love to them, as before God, even by requesting that he might be able to advance their interest. That you may, therefore, perceive the full meaning, read the words as though the word *also* were inserted, *requesting also, if by any means*, &c. By saying, *A prosperous journey*

---

[1] The order of the words, as arranged by *Calvin*, is better than that of our version; he connects "always in my prayers," or, "in all my prayers," with "requesting." The simpler rendering would be as follows:—
9. My witness indeed is God, whom I serve with my spirit in the
10. gospel of his Son, that I unceasingly make mention of you, always requesting in my prayers, that by some means now at length I may, through the will of God, have a free course to come to you.
"In the gospel," may either mean "according to the gospel," or, "in preaching the gospel." *Hodge* prefers the first. The particle ͒ clearly means "that" in this connection. That it is used in this sense in the New Testament there can be no doubt; see Acts xxvi. 8, 23; Heb. vii. 15.

by the will of God, he shows, not only that he looked to the Lord's favour for success in his journey, but that he deemed his journey prosperous, if it was approved by the Lord. According to this model ought all our wishes to be formed.

11. *For I greatly desire to see you.* He might, indeed, while absent, have confirmed their faith by his doctrine; but as advice is better taken from one present, he had a desire to be with them. But he explains what his object was, and shows that he wished to undertake the toil of a journey, not for his own, but for their advantage.—*Spiritual gifts*[1] he calls those which he possessed, being either those of doctrine, or of exhortation, or of prophecy, which he knew had come to him through God's favour. He has here strikingly pointed out the use of gifts by the word, *imparting :* for different gifts are distributed to each individual, that all may in kindness mutually assist one another, and transfer to others what each one possesses. See chap. xii. 3; and 1 Cor. xii. 11.

To confirm you, &c. He modifies what he had said of imparting, lest he should seem to regard them such as were yet to be instructed in the first elements of religion, as though they were not hitherto rightly taught in Christ. He then says, that he wished so to lend his aid to them, that they who had for the most part made a proficiency, might be further assisted : for a confirmation is what we all want, until Christ be fully formed in us. (Eph. iv. 13.)

12. Being not satisfied with this modest statement, he qualifies it, and shows, that he did not so occupy the place of a teacher, but that he wished to learn also from them; as though he said, "I desire so to confirm you according to the measure of grace conferred on me, that your example

---

[1] The words, τι χάρισμα πνευματικὸν, some spiritual gift, or benefit, seem to be of a general import. Some, such as *Chalmers* and *Haldane,* have supposed that a miraculous power is intended, which the Apostles alone conveyed, such as the power of speaking with tongues : but most Commentators agree in the view here given. The phrase is not found in any other place : χάρισμα, in the plural number, is used to designate miraculous powers, 1 Cor. xii. 9; and τὰ πνευματικά mean the same, 1 Cor. xiv. 1. But here, no doubt, the expression includes any gift or benefit, whether miraculous or ordinary, which the Apostle might have been made the means of conveying.—*Ed.*

may also add courage (*alacritatem*—alacrity) to my faith, and that we may thus mutually benefit one another."

See to what degree of modesty his pious heart submitted itself, so that he disdained not to seek confirmation from unexperienced beginners: nor did he speak dissemblingly, for there is no one so void of gifts in the Church of Christ, who is not able to contribute something to our benefit: but we are hindered by our envy and by our pride from gathering such fruit from one another. Such is our high-mindedness, such is the inebriety produced by vain reputation, that despising and disregarding others, every one thinks that he possesses what is abundantly sufficient for himself. I prefer to read with BUCER, *exhortation* (*exhortationem*—encouragement) rather than *consolatim*; for it agrees better with the former part.[1]

13. Now I would not have you ignorant, brethren, that oftentimes I purposed to come unto you, (but

13. Nolo verò vos ignorare, fratres, quod sæpe proposui venire ad vos, et impeditus sum hactenus, ut

---

[1] The verb is συμπαρακληθῆναι, which *Grotius* connects with ἐπιποθῶ in the preceding verse; and adds, "He softens what he had said, by showing, that he would not only bring some joy to them, but they also to him."
"Ut percipiam consolationem—that I may receive consolation," *Piscator*;
—"Ut unà recreemur—that we may be together refreshed," *Castelio*;
"Ad communem exhortationem percipiendam—in order to receive common exhortation," *Beza*; "Ut gaudium et voluptatem ex vobis percipiam —that I may receive joy and pleasure from you;" vel, "Ut mutuo solatio invicem nos erigamus atque firmemus—that by mutual comfort we may console and strengthen one another," *Schleusner*.

The verb with the prefix, συν, is only found here; but the verb παρακαλέω frequently occurs, and its common meaning is, to beseech, to exhort, to encourage, and by these means to comfort.

With regard to this passage, Professor *Stuart* says, "I have rendered the word, *comfort*, only because I cannot find any English word which will convey the full sense of the original."

"The word rendered *to comfort*," says Professor *Hodge*, "means *to invite, to exhort, to instruct, to console*, &c. Which of these senses is to be preferred here, it is not easy to decide. Most probably the Apostle intended to use the word in a wide sense, as expressing the idea, that he might be excited, encouraged, and comforted by his intercourse with his Christian brethren."—The two verses may be thus rendered:—

11. For I desire much to see you, that I may impart to you some spi-
12. ritual benefit, so that you may be strengthened: this also is *what I desire*, to be encouraged together with you, through the faith which is in both, even in you and in me.

Grotius observes, "ἐν ἀλλήλοις impropriè dixit pro *in utrisque*, in me et vobis. Dixit sic et Demosthenes, τα πρὸς ἀλλήλοις."—*Ed.*

was let hitherto,) that I might have some fruit among you also, even as among other Gentiles.

14. I am debtor both to the Greeks and to the Barbarians, both to the wise and to the unwise.

15. So, as much as in me is, I am ready to preach the gospel to you that are at Rome also.

fructum aliquem haberem in vobis, sicut et in reliquis gentibus.

14. Et Græcis et Barbaris et sapientibus et stultis debitor sum.

15. Itaque quantum in me est, paratus sum vobis quoque qui Romæ estis Evangelizare.

13. *I would not that you should be ignorant.* What he has hitherto testified—that he continually requested of the Lord that he might visit them, might have appeared a vain thing, and could not have obtained credit, had he neglected to seize the occasion when offered: he therefore says, that the effort had not been wanting, but the opportunity; for he had been prevented from executing a purpose often formed.

We hence learn that the Lord frequently upsets the purposes of his saints, in order to humble them, and by such humiliation to teach them to regard his Providence, that they may rely on it; though the saints, who design nothing without the Lord's will, cannot be said, strictly speaking, to be driven away from their purposes. It is indeed the presumption of impiety to pass by God, and without him to determine on things to come, as though they were in our own power; and this is what James sharply reprehends in chap. iv. 13.

But he says that he was *hindered:* you must take this in no other sense, but that the Lord employed him in more urgent concerns, which he could not have neglected without loss to the Church. Thus the hinderances of the godly and of the unbelieving differ: the latter perceive only that they are hindered, when they are restrained by the strong hand of the Lord, so as not to be able to move; but the former are satisfied with an hinderance that arises from some approved reason; nor do they allow themselves to attempt any thing beyond their duty, or contrary to edification.

That I might obtain some fruit, &c. He no doubt speaks of that fruit, for the gathering of which the Lord sent his Apostles, " I have chosen you, that ye may go and bring forth fruit, and that your fruit may remain." (John xv. 16.)

Though he gathered it not for himself, but for the Lord, he yet calls it his own; for the godly have nothing more as their own than the work of promoting the glory of the Lord, with which is connected all their happiness. And he records what had happened to him with respect to *other nations*, that the Romans might entertain hope, that his coming to them would not be unprofitable, which so many nations had found to have been attended with so much benefit.

14. *I am a debtor both to the Greeks and to the Barbarians*, &c. Those whom he means by the Greeks and the Barbarians, he afterwards explains by adding, *both to the wise and to the foolish;* which words Erasmus has not rendered amiss by " learned and unlearned," (*eruditos et rudes*,) but I prefer to retain the very words of Paul. He then takes an argument from his own office, and intimates that it ought not to be ascribed to his arrogance, that he thought himself in a manner capable of teaching the Romans, however much they excelled in learning and wisdom and in the knowledge of things, inasmuch as it had pleased the Lord to make him a debtor even to the wise.[1]

Two things are to be here considered—that the gospel is by a heavenly mandate destined and offered to the wise, in order that the Lord may subject to himself all the wisdom of this world, and make all variety of talents, and every kind of science, and the loftiness of all arts, to give way to the simplicity of his doctrine; and what is more, they are to be reduced to the same rank with the unlearned, and to be made so meek, as to be able to bear those to be their fellow-disciples under their master, Christ, whom they would not have deigned before to take as their scholars; and then, that the unlearned are by no means to be driven away from

---

[1] *Chalmers* paraphrases the text thus—" I am bound, or I am under obligation, laid upon me by the duties of my office, to preach both to Greeks and Barbarians, both to the wise and the unwise."

In modern phraseology, the words may be rendered, " Both to the civilized and to the uncivilized, both to the learned and to the unlearned, am I a debtor." The two last terms are not exactly parallel to the two first, as many unlearned were among the Greeks, or the civilized, as well as among the Barbarians.—*Ed*.

this school, nor are they to flee away from it through groundless fear; for if Paul was indebted to them, being a faithful debtor, he had doubtless discharged what he owed; and thus they will find here what they will be capable of enjoying. All teachers have also a rule here which they are to follow, and that is, modestly and kindly to accommodate themselves to the capacities of the ignorant and unlearned. Hence it will be, that they will be able, with more evenness of mind, to bear with many absurdities and almost innumerable things that may disgust them, by which they might otherwise be overcome. They are, however, to remember, that they are not so indebted to the foolish, as that they are to cherish their folly by immoderate indulgence.

15. *I am therefore ready*,[1] &c. He concludes what he had before said of his desire—that as he knew it to be his duty to spread the gospel among them, in order to gather fruit for the Lord, he was anxious to fulfil God's calling, as far as he was allowed to do so by the Lord.

16. For I am not ashamed of the gospel of Christ: for it is the power of God unto salvation to every one that believeth; to the Jew first, and also to the Greek.	16. Non enim pudet me Evangelii Christi, quandoquidem potentia est Dei, in salutem omni credenti, Iudæo primum, deinde Græco.
17. For therein is the righteousness of God revealed from faith to faith: as it is written, The just shall live by faith.	17. Nam justitia Dei in eo revelatur ex fide in fidem, sicut scriptum est, Justus ex fide sua vivet.

16. *I am not indeed ashamed*, &c. This is an anticipation of an objection; for he declares beforehand, that he cared not for the taunts of the ungodly; and he thus provides a way for himself, by which he proceeds to pronounce an eulogy on the value of the gospel, that it might not appear contemptible to the Romans. He indeed intimates that it *was* contemptible in the eyes of the world; and he

---

[1] τὸ κατ' ἐμὲ πρόθυμον, literally, "As to me *there is* readiness;" or, according to *Stuart*, "*There is* a readiness so far as it respects me." But, "I am ready," or, "I am prepared," conveys the meaning sufficiently, without the other words, "As much as in me is." By saying that *he* was prepared, he intimates that the event depended on another, even on God.—*Ed.*

does this by saying, that he was not ashamed of it. And thus he prepares them for bearing the reproach of the cross of Christ, lest they should esteem the gospel of less value by finding it exposed to the scoffs and reproaches of the ungodly; and, on the other hand, he shows how valuable it was to the faithful. If, in the first place, the power of God ought to be extolled by us, that power shines forth in the gospel; if, again, the goodness of God deserves to be sought and loved by us, the gospel is a display of his goodness. It ought then to be reverenced and honoured, since veneration is due to God's power; and as it avails to our salvation, it ought to be loved by us.

But observe how much Paul ascribes to the ministry of the word, when he testifies that God thereby puts forth his power to save; for he speaks not here of any secret revelation, but of vocal preaching. It hence follows, that those as it were wilfully despise the power of God, and drive away from them his delivering hand, who withdraw themselves from the hearing of the word.

At the same time, as he works not effectually in all, but only where the Spirit, the inward Teacher, illuminates the heart, he subjoins, *To every one who believeth.* The gospel is indeed offered to all for their salvation, but the power of it appears not everywhere: and that it is the savour of death to the ungodly, does not proceed from what it is, but from their own wickedness. By setting forth but one salvation he cuts off every other trust. When men withdraw themselves from this one salvation, they find in the gospel a sure proof of their own ruin. Since then the gospel invites all to partake of salvation without any difference, it is rightly called the doctrine of salvation: for Christ is there offered, whose peculiar office is to save that which was lost; and those who refuse to be saved by him, shall find him a Judge. But everywhere in Scripture the word salvation is simply set in opposition to the word destruction: and hence we must observe, when it is mentioned, what the subject of the discourse is. Since then the gospel delivers from ruin and the curse of endless death, its salvation is eternal life.[1]

---

[1] On *the power of God, Pareus* observes, that the abstract, after the

First to the Jew and then to the Greek. Under the word *Greek*, he includes all the Gentiles, as it is evident from the comparison that is made; for the two clauses comprehend all mankind. And it is probable that he chose especially this nation to designate other nations, because, in the first place, it was admitted, next to the Jews, into a participation of the gospel covenant; and, secondly, because the Greeks, on account of their vicinity, and the celebrity of their language, were more known to the Jews. It is then a mode of speaking, a part being taken for the whole, by which he connects the Gentiles universally with the Jews, as participators of the gospel: nor does he thrust the Jews from their own eminence and dignity, since they were the first partakers of God's promise and calling. He then reserves for them their prerogative; but he immediately joins the Gentiles, though in the second place, as being partakers with them.

17. *For*[1] *the righteousness of God,* &c. This is an explanation and a confirmation of the preceding clause—that the gospel is the power of God unto salvation. For if we seek salvation, that is, life with God, righteousness must be first sought, by which being reconciled to him, we may, through him being propitious to us, obtain that life which consists only in his favour; for, in order to be loved by God, we must first become righteous, since he regards unrighteousness with hatred. He therefore intimates, that we cannot obtain salvation otherwise than from the gospel, since nowhere else does God reveal to us his righteousness, which

Hebrew manner, is put for the concrete. *Power* means the instrument of God's power; that is, the gospel is an instrument rendered efficacious by divine power to convey salvation to believers: or, as *Stuart* says, "It is powerful through the energy which he imparts, and so it is called his power." *Chalmers* gives this paraphrase, "It is that, which however judged and despised as a weak instrument by the men of this world—it is that, to which he, by his own power, gives effect for the recovery of that life which all men had forfeited and lost by sin."

" The gospel is a *divine act*, which continues to operate through all ages of the world, and that not in the first place outwardly, but inwardly, in the depths of the soul, and for eternal purposes."—*Dr. Olshausen.*

[1] "The causative, γὰρ, indicates a connexion with the preceding, that the gospel is the power of God: the reason is, because by the gospel is revealed the righteousness of God, that is, made known by it is a way of righteousness and of obtaining life before God, which neither the law, nor philosophy, nor any other doctrine, was able to show."—*Pareus.*

alone delivers us from perdition. Now this righteousness, which is the groundwork of our salvation, is revealed in the gospel: hence the gospel is said to be the power of God unto salvation. Thus he reasons from the cause to the effect.

Notice further, how extraordinary and valuable a treasure does God bestow on us through the gospel, even the communication of his own righteousness. I take the righteousness of God to mean, that which is approved before his tribunal;[1] as that, on the contrary, is usually called the righteousness of men, which is by men counted and supposed to be righteousness, though it be only vapour. Paul, however, I doubt not, alludes to the many prophecies in which the Spirit makes known everywhere the righteousness of

---

[1] "The righteousness of God," δικαιοσύνη θεοῦ, has been the occasion of much toil to critics, but without reason: the very context is sufficient to show its meaning, it being what the gospel reveals, and what the gospel reveals is abundantly known from other passages. Whether we say, it is the righteousness which is approved of God, as *Calvin* says, or provided by God, or contrived by God, or imputed by God, the meaning does not materially differ, and indeed all these things, as it is evident from Scripture, are true respecting it.

There is more difficulty connected with the following words, ἐκ πίστεως εἰς πίστιν. The view which *Calvin* gives was adopted by some of the Fathers, such as *Theophylact* and *Clemens Alexandrinus;* and it is that of *Melancthon, Beza, Scaliger, Locke,* and many others. From *Poole* we find that *Chrysostom* gave this exposition, "From the obscure and inchoate faith of the Old Testament to the clear and full faith of the New;" and that *Ambrose's* exposition was the following, "From the faith or fidelity of God who promises to the faith of him who believes." But in all these views there is not that which comports with the context, nor is the construction very intelligible—" revealed from faith," what can it mean? To render the passage intelligibly, ἐκ πίστεως must be connected with δικαιοσύνη θεοῦ, as suggested by *Hammond*, and followed by *Doddridge* and *Macknight*. Then it would be, "The righteousness of God by faith, or, *which is* by faith:" this is revealed in the gospel "to faith," that is, in order that it may be believed; which is often the force of εἰς before a noun; as, εἰς τὴν ἀνομίαν—in order to do wickedness; or, εἰς ἁγιασμόν—in order to practise holiness, Rom vi. 19. *Chalmers, Stuart, Barnes,* and *Haldane* take this view. The verse may be thus rendered,—

    For the righteousness of God by faith is in it revealed in order to
    be believed, as it is written, "The just shall by faith live."

The same truth is conveyed in chap. iii. 22; and similar phraseology is found in Phil. iii. 9.

Barnes seems fully to express the import of the passage in these words, "God's plan of justifying men is revealed in the gospel, which plan is by faith, and the benefits of which plan shall be extended to all that have faith or that believe."—*Ed.*

God in the future kingdom of Christ. Some explain it as the righteousness which is freely given us by God: and I indeed confess that the words will bear this sense; for God justifies us by the gospel, and thus saves us: yet the former view seems to me more suitable, though it is not what I make much of. Of greater moment is what some think, that this righteousness does not only consist in the free remission of sins, but also, in part, includes the grace of regeneration. But I consider, that we are restored to life because God freely reconciles us to himself, as we shall hereafter show in its proper place.

But instead of the expression he used before, "to every one who believeth," he says now, *from faith;* for righteousness is offered by the gospel, and is received by faith. And he adds, *to faith:* for as our faith makes progress, and as it advances in knowledge, so the righteousness of God increases in us at the same time, and the possession of it is in a manner confirmed. When at first we taste the gospel, we indeed see God's smiling countenance turned towards us, but at a distance: the more the knowledge of true religion grows in us, by coming as it were nearer, we behold God's favour more clearly and more familiarly. What some think, that there is here an implied comparison between the Old and New Testament, is more refined than well-founded; for Paul does not here compare the Fathers who lived under the law with us, but points out the daily progress that is made by every one of the faithful.

As it is written, &c. By the authority of the Prophet Habakkuk he proves the righteousness of faith; for he, predicting the overthrow of the proud, adds this—that the life of the righteous consists in faith. Now we live not before God, except through righteousness: it then follows, that our righteousness is obtained by faith; and the verb being future, designates the real perpetuity of that life of which he speaks; as though he had said,—that it would not be momentary, but continue for ever. For even the ungodly swell with the false notion of having life; but when they say, "Peace and safety," a sudden destruction comes upon them, (1 Thess. v. 3.) It is therefore a shadow, which endures only for a moment. Faith alone is that which secures the perpetuity of life; and whence is this, except that it leads us to God, and makes our life to depend on him? For Paul would not have aptly quoted this testimony had not the meaning of the Prophet been, that we then only stand, when by faith we recumb on God: and he has not certainly ascribed life to the faith of the godly, but in as far as they, having renounced the arrogance of the world, resign themselves to the protection of God alone.[1]

He does not indeed professedly handle this subject; and hence he makes no mention of gratuitous justification: but it is sufficiently evident from the nature of faith, that this testimony is rightly applied to the present subject. Besides, we necessarily gather from his reasoning, that there is a mutual connection between faith and the gospel: for as the just is said to live by faith, he concludes that this life is received by the gospel.

We have now the principal point or the main hinge of the first part of this Epistle,—that we are justified by faith through the mercy of God alone. We have not this, indeed, as yet distinctly expressed by Paul; but from his own words it will hereafter be made very clear—that the righteousness, which is grounded on faith, depends entirely on the mercy of God.

18. For the wrath of God is revealed from heaven against all ungodliness and unrighteousness of men, who hold the truth in unrighteousness;	18. Revelatur enim ira Dei e cœlo, super omnem impietatem et injustitiam hominum, veritatem Dei injuste continentium;
19. Because that which may be known of God is manifest in them: for God hath shewed it unto them.	19. Quia quod cognoscitur de Deo manifestum est in ipsis: Deus enim illis manifestavit.

[1] Here is an instance in which Paul quotes the Old Testament, neither exactly from the Hebrew nor the Septuagint. The Hebrew is, "The just,—by his faith shall he live," צדיק באמונתו יחיה: and the Septuagint turns "his" into "my," ὁ δὲ δίκαιος ἐκ πίστεως μοῦ ζήσεται—"The just shall by my faith live;"—"by my faith," that is, according to the tenor of the passage, "by faith in me." The passage is quoted by him twice besides, in Gal. iii. 11, and in Heb. x. 38, but exactly in the same words, without the pronoun "his" or "my." His object in this, as in some similar instances, was to state the general truth contained in the passage, and not to give a strictly verbal quotation.—*Ed.*

CHAP. I. 18.   EPISTLE TO THE ROMANS.   67

20. For the invisible things of him from the creation of the world are clearly seen, being understood by the things that are made, *even* his eternal power and Godhead; so that they are without excuse:
21. Because that, when they knew God, they glorified *him* not as God, neither were thankful; but became vain in their imaginations, and their foolish heart was darkened.
22. Professing themselves to be wise, they became fools,
23. And changed the glory of the uncorruptible God into an image made like to corruptible man, and to birds, and four-footed beasts, and creeping things.

20. Si quidem invisibilia ipsius, ex creatione mundi operibus intellecta, conspiciuntur, æterna quoque ejus potentia, et divinitas; ut sint inexcusabiles.
21. Quoniam quum Deum cognovissent, non tanquam Deo gloriam dederunt, aut grati fuerunt; exinaniti sunt in cogitationibus suis, et obtenebratum est stultum cor eorum.
22. Quum se putarent sapientes, stulti facti sunt,
23. Et mutaverunt gloriam incorruptibilis Dei similitudine imaginis corruptibilis hominis, et volucrum, et quadrupedum, et serpentum.

18. *For*[1] *revealed,* &c. He reasons now by stating things of a contrary nature, and proves that there is no righteousness except what is conferred, or comes through the gospel; for he shows that without this all men are condemned: by it alone there is salvation to be found. And he brings, as the first proof of condemnation, the fact,—that though the structure of the world, and the most beautiful arrangement of the elements, ought to have induced man to glorify God, yet no one discharged his proper duty: it hence appears that all were guilty of sacrilege, and of wicked and abominable ingratitude.

[1] The connection here is not deemed very clear. *Stuart* thinks that this verse is connected, as the former one, with the 16th, and that it includes a reason why the Apostle was not ashamed of the gospel: and *Macknight* seems to have been of the same opinion, for he renders γὰρ, *besides.* In this case the revelation of wrath from heaven is that which is made by the gospel. This certainly gives a meaning to the words, "from heaven," which is hardly done by any other view. That the gospel reveals "wrath," as well as righteousness to be obtained by faith, is what is undeniable. Salvation to the believer, and condemnation to the unbeliever, is its sum and substance. The objection made by *Haldane* is of no force,—that the Apostle subsequently shows the sins of mankind as committed against the light of nature, and not against the gospel; for he seems to have brought forward the evidence from the light of nature, in order to confirm the evidence from the light of revelation. The expression is, "Revealed *is* the wrath of God," and not *has been.* See Acts xvii. 30, 31.

This is the view taken by *Turrettin;* and *Pareus* says, "There is nothing to prevent us from referring the revelation of wrath, as well as the revelation of righteousness, to the gospel."—*Ed.*

To some it seems that this is a main subject, and that Paul forms his discourse for the purpose of enforcing repentance; but I think that the discussion of the subject begins here, and that the principal point is stated in a former proposition; for Paul's object was to teach us where salvation is to be found. He has already declared that we cannot obtain it except through the gospel: but as the flesh will not willingly humble itself so far as to assign the praise of salvation to the grace of God alone, Paul shows that the whole world is deserving of eternal death. It hence follows, that life is to be recovered in some other way, since we are all lost in ourselves. But the words, being well considered, will help us much to understand the meaning of the passage.

Some make a difference between *impiety* and *unrighteousness*, and think, that by the former word is meant the profanation of God's worship, and by the latter, injustice towards men; but as the Apostle immediately refers this unrighteousness to the neglect of true religion, we shall explain both as referring to the same thing.[1] And then, *all the impiety of men* is to be taken, by a figure in language, as meaning "the impiety of all men," or, the impiety of which all men are guilty. But by these two words one thing is designated, and that is, ingratitude towards God; for we thereby offend in two ways: it is said to be ἀσέβεια, impiety, as it is a dishonouring of God; it is ἀδικία, unrighteousness, because man, by transferring to himself what belongs to God, unjustly deprives God of his glory. The word *wrath*, according to the usage of Scripture, speaking after the manner of men, means the vengeance of God; for God, in punishing, has, according to our notion, the appearance of one in wrath. It imports, therefore, no such emotion in God, but only has a reference to the perception and feeling of the sinner who is punished. Then he says that it is *revealed from heaven;* though the expression, *from heaven,* is taken by some in the sense of an adjective, as though he had said, "the wrath of the celestial God;" yet I think it more em-

---

[1] It is true that the immediate subject is the neglect of religion; but then injustice towards men is afterwards introduced, and most critics take it in this sense.—*Ed.*

phatical, when taken as having this import, " Wheresoever a man may look around him, he will find no salvation; for the wrath of God is poured out on the whole world, to the full extent of heaven."

The truth of God means, the true knowledge of God; and to *hold in* that, is to suppress or to obscure it: hence they are charged as guilty of robbery.—What we render *unjustly*, is given literally by Paul, *in unrighteousness*, which means the same thing in Hebrew: but we have regard to perspicuity.[1]

19. *Inasmuch as what may be known of God,* &c. He thus designates what it behoves us to know of God; and he means all that appertains to the setting forth of the glory of the Lord, or, which is the same thing, whatever ought to move and excite us to glorify God. And by this expression he intimates, that God in his greatness can by no means be fully comprehended by us, and that there are certain limits within which men ought to confine themselves, inasmuch as God accommodates to our small capacities what he testifies of himself. Insane then are all they who seek to know of themselves what God is: for the Spirit, the teacher of perfect wisdom, does not in vain invite our attention to what *may be known,* τὸ γνωστὸν; and by what means this is known, he immediately explains. And he said, *in them* rather than *to them,* for the sake of greater emphasis: for though the Apostle adopts everywhere Hebrew phrases, and ב, *beth,* is often redundant in that language, yet he seems here to have

---

[1] This clause, τῶν τὴν ἀλήθειαν ἐν ἀδικίᾳ κατεχόντων, is differently rendered, " Veritatem injuste detinentes—unjustly detaining the truth," *Turrettin;* " Who stifle the truth in unrighteousness," *Chalmers;* " Who hinder the truth by unrighteousness," *Stuart;* " Who wickedly oppose the truth," *Hodge;* " Who confine the truth by unrighteousness," *Macknight.*

" They rushed headlong," says *Pareus,* " into impiety against God and into injustice against one another, not through ignorance, but knowingly, not through weakness, but wilfully and maliciously: and this the Apostle expresses by a striking metaphor, taken from tyrants, who, against right and justice, by open violence, oppress the innocent, bind them in chains, and detain them in prison."

The sense given by *Schleusner* and some others, " Qui cum veri Dei cognitione pravitatem vitæ conjungunt—who connect with a knowledge of the true God a wicked life," seems not to comport with the context.

" The truth" means that respecting the being and power of God afterwards specified.—*Ed.*

intended to indicate a manifestation, by which they might be so closely pressed, that they could not evade ; for every one of us undoubtedly finds it to be engraven on his own heart.[1] By saying, that *God has made it manifest*, he means, that man was created to be a spectator of this formed world, and that eyes were given him, that he might, by looking on so beautiful a picture, be led up to the Author himself.

20. *Since his invisible things*,[2] &c. God is in himself invisible ; but as his majesty shines forth in his works and in his creatures everywhere, men ought in these to acknowledge him, for they clearly set forth their Maker: and for this reason the Apostle in his Epistle to the Hebrews says, that this world is a mirror, or the representation of invisible things. He does not mention all the particulars which may be thought to belong to God ; but he states, that we can arrive at the knowledge of his eternal power and divinity ;[3] for he who is the framer of all things, must necessarily be without beginning and from himself. When we arrive at this point, the divinity becomes known to us, which cannot exist except accompanied with all the attributes of a God, since they are all included under that idea.

---

[1] Some take ἐν αὐτοῖς, to mean *among them, i.e.*, as *Stuart* says, " in the midst of them, or before their eyes," that is, in the visible world; though many refer it with *Calvin*, to the moral sense, and that the expression is the same with " written in their hearts," in ch. ii. 15.—*Ed.*

[2] There is a passage quoted by *Wolfius* from *Aristotle* in his book *De Mundo*, which remarkably coincides with a part of this verse—" πάσῃ θνητῇ φύσει γινομένος ἀθεώρητος ἀπ' αὐτῶν τῶν ἔργων θεωρεῖται ὁ θεός—God, unseen by any mortal nature, is to be seen by the works themselves."—*Ed.*

[3] *Divinitas, θειότης*, here only, and not θεότης as in Col. i. 9. *Elsner* and others make a difference between these two words, and say, that the former means the divinity or majesty of God, and the latter his nature or being. There seems to be the idea of goodness conveyed in the word, θειότης : for in the following verse there are two things laid to the charge of the Gentiles which bear a reference to the two things said here— they did not glorify him as God, and they were not thankful. He made himself known by *power* as God, and by the beneficent exercise of that power, he had laid a claim to the gratitude of his creatures. See Acts xiv. 15; and xvii. 25, 27.

Venema, in his note on this passage, shows, that goodness was regarded by many of the heathens as the primary attribute of Deity. Among the Greeks, *goodness—τὸ ἀγαθὸν*, was the expression by which the Supreme Being was distinguished. And it appears evident from the context that the Apostle included this idea especially in the word θειότης.—*Ed.*

So that they are inexcusable. It hence clearly appears what the consequence is of having this evidence—that men cannot allege any thing before God's tribunal for the purpose of showing that they are not justly condemned. Yet let this difference be remembered, that the manifestation of God, by which he makes his glory known in his creation, is, with regard to the light itself, sufficiently clear ; but that on account of our blindness, it is not found to be sufficient. We are not however so blind, that we can plead our ignorance as an excuse for our perverseness. We conceive that there is a Deity; and then we conclude, that whoever he may be, he ought to be worshipped: but our reason here fails, because it cannot ascertain who or what sort of being God is. Hence the Apostle in Heb. xi. 3, ascribes to faith the light by which man can gain real knowledge from the work of creation, and not without reason ; for we are prevented by our blindness, so that we reach not to the end in view; we yet see so far, that we cannot pretend any excuse. Both these things are strikingly set forth by Paul in Acts xiv. 17, when he says, that the Lord in past times left the nations in their ignorance, and yet that he left them not without witness (ἀμάρτυρον,) since he gave them rain and fertility from heaven. But this knowledge of God, which avails only to take away excuse, differs greatly from that which brings salvation, which Christ mentions in John xvii. 3, and in which we are to glory, as Jeremiah teaches us, ch. ix. 24.

21. *For when they knew God,* &c. He plainly testifies here, that God has presented to the minds of all the means of knowing him, having so manifested himself by his works, that they must necessarily see what of themselves they seek not to know—that there is some God ; for the world does not by chance exist, nor could it have proceeded from itself. But we must ever bear in mind the degree of knowledge in which they continued ; and this appears from what follows.

They glorified him not as God. No idea can be formed of God without including his eternity, power, wisdom, goodness, truth, righteousness, and mercy. His eternity appears evident, because he is the maker of all things—his power, because he holds all things in his hand and continues their existence—his wisdom, because he has arranged things in such an exquisite order—his goodness, for there is no other cause than himself, why he created all things, and no other reason, why he should be induced to preserve them—his justice, because in his government he punishes the guilty and defends the innocent—his mercy, because he bears with so much forbearance the perversity of men—and his truth, because he is unchangeable. He then who has a right notion of God ought to give him the praise due to his eternity, wisdom, goodness, and justice. Since men have not recognised these attributes in God, but have dreamt of him as though he were an empty phantom, they are justly said to have impiously robbed him of his own glory. Nor is it without reason that he adds, *that they were not thankful;*[1] for there is no one who is not indebted to him for numberless benefits: yea, even on this account alone, because he has been pleased to reveal himself to us, he has abundantly made us indebted to him. *But they became vain,*[2] &c.; that is, having forsaken the truth of God, they turned to the

---

[1] The conjunctive, ἤ, is for ὅτι, says *Piscator:* but it is a Hebraism, for 1 is sometimes used in Hebrew without the negative, which belongs to a former clause.—*Ed.*

[2] The original words are, ἐματαιώθησαν ἐν τοῖς διαλογισμοῖς αὐτῶν,—" Vani facti sunt in ratiocinationibus suis—they became vain in their reasonings," *Pareus, Beza, Turrettin,* and *Doddridge;* " They became foolish by their own reasonings," *Macknight.*

" Whatever the right reason within," says Pareus, " or the frame of the world without, might have suggested respecting God, they indulged in pleasing speculations, specious reasonings, and in subtle and frivolous conclusions; some denied the existence of a God, as Epicurus and Democritus—others doubted, as Protagoras and Diagoras—others affirmed the existence of many gods; and these, as the Platonics, maintained that they are not corporeal, while the Greeks and Romans held them to be so, who worshipped dead men, impious, cruel, impure, and wicked. There were also the Egyptians, who worshipped as gods, brute animals, oxen, geese, birds, crocodiles, yea, what grew in their gardens, garlics and onions. A very few, such as Plato and Aristotle, acknowledged one supreme Being; but even these deprived him of his providence. These, and the like, were the monstrous opinions which the Gentiles deduced from their reasonings. They became *vain,* foolish, senseless."

" And darkened became their foolish heart,"—ἡ ἀσύνετος αὐτῶν καρδία; " cor eorum intelligentia carens—their heart void of understanding;" " their unintelligent heart," *Doddridge.* Perhaps " undiscerning heart" would be the most suitable. See Math. xv. 16. Heart, after the manner of the Hebrews, is to be taken here for the whole soul, especially the mind.—*Ed.*

vanity of their own reason, all the acuteness of which is fading and passes away like vapour. And thus their foolish mind, being involved in darkness, could understand nothing aright, but was carried away headlong, in various ways, into errors and delusions. Their unrighteousness was this—they quickly choked by their own depravity the seed of right knowledge, before it grew up to ripeness.

22. *While they were thinking,* &c. It is commonly inferred from this passage, that Paul alludes here to those philosophers, who assumed to themselves in a peculiar manner the reputation of wisdom; and it is thought that the design of his discourse is to show, that when the superiority of the great is brought down to nothing, the common people would have no reason to suppose that they had any thing worthy of being commended: but they seem to me to have been guided by too slender a reason; for it was not peculiar to the philosophers to suppose themselves wise in the knowledge of God, but it was equally common to all nations, and to all ranks of men. There were indeed none who sought not to form some ideas of the majesty of God, and to make him such a God as they could conceive him to be according to their own reason. This presumption I hold is not learned in the schools, but is innate, and comes with us, so to speak, from the womb. It is indeed evident, that it is an evil which has prevailed in all ages—that men have allowed themselves every liberty in coining superstitions. The arrogance then which is condemned here is this—that men sought to be of themselves wise, and to draw God down to a level with their own low condition, when they ought humbly to have given him his own glory. For Paul holds this principle, that none, except through their own fault, are unacquainted with the worship due to God; as though he said, " As they have proudly exalted themselves, they have become infatuated through the righteous judgment of God." There is an obvious reason, which contravenes the interpretation which I reject; for the error of forming an image of God did not originate with the philosophers; but they, by their consent, approved of it as received from others.[1]

---

[1] *Calvin* is peculiar in his exposition of this verse. Most critics agree

23. *And changed,* &c. Having feigned such a God as they could comprehend according to their carnal reason, they were very far from acknowledging the true God: but devised a fictitious and a new god, or rather a phantom. And what he says is, that they *changed* the glory of God; for as though one substituted a strange child, so they departed from the true God. Nor are they to be excused for this pretence, that they believe that God dwells in heaven, and that they count not the wood to be God, but his image; for it is a high indignity to God, to form so gross an idea of his majesty as to dare to make an image of him. But from the wickedness of such a presumption none were exempt, neither priests, nor statesmen, nor philosophers, of whom the most sound-minded, even Plato himself, sought to find out some likeness of God.

The madness then here noticed, is, that all attempted to make for themselves an image of God; which was a certain proof that their notions of God were gross and absurd. And, first, they befouled the majesty of God by forming him in the likeness of a *corruptible man:* for I prefer this rendering to that of *mortal man,* which is adopted by *Erasmus;* for Paul sets not the immortality of God in opposition to the mortality of man, but that glory, which is subject to no defects, to the most wretched condition of man. And then, being not satisfied with so great a crime, they descended even to beasts and to those of the most filthy kind; by

---

in thinking that those referred to here were those reputed learned among all nations, as Beza says, " Such as the Druids of the Gauls, the soothsayers of the Tuscans, the philosophers of the Greeks, the priests of the Egyptians, the magi of the Persians, the gymnosophists of the Indians, and the Rabbins of the Jews." He considers that the Apostle refers especially to such as these, though he speaks of all men as appearing to themselves very wise in their insane devices as to the worship of God. The wiser they thought themselves, the more foolish they became. See Jer. viii. 8, 9; 1 Cor. i. 19-22.

" This is the greatest unhappiness of man, not only not to feel his malady, but to extract matter of pride from what ought to be his shame. What they deemed to be their wisdom was truly their folly."—*Haldane.*

It is a just remark of *Hodge,* " That the higher the advancement of the nations in refinement and philosophy, the greater, as a general rule, the degradation and folly of their systems of religion." As a proof he mentions the ancient Egyptians, Greeks, and Romans, as compared with the aborigines of America.—*Ed.*

which their stupidity appeared still more evident. You may see an account of these abominations in *Lactantius*, in *Eusebius*, and in *Augustine* in his book *on the city of God*.

24. Wherefore God also gave them up to uncleanness, through the lusts of their own hearts, to dishonour their own bodies between themselves:	24. Propterea tradidit illos Deus in cupiditates cordium suorum in immunditiem, ut ignominia afficerent corpora sua in seipsis:
25. Who changed the truth of God into a lie, and worshipped and served the creature more than the Creator, who is blessed for ever. Amen.	25. Qui transmutarunt veritatem ejus in mendacium et coluerunt ac venerati sunt creaturam supra Creatorem, qui est benedictus in secula: Amen.
26. For this cause God gave them up unto vile affections: for even their women did change the natural use into that which is against nature:	26. Propterea, *inquam*, tradidit illos Deus in passiones ignominiosas: ac enim feminæ ipsorum transmutarunt naturalem usum in eum qui est præter naturam:
27. And likewise also the men, leaving the natural use of the woman, burned in their lust one toward another: men with men working that which is unseemly, and receiving in themselves that recompence of their error which was meet.	27. Similiter et viri quoque, amisso naturali usu feminæ, exarserunt mutua libidine, alii in alios; masculi in masculis fœditatem perpetrantes et quam decebat erroris sui mercedem in seipsis recipientes.
28. And even as they did not like to retain God in *their* knowledge, God gave them over to a reprobate mind, to do those things which are not convenient;	28. Et quemadmodum non probaverunt Deum habere in notitia, tradidit illos Deus in reprobam mentem, ad facienda quæ non decerent;
29. Being filled with all unrighteousness, fornication, wickedness, covetousness, maliciousness; full of envy, murder, debate, deceit, malignity; whisperers,	29. Ut essent pleni omni injustitia, nequitia, libidine, avaritia, malitia; referti invidia, homicidio, contentione, dolo, perversitate; susurrones,
30. Backbiters, haters of God, despiteful, proud, boasters, inventors of evil things, disobedient to parents,	30. Obtrectatores, osores Dei, malefici, contumeliosi, fastuosi, repertores malorum, parentibus immorigeri,
31. Without understanding, covenant-breakers, without natural affection, implacable, unmerciful:	31. Intelligentiæ expertes, insociabiles, affectu humanitatis carentes, fœdifragi, sine misericordiæ sensu;
32. Who, knowing the judgment of God, that they which commit such things are worthy of death, not only do the same, but have pleasure in them that do them.	32. Qui, quum Dei judicium cognoverint, quod qui talia agunt, digni sunt morte, non tantum ea faciunt, sed assentiuntur facientibus.

24. *God therefore gave them up*, &c. As impiety is a hidden evil, lest they should still find an evasion, he shows, by a more palpable demonstration, that they cannot escape, but

must be held fast by a just condemnation, since such fruits have followed this impiety as cannot be viewed otherwise than manifest evidences of the Lord's wrath. As the Lord's wrath is always just, it follows, that what has exposed them to condemnation, must have preceded it. By these evidences then he now proves the apostacy and defection of men: for the Lord indeed does so punish those, who alienate themselves from his goodness, that he casts them headlong into various courses which lead to perdition and ruin. And by comparing the vices, of which they were guilty, with the impiety, of which he had before accused them, he shows that they suffered punishment through the just judgment of God: for since nothing is dearer to us than our own honour, it is extreme blindness, when we fear not to bring disgrace on ourselves; and it is the most suitable punishment for a reproach done to the Divine Majesty. This is the very thing which he treats of to the end of the chapter; but he handles it in various ways, for the subject required ample illustration.

What then, in short, he proves to us is this,—that the ingratitude of men to God is incapable of being excused; for it is manifest, by unequivocal evidences, that the wrath of God rages against them: they would have never rolled themselves in lusts so filthy, after the manner of beasts, had not the majesty of God been provoked and incensed against them. Since, then, the worst abominations abounded everywhere, he concludes that there existed among them evidences of divine vengeance. Now, as this never rages without reason, or unjustly, but ever keeps within the limits of what is right, he intimates that it hence appears that perdition, not less certain than just, impended over all.

As to the manner in which God gives up or delivers men to wickedness, it is by no means necessary in this place to discuss a question so intricate, (*longam*—tedious.) It is indeed certain, that he not only permits men to fall into sin, by allowing them to do so, and by conniving at them; but that he also, by his equitable judgment, so arranges things, that they are led and carried into such madness by their own lusts, as well as by the devil. He therefore adopts the word, *give up*, according to the constant usage of Scripture; which word they forcibly wrest, who think that we are led into sin only by the permission of God: for as Satan is the minister of God's wrath, and as it were the executioner, so he is armed against us, not through the connivance, but by the command of his judge. God, however, is not on this account cruel, nor are we innocent, inasmuch as Paul plainly shows, that we are not delivered up into his power, except when we deserve such a punishment. Only we must make this exception, that the cause of sin is not from God, the roots of which ever abide in the sinner himself; for this must be true, " Thine is perdition, O Israel; in me only is thy help." (Hos. xiii. 9.)[1]

By connecting the *desires* or *lusts* of man's heart with uncleanness, he indirectly intimates what sort of progeny our heart generates, when left to itself. The expression, *among themselves*, is not without its force; for it significantly ex-

---

[1] On this subject *Augustine*, as quoted by Poole, uses a stronger language than which we find here:—*Tradidit non solum per patientiam et permissionem, sed per potentiam et quasi actionem; non faciendo voluntates malas, sed eis jam malis utendo ut voluerit; multa et intra ipsos et extra ipsos operando, à quibus illi occasionem capiunt graviùs peccandi; largiendo illis admonitiones, flagella, beneficia, &c., quibus quoque eos scivit Deus ad suam perniciem abusuros*—" He delivered them up, not only by sufferance and permission, but by power, and as it were by an efficient operation; not by making evil their wills, but by using them, being already evil, as he pleased; by working many things both within and without them, from which they take occasion to sin more grievously; by giving them warnings, scourges, benefits, &c., which God knew they would abuse to their own destruction."—This is an awful view of God's proceedings towards those who wilfully resist the truth, but no doubt a true one. Let all who have the opportunity of knowing the truth tremble at the thought of making light of it.

The preposition ἐν before *desires* or lusts, is used after the Hebrew manner, in the sense of *to* or *into;* for ב *beth*, means *in*, and *to*, and also *by* or *through;* and such is the import of ἐν as frequently used by the Apostle. It is so used in the preceding verse,—ἐν ὁμοιώματι—into the likeness, &c. Then the verse would be, as Calvin in sense renders it,—

God also on this account delivered them up to the lusts of their own hearts to work uncleanness, that they might dishonour their bodies among themselves.

The import of εἰς ἀκαθαρσίαν, in order to uncleanness, is no doubt, to work uncleanness; the Apostle frequently uses this kind of expression. *Stuart* labours here unnecessarily to show, that God gave them up, *being* in their lusts, &c., taking the clause as a description of those who were given up; but the plainest meaning is that which Calvin gives.—*Ed.*

presses how deep and indelible are the marks of infamy imprinted on our bodies.

25. *Who changed,* &c. He repeats what he had said before, though in different words, in order to fix it deeper in our minds. When the truth of God is turned to a lie, his glory is obliterated. It is then but just, that they should be besprinkled with every kind of infamy, who strive to take away from God his honour, and also to reproach his name.—*And worshipped,* &c. That I might include two words in one, I have given this rendering. He points out especially the sin of idolatry; for religious honour cannot be given to a creature, without taking it away, in a disgraceful and sacrilegious manner, from God: and vain is the excuse that images are worshipped on God's account, since God acknowledges no such worship, nor regards it as acceptable; and the true God is not then worshipped at all, but a fictitious God, whom the flesh has devised for itself.[1]—What is added, *Who is blessed for ever,* I explain as having been said for the purpose of exposing idolaters to greater reproach, and in this way, "He is one whom they ought alone to have honoured and worshipped, and from whom it was not right to take away any thing, no, not even the least."

26. *God therefore gave them up,* &c. After having introduced as it were an intervening clause, he returns to what he had before stated respecting the judgment of God: and

---

[1] The words, "the truth of God," and "falsehood," or, a lie, are Hebraistic in their meaning, signifying "the true God," and "an idol." The word, which means a lie, is often in Hebrew applied to any thing made to be worshipped. See Is. xliv. 17, compared with 20; Jer. xiii. 25. *Stuart* renders the sentence, "Who exchanged the true God for a false one." *Wolfius* objects to this view, and says, "I prefer to take ἀλήθειαν τοῦ θεοῦ, *for the truth* made known by *God* to the Gentiles, of which see ver. 18, and the following verses: they *changed* this into *a lie, i.e.,* into those insane and absurd notions, into which they were led by their διαλογισμοῖς—reasonings, ver. 21." The expression—παρὰ τὸν κτίσαντα, has been rendered by *Erasmus,* "above the Creator;" by *Luther,* "rather than the Creator;" by *Beza,* "to the neglect of the Creator—præterito conditore;" and by *Grotius,* "in the place of the Creator." The two last are more consonant with the general tenor of the context; for the persons here spoken of, according to the description given of them, did not worship God at all; παρὰ is evidently used in the sense of exclusion and opposition, παρὰ τὸν νόμον —contrary to the law, Acts xviii. 13; παρὰ φύσιν—contrary to nature, ver. 26. See Gal. i. 8.—*Ed.*

he brings, as the first example, the dreadful crime of unnatural lust; and it hence appears that they not only abandoned themselves to beastly lusts, but became degraded beyond the beasts, since they reversed the whole order of nature. He then enumerates a long catalogue of vices which had existed in all ages, and then prevailed everywhere without any restraint.

It is not to the purpose to say, that every one was not laden with so great a mass of vices; for in arraigning the common baseness of men, it is proof enough if all to a man are constrained to acknowledge some faults. So then we must consider, that Paul here records those abominations which had been common in all ages, and were at that time especially prevalent everywhere; for it is marvellous how common then was that filthiness which even brute beasts abhor; and some of these vices were even popular. And he recites a catalogue of vices, in some of which the whole race of man were involved; for though all were not murderers, or thieves, or adulterers, yet there were none who were not found polluted by some vice or another. He calls those *disgraceful passions*, which are shameful even in the estimation of men, and redound to the dishonouring of God.

27. *Such a reward for their error as was meet.* They indeed deserved to be blinded, so as to forget themselves, and not to see any thing befitting them, who, through their own malignity, closed their eyes against the light offered them by God, that they might not behold his glory: in short, they who were not ashamed to extinguish, as much as they could, the glory of God, which alone gives us light, deserved to become blind at noonday.

28. *And as they chose not*, &c. There is an evident comparison to be observed in these words, by which is strikingly set forth the just relation between sin and punishment. As they chose not to continue in the knowledge of God, which alone guides our minds to true wisdom, the Lord gave them a perverted mind, which can choose nothing that is right.[1]

---

[1] There is a correspondence between the words οὐκ ἐδοκίμασαν—they did not approve, or think worthy, and ἀδόκιμον—unapproved, or worthless, which is connected with νοῦν, mind. The verb means to *try* or *prove* a

And by saying, that they chose not, (*non probasse*—approved not,) it is the same as though he had said, that they pursued not after the knowledge of God with the attention they ought to have done, but, on the contrary, turned away their thoughts designedly from God. He then intimates, that they, making a depraved choice, preferred their own vanities to the true God; and thus the error, by which they were deceived, was voluntary.

To do those things which were not meet. As he had hitherto referred only to one instance of abomination, which prevailed indeed among many, but was not common to all, he begins here to enumerate vices from which none could be found free: for though every vice, as it has been said, did not appear in each individual, yet all were guilty of some vices, so that every one might separately be accused of manifest depravity. As he calls them in the first instance *not meet*, understand him as saying, that they were inconsistent with every decision of reason, and alien to the duties of men: for he mentions it as an evidence of a perverted mind, that men addicted themselves, without any reflection, to those vices, which common sense ought to have led them to renounce.

But it is labour in vain so to connect these vices, as to make them dependent one on another, since this was not

---

thing, as metal by fire, then to *distinguish* between what is genuine or otherwise, and also to *approve* of what is good and valuable. To *approve*, or think fit or worthy, seems to be the meaning here. Derived from this verb is ἀδόκιμος, which is applied to unapproved or adulterated money,—to men *unsound*, not able to bear the test, not genuine as Christians, 2 Cor. xiii. 5,—to the earth that is *unfit* to produce fruits, Heb. vi. 8. The nearest alliteration that can perhaps be presented is the following, " And as they did not deem it worth while to acknowledge God, God delivered them up to a worthless mind," that is, a mind unfit to discern between right and wrong. *Beza* gives this meaning, " Mentem omnis judicii expertem—a mind void of all judgment." *Locke's* " unsearching mind," and *Macknight's* " unapproving mind," and *Doddridge's* " undiscerning mind," do not exactly convey the right idea, though the last comes nearest to it. It is an unattesting mind, not capable of bringing things to the test—δοκίμιον, not able to distinguish between things of the most obvious nature.

" To acknowledge God" is literally " to have God in recognition—τὸν θεὸν ἔχειν ἐν ἐπιγνώσει." *Venema* says, that this is a purely Greek idiom, and adduces passages from *Herodotus* and *Xenophon*; from the first, the following phrase, ἐν ἀλογίῃ ἔχειν—to have in contempt, *i.e.*, to contemn or despise.—*Ed.*

Paul's design; but he set them down as they occurred to his mind. What each of them signifies, we shall very briefly explain.

29. Understand by *unrighteousness,* the violation of justice among men, by not rendering to each his due. I have rendered πονηρίαν, according to the opinion of AMMONIUS, *wickedness;* for he teaches us that πονηρον, the wicked, is δραστίκον κακου, the doer of evil. The word (*nequitia*) then means practised wickedness, or licentiousness in doing mischief: but maliciousness (*malitia*) is that depravity and obliquity of mind which leads us to do harm to our neighbour.[1] For the word, πορνείαν, which Paul uses, I have put *lust,* (*libidinem.*) I do not, however, object, if one prefers to render it fornication; but he means the inward passion as well as the outward act.[2] The words *avarice, envy,* and *murder,* have nothing doubtful in their meaning. Under the word *strife,* (*contentione,*)[3] he includes quarrels, fightings, and seditions. We have rendered κακοηθείαν, *perversity,* (*perversitatem;*)[4] which is a notorious and uncommon wickedness; that is, when a man, covered over, as it were, with hardness, has become hardened in a corrupt course of life by custom and evil habit.

30. The word θεοστυγείς means, no doubt, *haters of God;* for there is no reason to take it in a passive sense, (hated of God,) since Paul here proves men to be guilty by manifest vices. Those, then, are designated, who hate God, whose justice they seem to resist by doing wrong. *Whisperers* (*susurrones*) and *slanderers* (*obtrectatores*)[5] are to be thus distinguished; the former, by secret accusations, break off

---

[1] The two words are πονηρία and κακία. Doddridge renders them "mischief and malignity." *Pareus* says that κακία is vice, opposed to τη αριστη —virtue.—*Ed.*

[2] " Πορνεία has an extended sense, comprehending *all illicit intercourse,* whether fornication, adultery, incest, or any other *venus illicita.*"—*Stuart.*

[3] Improperly rendered "debate" in our version—ἔριδος, "strife," by *Macknight,* and "contention," by *Doddridge.*—*Ed.*

[4] In our version, "malignity;" by *Macknight,* "bad disposition;" and by *Doddridge,* "inveteracy of evil habits." *Schleusner* thinks that it means here "malevolence."—*Ed.*

[5] Καταλάλους, literally gainsayers, or those who speak against others,— defamers, calumniators; rendered "revilers," by *Macknight.*—*Ed.*

the friendships of good men, inflame their minds with anger, defame the innocent, and sow discords; and the latter, through an innate malignity, spare the reputation of no one, and, as though they were instigated by the fury of evil-speaking, they revile the deserving as well as the undeserving. We have translated ὑβριστὰς, *villanous,* (*maleficos;*) for the Latin authors are wont to call notable injuries villanies, such as plunders, thefts, burnings, and sorceries; and these were the vices which Paul meant to point out here.[1] I have rendered the word ὑπερήφανους, used by Paul, *insolent,* (*contumeliosos;*) for this is the meaning of the Greek word: and the reason for the word is this,—because such being raised, as it were, on high, look down on those who are, as it were, below them with contempt, and they cannot bear to look on their equals. *Haughty* are they who swell with the empty wind of overweeningness. *Unsociable*[2] are those who, by their iniquities, unloose the bands of society, or those in whom there is no sincerity or constancy of faith, who may be called truce-breakers.

31. Without *the feelings of humanity* are they who have put off the first affections of nature towards their own relations. As he mentions the want of *mercy* as an evidence of human nature being depraved, *Augustine,* in arguing against the Stoics, concludes, that mercy is a Christian virtue.

32. *Who, knowing the judgment*[3] *of God,* &c. Though this passage is variously explained, yet the following appears to

---

[1] The three words, ὑβριστὰς, ὑπερηφάνους, and ἀλαζόνας, seem to designate three properties of a proud spirit—disdainful or insolent, haughty and vainglorious. The ὑβρισται are those who treat others petulantly, contumeliously, or insultingly. "Insolent," as given by *Macknight,* is the most suitable word. The ὑπερηφάνος is one who sets himself to view above others, the high and elevated, who exhibits himself as superior to others. The ἀλαζων is the boaster, who assumes more than what belongs to him, or promises more than what he can perform. These three forms of pride are often seen in the world.—*Ed.*

[2] *Unsociabiles*—ἀσυνθέτους. "Faithless," perhaps, would be the most suitable word. "Who adhere not to compacts," is the explanation of *Hesychius.*

To preserve the same negative according to what is done in Greek, we may render the 31st verse as follows:—

31. Unintelligent, unfaithful, unnatural, unappeasable, unmerciful.—*Ed.*

[3] *Calvin* has "justitiam" here, though "judicium" is given in the text.—*Ed.*

me the correctest interpretation,—that men left nothing undone for the purpose of giving unbridled liberty to their sinful propensities; for having taken away all distinction between good and evil, they approved in themselves and in others those things which they knew displeased God, and would be condemned by his righteous judgment. For it is the summit of all evils, when the sinner is so void of shame, that he is pleased with his own vices, and will not bear them to be reproved, and also cherishes them in others by his consent and approbation. This desperate wickedness is thus described in Scripture: "They boast when they do evil," (Prov. ii. 14.) "She has spread out her feet, and gloried in her wickedness," (Ezek. xvi. 25.) For he who is ashamed is as yet healable; but when such an impudence is contracted through a sinful habit, that vices, and not virtues, please us, and are approved, there is no more any hope of reformation. Such, then, is the interpretation I give; for I see that the Apostle meant here to condemn something more grievous and more wicked than the very doing of vices: what that is I know not, except we refer to that which is the summit of all wickedness,—that is, when wretched men, having cast away all shame, undertake the patronage of vices in opposition to the righteousness of God.

CHAPTER II.

1. Therefore thou art inexcusable, O man, whosoever thou art that judgest: for wherein thou judgest another, thou condemnest thyself; for thou that judgest doest the same things.

2. But we are sure that the judgment of God is according to truth against them which commit such things.

1. Propterea inexcusabilis es, O homo, quicunque judicas: in quo enim judicas alterum, teipsum condemnas; eadem enim facis dum judicas.

2. Novimus autem quod judicium Dei est secundum veritatem in eos qui talia agunt.

THIS reproof is directed against hypocrites, who dazzle the eyes of men by displays of outward sanctity, and even think themselves to be accepted before God, as though they had given him full satisfaction. Hence Paul, after having stated the grosser vices, that he might prove that none are just before God, now attacks saintlings (*sanctulos*) of this kind, who could not have been included in the first catalogue. Now the inference is too simple and plain for any one to wonder how the Apostle derived his argument; for he makes them *inexcusable*, because they themselves knew the judgment of God, and yet transgressed the law; as though he said, " Though thou consentest not to the vices of others, and seemest to be avowedly even an enemy and a reprover of vices; yet as thou art not free from them, if thou really examinest thyself, thou canst not bring forward any defence."

For in what thou judgest another, &c. Besides the striking resemblance there is between the two Greek verbs, κρίνειν and κατακρίνειν, (to judge and to condemn,) the enhancing of their sin ought to be noticed; for his mode of speaking is the same, as though he said, " Thou art doubly deserving of condemnation; for thou art guilty of the same vices which thou blamest and reprovest in others." It is, indeed, a well-known saying,—that they who scrutinize the life of others lay claim themselves to innocence, temperance, and all virtues; and that those are not worthy of any indulgence who allow in themselves the same things which they undertake to correct in others. *For thou, judging, doest the same things:* so it is literally; but the meaning is, " Though thou judgest, thou yet doest the same things." And he says that they *did* them, because they were not in a right state of mind; for sin properly belongs to the mind. They then condemned themselves on this account,—because, in reproving a thief, or an adulterer, or a slanderer, they did not merely condemn the persons, but those very vices which adhered to themselves.[1]

---

[1] It is confessed by most that the illative, διὸ, at the beginning of the verse, can hardly be accounted for. The inference from the preceding is not very evident. It is, in my view, an instance of Hebraism; and the reference is not to what has preceded, but to what is to come. It is not properly an illative, but it anticipates a reason afterwards given, conveyed by *for*, or, *because*. Its meaning will be seen in the following version:—

On this account, inexcusable art thou, O man, whosoever thou be who condemnest another, because, in what thou condemnest another thou condemnest thyself; for thou who condemnest doest the same things.

The verb, κρίνω, has here the idea of condemning, or of passing judgment; to *judge* is not sufficiently distinct.—*Ed.*

2. *But we know that the judgment of God,* &c. The design of Paul is to shake off from hypocrites their self-complacencies, that they may not think that they can really gain any thing, though they be applauded by the world, and though they regard themselves guiltless; for a far different trial awaits them in heaven. But as he charges them with inward impurity, which, being hid from the eyes of men, cannot be proved and convicted by human testimonies, he summons them to the tribunal of God, to whom darkness itself is not hid, and by whose judgment the case of sinners, be they willing or unwilling, must be determined.

Moreover, *the truth* of judgment will in two ways appear, because God will punish sin without any respect of persons, in whomsoever it will be found; and he will not heed outward appearances, nor be satisfied with any outward work, except what has proceeded from real sincerity of heart. It hence follows, that the mask of feigned sanctity will not prevent him from visiting secret wickedness with judgment. It is, no doubt, a Hebrew idiom; for *truth* in Hebrew means often the inward integrity of the heart, and thus stands opposed not only to gross falsehood, but also to the outward appearance of good works. And then only are hypocrites awakened, when they are told that God will take an account, not only of their disguised righteousness, but also of their secret motives and feelings.[1]

3. And thinkest thou this, O man, that judgest them which do such things, and doest the same, that thou shalt escape the judgment of God?
4. Or despisest thou the riches of his goodness, and forbearance, and long-suffering;[2] not knowing that the goodness of God leadeth thee to repentance?

3. Existimas autem, O homo, qui judicas eos qui talia faciunt, et eadem facis, quod ipse effugies judicium Dei?
4. An divitias bonitatis ipsius tolerantiæque, ac lenitatis contemnis; ignorans quod bonitas Dei te ad pœnitentiam deducit?

---

[1] "According to truth"—κατὰ ἀλήθειαν, means, according to the true state of the case, without any partiality, or according to what is just and equitable; so *Grotius* takes it. Its corresponding word in Hebrew, אמת, is sometimes rendered δικαιοσύνη. It is found opposed to ἀδικία in 1 Cor. xiii. 6. The expression here may be deemed to be the same in meaning with δικαιοκρισία— righteous judgment, in verse 5.—*Ed.*

[2] *Lenitatis*—μακροθυμίας, tarditatis ad iram. "Long-suffering" expresses

5. But, after thy hardness and impenitent heart, treasurest up unto thyself wrath against the day of wrath and revelation of the righteous judgment of God;
6. Who will render to every man according to his deeds:
7. To them who, by patient continuance in well-doing, seek for glory, and honour, and immortality, eternal life;
8. But unto them that are contentious, and do not obey the truth, but obey unrighteousness, indignation and wrath,
9. Tribulation and anguish, upon every soul of man that doeth evil, of the Jew first, and also of the Gentile:
10. But glory, honour, and peace, to every man that worketh good; to the Jew first, and also to the Gentile.

5. Sed, juxta duritiam tuam, et cor pœnitere nescium, thesaurizas tibi iram in diem iræ et revelationis justi judicii Dei;
6. Qui redditurus est unicuique secundam ipsius opera:
7. Iis quidem, qui per boni operis perseverantiam, gloriam et honorem et immortalitatem quærunt, vitam æternam;
8. Iis vero qui sunt contentiosi, ac veritati immorigeri, injustitiæ autem obtemperant, excandescentia, ira, tribulatio,
9. Et anxietas in omnem animam hominis perpetrantis malum, Iudæi primum simul et Græci:
10. At gloria et honor et pax omni operanti bonum, Iudæo primum simul et Græco.

3. *And thinkest thou, O man,* &c. As rhetoricians teach us, that we ought not to proceed to give strong reproof before the crime be proved, Paul may seem to some to have acted unwisely here for having passed so severe a censure, when he had not yet proved the accusation which he had brought forward. But the fact is otherwise; for he adduced not his accusation before men, but appealed to the judgment of conscience; and thus he deemed that proved which he had in view—that they could not deny their iniquity, if they examined themselves and submitted to the scrutiny of God's tribunal. And it was not without urgent necessity, that he with so much sharpness and severity rebuked their fictitious sanctity; for men of this class will with astonishing security trust in themselves, except their vain confidence be forcibly shaken from them. Let us then remember, that this is the best mode of dealing with hypocrisy, in order to awaken it from its inebriety, that is, to draw it forth to the light of God's judgment.

the meaning very exactly. There is here a gradation—" goodness "—$\chi\rho\eta\sigma\tau\acute{o}\tau\eta\varsigma$, benevolence, kindness, bounty;—" forbearance "—$\mathring{\alpha}\nu o\chi\grave{\eta}$, withholding, *i.e.*, of wrath;—then " long-suffering," that is, bearing long with the sins of men. " Riches " mean abundance; the same as though the expression was, " the abounding goodness," &c.—*Ed.*

That thou shalt escape, &c. This argument is drawn from the less; for since our sins are subject to the judgment of men, much more are they to that of God, who is the only true Judge of all. Men are indeed led by a divine instinct to condemn evil deeds; but this is only an obscure and faint resemblance of the divine judgment. They are then extremely besotted, who think that they can escape the judgment of God, though they allow not others to escape their own judgment. It is not without an emphatical meaning that he repeats the word *man;* it is for the purpose of presenting a comparison between man and God.

4. *Dost thou despise the riches?* &c. It does not seem to me, as some think, that there is here an argument, conclusive on two grounds, (*dilemma*,) but an anticipation of an objection: for as hypocrites are commonly transported with prosperity, as though they had merited the Lord's kindness by their good deeds, and become thus more hardened in their contempt of God, the Apostle anticipates their arrogance, and proves, by an argument taken from a reason of an opposite kind, that there is no ground for them to think that God, on account of their outward prosperity, is propitious to them, since the design of his benevolence is far different, and that is, to convert sinners to himself. Where then the fear of God does not rule, confidence, on account of prosperity, is a contempt and a mockery of his great goodness. It hence follows, that a heavier punishment will be inflicted on those whom God has in this life favoured; because, in addition to their other wickedness, they have rejected the fatherly invitation of God. And though all the gifts of God are so many evidences of his paternal goodness, yet as he often has a different object in view, the ungodly absurdly congratulate themselves on their prosperity, as though they were dear to him, while he kindly and bountifully supports them.

Not knowing that the goodness of God, &c. For the Lord by his kindness shows to us, that it is he to whom we ought to turn, if we desire to secure our wellbeing, and at the same time he strengthens our confidence in expecting mercy. If we use not God's bounty for this end, we abuse it. But yet it is not to be viewed always in the same light; for when the Lord deals favourably with his servants and gives them earthly blessings, he makes known to them by symbols of this kind his own benevolence, and trains them up at the same time to seek the sum and substance of all good things in himself alone: when he treats the transgressors of his law with the same indulgence, his object is to soften by his kindness their perverseness; he yet does not testify that he is already propitious to them, but, on the contrary, invites them to repentance. But if any one brings this objection—that the Lord sings to the deaf as long as he does not touch inwardly their hearts; we must answer—that no fault can be found in this case except with our own depravity. But I prefer rendering the word which Paul here uses, *leads*, rather than *invites*, for it is more significant; I do not, however, take it in the sense of driving, but of leading as it were by the hand.

5. *But according to thy hardness*, &c. When we become hardened against the admonitions of the Lord, impenitence follows; and they who are not anxious about repentance openly provoke the Lord.[1]

This is a remarkable passage: we may hence learn what I have already referred to—that the ungodly not only accumulate for themselves daily a heavier weight of God's judgments, as long as they live here, but that the gifts of God also, which they continually enjoy, shall increase their condemnation; for an account of them all will be required: and it will then be found, that it will be justly imputed to them as an extreme wickedness, that they had been made worse through God's bounty, by which they ought surely to have been improved. Let us then take heed, lest by unlawful use of blessings we lay up for ourselves this cursed treasure.

For the day, &c.; literally, *in the day;* but it is put for εἰς ἡμέραν, for the day. The ungodly gather now the indigna-

---

[1] What follows in the text, according to *Calvin*, is this, " et cor pœnitere nescium—and a heart that knoweth not to repent;" καὶ ἀμετανόητον καρδίαν; which *Schleusner* renders thus, " animus, qui omnem emendationem respuit—a mind which rejects every improvement." It is an impenitable rather than " an impenitent heart," that is, a heart incapable of repenting. See Eph. iv. 19.—*Ed.*

tion of God against themselves, the stream of which shall then be poured on their heads: they accumulate hidden destruction, which then shall be drawn out from the treasures of God. The day of the last judgment is called the day of wrath, when a reference is made to the ungodly; but it will be a day of redemption to the faithful. And thus all other visitations of God are ever described as dreadful and full of terror to the ungodly; and on the contrary, as pleasant and joyful to the godly. Hence whenever the Scripture mentions the approach of the Lord, it bids the godly to exult with joy; but when it turns to the reprobate, it proclaims nothing but dread and terror. "A day of wrath," saith Zephaniah, " shall be that day, a day of tribulation and distress, a day of calamity and wretchedness, a day of darkness and of thick darkness, a day of mist and of whirlwind." (Zeph. i. 15.) You have a similar description in Joel ii. 2, &c. And Amos exclaims, "Woe to you who desire the day of the Lord! what will it be to you? The day of the Lord will be darkness, and not light." (Amos v. 18.) Farther, by adding the word *revelation,* Paul intimates what this day of wrath is to be,—that the Lord will then manifest his judgment: though he gives daily some indications of it, he yet suspends and holds back, till that day, the clear and full manifestation of it; for the books shall then be opened; the sheep shall then be separated from the goats, and the wheat shall be cleansed from the tares.

6. *Who will render to every one,* &c. As he had to do with blind saintlings, who thought that the wickedness of their hearts was well covered, provided it was spread over with some disguises, I know not what, of empty works, he pointed out the true character of the righteousness of works, even that which is of account before God; and he did this, lest they should feel confident that it was enough to pacify him, if they brought words and trifles, or leaves only. But there is not so much difficulty in this verse, as it is commonly thought. For the Lord, by visiting the wickedness of the reprobate with just vengeance, will recompense them with what they have deserved: and as he sanctifies those whom he has previously resolved to glorify, he will also crown their

good works, but not on account of any merit: nor can this be proved from this verse; for though it declares what reward good works are to have, it does yet by no means show what they are worth, or what price is due to them. And it is an absurd inference, to deduce merit from reward.

7. *To them indeed, who by perseverance,* &c.; literally, *patience;* by which word something more is expressed. For it is perseverance, when one is not wearied in constantly doing good; but patience also is required in the saints, by which they may continue firm, though oppressed with various trials. For Satan suffers them not by a free course to come to the Lord; but he strives by numberless hinderances to impede them, and to turn them aside from the right way. And when he says, that the faithful, by continuing in good works, *seek glory and honour,* he does not mean that they aspire after any thing else but the favour of God, or that they strive to attain any thing higher, or more excellent: but they cannot seek him, without striving, at the same time, for the blessedness of his kingdom, the description of which is contained in the paraphrase given in these words. The meaning then is,—that the Lord will give eternal life to those who, by attention to good works, strive to attain immortality.[1]

[1] It has appeared to some difficult to reconcile this language with the free salvation which the gospel offers, and to obviate the conclusion which many are disposed to draw from this passage—that salvation is by works as well as by faith.

To this objection *Pareus* answers, that the Apostle speaks here of salvation by the works of the law, not indeed as a thing possible, which he subsequently denies, but as a declaration of what it is, that he might thereby show the necessity of a gratuitous salvation which is by faith only. And this is the view which Mr. *Haldane* takes.

But there is no need of having recourse to this hypothesis: for whenever *judgment* is spoken of even in the New Testament, it is ever represented in the same way, as being regulated in righteousness, according to the *works* of every individual. See Acts xvii. 31; 2 Cor. v. 10; Col. iii. 24, 25; Rev. xx. 12; xxii. 12.

It will be a *judgment,* conducted according to the perfect rule of justice, with no respect of persons, with no regard to individuals as such, whether high or low, much or little favoured as to outward privileges, but according to what their conduct has been, under the circumstances of their case. The rule, if heathens, will be the law of nature; if Jews, the law which had been given them. Judgment, as to its character, will be still the same to those under the gospel; it will be according to what the gospel requires.—*Ed.*

8. *But to those who are contentious,* &c. There is some irregularity in the passage; first, on account of its tenor being interrupted, for the thread of the discourse required, that the second clause of the contrast should be thus connected,—"The Lord will render to them, who by perseverance in good works, seek glory, and honour, and immortality, eternal life; but to the contentious and the disobedient, eternal death." Then the conclusion might be joined,—" That for the former are prepared glory, and honour, and incorruption; and that for the latter are laid up wrath and misery." There is another thing,—These words, *indignation, wrath, tribulation, and anguish,* are joined to two clauses in the context. However, the meaning of the passage is by no means obscure; and with this we must be satisfied in the Apostolic writings. From other writings must eloquence be learnt: here spiritual wisdom is to be sought, conveyed in a plain and simple style.[1]

[1] With regard to the construction of this passage, 6-10, it may be observed, that it is formed according to the mode of Hebrew parallelism, many instances of which we meet with even in the prose writings of the New Testament. None of the ancients, nor any of the moderns, before the time of Bishop *Lowth,* understood much of the peculiar character of the Hebrew style. All the anomalies, noticed by *Calvin,* instantly vanish, when the passage is so arranged, as to exhibit the correspondence of its different parts. It consists of two general portions; the first includes three verses, 6, 7, and 8; the other, the remaining three verses. The same things are mainly included in both portions, only in the latter there are some things additional, and explanatory, and the order is reversed; so that the passage ends with what corresponds with its beginning. To see the whole in a connected form, it is necessary to set it down in lines, in the following manner:—
  6. Who will render to each according to his works,—
  7. To those indeed, who, by perseverance in well-doing,
    Seek glory and honour and immortality,—
    Eternal life;
  8. But *there shall be* to them who are contentious,
    And obey not the truth, but obey iniquity,—
    Indignation and wrath:
Then follow the same things, the order being reversed,—
  9. Distress and anguish *shall be*
    On every soul of man that worketh evil,—
    On the Jew first, and then on the Greek;
  10. But glory and honour and peace,
    To every one who worketh good,—
    To the Jew first and then to the Greek;
  11. For there is no respect of persons with God.
The idea in the last and the first line is essentially the same. This re-

Contention is mentioned here for rebellion and stubbornness; for Paul was contending with hypocrites who, by their gross and supine self-indulgence, trifled with God. By the word *truth*, is simply meant the revealed will of God, which alone is the light of truth: for it is what belongs to all the ungodly, that they ever prefer to be in bondage to iniquity, rather than to receive the yoke of God; and whatever obedience they may pretend, yet they never cease perversely to clamour and struggle against God's word. For as they who are openly wicked scoff at the truth, so hypocrites fear not to set up in opposition to it their artificial modes of worship. The Apostle further adds, that such disobedient persons *obey* or serve iniquity; for there is no middle course, which those who are unwilling to be in subjection to the law of the Lord can take, so as to be kept from falling immediately into the service of sin. And it is the just reward of outrageous licentiousness, that those become the bondslaves of sin who cannot endure the service of God. *Indignation and wrath,* so the character of the words induces me to render them; for θυμος in Greek means what the Latins call *excandescentia*—indignation, as *Cicero* teaches us, (Tusc. 4,) even a sudden burning of anger. As to the other words I follow *Erasmus.* But observe, that of the four which are mentioned, the two last are, as it were, the effects of the two first; for they who perceive that God is displeased and angry with them are immediately filled with confusion.

We may add, that though he might have briefly described, even in two words, the blessedness of the godly and also the misery of the reprobate, he yet enlarges on both subjects, and for this end—that he might more effectually strike men

petition is for the sake of producing an impression. The character of the righteous, in the first part, is, that by persevering in doing good they seek glory, honour, and immortality; and their reward is to be eternal life: the character of the wicked is that of being contentious, disobedient to the truth, and obedient to unrighteousness; and their reward is to be indignation and wrath. The character of the first, in the second part, is, that they work good; and of the other, that they work evil: and the reward of the first is glory, honour, and peace; and the reward of the other, distress and anguish; which are the effects of indignation and wrath, as glory, honour, and peace are the fruits or the constituent parts of eternal life. It is to be observed that priority in happiness, as well as priority in misery, is ascribed to the Jew.—*Ed.*

with the fear of God's wrath, and sharpen their desire for obtaining grace through Christ: for we never fear God's judgment as we ought, except it be set as it were by a lively description before our eyes ; nor do we really burn with desire for future life, except when roused by strong incentives, (*multis flabellis incitati*—incited by many fans.)

9. *To the Jew first*, &c. He simply places, I have no doubt, the Jew in opposition to the Gentile; for those whom he calls Greeks he will presently call Gentiles. But the Jews take the precedence in this case, for they had, in preference to others, both the promises and the threatenings of the law ; as though he had said, " This is the universal rule of the divine judgment ; it shall begin with the Jews, and it shall include the whole world."

11. For there is no respect of persons with God.
12. For as many as have sinned without law, shall also perish without law; and as many as have sinned in the law, shall be judged by the law;
13. (For not the hearers of the law *are* just before God, but the doers of the law shall be justified.

11. Siquidem non est acceptio personarum apud Deum.
12. Quicunque enim sine Lege peccaverunt sine Lege etiam peribunt; quicunque vero in Lege peccaverunt per Legem judicabuntur.
13. Non enim Legis auditores justi sunt apud Deum, sed qui Legem faciunt justificabuntur.

11. *There is no respect of persons*, &c. He has hitherto generally arraigned all mortals as guilty; but now he begins to bring home his accusation to the Jews and to the Gentiles separately : and at the same time he teaches us, that it is no objection that there is a difference between them, but that they are both without any distinction exposed to eternal death. The Gentiles pretended ignorance as their defence; the Jews gloried in the honour of having the law: from the former he takes away their subterfuge, and he deprives the latter of their false and empty boasting.

There is then a division of the whole human race into two classes; for God had separated the Jews from all the rest, but the condition of all the Gentiles was the same. He now teaches us, that this difference is no reason why both should not be involved in the same guilt. But the word *person* is taken in Scripture for all outward things, which are wont to be regarded as possessing any value or esteem. When therefore thou readest, that God is no respecter of persons, understand that what he regards is purity of heart or inward integrity; and that he hath no respect for those things which are wont to be highly valued by men, such as kindred, country, dignity, wealth, and similar things; so that respect of persons is to be here taken for the distinction or the difference there is between one nation and another.[1] But if any hence objects and says, " That then there is no such thing as the gratuitous election of God;" it may be answered, That there is a twofold acceptation of men before God; the first, when he chooses and calls us from nothing, through gratuitous goodness, as there is nothing in our nature which can be approved by him; the second, when after having regenerated us, he confers on us his gifts, and shows favour to the image of his Son which he recognises in us.

12. *Whosoever have sinned without law,*[2] &c. In the former part of this section he assails the Gentiles; though no Moses was given them to publish and to ratify a law from the Lord, he yet denies this omission to be a reason why they deserved

---

[1] The word προσωποληψία, respect of persons, is found in three other places, Eph. vi. 9; Col. iii. 25; and James ii. 1; and in these the reference is to conditions in life. In Acts x. 34, the word is in another form, προσωπολήπτης, a respecter of persons, and as a verb in James ii. 9. The full phrase is πρόσωπον λαμβάνω, as found in Luke xx. 21, and Gal. ii. 6. It is a phrase peculiar to the Hebrew language, and means literally, to *lift up* or *regard faces*, that is, *persons*, נשׂא פנים. See Lev. xix. 15; Deut. x. 17; 2 Chron. xix. 7.

An argument has been hence taken to oppose the doctrine of election; but this is to apply to a particular thing what belongs entirely and exclusively to another. This belongs to the administration of justice, but election is the exercise of mercy. Even *Grotius* admits, that God manifests a difference in bestowing benefits, but not in exercising judgment. Indeed, in the present instance, with regard to the subject handled by the Apostle, there was a manifest difference; the Gentile had only the law of nature, but the Jew had a revealed law. Yet when brought to judgment there was to be no respect of persons; each was to be judged impartially according to the circumstances of his condition. And further, election does not proceed on the principle of showing respect of persons, that is, of regarding men according to their privileges or outward circumstances, or kindred or relation in life, or any thing in man; but its sole and exclusive ground or reason is the good pleasure of God.—*Ed.*

[2] Ἀνόμως commonly means *unlawfully, wickedly, lawlessly;* but here, as it is evident from the context, it signifies *to be without law.* The adjective ἄνομος is also used once in this sense in 1 Cor. ix. 21.—*Ed.*

not the just sentence of death for their sins; as though he had said—that the knowledge of a written law was not necessary for the just condemnation of a sinner. See then what kind of advocacy they undertake, who through misplaced mercy, attempt, on the ground of ignorance, to exempt the nations who have not the light of the gospel from the judgment of God.

Whosoever have sinned under the law, &c. As the Gentiles, being led by the errors of their own reason, go headlong into ruin, so the Jews possess a law by which they are condemned;[1] for this sentence has been long ago pronounced, "Cursed are all they who continue not in all its precepts." (Deut. xxvii. 26.) A worse condition then awaits the Jewish sinners, since their condemnation is already pronounced in their own law.

13. *For the hearers of the law,* &c. This anticipates an objection which the Jews might have adduced. As they had heard that the law was the rule of righteousness, (Deut. iv. 1,) they gloried in the mere knowledge of it: to obviate this mistake, he declares that the hearing of the law or any knowledge of it is of no such consequence, that any one should on that account lay claim to righteousness, but that works must be produced, according to this saying, "He who will do these shall live in them." The import then of this verse is the following,—"That if righteousness be sought from the law, the law must be fulfilled; for the righteousness of the law consists in the perfection of works." They who pervert this passage for the purpose of building up justification by works, deserve most fully to be laughed at even by children. It is therefore improper and beyond what is needful, to introduce here a long discussion on the subject, with the view of exposing so futile a sophistry: for the Apostle only urges here on the Jews what he had mentioned, the decision of the law,—That by the law they could not be justified, except they fulfilled the law, that if they trans-

---

[1] The word "condemned" would be better in the text than "judged;" it would then more plainly correspond with the former part, where the word "perished" is used: and that it means "condemned" is evident, for those who have "sinned" are the persons referred to.—*Ed.*

gressed it, a curse was instantly pronounced on them. Now we do not deny but that perfect righteousness is prescribed in the law: but as all are convicted of transgression, we say that another righteousness must be sought. Still more, we can prove from this passage that no one is justified by works; for if they alone are justified by the law who fulfil the law, it follows that no one is justified; for no one can be found who can boast of having fulfilled the law.[1]

14. For when the Gentiles, which have not the law, do by nature the things contained in the law, these, having not the law, are a law unto themselves:	14. Quum enim Gentes, quæ Legem non habent, natura quæ Legis sunt faciant, ipsæ, Legem non habentes, sibi ipsæ sunt Lex:
15. Which shew the work of the law written in their hearts, their conscience also bearing witness, and *their* thoughts the mean while accusing or else excusing one another;	15. Quæ ostendunt opus Legis scriptum in cordibus suis, simul attestante ipsorum conscientia et cogitationibus inter se accusantibus aut etiam excusantibus,
16. In the day when God shall judge the secrets of men by Jesus Christ, according to my gospel.	16. In die qua judicabit Deus occulta hominum, secundum Evangelium meum, per Iesum Christum.

14. *For when the Gentiles,* &c. He now states what proves the former clause; for he did not think it enough to condemn us by mere assertion, and only to pronounce on us the just judgment of God; but he proceeds to prove this by reasons, in order to excite us to a greater desire for Christ, and to a greater love towards him. He indeed shows that ignorance is in vain pretended as an excuse by the Gentiles, since they prove by their own deeds that they have some rule of righteousness: for there is no nation so lost to every thing human, that it does not keep within the limits of some laws. Since then all nations, of themselves and without a monitor, are disposed to make laws for themselves, it is beyond all question evident that they have some notions of justice and rectitude, which the Greeks call preconceptions, προληψεις, and which are implanted by nature in the

---

[1] On the expression "hearers of the law," *Stuart* has these remarks,—"The Apostle here speaks of οἱ ἀκροαταὶ τοῦ νόμου, because the Jews were accustomed to *hear* the Scriptures read in public; but many of them did not individually possess copies of the sacred volume which they could read."

hearts of men. They have then a law, though they are without law: for though they have not a written law, they are yet by no means wholly destitute of the knowledge of what is right and just; as they could not otherwise distinguish between vice and virtue; the first of which they restrain by punishment, and the latter they commend, and manifest their approbation of it by honouring it with rewards. He sets nature in opposition to a written law, meaning that the Gentiles had the natural light of righteousness, which supplied the place of that law by which the Jews were instructed, so that they were a law to themselves.[1]

15. *Who show the work of the law*[2] *written*, &c.; that is, they prove that there is imprinted on their hearts a discrimination and judgment by which they distinguish between what is just and unjust, between what is honest and dishonest. He means not that it was so engraven on their will, that they sought and diligently pursued it, but that they were so mastered by the power of truth, that they could not disapprove of it. For why did they institute religious rites, except that they were convinced that God ought to be worshipped? Why were they ashamed of adultery and theft, except that they deemed them evils?

Without reason then is the power of the will deduced from this passage, as though Paul had said, that the keeping of the law is within our power; for he speaks not of the power to fulfil the law, but of the knowledge of it. Nor is the word *heart* to be taken for the seat of the affections, but

---

[1] As to the phrase, "these are a law unto themselves," *Venema* adduces classical examples,—" πᾶν τὸ βέλτιστον φαινόμενον ἔστω σοι νόμος ἀπαράβατος—Whatever seems best, let it be to thee a perpetual law."—*Epict. in Ench.*, c. 75. " τὸ μὲν ὀρθὸν νόμος ἐστὶ βασιληκός—What is indeed right, i a royal law."—*Plato in Min.*, p. 317.

The heathens themselves acknowledged a law of nature. *Turrettin* quotes a passage from a lost work of *Cicero*, retained by *Lactantius*, which remarkably coincides with the language of Paul here.—*Ed.*

[2] By the work of the law, τὸ ἔργον τοῦ νόμου, is to be understood what the law requires. The "work of God," in John vi. 29, is of the same import, that is, the work which God requires or demands; and the same word is plural in the former verse, τὰ ἔργα—" the works of God." So here, in the former verse, it is τὰ τοῦ νόμου—" the things of the law," where we may suppose ἔργα to be understood. The common expression, "the works of the law," has the same meaning, that is, such works as the law prescribes and requires.—*Ed.*

only for the understanding, as it is found in Deut. xxix. 4, "The Lord hath not given thee a heart to understand;" and in Luke xxiv. 25, "O foolish men, and slow in heart to believe."

Nor can we conclude from this passage, that there is in men a *full* knowledge of the law, but that there are only some seeds of what is right implanted in their nature, evidenced by such acts as these—All the Gentiles alike instituted religious rites, they made laws to punish adultery, and theft, and murder, they commended good faith in bargains and contracts. They have thus indeed proved, that God ought to be worshipped, that adultery, and theft, and murder are evils, that honesty is commendable. It is not to our purpose to inquire what sort of God they imagined him to be, or how many gods they devised; it is enough to know, that they thought that there is a God, and that honour and worship are due to him. It matters not whether they permitted the coveting of another man's wife, or of his possessions, or of any thing which was his,—whether they connived at wrath and hatred; inasmuch as it was not right for them to covet what they knew to be evil when done.

Their conscience at the same time attesting, &c. He could not have more forcibly urged them than by the testimony of their own conscience, which is equal to a thousand witnesses. By the consciousness of having done good, men sustain and comfort themselves; those who are conscious of having done evil, are inwardly harassed and tormented. Hence came these sayings of the heathens—"A good conscience is the widest sphere; but a bad one is the cruellest executioner, and more fiercely torments the ungodly than any furies can do." There is then a certain knowledge of the law by nature, which says, "This is good and worthy of being desired; that ought to be abhorred."

But observe how intelligently he defines conscience: he says, that reasons come to our minds, by which we defend what is rightly done, and that there are those which accuse and reprove us for our vices;[1] and he refers this process of

[1] *Calvin* seems to consider that the latter part of the verse is only an expansion or an exposition of the preceding clause respecting "conscience:"

accusation and defence to the day of the Lord; not that it will then first commence, for it is now continually carried on, but that it will then also be in operation; and he says this, that no one should disregard this process, as though it were vain and evanescent. And he has put, *in the day*, instead of, *at the day*,—a similar instance to what we have already observed.

16. *In which God shall judge the secrets of men.*[1] Most suitable to the present occasion is this periphrastic definition of judgment: it teaches those, who wilfully hide themselves in the recesses of insensibility, that the most secret thoughts and those now completely hid in the depths of their hearts, shall then be brought forth to the light. So he speaks in another place; in order to show to the Corinthians what little value belongs to human judgment, which regards only the outward action, he bids them to wait until the Lord came, who would bring to light the hidden things of dark-

---

but it seems to contain a distinct idea. The testimony of conscience is one thing, which is instantaneous, without reflection: and the thoughts or the reasonings—λογισμῶν, which alternately or mutually accuse or excuse, seem to refer to a process carried on by the mind, by which the innate voice of conscience is confirmed. This is the view taken by *Stuart* and *Barnes*, and to which *Hodge* is inclined.

Another view of the latter clause is given by *Doddridge*, *Macknight*, *Haldane*, and *Chalmers*. The last gives this paraphrase of the whole verse,—" For they show that the matter of the law is written in their hearts—both from their conscience testifying what is right and wrong in their own conduct, and from their reasonings in which they either accuse or vindicate one another."

But to regard the two clauses as referring to conscience and the inward workings of the mind, appears more consistent with the context. The Gentiles are those spoken of: God gave them no outward law, but the law of nature which is inward. Hence in the following verse he speaks of God as judging " the secrets of men," as the inward law will be the rule of judgment to the Gentiles.—*Ed.*

[1] In accordance with some of the fathers, *Jerome*, *Chrysostom*, *Theophylact*, and others, *Calvin* connects this with the immediately preceding verse: but almost all modern critics connect it with the 12th verse, and consider what intervenes as parenthetic. This is according to our version. In the 12th verse both the Gentile and the Jew are spoken of, and that with reference to judgment. In this verse the time and the character of that judgment are referred to, and its character especially as to the Gentile, as his case is particularly delineated in the parenthesis. The Apostle then, in what follows, turns to the Jew. " According to my gospel" must be understood, not as though the gospel is to be the rule of judgment to the Gentile, but as to the fact, that Christ is appointed to be the Judge of all. See Acts xvii. 31.—*Ed.*

ness, and reveal the secrets of the heart. (1 Cor. iv. 5.) When we hear this, let it come to our minds, that we are warned that if we wish to be really approved by our Judge, we must strive for sincerity of heart.

He adds, *according to my gospel*, intimating, that he announced a doctrine, to which the judgments of men, naturally implanted in them, gave a response: and he calls it *his* gospel, on account of the ministry; for the authority for setting forth the gospel resides in the true God alone; and it was only the dispensing of it that was committed to the Apostles. It is indeed no matter of surprise, that the gospel is in part called the messenger and the announcer of future judgment: for if the fulfilment and completion of what it promises be deferred to the full revelation of the heavenly kingdom, it must necessarily be connected with the last judgment: and further, Christ cannot be preached without being a resurrection to some, and a destruction to others; and both these things have a reference to the day of judgment. The words, *through Jesus Christ*, I apply to the day of judgment, though they are regarded otherwise by some; and the meaning is,—that the Lord will execute judgment by Christ, for he is appointed by the Father to be the Judge of the living and of the dead,—which the Apostles always mention among the main articles of the gospel. Thus the sentence will be full and complete, which would otherwise be defective.

17. Behold, thou art called a Jew, and restest in the law, and makest thy boast of God,	17. Ecce, tu Iudæus cognominaris, et acquiescis in Lege, et gloriaris in Deo,
18. And knowest *his* will, and approvest the things that are more excellent, being instructed out of the law;	18. Et nosti voluntatem, et probas eximia, institutus ex Lege;
19. And art confident that thou thyself art a guide of the blind, a light of them which are in darkness,	19. Confidisque teipsum esse ducem cæcorum, lumen eorum qui sunt in tenebris,
20. An instructer of the foolish, a teacher of babes, which hast the form of knowledge and of the truth in the law.	20. Eruditorem insipientium, doctorem imperitorum, habentem formam cognitionis ac veritatis in Lege:
21. Thou therefore which teachest another, teachest thou not thyself? thou that preachest a man should not steal, dost thou steal?	21. Qui igitur doces alterum, teipsum non doces; qui concionaris, non furandum, furaris;

22. Thou that sayest a man should not commit adultery, dost thou commit adultery? thou that abhorrest idols, dost thou commit sacrilege?	22. Qui dicis, non mœchandum, mœcharis; qui detestaris idola, sacrilegium perpetras;
23. Thou that makest thy boast of the law, through breaking the law dishonourest thou God?	23. Qui de Lege gloriaris, Deum per Legis transgressionem dehonestas:
24. For the name of God is blasphemed among the Gentiles through you, as it is written.[1]	24. Nomen enim Dei propter vos probro afficitur inter gentes, quemadmodum scriptum est.

17. *Behold, thou art named a Jew,* &c. Some old copies read εἰ δὲ, *though indeed;* which, were it generally received, would meet my approbation; but as the greater part of the manuscripts is opposed to it, and the sense is not unsuitable, I retain the old reading, especially as it is only a small difference of one letter.[2]

Having now completed what he meant to say of the Gentiles, he returns to the Jews; and that he might, with greater force, beat down their great vanity, he allows them all those privileges, by which they were beyond measure transported and inflated: and then he shows how insufficient they were for the attainment of true glory, yea, how they turned to their reproach. Under the name *Jew* he includes all the privileges of the nation, which they vainly pretended were derived from the law and the prophets; and so he comprehends all the Israelites, all of whom were then, without any difference, called Jews.

But at what time this name first originated it is uncertain, except that it arose, no doubt, after the dispersion.[3] *Josephus,* in the eleventh book of his Antiquities, thinks that it was taken from Judas Maccabæus, under whose auspices the liberty and honour of the people, after having for

---

[1] These texts are referred to, Is. lii. 5; Ezek. xxxvi. 20.

[2] *Griesbach* has since found a majority of MSS. in favour of this reading, and has adopted it. But the difficulty is to find a corresponding clause. There is none, except what begins in verse 21; εἰ δὲ and οὐ do not well respond, except we render the first, *though indeed,* and the other, *yet,* or *nevertheless,* somewhat in the sense of an adversative. It will admit this meaning in some passages. See Matt. xii. 12; xxvi. 54; Rom. x. 14.—*Ed.*

[3] This is not quite correct. They were called *Jews* even before the captivity, and during the captivity, but most commonly and regularly after it. The word, Jews, first occurs in 2 Kings xvi. 6. See Esth. iv. 3; Jer. xxxviii. 19; Dan. iii. 8; Ezra iv. 12; Neh. ii. 16.—*Ed.*

some time fallen, and been almost buried, revived again. Though I allow this opinion to be probable, yet, if there be some to whom it is not satisfactory, I will offer them a conjecture of my own. It seems, indeed, very likely, that after having been degraded and scattered through so many disasters, they were not able to retain any certain distinction as to their tribes; for a census could not have been made at that time, nor did there exist a regular government, which was necessary to preserve an order of this kind; and they dwelt scattered and in disorder; and having been worn out by adversities, they were no doubt less attentive to the records of their kindred. But though you may not grant these things to me, yet it cannot be denied but that a danger of this kind was connected with such disturbed state of things. Whether, then, they meant to provide for the future, or to remedy an evil already received, they all, I think, assumed the name of that tribe, in which the purity of religion remained the longest, and which, by a peculiar privilege, excelled all the rest, as from it the Redeemer was expected to come; for it was their refuge in all extremities, to console themselves with the expectation of the Messiah. However this may be, by the name of Jews they avowed themselves to be the heirs of the covenant which the Lord had made with Abraham and his seed.

And restest in the law, and gloriest in God, &c. He means not that they rested in attending to the law, as though they applied their minds to the keeping of it; but, on the contrary, he reproves them for not observing the end for which the law had been given; for they had no care for its observance, and were inflated on this account only,—because they were persuaded that the oracles of God belonged to them. In the same way they *gloried in God,* not as the Lord commands by his Prophet,—to humble ourselves, and to seek our glory in him alone, (Jer. ix. 24,)—but being without any knowledge of God's goodness, they made him, of whom they were inwardly destitute, peculiarly their own, and assumed to be his people, for the purpose of vain ostentation before men. This, then, was not the glorying of the heart, but the boasting of the tongue.

18. *And knowest his will, and approvest things excellent,* &c. He now concedes to them the knowledge of the divine will, and the approval of things useful; and this they had attained from the doctrine of the law. But there is a twofold approval,—one of choice, when we embrace the good we approve; the other of judgment, by which indeed we distinguish good from evil, but by no means strive or desire to follow it. Thus the Jews were so learned in the law that they could pass judgment on the conduct of others, but were not careful to regulate their life according to that judgment. But as Paul reproves their hypocrisy, we may, on the other hand, conclude, that excellent things are then only rightly approved (provided our judgment proceeds from sincerity) when God is attended to; for his will, as it is revealed in the law, is here appointed as the guide and teacher of what is to be justly approved.[1]

19. *And believest thyself,* &c. More is still granted to them; as though they had not only what was sufficient for themselves, but also that by which they could enrich others. He grants, indeed, that they had such abundance of learning, as that others might have been supplied.[2]

20. I take what follows, *having the form of knowledge,* as a

---

[1] There are two expositions of the words, δοκιμάζεις τὰ διαφέροντα, which may be sustained according to what the words signify in other places. The first word means to prove, or test, or examine, and also to approve; and the second signifies things which differ, or things which are excellent. "Thou provest, or, distinguishest things which differ," is the rendering of *Beza, Pareus, Doddridge,* and *Stuart:* "Thou approvest things excellent or useful," is the rendering of *Erasmus, Macknight,* and others. The first is the most suitable to the context, as knowledge, and not approval, is evidently intended, as proved by the explanatory clause which follows,— "being instructed out of the law."—*Ed.*

[2] Calvin has passed over here several clauses: they are so plain as to require no remarks, except the two last. "The instructor of the unwise —insipientium," ἀφρόνων, of such as were foolish from not understanding things rightly. "The teacher of the ignorant—imperitorum," νηπίων, babes, that is, of such as were ignorant like babes. But these and the foregoing titles, "the guide of the blind," and, "light to those in darkness," were such as the Jewish doctors assumed, and are not to be considered as having any great difference in their real meaning. There seems to be no reason to suppose, with *Doddridge* and some others, that "the blind, foolish, ignorant," were the Gentiles, for the Jews did not assume the office of teaching them. It is to be observed that Paul here takes the case, not of the common people, but of the learned—the teachers.

reason for the preceding; and it may be thus explained,—
"because thou hast the form of knowledge." For they professed to be the teachers of others, because they seemed to
carry in their breasts all the secrets of the law. The word
form is put for model (*exemplar*—pattern);[1] for Paul has
adopted μόρφωσιν and not τύπον: but he intended, I think,
to point out the conspicuous pomp of their teaching, and
what is commonly called display; and it certainly appears
that they were destitute of that knowledge which they pretended. But Paul, by indirectly ridiculing the perverted
use of the law, intimates, on the other hand, that right
knowledge must be sought from the law, in order that the
truth may have a solid basis.

21. *Thou, who then teachest another, teachest not thyself,*
&c.[2] Though the excellencies (*encomia*—commendations)

---

[1] The same word occurs only in 2 Tim. iii. 5, "μόρφωσιν εὐσεβείας—the form of godliness." It is taken here in a good sense, as meaning a sketch, a delineation, an outline, a representation, or a summary. *Chalmers* renders the words thus,—" The whole summary of knowledge and truth which is in the law." Some understand by *knowledge* what refers to morals or outward conduct, and by *truth* what is to be believed. Others regard them as an instance of Hebrewism, two substantives being put, instead of a substantive and an adjective; the phrase would then be, " true knowledge."—*Ed.*

[2] This clause, and those which follow, are commonly put in an interrogatory form, that is, as questions: but some, as *Theophylact, Erasmus,* and *Luther,* have rendered the clauses in the form here adopted. There is no difference in the meaning.

It is worthy of notice, that the Apostle, after the Hebrew manner, reverses the order as to the points he mentions; he, as it were, retrogrades, and begins to do so at this verse, the 21st. The passage may be thus rendered,—

17. Seeing then, thou art named a Jew,
   And reliest on the law, and gloriest in God,
18. And knowest his will,
   And decernest things which differ, being taught by the law,
19. And art confident that thou art
   A leader to the blind, a light to those in darkness,
20. An instructor to the foolish, a teacher to babes,
   Having the form of knowledge and of truth according to the law:
21. Yet thou, who teachest another, teachest not thyself,
   Thou, who preachest, " Steal not," stealest,
22. Thou, who sayest, " Commit no adultery," committest adultery,
   Thou who detestest idols, committest sacrilege,
23. Thou who gloriest in the law, by transgressing the law dishonourest God;
   For the name of God, as it is written, is through you blasphemed by the Gentiles.

which he has hitherto stated respecting the Jews, were such as might have justly adorned them, provided the higher ornaments were not wanting; yet as they included qualifications of a neutral kind, which may be possessed even by the ungodly and corrupted by abuse, they are by no means sufficient to constitute true glory. And hence Paul, not satisfied with merely reproving and taunting their arrogance in trusting in these things alone, employs them for the purpose of enhancing their disgraceful conduct; for he exposes himself to no ordinary measure of reproach, who not only renders useless the gifts of God, which are otherwise valuable and excellent, but by his wickedness vitiates and contaminates them. And a strange counsellor is he, who consults not for his own good, and is wise only for the benefit of others. He shows then that the praise which they appropriated to themselves, turned out to their own disgrace.

Thou who preachest, steal not, &c. He seems to have alluded to a passage in Psalm l. 16, where God says to the wicked, " Why dost thou declare my statutes, and takest my covenant in thy mouth? And thou hatest reform, and hast cast my words behind thee: when thou seest a thief, thou joinest him, and with adulterers is thy portion." And as this reproof was suitable to the Jews in old time, who, relying on the mere knowledge of the law, lived in no way better than if they had no law; so we must take heed, lest it should be turned against us at this day: and indeed it may be well applied to many, who, boasting of some extraordinary knowledge of the gospel, abandon themselves to every kind of uncleanness, as though the gospel were not a rule of life. That we may not then so heedlessly trifle with the Lord, let us remember what sort of judgment impends over such prattlers, (*logodædalis*—word-artificers,) who make a show of God's word by mere garrulity.

The 21st, and part of the 22d, refer to what is contained in the 19th and the 20th; and the latter part of the 22d to the 18th verse; and the 23d to the 17th. The latter part of the 22d helps us to fix the meaning of the latter part of the 18th; the man who hated idols and committed sacrilege proved that he did not exercise his boasted power of making a proper distinction between right and wrong. Then the man who is said, in verse 17, to rely on the law and glory in God, is charged, in the 23d verse, with the sin of dishonouring God by transgressing the law.—*Ed.*

22. *Thou who abhorrest idols,* &c. He fitly compares sacrilege to idolatry, as it is a thing of the same kind; for sacrilege is simply a profanation of the Divine Majesty, a sin not unknown to heathen poets. On this account *Ovid* (Metamor. 3,) calls *Lycurgus* sacrilegious for despising the rites of Bacchus; and in his *Fasti* he calls those sacrilegious hands which violated the majesty of Venus. But as the Gentiles ascribed the majesty of their gods to idols, they only thought it a sacrilege when any one plundered what was dedicated to their temples, in which, as they believed, the whole of religion centred. So at this day, where superstition reigns, and not the word of God, they acknowledge no other kind of sacrilege than the stealing of what belongs to churches, as there is no God but in idols, no religion but in pomp and magnificence.[1]

Now we are here warned, first, not to flatter ourselves and to despise others, when we have performed only some portions of the law,—and, secondly, not to glory in having outward idolatry removed, while we care not to drive away and to eradicate the impiety that lieth hid in our hearts.

23. *Thou who gloriest in the law,* &c. Though every transgressor dishonours God, (for we are all born for this end—to serve him in righteousness and holiness;) yet he justly imputes in this respect a special fault to the Jews; for as they

---

[1] "Sacrilege," mentioned here, is by some taken literally as meaning the robbing of God as to the sacrifices he required, and the profanation of sacred rites; "many examples of which," says *Turrettin*, "are recorded by the Prophets, and also by *Josephus*, both before and during the last war." But some extend its meaning to acts of hypocrisy and ungodliness, by which God's honour was profaned, and the glory due to him was denied. The highest sacrilege, no doubt, is to deprive God of that sincere service and obedience which he justly requires. "They caused," says *Pareus*, "the name and honour of God to be in various ways blasphemed by their wicked hypocrisy; and hence they were justly said by the Apostle to be guilty of sacrilege." He then adds, "We must notice, that idolatry is not opposed to sacrilege, but mentioned as a thing closely allied to it. Indeed all idolatry is sacrilegious. How then can the Monks, Priests, and Jesuits clear themselves from the charge of sacrilege? for they not only do not detest idolatry, being in this respect much worse than these hypocrites, but also greedily seek, like them, sacred offerings, and under the pretence of sanctity devour widows' houses, pillage the coffers of kings, and, what is most heinous, sacrilegiously rob God of his due worship and honour, and transfer them to saints." Yet the world is so blind as not to see the real character of such men!—*Ed.*

avowed God as their Lawgiver, and yet had no care to form their life according to his rule, they clearly proved that the majesty of their God was not so regarded by them, but that they easily despised him. In the same manner do they at this day dishonour Christ, by transgressing the gospel, who prattle idly about its doctrine, while yet they tread it under foot by their unbridled and licentious mode of living.

24. *For the name of God,* &c. I think this quotation is taken from Ezek. xxxvi. 20, rather than from Isaiah lii. 5; for in Isaiah there are no reproofs given to the people, but that chapter in Ezekiel is full of reproofs. But some think that it is a proof from the less to the greater, according to this import, "Since the Prophet upbraided, not without cause, the Jews of his time, that on account of their captivity, the glory and power of God were ridiculed among the Gentiles, as though he could not have preserved the people, whom he had taken under his protection, much more are ye a disgrace and dishonour to God, whose religion, being judged of by your wicked life, is blasphemed." This view I do not reject, but I prefer a simpler one, such as the following,— "We see that all the reproaches cast on the people of Israel do fall on the name of God; for as they are counted, and are said to be the people of God, his name is as it were engraven on their foreheads: it must hence be, that God, whose name they assume, is in a manner defamed by men, through their wicked conduct." It was then a monstrous thing, that they who derived their glory from God should have disgraced his holy name; for it behoved them surely to requite him in a different manner.[1]

---

[1] On this remarkable passage *Haldane* has these very appropriate, just, and striking observations,—

"The Apostle, in these verses, exhibits the most lively image of hypocrisy. Was there ever a more beautiful veil than that under which the Jew presents himself? He is a man of confession, of praise, of thanksgiving—a man, whose trust is in the law, whose boast is of God, who knows his will, who approves of things that are excellent; a man who calls himself a conductor of the blind, a light of those who are in darkness, an instructor of the ignorant, a teacher of babes; a man who directs others, who preaches against theft, against adultery, against idolatry, and to sum up the whole, a man who glories in the commandments of the Lord. Who would not say that this is an angel arrayed in human form—a star detached from the firmament, and brought nearer to enlighten the earth?

25. For circumcision verily profiteth, if thou keep the law: but if thou be a breaker of the law, thy circumcision is made uncircumcision.
26. Therefore, if the uncircumcision keep the righteousness of the law, shall not his uncircumcision be counted for circumcision?
27. And shall not uncircumcision which is by nature, if it fulfil the law, judge thee, who by the letter and circumcision dost transgress the law?
28. For he is not a Jew which is one outwardly; neither *is that* circumcision which is outward in the flesh:
29. But he *is* a Jew which is one inwardly: and circumcision *is that* of the heart, in the spirit, *and* not in the letter; whose praise *is* not of men, but of God.

25. Nam circumcisio quidem prodest, si Legem observes; quod si transgressor Legis fueris, circumcisio tua in præputium versa est.
26. Si ergo præputium justitias Legis servaverit, nonne præputium ejus pro circumcisione censebitur?
27. Et judicabit quod ex natura est præputium (si Legem servaverit) te qui per literam et circumcisionem transgressor es Legis?
28. Non enim qui est in aperto Iudæus est; nec quæ in aperto est circumcisio in carne, ea est circumcisio:
29. Sed qui est in occulto Iudæus; et circumcisio cordis in spiritu non litera; cujus laus non ex hominibus est sed ex Deo.

25. *For circumcision indeed profits,* &c. He dissipates by anticipation what the Jews might have objected in opposition to him in the defence of their own cause: for since circumcision was a symbol of the Lord's covenant, by which he had chosen Abraham and his seed as his peculiar people, they seemed not to have gloried in vain; but as they neglected what the sign signified, and regarded only the outward form, he gives this answer—That they had no reason to lay claim to any thing on account of the bare sign. The true character of circumcision was a spiritual promise, which required faith: the Jews neglected both, the promise as well as faith. Then foolish was their confidence. Hence it is, that he omits

But observe what is concealed under this mask. It is a man who is himself untaught; it is a thief, an adulterer, a sacrilegious person; in one word, a wicked man, who continually dishonours God by the transgression of his law. Is it possible to imagine a contrast more monstrous than between these fair appearances and this awful reality?"
No, certainly; but it is a contrast which still exists, with various modifications, in many instances.—It ought to be observed, that when the author calls the Jew "a man of confession, of praise, of thanksgiving," he alludes to the import of the word, Jew, in Hebrew, which is derived from a verb, which includes these ideas: and it is supposed by some, that there is an allusion in the last words of this chapter, "whose praise," &c., to what the name signifies.—*Ed.*

to state here the main use of circumcision, and proceeds to expose their gross error, as he does in his Epistle to the Galatians. And this ought to be carefully noticed; for if he were explaining the whole character and design of circumcision, it would have been inconsistent in him not to have made mention of grace and free promise: but in both instances he spoke according to what the subject he had in hand required, and therefore he only discussed that part which was controverted.

They thought that circumcision was of itself sufficient for the purpose of obtaining righteousness. Hence, speaking according to such an opinion, he gives this reply—That if this benefit be expected from circumcision, it is on this condition, that he who is circumcised, must serve God wholly and perfectly. Circumcision then requires perfection. The same may be also said of our baptism: when any one confidently relies on the water of baptism alone, and thinks that he is justified, as though he had obtained holiness by that ordinance itself, the end of baptism must be adduced as an objection; which is, that the Lord thereby calls us to holiness of life: the grace and promise, which baptism testifies (*testificatur*) and seals, (*obsignat*,) need not in this case to be mentioned; for our business is with those who, being satisfied with the empty shadow of baptism, care not for nor consider what is material (*solidum*—substantial) in it. And this very thing you may observe in Paul—that when he speaks to the faithful of signs, apart from controversy, he connects them with the efficacy and fulfilment of the promises which belong to them; but when he contends with the absurd and unskilful interpreters of signs, he omits all mention of the proper and true character of signs, and directs his whole discourse against their perverted interpretation.

Now many, seeing that Paul brings forward circumcision rather than any other part of the law, suppose that he takes away justification only from ceremonies: but the matter is far otherwise; for it always happens, that those who dare to set up their own merits against the righteousness of God, glory more in outward observances than in real goodness;

for no one, who is seriously touched and moved by the fear of God, will ever dare to raise up his eyes to heaven, since the more he strives after true righteousness, the clearer he sees how far he is from it. But as to the Pharisees, who were satisfied with imitating holiness by an outward disguise, it is no wonder that they so easily deluded themselves. Hence Paul, after having left the Jews nothing, but this poor subterfuge of being justified by circumcision, does now also take from them even this empty pretence.

26. *If then the uncircumcision,* &c. This is a very strong argument. Every thing is below its end and subordinate to it. Circumcision looks to the law, and must therefore be inferior to it: it is then a greater thing to keep the law than circumcision, which was for its sake instituted. It hence follows, that the uncircumcised, provided he keeps the law, far excels the Jew with his barren and unprofitable circumcision, if he be a transgressor of the law: and though he is by nature polluted, he shall yet be so sanctified by keeping the law, that uncircumcision shall be imputed to him for circumcision. The word *uncircumcision*, is to be taken in its proper sense in the second clause; but in the first, figuratively, for the Gentiles, the thing for the persons.

It must be added—that no one ought anxiously to inquire what observers of the law are those of which Paul speaks here, inasmuch no such can be found; for he simply intended to lay down a supposed case—that if any Gentile could be found who kept the law, his righteousness would be of more value without circumcision, than the circumcision of the Jew without righteousness. And hence I refer what follows, *And what is by nature uncircumcision shall judge thee,* &c., not to persons, but to the case that is supposed, according to what is said of the Queen of the south, that she shall come, &c., (Matt. xii. 42,) and of the men of Nineveh, that they shall rise up in judgment, &c., (Luke xi. 32.) For the very words of Paul lead us to this view—" The Gentile," he says, " being a keeper of the law, shall judge thee, who art a transgressor, though he is uncircumcised, and thou hast the literal circumcision."

27. *By the letter and circumcision*, &c. A construction[1] which means a literal circumcision. He does not mean that they violated the law, because they had the literal circumcision; but because they continued, though they had the outward rite, to neglect the spiritual worship of God, even piety, justice, judgment, and truth, which are the chief matters of the law.[2]

28. *For a Jew is not he*, &c. The meaning is, that a real Jew is not to be ascertained, either by natural descent, or by profession, or by an external symbol; that the circumcision which constitutes a Jew, does not consist in an outward sign only, but that both are inward. And what he subjoins with regard to true circumcision, is taken from various passages of Scripture, and even from its general teaching; for the people are everywhere commanded to circumcise their hearts, and it is what the Lord promises to do. The fore-skin was cut off, not indeed as the small corruption of one part, but as that of the whole nature. Circumcision then signified the mortification of the whole flesh.

29. What he then adds, *in the spirit, not in the letter*, understand thus: He calls the outward rite, without piety, the *letter*, and the spiritual design of this rite, the *spirit;* for

---

[1] *Hypallage*, substitution, a figure of speech, by which a noun or an adjective is put in a form different from its obvious import.—*Ed.*

[2] The rendering of this clause is rather obscure, " who by the letter and circumcision dost transgress the law." The preposition, διὰ, has no doubt the meaning of ἐν or σύν, as in some other passages, as in ch. iv. 11, δι' ἀκροβυστίας—in uncircumcision, and in ch. viii. 25, δι' ὑπομονῆς—in or with patience. Then the version should be, " who, *being* with, or having, the letter and circumcision, dost transgress the law." The " letter" means the written law. That this is the meaning is evident from the context. Both *Grotius* and *Macknight* give the same construction. It is better to take " letter," *i.e.*, the law, and " circumcision" separate, than to amalgamate them by a rhetorical figure, as is done by *Calvin* and others. *Hodge* justly says, that this is " more suited to the context, as nothing is said here of spiritual circumcision."

The word γράμμα, letter, has various meanings—1. What is commonly called letter, the character, Luke xxiii. 38;—2. What is written, a bond or contract, Luke xvi. 6;—3. In the plural, letters, epistles, Acts xxviii. 21;—4. The written law, as here, and in the plural, the Old Testament Scriptures, 2 Tim. iii. 15;—5. What is conveyed by writing, learning, John vii. 15; Acts xxvi. 24;—and, 6. The outward performance of the law, it being written, as opposed to what is spiritual or inward, as in the last verse of this chapter, and in 2 Cor. iii. 6.—*Ed.*

the whole importance of signs and rites depends on what is designed; when the end in view is not regarded, the letter alone remains, which in itself is useless. And the reason for this mode of speaking is this,—where the voice of God sounds, all that he commands, except it be received by men in sincerity of heart, will remain in the letter, that is, in the dead writing; but when it penetrates into the heart, it is in a manner transformed into spirit. And there is an allusion to the difference between the old and the new covenant, which Jeremiah points out in ch. xxxi. 33; where the Lord declares that his covenant would be firm and permanent when engraven on the inward parts. Paul had also the same thing in view in another place, (2 Cor. iii. 6,) where he compares the law with the gospel, and calls the former "the letter," which is not only dead but killeth; and the latter he signalizes with the title of "spirit." But extremely gross has been the folly of those who have deduced a double meaning from the "letter," and allegories from the "spirit."

Whose praise is not from men, &c. As men fix their eyes only on those things which are visible, he denies that we ought to be satisfied with what is commendable in the estimation of men, who are often deceived by outward splendour; but that we ought to be satisfied with the all-seeing eyes of God, from which the deepest secrets of the heart are not hid. He thus again summons hypocrites, who soothe themselves with false opinions, to the tribunal of God.

CHAPTER III.

1. What advantage[1] then hath the Jew? or what profit *is there* of circumcision?
2. Much every way: chiefly, because that unto them were committed the oracles of God.

1. Quæ igitur prærogativa Iudæi, aut quæ utilitas circumcisionis?
2. Multa per omnem modum; ac primùm quidem, quòd illis credita sunt oracula Dei.

1. Though Paul has clearly proved that bare circumcision

[1] "Prærogativa—prerogative," τὸ περισσὸν, rendered "pre-eminence" by *Macknight;* "præstantia—superiority" by *Beza* and *Pareus;* and "advantage" in our version, and by *Doddridge* and *Stuart.—Ed.*

brought nothing to the Jews, yet since he could not deny but that there was some difference between the Gentiles and the Jews, which by that symbol was sealed to them by the Lord, and since it was inconsistent to make a distinction, of which God was the author, void and of no moment, it remained for him to remove also this objection. It was indeed evident, that it was a foolish glorying in which the Jews on this account indulged; yet still a doubt remained as to the design of circumcision; for the Lord would not have appointed it had not some benefit been intended. He therefore, by way of an objection, asks, what it was that made the Jew superior to the Gentile; and he subjoins a reason for this by another question, *What is the benefit of circumcision?* For this separated the Jews from the common class of men; it was a partition-wall, as Paul calls ceremonies, which kept parties asunder.

2. *Much in every way,* &c.; that is, very much. He begins here to give the sacrament its own praise; but he concedes not, that on this account the Jews ought to have been proud; for when he teaches that they were sealed by the symbol of circumcision, by which they were counted the children of God, he does not allow that they became superior to others through any merit or worthiness of their own, but through the free mercy of God. If then regard be had to them as men, he shows that they were on a level with others; but if the favours of God be taken to the account, he admits that they possessed what made them more eminent than other men.

First, indeed, because intrusted to them, &c. Some think there is here an unfinished period, for he sets down what he does not afterwards complete. But the word *first* seems not to me to be a note of number, but means "chiefly" or especially,[1] and is to be taken in this sense—" Though it were but this one thing, that they have the oracles[2] of God com-

---

[1] The word πρῶτον is thus used in other places. See Matt. vi. 33; Mark vii. 27; 2 Peter i. 20.—*Ed.*

[2] Λόγια, *oracula*, mean, in Greek authors, divine responses. *Hesychius* explains it by Θέσφατα—divine dictates. The word is used four times in the New Testament. In Acts vii. 38, it means specifically the law of Moses; here it includes the whole of the Old Testament; in Heb. v. 12,

mitted to them, it might be deemed sufficient to prove their superiority." And it is worthy of being noticed, that the advantage of circumcision is not made to consist in the naked sign, but its value is derived from the word; for Paul asks here what benefit the sacrament conferred on the Jews, and he answers, that God had deposited with them the treasure of celestial wisdom. It hence follows, that, apart from the word, no excellency remained. By *oracles* he means the covenant which God revealed first to Abraham and to his posterity, and afterwards sealed and unfolded by the law and the Prophets.

Now the oracles were committed to them, for the purpose of preserving them as long as it pleased the Lord to continue his glory among them, and then of publishing them during the time of their stewardship through the whole world: they were first depositaries, and secondly dispensers. But if this benefit was to be so highly esteemed when the Lord favoured one nation only with the revelation of his word, we can never sufficiently reprobate our ingratitude, who receive his word with so much negligence or with so much carelessness, not to say disdain.

3. For what if some did not believe? shall their unbelief make the faith of God without effect?
4. God forbid: yea, let God be true, but every man a liar; as it is written, That thou mightest be justified in thy sayings, and mightest overcome when thou art judged.

3. Quid enim si quidem fuerunt increduli? num incredulitas eorum fidem Dei faciet irritam?
4. Ne ita sit; quin sit Deus verax, omnis autem homo mendax; quemadmodum scriptum est, ut justificeris in sermonibus tuis, et vincas quum judicaris.[1]

3. *What indeed if some,* &c. As before, while regarding the Jews as exulting in the naked sign, he allowed them no not even a spark of glory; so now, while considering the nature of the sign, he testifies that its virtue (*virtutem, efficacy*) is not destroyed, no, not even by their inconstancy.

and in 1 Peter iv. 11, it embraces the truths of the Gospel. The divine character of the Scriptures is by this word attested; they are the oracles of God, his dictates, or communications from him.—*Ed.*

[1] The references in the margin are the following:—Rom. ix. 6; 2 Tim. ii. 13; John iii. 33; Ps. cxvi. 11; li. 4.

As then he seemed before to have intimated that whatever grace there might have been in the sign of circumcision, it had wholly vanished through the ingratitude of the Jews, he now, anticipating an objection, again asks what opinion was to be formed of it. There is here indeed a sort of reticence, as he expresses less than what he intended to be understood; for he might have truly said that a great part of the nation had renounced the covenant of God; but as this would have been very grating to the ears of the Jews, he mitigated its severity, and mentioned only some.

Shall their unbelief, &c. Καταργεῖν is properly to render void and ineffectual; a meaning most suitable to this passage. For Paul's inquiry is not so much whether the unbelief of men neutralizes the truth of God, so that it should not in itself remain firm and constant, but whether it hinders its effect and fulfilment as to men. The meaning then is, "Since most of the Jews are covenant-breakers, is God's covenant so abrogated by their perfidiousness that it brings forth no fruit among them? To this he answers, that it cannot be that the truth of God should lose its stability through man's wickedness. Though then the greater part had nullified and trodden under foot God's covenant, it yet retained its efficacy and manifested its power, not indeed as to all, but with regard to a few of that nation: and it is then efficacious, when the grace or the blessing of the Lord avails to eternal salvation. But this cannot be, except when the promise is received by faith; for it is in this way that a mutual covenant is on both sides confirmed. He then means that some ever remained in that nation, who by continuing to believe in the promise, had not fallen away from the privileges of the covenant.

4. *But let God be true,* &c. Whatever may be the opinion of others, I regard this as an argument taken from the necessary consequence of what is opposed to it, by which Paul invalidates the preceding objection. For since these two things stand together, yea, necessarily accord, that God is true and that man is false, it follows that the truth of God is not nullified by the falsehood of men; for except he did now set these two things in opposition, the one to the other,

he would afterwards have in vain laboured to refute what was absurd, and show how God is just, though he manifests his justice by our unjustice. Hence the meaning is by no means ambiguous,—that the faithfulness of God is so far from being nullified by the perfidy and apostasy of men, that it thereby becomes more evident. "*God*," he says, "*is true*, not only because he is prepared to stand faithfully to his promises, but because he also really fulfils whatever he declares; for he so speaks, that his command becomes a reality. On the other hand, *man is false*, not only because he often violates his pledged faith, but because he naturally seeks falsehood and shuns the truth."

The first clause contains the primary axiom of all Christian philosophy; the latter is taken from Ps. cxvi. 11, where David confesses that there is nothing certain from man or in man.

Now this is a remarkable passage, and contains a consolation that is much needed; for such is the perversity of men in rejecting and despising God's word, that its truth would be often doubted were not this to come to our minds, that God's verity depends not on man's verity. But how does this agree with what has been said previously—that in order to make the divine promise effectual, faith, which receives it, is on the part of men necessary? for faith stands opposed to falsehood. This seems, indeed, to be a difficult question; but it may with no great difficulty be answered, and in this way—the Lord, notwithstanding the lies of men, and though these are hinderances to his truth, does yet find a way for it through a pathless track, that he may come forth a conqueror, and that is, by correcting in his elect the inbred unbelief of our nature, and by subjecting to his service those who seem to be unconquerable. It must be added, that the discourse here is concerning the corruption of nature, and not the grace of God, which is the remedy for that corruption.

That thou mightest be justified, &c. The sense is, So far is it that the truth of God is destroyed by our falsehood and unfaithfulness, that it thereby shines forth and appears more evident, according to the testimony of David, who says, that as he was a sinner, God was a just and righteous Judge in whatever he determined respecting him, and that he would overcome all the calumnies of the ungodly who murmured against his righteousness. By the *words* of God, David means the judgments which he pronounces upon us; for the common application of these to promises is too strained: and so the particle *that*, is not so much final, nor refers to a far-fetched consequence, but implies an inference according to this purport, "Against thee have I sinned; justly then dost thou punish me." And that Paul has quoted this passage according to the proper and real meaning of David, is clear from the objection that is immediately added, "How shall the righteousness of God remain perfect if our iniquity illustrates it?" For in vain, as I have already observed, and unseasonably has Paul arrested the attention of his readers with this difficulty, except David meant, that God, in his wonderful providence, elicited from the sins of men a praise to his own righteousness. The second clause in Hebrew is this, "And that thou mightest be pure in thy judgment;" which expression imports nothing else but that God in all his judgments is worthy of praise, how much soever the ungodly may clamour and strive by their complaints disgracefully to efface his glory. But Paul has followed the Greek version, which answered his purpose here even better. We indeed know that the Apostles in quoting Scripture often used a freer language than the original; for they counted it enough to quote what was suitable to their subject: hence they made no great account of words.

The application then of this passage is the following: Since all the sins of mortals must serve to illustrate the glory of the Lord, and since he is especially glorified by his truth, it follows, that even the falsehood of men serves to confirm rather than to subvert his truth. Though the word κρίνεσθαι, may be taken actively as well as passively, yet the Greek translators, I have no doubt, rendered it passively, contrary to the meaning of the Prophet.[1]

---

[1] Whenever there is a material agreement between the Greek and the Hebrew, we ought not to make it otherwise. If the verb κρίνεσθαι, as admitted by most critics, may be taken actively, and be thus made to agree

5. But if our unrighteousness commend the righteousness of God, what shall we say? *Is* God unrighteous who taketh vengeance? (I speak as a man)
6. God forbid: for then how shall God judge the world?
7. For if the truth of God hath more abounded through my lie unto his glory; why yet am I also judged as a sinner?
8. And not *rather*, (as we be slanderously reported, and as some affirm that we say,) Let us do evil, that good may come? whose damnation is just.

5. Quòd si injustitia nostra Dei justitiam commendat, quid dicemus? num injustus est Deus qui infert iram? Secundum hominem dico.
6. Ne ita sit: nam quomodo judicabit Deus mundum?
7. Si enim veritas Dei per meum mendacium excelluit in ejus gloriam; quid etiamnum et ego velut peccator judicor;
8. Et non (quemadmodum exprobratur nobis, et quemadmodum aiunt quidam nos dicere) Faciamus mala, ut veniant bona? quorum judicium justum est.

5. *But if our unrighteousness,* &c. Though this is a digression from the main subject, it was yet necessary for the Apostle to introduce it, lest he should seem to give to the ill-disposed an occasion to speak evil, which he knew would be readily laid hold on by them. For since they were watching for every opportunity to defame the gospel, they had, in the testimony of David, what they might have taken for the purpose of founding a calumny,—" If God seeks nothing

with the Hebrew, what reason can there be to take it in another sense? The only real difference is in one word, between νικήσης, " overcomest," and תזכה, " art clear:" but the meaning is the same, though the words are different. To overcome in judgment, and to be clear in judgment, amounts to the same thing. The parallelism of the Hebrew requires κρίνεσθαι to be a verb in the middle voice, and to have an active meaning. The two lines in Hebrew, as it is often the case in Hebrew poetry, contain the same sentiment in different words, the last line expressing it more definitely; so that to be " justified," and to be " cleared," convey the same idea; and also " in thy word," or saying—בדברך, and " in thy judgment"—בשפטך. In *many* copies both these last words are in the plural number, so that the first would be strictly what is here expressed, " in thy words," that is, the words which thou hast declared; and " in thy judgments," that is, those which thou hast announced, would be fully rendered by " when thou judgest."

Commentators, both ancient and modern, have differed on the meaning of the verb in question. *Pareus, Beza, Macknight,* and *Stuart,* take it in an active sense; while *Erasmus, Grotius, Venema,* and others, contend for the passive meaning. *Drusius, Hammond,* and *Doddridge* render it, " when thou contendest in judgment," or, " when thou art called to judgment:" and such a meaning no doubt the verb has according to Matt. v. 40, and 1 Cor. vi. 1, 6. But in this case regard must be had especially to the meaning which corresponds the nearest with the original Hebrew. Some have maintained that "in thy judgment"—בשפטך, may be rendered " in judging thee;" but this would not only be unusual and make the sen-

else, but to be glorified by men, why does he punish them, when they offend, since by offending they glorify him? Without cause then surely is he offended, if he derives the reason of his displeasure from that by which he is glorified." There is, indeed, no doubt, but that this was an ordinary, and everywhere a common calumny, as it will presently appear. Hence Paul could not have covertly passed it by; but that no one should think that he expressed the sentiments of his own mind, he premises that he assumes the person of the ungodly; and at the same time, he sharply touches, by a single expression, on human reason; whose work, as he intimates, is ever to bark against the wisdom of God; for he says not, " according to the ungodly," but " according to man," or as man. And thus indeed it is, for all the mysteries of God are paradoxes to the flesh: and at the same time it possesses so much audacity, that it fears not to oppose them, and insolently to assail what it cannot comprehend. We are hence reminded, that if we desire to become capable of understanding them, we must especially labour to become freed from our own reason, (*proprio sensu,*) and to give up ourselves, and unreservedly to submit to his

tence hardly intelligible, but also destroy the evident parallelism of the two lines. The whole verse may be thus literally rendered from the Hebrew,—

  Against thee, against thee only have I sinned;
  And the evil before thine eyes have I done;
  So that thou art justified in thy words,
  And clear in thy judgments.

The conjunction למען, admits of being rendered *so that;* see Ps. xxx. 12; Is. xli. 20; Amos ii. 7; and ὅπως in many instances may be thus rendered; see Luke ii. 35; Philem. 6; 1 Pet. ii. 9. It is what *Schleusner* designates ἐκβατικῶς, signifying the issue or the event.

 Pareus connects the passage differently. He considers the former part of the verse parenthetic, or as specifying what is generally stated in the previous verse, the third; and with that verse he connects this passage: so that the rendering of the two verses would be the following,—

  3. For my transgression I acknowledge,
   And my sin is before me continually,—
  4. (Against thee, against thee only have I sinned,
   And the evil before thine eyes have I done,)
   That thou mightest be justified in thy saying,
   And clear in thy judgment.

This is certainly more probable than what *Vatablus* and *Houbigant* propose, who connect the passage with the second verse, " Wash me thoroughly," &c. But the sense given by *Calvin* is the most satisfactory.—*Ed.*

word.—The word *wrath,* taken here for judgment, refers to punishment; as though he said, " Is God unjust, who punishes those sins which set forth his righteousness?"

6. *By no means,* &c. In checking this blasphemy he gives not a direct reply to the objection, but begins with expressing his abhorrence of it, lest the Christian religion should even appear to include absurdities so great. And this is more weighty than if he adopted a simple denial; for he implies, that this impious expression deserved to be regarded with horror, and not to be heard. He presently subjoins what may be called an indirect refutation; for he does not distinctly refute the calumny, but gives only this reply,— that the objection was absurd. Moreover, he takes an argument from an office which belongs to God, by which he proves it to be impossible,—*God shall judge the world;* he cannot then be unjust.

This argument is not derived, so to speak, from the mere power of God, but from his exercised power, which shines forth in the whole arrangement and order of his works; as though he said,—"It is God's work to judge the world, that is, to rectify it by his own righteousness, and to reduce to the best order whatever there is in it out of order: he cannot then determine any thing unjustly." And he seems to allude to a passage recorded by Moses, in Gen. xviii. 25, where it is said, that when Abraham prayed God not to deliver Sodom wholly to destruction, he spoke to this purpose,—" It is not meet, that thou who art to judge the earth, shouldest destroy the just with the ungodly: for this is not thy work, nor can it be done by thee." A similar declaration is found in Job xxxiv. 17,—" Should he who hates judgment exercise power?" For though there are found among men unjust judges, yet this happens, because they usurp authority contrary to law and right, or because they are inconsiderately raised to that eminence, or because they degenerate from themselves. But there is nothing of this kind with regard to God. Since, then, he is by nature judge, it must be that he is just, for he cannot deny himself. Paul then proves from what is impossible, that God is absurdly accused of unrighteousness; for to him peculiarly and naturally belongs the work of justly governing the world. And though what Paul teaches extends to the constant government of God, yet I allow that it has a special reference to the last judgment; for then only a real restoration of just order will take place. But if you wish for a direct refutation, by which profane things of this kind may be checked, take this, and say, "That it comes not through what unrighteousness is, that God's righteousness becomes more illustrious, but that our wickedness is so surpassed by God's goodness, that it is turned to serve an end different from that to which it tends."

7. *If indeed*[1] *the truth of God*, &c. This objection, I have no doubt, is adduced in the person of the ungodly; for it is a sort of an explanation of the former verse, and would have been connected with it, had not the Apostle, moved with indignation, broken off the sentence in the middle. The meaning of the objection is,—" If by our unfaithfulness the truth of God becomes more conspicuous, and in a manner confirmed, and hence more glory redounds to him, it is by no means just, that he, who serves to display God's glory, should be punished as a sinner."[2]

8. *And not*, &c. This is an elliptical sentence, in which a word is to be understood. It will be complete, if you read it thus,—"and why is it not rather said, (as we are reproached, &c.) that we are to do evils, that good things may

---

[1] Or, "For if"—*Si enim*—εἰ γὰρ. The particle γὰρ here gives no reason, but is to be viewed as meaning *then*, or *indeed*, *verily;* see Luke xii. 58; John ix. 30; Acts xvi. 37; Phil. ii. 27. Stuart renders it, *still*, and says, that it "points to a connection with ver. 5, and denotes a *continuance* of the same theme." Macknight often renders it by *further*, *besides*, and no doubt rightly.—*Ed.*

[2] It is remarkable how the Apostle changes his words from the third verse to the end of this, while the same things are essentially meant. His style is throughout Hebraistic. Stuart makes these just remarks, " Ἀδικία is here [ver. 5] the *generic* appellation of sin, for which a specific name, ἀπιστία, was employed in ver. 3, and ψεῦσμα, in ver. 7. In like manner the δικαιοσύνη, in ver. 5, which is a *generic* appellation, is expressed by a specific one, πίστιν, in ver. 3, and by ἀλήθεια, in ver. 7. The idea is substantially the same, which is designated by these respectively corresponding appellations. *Fidelity, uprightness, integrity*, are designated by πίστιν, δικαιοσύνην, and ἀλήθεια; while ἀπιστία, ἀδικία, and ψεύσματι, designate *unfaithfulness, want of uprightness*, and *false dealing.* All of these terms have more or less reference to the ברית, *covenant* or *compact* (so to speak) which existed between God and his ancient people."—*Ed.*

come?" But the Apostle deigns not to answer the slander; which yet we may check by the most solid reason. The pretence, indeed, is this,—" If God is by our iniquity glorified, and if nothing can be done by man in this life more befitting than to promote the glory of God, then let us sin to advance his glory!" Now the answer to this is evident,— " That evil cannot of itself produce any thing but evil; and that God's glory is through our sin illustrated, is not the work of man, but the work of God; who, as a wonderful worker, knows how to overcome our wickedness, and to convert it to another end, so as to turn it contrary to what we intend, to the promotion of his own glory." God has prescribed to us the way, by which he would have himself to be glorified by us, even by true piety, which consists in obedience to his word. He who leaps over this boundary, strives not to honour God, but to dishonour him. That it turns out otherwise, is to be ascribed to the Providence of God, and not to the wickedness of man; through which it comes not, that the majesty of God is not injured, nay, wholly overthrown.[1]

(*As we are reproached,*) &c. Since Paul speaks so reverently of the secret judgments of God, it is a wonder that his enemies should have fallen into such wantonness as to calumniate him: but there has never been so much reverence and seriousness displayed by God's servants as to be sufficient to check impure and virulent tongues. It is not then a new thing, that adversaries at this day load with so many false accusations, and render odious our doctrine, which we ourselves know to be the pure gospel of Christ, and all the angels, as well as the faithful, are our witnesses. Nothing can be imagined more monstrous than what we read here was laid to the charge of Paul, to the end, that his preach-

---

[1] *Grotius* thinks, that in the beginning of this verse there is a transposition, and that ὅτι, after the parenthesis, ought to be construed before μὴ which precedes it, and that ὅτι is for *cur*, why,—as in Mark ix. 11, and 28. The version would then be, " and why not, (as we are reproached, and as some declare that we say,) Let us do evil that good may come?" This is the rendering of *Luther*. But *Limborch* and *Stuart* consider λέγωμεν to be understood after μὴ; and the latter takes μὴ, not as a negative, but an interrogative, " and shall we say," &c. ? Amidst these varieties, the main drift of the passage remains the same.—*Ed.*

ing might be rendered hateful to the inexperienced. Let us then bear this evil, when the ungodly abuse the truth which we preach by their calumnies: nor let us cease, on this account, constantly to defend the genuine confession of it, inasmuch as it has sufficient power to crush and to dissipate their falsehoods. Let us, at the same time, according to the Apostle's example, oppose, as much as we can, all malicious subtilties, (*technis*—crafts, wiles,) that the base and the abandoned may not, without some check, speak evil of our Creator.

Whose judgment is just. Some take this in an active sense, as signifying that Paul so far assents to them, that what they objected was absurd, in order that the doctrine of the gospel might not be thought to be connected with such paradoxes : but I approve more of the passive meaning; for it would not have been suitable simply to express an approval of such a wickedness, which, on the contrary, deserved to be severely condemned ; and this is what Paul seems to me to have done. And their perverseness was, on two accounts, to be condemned,—first, because this impiety had gained the assent of their minds ; and secondly, because, in traducing the gospel, they dared to draw from it their calumny.

9. What then? are we better *than they?* No, in no wise: for we have before proved both Jews and Gentiles, that they are all under sin.

9. Quid ergo? præcellimus?[1] Nequaquam: ante enim constituimus tàm Judæos quàm Græcos, omnes sub peccato esse.

9. *What then?* He returns from his digression to his subject. For lest the Jews should object that they were deprived of their right, as he had mentioned those distinctions of honour, for which they thought themselves superior to the Gentiles, he now at length replies to the question—in what

---

[1] " Præcellimus?" προεχόμεθα; " Have we the advantage?" *Doddridge;* " Do we excel?" *Macknight;* " Have we any preference?" *Stuart.* It is thus paraphrased by *Theodoret,* τί οὖν κατέχομεν περισσόν—" What advantage, then, have we?" " Præcellimus" is the rendering of *Erasmus, Pareus,* and *Beza. Venema* says, that this verb, in the active voice only, has this meaning in Greek authors; but the context can allow it no other sense here. *Wetstein* indeed gives it a passive meaning, " an antecellimur —are we surpassed?" but it can hardly comport with the drift of the passage.—*Ed.*

respect they excelled the Gentiles. And though his answer seems in appearance to militate against what he had said before, (for he now strips those of all dignity to whom he had attributed so much,) there is yet no discord; for those privileges in which he allowed them to be eminent, were separate from themselves, and dependent on God's goodness, and not on their own merit: but here he makes inquiry as to their own worthiness, whether they could glory in any respect in themselves. Hence the two answers he gives so agree together, that the one follows from the other; for while he extols their privileges, by including them among the free benefits of God, he shows that they had nothing of their own. Hence, what he now answers might have been easily inferred; for since it was their chief superiority, that God's oracles were deposited with them, and they had it not through their own merit, there was nothing left for them, on account of which they could glory before God. Now mark the holy contrivance (*sanctum artificium*) which he adopts; for when he ascribes pre-eminency to them, he speaks in the third person; but when he strips them of all things, he puts himself among them, that he might avoid giving offence.

For we have before brought a charge, &c. The Greek verb which Paul adopts, αἰτιᾶσθαι, is properly a forensic term; and I have therefore preferred to render it, "We have brought a charge;"[1] for an accuser in an action is said to charge a crime, which he is prepared to substantiate by testimonies and other proofs. Now the Apostle had summoned all mankind universally before the tribunal of God, that he might include all under the same condemnation: and it is to no purpose for any one to object, and say that the Apostle here not only brings a charge, but more especially proves it; for a charge is not true except it depends on solid and strong evidences, according to what *Cicero* says, who, in a certain place, distinguishes between a charge and a slander. We

---

[1] So do *Grotius, Beza*, and *Stuart* render the verb. *Doddridge* and *Macknight* have preserved our common version. "We have before charged," *Chalmers*. "Antea idoneis argumentis demonstravimus—we have before proved by sufficient arguments," *Schleusner*. It is charge rather than conviction that the verb imports, though the latter idea is also considered to be included.—*Ed.*

must add, that to be *under sin* means that we are justly condemned as sinners before God, or that we are held under the curse which is due to sin; for as righteousness brings with it absolution, so sin is followed by condemnation.

10. As it is written, There is none righteous, no, not one:	10. Sicut scriptum, Quòd non est justus quisquam, ne unus quidem;
11. There is none that understandeth, there is none that seeketh after God.	11. Non est intelligens, non est qui requirat Deum;
12. They are all gone out of the way, they are together become unprofitable; there is none that doeth good, no, not one.	12. Omnes declinarunt, simul facti sunt inutiles; non est qui exerceat benignitatem, ne ad unum quidem:
13. Their throat *is* an open sepulchre: with their tongues they have used deceit: the poison of asps *is* under their lips:	13. Sepulchrum apertum guttur eorum; linguis dolosè egerunt: venenum aspidum sub labiis eorum:
14. Whose mouth *is* full of cursing and bitterness:	14. Quorum os execratione et amarulentia plenum:
15. Their feet *are* swift to shed blood:	15. Veloces pedes eorum ad effundendum sanguinem;
16. Destruction and misery *are* in their ways:	16. Contritio et calamitas in viis eorum;
17. And the way of peace have they not known:	17. Et viam pacis non noverunt:
18. There is no fear of God before their eyes.	18. Non est timor Dei præ oculis eorum.[1]

10. *As it is written,* &c. He has hitherto used proofs or arguments to convince men of their iniquity; he now begins to reason from authority; and it is to Christians the strongest kind of proof, when authority is derived from the only true God. And hence let ecclesiastical teachers learn what their office is; for since Paul asserts here no truth but what he confirms by the sure testimony of Scripture, much less ought such a thing to be attempted by those, who have no other commission but to preach the gospel, which they have received through Paul and others.

There is none righteous, &c. The Apostle, who gives the meaning rather than the entire words, seems, in the first place, before he comes to particulars, to state generally the substance of what the Prophet declares to be in man, and

---

[1] The references given in the margin are these,—Ps. xiv. 1-3; liii. 3 v. 9; xiv. 3; ix. 7; Is. lvi. 7; Prov. i. 16; Ps. xxxvi. 1.

that is—that *none is righteous :*[1] he afterwards particularly enumerates the effects or fruits of this unrighteousness.

11. The first effect is, that *there is none that understands :* and then this ignorance is immediately proved, for they *seek not God;* for empty is the man in whom. there is not the knowledge of God, whatever other learning he may possess; yea, the sciences and the arts, which in themselves are good, are empty things, when they are without this groundwork.

12. It is added,[2] *There is no one who doeth kindness.* By this we are to understand, that they had put off every feeling of humanity. For as the best bond of mutual concord among us is the knowledge of God, (as he is the common Father of all, he wonderfully unites us, and without him there is nothing but disunion,) so inhumanity commonly follows where there is ignorance of God, as every one, when he despises others, loves and seeks his own good.

13. It is further added, *Their throat is an open grave ;*[3] that is, a gulf to swallow up men. It is more than if he had said, that they were devourers ($ἀνθρωποφάγους$—men-eaters;)

---

[1] Ps. xiv. 1. The Hebrew is, "There is none that doeth good;" and the *Septuagint,* "There is none doing kindness, ($χρηστότητα$), there is not even one, ($οὐκ ἔστιν ἕως ἑνός.$)" So that the Apostle quotes the meaning, not the words.

The *eleventh* verse is from the same Psalm; the Hebrew, with which the *Septuagint* agree, except that there is the disjunctive $ἢ$ between the participles, is the following,—"Whether there is any one who understands, who seeks after God."—*Ed.*

[2] This verse is literally the *Septuagint,* and as to meaning, a correct version of the Hebrew. "All have gone out of the way—$πάντες ἐξέκλιναν,$" is in Hebrew הכל סר, "the whole (or every one) has turned aside," or revolted, or apostatized. Then, "they have become unprofitable" or useless, is נאלחו, "they are become putrid," or corrupted, like putrified fruit or meat, therefore useless, not fit for what they were designed—to serve God and to promote their own and the good of others. Idolatry was evidently this putrescence.—*Ed.*

[3] This is from Ps. v. 9, that is, the first part, and is literally the *Septuagint,* which correctly represents the Hebrew. The last clause is from Ps. cxl. 3, and is according to the *Septuagint,* and the Hebrew, too, except that "asps," or adders, is in the singular number. *Stuart* gives the import of this figurative language different from *Calvin:* "As from the sepulchre," he says, "issues forth an offensive and pestilential vapour; so from the mouths of slanderous persons issue noisome and pestilential words. Their words are like poison, they utter the poisonous breath of slander."—*Ed.*

for it is an intimation of extreme barbarity, when the throat is said to be so great a gulf, that it is sufficient to swallow down and devour men whole and entire. Their *tongues are deceitful,* and, *the poison of asps is under their lips,* import the same thing.

14. Then he says, that *their mouth is full of cursing and bitterness,*[1]—a vice of an opposite character to the former; but the meaning is, that they are in every way full of wickedness; for if they speak fair, they deceive and blend poison with their flatteries; but if they draw forth what they have in their hearts, bitterness and cursing stream out.

16. Very striking is the sentence that is added from Isaiah, *Ruin and misery are in all their ways;*[2] for it is a representation of ferociousness above measure barbarous, which produces solitude and waste by destroying every thing wherever it prevails: it is the same as the description which *Pliny* gives of *Domitian.*

17. It follows, *The way of peace they have not known:* they are so habituated to plunders, acts of violence and wrong, to savageness and cruelty, that they know not how to act kindly and courteously.

18. In the last clause[3] he repeats again, in other words,

---

[1] Ps. x. 7. Paul corrects the order of the words as found in the *Septuagint,* and gives the Hebrew more exactly; but retains the word "bitterness," by which the *Septuagint* have rendered מרמות, which means *deceit,* or rather, mischievous deceit. Some think that it ought to be מררות, "bitterness;" but there is no copy in its favour.—*Ed.*

[2] The 15th, 16th, and 17th verses are taken from Isaiah lix. 7, 8. Both the Hebrew and the *Septuagint* are alike, but Paul has abbreviated them, and changed two words in the Greek version, having put ἐξεῖς for ταχινοὶ, and ἔγνωσαν for ἴδασι, and has followed that version in leaving out "innocent" before "blood."—*Ed.*

[3] It is taken from Ps. xxxvi. 1, and verbatim from the Greek version, and strictly in accordance with the Hebrew. It is evident from several of these quotations, that Paul's object, as *Calvin* says, was to represent the general meaning, and not to keep strictly to the expressions.

There is a difference of opinion as to the precise object of the Apostle; whether in these quotations he had regard to the Jews only, or to both Jews and Gentiles. In the introduction, verse 9, he mentions both, and in the conclusion, verse 19, he evidently refers to both, in these words, " that every mouth may be stopped, and *all the world* may become guilty before God."

The most consistent view seems to be, that the passages quoted refer both to Jews and Gentiles; the last, more especially, to the Jews, while what we have noticed at the beginning—that every wickedness flows from a disregard of God: for as the principal part of wisdom is the fear of God, when we depart from that, there remains in us nothing right or pure. In short, as it is a bridle to restrain our wickedness, so when it is wanting, we feel at liberty to indulge every kind of licentiousness.

And that these testimonies may not seem to any one to have been unfitly produced, let us consider each of them in connection with the passages from which they have been taken. David says in Ps. xiv. 1, that there was such perverseness in men, that God, when looking on them all in their different conditions, could not find a righteous man, no, not one. It then follows, that this evil pervaded mankind universally; for nothing is hid from the sight of God. He speaks indeed at the end of the Psalm of the redemption of Israel: but we shall presently show how men become holy, and how far they are exempt from this condition. In the other Psalms he speaks of the treachery of his enemies, while he was exhibiting in himself and in his descendants a type of the kingdom of Christ: hence we have in his adversaries the representatives of all those, who being alienated from Christ, are not led by his Spirit. Isaiah expressly mentions Israel; and therefore his charge applies with still greater force against the Gentiles. What, then? There is no doubt but that the character of men is described in those words, in order that we may see what man is when left to himself; for Scripture testifies that all men are in this state, who are not regenerated by the grace of God. The condition of the saints would be nothing better, were not this depravity corrected in them: and that they may still remember that they differ nothing from others by nature, they do find in the relics of their flesh (by which they are always encompassed) the seeds of those evils, which would constantly produce fruits, were they not prevented by being mortified; and for this mortification they are indebted to God's mercy and not to their own nature. We may add,

some of the preceding have a special reference to the Gentile world, particularly Ps. xiv., as it describes the character of the enemies of God and his people, to whose liberation the Psalmist refers in the last verse.—*Ed.*

that though all the vices here enumerated are not found conspicuously in every individual, yet they may be justly and truly ascribed to human nature, as we have already observed on chap. i. 26.

19. Now we know, that what things soever the law saith, it saith to them who are under the law; that every mouth may be stopped, and all the world may become guilty before God.	19. Scimus autem quòd quæcunque Lex dicit, iis qui in Lege sunt loquitur; ut omne os obstruatur, et obnoxius fiat omnis mundus Deo.[1]
20. Therefore by the deeds of the law there shall no flesh be justified in his sight: for by the law *is* the knowledge of sin.	20. Quoniam ex operibus Legis non justificabitur omnis caro coram ipso; per Legem enim agnitio peccati.

19. *Now we know,* &c. Leaving the Gentiles, he distinctly addresses his words to the Jews; for he had a much more difficult work in subduing them, because they, though no less destitute of true righteousness than the Gentiles, yet covered themselves with the cloak of God's covenant, as though it was a sufficient holiness to them to have been separated from the rest of the world by the election of God. And he indeed mentions those evasions, which he well understood the Jews were ready to bring forward; for whatever was said in the law unfavourably of mankind, they usually applied to the Gentiles, as though they were exempt from the common condition of men, and no doubt they would have been so, had they not fallen from their own dignity. Hence, that no false conceit as to their own worthiness should be a hinderance to them, and that they might not confine to the Gentiles alone what applied to them in common with others, Paul here anticipates them, and shows, from what Scripture declares, that they were not only blended with the multitude, but that condemnation was peculiarly denounced on them. And we indeed see the discretion of the Apostle in under-

---

[1] *Obnoxius Deo*—ὑπόδικος .. τῷ θεῷ: " Obnoxius condemnationi Dei— subject to the condemnation of God," *Beza;* " Liable to punishment before God," *Macknight;* " Stand convicted before God," *Doddridge.* The word means to be " under sentence" or under condemnation, and thus " to God," *i.e.,* before God. *Tillotson* gives this paraphrase, " Liable to the Divine justice." It may be rendered " condemned before God." The meaning is that the world is under condemnation.—*Ed.*

taking to refute these objections; for to whom but to the Jews had the law been given, and to whose instruction but theirs ought it to have served? What then it states respecting others is as it were accidental; or as they say, πάρεργον, an appendage; but it applies its teaching mainly to its own disciples.

Under the law. He says that the Jews were those to whom the law was destined, it hence follows, that it especially regards them; and under the word law he includes also the Prophets, and so the whole of the Old Testament.—*That every mouth may be stopped,* &c.; that is, that every evasion may be cut off, and every occasion for excuse. It is a metaphor taken from courts of law, where the accused, if he has anything to plead as a lawful defence, demands leave to speak, that he might clear himself from the things laid to his charge; but if he is convicted by his own conscience, he is silent, and without saying a word waits for his condemnation, being even already by his own silence condemned. Of the same meaning is this saying in Job xl. 4, "I will lay my hand on my mouth." He indeed says, that though he was not altogether without some kind of excuse, he would yet cease to justify himself, and submit to the sentence of God. The next clause contains the explanation; for his mouth is stopped, who is so fast held by the sentence of condemnation, that he can by no means escape. According to another sense, to be silent before the Lord is to tremble at his majesty, and to stand mute, being astonished at his brightness.[1]

20. *Therefore by the works of the law,* &c. It is a matter of doubt, even among the learned, what the works of the law mean. Some extend them to the observance of the whole law, while others confine them to the ceremonies alone.

---

[1] To see the force and meaning of this verse, we must bear in mind that the former part was said to prevent the Jews from evading the application of the preceding testimonies; and then the words "that every mouth," &c., and "that all the world," &c., were added, not so much to include the Gentiles, as to include the Jews, who thought themselves exempted. No doubt the Gentiles are included, but the special object of the Apostle evidently seems to prevent the Jews from supposing that they were not included. In no other way can the connection between the two parts of the verse be understood.—*Ed.*

The addition of the word *law* induced *Chrysostom, Origen,* and *Jerome* to assent to the latter opinion;[1] for they thought that there is a peculiar intimation in this appendage, that the expression should not be understood as including all works. But this difficulty may be very easily removed: for seeing works are so far just before God as we seek by them to render to him worship and obedience, in order expressly to take away the power of justifying from all works, he has mentioned those, if there be any, which can possibly justify; for the law hath promises, without which there would be no value in our works before God. You hence see the reason why Paul expressly mentioned the works of the law; for it is by the law that a reward is apportioned to works. Nor was this unknown to the schoolmen, who held it as an approved and common maxim, that works have no intrinsic worthiness, but become meritorious by covenant. And though they were mistaken, inasmuch as they saw not that works are ever polluted with vices, which deprive them of any merit, yet this principle is still true, that the reward for works depends on the free promise of the law. Wisely then and rightly does Paul speak here; for he speaks not of mere works, but distinctly and expressly refers to the keeping of the law, the subject which he is discussing.[2]

[1] The original is " ut in priorem opinionem concederent:" but the context shows clearly that "priorem" is a misprint for "posteriorem." In addition to the authors mentioned here may be added *Ambrose, Theodoret, Pelagius, Erasmus,* and *Grotius.* And yet, notwithstanding all those authorities, the opinion referred to is wholly inconsistent with the reasoning of the Apostle here and throughout the whole Epistle. It has indeed been given up as untenable by modern authors of the same school, such as *Locke, Whitby,* and *Macknight.*

To disprove this notion it is sufficient to notice the sins which the Apostle had referred to; they are not those against the ceremonial but the moral law, and it is because the moral law is transgressed that it cannot justify.

" If there be any law which man has perfectly kept, he may doubtless be justified by it; and surely no man can be justified by a law which condemns him for breaking it. But there is no law of God which any man has kept; therefore no law by the deeds of which a man can be justified. The Gentile broke the law of his reason and conscience; the Jew broke the moral law; and even the attempt to justify himself by observing the ceremonial law, contradicted the very nature and intent of it."—*Scott.*

[2] The argument and the reasoning of the Apostle seem to require that ἐξ ἔργων νόμου should be rendered here literally, "by works of law," without the article, as the word "law" seems here, according to the drift of the

As to those things which have been adduced by learned men in defence of this opinion, they are weaker than they might have been. They think that by mentioning circumcision, an example is propounded, which belonged to ceremonies only: but why Paul mentioned circumcision, we have alredy explained; for none swell more with confidence in works than hypocrites, and we know that they glory only in external masks; and then circumcision, according to their view, was a sort of initiation into the righteousness of the law; and hence it seemed to them a work of primary excellence, and indeed the basis as it were of the righteousness of works.—They also allege what is said in the Epistle to the Galatians, where Paul handles the same subject, and refers to ceremonies only; but that also is not sufficiently strong to support what they wish to defend. It is certain that Paul had a controversy with those who inspired the people with a false confidence in ceremonies; that he might cut off this confidence, he did not confine himself to ceremonies, nor did he speak specifically of what value they were; but he included the whole law, as it is evident from those passages which are derived from that source. Such also was the character of the disputation held at Jerusalem by the disciples.

But we contend, not without reason, that Paul speaks here of the whole law; for we are abundantly supported by the thread of reasoning which he has hitherto followed and continues to follow, and there are many other passages which will not allow us to think otherwise. It is therefore a truth, which deserves to be remembered as the first in importance,—that by keeping the law no one can attain righteousness. He had before assigned the reason, and he will repeat it presently again, and that is, that all, being to a man guilty of transgression, are condemned for unrighteousness by the law. And these two things—to be justified by

argument, to mean law in general, both natural and revealed; and διὰ νόμου in the next clause must be regarded as having the same meaning; the law of nature as well as the written law, though not to the same extent, makes sin known. This is the view taken by *Pareus, Doddridge, Macknight, Stuart,* and *Haldane.—Ed.*

works—and to be guilty of transgressions, (as we shall show more at large as we proceed,) are wholly inconsistent the one with the other.—The word *flesh*, without some particular specification, signifies men;[1] though it seems to convey a meaning somewhat more general, as it is more expressive to say, "All mortals," than to say, "All men," as you may see in *Gallius*.

For by the law, &c. He reasons from what is of an opposite character,—that righteousness is not brought to us by the law, because it convinces us of sin and condemns us; for life and death proceed not from the same fountain. And as he reasons from the contrary effect of the law, that it cannot confer righteousness on us, let us know, that the argument does not otherwise hold good, except we hold this as an inseparable and unvarying circumstance,—that by showing to man his sin, it cuts off the hope of salvation. It is indeed by itself, as it teaches us what righteousness is, the way to salvation: but our depravity and corruption prevent it from being in this respect of any advantage to us. It is also necessary in the second place to add this,—that whosoever is found to be a sinner, is deprived of righteousness; for to devise with the sophisters a half kind of righteousness, so that works in part justify, is frivolous: but nothing is in this respect gained, on account of man's corruption.

21. But now the righteousness of God without the law[2] is manifested, being witnessed by the law and the prophets;

21. Nunc autem sine Lege justitia Dei manifesta est, testimonio comprobata Legis et prophetarum;

---

[1] The expression is, *ὀυ...πᾶσα σὰρξ*—not all, that is, not any flesh, &c.: the word *πᾶσα*, like כל in Hebrew, is used here in the sense of "any." The sentence bears a resemblance to what is contained in Ps. cxliii. 2, "for justified before thee shall not all living," or, not any one living, לא...כל חי. The sentence here is literally, "Hence by works of law shall not be justified any flesh before Him."—*Ed.*

[2] Here again it is better, and indeed necessary for the Apostle's argument, to render *χωρὶς νόμου*, "without law," that is, without any law, either natural or revealed. The same sentiment is found in Gal. iii. 21— "For if a law had been given, capable of giving life, truly righteous would have been by law (*ἐκ νόμου*.)" The version of *Macknight* seems just, "But now a righteousness of God without law is discovered." But we may retain the tense (*πιφανίρωται*) "has been discovered," or manifested, or made known. "A righteousness of God without law," is a similar

22. Even the righteousness of God *which is* by faith of Jesus Christ unto all and upon all them that believe; for there is no difference:

22. Justitia, inquam, Dei per fidem Iesu Christi, in omnes et super omnes credentes; non est sanè distinctio:

21. *But now without the law,* &c. It is not certain for what distinct reason he calls that the righteousness of God, which we obtain by faith; whether it be, because it can alone stand before God, or because the Lord in his mercy confers it on us. As both interpretations are suitable, we contend for neither. This righteousness then, which God communicates to man, and accepts alone, and owns as righteousness, has been revealed, he says, *without the law,* that is, without the aid of the law; and the law is to be understood as meaning works; for it is not proper to refer this to its teaching, which he immediately adduces as bearing witness to the gratuitous righteousness of faith. Some confine it to ceremonies; but this view I shall presently show to be unsound and frigid. We ought then to know, that the merits of works are excluded. We also see that he blends not works with the mercy of God; but having taken away and wholly removed all confidence in works, he sets up mercy alone.

It is not unknown to me, that *Augustine* gives a different explanation; for he thinks that the righteousness of God is the grace of regeneration; and this grace he allows to be free, because God renews us, when unworthy, by his Spirit; and from this he excludes the works of the law, that is, those works, by which men of themselves endeavour, without renovation, to render God indebted to them. (*Deum promereri*—to oblige God.) I also well know, that some new speculators proudly adduce this sentiment, as though it were at this day revealed to them. But that the Apostle includes all works without exception, even those which the Lord produces in his own people, is evident from the context.

For no doubt Abraham was regenerated and led by the Spirit of God at the time when he denied that he was justi-

---

phrase to " the righteousness of God by faith," in ch. i. 17.—Then in the following clause the "law" means not specifically the law of Moses, but the Old Testament, excepting the Prophets.—*Ed.*

fied by works. Hence he excluded from man's justification not only works morally good, as they commonly call them, and such as are done by the impulse of nature, but also all those which even the faithful can perform.¹ Again, since this is a definition of the righteousness of faith, " Blessed are they whose iniquities are forgiven," there is no question to be made about this or that kind of work; but the merit of works being abolished, the remission of sins alone is set down as the cause of righteousness.

They think that these two things well agree,—that man is justified by faith through the grace of Christ,—and that he is yet justified by the works, which proceed from spiritual regeneration; for God gratuitously renews us, and we also receive his gift by faith. But Paul takes up a very different principle,—that the consciences of men will never be tranquillized until they recumb on the mercy of God alone.² Hence, in another place, after having taught us that God is in Christ justifying men, he expresses the manner,—" By not imputing to them their sins." In like manner, in his Epistle to the Galatians, he puts the law in opposition to faith with regard to justification; for the law promises life to those who do what it commands, (Gal. iii. 12;) and it requires not only the outward performance of works, but also sincere love to God. It hence follows, that in the righteousness of faith, no merit of works is allowed. It then appears

¹ Professor *Hodge* very justly observes, " It never was the doctrine of the Reformation, or of the Lutheran and Calvinistic divines, that the imputation of righteousness affected the moral character of those concerned. It is true," he adds, " whom God justifies he also sanctifies; but justification is not sanctification, and the imputation of righteousness is not the infusion of righteousness."—*Ed.*

² " The foundation of your trust before God, must be either your own righteousness out and out, or the righteousness of Christ out and out... If you are to lean upon your own merit, lean upon it wholly—if you are to lean upon Christ, lean upon him wholly. The two will not amalgamate together; and it is the attempt to do so, which keeps many a weary and heavy-laden inquirer at a distance from rest, and at a distance from the truth of the gospel. Maintain a clear and consistent posture. Stand not before God with one foot upon a rock and the other upon a treacherous quicksand...We call upon you not to lean so much as the weight of one grain or scruple of your confidence upon your own doings—to leave this ground entirely, and to come over entirely to the ground of a Redeemer's blood and a Redeemer's righteousness."—*Dr. Chalmers.*

evident, that it is but a frivolous sophistry to say, that we are justified in Christ, because we are renewed by the Spirit, inasmuch as we are the members of Christ,—that we are justified by faith, because we are united by faith to the body of Christ,—that we are justified freely, because God finds nothing in us but sin.

But we are *in Christ*, because we are out of ourselves; and justified by *faith*, because we must recumb on the mercy of God alone, and on his gratuitous promises; and *freely*, because God reconciles us to himself by burying our sins. Nor can this indeed be confined to the commencement of justification, as they dream; for this definition—" Blessed are they whose iniquities are forgiven"—was applicable to David, after he had long exercised himself in the service of God; and Abraham, thirty years after his call, though a remarkable example of holiness, had yet no works for which he could glory before God, and hence his faith in the promise was imputed to him for righteousness; and when Paul teaches us that God justifies men by not imputing their sins, he quotes a passage, which is daily repeated in the Church. Still more, the conscience, by which we are disturbed on the score of works, performs its office, not for one day only, but continues to do so through life. It hence follows that we cannot remain, even to death, in a justified state, except we look to Christ only, in whom God has adopted us, and regards us now as accepted. Hence also is their sophistry confuted, who falsely accuse us of asserting, that according to Scripture we are justified by faith only, while the exclusive word *only*, is nowhere to be found in Scripture. But if justification depends not either on the law, or on ourselves, why should it not be ascribed to mercy alone? and if it be from mercy only, it is then by faith only.

The particle *now* may be taken adversatively, and not with reference to time; as we often use *now* for *but*.[1] But if you prefer to regard it as an adverb of time, I willingly admit it,

---

[1] "The words *but now* may be regarded merely as marking the transition from one paragraph to another, or as a designation of tense; *now*, *i.e.*, under the gospel dispensation. In favour of this view is the phrase, " to declare *at this time* his righteousness, verse 26."—*Hodge.*

so that there may be no room to suspect an evasion; yet the abrogation of ceremonies alone is not to be understood; for it was only the design of the Apostle to illustrate by a comparison the grace by which we excel the fathers. Then the meaning is, that by the preaching of the gospel, after the appearance of Christ in the flesh, the righteousness of faith was revealed. It does not, however, hence follow, that it was hid before the coming of Christ; for a twofold manifestation is to be here noticed: the first in the Old Testament, which was by the word and sacraments; the other in the New, which contains the completion of ceremonies and promises, as exhibited in Christ himself: and we may add, that by the gospel it has received a fuller brightness.

Being proved [*or approved*] *by the testimony,*[1] &c. He adds this, lest in the conferring of free righteousness the gospel should seem to militate against the law. As then he has denied that the righteousness of faith needs the aid of the law, so now he asserts that it is confirmed by its testimony. If then the law affords its testimony to gratuitous righteousness, it is evident that the law was not given for this end, to teach men how to obtain righteousness by works. Hence they pervert it, who turn it to answer any purpose of this kind. And further, if you desire a proof of this truth, examine in order the chief things taught by Moses, and you will find that man, being cast from the kingdom of God, had no other restoration from the beginning than that contained in the evangelical promises through the blessed seed, by whom, as it had been foretold, the serpent's head was to be bruised, and through whom a blessing to the nations had been promised: you will find in the commandments a demonstration of your iniquity, and from the sacrifices and oblations you may learn that satisfaction and cleansing are to be obtained in Christ alone.[2] When you come to the *Pro*-

---

[1] "Testimonio comprobata," &c., so *Beza* and *Pareus* render μαρτυρουμένη; "Being attested," *Doddridge;* "Being testified," *Macknight*. *Schleusner* gives a paraphrase, "Being predicted and promised;" and this no doubt is the full meaning.—*Ed.*

[2] Concurrent with what is said here is this striking and condensed passage from *Scott,*—"It has been witnessed by the law and the Prophets; the ceremonies typified it; the very strictness of the moral law and its awful

phets you will find the clearest promises of gratuitous mercy. On this subject see my Institutes.

22. *Even the righteousness of God*, &c.[1] He shows in few words what this justification is, even that which is found in Christ and is apprehended by faith. At the same time, by introducing again the name of God, he seems to make God the founder, (*autorem*, the author,) and not only the approver of the righteousness of which he speaks; as though he had said, that it flows from him alone, or that its origin is from heaven, but that it is made manifest to us in Christ.

When therefore we discuss this subject, we ought to proceed in this way: *First,* the question respecting our justification is to be referred, not to the judgment of men, but to the judgment of God, before whom nothing is counted righteousness, but perfect and absolute obedience to the law; which appears clear from its promises and threatenings: if no one is found who has attained to such a perfect measure of holiness, it follows that all are in themselves destitute of righteousness. *Secondly,* it is necessary that Christ should come to our aid; who, being alone just, can render us just by transferring to us his own righteousness. You now see how the righteousness of faith is the righteousness of Christ. When therefore we are justified, the efficient cause is the mercy of God, the meritorious is Christ, the instrumental is the word in connection with faith.[2] Hence faith is said to justify, because it is the instrument by which we receive Christ, in whom righteousness is conveyed to us. Having

---

curses, being compared with the promises of mercy to sinners, implied it; the promises and predictions of the Messiah bore witness to it; the faith and hope of ancient believers recognised it; and the whole Old Testament, rightly understood, taught men to expect and depend on it."—*Ed.*

[1] The words which follow, διὰ πίστεως Ἰησοῦ Χριστοῦ, " by or through the faith of Jesus Christ," mean not the faith which is his, but the faith of which he is the object. They ought to be rendered " through faith in Jesus Christ." The genitive case has often this meaning: " Εχιτι πίστιν Θεοῦ—Have faith in (of) God," Mark xi. 22; " Εν πίστει ζῶ τῇ τοῦ υἱοῦ τοῦ Θεοῦ—I live by the faith of the Son of God;" it should be in our language, " I live by faith in the Son of God." This genitive case of the object is an Hebraism, and is of frequent occurrence.—*Ed.*

[2] The original is this, " Ut ergo justificemur, causa efficiens est misericordia Dei, Christus materia, verbum cum fide instrumentum—When therefore we are justified, the efficient cause is God's mercy, Christ is the material, the word with faith is the instrument."—*Ed.*

been made partakers of Christ, we ourselves are not only just, but our works also are counted just before God, and for this reason, because whatever imperfections there may be in them, are obliterated by the blood of Christ; the promises, which are conditional, are also by the same grace fulfilled to us; for God rewards our works as perfect, inasmuch as their defects are covered by free pardon.

Unto all and upon all,[1] &c. For the sake of amplifying, he repeats the same thing in different forms; it was, that he might more fully express what we have already heard, that faith alone is required, that the faithful are not distinguished by external marks, and that hence it matters not whether they be Gentiles or Jews.

23. For all have sinned, and come short of the glory of God:
24. Being justified freely by his grace, through the redemption that is in Christ Jesus;
25. Whom God hath set forth *to be* a propitiation through faith in his blood, to declare his righteousness for the remission of sins that are past, through the forbearance of God;
26. To declare, *I say*, at this time his righteousness; that he might be just, and the justifier of him which believeth in Jesus.

23. Omnes enim peccaverunt, et destituuntur gloriâ Dei;
24. Justificati gratis ipsius gratiâ per redemptionem quæ est in Christo Iesu:
25. Quem proposuit Deus propitiatorium per fidem in sanguine ipsius, in demonstrationem justitiæ suæ, propter remissionem delictorum,
26. Quæ priùs extiterunt in tolerantiâ Dei; ad demonstrationem justitiæ suæ, in hoc tempore; ut sit ipse justus et justificans eum qui est ex fide Iesu.

There is indeed no difference, &c. He urges on all, without exception, the necessity of seeking righteousness in Christ; as though he had said, "There is no other way of attaining righteousness; for some cannot be justified in this

---

[1] Εἰς πάντας καὶ ἐπὶ πάντας. He makes a similar difference in his expressions in verse 30. This righteousness, as some say, came *to* the Jews, as it had been promised to them, and *upon* the Gentiles, as a gift with which they were not acquainted, and it was conferred on them. But the possession was equal and belonged to all who believed, and to none else, whether Jews or Gentiles.

Stuart connects these words with "manifested," or revealed, in verse 21. It is manifested *to* all, and manifested *for* all; that is, for the real benefit of all who believe; in other words, it is offered to all, but becomes of real advantage only to those who believe. But the simpler mode is to consider the words *which is*, as in our version, to be understood. Ἐρχομένη is the word which Luther adopts.—*Ed.*

and others in that way; but all must alike be justified by faith, because all are sinners, and therefore have nothing for which they can glory before God." But he takes as granted that every one, conscious of his sin, when he comes before the tribunal of God, is confounded and lost under a sense of his own shame; so that no *sinner* can bear the presence of God, as we see an example in the case of Adam. He again brings forward a reason taken from the opposite side; and hence we must notice what follows. Since we are all sinners, Paul concludes, that we are deficient in, or *destitute of*, the praise due to righteousness. There is then, according to what he teaches, no righteousness but what is perfect and absolute. Were there indeed such a thing as half righteousness, it would yet be necessary to deprive the sinner entirely of all glory: and hereby the figment of partial righteousness, as they call it, is sufficiently confuted; for if it were true that we are justified in part by works, and in part by grace, this argument of Paul would be of no force—that all are deprived of the glory of God because they are sinners. It is then certain, there is no righteousness where there is sin, until Christ removes the curse; and this very thing is what is said in Gal. iii. 10, that all who are under the law are exposed to the curse, and that we are delivered from it through the kindness of Christ. *The glory of God* I take to mean the approbation of God, as in John xii. 43, where it is said, that "they loved the glory of men more than the glory of God." And thus he summons us from the applause of a human court to the tribunal of heaven.[1]

24. *Being justified freely*, &c. A participle is here put for a verb according to the usage of the Greek language.

---

[1] *Beza* gives another view, that the verb ὑστεροῦνται, refers to those who run a race, and reach not the goal, and lose the prize. The "glory of God" is the happiness which he bestows; (see ch. v. 2;) of this all mankind come short, however much some seemed to labour for it; and it can only be attained by faith. *Pareus, Locke,* and *Whitby* give the same view. Others consider it to be "the glory" due to God,—that all come short of rendering him the service and honour which he justly demands and requires. So *Doddridge, Scott,* and *Chalmers.* But *Melancthon, Grotius,* and *Macknight* seemed to have agreed with *Calvin* in regarding "glory" here as the praise or approbation that comes from God. The second view seems the most appropriate, according to what is said in ch. i. 21, "they glorified him not as God."—*Ed.*

The meaning is,—that since there remains nothing for men, as to themselves, but to perish, being smitten by the just judgment of God, they are to be justified freely through his mercy; for Christ comes to the aid of this misery, and communicates himself to believers, so that they find in him alone all those things in which they are wanting. There is, perhaps, no passage in the whole Scripture which illustrates in a more striking manner the efficacy of his righteousness; for it shows that God's mercy is the efficient cause, that Christ with his blood is the meritorious cause, that the formal or instrumental cause is faith in the word, and that, moreover, the final cause is the glory of the divine justice and goodness.

With regard to the efficient cause, he says, that we are *justified freely*, and further, by his grace; and he thus repeats the word to show that the whole is from God, and nothing from us. It might have been enough to oppose grace to merits; but lest we should imagine a half kind of grace, he affirms more strongly what he means by a repetition, and claims for God's mercy alone the whole glory of our righteousness, which the sophists divide into parts and mutilate, that they may not be constrained to confess their own poverty.—*Through the redemption*, &c. This is the material, —Christ by his obedience satisfied the Father's justice, (*judicium*—judgment,) and by undertaking our cause he liberated us from the tyranny of death, by which we were held captive; as on account of the sacrifice which he offered is our guilt removed. Here again is fully confuted the gloss of those who make righteousness a quality; for if we are counted righteous before God, because we are redeemed by a price, we certainly derive from another what is not in us. And Paul immediately explains more clearly what this redemption is, and what is its object, which is to reconcile us to God; for he calls Christ a propitiation, (or, if we prefer an allusion to an ancient type,) a propitiatory. But what he means is, that we are not otherwise just than through Christ propitiating the Father for us. But it is necessary for us to examine the words.[1]

[1] On this word ἱλαστήριον, both *Venema*, in his Notes on the Comment of

25. *Whom God hath set forth,* &c. The Greek verb, προτιθέναι, means sometimes to determine beforehand, and sometimes to set forth. If the first meaning be taken, Paul refers to the gratuitous mercy of God, in having appointed Christ as our Mediator, that he might appease the Father by the sacrifice of his death: nor is it a small commendation of God's grace that he, of his own good will, sought out a way by which he might remove our curse. According to this view, the passage fully harmonizes with that in John iii. 16, "God so loved the world, that he gave his only-begotten Son." Yet if we embrace this meaning, it will remain still true, that God hath set him forth in due time, whom he had appointed as a Mediator. There seems to be an allusion in the word, ἱλαστήριον, as I have said, to the ancient propitiatory; for he teaches us that the same thing was really exhibited in Christ, which had been previously typified. As, however, the other view cannot be disproved, should any

Stephanus de Brais on this Epistle, and Professor *Stuart*, have long remarks. They both agree as to the meaning of the word as found in the Septuagint and in Greek authors, but they disagree as to its import here. It means uniformly in the Septuagint, the mercy-seat, כפרת, and, as it is in the form of an adjective, it has at least once, (Ex. xxv. 17,) ἐπίθεμα, *cover,* added to it. But in the Classics it means a propitiatory sacrifice, the word θῦμα, a sacrifice, being understood; but it is used by itself as other words of similar termination are. It is found also in *Josephus* and in *Maccabees* in this sense. It appears that *Origen, Theodoret,* and other Fathers, and also *Erasmus, Luther,* and *Locke,* take the first meaning— *mercy-seat;* and that *Grotius, Elsner, Turrettin, Bos,* and *Tholuck,* take the second meaning—*a propitiatory sacrifice.* Now as both meanings are legitimate, which of them are we to take? *Venema* and *Stuart* allude to one thing which much favours the latter view, that is, the phrase ἐν τῳ αἵματι αὐτοῦ; and the latter says, that it would be incongruous to represent Christ himself as the mercy-seat, and to represent him also as sprinkled by his own blood; but that it is appropriate to say that a propitiatory sacrifice was made by his blood. The verb προέθετο, *set forth,* it is added, seems to support the same view. To exhibit a *mercy-seat* is certainly not suitable language in this connection.

Pareus renders it "placamentum—atonement," *hoc est,* "placatorem," that is, "atoner, or expiator." *Beza's* version is the same—"placamentum:" *Doddridge* has "propitiation," and *Macknight,* "a propitiatory," and *Schleusner,* "expiatorem—expiator."

The word occurs in one other place with the neuter article, τὸ ἱλαστήριον, Heb. ix. 5; where it clearly means the mercy-seat. It is ever accompanied with the article in the Septuagint, when by itself, see Lev. xvi. 2, 13-15; but here it is without the article, and may be viewed as an adjective dependent on ὃν, "whom," and rendered propitiator. Had the mercy-seat been intended, it would have been τὸ ἱλαστήριον.—*Ed.*

prefer it, I shall not undertake to decide the question. What Paul especially meant here is no doubt evident from his words; and it was this,—that God, without having regard to Christ, is always angry with us,—and that we are reconciled to him when we are accepted through his righteousness. God does not indeed hate in us his own workmanship, that is, as we are formed men; but he hates our uncleanness, which has extinguished the light of his image. When the washing of Christ cleanses this away, he then loves and embraces us as his own pure workmanship.

A propitiatory through faith in his blood, &c. I prefer thus literally to retain the language of Paul; for it seems indeed to me that he intended, by one single sentence, to declare that God is propitious to us as soon as we have our trust resting on the blood of Christ; for by faith we come to the possession of this benefit. But by mentioning *blood* only, he did not mean to exclude other things connected with redemption, but, on the contrary, to include the whole under one word: and he mentioned "blood," because by it we are cleansed. Thus, by taking a part for the whole, he points out the whole work of expiation. For, as he had said before, that God is reconciled in Christ, so he now adds, that this reconciliation is obtained by faith, mentioning, at the same time, what it is that faith ought mainly to regard in Christ—his blood.

For (propter) the remission of sins,[1] &c. The causal pre-

---

[1] The words are, διὰ τὴν πάρεσιν. They seem connected, not with the first clause, but with the one immediately preceding; and διὰ may be rendered here *in*; see a note on ch. ii. 26; or more properly, perhaps, *on account of*. "For a proof of his own righteousness *in* passing by the sins," &c., *Macknight;* "In order to declare his justification *with respect to* the remission of sins," *Stuart*.

What is God's "righteousness" here has been variously explained. Some regard it his righteousness in fulfilling his promises, as *Beza;* others, his righteousness in Christ to believers, mentioned in ch. i. 17, as *Augustine;* and others, his righteousness as the God of rectitude and justice, as *Chrysostom*. Some, too, as *Grotius*, view it as meaning goodness or mercy, regarding the word as having sometimes this sense.

It is the context that can help us to the right meaning. God exhibited his Son as a propitiation, to set forth this righteousness; and this righteousness is connected with the remission of, or rather, as the word means, the preterition of or connivance at sins committed under the old dispensation: and those sins were connived at through the forbearance of God, he

position imports as much as though he had said, "for the sake of remission," or, "to this end, that he might blot out sins." And this definition or explanation again confirms what I have already often reminded you,—that men are pronounced just, not because they are such in reality, but by imputation: for he only uses various modes of expression, that he might more clearly declare, that in this righteousness there is no merit of ours; for if we obtain it by the remission of sins, we conclude that it is not from ourselves; and further, since remission itself is an act of God's bounty alone, every merit falls to the ground.

It may, however, be asked, why he confines pardon to preceding sins? Though this passage is variously explained, yet it seems to me probable that Paul had regard to the legal expiations, which were indeed evidences of a future satisfaction, but could by no means pacify God. There is a similar passage in Heb. ix. 15, where it is said, that by Christ a redemption was brought from sins, which remained under the former Testament. You are not, however, to understand that no sins but those of former times were expiated by the death of Christ—a delirious notion, which some fanatics

not executing the punishment they deserved; and the purpose is stated to be,—that God might be or appear *just*, while he is the justifier of those who believe in Christ. Now, what can this righteousness be but his administrative justice? As the law allowed no remission, and God did remit sins, there appeared to be a stain on divine justice. The exhibition of Christ as an atonement is what alone removes it. And there is a word in the former verse, as *Venema* justly observes, which tends to confirm this view, and that word is redemption, ἀπολυτρώσις, which is a deliverance obtained by a ransom, or by a price, such as justice requires.

Both *Doddridge* and *Scott* regard the passage in this light; and the latter gives the following version of it,—

"Whom God hath before appointed to be a propitiation, through faith in his blood, for a demonstration of his justice, on account of the passing by of sins, that had been committed in former times, through the forbearance of God; *I say*, for a demonstration of his justice, in this present time, in order that he might be just, and the justifier of him that believeth in Jesus."—Nothing can be clearer than this version.

The last words are rightly rendered, though not literally; τὸν ἐκ πίστεως Ἰησοῦ—"him of the faith of Jesus," or, "him of faith in Jesus." Him of faith is him who believes, as τοῖς οὐκ ἐκ περιτομῆς—"them not of circumcision," means "them who are not circumcised," ch. iv. 12; and τοῖς ἐξ ἐριθείας—"those of contention," signifies, "those who contend," or, are contentious, ch. ii. 8.—*Ed.*

have drawn from a distorted view of this passage. For Paul teaches us only this,—that until the death of Christ there was no way of appeasing God, and that this was not done or accomplished by the legal types: hence the reality was suspended until the fulness of time came. We may further say, that those things which involve us daily in guilt must be regarded in the same light; for there is but one true expiation for all.

Some, in order to avoid what seems inconsistent, have held that former sins are said to have been forgiven, lest there should seem to be a liberty given to sin in future. It is indeed true that no pardon is offered but for sins committed; not that the benefit of redemption fails or is lost, when we afterwards fall, as *Novatus* and his sect dreamed, but that it is the character of the dispensation of the gospel, to set before him who will sin the judgment and wrath of God, and before the sinner his mercy. But what I have already stated is the real sense.

He adds, that this remission was *through forbearance;* and this I take simply to mean gentleness, which has stayed the judgment of God, and suffered it not to burst forth to our ruin, until he had at length received us into favour. But there seems to be here also an implied anticipation of what might be said; that no one might object, and say that this favour had only of late appeared. Paul teaches us, that it was an evidence of forbearance.

26. *For a demonstration,*[1] &c. The repetition of this clause

---

[1] There is a different preposition used here, πρὸς, while εἰς is found in the preceding verse. The meaning seems to be the same; for both prepositions are used to designate the design, end, or object of any thing. This variety seems to have been usual with the Apostle; similar instances are found in ver. 22, as to εἰς and ἐπὶ, and in ver. 30, as to ἐκ and διὰ. "By both," says *Wolfius*, "the final cause (*causa finalis*) is indicated." *Beza* renders them both by the same preposition, *ad*, in Latin; and *Stuart* regards the two as equivalent. There is, perhaps, more refinement than truth in what *Pareus* says,—that εἰς intimates the proximate end—the forgiveness of sins; and πρὸς, the final end—the glory of God in the exhibition of his justice as well as of his mercy. There is, at the same time, something in the passage which seems favourable to this view. Two objects are stated at the end of the passage,—that God might appear just, and be also the justifier of such as believe. The last may refer to εἰς, and the former to πρὸς; and this is consistent with the usual style of the Apostle;

is emphatical; and Paul designedly made it, as it was very needful; for nothing is more difficult than to persuade man that he ought to disclaim all things as his own, and to ascribe them all to God. At the same time mention was intentionally made twice of this demonstration, that the Jews might open their eyes to behold it.—*At this time,* &c. What had been ever at all times, he applies to the time when Christ was revealed, and not without reason; for what was formerly known in an obscure manner under shadows, God openly manifested in his Son. So the coming of Christ was the time of his good pleasure, and the day of salvation. God had indeed in all ages given some evidence of his righteousness; ebut it appeared far brighter when the sun of righteousness shone. Noticed, then, ought to be the comparison between the Old and the New Testament; for then only was revealed the righteousness of God when Christ appeared.

That he might be just, &c. This is a definition of that righteousness which he has declared was revealed when Christ was given, and which, as he has taught us in the first chapter, is made known in the gospel: and he affirms that it consists of two parts—The first is, that God is just, not indeed as one among many, but as one who contains within himself all fulness of righteousness; for complete and full praise, such as is due, is not otherwise given to him, but when he alone obtains the name and the honour of being just, while the whole human race is condemned for injustice: and then the other part refers to the communication of righteousness; for God by no means keeps his riches laid up in himself, but pours them forth upon men. Then the righteousness of God shines in us, whenever he justifies us by faith in Christ; for in vain were Christ given us for righteousness, unless there was the fruition of him by faith. It hence follows, that all were unjust and lost in themselves, until a remedy from heaven was offered to them.[1]

for, in imitation of the Prophets, where two things are mentioned in a former clause, the order is reversed in the second.—*Ed.*

A parallel passage to this, including the two verses, 25 and 26, is found in Heb. ix. 15; where a reference, as here, is made to the effect of Christ's death as to the saints under the Old Testament. The same truth is implied in other parts of Scripture, but not so expressly declared.

27. Where *is* boasting then? It is excluded. By what law? of works? Nay: but by the law of faith.
28. Therefore we conclude, that a man is justified by faith without the deeds of the law.

27. Ubi ergo gloriatio?[1] exclusa est. Per quam legem? operum? Nequaquam; sed per legem fidei.
28. Constituimus ergo, fide justificari hominem sine operibus Legis.

27. *Where then is glorying?* The Apostle, after having, with reasons abundantly strong, cast down men from their confidence in works, now triumphs over their folly: and this exulting conclusion was necessary; for on this subject, to teach us would not have been enough; it was necessary that the Holy Spirit should loudly thunder, in order to lay prostrate our loftiness. But he says that glorying is beyond all doubt excluded, for we cannot adduce anything of our own, which is worthy of being approved or commended by God. If the material of glorying be merit, whether you name that of congruity or of condignity, by which man would conciliate God, you see that both are here annihilated; for he treats not of the lessening or the modifying of merit, but Paul leaves not a particle behind. Besides, since by faith glorying in works is so taken away, that faith cannot be truly preached, without wholly depriving man of all praise by ascribing all to God's mercy—it follows, that we are assisted by no works in obtaining righteousness.

Of works? In what sense does the Apostle deny here, that our merits are excluded by the law, since he has before proved that we are condemned by the law? for if the law delivers us over to death, what glorying can we obtain from it? Does it not on the contrary deprive us of all glorying and cover us with shame? He then indeed showed, that our sin is laid open by what the law declares, for the keeping of it is what we have all neglected: but he means here, that were righteousness to be had by the law of works, our

---

Stuart makes here an important remark—that if the death of Christ be regarded only as that of a martyr or as an example of constancy, how then could its efficacy be referred to "sins that are past?" In no other way than as a vicarious death could it possibly have any effect on past sins, not punished through God's forbearance.—*Ed.*

[1] *Gloriatio—καύχησις*—glorying—boasting or rejoicing. "The result of the gospel plan of salvation is to prevent all self-approbation, self-gratulation and exaltation on the part of the sinner."—*Hodge.*

glorying would not be excluded ; but as it is by faith alone, there is nothing that we can claim for ourselves ; for faith receives all from God, and brings nothing except an humble confession of want.

This contrast between faith and works ought to be carefully noticed: works are here mentioned without any limitation, even works universally. Then he neither speaks of ceremonies only, nor specifically of any external work, but includes all the merits of works which can possibly be imagined.

The name of *law* is here, with no strict correctness, given to faith: but this by no means obscures the meaning of the Apostle ; for what he understands is, that when we come to the rule of faith, the whole glorying in works is laid prostrate ; as though he said—" The righteousness of works is indeed commended by the law, but that of faith has its own law, which leaves to works, whatever they may be, no righteousness."[1]

28. *We then conclude,* &c. He now draws the main proposition, as one that is incontrovertible, and adds an explanation. Justification by faith is indeed made very clear, while works are expressly excluded. Hence, in nothing do our adversaries labour more in the present day than in attempts to blend faith with the merits of works. They indeed allow that man is justified by faith ; but not by faith alone ; yea, they place the efficacy of justification in love, though in words they ascribe it to faith. But Paul affirms in this passage that justification is so gratuitous, that he makes it quite evident, that it can by no means be associated with the merit of works. Why he names the works of the law, I

---

[1] *Grotius* explains " law" here by " vivendi regula—rule of living ;" *Beza*, by " doctrina—doctrine or teaching," according to the import of the word תורה in Hebrew; and *Pareus* takes " the law of works," metonymically, for works themselves, and " the law of faith," for faith itself; and he quotes these words of *Theophylact,* " The Apostle calls faith a law, because the word, law, was in high veneration among the Jews." He uses the term, law, in a similar manner in chap. viii. 2, " The law of the spirit of life," &c. " He calls here the gospel ' the law of faith,' because faith is the condition of the gospel covenant, as perfect obedience was the condition of the covenant of nature and of that of Moses, (conditio fœderis naturalis et fœderis Mosaici.)"—*Turrettin.*

have already explained; and I have also proved that it is quite absurd to confine them to ceremonies. Frigid also is the gloss, that works are to be taken for those which are outward, and done without the Spirit of Christ. On the contrary, the word *law* that is added, means the same as though he called them meritorious; for what is referred to is the reward promised in the law.¹

What James says, that man is not justified by faith alone, but also by works, does not at all militate against the preceding view. The reconciling of the two views depends chiefly on the drift of the argument pursued by James. For the question with him is not, how men attain righteousness before God, but how they prove to others that they are justified; for his object was to confute hypocrites, who vainly boasted that they had faith. Gross then is the sophistry, not to admit that the word, to justify, is taken in a different sense by James, from that in which it is used by Paul; for they handle different subjects. The word, faith, is also no doubt capable of various meanings. These two things must be taken to the account, before a correct judgment can be formed on the point. We may learn from the context, that James meant no more than that man is not made or proved to be just by a feigned or dead faith, and that he must prove his righteousness by his works. See on this subject my Institutes.

29. *Is he* the God of the Jews only? *is he* not also of the Gentiles? Yes, of the Gentiles also:
30. Seeing *it is* one God² which shall justify the circumcision by faith, and uncircumcision through faith.

29. Num Iudæorum Deus tantùm? an non et Gentium? certè et Gentium.
30. Quandoquidem unus Deus, qui justificabit circumcisionem ex fide, et præputium per fidem.

29. *Is he the God of the Jews only?* The second proposition is, that this righteousness belongs no more to the Jews than to the Gentiles: and it was a great matter that this

---

¹ The phrase, χωρίς ἔργων νόμου, may be rendered, " without the works of law," that is, either natural or revealed; for Gentiles as well as Jews are here contemplated.—*Ed.*

² Εἷς ὁ Θεός—*unus Deus.* Εἷς here means the *same*, see 1 Cor. iii. 8; or if it be rendered *one*, it refers to God as being one in his purpose, and as to the way of salvation. See Zech. xiv. 9.—*Ed.*

point should be urged, in order that a free passage might be made for the kingdom of Christ through the whole world. He does not then ask simply or expressly, whether God was the Creator of the Gentiles, which was admitted without any dispute; but whether he designed to manifest himself as a Saviour also to them. As he had put all mankind on a level, and brought them to the same condition, if there be any difference between them, it is from God, not from themselves, who have all things alike: but if it be true that God designs to make all the nations of the earth partakers of his mercy, then salvation, and righteousness, which is necessary for salvation, must be extended to all. Hence under the name, *God*, is conveyed an intimation of a mutual relationship, which is often mentioned in Scripture,—" I shall be to you a God, and you shall be to me a people." (Jer. xxx. 22.) For the circumstance, that God, for a time, chose for himself a peculiar people, did not make void the origin of mankind, who were all formed after the image of God, and were to be brought up in the world in the hope of a blessed eternity.

30. *Who shall justify*,[1] &c. In saying that some are justified by faith, and some through faith, he seems to have indulged himself in varying his language, while he expresses the same thing, and for this end,—that he might, by the way, touch on the folly of the Jews, who imagined a difference between themselves and the Gentiles, though on the subject of justification there was no difference whatever; for since men became partakers of this grace by faith only, and since faith in all is the same, it is absurd to make a distinction in what is so much alike. I am hence led to think that there is something ironical in the words, as though he said,—" If any wishes to have a difference made between the Gentile and the Jew, let him take this,—that the one obtains righteousness *by* faith, and the other *through* faith." But it may be, that some will prefer this distinction,—that

---

[1] The future is used for the present—" who justifies," after the manner of the Hebrew language, though some consider that the day of judgment is referred to; but he seems to speak of a present act, or as *Grotius* says, of a continued act, which the Hebrews expressed by the future tense.—*Ed.*

the Jews were justified by faith, because they were born the heirs of grace, as the right of adoption was transmitted to them from the Fathers,—and that the Gentiles were justified through faith, because the covenant to them was adventitious.

31. Do we then make void the law through faith? God forbid: yea, we establish the law.	31. Legem igitur irritam facimus per fidem? Ne ita sit: sed Legem stabilimus.

31. *Do we then make*, &c. When the law is opposed to faith, the flesh immediately suspects that there is some contrariety, as though the one were adverse to the other : and this false notion prevails, especially among those who are imbued with wrong ideas as to the law, and leaving the promises, seek nothing else through it but the righteousness of works. And on this account, not only Paul, but our Lord himself, was evil spoken of by the Jews, as though in all his preaching he aimed at the abrogation of the law. Hence it was that he made this protest,—" I came not to undo, but to fulfil the law." (Matt. v. 17.)

And this suspicion regards the moral as well as the ceremonial law; for as the gospel has put an end to the Mosaic ceremonies, it is supposed to have a tendency to destroy the whole dispensation of Moses. And further, as it sweeps away all the righteousness of works, it is believed to be opposed to all those testimonies of the law, by which the Lord has declared, that he has thereby prescribed the way of righteousness and salvation. I therefore take this defence of Paul, not only as to ceremonies, nor as to the commandments which are called moral, but with regard to the whole law universally.[1]

[1] The law here, no doubt means, the law of which mention is made in the preceding verses—the law by the works of which we cannot be justified—the law that is in this respect opposed to faith. To refer us for its meaning to verses 20 and 21, as is done by *Stuart*, "is wholly unwarrantable," and to say that it means the Old Testament; for this is to separate it from its immediate connection without any satisfactory reason. Besides, such an interpretation obliterates an important doctrine, that faith does not render void, or nullify the authority, the use and sanctions of the moral law, but on the contrary, sustains and confirms them. Though it does what the law does not, and cannot do, inasmuch as it saves the sinner whom

For the *moral* law is in reality confirmed and established through faith in Christ, inasmuch as it was given for this end—to lead man to Christ by showing him his iniquity; and without this it cannot be fulfilled, and in vain will it require what ought to be done; nor can it do anything but irritate lust more and more, and thus finally increase man's condemnation; but where there is a coming to Christ, there is first found in him the perfect righteousness of the law, which becomes ours by imputation, and then there is sanctification, by which our hearts are prepared to keep the law; it is indeed imperfectly done, but there is an aiming at the work. Similar is the case with *ceremonies*, which indeed cease and vanish away when Christ comes, but they are in reality confirmed by him; for when they are viewed in themselves they are vain and shadowy images, and then only do they attain anything real and solid, when their end is regarded. In this then consists their chief confirmation, when they have obtained their accomplishment in Christ. Let us then also bear in mind, so to dispense the gospel that by our mode of teaching the law may be confirmed; but let it be sustained by no other strength than that of faith in Christ.

CHAPTER IV.

1. What shall we then say that Abraham, our father as pertaining to the flesh, hath found?
2. For if Abraham were justified by works, he hath *whereof* to glory, but not before God.
3. For what saith the scripture? Abraham believed God, and it was counted unto him for righteousness.[1]

1. Quid ergo dicemus, invenisse Abraham patrem nostrum secundum carnem?
2. Si enim Abraham ex operibus justificatus est, habet quo glorietur, sed non apud Deum.
3. Quid enim Scriptura dicit? Credidit Abraham Deo, et imputatum est illi in justitiam.

the law condemns; it yet effects this without relaxing or dishonouring the law, but in a way that renders it, if possible, more binding, and more honourable, and more illustrious. It only renders the passage more intricate to include the ceremonial law, (for that has more of faith than of law in it,) to which no reference is made in the context: but there seems to be no objection to include the law of conscience, as well as the written law; for faith confirms both, and the word "law," is here without the article, though this indeed of itself is not decisive. The moral law, then, as well as the law of conscience, is what is here intended: for the authority of both is confirmed and strengthened by faith.—*Ed.*

[1] This chapter, as *Turrettin* observes, divides itself into three parts.

1. *What then*, &c. This is a confirmation by example; and it is a very strong one, since all things are alike with regard to the subject and the person; for he was the father of the faithful, to whom we ought all to be conformed; and there is also but one way and not many ways by which righteousness may be obtained by all. In many other things one example would not be sufficient to make a common rule; but as in the person of Abraham there was exhibited a mirror and pattern of righteousness, which belongs in common to the whole Church, rightly does Paul apply what has been written of him alone to the whole body of the Church, and at the same time he gives a check to the Jews, who had nothing more plausible to glory in than that they were the children of Abraham; and they could not have dared to claim to themselves more holiness than what they ascribed to the holy patriarch. Since it is then evident that he was justified freely, his posterity, who claimed a righteousness of their own by the law, ought to have been made silent even through shame.

According to the flesh, &c. Between this clause and the word *father* there is put in Paul's text the verb εὑρηκέναι, in this order—" What shall we say that Abraham our father has found according to the flesh?" On this account, some interpreters think that the question is—" What has Abraham obtained according to the flesh?" If this exposition be approved, the words *according to the flesh* mean naturally or from himself. It is, however, probable that they are to be connected with the word *father*.[1] Besides, as we are wont to be more touched by domestic examples, the dignity of their race, in which the Jews took too much pride, is here

The *first* from 1 to 12 inclusive; the *second* from 13 to 17 inclusive, in which it is proved that the promises made to Abraham did not depend on the law; and the *third* from 18 to the end, in which the faith of Abraham is commended, and the Christian faith briefly referred to.

But *Pareus* makes a different division: 1, Four proofs of justification by faith, from 1 to 16; 2, The dispensation of Abraham, from 17 to 22; 3, The application of the subject, from 23 to 25.—*Ed.*

[1] So did all the fathers according to *Pareus*, and so does the *Vulgate*. But later commentators have taken the words as they stand, and with good reason, for otherwise the correspondence between this and the following verse would not be apparent. *Beza, Hammond,* and *Macknight* take the

again expressly mentioned. But some regard this as spoken
in contempt, as they are elsewhere called the carnal children
of Abraham, being not so spiritually or in a legitimate sense.
But I think that it was expressed as a thing peculiar to the
Jews; for it was a greater honour to be the children of
Abraham by nature and descent, than by mere adoption,
provided there was also faith. He then concedes to the Jews
a closer bond of union, but only for this end—that he might
more deeply impress them that they ought not to depart
from the example of their father.

2. *For if Abraham,* &c. This is an incomplete argument,[1]
which may be made in this form—" If Abraham was justified
by works, he might justly glory : but he had nothing for
which he could glory before God ; then he was not justified
by works." Thus the clause *but not before God*, is the minor
proposition ; and to this must be added the conclusion which
I have stated, though it is not expressed by Paul. He calls
that glorying when we pretend to have anything of our own
to which a reward is supposed to be due at God's tribunal.

words in their proper order; and this is what is done by the Syriac and
Arabic versions.

Κατὰ σάρκα is rendered by *Grotius* and *Macknight*, " by *(per)* the flesh."
Some understand by the word " flesh," circumcision, as *Vatablus;* others,
natural powers, as *Grotius*. But *Beza* and *Hammond* think that it is the
same as what is meant " by works" in the next verse; and " flesh " evidently has this meaning : it signifies often the performance of what the
law requires, the observance not only of ceremonial but also of moral duties.
See Gal. iii. 3 ; vi. 12 ; and especially Phil. iii. 3, 4 ; where Paul gives up
" all confidence in the *flesh*," and enumerates, among other things, his strict
conformity to the law.—*Ed.*

[1] *Epicheirema;* in Greek ἐπιχείρημα, an attempted but an unfinished
process of reasoning. It is not necessary to introduce this sort of syllogism,
it being not the character of Scripture nor of any other writing to discuss
matters in this form.

The word for " glorying " here, καύχημα, is different from that in ch.
iii. 27, καύχησις, and means reason, ground, or cause for glorying, and is
rendered by *Grotius* " unde laudem speret —whereby he may hope for
praise ;" and by *Beza* and *Piscator* " unde glorietur—whereby he may
glory." To complete the following clause, most repeat the words ἔχω
καύχημα—" But he has no ground for glorying before God." *Vatablus*
gives another meaning, " But not with regard to God," that is, with regard
to what he has said in his word; and this view is confirmed by what immediately follows, " For what saith the Scripture ? " In this case there is
nothing understood. That πρὸς θεόν is used in a similar manner, is evident
from other passages : τὰ πρὸς θεόν—" things which pertain to God," *i.e.*, to
God's work or service. See Heb. ii. 17 ; v. 1.—*Ed.*

Since he takes this away from Abraham, who of us can claim for himself the least particle of merit?

3. *For what saith the Scripture?* This is a proof of the minor proposition, or of what he assumed, when he denied that Abraham had any ground for glorying: for if Abraham was justified, because he embraced, by faith, the bountiful mercy of God, it follows, that he had nothing to glory in; for he brought nothing of his own, except a confession of his misery, which is a solicitation for mercy. He, indeed, takes it as granted, that the righteousness of faith is the refuge, and, as it were, the asylum of the sinner, who is destitute of works. For if there be any righteousness by the law or by works, it must be in men themselves; but by faith they derive from another what is wanting in themselves; and hence the righteousness of faith is rightly called imputative.

The passage, which is quoted, is taken from Gen. xv. 6; in which the word *believe* is not to be confined to any particular expression, but it refers to the whole covenant of salvation, and the grace of adoption, which Abraham apprehended by faith. There is, indeed, mentioned there the promise of a future seed; but it was grounded on gratuitous adoption:[1] and it ought to be observed, that salvation without the grace of God is not promised, nor God's grace without salvation; and again, that we are not called to the grace of God nor to the hope of salvation, without having righteousness offered to us.

Taking this view, we cannot but see that those understand not the principles of theology, who think that this testimony recorded by Moses, is drawn aside from its obvious meaning by Paul: for as there is a particular promise there stated, they understand that he acted rightly and faithfully in believing it, and was so far approved by God. But they are in this mistaken; first, because they have not considered that *believing* extends to the whole context, and ought not

---

[1] The adoption is evidently included in the words, found in the first verse of this chapter, "I am thy shield and thy exceeding great reward." What follows is connected with this, and the promise of a numerous seed arose from what Abraham said respecting an heir. His *believing* them had an especial regard to the first promise, as the second, respecting his "seed," was only, as it were, an enlargement of the first, or an addition to it.—*Ed.*

to be confined to one clause. But the principal mistake is, that they begin not with the testimony of God's favour. But God gave this, to make Abraham more assured of his adoption and paternal favour; and included in this was eternal salvation by Christ. Hence Abraham, by believing, embraced nothing but the favour offered to him, being persuaded that it would not be void. Since this was imputed to him for righteousness, it follows, that he was not otherwise just, than as one trusting in God's goodness, and venturing to hope for all things from him. Moses does not, indeed, tell us what men thought of him, but how he was accounted before the tribunal of God. Abraham then laid hold on the benignity of God offered to him in the promise, through which he understood that righteousness was communicated to him. It is necessary, in order to form an opinion of righteousness, to understand this relation between the promise and faith; for there is in this respect the same connection between God and us, as there is, according to the lawyers, between the giver and the person to whom any thing is given, (*datorem et donatarium*—the donor and the donee:) for we can no otherwise attain righteousness, than as it is brought to us, as it were, by the promise of the gospel; and we realize its possession by faith.[1]

How to reconcile what James says, which seems some-

---

[1] The foregoing observations contain a lucid and a satisfactory view of the character of Abraham's faith, perfectly consistent with what is said of it by Paul in this chapter, and in the epistle to the Galatians. Some think that the *principle* of faith was the only thing which the Apostle had in view in referring to Abraham's faith, and that he had no special regard to the object of justifying faith, that is, Christ. But that Christ was, in a measure, revealed to him, is evident from the account given in Genesis, and from what Christ himself has said,—that Abraham saw his day and rejoiced, John viii. 56. At the same time it was the promise of gratuitous mercy, as Calvin intimates, that formed the most distinctive object of Abraham's faith, the promise of a free acceptance, without any regard to works. There are two things which the Apostle clearly intended to show, —that imputation of righteousness is an act of gratuitous favour,—and that it is alone by faith.

There is some difference in the wording, though not in the meaning, of the sentence from Gen. xv. 6. Paul gives it literally according to the Septuagint. The word "Abraham," is put in; instead of "Jehovah," it is "God;" the verb "count," is made passive, and a preposition is placed before "righteousness." The Hebrew is this,—"And he believed on Jehovah, and he counted it to him righteousness." The "it," no doubt, refers

what contrary to this view, I have already explained, and intend to explain more fully, when I come, if the Lord will permit, to expound that Epistle.

Only let us remember this,—that those to whom righteousness is imputed, are justified; since these two things are mentioned by Paul as being the same. We hence conclude, that the question is not, what men are in themselves, but how God regards them? not that purity of conscience and integrity of life are to be separated from the gratuitous favour of God; but that when the reason is asked, why God loves us and owns us as just, it is necessary that Christ should come forth as one who clothes us with his own righteousness.

4. Now to him that worketh is the reward not reckoned of grace, but of debt.	4. Ei quidem qui operatur merces non imputatur secundum gratiam, sed secundum debitum :
5. But to him that worketh not, but believeth on him that justifieth the ungodly, his faith is counted for righteousness.	5. Ei verò qui non operatur, credit autem in eum qui justificat impium, imputatur fides sua in justitiam.

4. *To him indeed who works*, &c. It is not he, whom he calls a worker, who is given to good works, to which all the children of God ought to attend, but the person who seeks to merit something by his works: and in a similar way he calls him no worker who depends not on the merit of what he does. He would not, indeed, have the faithful to be idle; but he only forbids them to be mercenaries, so as to demand any thing from God, as though it were justly their due.

to what is included in the word "believed." So Paul explains it in ver. 9, where he expressly puts down πίστις, faith.

It has been said that this faith of Abraham was not faith in Christ, according to what the context shows in Genesis. And it was not so specifically; nor does Paul represent it as such; for this was not his object. He states it throughout as faith in God; it was believing the testimony of God; but that testimony embraced a promise respecting Christ; so that it included the Saviour within its compass. We must remember that Paul's object is to establish this truth,—that righteousness is attained by faith and not by works; and that for this end he adduces the examples both of Abraham and David. It was not his design to point out specifically the object of justifying faith. We must keep this in view, in order to understand the reasoning of the Apostle in this chapter: it is the power and efficacy of faith, in opposition to all works, that he particularly dwells upon; and the gracious promise of God was its object.—*Ed.*

We have before reminded you, that the question is not here how we are to regulate our life, but how we are to be saved : and he argues from what is contrary,—that God confers not righteousness on us because it is due, but bestows it as a gift. And indeed I agree with *Bucer*, who proves that the argument is not made to depend on one expression, but on the whole passage, and formed in this manner, "If one merits any thing by his work, what is merited is not freely imputed to him, but rendered to him as his due. Faith is counted for righteousness, not that it procures any merit for us, but because it lays hold on the goodness of God : hence righteousness is not due to us, but freely bestowed." For as Christ of his own good-will justifies us through faith, Paul always regards this as an evidence of our emptiness ; for what do we believe, except that Christ is an expiation to reconcile us to God ? The same truth is found in other words in Gal. iii. 11, where it is said, "That no man is justified by the law, it is evident, for the just shall by faith live : but the law is not by faith ; but he who doeth these things shall live in them." Inasmuch, then, as the law promises reward to works, he hence concludes, that the righteousness of faith, which is free, accords not with that which is operative : this could not be were faith to justify by means of works.—We ought carefully to observe these comparisons, by which every merit is entirely done away.

5. *But believes on him,* &c. This is a very important sentence, in which he expresses the substance and nature both of faith and of righteousness. He indeed clearly shews that faith brings us righteousness, not because it is a meritorious act, but because it obtains for us the favour of God.[1] Nor does he declare only that God is the giver of righteousness,

---

[1] Some have stumbled at this sentence,—" his faith is counted for righteousness," and have misapplied it, as though faith were in itself the cause of righteousness, and hence a meritorious act, and not the way and means of attaining righteousness. Condensed sentences will not submit to the rules of logic, but must be interpreted according to the context and explanations elsewhere found. "His faith" means, no doubt, his faith in the Promise, or in God who promises, or in him who, as is said in this verse, "justifies the ungodly:" hence what is believed, or the object of faith, is what is counted for righteousness. This accords with the declarations,—that "man is justified by faith," ch. iii. 28,—and that "the

but he also arraigns us of unrighteousness, in order that the bounty of God may come to aid our necessity: in short, no one will seek the righteousness of faith except he who feels that he is ungodly; for this sentence is to be applied to what is said in this passage,—that faith adorns us with the righteousness of another, which it seeks as a gift from God. And here again, God is said to justify us when he freely forgives sinners, and favours those, with whom he might justly be angry, with his love, that is, when his mercy obliterates our unrighteousness.

6. Even as David also describeth the blessedness of the man, unto whom God imputeth righteousness without works,	6. Quemadmodum etiam David finit beatudinem hominis, cui Deus imputat justitiam absque operibus,
7. *Saying*, Blessed *are* they whose iniquities are forgiven, and whose sins are covered.	7. Beati quorum remissæ sunt iniquitates, et quorum tecta sunt peccata:
8. Blessed *is* the man to whom the Lord will not impute sin.	8. Beatus vir, cui non imputavit Dominus peccatum.

6. *As David also defines,* &c. We hence see the sheer sophistry of those who limit the works of the law to ceremonies; for he now simply calls those works, without anything added, which he had before called the works of the law. Since no one can deny that a simple and unrestricted mode of speaking, such as we find here, ought to be understood of every work without any difference, the same view must be held throughout the whole argument. There is indeed nothing less reasonable than to remove from ceremonies only the power of justifying, since Paul excludes all works indefinitely. To the same purpose is the negative clause,—that God justifies men by *not* imputing sin: and by these words we are taught that righteousness, according

righteousness of God" is "by faith," ch. iii. 22. If *by* faith, then faith itself is not that righteousness.

"Beware," says *Chalmers*, "of having any such view of faith as will lead you to annex to it the kind of merit, or of claim, or of glorying under the gospel, which are annexed to works under the law. This, in fact, were just animating with a legal spirit the whole phraseology and doctrine of the gospel. It is God who justifies. He drew up the title-deed, and he bestowed the title-deed. It is ours simply to lay hold of it...Any other view of faith than that which excludes boasting must be altogether unscriptural."—*Ed.*

to Paul, is nothing else than the remission of sins; and further, that this remission is gratuitous, because it is imputed without works, which the very name of remission indicates; for the creditor who is paid does not remit, but he who spontaneously cancels the debt through mere kindness. Away, then, with those who teach us to redeem pardon for our sins by satisfactions; for Paul borrows an argument from this pardon to prove the gratuitous gift of righteousness.[1] How then is it possible for them to agree with Paul? They say, "We must satisfy by works the justice of God, that we may obtain the pardon of our sins:" but he, on the contrary, reasons thus,—"The righteousness of faith is gratuitous, and without works, because it depends on the remission of sins." Vicious, no doubt, would be this reasoning, if any works interposed in the remission of sins.

Dissipated also, in like manner, by the words of the Prophet, are the puerile fancies of the schoolmen respecting half remission. Their childish fiction is,—that though the fault is remitted, the punishment is still retained by God. But the Prophet not only declares that our sins are covered, that is, removed from the presence of God; but also adds, that they are not imputed. How can it be consistent, that God should punish those sins which he does not impute? Safe then does this most glorious declaration remain to us— "That he is justified by faith, who is cleared before God by a gratuitous remission of his sins." We may also hence learn, the unceasing perpetuity of gratuitous righteousness

---

[1] Speaking of this righteousness, *Pareus* says, "It is not ours, otherwise God would not gratuitously impute it, but bestow it as a matter of right; nor is it a habit or quality, for it is without works, and imputed to the *ungodly*, who have habitually nothing but iniquities; but it is a gratuitous remission, a covering, a non-imputation of sins."

It is a striking proof of what the Apostle had in view here, that he stops short and does not quote the whole verse from Ps. xxxii. 2. He leaves out, "and in whose spirit there is no guile:" and why? Evidently because his subject is justification, and not sanctification. He has thus most clearly marked the difference between the two.

Sins may be said to be "forgiven" or remitted, because they are debts, and "covered," because they are filthy and abominable in the sight of God: and they are said to be "not imputed," or not put to one's account, in order to convey an assurance, that they are wholly removed, and shall be no more remembered.—*Ed.*

through life: for when David, being wearied with the continual anguish of his own conscience, gave utterance to this declaration, he no doubt spoke according to his own experience; and he had now served God for many years. He then had found by experience, after having made great advances, that all are miserable when summoned before God's tribunal; and he made this avowal, that there is no other way of obtaining blessedness, except the Lord receives us into favour by not imputing our sins. Thus fully refuted also is the romance of those who dream, that the righteousness of faith is but initial, and that the faithful afterwards retain by works the possession of that righteousness which they had first attained by no merits.

It invalidates in no degree what Paul says, that works are sometimes imputed for righteousness, and that other kinds of blessedness are mentioned. It is said in Ps. cvi. 30, that it was imputed to Phinehas, the Lord's priest, for righteousness, because he took away reproach from Israel by inflicting punishment on an adulterer and a harlot. It is true, we learn from this passage, that he did a righteous deed; but we know that a person is not justified by one act. What is indeed required is perfect obedience, and complete in all its parts, according to the import of the promise,—" He who shall do these things shall live in them." (Deut. iv. 1.) How then was this judgment which he inflicted imputed to him for righteousness? He must no doubt have been previously justified by the grace of God: for they who are already clothed in the righteousness of Christ, have God not only propitious to them, but also to their works, the spots and blemishes of which are covered by the purity of Christ, lest they should come to judgment. As works, infected with no defilements, are alone counted just, it is quite evident that no human work whatever can please God, except through a favour of this kind. But if the righteousness of faith is the only reason why our works are counted just, you see how absurd is the argument,—" That as righteousness is ascribed to works, righteousness is not by faith only." But I set against them this invincible argument, that all works are to be condemned as those of unrighteousness, except a man be justified solely by faith.

The like is said of blessedness: they are pronounced blessed who fear the Lord, who walk in his ways, (Ps. cxxviii. 1,) who meditate on his law day and night, (Ps. i. 2:) but as no one doeth these things so perfectly as he ought, so as fully to come up to God's command, all blessedness of this kind is nothing worth, until we be made blessed by being purified and cleansed through the remission of sins, and thus cleansed, that we may become capable of enjoying that blessedness which the Lord promises to his servants for attention to the law and to good works. Hence the righteousness of works is the effect of the righteousness of God, and the blessedness arising from works is the effect of the blessedness which proceeds from the remission of sins. Since the cause ought not and cannot be destroyed by its own effect, absurdly do they act, who strive to subvert the righteousness of faith by works.

But some one may say, "Why may we not maintain, on the ground of these testimonies, that man is justified and made blessed by works? for the words of Scripture declare that man is justified and made blessed by works as well as by faith." Here indeed we must consider the order of causes as well as the dispensation of God's grace: for inasmuch as whatever is declared, either of the righteousness of works or of the blessedness arising from them, does not exist, until this only true righteousness of faith has preceded, and does alone discharge all it's offices, this last must be built up and established, in order that the other may, as a fruit from a tree, grow from it and flourish.

9. *Cometh* this blessedness then upon the circumcision *only*,[1] or upon

9. Beatudo ergo ista in circumcisionem modò, an et in præputium

[1] This "only" is not in the original, but is supplied by most commentators: yet it is not necessary, nor makes the meaning consistent with what follows in ver. 10. The Καὶ in the next clause is omitted in many copies; but if retained, it will not alter the sense. We may render this part of the verse thus,

"*Came* then this blessedness on the circumcision, or even on the uncircumcision?"

Then in the tenth verse he answers in the negative,—that it was not

the uncircumcision also? for we say that faith was reckoned to Abraham for righteousness. 10. How was it then reckoned? when he was in circumcision, or in uncircumcision? Not in circumcision, but in uncircumcision.	competit? Dicimus enim quòd imputata fuit Abrahæ fides in justitiam. 10. Quomodo igitur imputata fuit? in circumcisione quum esset, an in præputio? non in circumcisione, sed in præputio.

As circumcision and uncircumcision are alone mentioned, some unwisely conclude, that the only question is, that righteousness is not attained by the ceremonies of the law. But we ought to consider what sort of men were those with whom Paul was reasoning; for we know that hypocrites, whilst they generally boast of meritorious works, do yet disguise themselves in outward masks. The Jews also had a peculiar way of their own, by which they departed, through a gross abuse of the law, from true and genuine righteousness. Paul had said, that no one is blessed but he whom God reconciles to himself by a gratuitous pardon; it hence follows, that all are accursed, whose works come to judgment. Now then this principle is to be held, that men are justified, not by their own worthiness, but by the mercy of God. But still, this is not enough, except remission of sins precedes all works, and of these the first was circumcision, which initiated the Jewish people into the service of God. He therefore proceeds to demonstrate this also.

We must ever bear in mind, that circumcision is here mentioned as the initial work, so to speak, of the righteousness of the law: for the Jews gloried not in it as the symbol of God's favour, but as a meritorious observance of the law: and on this account it was that they regarded themselves better than others, as though they possessed a higher excellency before God. We now see that the dispute is not about one rite, but that under one thing is included every work of the law; that is, every work to which reward can be due. Circumcision then was especially mentioned, because it was the basis of the righteousness of the law.

to Abraham while " in circumcision," but while he was "in uncircumcision." The reference is evidently to the first state of things, to the case of Abraham himself. Abraham is supposed to have been justified by faith about *fourteen* years before he was circumcised.—*Ed.*

But Paul maintains the contrary, and thus reasons: "If Abraham's righteousness was the remission of sins, (which he safely takes as granted,) and if Abraham attained this before circumcision, it then follows that remission of sins is not given for preceding merits." You see that the argument rests on the order of causes and effects; for the cause is always before its effect; and righteousness was possessed by Abraham before he had circumcision.

11. And he received the sign of circumcision, a seal of the righteousness of the faith which *he had yet* being uncircumcised: that he might be the father of all them that believe, though they be not circumcised; that righteousness might be imputed unto them also:	11. Et signum accepit circumcisionis, sigillum justitiæ fidei quæ fuerat in præputio; ut esset pater omnium credentium per præputium, quo ipsis quoque imputetur justitia;
12. And the father of circumcision to them who are not of the circumcision only, but who also walk in the steps of that faith of our father Abraham, which *he had* being *yet* uncircumcised.	12. Et pater circumcisionis, non iis qui sunt ex circumcisione tantum, sed qui insistunt vestigiis fidei, quæ fuit in præputio patris nostri Abrahæ.

11. *And he received the sign*, &c. In order to anticipate an objection, he shows that circumcision was not unprofitable and superfluous, though it could not justify; but it had another very remarkable use, it had the office of sealing, and as it were of ratifying the righteousness of faith. And yet he intimates at the same time, by stating what its object was, that it was not the cause of righteousness, it indeed tended to confirm the righteousness of faith, and that already obtained in uncircumcision. He then derogates or takes away nothing from it.

We have indeed here a remarkable passage with regard to the general benefits of sacraments. According to the testimony of Paul, they are seals by which the promises of God are in a manner imprinted on our hearts, (*Dei promissiones cordibus nostris quodammodo imprimuntur,*) and the certainty of grace confirmed (*sancitur gratiæ certitudo.*) And though by themselves they profit nothing, yet God has designed them to be the instruments (*instrumenta*) of his grace; and he effects by the secret grace of his Spirit, that they should not be without benefit in the elect. And though they are dead and unprofitable symbols to the reprobate, they yet ever retain their import and character (*vim suam et naturam :*) for though our unbelief may deprive them of their effect, yet it cannot weaken or extinguish the truth of God. Hence it remains a fixed principle, that sacred symbols are testimonies, by which God seals his grace on our hearts.

As to the symbol of circumcision, this especially is to be said, that a twofold grace was represented by it. God had promised to Abraham a blessed seed, from whom salvation was to be expected by the whole world. On this depended the promise—" I will be to thee a God." (Gen. xvii. 7.) Then a gratuitous reconciliation with God was included in that symbol: and for this reason it was necessary that the faithful should look forward to the promised seed. On the other hand, God requires integrity and holiness of life ; he indicated by the symbol how this could be attained, that is, by cutting off in man whatever is born of the flesh, for his whole nature had become vicious. He therefore reminded Abraham by the external sign, that he was spiritually to cut off the corruption of the flesh ; and to this Moses has also alluded in Deut. x. 16. And to show that it was not the work of man, but of God, he commanded tender infants to be circumcised, who, on account of their age, could not have performed such a command. Moses has indeed expressly mentioned spiritual circumcision as the work of divine power, as you will find in Deut. xxx. 6, where he says, " The Lord will circumcise thine heart:" and the Prophets afterwards declared the same thing much more clearly.

As there are two points in baptism now, so there were formerly in circumcision ; for it was a symbol of a new life, and also of the remission of sins. But the fact as to Abraham himself, that righteousness preceded circumcision, is not always the case in sacraments, as it is evident from the case of Isaac and his posterity: but God intended to give such an instance once at the beginning, that no one might ascribe salvation to external signs.[1]

[1] The word " sign" in this passage, σημεῖον, seems not to mean an out-

That he might be the father, &c. Mark how the circumcision of Abraham confirms our faith with regard to gratuitous righteousness; for it was the sealing of the righteousness of faith, that righteousness might also be imputed to us who believe. And thus Paul, by a remarkable dexterity, makes to recoil on his opponents what they might have adduced as an objection: for since the truth and import (*veritas et vis*) of circumcision were found in an uncircumcised state, there was no ground for the Jews to elevate themselves so much above the Gentiles.

But as a doubt might arise, whether it behoves us, after the example of Abraham, to confirm also the same righteousness by the sign of circumcision, how came the Apostle to make this omission? Even because he thought that the question was sufficiently settled by the drift of his argument: for as this truth had been admitted, that circumcision availed only to seal the grace of God, it follows, that it is now of no benefit to us, who have a sign instituted in its place by our Lord. As then there is no necessity now for circumcision, where baptism is, he was not disposed to contend unnecessarily for that respecting which there was no doubt, that is, why the righteousness of faith was not sealed to the Gentiles in the same way as it was to Abraham. *To believe in uncircumcision* means, that the Gentiles, being satisfied with their own condition, did not introduce the seal of circumcision: and so the proposition διὰ, *by*, is put for ἐν, *in*.[1]

---

ward token of something inward, but a mark, circumcision itself, which was imprinted, as it were, as a mark in the flesh. So *Macknight* renders it, "The mark of circumcision." That circumcision was a sign or a symbol of what was spiritual, is evident: but this is not what is taught here. Circumcision is expressly called "a token," or a sign, in Gen. xvii. 11; but it is said to have been "a token of the covenant," that is, a proof and an evidence of it. The *design* of circumcision is expressed by the next word, σφραγῖδα—seal. This sometimes signified the instrument, 1 Kings xxi. 8; and sometimes the impression, Rev. v. 1: and the impression was used for various purposes,—to close up a document, to secure a thing, and also to confirm an agreement. It is taken here in the latter sense; circumcision was a "seal," a confirmation, an evidence, a proof, or a pledge, "of the righteousness" obtained "by faith." We meet not with any distinct statement of this kind in Genesis: it is what the Apostle had gathered, and rightly gathered, from the account given us of what took place between God and Abraham.—*Ed.*

[1] See a similar instance in chap. ii. 27.—*Ed.*

12. *To them who are not,* &c. The verb, *are,* is in this place to be taken for, " are deemed to be:" for he touches the carnal descendants of Abraham, who, having nothing but outward circumcision, confidently gloried in it. The other thing, which was the chief matter, they neglected; for the faith of Abraham, by which alone he obtained salvation, they did not imitate. It hence appears, how carefully he distinguished between faith and the sacrament; not only that no one might be satisfied with the one without the other, as though it were sufficient for justifying; but also that faith alone might be set forth as accomplishing everything: for while he allows the circumcised Jews to be justified, he expressly makes this exception—provided in true faith they followed the example of Abraham; for why does he mention faith while in uncircumcision, except to show, that it is alone sufficient, without the aid of anything else? Let us then beware, lest any of us, by halving things, blend together the two modes of justification.

What we have stated disproves also the scholastic dogma respecting the difference between the sacraments of the Old and those of the New Testament; for they deny the power of justifying to the former, and assign it to the latter. But if Paul reasons correctly, when he argues that circumcision does not justify, because Abraham was justified by faith, the same reason holds good for us, while we deny that men are justified by baptism, inasmuch as they are justified by the same faith with that of Abraham.

13. For the promise, that he should be the heir of the world, *was* not to Abraham, or to his seed, through the law, but through the righteousness of faith.	13. Non enim per Legem promissio Abrahæ et semini ejus data est, ut esset hæres mundi; sed per justitiam fidei.

13. *For the promise,* &c. He now more clearly sets the law and faith in opposition, the one to the other, which he had before in some measure done; and this ought to be carefully observed: for if faith borrows nothing from the law in order to justify, we hence understand, that it has respect to nothing else but to the mercy of God. And further, the romance of those who would have this to have been said of

ceremonies, may be easily disproved; for if works contributed anything towards justification, it ought not to have been said, through the written law, but rather, through the law of nature. But Paul does not oppose spiritual holiness of life to ceremonies, but faith and its righteousness. The meaning then is, that heirship was promised to Abraham, not because he deserved it by keeping the law, but because he had obtained righteousness by faith. And doubtless (as Paul will presently show) consciences can then only enjoy solid peace, when they know that what is not justly due is freely given them.[1]

Hence also it follows, that this benefit, the reason for which applies equally to both, belongs to the Gentiles no less than to the Jews; for if the salvation of men is based on the goodness of God alone, they check and hinder its course, as much as they can, who exclude from it the Gentiles.

That he should be the heir of the world,[2] &c. Since he now

---

[1] Critics have differed as to the disjunctive ἤ, *or*, " or to his seed." Some think it is put for καὶ, *and:* but *Pareus* thinks that it has a special meaning, intended to anticipate an objection. The Jews might have said, " If the case with Abraham is as stated, it is not so with his seed who received the law." Yes, says Paul, there is no difference, " The promise to Abraham, or to his seed, to whom the law was actually given, was not by the law."

Hammond renders the whole verse more literally than in our version,—
" The promise to Abraham or to his seed, that he should be the heir of the world, was not by the law, but through the righteousness of faith."—*Ed.*

[2] There is in Genesis no expression conveyed in these words; but the probability is, that he intended to express in another form what he distinctly quotes in verse 17th, " I have made thee a father of many nations."

The word " father," in this case, has been commonly understood to mean a leader, a pattern, a model, an exemplar, a forerunner, as Abraham was the first believer justified by faith, of whom there is an express record. But the idea seems to be somewhat different. He was a father as the first possessor of an inheritance which was to descend to all his children. The inheritance was given him by grace through faith; it was to descend, as it were, to all his lawful posterity, to all his legitimate seed, that is, to all who possessed the like faith with himself. He is therefore called the father of many nations, because many nations would become his legitimate heirs by becoming believers; and in the same sense must be regarded the expression here, " the heir of the world;" he was the representative of all the believing world, and made an heir of an inheritance which was to come to the world in general, to the believing Jews and to the believing Gentiles. He was the heir, the first possessor, of what was to descend to the world

speaks of eternal salvation, the Apostle seems to have somewhat unseasonably led his readers to the world; but he includes generally under this word *world,* the restoration which was expected through Christ. The chief thing was indeed the restoration of life; it was yet necessary that the fallen state of the whole world should be repaired. The Apostle, in Heb. i. 2, calls Christ the heir of all the good things of God; for the adoption which we obtain through his favour restores to us the possession of the inheritance which we lost in Adam; and as under the type of the land of Canaan, not only the hope of a heavenly life was exhibited to Abraham, but also the full and complete blessing of God, the Apostle rightly teaches us, that the dominion of the world was promised to him. Some taste of this the godly have in the present life; for how much soever they may at times be oppressed with want, yet as they partake with a peaceable conscience of those things which God has created for their use, and as they enjoy through his mercy and good-will his earthly benefits no otherwise than as pledges and earnests of eternal life, their poverty does in no degree prevent them from acknowledging heaven, and the earth, and the sea, as their own possessions.

Though the ungodly swallow up the riches of the world, they can yet call nothing as their own; but they rather snatch them as it were by stealth; for they possess them under the curse of God. It is indeed a great comfort to the godly in their poverty, that though they fare slenderly, they yet steal nothing of what belongs to another, but receive their lawful allowance from the hand of their celestial Father, until they enter on the full possession of their inheritance, when all creatures shall be made subservient to their glory; for both heaven and earth shall be renewed for this end,—that according to their measure they may contribute to render glorious the kingdom of God.

without any difference. He was the heir of the world in the same sense as he was "the father of all who believe," as he is said to have been in verse eleventh.

The inheritance was doubtless eternal life or the heavenly kingdom, the country above, of which the land of Canaan was a type and a pledge. See Heb. xi. 12, 13, 16.—*Ed.*

14. For if they which are of the law *be* heirs, faith is made void, and the promise made of none effect:

15. Because the law worketh wrath: for where no law is, *there is* no transgression.

14. Si enim ii qui sunt ex Lege hæredes sunt, exinanita est fides et abolita est promissio:

15. Nam Lex iram efficit; siquidem ubi non est Lex, neque etiam transgressio.

14. *For if they who are of the law,* &c. He takes his argument from what is impossible or absurd, that the favour which Abraham obtained from God, was not promised to him through any legal agreement, or through any regard to works; for if this condition had been interposed—that God would favour those only with adoption who deserved, or who performed the law, no one could have dared to feel confident that it belonged to him: for who is there so conscious of so much perfection that he can feel assured that the inheritance is due to him through the righteousness of the law? Void then would faith be made; for an impossible condition would not only hold the minds of men in suspense and anxiety, but fill them also with fear and trembling: and thus the fulfilment of the promises would be rendered void; for they avail nothing but when received by faith. If our adversaries had ears to hear this one reason, the contest between us might easily be settled.

The Apostle assumes it as a thing indubitable, that the promises would by no means be effectual except they were received with full assurance of mind. But what would be the case if the salvation of men was based on the keeping of the law? consciences would have no certainty, but would be harassed with perpetual inquietude, and at length sink in despair; and the promise itself, the fulfilment of which depended on what is impossible, would also vanish away without producing any fruit. Away then with those who teach the common people to seek salvation for themselves by works, seeing that Paul declares expressly, that the promise is abolished if we depend on works. But it is especially necessary that this should be known,—that when there is a reliance on works, faith is reduced to nothing. And hence we also learn what faith is, and what sort of righteousness ought that of works to be, in which men may safely trust.

The Apostle teaches us, that faith perishes, except the

soul rests on the goodness of God. Faith then is not a naked knowledge either of God or of his truth; nor is it a simple persuasion that God is, that his word is the truth; but a sure knowledge of God's mercy, which is received from the gospel, and brings peace of conscience with regard to God, and rest to the mind. The sum of the matter then is this,—that if salvation depends on the keeping of the law, the soul can entertain no confidence respecting it, yea, that all the promises offered to us by God will become void: we must thus become wretched and lost, if we are sent back to works to find out the cause or the certainty of salvation.

15. *For the law causeth wrath,* &c. This is a confirmation of the last verse, derived from the contrary effect of the law; for as the law generates nothing but vengeance, it cannot bring grace. It can indeed show to the good and the perfect the way of life: but as it prescribes to the sinful and corrupt what they ought to do, and supplies them with no power for doing, it exhibits them as guilty before the tribunal of God. For such is the viciousness of our nature, that the more we are taught what is right and just, the more openly is our iniquity discovered, and especially our contumacy, and thus a heavier judgment is incurred.

By *wrath,* understand God's judgment, which meaning it has everywhere. They who explain it of the wrath of the sinner, excited by the law, inasmuch as he hates and execrates the Lawgiver, whom he finds to be opposed to his lusts, say what is ingenious, but not suitable to this passage; for Paul meant no other thing, than that condemnation only is what is brought on us all by the law, as it is evident from the common use of the expression, and also from the reason which he immediately adds.

Where there is no law, &c. This is the proof, by which he confirms what he had said; for it would have been difficult to see how God's *wrath* is kindled against us through the law, unless it had been made more apparent. And the reason is, that as the knowledge of God's justice is discovered by the law, the less excuse we have, and hence the more grievously we offend against God; for they who despise the known will of God, justly deserve to sustain a heavier punishment, than those who offend through ignorance. But the Apostle speaks not of the mere transgression of what is right, from which no man is exempt; but he calls that a transgression, when man, having been taught what pleases and displeases God, knowingly and wilfully passes over the boundaries fixed by God's word; or, in other words, transgression here is not a mere act of sin, but a wilful determination to violate what is right.[1] The particle, *οὗ, where*, which I take as an adverb, some consider to be a relative, *of which;* but the former reading is the most suitable, and the most commonly received. Whichever reading you may follow, the meaning will be the same,—that he who is not instructed by the written law, when he sins, is not guilty of so great a transgression, as he is who knowingly breaks and transgresses the law of God.

16. Therefore *it is* of faith, that *it might be* by grace; to the end the promise might be sure to all the seed; not to that only which is of the law, but to that also which is of the faith of Abraham; who is the father of us all,

17. (As it is written, I have made thee a father of many nations,) before him whom he believed, *even* God, who quickeneth the dead, and calleth those things which be not as though they were.

16. Propterea ex fide, ut secundum gratiam, quo firma sit promissio universo semini non ei quod est ex Lege solùm, sed quod est ex fide Abrahæ, qui est pater omnium nostrûm,

17. (Sicut scriptum est, Quòd patrem multarum gentium posui te,) coram Deo, cui credidit, qui vivificat mortuos et vocat ea quæ non sunt tanquàm sint.

16. *It is therefore of faith*, &c. This is the winding up of the argument; and you may summarily include the whole

---

[1] It is better to take this sentence, "Where there is no law, there is no transgression," according to its obvious meaning; as it comports better with the former clause. The reasoning seems to be this,—" The promise is by faith, and not by the law; for the law brings wrath or condemnation: but where there is no law, there is no transgression to occasion wrath." The same idea is essentially conveyed in ver. 16, where it is said, that the promise is sure, because it is through faith and by grace. Had it been by the law, there would have been transgression and wrath, and hence the loss of the promise.

This verse is connected with the 13th rather than with the 14th. It contains another reason, besides what the 14th gives, in confirmation of what is said in the 13th. Hence *Macknight* renders γὰρ, in this verse, "farther," which renders the connection more evident. "Where no law is, there is no transgression, and therefore no wrath or punishment; but where law is, there is transgression, wrath, and punishment."—*Pareus.*

of it in this statement,—" If the heirship of salvation comes to us by works, then faith in it vanishes, the promise of it is abolished; but it is necessary that both these should be sure and certain; hence it comes to us by faith, so that its stability, being based on the goodness of God alone, may be secured." See how the Apostle, regarding faith as a thing firm and certain, considers hesitancy and doubt as unbelief, by which faith is abolished, and the promise abrogated. And yet this doubting is what the schoolmen call a moral conjecture, and which, alas! they substitute for faith.

That it might be by grace, &c. Here, in the first place, the Apostle shows, that nothing is set before faith but mere grace; and this, as they commonly say, is its object: for were it to look on merits, absurdly would Paul infer, that whatever it obtains for us is gratuitous. I will repeat this again in other words,—" If grace be everything that we obtain by faith, then every regard for works is laid in the dust." But what next follows more fully removes all ambiguity,— that the promise then only stands firm, when it recumbs on grace: for by this expression Paul confirms this truth, that as long as men depend on works, they are harassed with doubts; for they deprive themselves of what the promises contain. Hence, also, we may easily learn, that grace is not to be taken, as some imagine, for the gift of regeneration, but for a gratuitous favour: for as regeneration is never perfect, it can never suffice to pacify souls, nor of itself can it make the promise certain.

Not to that only which is of the law, &c. Though these words mean in another place those who, being absurd zealots of the law, bind themselves to its yoke, and boast of their confidence in it, yet here they mean simply the Jewish nation, to whom the law of the Lord had been delivered. For Paul teaches us in another passage, that all who remain bound to the dominion of the law, are subject to a curse; it is then certain that they are excluded from the participation of grace. He does not then call them the servants of the law, who, adhering to the righteousness of works, renounce Christ; but they were those Jews who had been brought up in the law, and yet professed the name of Christ. But that the sentence may be made clearer, let it be worded thus,—" Not to those only who are of the law, but to all who imitate the faith of Abraham, though they had not the law before."

Who is the father of us all, &c. The relative has the meaning of a causative particle ; for he meant to prove, that the Gentiles were become partakers of this grace, inasmuch as by the same oracle, by which the heirship was conferred on Abraham and his seed, were the Gentiles also constituted his seed: for he is said to have been made the father, not of one nation, but of many nations ; by which was presignified the future extension of grace, then confined to Israel alone. For except the promised blessing had been extended to them, they could not have been counted as the offspring of Abraham. The past tense of the verb, according to the common usage of Scripture, denotes the certainty of the Divine counsel ; for though nothing then was less apparent, yet as God had thus decreed, he is rightly said to have been made the father of many nations. Let the testimony of Moses be included in a parenthesis, that this clause, " Who is the father of us all," may be connected with the other, "before God," &c. : for it was necessary to explain also what that relationship was, that the Jews might not glory too much in their carnal descent. Hence he says, " He is our *father before God ;*" which means the same as though he had said, " He is our spiritual father;" for he had this privilege, not from his own flesh, but from the promise of God.[1]

[1] It appears from *Pareus* and *Hammond*, that some of the Fathers, such as *Chrysostom* and *Theophylact*, regarded κατίναντι in the sense of ὁμοίως, *like,* and have rendered the passage, " like God, in whom he believed;" that is, that as God is not partial, but the Father of all, so Abraham was. But this meaning is not consistent with the import of κατίναντι, nor with the context. The preposition is found in four other places, Mark xi. 2 ; xii. 41 ; xiii. 3 ; Luke xix. 30, and invariably means *before,* or, *over against.* The *Septuagint* use it in Num. xxv. 4, in the sense of *before,* κατίναντι τοῦ ἡλίου—" before the sun," not " *against* the sun," as in our version ; for the word in Hebrew is נגד, *coram, in conspectu.* The context also requires this meaning: Abraham was a father of many nations *before* God, or, in the view or estimation of God, and not in the view or estimation of men, because God, as it is said at the end of the verse, regards things which are not, as though they were. Hence Abraham was already in God's view, according to his purpose, the father of many nations.

The collocation of the words is said by *Wolfius* to be an instance of Atti-

17. *Whom he believed, who quickens the dead,* &c. In this circuitous form is expressed the very substance of Abraham's faith, that by his example an opening might be made for the Gentiles. He had indeed to attain, in a wonderful way, the promise which he had heard from the Lord's mouth, since there was then no token of it. A seed was promised to him as though he was in vigour and strength; but he was as it were dead. It was hence necessary for him to raise up his thoughts to the power of God, by which the dead are quickened. It was therefore not strange that the Gentiles, who were barren and dead, should be introduced into the same society. He then who denies them to be capable of grace, does wrong to Abraham, whose faith was sustained by this thought,—that it matters not whether he was dead or not who is called by the Lord; to whom it is an easy thing, even by a word, to raise the dead through his own power.

We have here also a type and a pattern of the call of us all, by which our beginning is set before our eyes, not as to our first birth, but as to the hope of future life,—that when we are called by the Lord we emerge from nothing; for whatever we may seem to be we have not, no, not a spark of anything good, which can render us fit for the kingdom of God. That we may indeed on the other hand be in a suitable state to hear the call of God, we must be altogether dead in ourselves. The character of the divine calling is, that they who are dead are raised by the Lord, that they who are nothing begin to be something through his power. The word *call* ought not to be confined to preaching, but it is to be taken, according to the usage of Scripture, for raising up; and it is intended to set forth more fully the power of God, who raises up, as it were by a nod only, whom he wills.[1]

cism, the word Θεοῦ, being separated from its preposition: and οὗ is put for ᾧ by the grammatical law of attraction; and *Stuart* brings three similar instances of the relative being regulated by the case of its noun, though preceding it in the sentence, Mark vi. 16; Acts xxi. 16; and Rom. vi. 17.

[1] The idea of commanding to existence, or of effecting, is given by many commentators to the word καλοῦντος; but this seems not necessary. The simple notion of calling, naming, regarding, or representing, is more consistent with the passage, and with the construction of the sentence: and the various modes of rendering it, which critics have proposed, have arisen

18. Who against hope believed in hope, that he might become the father of many nations, according to that which was spoken, So shall thy seed be.	18. Qui præter (*vel* supra) spem super spe credidit, ut esset[1] pater multarum gentium, secundum quod dictum erat, Sic erit semen tuum.

18. *Who against hope,* &c. If we thus read, the sense is, that when there was no probable reason, yea, when all things were against him, he yet continued to believe. And, doubtless, there is nothing more injurious to faith than to fasten our minds to our eyes, that we may from what we see, seek a reason for our hope. We may also read, " above hope," and perhaps more suitably; as though he had said that by his faith he far surpassed all that he could conceive; for except faith flies upward on celestial wings, so as to look down on all the perceptions of the flesh as on things far below, it will stick fast in the mud of the world. But Paul uses the word hope twice in this verse: in the first instance, he means a probable evidence for hoping, such as can be derived from nature and carnal reason; in the second, he refers to faith given by God;[2] for when he had no ground

---

from not taking the word in its most obvious meaning. The literal version is, " and who calls things not existing as existing,"—καὶ καλοῦντος τὰ μὴ ὄντα ὡς ὄντα. The reference is evidently to the declaration, " I have made thee the father of many nations." This had then no real existence; but God represents it as having an existence already. Far-fetched meanings are sometimes adopted, when the plainest and the most obvious is passed by.—*Ed.*

[1] " *Ut esset:*" this may indeed be rendered according to our version, " that he might become;" but the drift of the comment seems to favour the other view, that he believed that he should be, and not that he believed in order to be, or that he might be, the father of many nations εἰς τὸ γινέσθαι αὐτόν; " that he should be," is the rendering of *Hammond, Doddridge,* and *Stuart;* and it is indeed what is consistent with the drift of the passage, and with what is recorded in Genesis. *Wolfius* says, that εἰς here does not signify the final cause, but the subject or the object of faith and hope; Abraham believed the promise, that he should be the father of many nations.— *Ed.*

[2] This is a striking instance of the latitude of meaning which some words have in Scripture. Here hope, in the first instance, means the *ground* of hope; and in the second, the *object* of hope. So faith, in verse 5, and in other places, must be considered as including its object, the gracious promise of God; for otherwise it will be a meritorious act, the very thing which the Apostle throughout repudiates with regard to man's justification. Faith, as it lays hold on God's promise of free acceptance and forgiveness, can alone, in the very nature of things, be imputed for righteousness: it is not indispensably necessary that the way, or medium, or the meritorious cause of acceptance and forgiveness, should be clearly

for hoping he yet in hope relied on the promise of God; and he thought it a sufficient reason for hoping, that the Lord had promised, however incredible the thing was in itself.

According to what had been said, &c. So have I preferred to render it, that it may be applied to the time of Abraham; for Paul meant to say, that Abraham, when many temptations were drawing him to despair, that he might not fail, turned his thoughts to what had been promised to him, "Thy seed shall equal the stars of heaven and the sands of the sea;" but he designedly adduced this quotation incomplete, in order to stimulate us to read the Scriptures. The Apostles, indeed, at all times, in quoting the Scriptures, took a scrupulous care to rouse us to a more diligent reading of them.

19. And being not weak in faith, he considered not his own body now dead, when he was about an hundred years old, neither yet the deadness of Sarah's womb:

20. He staggered not at the promise of God through unbelief; but was strong in faith, giving glory to God;

21. And being fully persuaded, that what he had promised, he was able also to perform.

22. And therefore it was imputed to him for righteousness.

19. Ac fide minimè debilitatus, non consideravit suum ipsius corpus jam emortuum, centenarius quum ferè esset, nec emortuam vulvam Saræ:

20. Nec vero in Dei promissionem per incredulitatem disquisivit; sed roboratus est fide, tribuens gloriam Deo;

21. Ac certè persuasus, quod ubi quid promisit, possit etiam præstare.

22. Ideo et imputatum illi est in justitiam.

19. *In faith,* &c. If you prefer to omit one of the negatives you may render it thus, "Being weak in faith, he considered not his own body," &c.; but this makes no sense. He indeed shows now more fully what might have hindered, yea, and wholly turned Abraham aside from receiving the promise. A seed from Sarah was promised to him at a time when he was not by nature fit for generating, nor Sarah for conceiving. Whatever he could see as to himself was opposed to the accomplishment of the promise. Hence, that he might yield to the truth of God, he withdrew his mind from those things which presented themselves to his own view, and as

known and distinctly seen; the gracious promise of God is enough, so that faith may become a justifying faith.

it were forgot himself. You are not however to think, that he had no regard whatever to his own body, now dead, since Scripture testifies to the contrary; for he reasoned thus with himself, "Shall a child be born to a man an hundred years old? and shall Sarah, who is ninety, bear a son?" But as he laid aside the consideration of all this, and resigned his own judgment to the Lord, the Apostle says, that he *considered not*, &c.; and truly it was a greater effort to withdraw his thoughts from what of itself met his eyes, than if such a thing came into his mind.

And that the body of Abraham was become through age incapable of generating, at the time he received the Lord's blessing, is quite evident from this passage, and also from Gen. xvii. and xviii., so that the opinion of *Augustine* is by no means to be admitted, who says somewhere, that the impediment was in Sarah alone. Nor ought the absurdity of the objection to influence us, by which he was induced to have recourse to this solution; for he thought it inconsistent to suppose that Abraham in his hundredth year was incapable of generating, as he had afterwards many children. But by this very thing God rendered his power more visible, inasmuch as he, who was before like a dry and barren tree, was so invigorated by the celestial blessing, that he not only begot Isaac, but, as though he was restored to the vigour of age, he had afterwards strength to beget others. But some one may object and say, that it is not beyond the course of nature that a man should beget children at that age. Though I allow that such a thing is not a prodigy, it is yet very little short of a miracle. And then, think with how many toils, sorrows, wanderings, distresses, had that holy man been exercised all his life; and it must be confessed, that he was no more debilitated by age, than worn out and exhausted by toils. And lastly, his body is not called barren simply but comparatively; for it was not probable that he, who was unfit for begetting in the flower and vigour of age, should begin only now when nature had decayed.

The expression, *being not weak in faith*, take in this sense—that he vacillated not, nor fluctuated, as we usually do under difficult circumstances. There is indeed a twofold weakness of faith—one is that which, by succumbing to trying adversities, occasions a falling away from the supporting power of God—the other arises from imperfection, but does not extinguish faith itself: for the mind is never so illuminated, but that many relics of ignorance remain; the heart is never so strengthened, but that much doubting cleaves to it. Hence with these vices of the flesh, ignorance and doubt, the faithful have a continual conflict, and in this conflict their faith is often dreadfully shaken and distressed, but at length it comes forth victorious; so that they may be said to be strong even in weakness.

20. *Nor did he through unbelief make an inquiry*, &c. Though I do not follow the old version, nor *Erasmus*, yet my rendering is not given without reason. The Apostle seems to have had this in view,—That Abraham did not try to find out, by weighing the matter in the balance of unbelief, whether the Lord was able to perform what he had promised. What is properly to inquire or to search into anything, is to examine it through diffidence or mistrust, and to be unwilling to admit what appears not credible, without thoroughly sifting it.[1] He indeed asked, how it could come to pass, but that was the asking of one astonished; as the case was with the Virgin Mary, when she inquired of the angel how could that be which he had announced; and there are other similar instances. The saints then, when a message is brought them respecting the works of God, the greatness of which exceeds their comprehension, do indeed burst forth into expressions of wonder; but from this wonder they soon pass on to lay hold on the power of God: on the contrary, the wicked, when they examine a message, scoff at and reject it as a fable. Such, as you will find, was the case with the Jews, when they asked Christ how he could give his

[1] The verb is διεκρίθη, which *Calvin* renders " disquisivit." The most common meaning of the verb is to hesitate, to doubt: it has the sense of exploring and examining, in the active voice, as in 1 Cor. xi. 31, but not in the passive.—See Matt. xxi. 21; Mark xi. 23; Acts x. 20. The version of *Pareus* is, " non disceptavit—he disputed not," and also of *Macknight*. But the fathers, and many moderns, such as *Beza, Hammond, Stuart*, and others, have rendered the sentence, " He doubted not." *Phavorinus* says, as quoted by *Poole*, that διακρίνεσθαι, is to doubt, to hesitate, to dispute, to distrust, (*diffidere*.)—*Ed*.

flesh to be eaten. For this reason it was, that Abraham was not reproved when he laughed and asked, how could a child be born to a man an hundred years old, and to a woman of ninety; for in his astonishment he fully admitted the power of God's word. On the other hand, a similar laughter and inquiry on the part of Sarah were not without reproof, because she regarded not the promise as valid.

If these things be applied to our present subject, it will be evident, that the justification of Abraham had no other beginning than that of the Gentiles. Hence the Jews reproach their own father, if they exclaim against the call of the Gentiles as a thing unreasonable. Let us also remember, that the condition of us all is the same with that of Abraham. All things around us are in opposition to the promises of God: He promises immortality; we are surrounded with mortality and corruption: He declares that he counts us just; we are covered with sins: He testifies that he is propitious and kind to us; outward judgments threaten his wrath. What then is to be done? We must with closed eyes pass by ourselves and all things connected with us, that nothing may hinder or prevent us from believing that God is true.

But he was strengthened, &c. This is of the same import with a former clause, when it is said, that he was not weak in faith. It is the same as though he had said, that he overcame unbelief by the constancy and firmness of faith.[1] No one indeed comes forth a conqueror from this contest, but he who borrows weapons and strength from the word of God. From what he adds, *giving glory to God,* it must be observed, that no greater honour can be given to God, than by faith to seal his truth; as, on the other hand, no greater dishonour can be done to him, than to refuse his offered favour, or to discredit his word. It is hence the chief thing in honouring God, obediently to embrace his promises: and true religion begins with faith.

21. *That what he had promised,* &c. As all men acknow-

---

[1] " Doubt," says *Pareus,* " has two arguments—*will* God do this? and *can* God do this? Faith has also two arguments—God *will* do it, because he has promised; and he *can* do it, because he is omnipotent."

ledge God's power, Paul seems to say nothing very extraordinary of the faith of Abraham; but experience proves, that nothing is more uncommon, or more difficult, than to ascribe to God's power the honour which it deserves. There is indeed no obstacle, however small and insignificant, by which the flesh imagines the hand of God is restrained from working. Hence it is, that in the slightest trials, the promises of God slide away from us. When there is no contest, it is true, no one, as I have said, denies that God can do all things; but as soon as anything comes in the way to impede the course of God's promise, we cast down God's power from its eminence. Hence, that it may obtain from us its right and its honour, when a contest comes, we ought to determine thus,—That it is no less sufficient to overcome the obstacles of the world, than the strong rays of the sun are to dissipate the mists. We are indeed wont ever to excuse ourselves, that we derogate nothing from God's power, whenever we hesitate respecting his promises, and we commonly say, " The thought, that God promises more in his word than he can perform, (which would be a falsehood and blasphemy against him,) is by no means the cause of our hesitation; but that it is the defect which we feel in ourselves." But we do not sufficiently exalt the power of God, unless we think it to be greater than our weakness. Faith then ought not to regard our weakness, misery, and defects, but to fix wholly its attention on the power of God alone; for if it depends on our righteousness or worthiness, it can never ascend to the consideration of God's power. And it is a proof of the unbelief, of which he had before spoken, when we mete the Lord's power with our own measure. For faith does not think that God can do all things, while it leaves him sitting still, but when, on the contrary, it regards his power in continual exercise, and applies it, especially, to the accomplishment of his word: for the hand of God is ever ready to execute whatever he has declared by his mouth.

It seems strange to me, that *Erasmus* approved of the relative in the masculine gender; for though the sense is not changed, we may yet come nearer to the Greek words of

Paul. The verb, I know, is passive;[1] but the abruptness may be lessened by a little change.

22. *And it was therefore imputed*,[2] &c. It becomes now more clear, how and in what manner faith brought righteousness to Abraham; and that was, because he, leaning on God's word, rejected not the promised favour. And this connection of faith with the word ought to be well understood and carefully remembered; for faith can bring us nothing more than what it receives from the word. Hence he does not become immediately just, who is imbued only with a general and confused idea that God is true, except he reposes on the promise of his favour.

23. Now, it was not written for his sake alone, that it was imputed to him;
24. But for us also, to whom it shall be imputed, if we believe on him that raised up Jesus our Lord from the dead;
25. Who was delivered for our offences, and was raised again for our justification.

23. Non est autem scriptum propter ipsum tantùm, imputatum fuisse illi;
24. Sed etiam propter nos, quibus imputabitur credentibus in eum, qui excitavit Iesum Dominum nostrum ex mortuis:
25. Qui traditus fuit propter delicta nostra, et excitatus propter nostram justificationem.

23. *Now it was not written*, &c. A proof from example is not always valid, of which I have before reminded you; lest this should be questioned, Paul expressly affirms, that in the person of Abraham was exhibited an example of a common righteousness, which belongs equally to all.

We are, by this passage, reminded of the duty of seeking profit from the examples recorded in Scripture. That history is the teacher of what life ought to be, is what heathens

---

[1] The verb is, ἐπήγγιλται, used here, and perhaps in one other place, Heb. xii. 26, in an active sense. It is usually found, in the sense of promising, in the middle voice, as in Mark xiv. 11; Acts vii. 5; Heb. vi. 13, &c. It is an anomaly that is to be met with sometimes in Greek authors. —*Ed.*

[2] As in a former instance in verse 3, there is no nominative case to this verb: it is supplied by the sentence. This is the case not unfrequently in languages, such as Greek and Hebrew, in which the person is included in the verb itself. There is no nominative in the Welsh version, and there seems to be no need of it, *Amhyny y cyvrivwyd iddo yn gyviawnder.*

"It is most true, as Paul says to the Romans, that by faith Abraham was justified, and not by *obedience*: but it is just as true what he says to the Hebrews, that it was by faith that Abraham *obeyed*."—*Chalmers.*

have with truth said; but as it is handed down by them, no one can derive from it sound instruction. Scripture alone justly claims to itself an office of this kind. For in the first place it prescribes general rules, by which we may test every other history, so as to render it serviceable to us: and in the second place, it clearly points out what things are to be followed, and what things are to be avoided. But as to doctrine, which it especially teaches, it possesses this peculiarity, —that it clearly reveals the providence of God, his justice and goodness towards his own people, and his judgments on the wicked.

What then is recorded of Abraham is by Paul denied to have been written only for his sake; for the subject is not what belongs to the special call of one or of any particular person; but that way of obtaining righteousness is described, which is ever the same with regard to all; and it is what belonged to the common father of the faithful, on whom the eyes of all ought to be fixed.

If then we would make a right and proper use of sacred histories, we must remember so to use them as to draw from them sound doctrine. They instruct us, in some parts, how to frame our life; in others, how to strengthen faith; and then, how we are to be stirred up to serve the Lord. In forming our life, the example of the saints may be useful; and we may learn from them sobriety, chastity, love, patience, moderation, contempt of the world, and other virtues. What will serve to confirm faith is the help which God ever gave them, the protection which brought comfort in adversities, and the paternal care which he ever exercised over them. The judgments of God, and the punishments inflicted on the wicked, will also aid us, provided they fill us with that fear which imbues the heart with reverence and devotion.

But by saying, *not on his account only*, he seems to intimate, that it was written partly for his sake. Hence some think, that what Abraham obtained by faith was commemorated to his praise, because the Lord will have his servants to be for ever remembered, according to what Solomon says, that their name will be blessed. (Prov. x. 7.) But what if you take the words, *not on his account only*, in a simpler form, as though it were some singular privilege, not fit to be made an example of, but yet suitable to teach us, who must be justified in the same manner? This certainly would be a more appropriate sense.

24. *Who believe on him*, &c. I have already reminded you of the design of those periphrastic expressions: Paul introduced them, that he might, according to what the passages may require, describe in various ways the real character of faith—of which the resurrection of Christ is not the smallest part; for it is the ground of our hope as to eternal life. Had he said only, that we believe in God, it could not have been so readily learnt how this could serve to obtain righteousness; but when Christ comes forth and presents to us in his own resurrection a sure pledge of life, it then appears evident from what fountain the imputation of righteousness flows.

25. *Who was delivered for our offences*,[1] &c. He expands and illustrates more at large the doctrine to which I have just referred. It indeed greatly concerns us, not only to have our minds directed to Christ, but also to have it distinctly made known how he attained salvation for us. And

---

[1] It is διὰ τὰ παραπτώματα ἡμῶν, "for our offences," and διὰ τὴν δικαίωσιν ἡμῶν, "for our justification." The preposition διὰ, has here clearly two meanings: the first signifies the *reason* why; and the second, the *end* for which. How is this to be known? By the character of the sentence, and by what is taught elsewhere. *For*, to which *Johnson* attaches forty meanings, is commonly understood here as having a different sense; and this is sufficiently indicated by what is connected with it. But in case a doubt arises, we have only to consult other passages in which the subject is handled.

Take the first instance—" for our offences." There are those who say that διὰ here means *because of*, or, *on account of;* and this, in order to evade the idea of a propitiation. The preposition, no doubt, has this sense; but is this its sense here? If the sentence itself be deemed insufficient to determine the question, (though to a plain reader it is,) let us see what is said elsewhere of Christ's death in connection with our sins or offences. He himself said, that he came " to give his life a ransom (λύτρον—a redeeming price) for many," Matt. xx. 28. It is said, that he "gave himself a ransom (ἀντίλυτρον—a redeeming price for another) for all," 1 Tim. ii. 6. It is expressly declared, that " Christ was once *offered* to bear the *sins* of many," Heb. ix. 28. And more to the purpose still, if possible, is the testimony of John, when he says that Christ " is the propitiation (ἱλασμός—expiation) for our sins," 1 John ii. 2. Now, can it be that we can give any other meaning to the text, than that God delivered his Son as a sacrifice for our offences? This is the doctrine of Scripture throughout. —*Ed.*

though Scripture, when it treats of our salvation, dwells especially on the death of Christ, yet the Apostle now proceeds farther: for as his purpose was more explicitly to set forth the cause of our salvation, he mentions its two parts; and says, first, that our sins were expiated by the death of Christ,—and secondly, that by his resurrection was obtained our righteousness. But the meaning is, that when we possess the benefit of Christ's death and resurrection, there is nothing wanting to the completion of perfect righteousness. By separating his death from his resurrection, he no doubt accommodates what he says to our ignorance; for it is also true that righteousness has been obtained for us by that obedience of Christ, which he exhibited in his death, as the Apostle himself teaches us in the following chapter. But as Christ, by rising from the dead, made known how much he had effected by his death, this distinction is calculated to teach us that our salvation was begun by the sacrifice, by which our sins were expiated, and was at length completed by his resurrection: for the beginning of righteousness is to be reconciled to God, and its completion is to attain life by having death abolished. Paul then means, that satisfaction for our sins was given on the cross: for it was necessary, in order that Christ might restore us to the Father's favour, that our sins should be abolished by him; which could not have been done had he not on their account suffered the punishment, which we were not equal to endure. Hence Isaiah says, that the chastisement of our peace was upon him. (Isa. liii. 5.) But he says that he was delivered, and not, that he died; for expiation depended on the eternal goodwill of God, who purposed to be in this way pacified.

And was raised again for our justification. As it would not have been enough for Christ to undergo the wrath and judgment of God, and to endure the curse due to our sins, without his coming forth a conqueror, and without being received into celestial glory, that by his intercession he might reconcile God to us, the efficacy of justification is ascribed to his resurrection, by which death was overcome; not that the sacrifice of the cross, by which we are reconciled to God, contributes nothing towards our justification, but that the completeness of his favour appears more clear by his coming to life again.¹

But I cannot assent to those who refer this second clause to newness of life; for of that the Apostle has not begun to speak; and further, it is certain that both clauses refer to the same thing. For if justification means renovation, then that he died for our sins must be taken in the same sense, as signifying, that he acquired for us grace to mortify the flesh; which no one admits. Then, as he is said to have died for our sins, because he delivered us from the evil of death by suffering death as a punishment for our sins; so he is now said to have been raised for our justification, because he fully restored life to us by his resurrection: for he was first smitten by the hand of God, that in the person of the sinner he might sustain the misery of sin; and then he was raised to life, that he might freely grant to his people righteousness and life.² He therefore still speaks of imputative justification; and this will be confirmed by what immediately follows in the next chapter.

CHAPTER V.

1. Therefore, being justified by faith, we have peace with God, through our Lord Jesus Christ:	1. Iustificatus ergo ex fide, pacem habemus apud Deum per Dominum nostrum Iesum Christum;

¹ Christ is said here to have been raised from the dead *by God*, as well as delivered into death. "However much the import of this," says *Chalmers*, "may have escaped the notice of an ordinary reader, it is pregnant with meaning of the weightiest importance. You know that when the prison door is opened to a criminal, and that by the very authority which lodged him there, it evinces that the debt of his transgression has been rendered, and that he stands acquitted of all its penalties. It was not for his own, but for our offences that Jesus was delivered unto the death, and that his body was consigned to the imprisonment of the grave. And when an angel descended from heaven, and rolled back the great stone from the door of the sepulchre, this speaks to us, that the justice of God is satisfied, that the ransom of our iniquity has been paid, that Christ has rendered a full discharge of all the debt for which he undertook as the great surety between God and the sinners who believe in him."—*Ed.*

² "Either therefore as the evidence of the acceptance of his sufferings as our substitute, or as a necessary step towards securing the application of their merit to our benefit, the resurrection of Christ was essential to our justification."—Professor *Hodge*.

2. By whom also we have access by faith into this grace wherein we stand, and rejoice in hope of the glory of God.

2. Per quem accessum habuimus fide in gratiam istam in qua stetimus, et gloriamur super spe gloriæ Dei.

1. *Being then justified,* &c. The Apostle begins to illustrate by the effects, what he has hitherto said of the righteousness of faith: and hence the whole of this chapter is taken up with amplifications, which are no less calculated to explain than to confirm. He had said before, that faith is abolished, if righteousness is sought by works; and in this case perpetual inquietude would disturb miserable souls, as they can find nothing substantial in themselves: but he teaches us now, that they are rendered quiet and tranquil, when we have obtained righteousness by faith, *We have peace with God;* and this is the peculiar fruit of the righteousness of faith. When any one strives to seek tranquillity of conscience by works, (which is the case with profane and ignorant men,) he labours for it in vain; for either his heart is asleep through his disregard or forgetfulness of God's judgment, or else it is full of trembling and dread, until it reposes on Christ, who is alone our peace.

Then peace means tranquillity of conscience, which arises from this,—that it feels itself to be reconciled to God. This the Pharisee has not, who swells with false confidence in his own works; nor the stupid sinner, who is not disquieted, because he is inebriated with the sweetness of vices: for though neither of these seems to have a manifest disquietude, as he is who is smitten with a consciousness of sin; yet as they do not really approach the tribunal of God, they have no reconciliation with him; for insensibility of conscience is, as it were, a sort of retreating from God. Peace with God is opposed to the dead security of the flesh, and for this reason,—because the first thing is, that every one should become awakened as to the account he must render of his life; and no one can stand boldly before God, but he who relies on a gratuitous reconciliation; for as long as he is God, all must otherwise tremble and be confounded. And this is the strongest of proofs, that our opponents do nothing but prate to no purpose, when they ascribe righteousness to works; for this conclusion of Paul is derived from this fact,—that miserable souls always tremble, except they repose on the grace of Christ.

2. *Through whom we have access,*[1] &c. Our reconciliation with God depends only on Christ; for he only is the beloved Son, and we are all by nature the children of wrath. But this favour is communicated to us by the gospel; for the gospel is the ministry of reconciliation, by the means of which we are in a manner brought into the kingdom of God. Rightly then does Paul set before our eyes in Christ a sure pledge of God's favour, that he might more easily draw us away from every confidence in works. And as he teaches us by the word *access,* that salvation begins with Christ, he excludes those preparations by which foolish men imagine that they can anticipate God's mercy; as though he said,

[1] *Calvin* leaves out καὶ, " also." *Griesbach* retains it. The omission is only in one MS., and in the *Syriac* and *Ethiopic* versions: it is rendered νυν by *Theodoret*. But its meaning here seems not to be " also," but " even" or " yea:" for this verse contains in part the same truth as the former. The style of Paul is often very like that of the Prophets, that is, the arrangement of his sentences is frequently on their model. In the Prophets, and also in the Psalms, we find often two distichs and sometimes two verses containing the same sentiment, only the latter distich states it differently, and adds something to it. See, for example, Ps. xxxii. 1, 2. Such is exactly the case here. " Justified by faith," and " this grace in which we stand," are the same. " Through our Lord Jesus Christ," and " through whom we have access," are identical in their import. The additional idea in the second verse is the last clause. That we may see how the whole corresponds with the Prophetic style, the two verses shall be presented in lines:—

  1. Having then been justified by faith,
     We have peace with God,
     Through our Lord Jesus Christ;
  2. Through whom we have had, yea, the access by faith
     To this grace, in which we stand,
     And exult in the hope of the glory of God.

The illative, *then,* is to be preferred to *therefore,* as it is an inference, not from a particular verse or a clause, but from what the Apostle had been teaching. By the phrase, " the glory of God," is meant the glory which God bestows: it is, to use the words of Professor *Stuart,* " genitivus auctoris."

The word "access," προσαγωγὴν, has two meanings,—introduction (adductio)—and access (accessio.) The verb προσάγειν, is used in 1 Pet. iii. 18, in the sense of introducing, leading or bringing to. So Christ, as *Wolfius* remarks, may be considered to be here represented as the introducer and reconciler, through whom believers come to God and hold intercourse with him. " Introduction" is the version of *Macknight;* and *Doddridge* has also adopted this idea.—*Ed.*

"Christ comes not to you, nor helps you, on account of your merits." He afterwards immediately subjoins, that it is through the continuance of the same favour that our salvation becomes certain and sure; by which he intimates, that perseverance is not founded on our power and diligence, but on Christ; though at the same time by saying, that we *stand*, he indicates that the gospel ought to strike deep roots into the hearts of the godly, so that being strengthened by its truth, they may stand firm against all the devices of Satan and of the flesh. And by the word *stand*, he means, that faith is not a changeable persuasion, only for one day; but that it is immutable, and that it sinks deep into the heart, so that it endures through life. It is then not he, who by a sudden impulse is led to believe, that has faith, and is to be reckoned among the faithful; but he who constantly, and, so to speak, with a firm and fixed foot, abides in that station appointed to him by God, so as to cleave always to Christ.

And glory in the hope, &c. The reason that the hope of a future life exists and dares to exult, is this,—because we rest on God's favour as on a sure foundation: for Paul's meaning is, that though the faithful are now pilgrims on the earth, they yet by hope scale the heavens, so that they quietly enjoy in their own bosoms their future inheritance. And hereby are subverted two of the most pestilent dogmas of the sophists. What they do in the first place is, they bid Christians to be satisfied with moral conjecture as to the perception of God's favour towards them; and secondly, they teach that all are uncertain as to their final perseverance. But except there be at present a sure knowledge, and a firm and undoubting persuasion as to the future, who would dare to glory? The hope of the glory of God has shone upon us through the gospel, which testifies that we shall be participators of the Divine nature; for when we shall see God face to face, we shall be like him. (2 Peter i. 4; 1 John iii. 2.)

3. And not only *so*, but we glory in tribulations also: knowing that tribulation worketh patience;

3. Neque id modò, sed gloriamur[1] etiam in afflictionibus; scientes quòd tribulatio patientiam efficiat;

[1] Gloriamur—καυχώμεθα. The same as in the preceding verse, and

4. And patience, experience; and experience, hope:

5. And hope maketh not ashamed; because the love of God is shed abroad in our hearts by the Holy Ghost, which is given unto us.

4. Patientia verò probationem; probatio autem spem:

5. Porrò spes non pudefacit, quoniam dilectio Dei diffusa est in cordibus nostris per Spiritum sanctum, qui datus est nobis.

3. *Not only so,* &c. That no one might scoffingly object and say, that Christians, with all their glorying, are yet strangely harassed and distressed in this life, which condition is far from being a happy one,—he meets this objection, and declares, not only that the godly are prevented by these calamities from being blessed, but also that their glorying is thereby promoted. To prove this he takes his argument from the effects, and adopts a remarkable gradation, and at last concludes, that all the sorrows we endure contribute to our salvation and final good.

By saying that the saints glory in tribulations, he is not to be understood, as though they dreaded not, nor avoided adversities, or were not distressed with their bitterness when they happened, (for there is no patience when there is no feeling of bitterness ;) but as in their grief and sorrow they are not without great consolation, because they regard that whatever they bear is dispensed to them for good by the hand of a most indulgent Father, they are justly said to glory: for whenever salvation is promoted, there is not wanting a reason for glorying.

We are then taught here what is the design of our tribulations, if indeed we would prove ourselves to be the children of God. They ought to habituate us to patience ; and if they do not answer this end, the work of the Lord is rendered void and of none effect through our corruption: for how does he prove that adversities do not hinder the glorying of the faithful, except that by their patience in enduring them, they feel the help of God, which nourishes and confirms their hope ? They then who do not learn patience, do not, it is certain, make good progress. Nor is it any

---

rendered " boast" by *Macknight*, and in the former verse by *Doddridge*, and here, " glory." " Boast" is certainly not a proper word, for it is commonly used in a bad sense. " Rejoice" is too feeble, for it means exultation and triumph.—*Ed.*

objection, that there are recorded in Scripture some complaints full of despondency, which the saints had made: for the Lord sometimes so depresses and straitens for a time his people, that they can hardly breathe, and can hardly remember any source of consolation; but in a moment he brings to life those whom he had nearly sunk in the darkness of death. So that what Paul says is always accomplished in them—" We are in every way oppressed, but not made anxious; we are in danger, but we are not in despair; we suffer persecution, but we are not forsaken; we are cast down, but we are not destroyed." (2 Cor. iv. 8.)

Tribulation produces (efficiat) *patience,* &c. This is not the natural effect of tribulation; for we see that a great portion of mankind are thereby instigated to murmur against God, and even to curse his name. But when that inward meekness, which is infused by the Spirit of God, and the consolation, which is conveyed by the same Spirit, succeed in the place of our stubbornness, then tribulations become the means of generating patience; yea, those tribulations, which in the obstinate can produce nothing but indignation and clamorous discontent.

4. *Patience, probation,* &c. James, adopting a similar gradation, seems to follow a different order; for he says, that patience proceeds from probation: but the different meaning of the word is what will reconcile both. Paul takes probation for the experience which the faithful have of the sure protection of God, when by relying on his aid they overcome all difficulties, even when they experience, whilst in patiently enduring they stand firm, how much avails the power of the Lord, which he has promised to be always present with his people. James takes the same word for tribulation itself, according to the common usage of Scripture; for by these God proves and tries his servants: and they are often called trials.[1]

---

[1] The word in James is δοκίμιον, while here it is δοκιμή. The first means a test, or the act of testing—trial; and the second, the result of testing—experience, and is rendered in our version "proof," 2 Cor. ii. 9,—" experiment," 2 Cor. ix. 13,—and in 2 Cor. viii. 2, " trial," which ought to be experience. *Beza* says, that the first bears to the second a similar rela-

According then to the present passage, we then only make advances in patience as we ought, when we regard it as having been continued to us by God's power, and thus entertain hope as to the future, that God's favour, which has ever succoured us in our necessities, will never be wanting to us. Hence he subjoins, that from probation arises hope; for ungrateful we should be for benefits received, except the recollection of them confirms our hope as to what is to come.

5. *Hope maketh not ashamed*, &c.;[1] that is, it regards salvation as most certain. It hence appears, that the Lord tries us by adversities for this end,—that our salvation may thereby be gradually advanced. Those evils then cannot render us miserable, which do in a manner promote our happiness. And thus is proved what he had said, that the godly have reasons for glorying in the midst of their afflictions.

For the love of God, &c. I do not refer this only to the last sentence, but to the whole of the preceding passage. I therefore would say,—that by tribulations we are stimulated to patience, and that patience finds an experiment of divine help, by which we are more encouraged to entertain hope; for however we may be pressed and seem to be nearly consumed, we do not yet cease to feel God's favour towards us, which affords the richest consolation, and much more abundant than when all things happen prosperously. For as that happiness, which is so in appearance, is misery itself, when God is adverse to and displeased with us; so when he

---

tion as cause bears to effect: the one thing is testing or probation, and the other is the experience that is thereby gained.

The word is rendered here, not very intelligibly, "approbation," both by *Macknight* and *Stuart;* but more correctly, "experience," by *Beza* and *Doddridge*.—*Ed.*

[1] *Chalmers* observes, that there are two hopes mentioned in this passage,—the hope of faith in the second verse, and the hope of experience in this. "The hope of the fourth verse," he says, "is distinct from and posterior to the hope of the second; and it also appears to be derived from another source. The first hope is hope in believing, a hope which hangs direct on the testimony of God...The second hope is grounded on distinct considerations—not upon what the believer sees to be in the testimony of God, but upon what he finds to be in himself.—It is the fruit not of faith, but of experience; and is gathered not from the word that is without, but from the feeling of what passes within."—*Ed.*

is propitious, even calamities themselves will surely be turned to a prosperous and a joyful issue. Seeing all things must serve the will of the Creator, who, according to his paternal favour towards us, (as Paul declares in the eighth chapter,) overrules all the trials of the cross for our salvation, this knowledge of divine love towards us is instilled into our hearts by the Spirit of God; for the good things which God has prepared for his servants are hid from the ears and the eyes and the minds of men, and the Spirit alone is he who can reveal them. And the word *diffused*, is very emphatical; for it means that the revelation of divine love towards us is so abounding that it fills our hearts; and being thus spread through every part of them, it not only mitigates sorrow in adversities, but also, like a sweet seasoning, it renders tribulations to be loved by us.[1]

He says further, that the Spirit is *given*, that is, bestowed through the gratuitous goodness of God, and not conferred for our merits; according to what *Augustine* has well observed, who, though he is mistaken in his view of the love of God,

---

[1] "The love of God" in this passage may mean either the love of which God is the object—love to God, or the love which he possesses—God's love to us: the *usus loquendi* would admit either of these meanings; and hence commentators have differed on the point. The expression, τὴν ἀγάπην τοῦ Θεοῦ, in Luke xii. 42, John v. 42, and in other places, means "love to God;" and ἡ ἀγάπη τοῦ Θεοῦ, in 1 John iv. 9, signifies clearly the love of God to us. The meaning then can alone be ascertained by the context, and by the wording of the sentence. It stands connected with christian graces, patience and hope; and this favours the first view, that it is love to God produced within by the Spirit. Then the verb, ἐκκέχυ-ται—is poured out or poured forth, seems more suitable to the idea of love being communicated as a gift, or as a holy feeling within. It is further what prevents hope from being disappointed; it is some good or enjoyment that now strengthens and satisfies hope; and to love God who first loved us is to realize in a measure what hope expects; and when it is said that it is diffused by the Spirit, we are reminded of what Paul says in Gal. v. 22, that "love" is one of the fruits of the Spirit. But it may, on the other hand, be alleged, that the verse stands connected with what follows, as the next verse begins with "for," and that the subsequent context most clearly refers to the love of God to us; and this evidently decides the question.

The first view, our love to God, has been adopted by *Augustine*, *Mede*, *Doddridge*, *Scott*, and *Stuart;* and the other, God's love to us, by *Chrysostom*, *Beza*, *Pareus*, *Grotius*, *Hodge*, and *Chalmers*, and also by *Schleusner*, who gives this paraphrase, "Amor Dei abundè nobis declaratus est—the love of God is abundantly declared to us."—*Ed.*

gives this explanation,—that we courageously bear adversities, and are thus confirmed in our hope, because we, having been regenerated by the Spirit, do love God. It is indeed a pious sentiment, but not what Paul means: for love is not to be taken here in an active but a passive sense. And certain it is, that no other thing is taught by Paul than that the true fountain of all love is, when the faithful are convinced that they are loved by God, and that they are not slightly touched with this conviction, but have their souls thoroughly imbued with it.

6. For when we were yet without strength, in due time Christ died for the ungodly.
7. For scarcely for a righteous man will one die; yet peradventure for a good man some would even dare to die.
8. But God commendeth his love toward us, in that, while we were yet sinners, Christ died for us.
9. Much more then, being now justified by his blood, we shall be saved from wrath through him.

6. Christus enim, quum adhuc essemus infirmi secundum rationem temporis, pro impiis mortuus est:
7. Vix sanè pro justo quis moriatur; nam pro bono forsan aliquis etiam mori audeat.
8. Confirmat autem erga nos charitatem Deus quòd peccatores quum adhuc essemus, Christus pro nobis mortuus est:
9. Multo igitur magis, justificati nunc per sanguinem ejus, servabimur per ipsum ab ira.

6. *For Christ,* &c. I ventured not in my version to allow myself so much liberty as to give this rendering, "In the time in which we were weak;" and yet I prefer this sense. An argument begins here, which is from the greater to the less, and which he afterwards pursues more at large: and though he has not woven the thread of his discourse so very distinctly, yet its irregular structure does not disturb the meaning. "If Christ," he says, "had mercy on the ungodly, if he reconciled enemies to his Father, if he has done this by the virtue of his death, much more easily will he save them when justified, and keep those restored to favour in the possession of it, especially when the influence of his life is added to the virtue of his death."[1] The time of weakness

[1] On the argument of this verse, and on what follows to the tenth verse, Professor *Stuart* makes this remark,—" The passage before us seems to be more direct, in respect to *the perseverance of the saints,* than almost any other passage in the Scriptures which I can find. The sentiment here is not dependent on the *form* of a particular expression, (as it appears to

some consider to be that, when Christ first began to be manifested to the world, and they think that those are called weak, who were like children under the tuition of the law. I apply the expression to every one of us, and I regard that time to be meant, which precedes the reconciliation of each one with God. For as we are all born the children of wrath, so we are kept under that curse until we become partakers of Christ. And he calls those weak, who have nothing in themselves but what is sinful; for he calls the same immediately afterwards ungodly. And it is nothing new, that weakness should be taken in this sense. He calls, in 1 Cor. xii. 22, the covered parts of the body weak; and, in 2 Cor. x. 10, he designates his own bodily presence weak, because it had no dignity. And this meaning will soon again occur. When, therefore, we were weak, that is, when we were in no way worthy or fit that God should look on us, at this very time Christ died for the ungodly: for the beginning of religion is faith, from which they were all alienated, for whom Christ died. And this also is true as to the ancient fathers, who obtained righteousness before he died; for they derived this benefit from his future death.[1]

7. *For a just man*, &c. The meaning of the passage has constrained me to render the particle γὰρ as an affirmative or declarative rather than as a causative. The import of the sentence is this, "Most rare, indeed, is such an example to be found among men, that one dies for a just man, though this may sometimes happen: but let this be granted, yet for an ungodly man none will be found willing to die: this

be in some other passages); but it is fundamentally connected with the very nature of the argument."—*Ed.*

[1] Others, as well as *Calvin*, such as *Chrysostom* and *Erasmus*, have connected κατὰ καιρὸν with the preceding, and not with the following words. And *Pareus*, who inclined to the same view, gives this explanation,—" He distinguishes the former from the present state, as though he said, 'We who are now justified by faith were formerly ungodly.'" *Chrysostom* refers to the time of the law, and considers the weakness here to be that of man under the law. This gives an emphatic meaning to "weak," which otherwise it seems not to have, and is countenanced by what is said in ch. viii. 3, where the law is said to be weak, but weak on account of the weakness of the flesh. At the same time it must be observed, that most commentators, like *Beza*, connect these words, κατὰ καιρὸν, with the death of Christ, as having taken place "in due time," appointed by God, and pre-signified by the prophets, according to what is said in Gal. iv. 4.—*Ed.*

is what Christ has done."[1] Thus it is an illustration, derived from a comparison; for such an example of kindness, as Christ has exhibited towards us, does not exist among men.

8. *But God confirms,* &c. The verb, συνίστησι, has various meanings; that which is most suitable to this place is that of confirming; for it was not the Apostle's object to excite our gratitude, but to strengthen the trust and confidence of our souls. He then *confirms,* that is, exhibits his love to us as most certain and complete, inasmuch as for the sake of the ungodly he spared not Christ his own Son. In this, indeed, his love appears, that being not moved by love on our part, he of his own good will first loved us, as John tells us. (1 John iii. 16.)—Those are here called *sinners,* (as in many other places,) who are wholly vicious and given up to sin, according to what is said in John ix. 31, "God hears not sinners," that is, men abandoned and altogether wicked. The woman called "a sinner," was one of a shameful character. (Luke vii. 37.) And this meaning appears more evident from the contrast which immediately follows,—*for being now justified through his blood:* for since he sets the two in oppo-

---

[1] *Calvin* has omitted what is said of the "good" man; for whom, it is said, one would perhaps even dare to die. The "just," δίκαιος, is he who acts according to what justice requires, and according to what the Rabbins say, "What is mine is mine, and what is thine is thine," שלי שלי ושלך שלך: but the "good," ἀγαθός, is the kind, the benevolent, the beneficent, called טוב in Hebrew; who is described by *Cicero* as one who does good to those to whom he can, (vir bonus est is, qui prodest quibus potest.)

There is here an evident contrast between these words and those employed in verses 6 and 8, to designate the character of those for whom Christ died. The just, δίκαιος, is the opposite of the "ungodly," ἀσεβής, who, by not worshipping and honouring God, is guilty of injustice of the highest kind, and in this sense of being unjust it is found in ch. iv. 5, where God is said to "justify the ungodly," that is, him who is unjust by withholding from God the homage which rightly belongs to him. *Phavorinus* gives ἀθέμιτος, unlawful, unjust, as one of its meanings.—What forms a contrast with "good" is sinner, ἁμαρτωλός, which often means wicked, mischievous, one given to vice and the doing of evil. *Suidas* describes ἁμαρτωλοί as those who determine to live in transgression, οἱ παρανομίᾳ συζῆν προαιρούμενοι; and *Schleusner* gives "scelestus—wicked," "flagitiosus—full of mischief," as being sometimes its meaning.

But the description goes farther, for in ver. 10 the word "enemies, ἐχθροί," is introduced in order to complete the character of those for whom Christ died. They were not only "ungodly," and therefore unjust towards God, and "wicked," given to all evils; but also "enemies," entertaining hatred to God, and carrying on war, as it were, against him.—*Ed.*

sition, the one to the other, and calls those justified who are delivered from the guilt of sin, it necessarily follows that those are sinners who, for their evil deeds, are condemned.[1]

The import of the whole is,—since Christ has attained righteousness for sinners by his death, much more shall he protect them, being now justified, from destruction. And in the last clause he applies to his own doctrine the comparison between the less and the greater: for it would not have been enough for salvation to have been once procured for us, were not Christ to render it safe and secure to the end. And this is what the Apostle now maintains; so that we ought not to fear, that Christ will cut off the current of his favour while we are in the middle of our course: for inasmuch as he has reconciled us to the Father, our condition is such, that he purposes more efficaciously to put forth and daily to increase his favour towards us.

10. For if, when we were enemies, we were reconciled to God by the death of his Son; much more, being reconciled, we shall be saved by his life.

10. Si enim quum inimici essemus, reconciliati sumus Deo per mortem Filii ejus; multo magis, reconciliati, servabimur per vitam ipsius.

This is an explanation of the former verse, amplified by introducing a comparison between life and death. We were enemies, he says, when Christ interposed for the purpose of propitiating the Father: through this reconciliation we are now friends; since this was effected by his death; much more influential and efficacious will be his life.[2] We hence

---

[1] The meaning given to συνίστησι is not peculiar. It is used with an accusative in two senses,—to recommend, to commend, to praise, as in ch. xvi. 1; 2 Cor. iii. 1; v. 12; x. 12, 18; and also, to prove, to demonstrate, to shew, to render manifest or certain, and thus to confirm, as in ch. iii. 5; 2 Cor. vi. 4; vii. 11; Gal. ii. 18; *Schleusner* refers to this passage as an instance of the latter meaning. That God proved, or rendered manifest, or conspicuously shewed, his love, seems to be the most suitable idea, as the proof or the evidence is stated in the words which follow. The *Syriac* version gives the sense of shewing or proving. *Vatablus* has "proves" or verifies; *Grotius*, "renders conspicuous;" *Beza*, "commends," as our version and *Macknight; Doddridge*, "recommends;" *Hodge*, "renders conspicuous."—*Ed.*

[2] "By his life," the abstract for the concrete; it means, "through him being alive," being at God's right hand, having every power committed to him, and making intercession for us, chap. viii. 34. "Because *I live*, ye shall live also," John xiv. 19.—*Ed.*

have ample proofs to strengthen our hearts with confidence respecting our salvation. By saying that we were reconciled to God by the death of Christ, he means, that it was the sacrifice of expiation, by which God was pacified towards the world, as I have showed in the fourth chapter.

But the Apostle seems here to be inconsistent with himself; for if the death of Christ was a pledge of the divine love towards us, it follows that we were already acceptable to him; but he says now, that we were enemies. To this I answer, that as God hates sin, we are also hated by him as far as we are sinners; but as in his secret counsel he chooses us into the body of Christ, he ceases to hate us: but restoration to favour is unknown to us, until we attain it by faith. Hence with regard to us, we are always enemies, until the death of Christ interposes in order to propitiate God. And this twofold aspect of things ought to be noticed; for we do not know the gratuitous mercy of God otherwise than as it appears from this—that he spared not his only-begotten Son; for he loved us at a time when there was discord between him and us: nor can we sufficiently understand the benefit brought to us by the death of Christ, except this be the beginning of our reconciliation with God, that we are persuaded that it is by the expiation that has been made, that he, who was before justly angry with us, is now propitious to us. Since then our reception into favour is ascribed to the death of Christ, the meaning is, that guilt is thereby taken away, to which we should be otherwise exposed.

| 11. And not only *so*, but we also joy in God, through our Lord Jesus Christ, by whom we have now received the atonement. | 11. Non solùm autem, sed etiam gloriamur in Deo per Dominum Iesum Christum, per quem nunc reconciliationem accepimus. |

11. *And not this only*, &c. He now ascends into the highest strain of glorying; for when we glory that God is ours, whatever blessings can be imagined or wished, ensue and flow from this fountain; for God is not only the chief of all good things, but also possesses in himself the sum and substance of all blessings; and he becomes ours through Christ. We then attain this by faith,—that nothing is

wanting to us as to happiness. Nor is it in vain that he so often mentions reconciliation: it is, first, that we may be taught to fix our eyes on the death of Christ, whenever we speak of our salvation; and, secondly, that we may know that our trust must be fixed on nothing else, but on the expiation made for our sins.

12. Wherefore, as by one man sin entered into the world, and death by sin; and so death passed upon all men, for that all have sinned:

13. (For until the law sin was in the world: but sin is not imputed when there is no law.

14. Nevertheless death reigned from Adam to Moses, even over them that had not sinned after the similitude of Adam's transgression, who is the figure of him that was to come.

12. Quamobrem sicut per unum hominem peccatum in mundum introiit, et per peccatum mors; atque ita in omnes homines mors pervagata est, quandoquidem omnes peccaverunt:

13. (Nam usque ad legem peccatum erat in mundo; peccatum autem non imputatur, quum non est lex:

14. Sed regnavit mors ab Adam usque ad Mosen, etiam in eos qui non peccaverunt ad similitudinem prævericationis Adam, qui est figura futuri.

12. *Wherefore as,* &c. He now begins to enlarge on the same doctrine, by comparing with it what is of an opposite character. For since Christ came to redeem us from the calamity into which Adam had fallen, and had precipitated all his posterity with him, we cannot see with so much clearness what we have in Christ, as by having what we have lost in Adam set before us, though all things on both sides are not similar: hence Paul subjoins an exception, which we shall notice in its place; and we shall also point out any other difference that may occur. The incompleteness of the sentence sometimes renders it obscure, as when the second clause, which answers to the former, is not expressed. But we shall endeavour to make both plain when we come to those parts.[1]

[1] The beginning of this verse has occasioned a vast number of conjectures, both as to the connection and as to the corresponding clause to the first sentence. Most agree in the main with *Calvin* on these two points. *Hodge* announces a similar view as to the connection in these words,— "The idea of men being regarded and treated, not according to their own merits, but the merit of another, is contrary to the common mode of thinking among men. The Apostle illustrates and enforces it by an appeal to the great analogous fact in the history of the world."

As to the corresponding clause, that it is found in the 18th verse, there

Sin entered into the world, &c. Observe the order which he keeps here; for he says, that sin preceded, and that from sin death followed. There are indeed some who contend, that we are so lost through Adam's sin, as though we perished through no fault of our own, but only, because he had sinned for us. But Paul distinctly affirms, that sin extends to all who suffer its punishment: and this he afterwards more fully declares, when subsequently he assigns a reason why all the posterity of Adam are subject to the dominion of death; and it is even this—because we have all, he says, sinned. But to sin in this case, is to become corrupt and vicious; for the natural depravity which we bring from our mother's womb, though it brings not forth immediately its own fruits, is yet sin before God, and deserves his vengeance: and this is that sin which they call original. For as Adam at his creation had received for us as well as for himself the gifts of God's favour, so by falling away from the Lord, he in himself corrupted, vitiated, depraved, and ruined our nature; for having been divested of God's likeness, he could

---

is a common consent,—*Pareus, Willet, Grotius, Doddridge, Scott, Stuart, Chalmers,* &c.; the intervening verses are viewed as parenthetic.

The phrase, διὰ τοῦτο, and also διὸ and οὖν, are sometimes used anticipatively as well as retrospectively, as their corresponding particles are often in Hebrew. See note on chap. ii. 1. That Paul uses διὰ τοῦτο in this way appears evident from chap. iv. 16; xiii. 6; 1 Cor. xi. 10. It anticipates here, as I think, what is afterwards expressed by ἐφ' ᾧ, as in chap. iv. 16, by ἵνα, in chap. xiii. 6, by γὰρ, and in 1 Cor. xi. 10, by διὰ before angels. Then the meaning of the verse would be conveyed by the following rendering,—

12. For this reason—as through one man sin entered into the world, and through sin death, even so death came on all men, because all have sinned.

According to this view, the corresponding clause is in the verse itself. The sentiment of the passage is this,—through one man sin entered and death followed; and death followed as to all mankind, because all had sinned. Then, according to his usual manner, the Apostle takes up the last subject, "sin," issuing in the death of all; and at the end of the 14th verse he goes back to "the one man," Adam, who he says was a type of another: and this sentence is made the text of what follows till the end of the 19th verse. Having before referred to the state of things before the "law," in the two remaining verses he refers to the bearing of the law on his subject, and shows that there is in Christ an abundant provision for the increase of sin occasioned by the law.

So abundant is grace that it is fully sufficient to remove *original* sin, *actual* sins—its fruits, and the sins discovered by the law, and by its means increased and enhanced. Hence superabundance is ascribed to it.—*Ed.*

not have generated seed but what was like himself. Hence we have all sinned; for we are all imbued with natural corruption, and so are become sinful and wicked. Frivolous then was the gloss, by which formerly the Pelagians endeavoured to elude the words of Paul, and held, that sin descended by imitation from Adam to the whole human race; for Christ would in this case become only the exemplar and not the cause of righteousness. Besides, we may easily conclude, that he speaks not here of actual sin; for if every one for himself contracted guilt, why did Paul form a comparison between Adam and Christ? It then follows that our innate and hereditary depravity is what is here referred to.[1]

[1] The particles ἰφ' ᾦ, at the end of this verse, have been variously rendered, without much change in the meaning. " In quo—in which," *i.e.*, sin, *Augustine;* " in quo—in whom," *i.e.*, man, *Chrysostom* and *Beza;* " per quem—by or through whom," *Grotius;* " propterea quod," vel, " quia," vel, " quoniam—because," *Luther, Pareus,* and *Raphelius;* which is the same with that of *Calvin.* See Matt. xxvi. 50; 2 Cor. v. 4; Phil. iii. 12.

Wolfius quotes a singular passage from a Jewish Rabbi, *Moses* Tranensis, " In the sin which the first man sinned, the whole world through him (or in him, בו) sinned; for he was every man, or all mankind—כי זה כל אדם." The idea is exactly the same with that of the Apostle.

" There are three things," says *Pareus,* " which are to be considered in Adam's sin,—the sinful act, the penalty of the law, and the depravity of nature; or in other words, the transgression of the command, the punishment of death, and natural corruption, which was the loss of God's image, and in its stead came deformity and disorder. From none of these his posterity are free, but all these have descended to them; there is a participation of the transgression, an imputation of guilt, and the propagation of natural depravity. There is a *participation* of the sin; for all his posterity were seminally in his loins, so that all sinned in his sin, as Levi paid tithes in the loins of Abraham; and as children are a part of their parents, so children are in a manner partakers of their parents' sin. There is also an *imputation* of guilt; for the first man so stood in favour, that when he sinned, not only he, but also all his posterity fell with him, and became with him subject to eternal death. And lastly, there is the *propagation* or the generation of a dreadful deformity of nature; for such as Adam became after the fall, such were the children he begat, being after his own image, and not after the image of God. Gen. v. 1....All these things, as to the first sin, apply to the parent and also to the children, with only this difference—that Adam sinning first transgressed, first contracted guilt, and first depraved his nature,—and that all these things belong to his posterity by participation, imputation, and propagation."

Both *Stuart* and *Barnes* stumble here; and though they denounce theorizing, and advocate adherence to the language of Scripture, they do yet theorize and attempt to evade the plain and obvious meaning

13. *For until the law,* &c. This parenthesis anticipates an objection: for as there seems to be no transgression without the law, it might have been doubted whether there were before the law any sin: that there was after the law admitted of no doubt. The question only refers to the time preceding the law. To this then he gives this answer—that though God had not as yet denounced judgment by a written law, yet mankind were under a curse, and that from the womb; and hence that they who led a wicked and vicious life before the promulgation of the law, were by no means exempt from the condemnation of sin; for there had always been some notion of a God, to whom honour was due, and there had ever been some rule of righteousness. This view is so plain and so clear, that of itself it disproves every opposite notion.

But sin is not imputed, &c. Without the law reproving us, we in a manner sleep in our sins; and though we are not ignorant that we do evil, we yet suppress as much as we can the knowledge of evil offered to us, at least we obliterate it by quickly forgetting it. While the law reproves and chides us, it awakens us as it were by its stimulating power, that we may return to the consideration of God's judgment. The Apostle then intimates that men continue in their perverseness when not roused by the law, and that when the difference between good and evil is laid aside, they securely and joyfully indulge themselves, as if there was no judgment to come. But that before the law iniquities were by God imputed to men is evident from the punishment of Cain, from the deluge by which the whole world was destroyed, from the fate of Sodom, and from the plagues inflicted on Pharaoh and Abimelech on account of Abraham, and also

of this passage. But in trying to avoid one difficulty, they make for themselves another still greater. The penalty, or the imputation of guilt, they admit; which is indeed undeniable, as facts, as well as Scripture, most clearly prove: but the participation they deny, though words could hardly be framed to express it more distinctly than the words of this verse; and thus, according to their view, a punishment is inflicted without a previous implication in an offence; while the Scriptural account of the matter is, according to what Calvin states, that "sin extends to all who suffer its punishment," though he afterwards explains this in a way that is not altogether consistent.—*Ed.*

from the plagues brought on the Egyptians. That men also imputed sin to one another, is clear from the many complaints and expostulations by which they charged one another with iniquity, and also from the defences by which they laboured to clear themselves from accusations of doing wrong. There are indeed many examples which prove that every man was of himself conscious of what was evil and of what was good: but that for the most part they connived at their own evil deeds, so that they imputed nothing as a sin to themselves unless they were constrained. When therefore he denies that sin without the law is imputed, he speaks comparatively; for when men are not pricked by the goads of the law, they become sunk in carelessness.[1]

But Paul wisely introduced this sentence, in order that the Jews might hence more clearly learn how grievously they offended, inasmuch as the law openly condemned them; for if they were not exempted from punishment whom God had never summoned as guilty before his tribunal, what would become of the Jews to whom the law, like a herald, had proclaimed their guilt, yea, on whom it denounced judgment? There may be also another reason adduced why he expressly says, that sin reigned before the law, but was not imputed, and that is, that we may know that the cause of death proceeds not from the law, but is only made known by it. Hence he declares, that all became miserably lost

[1] This verse, as bearing on the argument, may be viewed rather differently. This and the following verse contain an explanation or an illustration of the last, the 12th. He states in this verse two things: a fact and a general principle; the fact is, that sin, the first sin in its evident effects, (for he speaks throughout of *no other sin*, as to Adam, or as producing death,) was in the world before the law of Moses was given; and the general principle he avows is, that no sin is imputed where there is no law. Having made this last admission, he proceeds in the 14th to say, that "nevertheless," or notwithstanding, death, the effect of sin, prevailed in the world, and prevailed even as to those who did not *actually* or personally sin as Adam did. He takes no account of personal sins, for his object was to show the effects of the first sin. And then he says, that in this respect Adam was a kind of type, a figure, a representative of Christ who was to come; and in the three verses which follow, the 15th, the 16th, and 17th, he traces the similitude between the two, pointing out at the same time the difference, which in every instance is in favour of the last Adam. That τύπος signifies here likeness and not identity, is quite certain, whatever may be its common meaning, because its import is exemplified and illustrated in the verses which follow.—*Ed.*

immediately after the fall of Adam, though their destruction was only made manifest by the law. If you translate the adversative δε, *though*, the text would run better; for the meaning is, that though men may indulge themselves, they cannot yet escape God's judgment, even when there is no law to reprove them.

Death reigned from Adam, &c. He explains more clearly that it availed men nothing that from Adam to the time when the law was promulgated, they led a licentious and careless life, while the difference between good and evil was wilfully rejected, and thus, without the warning of the law, the remembrance of sin was buried; yea, that this availed them nothing, because sin did yet issue in their condemnation. It hence appears, that death even then reigned; for the blindness and obduracy of men could not stifle the judgment of God.

14. *Even over them*, &c. Though this passage is commonly understood of infants, who being guilty of no actual sin, die through original sin, I yet prefer to regard it as referring to all those who sinned without the law; for this verse is to be connected with the preceding clause, which says, that those who were without the law did not impute sin to themselves. Hence they sinned not after the similitude of Adam's transgression; for they had not, like him, the will of God made known to them by a certain oracle: for the Lord had forbidden Adam to touch the fruit of the tree of the knowledge of good and evil; but to them he had given no command besides the testimony of conscience. The Apostle then intended to imply, that it did not happen through the difference between Adam and his posterity that they were exempt from condemnation. Infants are at the same time included in their number.

Who is a type of him who was to come. This sentence is put instead of a second clause; for we see that one part only of the comparison is expressed, the other is omitted—an instance of what is called *anacoluthon*.[1] You are then to take the meaning as though it was said, "As by one man

---

[1] 'Ανακόλουθον, not consequent: a figure in grammar when a word or a clause, required by a former one, is not put down.—*Ed.*

sin entered into the whole world, and death through sin, so by one man righteousness returned, and life through righteousness." But in saying that Adam bore a resemblance to Christ, there is nothing incongruous; for some likeness often appears in things wholly contrary. As then we are all lost through Adam's sin, so we are restored through Christ's righteousness: hence he calls Adam not inaptly the type of Christ. But observe, that Adam is not said to be the type of sin, nor Christ the type of righteousness, as though they led the way only by their example, but that the one is contrasted with the other. Observe this, lest you should foolishly go astray with *Origen*, and be involved in a pernicious error; for he reasoned philosophically and profanely on the corruption of mankind, and not only diminished the grace of Christ, but nearly obliterated it altogether. The less excusable is *Erasmus*, who labours much in palliating a notion so grossly delirious.

15. But not as the offence, so also *is* the free gift. For if through the offence of one many be dead; much more the grace of God, and the gift by grace, *which is* by one man, Jesus Christ, hath abounded unto many.	15. Sed non sicut delictum, ita et donum; nam si unius delicto[1] multi mortui sunt, multo magis gratia Dei et donum Dei in gratia, quæ fuit unius hominis Christi, in multos abundavit.

15. *But not as the offence*, &c. Now follows the rectifying or the completion of the comparison already introduced. The Apostle does not, however, very minutely state the

---

[1] *Delicto*—fault, παράπτωμα—stumbling, fall, transgression. Perhaps the last would be the best word here. It is rendered sometimes in the plural number "trespasses," Matt. xviii. 35; 2 Cor. v. 19; Eph. ii. 1. *Macknight* renders it here "fall," but most "offence." The comparison here is between the sin of *one*, which produced death, and the grace of God through *one*, which brings the "gift" of life; and the difference, "much more," seems to refer to the exuberance of grace by which man is to be raised to a higher state than that from which Adam fell. "A little lower than the angels" was man in his first creation; he is by exuberance of grace to be raised to a state as high as that of angels, if not higher: or we may take "much more" as intimating the greater power of grace to recover than sin to destroy. Sin is the act of man, and issued in death; but grace is the act of God, and will therefore with greater certainty issue in life.

"Adam's life after his fall was even as a slow dying, that reached its completion in his physical death; Christ's ζωοποίησις of mankind is also gradual, the height of which is in the glorification of the body."—*Olshausen*.

points of difference between Christ and Adam, but he obviates errors into which we might otherwise easily fall, and what is needful for an explanation we shall add. Though he mentions oftentimes a difference, yet there are none of these repetitions in which there is not a want of a corresponding clause, or in which there is not at least an ellipsis. Such instances are indeed defects in a discourse; but they are not prejudicial to the majesty of that celestial wisdom which is taught us by the Apostle; it has, on the contrary, so happened through the providence of God, that the highest mysteries have been delivered to us in the garb of an humble style,[1] in order that our faith may not depend on the potency of human eloquence, but on the efficacious working of the Spirit alone.

He does not indeed even now expressly supply the deficiency of the former sentence, but simply teaches us, that there is a greater measure of grace procured by Christ, than of condemnation introduced by the first man. What some think, that the Apostle carries on here a chain of reasoning, I know not whether it will be deemed by all sufficiently evident. It may indeed be justly inferred, that since the fall of Adam had such an effect as to produce the ruin of many, much more efficacious is the grace of God to the benefit of many; inasmuch as it is admitted, that Christ is much more powerful to save, than Adam was to destroy. But as they cannot be disproved, who wish to take the passage without this inference, I am willing that they should

---

[1] "Sub contemptibili verborum humilitate." This sort of derogatory language as to the style of Scripture, *Calvin* had evidently learnt from the fathers. *Chrysostom* and *Jerome* did sometimes say most unwarrantable things in this respect, and that in a great measure because they did not understand the style of the New Testament, and in part with the view of taking away, by an admission, the force of objections alleged by admirers of Grecian and refined diction. The style of the New Testament is that of the Old; and hardly any of the fathers, except *Origen* and *Jerome*, knew Hebrew, and the latter learnt it only in his old age, so that he could have had no great insight into its peculiarities. One like *Chrysostom*, brought up in the refinements of Grecian literature, was a very unfit judge of the style of the New Testament, and hence it is that the criticisms of the Greek fathers in general are comparatively of very little value.

The whole of this passage, 12-19, is constructed according to the model of the Hebrew style; and when rightly understood, it will appear to contain none of those defects ascribed to it.—*Ed.*

choose either of these views; though what next follows cannot be deemed an inference, yet it is of the same meaning. It is hence probable, that Paul rectifies, or by way of exception modifies, what he had said of the likeness between Christ and Adam.

But observe, that a larger number (*plures*) are not here contrasted with many (*multis*,) for he speaks not of the number of men: but as the sin of Adam has destroyed many, he draws this conclusion,—that the righteousness of Christ will be no less efficacious to save many.[1]

When he says, *by the offence of one*, &c., understand him as meaning this,—that corruption has from him descended to us: for we perish not through his fault, as though we were blameless; but as his sin is the cause of our sin, Paul ascribes to him our ruin: our sin I call that which is implanted in us, and with which we are born.

The grace of God and the gift of God through grace, &c. Grace is properly set in opposition to offence; the gift which proceeds from grace, to death. Hence *grace* means the free goodness of God or gratuitous love, of which he has given us a proof in Christ, that he might relieve our misery: and *gift* is the fruit of this mercy, and hath come to us, even the

---

[1] It is evident that "the many," οἱ πολλοί, include those connected with the two parties—the many descendants of Adam, and the many believers in Christ. And "the many" was adopted to form a contrast with the "one."

"The many" are termed "all" in ver. 18, and again, "the many," in ver. 19. They are called "the many" and "all" alike with regard both to Adam and to Christ. Some maintain that the terms are coextensive in the two instances. That the whole race of man is meant in the one instance, cannot be doubted: and is there any reason why the whole race of man should not be included in the second? Most clearly there is. The Apostle speaks of *Adam* and his posterity, and also of *Christ* and his people, or those "who receive abundance of grace," or, "are made righteous;" and "the many" and the "all" are evidently those who belong to each separately. In no other way can the words with any consistency be understood. All who fell in Adam do not certainly "receive abundance of grace," and are not "made righteous." And it is not possible, as Professor *Hodge* observes, "so to eviscerate such declarations as these, as to make them to contain nothing more than that the chance of salvation is offered to all men." This is indeed contrary to evident facts. Nor can they mean, that a way of acceptance has been opened, which is suitable to all; for though this is true, it yet cannot be the meaning here. Hence "the many" and the "all," as to Adam, are all his descendants; and "the many" and the "all," as to Christ, are those who believe.—*Ed.*

reconciliation by which we have obtained life and salvation, righteousness, newness of life, and every other blessing. We hence see how absurdly the schoolmen have defined grace, who have taught that it is nothing else but a quality infused into the hearts of men: for grace, properly speaking, is in God; and what is in us is the effect of grace. And he says, that it is by *one man;* for the Father has made him the fountain out of whose fulness all must draw. And thus he teaches us, that not even the least drop of life can be found out of Christ,—that there is no other remedy for our poverty and want, than what he conveys to us from his own abundance.

16. And not as *it was* by one that sinned,[1] *so is* the gift: for the judgment *was* by one to condemnation, but the free gift *is* of many offences unto justification.	16. Et non sicut per unum qui peccaverat, ita donum; judicium enim ex uno in condemationem, donum autem ex multis delictis in justificationem.

16. This is especially an explanation of what he had said before,—that by one offence guilt issued in the condemnation of us all, but that grace, or rather the gratuitous gift, is efficacious to our justification from many offences. It is indeed an expansion of what the last verse contains; for he had not hitherto expressed, how or in what respect Christ excelled Adam. This difference being settled, it appears evident, that their opinion is impious, who have taught that we recover nothing else by Christ but a freedom from original sin, or the corruption derived from Adam. Observe also, that these many offences, from which he affirms we are freed through Christ, are not to be understood only of those which every one must have committed before baptism, but

[1] Many copies have ἁμαρτήματος—sin; but it is a reading deemed by *Griesbach* of less authority than the received text, ἁμαρτήσαντος—sinning: yet there being good MSS. in its favour, and several versions, especially the *Syriac* and the *Vulgate*, and the passage requiring it, this reading is to be preferred. Then the rendering would be the following,—

And not as through one sin, is the free gift—(δώρημα;) for judgment was indeed from one *sin* to condemnation, but the free favour (χάρισμα) is from many trespasses to justification.

It is the character of the Apostle's style to change his words, while the same idea is often intended. The comparison here is between the *one sin* which issued in condemnation, and the *many trespasses* or offences, from which a justification is the favour obtained.—*Ed.*

also of those by which the saints contract daily new guilt; and on account of which they would be justly exposed to condemnation, were they not continually relieved by this grace.

He sets gift in opposition to judgment: by the latter he means strict justice; by the former, gratuitous pardon. From strict justice comes condemnation; from pardon, absolution. Or, which is the same thing, were God to deal with us according to justice, we should be all undone; but he justifies us freely in Christ.

17. For if by one man's offence death reigned by one; much more they which receive abundance of grace, and of the gift of righteousness, shall reign in life by one, Jesus Christ.)[1]	17. Si enim unius delicto mors regnavit per unum; multò magis, qui exuberantiam gratiæ et doni justitiæ acceperunt, in vita regnabunt per unum Iesum Christum.)

17. *For if for the offence of one,* &c. He again subjoins a general explanation, on which he dwells still further; for it was by no means his purpose to explain every part of the subject, but to state the main points. He had before declared, that the power of grace had surpassed that of sin: and by this he consoles and strengthens the faithful, and, at the same time, stimulates and encourages them to meditate on the benignity of God. Indeed the design of so studious a repetition was,—that the grace of God might be worthily set forth, that men might be led from self-confidence to trust in Christ, that having obtained his grace they might enjoy full assurance; and hence at length arises gratitude. The sum of the whole is this—that Christ surpasses Adam; the sin of one is overcome by the righteousness of the other; the curse of one is effaced by the grace of the other; from one,

---

[1] This verse, according to the usual manner of the Apostle, whose style is that of the Prophets, includes the two main ideas of the two preceding verses, in another form, and in an inverted order, as it refers first to the *one offence* and then to the *one man*, in the first clause; and the same order is followed in the second; "the exuberance of grace" is to cover the *many offences* before mentioned, as opposed to the *one offence,* and to *one man* is opposed *one* Christ Jesus.

The reading ἐν τῷ ἑνί, though according to *Griesbach,* it is not, as to MSS., of equal authority with the received text, is yet to be preferred; for τοῦ ἑνὸς makes a tautology, and destroys the order which we find preserved in the second clause.—*Ed.*

death has proceeded, which is absorbed by the life which the other bestows.

But the parts of this comparison do not correspond; instead of adding, " the gift of life shall more fully reign and flourish through the exuberance of grace," he says, that "the faithful shall reign;" which amounts to the same thing; for the reign of the faithful is in life, and the reign of life is in the faithful.

It may further be useful to notice here the difference between Christ and Adam, which the Apostle omitted, not because he deemed it of no importance, but unconnected with his present subject.

The first is, that by Adam's sin we are not condemned through imputation alone, as though we were punished only for the sin of another; but we suffer his punishment, because we also ourselves are guilty; for as our nature is vitiated in him, it is regarded by God as having committed sin. But through the righteousness of Christ we are restored in a different way to salvation; for it is not said to be accepted for us, because it is in us, but because we possess Christ himself with all his blessings, as given to us through the bountiful kindness of the Father. Hence the gift of righteousness is not a quality with which God endows us, as some absurdly explain it, but a gratuitous imputation of righteousness; for the Apostle plainly declares what he understood by the word *grace*. The other difference is, that the benefit of Christ does not come to all men, while Adam has involved his whole race in condemnation; and the reason of this is indeed evident; for as the curse we derive from Adam is conveyed to us by nature, it is no wonder that it includes the whole mass; but that we may come to a participation of the grace of Christ, we must be ingrafted in him by faith. Hence, in order to partake of the miserable inheritance of sin, it is enough for thee to be man, for it dwells in flesh and blood; but in order to enjoy the righteousness of Christ it is necessary for thee to be a believer; for a participation of him is attained only by faith. He is communicated to infants in a peculiar way; for they have by covenant the right of adoption, by which they pass over unto a participation of Christ.[1] Of the children of the godly I speak, to whom the promise of grace is addressed; for others are by no means exempted from the common lot.

18. Therefore, as by the offence of one *judgment came* upon all men to condemnation; even so by the righteousness of one *the free gift came* upon all men unto justification of life.	18. Itaque quemadmodum, per unius delictum, in omnes homines in condemnationem; sic et per unius justificationem, in omnes homines in justificationem vitæ.

18. *Therefore,* &c. This is a defective sentence; it will be complete if the words *condemnation* and *justification* be read in the nominative case; as doubtless you must do in order to complete the sense. We have here the general conclusion from the preceding comparison; for, omitting the mention of the intervening explanation, he now completes the comparison, " As by the offence of one we were made (*constituti*) sinners; so the righteousness of Christ is efficacious to justify us." He does not say the righteousness—δικαιοσύνην, but the justification—δικαίωμα,[2] of Christ, in order to remind us that he was not as an individual just for himself, but that the righteousness with which he was endued reached farther, in order that, by conferring this gift, he might enrich the faithful. He makes this favour common to all, because it is propounded to all, and not because it is in reality extended to all; for though Christ suffered for the sins of the whole world, and is offered through God's benignity indiscriminately to all, yet all do not receive him.[3]

[1] The original is, " Habent enim in fœdere jus adoptionis, quo in Christi communionem transeunt."—*Ed.*

[2] The meaning of this word is evident here; for it stands in contrast with παράπτωμα—offence or transgression, in the former clause, and is identical in sense with ὑπακοή—obedience, in the next verse. It means what is *appointed* and adjudged as right; and hence it is rendered " ordinance," Luke i. 6; "judgment," Rom. i. 32; and, in verse 16 of this chapter, " justification," when it stands opposed to κατάκριμα—condemnation, and means absolution, acquittal, as the determination of the judge. It signifies here, that what Christ did was according to God's appointment; it was something directly contrary to offence or transgression; and what it was is explained in the next verse by the word " obedience." *Wolfius* says, that δικαίωμα is the satisfaction of Christ, or his active and passive obedience, verse 19,—that δικαιοσύνη is the merit of Christ, obtained by his death and applied to us by faith, chap. iii. 22,—and that δικαίωσις is the act of justification which follows from the satisfaction of Christ, apprehended by faith.—*Ed.*

[3] " Nam etsi passus est Christus pro peccatis totius mundi, atque omni-

These two words, which he had before used, *judgment* and *grace*, may be also introduced here in this form, " As it was through God's judgment that the sin of one issued in the condemnation of many, so grace will be efficacious to the justification of many." *Justification of life* is to be taken, in my judgment, for remission, which restores life to us, as though he called it life-giving.¹ For whence comes the hope of salvation, except that God is propitious to us; and we must be just, in order to be accepted. Then life proceeds from justification.²

19. For as by one man's disobedience many were made sinners; so by the obedience of one shall many be made righteous.

19. Quemadmodum enim per disobedientiam unius hominis peccatores constituti sunt multi; sic et per obedientiam unius justi constituentur multi.

This is no tautology, but a necessary explanation of the former verse. For he shows that we are guilty through the offence of one man, in such a manner as not to be ourselves innocent. He had said before, that we are condemned; but that no one might claim for himself innocency, he also subjoined, that every one is condemned because he is a sinner. And then, as he declares that we are made righteous through the obedience of Christ, we hence conclude that Christ, in satisfying the Father, has provided a righteousness for us.

bus indifferenter Dei benignitate offertur; non tamen omnes apprehendunt." It appears from this sentence that *Calvin* held general redemption.—*Ed*.

¹ It is an Hebraistic form of speaking, *genitivus effectûs*. Its meaning is, that it is a justification unto life, whose end is life, or, which issues in life, that is, eternal life, according to its import in verse 17, when reigning in life—ἐν ζωῇ, is spoken of; and the word "eternal," is added to it in the last verse. This life commences with justification, and therefore this view includes what *Calvin* says, though it extends farther.—*Ed*.

² In our version are introduced "judgment" and "free-gift," from verse 16; and it is what has been done by most interpreters. The words are found here in no MSS.; but there is another reading countenanced by four MSS., as given by *Griesbach*, and two of them ancient; the word for offence is put in the nominative case, τὸ παράπτωμα, and the word for righteousness the same, τὸ δικαίωμα. Then the reading would be—

18. So then, as through one the transgression *was*, as to all men, unto condemnation; so also through one the righteousness *is*, as to all men, unto justification of life.

This agrees better with the following verse, though the meaning is substantially the same with what is given in our version.—*Ed*.

It then follows, that righteousness is in Christ, and that it is to be received by us as what peculiarly belongs to him. He at the same time shows what sort of righteousness it is, by calling it obedience. And here let us especially observe what we must bring into God's presence, if we seek to be justified by works, even obedience to the law, not to this or to that part, but in every respect perfect; for when a just man falls, all his former righteousness will not be remembered. We may also hence learn, how false are the schemes which they take to pacify God, who of themselves devise what they obtrude on him. For then only we truly worship him when we follow what he has commanded us, and render obedience to his word. Away then with those who confidently lay claim to the righteousness of works, which cannot otherwise exist than when there is a full and complete observance of the law; and it is certain that this is nowhere to be found. We also learn, that they are madly foolish who vaunt before God of works invented by themselves, which he regards as the filthiest things; for obedience is better than sacrifices.

20. Moreover, the law entered, that the offence might abound:[1] but where sin abounded, grace did much more abound:
21. That as sin hath reigned unto death, even so might grace reign through righteousness unto eternal life by Jesus Christ our Lord.

20. Lex verò intervenit, ut abundaret delictum; ubi verò abundavit delictum, superabundavit et gratia:
21. Quò, sicut regnavit peccatum per mortem, sic et gratia regnet per justitiam in vitam æternam per Iesum Christum Dominum nostrum.

20. *But the law intervened,* &c. This subject depends on what he had said before,—that there was sin before the law was published. This being the case, then follows immediately this question—For what purpose was the law given? It was therefore necessary to solve this difficulty; but as a longer digression was not suitable, he deferred the subject

---

[1] Πλεονάση, which means to grow more and more, to increase, to multiply: it is a different verb from that in the last clause. What he calls "offence" or "fall" in this member of the sentence, he calls "sin" in the next. It is still "the fall" or "the sin" which caused it: for that is the parent of every other sin.—*Ed.*

and handled it in another place: and now by the way he only says, that the law entered,[1] that sin might abound; for he describes not here the whole office and use of the law, but only touches on one part, which served his present purpose. He indeed teaches us, that it was needful that men's ruin should be more fully discovered to them, in order that a passage might be opened for the favour of God. They were indeed shipwrecked before the law was given; as however they seemed to themselves to swim, while in their destruction, they were thrust down into the deep, that their deliverance might appear more evident, when they thence emerge beyond all human expectation. Nor was it unreasonable, that the law should be partly introduced for this end—that it might again condemn men already condemned; for nothing is more reasonable than that men should, through all means be brought, nay, forced, by being proved guilty, to know their own evils.

That offence might abound, &c. It is well known how some, following *Augustine,* usually explain this passage,—that lust is irritated the more, while it is checked by the restraints of the law; for it is man's nature to strive for what is forbidden. But I understand no other increase to be intended here than that of knowledge and of obstinacy; for sin is set by the law before the eyes of man, that he may be continually forced to see that condemnation is prepared for him. Thus sin disturbs the conscience, which, when cast

---

[1] " Intercessisse legem—that the law came between," *i.e.,* Adam and Christ; παρεισῆλθεν, from παρὰ, with, besides, or between, and εἰσέρχομαι, to enter. It occurs elsewhere only in Gal. ii. 4, where it is rendered, " came in privily," as required by the context. But it cannot be so rendered here. *Schleusner* says, that it simply means to enter, and that it is so used by *Philo.* It is thus rendered by the *Syriac* and *Arabic* versions. *Erasmus* has " obiter subiit, *vel,* irrepsit—came, *or,* crept in by the by;" *Hammond* has the same; but *Beza* attaches the idea of *besides* to παρὰ,— " præterea introiit—entered in besides," *i.e.,* in addition to the disease under which all men laboured, having been contaminated by that of the first sin. " Intervenit—intervened," is the rendering of *Grotius;* that is, the law intervened between the beginning of sin and the beginning of new righteousness. " The law," says *Hodge,* " was *superinduced* on a plan already laid. It was not designed for the accomplishment of man's salvation, that is, either for his justification or sanctification, but for the accomplishment of a very subordinate part in the great scheme of mercy." —*Ed.*

behind them, men forget. And farther, he who before only passed over the bounds of justice, becomes now, when the law is introduced, a despiser of God's authority, since the will of God is made known to him, which he now wantonly tramples under feet. It hence follows, that sin is increased by the law, since now the authority of the lawgiver is despised and his majesty degraded.[1]

Grace has superabounded. After sin has held men sunk in ruin, grace then comes to their help: for he teaches us, that the abundance of grace becomes for this reason more illustrious,—that while sin is overflowing, it pours itself forth so exuberantly, that it not only overcomes the flood of sin, but wholly absorbs it.[2] And we may hence learn, that our condemnation is not set before us in the law, that we may abide in it; but that having fully known our misery, we may be led to Christ, who is sent to be a physician to the sick, a deliverer to the captives, a comforter to the afflicted, a defender to the oppressed. (Is. lxi. 1.)

21. *That as sin has reigned,* &c. As sin is said to be the sting of death, and as death has no power over men, except on account of sin; so sin executes its power by death: it is hence said to exercise thereby its dominion. In the last clause the order of the words is deranged, but yet not without reason. The simple contrast might have been thus formed,—" That righteousness may reign through Christ." But Paul was not content to oppose what is contrary to what is contrary, but adds the word *grace,* that he might more deeply print this truth on the memory—that the whole is to be ascribed, not to our merit, but to the kindness of

---

[1] *Chrysostom* regarded ἵνα here as denoting not the *final cause,* but the *event,* and thought the meaning to be, that the law entered, so that the effect or event was, that sin increased. Its rendering would then be, *so that:* and this seems to be the meaning given to it by *Calvin.* The law did not create sin, but made it known, and by discovering it, increased its guilt when persisted in, and by discovering it showed the necessity of a Saviour.

[2] The superabounding has a reference to the increasing of sin by means of the law. Grace not only abounded so as to be sufficient to remedy the first sin and the sins which followed it; but it abounded still more, so as to be an adequate provision for sin when increased by the law, through the perverseness of human nature.—*Ed.*

God.[1] He had previously said, that death reigned; he now ascribes reigning to sin; but its end or effect is death. And he says, that it has reigned, in the past tense; not that it has ceased to reign in those who are born only of flesh, and he thus distinguishes between Adam and Christ, and assigns to each his own time. Hence as soon as the grace of Christ begins to prevail in any one, the reign of sin and death ceases.[2]

---

[1] The antithesis to "sin" is properly "righteousness;" but, as *Calvin* observes, "grace" is connected with it. To preserve the contrast, the sentence might be rendered, "grace through righteousness;" and then to show the medium or channel through which this "grace through righteousness" is to reign so as to issue in "eternal life," it is added, "through Jesus Christ our Lord." So that in this single sentence, we have the origin, "grace," the means or the meritorious cause, "righteousness," the agent, or the procurer of it, "Jesus Christ," and the end, "eternal life." Some take "grace" as antithetic to sin, and connect "righteousness" with "eternal life," and render it "justification;" but this does not so well preserve the antithetic character of the clause. Those who render it "holiness" completely misunderstand the drift of the passage.

The first part is differently rendered: instead of "unto death," *Hammond* renders it, like *Calvin*, "through death," and *Grotius*, "by (*per*) death." The preposition is ἐν and not εἰς, and its common meaning is "in," and it may be here translated, "in death;" *i.e.*, in a state of death. The reign of sin was that of death and misery; the reign of grace through Christ's righteousness is that of life and happiness, which is never to end.—*Ed.*

[2] That the antitheses of this remarkable passage, from verse 12 to the end, may be more clearly seen, it shall be presented in lines. The contrast in verses 12 and 20 will be found in the first and last line and in the second and the third; and as to all the other verses, in the first and the third line and in the second and the fourth, except the 13th and the 14th, which are an explanation of the 12th. The 17th includes the *two* ideas of the 15th and 16th, in an inverted order. The 18th and 19th contain the summing up of the argument,—

> 12. For this reason,—as by one man sin entered into the world,
> And death by sin,
> Even so death came upon all men,—
> Because all had sinned:
> 13. Sin indeed was until the law in the world,
> But sin is not imputed when there is no law;
> 14. Yet reign did death from Adam to Moses
> Even over those who had not sinned
> After the likeness of the transgression of Adam,
> Who is the type of him who was to come.
>
> 15. But not as the transgression,
> So also the free favour;
> For if through the transgression of one
> Many died,

CHAPTER VI.

1. What shall we say then? Shall we continue in sin, that grace may abound?	1. Quid ergo dicemus? manebimus in peccato, ut gratia abundet?
2. God forbid. How shall we, that are dead to sin, live any longer therein?	2. Ne sit ita: qui mortui sumus peccato, quomodo adhuc vivemus in eo?

1. *What then shall we say?* Throughout this chapter the Apostle proves, that they who imagine that gratuitous righteousness is given us by him, apart from newness of life, shamefully rend Christ asunder: nay, he goes further, and refers to this objection,—that there seems in this case to be an opportunity for the display of grace, if men continued

> Much more has God's grace, and his free gift through the
>   grace of one man, Jesus Christ,
> Abounded unto many:
> 16.   And not as through one sin,
>   *So* the free gift;
> For judgment *was* indeed
> Through one *sin* to condemnation,
> But the free favour
> *Is* from many transgressions to justification:—
> 17. For if for one transgression,
> Death reigned through one;
> Much more shall they, who receive abundance of grace
>   and of the gift of righteousness,
> Reign in life through one, Jesus Christ.
>
> 18. So then, as through one transgression,
> *Judgment was* on all men to condemnation;
> So also through one righteousness,
> *The free favour* is on all men to justification of life:
> 19. For as through the disobedience of one man,
> Sinful were made many;
> So also through the obedience of one,
> Righteous shall be made many.
>
> 20. But the law entered in,
> That multiplied might be transgression;
> But where sin multiplied,
> Superabounded has grace:
> So that as sin reigned
> Into death;
> So also grace shall reign through righteousness,
> Into eternal life, through Jesus Christ our Lord.—*Ed.*

fixed in sin. We indeed know that nothing is more natural than that the flesh should indulge itself under any excuse, and also that Satan should invent all kinds of slander, in order to discredit the doctrine of grace; which to him is by no means difficult. For since everything that is announced concerning Christ seems very paradoxical to human judgment, it ought not to be deemed a new thing, that the flesh, hearing of justification by faith, should so often strike, as it were, against so many stumbling-stones. Let us, however, go on in our course; nor let Christ be suppressed, because he is to many a stone of offence, and a rock of stumbling; for as he is for ruin to the ungodly, so he is to the godly for a resurrection. We ought, at the same time, ever to obviate unreasonable questions, lest the Christian faith should appear to contain anything absurd.

The Apostle now takes notice of that most common objection against the preaching of divine grace, which is this, —" That if it be true, that the more bountifully and abundantly will the grace of God aid us, the more completely we are overwhelmed with the mass of sin; then nothing is better for us than to be sunk into the depth of sin, and often to provoke God's wrath with new offences; for then at length we shall find more abounding grace; than which nothing better can be desired." The refutation of this we shall hereafter meet with.

2. *By no means.* To some the Apostle seems to have only intended indignantly to reprove a madness so outrageous; but it appears from other places that he commonly used an answer of this kind, even while carrying on a long argument; as indeed he does here, for he proceeds carefully to disprove the propounded slander. He, however, first rejects it by an indignant negative, in order to impress it on the minds of his readers, that nothing can be more inconsistent than that the grace of Christ, the repairer of our righteousness, should nourish our vices.

Who have died to sin, &c. An argument derived from what is of an opposite character. " He who sins certainly lives to sin; we have died to sin through the grace of Christ; then it is false, that what abolishes sin gives vigour to it."

The state of the case is really this,—that the faithful are never reconciled to God without the gift of regeneration; nay, we are for this end justified,—that we may afterwards serve God in holiness of life. Christ indeed does not cleanse us by his blood, nor render God propitious to us by his expiation, in any other way than by making us partakers of his Spirit, who renews us to a holy life. It would then be a most strange inversion of the work of God were sin to gather strength on account of the grace which is offered to us in Christ; for medicine is not a feeder of the disease, which it destroys.[1] We must further bear in mind, what I have already referred to—that Paul does not state here what God finds us to be, when he calls us to an union with his Son, but what it behoves us to be, after he has had mercy on us, and has freely adopted us; for by an adverb, denoting a future time, he shows what kind of change ought to follow righteousness.

[1] This phrase, " died to sin," is evidently misapprehended by *Haldane*. Having been offended, and justly so, by an unguarded and erroneous expression of *Stuart*, derived from *Chrysostom*, and by the false rendering of *Macknight*, he went to another extreme, and maintained, that to die, or to be dead to sin, means to be freed from its guilt, while the whole context proves, that it means deliverance from its power as a master, from the servitude or bondage of sin. To live in it, does not mean to live under its guilt, but in its service and under its ruling power; and this is what the Apostle represents as a contrast to being dead to sin. Not to " serve sin," in ver. 6, is its true explanation. See also verses 11, 12, and 14.

The very argument requires this meaning. The question in the first verse,—" Shall we continue in sin?" does not surely mean—shall we continue in or under the guilt of sin? but in its service, and in the practice of it. It was the charge of practical licentiousness that the Apostle rebuts; and he employs an argument suitable to the purpose, "If we are dead to sin, freed from it as our master, how absurd it is to suppose that we can live any longer in its service?" Then he shows in what follows how this had been effected. This is clearly the import of the passage, and so taken by almost all commentators.

But it must be added, that *Venema* and *Chalmers* materially agree with *Haldane*. The former says, that to " die to sin " is to give to sin what it demands, and that is, death; and that when this is given, it can require nothing more. In this sense, he adds, Christ died to sin (ver. 10); and in the same sense believers die to sin, being, as they are, united to Christ, his death being viewed as their death. However true this theology may be, (and *Chalmers* shows this in his own inimitable manner,) it does not seem to be taught here: though there may be something in one or two expressions to favour it; yet the whole tenor of the passage, and many of the phrases, seem clearly to constrain us to adopt the other view.—*Ed.*

3. Know ye not, that so many of us as were baptized into Jesus Christ were baptized into his death?

4. Therefore we are buried with him by baptism into death: that like as Christ was raised up from the dead by the glory of the Father, even so we also should walk in newness of life.

3. Num ignoratis quòd quicunque baptizati sumus in Christum, in mortem ejus baptizati sumus?

4. Consepulti ergo sumus ei per baptismum in mortem; ut quemadmodum suscitatus est Christus ex mortuis per gloriam Patris, sic et nos in novitate vitæ ambulemus.

3. *Know ye not,* &c. What he intimated in the last verse —that Christ destroys sin in his people, he proves here by mentioning the effect of baptism, by which we are initiated into his faith; for it is beyond any question, that we put on Christ in baptism, and that we are baptized for this end— that we may be one with him. But Paul takes up another principle—that we are then really united to the body of Christ, when his death brings forth in us its fruit; yea, he teaches us, that this fellowship as to death is what is to be mainly regarded in baptism; for not washing alone is set forth in it, but also the putting to death and the dying of the old man. It is hence evident, that when we become partakers of the grace of Christ, immediately the efficacy of his death appears. But the benefit of this fellowship as to the death of Christ is described in what follows.[1]

4. *We have then been buried with him,* &c. He now begins to indicate the object of our having been baptized into

---

[1] " Baptized into (εἰς) Christ," " baptized into (εἰς) Moses," 1 Cor. x. 2, " baptized into (εἰς) one body," 1 Cor. xii. 13, are all the same forms of expression, and must mean, that by the rite of baptism a professed union is made, and, in the two first instances, a submission to the authority exercised is avowed. By " baptized into his death," we are to understand, " baptized," in order to die with him, or to die as he died; not that the death is the same; for it is a like death, as it is expressed in ver. 5, as the resurrection is a like resurrection. His death was natural, ours is spiritual; the same difference holds as to the resurrection. It is the *likeness* that is throughout to be regarded; and this is the key to the whole passage. It is true, that through the efficacy of Christ's death alone the death of his people takes place, and through the operation of his Spirit; but to teach this is not the design of the Apostle here; his object seems to be merely to show that a change takes place in every true Christian, symbolized by baptism, and that this change bears a likeness to the death and resurrection of our Saviour. He speaks of baptism here not merely as a symbol, but as including what it symbolizes; as he does in a similar passage, Col. ii. 11, 12, where he refers to this change, first under the symbol of circumcision, and then of baptism; which clearly proves that the same thing is signified by both.—*Ed.*

the death of Christ, though he does not yet completely unfold it; and the object is—that we, being dead to ourselves, may become new creatures. He rightly makes a transition from a fellowship in death to a fellowship in life; for these two things are connected together by an indissoluble knot— that the old man is destroyed by the death of Christ, and that his resurrection brings righteousness, and renders us new creatures. And surely, since Christ has been given to us for life, to what purpose is it that we die with him except that we may rise to a better life? And hence for no other reason does he slay what is mortal in us, but that he may give us life again.

Let us know, that the Apostle does not simply exhort us to imitate Christ, as though he had said that the death of Christ is a pattern which all Christians are to follow; for no doubt he ascends higher, as he announces a doctrine, with which he connects, as it is evident, an exhortation; and his doctrine is this—that the death of Christ is efficacious to destroy and demolish the depravity of our flesh, and his resurrection, to effect the renovation of a better nature, and that by baptism we are admitted into a participation of this grace. This foundation being laid, Christians may very suitably be exhorted to strive to respond to their calling. Farther, it is not to the point to say, that this power is not apparent in all the baptized; for Paul, according to his usual manner, where he speaks of the faithful, connects the reality and the effect with the outward sign; for we know that whatever the Lord offers by the visible symbol is confirmed and ratified by their faith. In short, he teaches what is the real character of baptism when rightly received. So he testifies to the Galatians, that all who have been baptized into Christ, have put on Christ. (Gal. iii. 27.) Thus indeed must we speak, as long as the institution of the Lord and the faith of the godly unite together; for we never have naked and empty symbols, except when our ingratitude and wickedness hinder the working of divine beneficence.[1]

[1] That the *mode* of baptism, *immersion*, is intimated by " buried," has been thought by most, by *Chrysostom, Augustine, Hammond, Pareus, Mede, Grotius, Doddridge, Chalmers,* and others; while some, such as *Scott, Stuart,* and *Hodge,* do not consider this as necessarily intended, the

By the glory of the Father, that is, by that illustrious power by which he exhibited himself as really glorious, and as it were manifested the greatness of his glory. Thus often is the power of God, which was exercised in the resurrection of Christ, set forth in Scripture in sublime terms, and not without reason; for it is of great importance, that by so explicit a record of the ineffable power of God, not only faith in the last resurrection, which far exceeds the perception of the flesh, but also as to other benefits which we receive from the resurrection of Christ, should be highly commended to us.[1]

5. For if we have been planted together in the likeness of his death, we shall be also *in the likeness of his* resurrection:	5. Nam si insititii facti sumus similitudini mortis ejus, nimirum et resurrectionis participes erimus:
6. Knowing this, that our old man is crucified with *him,* that the body of sin might be destroyed, that henceforth we should not serve sin.	6. Illud scientes, quòd vetus noster homo simul cum ipso crucifixus est, ut aboleretur corpus peccati, ut non ultrà serviamus peccato.

5. *For if we have been ingrafted,* &c. He strengthens in plainer words the argument he has already stated; for the similitude which he mentions leaves now nothing doubtful, inasmuch as grafting designates not only a conformity of example, but a secret union, by which we are joined to him; so that he, reviving us by his Spirit, transfers his own virtue to us. Hence as the graft has the same life or death in common with the tree into which it is ingrafted, so it is

word "buried" having been adopted to express more fully what is meant by being "dead," and there being another word, "planted," used to convey the same idea, which cannot be applied to the rite of baptism.

"Buried with him," means buried like him, or in like manner; and so "crucified with him," in verse 6, is the same: συν prefixed to verbs, has clearly this meaning. See chap. viii. 17; Col. iii. 1; 2 Tim. ii. 11. "Into death" is not to be connected with "planted," but with "baptism;" it was "a baptism into death," that is, which represented death, even death unto sin.—*Ed.*

[1] *Beza* takes διὰ, *by,* before "glory," in the sense of εἰς, *to,* "to the glory of the Father;" but this is unusual. It seems to be a metonymy, the effect for the cause: it was done by power which manifested and redounded to the glory of God. The word "glory," δόξα, is used for power in John xi. 40. The Hebrew word, עז, strength, power, is sometimes rendered δόξα by the Septuagint; see Ps. lxvii. 34, (in our version, lxviii. 34;) Is. xii. 2; xlv. 24. God's power is often expressly mentioned in connection with the resurrection; See 1 Cor. vi. 14; 2 Cor. xiii. 4; Col. i. 11.—*Ed.*

reasonable that we should be partakers of the life no less than of the death of Christ; for if we are ingrafted according to the likeness of Christ's death, which was not without a resurrection, then our death shall not be without a resurrection. But the words admit of a twofold explanation,— either that we are ingrafted in Christ into the likeness of his death, or, that we are simply ingrafted in its likeness. The first reading would require the Greek dative ὁμοιώματι, to be understood as pointing out the manner; nor do I deny but that it has a fuller meaning: but as the other harmonizes more with simplicity of expression, I have preferred it; though it signifies but little, as both come to the same meaning. *Chrysostom* thought that Paul used the expression, " likeness of death," for death, as he says in another place, " being made in the likeness of men." But it seems to me that there is something more significant in the expression; for it not only serves to intimate a resurrection, but it seems also to indicate this—that we die not like Christ a natural death, but that there is a similarity between our and his death; for as he by death died in the flesh, which he had assumed from us, so we also die in ourselves, that we may live in him. It is not then the same, but a similar death; for we are to notice the connection between the death of our present life and spiritual renovation.

Ingrafted, &c. There is great force in this word, and it clearly shows, that the Apostle does not exhort, but rather teach us what benefit we derive from Christ; for he requires nothing from us, which is to be done by our attention and diligence, but speaks of the grafting made by the hand of God. But there is no reason why you should seek to apply the metaphor or comparison in every particular; for between the grafting of trees, and this which is spiritual, a disparity will soon meet us: in the former the graft draws its aliment from the root, but retains its own nature in the fruit; but in the latter not only we derive the vigour and nourishment of life from Christ, but we also pass from our own to his nature. The Apostle, however, meant to express nothing else but the efficacy of the death of Christ, which manifests itself in putting to death our flesh, and also the efficacy of his resurrection, in renewing within us a spiritual nature.¹

6. *That our old man,* &c. The old man, as the Old Testament is so called with reference to the New; for he begins to be old, when he is by degrees destroyed by a commencing regeneration. But what he means is the whole nature which we bring from the womb, and which is so incapable of the kingdom of God, that it must so far die as we are renewed to real life. This old man, he says, is fastened to the cross of Christ, for by its power he is slain: and he expressly referred to the cross, that he might more distinctly show, that we cannot be otherwise put to death than by partaking of his death. For I do not agree with those who think that he used the word crucified, rather than dead, because he still lives, and is in some respects vigorous. It is indeed a correct sentiment, but not suitable to this passage. *The body of sin,* which he afterwards mentions,

¹ The word σύμφυτοι, is rendered *insititii* by *Calvin,* and the same by *Erasmus, Pareus,* and *Hammond.* The *Vulgate* has " complantati—planted together;" *Beza,* " cum eo plantati coaluimus—being planted with him we grow together;" *Doddridge,* " grow together;" and *Macknight,* "planted together." The word properly means either to grow together, or to be born together; and φύω never means to graft. It is only found here; and it is applied by the *Septuagint,* in Zech. xi. 2, to a forest growing together. The verb συμφύω is once used in Luke viii. 7, and refers to the thorns which *sprang up with* the corn. It occurs as a participle in the same sense in the Wisdom of Solomon, xiii. 13. It appears from *Wolfius* that the word is used by Greek authors in a sense not strictly literal, to express congeniality, conjoining, union, as the sameness of disposition, or the joining together of a dismembered limb, or, as *Grotius* says, the union of friendship. It might be so taken here, and the verse might be thus rendered,—

For if we have been united (or, connected) by a similarity to his death, we shall certainly be also *united by a similarity* to *his* resurrection.

The genitive case here may be regarded as that of the object, as the love of God means sometimes love to God. Evidently the truth intended to be conveyed is, that as the Christian's death to sin bears likeness to Christ's death, so his rising to a spiritual life is certain to bear a similar likeness to Christ's resurrection. Then in the following verses this is more fully explained.

" The Apostle," says *Beza,* " uses the future tense, ' we shall be,' because we are not as yet wholly dead, or wholly risen, but are daily emerging." But the future here, as *Stuart* remarks, may be considered as expressing what is to follow the death previously mentioned, or as designating an *obligation,* as in Matt. iv. 10; Luke iii. 10, 12, 14; or a *certainty* as to the result.—*Ed.*

does not mean flesh and bones, but the corrupted mass; for man, left to his own nature, is a mass made up of sin.¹

He points out the end for which this destruction is effected, when he says, *so that we may no longer serve sin.* It hence follows, that as long as we are children of Adam, and nothing more than men, we are so in bondage to sin, that we can do nothing else but sin; but that being grafted in Christ, we are delivered from this miserable thraldom; not that we immediately cease entirely to sin, but that we become at last victorious in the contest.

7. For he that is dead is freed from sin.
8. Now, if we be dead with Christ, we believe that we shall also live with him:
9. Knowing that Christ, being raised from the dead, dieth no more; death hath no more dominion over him.
10. For in that he died, he died unto sin once: but in that he liveth, he liveth unto God.
11. Likewise reckon ye also yourselves to be dead indeed unto sin, but alive unto God through Jesus Christ our Lord.

7. Qui enim mortuus est, justificatus est à peccato.
8. Si verò mortui sumus cum Christo, credimus quòd et vivemus cum eo;
9. Scientes quòd Christus suscitatus ex mortuis, ampliùs non moritur, mors illi ampliùs non dominatur:
10. Quòd enim mortuus est, peccato mortuus est semel; quòd autem vivit, vivit Deo.
11. Sic et ipsi æstimate vosmet esse mortuos quidem peccato, viventes autem Deo in Christo Iesu Domino nostro.

7. *For he who has died,* &c. This is an argument derived from what belongs to death or from its effect. For if death destroys all the actions of life, we who have died to sin ought to cease from those actions which it exercised during its life. Take *justified* for freed or reclaimed from bondage; for as he is freed from the bond of a charge, who is absolved

¹ It is thought by *Pareus* and others, that "body" is here assigned to "sin," in allusion to the crucifixion that is mentioned, as a body in that case is fixed to the cross, and that it means the whole congeries, or, as Calvin calls it, the whole mass of sins, such as pride, passion, lust, &c. But the reason for using the word "body," is more probably this, because he called innate sin, man—" the old man;" and what properly belongs to man is a body. The " body of sin " is a Hebraism, and signifies a sinful body. It has no special reference to the material body, as *Origen* thought. The " man " here is to be taken in a spiritual sense, as one who has a mind, reason, and affections: therefore the body which belongs to him must be of the same character: it is the whole of what appertains to " the old man," as he is corrupt and sinful, the whole of what is earthly, wicked, and depraved in him. It is the sinful body of the old man.—*Ed.*

by the sentence of a judge; so death, by freeing us from this life, sets us free from all its functions.¹

But though among men there is found no such example, there is yet no reason why you should think, that what is said here is a vain speculation, or despond in your minds, because you find not yourselves to be of the number of those who have wholly crucified the flesh; for this work of God is not completed in the day in which it is begun in us; but it gradually goes on, and by daily advances is brought by degrees to its end. So then take this as the sum of the whole,—" If thou art a Christian, there must appear in thee an evidence of a fellowship as to the death of Christ; the fruit of which is, that thy flesh is crucified together with all its lusts; but this fellowship is not to be considered as not existing, because thou findest that the relics of the flesh still live in thee; but its increase ought to be diligently laboured for, until thou arrivest at the goal." It is indeed well with us, if our flesh is continually mortified; nor is it a small attainment, when the reigning power, being taken away from it, is wielded by the Holy Spirit. There is another fellowship as to the death of Christ, of which the Apostle often speaks, as he does in 2 Cor. iv., that is, the bearing of the cross, which is followed by a joint-participation also of eternal life.

8. *But if we have died,* &c. He repeats this for no other end but that he might subjoin the explanation which follows, that Christ, having once risen, dies no more. And

---

¹ This verse has occasioned various explanations. The most obvious meaning of the first clause is, that to " die " here means to die with or in a similar manner with Christ, for in the next verse, where the idea is resumed, " with " or like " Christ," is expressly stated. The verb, δεδικαίω-ται, " is," or has been " justified," has been considered by the early and most of the later commentators in the sense of being *freed* or delivered. This is the view, among others, of *Chrysostom, Basil, Œcumenius, Beza, Pareus, Hammond, Grotius, Doddridge,* and *Macknight.* But it must be added, that it is a meaning of which there is no other clear instance in the New Testament, though the verb occurs often. *Scott,* aware of this, gives it its common meaning, "justified;" and though he does not take the view of *Venema, Chalmers,* and *Haldane,* as to the general import of the former part of this chapter, he yet considers that to be " justified from sin" here, is to be justified from its guilt and penalty. Nor is it irrelevant to the subject in hand to refer to justification: for it is a very important truth to declare, that to die to sin is an evidence of being justified from its guilt.—*Ed.*

hereby he teaches us that newness of life is to be pursued by Christians as long as they live; for since they ought to represent in themselves an image of Christ, both by crucifying the flesh and by a spiritual life, it is necessary that the former should be done once for all, and that the latter should be carried on continually: not that the flesh, as we have already said, dies in us in a moment, but that we ought not to retrograde in the work of crucifying it. For if we roll again in our own filth, we deny Christ; of whom we cannot be the participators except through newness of life, inasmuch as he lives an incorruptible life.

9. *Death no more rules over him*, &c. He seems to imply that death once ruled over Christ; and indeed when he gave himself up to death for us, he in a manner surrendered and subjected himself to its power; it was however in such a way that it was impossible that he should be kept bound by its pangs, so as to succumb to or to be swallowed up by them. He, therefore, by submitting to its dominion, as it were, for a moment, destroyed it for ever. Yet, to speak more simply, the dominion of death is to be referred to the state of death voluntarily undergone, which the resurrection terminated. The meaning is, that Christ, who now vivifies the faithful by his Spirit, or breathes his own life into them by his secret power from heaven, was freed from the dominion of death when he arose, that by virtue of the same dominion he might render free all his people.

10. *He died once to sin*, &c. What he had said—that we, according to the example of Christ, are for ever freed from the yoke of death, he now applies to his present purpose, and that is this—that we are no more subject to the tyranny of sin, and this he proves from the designed object of Christ's death; for he died that he might destroy sin.

But we must observe what is suitable to Christ in this form of expression; for he is not said to die to sin, so as to cease from it, as the words must be taken when applied to us, but that he underwent death on account of sin, that having made himself $ἀντίλυτρον$, a ransom, he might annihilate the power and dominion of sin.[1] And he says that he

---

[1] This difference may be gathered from the general tenor of the whole

died *once,* not only because he has by having obtained eternal redemption by one offering, and by having made an expiation for sin by his blood, sanctified the faithful for ever; but also in order that a mutual likeness may exist between us. For though spiritual death makes continual advances in us, we are yet said properly to die only once, that is, when Christ, reconciling us by his blood to the Father, regenerates us at the same time by the power of his Spirit.

But that he lives, &c. Whether you add *with* or *in* God, it comes to the same meaning; for he shows that Christ lives a life subject to no mortality in the immortal and incorruptible kingdom of God; a type of which ought to appear in the regeneration of the godly. We must here remember the particle of likeness, *so;* for he says not that we shall now live in heaven, as Christ lives there; but he makes the new life, which after regeneration we live on earth, similar to his celestial life. When he says that we ought to *die to sin,* according to his example, we are not to suppose it to be the same kind of death; for we die to sin, when sin dies in us, but it was otherwise with Christ; by dying it was that he conquered sin. But he had just said before, that we believe that we shall have life in common with him, he fully shows by the word believing that he speaks of the grace of Christ: for if he only reminded us of a duty, his mode of speaking would have been this, "Since we die with Christ, we ought also to live with him." But the word believing denotes that he treats here of doctrine which is based on the promises; as though he had said, that the faithful ought to feel assured that they are through the kindness of Christ dead as to the flesh, and that the same Christ will preserve them in newness of life to the end.

passage; for his death and our death are said to have a *likeness,* and not to be same. And farther, in mentioning our death in this connection, in the next verse, he changes his phraseology; it is νεκροὺς εἶναι and not ἀποθάνειν, which means those deprived of life—the lifeless. "The dead (νεκροὺς) in trespasses and sins," are those who have no spiritual life; and to be dead *to* sin is not to have life for sin, to be freed from its ruling power. See verse 18.

It is usual with the Apostle to adopt the same form of words in different senses, which can only be distinguished by the context or by other parts of Scripture, as it has been noticed in a note on ch. iv. 25.—*Ed.*

But the future time of the verb *live*, refers not to the last resurrection, but simply denotes the continued course of a new life, as long as we peregrinate on the earth.

11. *So count ye also yourselves*, &c. Now is added a definition of that analogy to which I have referred. For having stated that Christ once died to sin and lives for ever to God, he now, applying both to us, reminds us how we now die while living, that is, when we renounce sin. But he omits not the other part, that is, how we are to live after having by faith received the grace of Christ: for though the mortifying of the flesh is only begun in us, yet the life of sin is destroyed, so that afterwards spiritual newness, which is divine, continues perpetually. For except Christ were to slay sin in us at once to the end, his grace would by no means be sure and durable.

The meaning, then, of the words may be thus expressed, "Take this view of your case,—that as Christ once died for the purpose of destroying sin, so you have once died, that in future you may cease from sin; yea, you must daily proceed with that work of mortifying, which is begun in you, till sin be wholly destroyed: as Christ is raised to an incorruptible life, so you are regenerated by the grace of God, that you may lead a life of holiness and righteousness, inasmuch as the power of the Holy Spirit, by which ye have been renewed, is eternal, and shall ever continue the same." But I prefer to retain the words of Paul, *in Christ Jesus*, rather than to translate with *Erasmus, through Christ Jesus;* for thus the grafting, which makes us one with Christ, is better expressed.

12. Let not sin therefore reign in your mortal body, that ye should obey it in the lusts thereof:
13. Neither yield ye your members *as* instruments of unrighteousness unto sin: but yield yourselves unto God, as those that are alive from the dead, and your members *as* instruments of righteousness unto God.

12. Ne ergo regnet peccatum in mortali vestro corpore, ut illi obediatis in cupiditatibus suis:
13. Neque exhibeatis membra vestra arma injustitiæ peccato; sed exhibeatis vosmetipsos Deo, tanquam ex mortuis viventes, et membra vestra arma justitiæ Deo.

12. *Let not sin then*, &c. He now begins with exhortation, which naturally arises from the doctrine which he had de-

livered respecting our fellowship with Christ. Though sin dwells in us, it is inconsistent that it should be so vigorous as to exercise its reigning power; for the power of sanctification ought to be superior to it, so that our life may testify that we are really the members of Christ.

I have already reminded you that the word *body* is not to be taken for flesh, and skin, and bones, but, so to speak, for the whole of what man is.[1] This may undoubtedly be inferred from the passage; for the other clause, which he immediately subjoins respecting the members of the body, includes the soul also: and thus in a disparaging manner does Paul designate earthly man, for owing to the corruption of our nature we aspire to nothing worthy of our original. So also does God say in Gen. vi. 3; where he complains that man was become flesh like the brute animals, and thus allows him nothing but what is earthly. To the same purpose is the declaration of Christ, "What is born of the flesh is flesh." (John iii. 6.) But if any makes this objection—that the case with the soul is different; to this the ready answer is—that in our present degenerate state our souls are fixed to the earth, and so enslaved to our bodies, that they have fallen from their own superiority. In a word, the nature of man is said to be corporeal, because he is destitute of celestial grace, and is only a sort of empty shadow or image. We may add, that the body, by way of contempt, is said by Paul to be *mortal*, and this to teach us, that the whole nature of man tends to death and ruin. Still further, he gives the name of sin to the original depravity which dwells in our hearts, and which leads us to sin, and from which indeed all evil deeds and abominations stream forth. In the middle, between sin and us, he places lusts, as the

---

[1] That is, as a corrupt being: literally it is "for the whole mass of man." The "body" here may be the same with that of "the old man" in ver. 6; and the word for "lusts," ἐπιθυμίαις, is often applied to designate the desires of the mind as well as the lusts of the natural body. The word, θνητῶ, "mortal," would in this case mean, doomed to die, having been crucified; it is a body in the process of dying. Innate sin is here personified as a king, a ruler, and as having a body, he being "the old man;" and this body is represented as belonging to Christians—"your," as the old man is—"*our* old man."—*Ed.*

former has the office of a king, while lusts are its edicts and commands.

13. *Nor present your members,* &c. When once sin has obtained dominion in our soul, all our faculties are continually applied to its service. He therefore describes here the reign of sin by what follows it, that he might more clearly show what must be done by us, if we would shake off its yoke. But he borrows a similitude from the military office, when he calls our members weapons or arms (*arma*);[1] as though he said, "As the soldier has ever his arms ready, that he may use them whenever he is ordered by his general, and as he never uses them but at his command; so Christians ought to regard all their faculties to be the weapons of the spiritual warfare: if then they employ any of their members in the indulgence of depravity, they are in the service of sin. But they have made the oath of soldiers to God and to Christ, and by this they are held bound: it hence behoves them to be far away from any intercourse with the camps of sin."—Those may also here see by what right they proudly lay claim to the Christian name, who have all their members, as though they were the prostitutes of Satan, prepared to commit every kind of abomination.

On the other hand, he now bids us to present ourselves wholly to God, so that restraining our minds and hearts from all wanderings into which the lusts of the flesh may draw us, we may regard the will of God alone, being ready to receive his commands, and prepared to execute his orders; and that our members also may be devoted and consecrated to his will, so that all the faculties both of our souls and of our bodies may aspire after nothing but his glory. The reason for this is also added—that the Lord, having destroyed our former life, has not in vain created us for another, which ought to be accompanied with suitable actions.

[1] The idea of a king, a ruler, or a tyrant, is preserved throughout. Innate sin is a ruler, carrying on a warfare, and therefore has weapons which he exploys. In the preceding verse are mentioned the gratifications with which he indulges his subjects—"lusts," here the weapons by which he defends his kingdom, and carries on an offensive warfare, committing acts of wickedness and wrong—"weapons of injustice, $ἀδικίας$." "He who sins," says an old author, "does wrong either to himself or to his neighbour, and always to God."—*Ed.*

14. For sin shall not have dominion over you:[1] for ye are not under the law, but under grace.
15. What then? shall we sin, because we are not under the law, but under grace? God forbid.
16. Know ye not, that to whom ye yield yourselves servants to obey, his servants ye are to whom ye obey; whether of sin unto death, or of obedience unto righteousness?
17. But God be thanked, that ye were the servants of sin; but ye have obeyed from the heart that form of doctrine which was delivered you.
18. Being then made free from sin, ye became the servants of righteousness.

14. Peccatum enim vobis non dominabitur, non enim estis sub Lege, sed sub gratiâ.
15. Quid ergo? peccabimus, quia non sumus sub Lege, sed sub gratiâ? Absit:
16. Nescitis quòd cui exhibuistis vos servos in obedientiam, ejus servi estis cui obeditis, sive peccati in mortem, sive obedientiæ in justitiam?
17. Gratia autem Deo, quòd fuistis servi peccati, obedistis verò ex animo typo doctrinæ in quem traducti estis:
18. Manumissi verò peccato, servi facti estis justitiæ.

14. *For sin shall not rule over you,* &c. It is not necessary to continue long in repeating and confuting expositions, which have little or no appearance of truth. There is one which has more probability in its favour than the rest, and it is this—that by *law* we are to understand the letter of the law, which cannot renovate the soul, and by *grace*, the grace of the Spirit, by which we are freed from depraved lusts. But this I do not wholly approve of; for if we take this meaning, what is the object of the question which immediately follows, " Shall we sin because we are not under the law?" Certainly the Apostle would never have put this question, had he not understood, that we are freed from the strictness of the law, so that God no more deals with us according to the high demands of justice. There is then no doubt but that he meant here to indicate some freedom from the very law of God. But laying aside controversy, I will briefly explain my view.

It seems to me, that there is here especially a consolation offered, by which the faithful are to be strengthened, lest they should faint in their efforts after holiness, through a

---

[1] " Vobis non dominabitur;" *ὀυ κυριεύσει*—shall not be a lord over you, shall not have power or authority or control over you; or, it may mean, shall not domineer over you, so as to retain you, as it were by force, under its power: and the reason given favours this idea; for he says, " Ye are not under law, but under grace." Law is the strength of sin; and by law it binds its subjects under its service.—*Ed.*

consciousness of their own weakness. He had exhorted them to devote all their faculties to the service of righteousness; but as they carry about them the relics of the flesh, they cannot do otherwise than walk somewhat lamely. Hence, lest being broken down by a consciousness of their infirmity they should despond, he seasonably comes to their aid, by interposing a consolation, derived from this circumstance—that their works are not now tested by the strict rule of the law, but that God, remitting their impurity, does kindly and mercifully accept them. The yoke of the law cannot do otherwise than tear and bruise those who carry it. It hence follows, that the faithful must flee to Christ, and implore him to be the defender of their freedom: and as such he exhibits himself; for he underwent the bondage of the law, to which he was himself no debtor, for this end—that he might, as the Apostle says, redeem those who were under the law.

Hence, *not to be under the law* means, not only that we are not under the letter which prescribes what involves us in guilt, as we are not able to perform it, but also that we are no longer subject to the law, as requiring perfect righteousness, and pronouncing death on all who deviate from it in any part. In like manner, by the word *grace*, we are to understand both parts of redemption—the remission of sins, by which God imputes righteousness to us,—and the sanctification of the Spirit, by whom he forms us anew unto good works. The adversative particle, [ἀλλὰ, *but*,] I take in the sense of alleging a reason, which is not unfrequently the case; as though it was said—"We who are under grace, are not therefore under the law."

The sense now is clear; for the Apostle intended to comfort us, lest we should be wearied in our minds, while striving to do what is right, because we still find in ourselves many imperfections. For how much soever we may be harassed by the stings of sin, it cannot yet overcome us, for we are enabled to conquer it by the Spirit of God; and then, being under grace, we are freed from the rigorous requirements of the law. We must further understand, that the Apostle assumes it as granted, that all who are without the grace of God, being bound under the yoke of the law, are under condemnation. And so we may on the other hand conclude, that as long as they are under the law, they are subject to the dominion of sin.[1]

15. *What then?* As the wisdom of the flesh is ever clamorous against the mysteries of God, it was necessary for the Apostle to subjoin what might anticipate an objection: for since the law is the rule of life, and has been given to guide men, we think that when it is removed all discipline immediately falls to the ground, that restraints are taken away, in a word, that there remains no distinction or difference between good and evil. But we are much deceived if we think, that the righteousness which God approves of in his law is abolished, when the law is abrogated; for the abrogation is by no means to be applied to the precepts which teach the right way of living, as Christ confirms and sanctions these and does not abrogate them; but the right view is, that nothing is taken away but the curse, to which all men without grace are subject. But though Paul does not distinctly express this, yet he indirectly intimates it.

16. *By no means: know ye not?* This is not a bare denial as some think, as though he preferred to express his abhorrence of such a question rather than to disprove it: for a confutation immediately follows, derived from a contrary supposition, and to this purpose, " Between the yoke of Christ and that of sin there is so much contrariety, that no one can bear them both; if we sin, we give ourselves up to the service of sin; but the faithful, on the contrary, have been redeemed from the tyranny of sin, that they may serve Christ: it is therefore impossible for them to remain bound to sin." But it will be better to examine more closely the course of reasoning, as pursued by Paul.

To whom we obey, &c. This relative may be taken in a causative sense, as it often is; as when one says,—there is no kind of crime which a parricide will not do, who has not

---

[1] The word "law" here, is taken by *Scott* and others, indefinitely, as meaning law as the ground of the covenant of works, written or unwritten; and the literal rendering is, " under law"—$\dot{\upsilon}\pi\grave{o}$ $\nu\acute{o}\mu o \upsilon$; and it is the same in the next verse, " under law."—*Ed.*

hesitated to commit the greatest crime of all, and so barbarous as to be almost abhorred even by wild beasts. And Paul adduces his reason partly from the effects, and partly from the nature of correlatives. For first, if they obey, he concludes that they are servants, for obedience proves that he, who thus brings one into subjection to himself, has the power of commanding. This reason as to service is from the effect, and from this the other arises. "If you be servants, then of course sin has the dominion."

Or of obedience, &c. The language is not strictly correct; for if he wished to have the clauses correspondent, he would have said, "or of righteousness unto life."[1] But as the change in the words does not prevent the understanding of the subject, he preferred to express what righteousness is by the word *obedience;* in which however there is a metonymy, for it is to be taken for the very commandments of God; and by mentioning this without addition, he intimated that it is God alone, to whose authority consciences ought to be subject. Obedience then, though the name of God is suppressed, is yet to be referred to him, for it cannot be a divided obedience.

17. *But thanks be to God,* &c. This is an application of the similitude of the present subject. Though they were only to be reminded that they were not now the servants of

---

[1] *Beza's* remark on this is,—that obedience is not the cause of life, as sin is of death, but is the way to life: and hence the want of correspondence in the two clauses. But others, such as *Venema, Turrettin,* and *Stuart,* consider that the clauses really correspond. They take εἰς θάνατον —" unto death," as signifying, unto condemnation; and εἰς δικαιοσύνην, they render " unto justification;" and ὑπακοὴ, " obedience," is in their view the obedience of faith. This construction might be admitted, were it not for the last clause of ver. 18, where we have, " Ye became the servants of righteousness," the same word, δικαιοσύνη; *except* we consider that also, as *Venema* does, as signifying the righteousness of faith, by a sort of personification: and if so, we must attach the same meaning to " righteousness," δικαιοσύνη, in ver. 19, which issues in, or leads to holiness; and also to " righteousness," δικαιοσύνη, in ver. 20. As the Apostle personifies sin, he may also be supposed to personify righteousness, that is, the righteousness of faith. In this case, we might as well retain the word " righteousness" in this verse, and not justification, which it never strictly means; for the correspondence in the terms would be still essentially preserved, as with the righteousness of faith eternal life is inseparably connected.—*Ed.*

sin, he yet adds a thanksgiving; first, that he might teach them, that this was not through their own merit, but through the special mercy of God; and secondly, that by this thanksgiving, they might learn how great was the kindness of God, and that they might thereby be more stimulated to hate sin. And he gives thanks, not as to that time during which they were the servants of sin, but for the liberation which followed, when they ceased to be what they were before. But this implied comparison between their former and present state is very emphatical; for the Apostle touches the calumniators of the grace of Christ, when he shows, that without grace the whole race of man is held captive under the dominion of sin; but that the kingdom of sin comes to an end, as soon as grace puts forth its power.[1]

We may hence learn, that we are not freed from the bondage of the law that we may sin; for the law does not lose its dominion, until the grace of God restores us to him, in order to renew us in righteousness: and it is hence impossible that we should be subject to sin, when the grace of God reigns in us: for we have before stated, that under this term grace, is included the spirit of regeneration.

You have obeyed from the heart, &c. Paul compares here the hidden power of the Spirit with the external letter of the law, as though he had said, "Christ inwardly forms our souls in a better way, than when the law constrains them by threatening and terrifying us." Thus is dissipated the following calumny, "If Christ frees us from subjection to the law, he brings liberty to sin." He does not indeed allow his people unbridled freedom, that they might frisk about without any restraint, like horses let loose in the fields; but he brings them to a regular course of life.—Though *Erasmus,* following the old version, has chosen to

---

[1] Our version of this verse conveys the idea, that the Apostle gave thanks that they had been the servants of sin; but ὅτι is often rendered *for,* as in Matt. v. 3, 4; Luke x. 13; and in Matt. vi. 5, followed by δὲ as here, in ver. 6. The rendering may be this,—

But thanks be to God; for ye have been the servants of sin, but have obeyed the form of doctrine, in which ye have been taught.—*Ed.*

translate it the "form" (*formam*) *of doctrine*, I have felt constrained to retain *type*, the word which Paul uses: some may perhaps prefer the word pattern.[1] It seems indeed to me to denote the formed image or impress of that righteousness which Christ engraves on our hearts: and this corresponds with the prescribed rule of the law, according to which all our actions ought to be framed, so that they deviate not either to the right or to the left hand.

18. *And having been made free from sin*, &c. The meaning is, " It is unreasonable that any one, after having been made free, should continue in a state of bondage; for he ought to maintain the freedom which he has received: it is not then befitting, that you should be brought again under the dominion of sin, from which you have been set at liberty by Christ." It is an argument derived from the efficient cause; another also follows, taken from the final cause, " Ye have been liberated from the bondage of sin, that ye might pass into the kingdom of righteousness; it is hence right that you should wholly turn away from sin, and turn your minds wholly to righteousness, into the service of which you have been transferred."

[1] The version of Calvin is, " Obedîstis verò et animo typo doctrinæ in quem traducti estis."

The word τύπος, is rendered in John xx. 25, *print*, that is, of the nails,—in Acts vii. 43, in the plural, *figures*, that is, images,—in Acts vii. 44, *fashion*, that is, pattern or model,—in Heb. viii. 5, *pattern*,—in Acts xxiii. 25, *manner*, that is, form,—in Rom. v. 14, *figure*, that is, representative,—in Tit. ii. 7, *pattern;* and in all other instances in which it occurs, except in this place, it is rendered *example*, and in the plural, *examples*, as afforded by the conduct of others, or by events; see 1 Cor. x. 6, 11; Phil. iii. 17; 1 Thess. i. 7; 2 Thess. iii. 9; 1 Tim. iv. 12; 1 Pet. v. 3. The idea of *mould*, which some give to it, is without an example in the New Testament.

Our version is that of *Castellio*, in the meaning of which most critics agree. *Grotius* gives this paraphrase, " Obedistis ad eum modum quem doctrina evangelii præscribit—Ye became obedient to that rule which the doctrine of the gospel prescribes." *Wolfius* quotes from *Iamblichus*, in his life of *Pythagoras*, passages in which τύπος is used for *form, model*, or *manner*,—" τῆς παιδεύσεως ὁ τύπος—the form of instruction ;" and " τύπος δι-δασκαλίας—the form or manner of teaching."

The grammatical difficulty is best removed by *Stuart*, who considers τύπον to be for τυπω, the case being changed by the preceding pronoun, no uncommon thing in Greek: the literal rendering would then be,— " Ye have obeyed the form of doctrine, respecting which (or, in which, see Mark v. 34) ye have been instructed."—*Ed.*

It must be observed, that no one can be a servant to righteousness except he is first liberated by the power and kindness of God from the tyranny of sin. So Christ himself testifies, "If the Son shall free you, you shall be free indeed." (John viii. 36.) What are then our preparations by the power of free will, since the commencement of what is good proceeds from this manumission, which the grace of God alone effects?

19. I speak after the manner of men, because of the infirmity of your flesh: for as ye have yielded your members servants to uncleanness, and to iniquity unto iniquity; even so now yield your members servants to righteousness unto holiness.	19. Humanum dico propter infirmitatem carnis vestræ, quemadmodum exhibuistis membra vestra serva immunditiæ et iniquitati in iniquitatem, sic et nunc exhibite membra vestra serva justitiæ in sanctificationem.

19. *I speak what is human,* &c. He says that he speaks after the manner of men, not as to the substance but as to the manner. So Christ says, in John iii. 12, that he announced earthly things, while yet he spoke of heavenly mysteries, though not so magnificently as the dignity of the things required, because he accommodated himself to the capacities of a people ignorant and simple. And thus the Apostle says, by way of preface, that he might more fully show how gross and wicked is the calumny, when it is imagined, that the freedom obtained by Christ gives liberty to sin. He reminds the faithful at the same time, that nothing is more unreasonable, nay, base and disgraceful, than that the spiritual grace of Christ should have less influence over them than earthly freedom; as though he had said, "I might, by comparing sin and righteousness, show how much more ardently ye ought to be led to render obedience to the latter, than to serve the former; but from regard to your infirmity I omit this comparison: nevertheless, though I treat you with great indulgence, I may yet surely make this just demand—that you should not at least obey righteousness more coldly or negligently than you served sin." It is a sort of reticence or silence, a withholding of something when we wish more to be understood than what we express. He does yet exhort them to render obedi-

ence to righteousness with so much more diligence, as that which they served is more worthy than sin, though he seems not to require this in so many words.[1]

As ye have presented, &c.; that is, " As ye were formerly ready with all your faculties to serve sin, it is hence sufficiently evident how wretchedly enslaved and bound did your depravity hold you to itself: now then ye ought to be equally prompt and ready to execute the commands of God; let not your activity in doing good be now less than it was formerly in doing evil." He does not indeed observe the same order in the antithesis, by adapting different parts to each other, as he does in 1 Thess. iv. 7, where he sets uncleanness in opposition to holiness; but the meaning is still evident.

He mentions first two kinds—uncleanness and iniquity; the former of which is opposed to chastity and holiness, the other refers to injuries hurtful to our neighbour. But he repeats iniquity twice, and in a different sense: by the first he means plunders, frauds, perjuries, and every kind of wrong; by the second, the universal corruption of life, as though he had said, " Ye have prostituted your members so as to perpetrate all wicked works, and thus the kingdom of iniquity became strong in you."[2] By *righteousness* I understand the law or the rule of a holy life, the design of which

---

[1] The phrase is taken differently: Ἀνθρώπινον λέγω—" I speak what is human," that is, what is proportionable to man's strength, says *Chrysostom*—what is done and known in common life, as in Gal. iii. 15, or, what is moderate, says *Hammond*—what is level to man's understanding, says *Vatablus*. The first proposed by *Hammond* is the meaning most suitable here; for the Apostle had previously used reasons and arguments, and sacred similitudes; but he comes now to what is known in common life among men, the connection between masters and servants, and he did this in condescension to their weakness, which he calls the weakness of the flesh, that is, the weakness of which flesh, the depravity of nature, was the cause; it was weakness arising from the flesh.—*Ed.*

[2] The different clauses of this verse have been a knotty point to all commentators. Probably the Apostle did not intend to keep up a regular course of antithesis, the subject not admitting of this; because the progress of evil and the progress of its remedy may be different, and it seems to be so in the present case. Sin is innate and inward, and its character, as here represented, is vileness and iniquity, and it breaks out into acts of iniquity: he does not repeat the other character, vileness; but when he comes to the contrast he mentions holiness, and does not add what is antithetic to iniquity. This is a striking instance of the elliptical style of the Apostle. It is not neglect or carelessness, but no doubt an intentional

is sanctification, as the case is when the faithful devote themselves to serve God in purity.

20. For when ye were the servants of sin, ye were free from righteousness.	20. Quando enim servi fuistis peccati, liberi fuistis justitiæ.
21. What fruit had ye then in those things whereof ye are now ashamed? for the end of those things *is* death.	21. Quem ergo fructum habuistis tunc in iis, de quibus nunc erubescitis? siquidem finis eorum mors.
22. But now, being made free from sin, and become servants to God, ye have your fruit unto holiness, and the end everlasting life.	22. Nunc vero manumissi a peccato, Deo autem in servitutem addicti, habetis fructum vestrum in sanctificationem, finem vero vitam æternam.
23. For the wages of sin *is* death; but the gift of God *is* eternal life through Jesus Christ our Lord.	23. Stipendia enim peccati, mors; donum vero Dei, vita æterna, in Christo Iesu Domino nostro.

20. *For when ye were,* &c. He still repeats the difference, which he had before mentioned, between the yoke of righteousness and that of sin; for these two things, sin and righteousness, are so contrary, that he who devotes himself to the one, necessarily departs from the other. And he thus represents both, that by viewing them apart we may see more clearly what is to be expected from each; for to set things thus apart enables us to understand better their distinctive character. He then sets sin on one side, and righteousness

omission; it being the character of his mode of writing, which he had in common with the ancient Prophets.

Then comes the word "righteousness," which I am disposed to think is that which all along has been spoken of, the righteousness of faith; this is not innate, not inward, but which comes from without, and is apprehended by faith, by which sins are forgiven, and God's favour obtained; and they who become the servants of this are to cultivate holiness both inward and outward; they ought to present all their members, that is, all their faculties, to the service of this master, so that they may become holy in all manner of conversation.

But if this idea of righteousness be disapproved of, we may still account for the apparent irregularity in the construction of the passage. It is an instance of an inverted order, many examples of which are found even in this Epistle. He begins with "uncleanness," he ends with "holiness," and then the intervening words which are in contrast correspond, "iniquity" and "righteousness." Here is also an inversion in the meaning; "uncleanness" is the principle, and "holiness" is the action; while "iniquity" is the action, and "righteousness" is the principle. If this view is right, we have here a singular instance of the inverted parallelism, both as to words and meaning.—*Ed.*

on the other; and having stated this distinction, he afterwards shows what results from each of them.

Let us then remember that the Apostle still reasons on the principle of contraries, and in this manner, " While ye were the servants of sin, ye were freed from righteousness; but now a change having taken place, it behoves you to serve righteousness; for you have been liberated from the yoke of sin. He calls those *free from righteousness* who are held by no bridle to obey righteousness. This is the liberty of the flesh, which so frees us from obedience to God, that it makes us slaves to the devil. Wretched then and accursed is this liberty, which with unbridled or rather mad frenzy, leads us exultingly to our destruction.

21. *What fruit, then,* &c. He could not more strikingly express what he intended than by appealing to their conscience, and by confessing shame as it were in their person. Indeed the godly, as soon as they begin to be illuminated by the Spirit of Christ and the preaching of the gospel, do freely acknowledge their past life, which they have lived without Christ, to have been worthy of condemnation; and so far are they from endeavouring to excuse it, that, on the contrary, they feel ashamed of themselves. Yea, further, they call to mind the remembrance of their own disgrace, that being thus ashamed, they may more truly and more readily be humbled before God.

Nor is what he says insignificant, *Of which ye are now ashamed;* for he intimates that we are possessed with extreme blind love for ourselves, when we are involved in the darkness of our sins, and think not that there is so much filth in us. The light of the Lord alone can open our eyes to behold the filthiness which lies hid in our flesh. He only then is imbued with the principles of Christian philosophy, who has well learnt to be really displeased with himself, and to be confounded with shame for his own wretchedness. He shows at last still more plainly from what was to follow, how much they ought to have been ashamed, that is, when they came to understand that they had been standing on the very precipice of death, and had been nigh destruction; yea, that they would have already entered the gates of death, had they not been reclaimed by God's mercy.

22. *Ye have your fruit unto holiness,* &c. As he had before mentioned a twofold end of sin, so he does now as to righteousness. Sin in this life brings the torments of an accusing conscience, and in the next eternal death. We now gather the fruit of righteousness, even holiness; we hope in future to gain eternal life. These things, unless we are beyond measure stupid, ought to generate in our minds a hatred and horror of sin, and also a love and desire for righteousness. Some render τελος, "tribute" or reward, and not "end," but not, as I think, according to the meaning of the Apostle; for though it is true that we bear the punishment of death on account of sin, yet this word is not suitable to the other clause, to which it is applied by Paul, inasmuch as life cannot be said to be the tribute or reward of righteousness.

23. *For the wages of sin,* &c. There are those who think that Paul, by comparing death to allowances of meat, (*obsoniis,*) points out in a disparaging manner the kind of wretched reward that is allotted to sinners, as this word is taken by the Greeks sometimes for portions allowed to soldiers. But he seems rather indirectly to condemn the blind appetites of those who are ruinously allured by the enticements of sin, as the fish are by the hook. It will however be more simple to render the word "wages," for surely death is a sufficiently ample reward to the wicked. This verse is a conclusion to the former, and as it were an epilogue to it. He does not, however, in vain repeat the same thing again; but by doubling the terror, he intended to render sin an object of still greater hatred.

But the gift of God. They are mistaken who thus render the sentence, "Eternal life is the gift of God," as though eternal life were the subject, and the gift of God the predicate; for this does not preserve the contrast. But as he has already taught us, that sin produces nothing but death; so now he subjoins, that this gift of God, even our justification and sanctification, brings to us the happiness of eternal life. Or, if you prefer, it may be thus stated,—"As the cause of death is sin, so righteousness, which we obtain through Christ, restores to us eternal life."

It may however be hence inferred with certainty, that our salvation is altogether through the grace and mere beneficence of God. He might indeed have used other words—that the wages of righteousness is eternal life; and then the two clauses would correspond: but he knew that it is through God's gift we obtain it, and not through our own merits; and that it is not one or a single gift; for being clothed with the righteousness of the Son, we are reconciled to God, and we are by the power of the Spirit renewed unto holiness. And he adds, *in Christ Jesus*, and for this reason, that he might call us away from every conceit respecting our own worthiness.

CHAPTER VII.

1. Know ye not, brethren, (for I speak to them that know the law,) how that the law hath dominion over a man as long as he liveth?
2. For the woman which hath an husband is bound by the law to *her* husband so long as he liveth; but if the husband be dead, she is loosed from the law of *her* husband.
3. So then if, while *her* husband liveth, she be married to another man, she shall be called an adulteress: but if her husband be dead, she is free from that law; so that she is no adulteress, though she be married to another man.
4. Wherefore, my brethren, ye also are become dead to the law by the body of Christ; that ye should be married to another, *even* to him who is raised from the dead, that we should bring forth fruit unto God.

1. Num ignoratis fratres (scientibus enim Legem loquor) quod Lex dominatur homini quamdiu vivit?
2. Nam viro subjecta mulier, viventi viro alligata est per Legem; quod si mortuus fuerit vir, soluta est a Lege viri.
3. Proinde vivente marito, si alteri viro conjuncta fuerit, adultera vocabitur: quod si mortuus fuerit vir, liberata est a Lege ne amplius sit adultera si alteri nupserit.
4. Itaque fratres mei, vos quoque mortui estis Legi per corpus Christi, ut posthac alterius sitis, ejus qui ex mortuis suscitatus est, ut fructificemus Deo.[1]

Though he had, in a brief manner, sufficiently explained the question respecting the abrogation of the law; yet as it

---

[1] That is, the law by which she was bound to her husband, or, the law by which he became her husband. It is an instance of the latitude in which the genitive case is used.—*Ed.*

was a difficult one, and might have given rise to many other questions, he now shows more at large how the law, with regard to us, is become abrogated; and then he sets forth what good is thereby done to us: for while it holds us separated from Christ and bound to itself, it can do nothing but condemn us. And lest any one should on this account blame the law itself, he takes up and confutes the objections of the flesh, and handles, in a striking manner, the great question respecting the use of the law.[1]

1. *Know ye not,* &c. Let the general proposition be, that the law was given to men for no other end but to regulate the present life, and that it belongs not to those who are dead: to this he afterwards subjoins this truth—that we are dead to it through the body of Christ. Some understand, that the dominion of the law continues so long to bind us as it remains in force. But as this view is rather obscure, and does not harmonize so well with the proposition which immediately follows, I prefer to follow those who regard what is said as referring to the life of man, and not to the law. The question has indeed a peculiar force, as it affirms the certainty of what is spoken; for it shows that it was not a thing new or unknown to any of them, but acknowledged equally by them all.

(*For to those who know the law I speak.*) This parenthesis is to be taken in the same sense with the question, as though he had said—that he knew that they were not so unskilful in the law as to entertain any doubt on the subject. And though both sentences might be understood of all laws, it is yet better to take them as referring to the law of God, which is the subject that is discussed. There are some who think that he ascribes knowledge of the law to the Romans, be-

---

[1] The connection of the beginning of this chapter with the 14th verse of the former chapter deserves to be noticed. He says there, that sin shall not rule over us, *because* we are not under law, but under grace. Then he asks, in verse 15, "Shall we sin, because we are not under law, but under grace?" This last subject, according to his usual mode, he takes up *first*, and discusses it till the end of the chapter: and then in this chapter he reassumes the first subject—freedom from the law. This is a striking instance of the Apostle's manner of writing, quite different from what is usual with us in the present day. He mentions two things; he proceeds with the last, and then goes back to the first.—*Ed.*

cause the largest part of the world was under their power and government; but this is puerile: for he addressed in part the Jews or other strangers, and in part common and obscure individuals; nay, he mainly regarded the Jews, with whom he had to do respecting the abrogation of the law: and lest they should think that he was dealing captiously with them, he declares that he took up a common principle, known to them all, of which they could by no means be ignorant, who had from their childhood been brought up in the teaching of the law.

2. *For a woman subject to a man,* &c. He brings a similitude, by which he proves, that we are so loosed from the law, that it does not any longer, properly and by its own right, retain over us any authority: and though he could have proved this by other reasons, yet as the example of marriage was very suitable to illustrate the subject, he introduced this comparison instead of evidence to prove his point. But that no one may be puzzled, because the different parts of the comparison do not altogether correspond, we are to be reminded, that the Apostle designedly intended, by a little change, to avoid the invidiousness of a stronger expression. He might have said, in order to make the comparison complete, "A woman after the death of her husband is loosed from the bond of marriage: the law, which is in the place of a husband to us, is to us dead; then we are freed from its power." But that he might not offend the Jews by the asperity of his expressions, had he said that the law was dead, he adopted a digression, and said, that we are dead to the law.[1] To some indeed he appears to reason from

[1] This is a plausible reason, derived from *Theodoret* and *Chrysostom;* but hardly necessary. Commentators have felt much embarrassed in applying the illustration given here. The woman is freed by the death of the husband; but the believer is represented as freed by dying himself. This does not correspond: and if we attend to what the Apostle says, we shall see that he did not contemplate such a correspondence. Let us notice how he introduces the illustration; "the law," he says in the first verse, "rules, or exercises authority, over a man while he lives;" and then let us observe the application in verse 4, where he speaks of our dying to the law. The main design of the illustration then was, to show that there is no freedom from a law but by *death;* so that there is no necessity of a correspondence in the other parts. As in the case of man and wife, death destroys the bond of marriage; so in the case of man and the law, that is,

the less to the greater: however, as I fear that this is too strained, I approve more of the first meaning, which is simpler. The whole argument then is formed in this manner, " The woman is bound to her living husband by the law, so that she cannot be the wife of another ; but after the death of her husband she is loosed from the bond of his law, so that she is free to marry whom she pleases."

Then follows the application,—

The law was, as it were our husband, under whose yoke we were kept until it became dead to us:

After the death of the law Christ received us, that is, he joined us, when loosed from the law, to himself:

Then being united to Christ risen from the dead, we ought to cleave to him alone:

And as the life of Christ after the resurrection is eternal, so hereafter there shall be no divorce.

But further, the word law is not mentioned here in every part in the same sense : for in one place it means the bond of marriage ; in another, the authority of a husband over his wife ; and in another, the law of Moses : but we must remember, that Paul refers here only to that office of the law which was peculiar to the dispensation of Moses ; for as far as God has in the ten commandments taught what is just and right, and given directions for guiding our life, no abrogation of the law is to be dreamt of ; for the will of God must stand the same forever. We ought carefully to remember that this is not a release from the righteousness which is taught in the law, but from its rigid requirements, and from the curse which thence follows. The law, then, as a rule of life, is not abrogated ; but what belongs to it as opposed to the liberty obtained through Christ, that is, as it requires absolute perfection : for as we render not this perfection, it

---

the law as the condition of life, there must be a death; else there is no freedom. But there is one thing more in the illustration, which the Apostle adopts, the liberty to marry another, when death has given a release : The bond of connection being broken, a union with another is legitimate. So far only is the example adduced to be applied—*death* puts an end to the right and authority of law ; and then the party released may justly form another connection. It is the attempt to make all parts of the comparison to correspond that has occasioned all the difficulty.—*Ed.*

binds us under the sentence of eternal death. But as it was not his purpose to decide here the character of the bond of marriage, he was not anxious to mention the causes which release a woman from her husband. It is therefore unreasonable that anything decisive on this point should be sought here.

4. *Through the body of Christ.* Christ, by the glorious victory of the cross, first triumphed over sin; and that he might do this, it was necessary that the handwriting, by which we were held bound, should be cancelled. This handwriting was the law, which, while it continued in force, rendered us bound to serve[1] sin; and hence it is called the power of sin. It was then by cancelling this handwriting that we were delivered through the body of Christ—through his body as fixed to the cross.[2] But the Apostle goes farther, and says, that the bond of the law was destroyed; not that we may live according to our own will, like a widow, who lives as she pleases while single; but that we may be now bound to another husband; nay, that we may pass from hand to hand, as they say, that is, from the law to Christ. He at the same time softens the asperity of the expression, by saying that Christ, in order to join us to his own body, made us free from the yoke of the law. For though Christ subjected himself for a time of his own accord to the law, it is not yet right to say that the law ruled over him. Moreover, he conveys to his own members the liberty which he himself possesses. It is then no wonder that he exempts those from the yoke of the law, whom he unites by a sacred bond to himself, that they may be one body in him.

Even *his who has been raised,* &c. We have already said, that Christ is substituted for the law, lest any freedom should be pretended without him, or lest any, being not yet dead to the law, should dare to divorce himself from it. But he adopts here a periphrastic sentence to denote the eternity of that life which Christ attained by his resurrection, that

---

[1] "Obæratos"—debtors bound to serve their creditors until payment is made.—*Ed.*

[2] That his crucified body is intended, is clear from what follows; for he is spoken of as having "been raised from the dead."—*Ed.*

Christians might know that this connection is to be perpetual. But of the spiritual marriage between Christ and his Church he speaks more fully in Eph. vi.

That we may bring forth fruit to God. He ever annexes the final cause, lest any should indulge the liberty of their flesh and their own lusts, under the pretence that Christ has delivered them from the bondage of the law; for he has offered us, together with himself, as a sacrifice to the Father, and he regenerates us for this end—that by newness of life we may bring forth fruit unto God: and we know that the fruits which our heavenly Father requires from us are those of holiness and righteousness. It is indeed no abatement to our liberty that we serve God; nay, if we desire to enjoy so great a benefit as there is in Christ, it will not henceforth be right in us to entertain any other thought but that of promoting the glory of God; for which purpose Christ has connected us with himself. We shall otherwise remain the bond-slaves, not only of the law, but also of sin and of death.

| 5. For when we were in the flesh, the motions of sins, which were by the law, did work in our members to bring forth fruit unto death. | 5. Quum enim essemus in carne, affectus peccatorum qui sunt per Legem, in membris nostris operabantur ad fructificandum morti: |
| 6. But now we are delivered from the law, that being dead wherein we were held; that we should serve in newness of spirit, and not *in* the oldness of the letter. | 6. Nunc verò soluti sumus a Lege, mortui ei in qua detinebamur; ut serviamus in novitate spiritus, et non in vetustate literæ. |

5. *For when we were,* &c. He shows still more clearly by stating the contrary effect, how unreasonably the zealots of the law acted, who would still detain the faithful under its dominion; for as long as the literal teaching of the law, unconnected with the Spirit of Christ, rules and bears sway, the wantonness of the flesh is not restrained, but, on the contrary, breaks out and prevails. It hence follows, that the kingdom of righteousness is not established, except when Christ emancipates us from the law. Paul at the same time reminds us of the works which it becomes us to do, when set free from the law. As long, then, as man is kept under the yoke of the law, he can, as he is sinning continually, procure nothing for himself but death. Since bondage to the law

produces sin only, then freedom, its opposite, must tend to righteousness; if the former leads to death, then the latter leads to life. But let us consider the very words of Paul.

In describing our condition during the time we were subject to the dominion of the law, he says, that we were *in the flesh*. We hence understand, that all those who are under the law attain nothing else but this—that their ears are struck by its external sound without any fruit or effect, while they are inwardly destitute of the Spirit of God. They must therefore necessarily remain altogether sinful and perverse, until a better remedy succeeds to heal their diseases. Observe also this usual phrase of Scripture, to *be in the flesh;* it means to be endued only with the gifts of nature, without that peculiar grace with which God favours his chosen people. But if this state of life is altogether sinful, it is evident that no part of our soul is naturally sound, and that the power of free will is no other than the power of casting evil emotions as darts into all the faculties of the soul.[1]

The emotions of sins,[2] *which are through the law,* &c.; that is, the law excited in us evil emotions, which exerted their

---

[1] To be "in the flesh" has two meanings,—to be unrenewed, and in our natural corrupt state, as *Calvin* says, see chap. viii. 8,—and to be subject to external rites and ceremonies, as the Jews were, see Gal. iii. 3; Phil. iii. 4. Its meaning here, according to *Beza* and *Pareus*, is the first; according to *Grotius* and *Hammond*, the second; and according to *Turrettin* and *Hodge*, both are included, as the context, in their view, evidently shows.—*Ed.*

[2] "Affectus peccatorum—affections of sins;" τα παθήματα, &c.,—"cupiditates—desires," or lusts, *Grotius*. The word is commonly taken passively, as signifying afflictions, sufferings; ch. viii. 18; 2 Cor. i. 5; Col. i. 24; but here, and in Gal. v. 24, it evidently means excitements, commotions, emotions, lusts or lustings. "Passion" in our language admits of two similar meanings,—suffering, and an excited feeling, or an inward commotion.

These "emotions" are said to be through the law,—"made known by the law," says *Chrysostom;* but "occasioned by the law," is more correct, as it appears from ver. 8, or, "made to abound by the law," as in ch. v. 20. The law, instead of making men holy, made them, through the perversity of human nature, to sin the more. "Emotions of sins" is an Hebraism for "sinful emotions."—"The members" are those of the "old man," and not those of the material body, though it is commonly thought that they are the latter, and mentioned, because they are employed as the instruments of sin: but there are many sins, and those of the worst kind, which are confined to the mind and heart. It is therefore more consistent to regard them as the members of "the body of sin," ch. vi. 6.—*Ed.*

influence through all our faculties; for there is no part which is not subject to these depraved passions. What the law does, in the absence of the inward teacher, the Spirit, is increasingly to inflame our hearts, so that they boil up with lusts. But observe here, that the law is connected with the vicious nature of man, the perversity of which, and its lusts, break forth with greater fury, the more they are checked by the restraints of righteousness. He further adds, that as long as the emotions of the flesh were under the dominion of the law they brought forth fruit to death; and he adds this to show that the law by itself is destructive. It hence follows, that they are infatuated, who so much desire this bondage which issues in death.

6. *But now we have been loosed from the law,* &c. He pursues the argument derived from the opposite effect of things, —" If the restraint of the law availed so little to bridle the flesh, that it became rather the exciter of sin; then, that we may cease from sin, we must necessarily be freed from the law." Again, " If we are freed from the bondage of the law for this end, that we may serve God; then, perversely do they act who hence take the liberty to indulge in sin; and falsely do they speak who teach, that by this means loose reins are given to lusts." Observe, then, that we are then freed from the law, when God emancipates us from its rigid exactions and curse, and endues us with his Spirit, through whom we walk in his ways.[1]

Having died to that, &c. This part contains a reason, or rather, indicates the manner in which we are made free; for the law is so far abrogated with regard to us, that we are not pressed down by its intolerable burden, and that its inexorable rigour does not overwhelm us with a curse.[2]—*In*

---

[1] That the moral, and not the ceremonial law, is meant here, is incontestably evident from what the Apostle adds in the following verses. He quotes the moral law in the next verse; he calls this law, in ver. 10, the commandment, τὴν ἐντολὴν, which was unto life, see Matt. xix. 16; and he says, that " by it " sin " slew " him, which could not have been said of the ceremonial law.—*Ed.*

[2] Our common version is evidently incorrect as to this clause. The pronoun αὐτῷ or ἐκείνῳ, is to be supplied. There is an exactly similar ellipsis in ch. vi. 21. *Beza* and several others, as well as our version, have followed a reading, ἀποθανόντος, which *Griesbach* disregards as of no

newness of spirit; He sets the spirit in opposition to the letter; for before our will is formed according to the will of God by the Holy Spirit, we have in the law nothing but the outward letter, which indeed bridles our external actions, but does not in the least restrain the fury of our lusts. And he ascribes *newness* to the Spirit, because it succeeds the *old* man; as the letter is called *old*, because it perishes through the regeneration of the Spirit.

7. What shall we say then? *Is* the law sin? God forbid. Nay, I had not known sin but by the law: for I had not known lust, except the law had said, Thou shalt not covet.[1]

8. But sin, taking occasion by the commandment, wrought in me all manner of concupiscence.

7. Quid ergo dicemus? Lex peccatum est? Absit: sed peccatum non cognovi nisi per Legem: concupiscentiam enim non noveram, nisi Lex diceret, Non concupisces.

8. Occasione autem sumpta, peccatum per mandatum effecit in me omnem concupiscentiam.

7. *What then shall we say?* Since it has been said that we must be freed from the law, in order that we may serve God in newness of spirit, it seemed as though this evil belonged to the law,—that it leads us to sin. But as this would be above measure inconsistent, the Apostle rightly undertook to disprove it. Now when he adds, *Is the law sin?* what he means is, "Does it so produce sin that its guilt ought to be imputed to the law?"—*But sin I knew not, except*

authority; and it is inconsistent with the usual phraseology of the Apostle. See ver. 4, and Gal. ii. 19.—*Ed.*

[1] Perhaps the sentence ought to have been rendered, For lust (concupiscentiam) I had not known, except the law had said, " Thou shalt not lust" (non concupisces.) Then the word "coveting" in the next verse should be "lust" (concupiscentiam.) But "Thou shalt not covet," is the commandment; and to retain a similarity of idea, for the lack of a more suitable word, it seems necessary to have coveting, as covetousness has not the meaning here intended. There is the same correspondence in the words in Greek as in *Calvin's* Latin. The noun is rendered first in our version "lust," and then "concupiscence;" and the same is done by *Doddridge;* the "strong desire" of *Macknight* is by no means suitable; the "inordinate desire" of *Stuart* is better, though "Thou shalt not lust," cannot be approved. By ἐπιθυμία, desire, is meant the inward propensity that is sinful. It is called "sin" in the preceding clause; and, according to the usual style of the Apostle, to show what sin was intended, it is called here desire: it is then sin in the wish, in the inclination or disposition within. And this very sinful *desire* the tenth commandment distinctly forbids.—*Ed.*

through the law; sin then dwells in us, and not in the law; for the cause of it is the depraved lust of our flesh, and we come to know it by the knowledge of God's righteousness, which is revealed to us in the law.[1] You are not indeed to understand, that no difference whatever can be known between right and wrong without the law; but that without the law we are either too dull of apprehension to discern our depravity, or that we are made wholly insensible through self-flattery, according to what follows,—

For coveting I had not known, &c. This is then an explanation of the former sentence, by which he proves that ignorance of sin, of which he had spoken, consisted in this— that he perceived not his own coveting. And he designedly referred to this one kind of sin, in which hypocrisy especially prevails, which has ever connected with itself supine self-indulgence and false assurance. For men are never so destitute of judgment, but that they retain a distinction in external works; nay, they are constrained even to condemn wicked counsels and sinister purposes: and this they cannot do, without ascribing to a right object its own praise. But coveting is more hidden and lies deeper; hence no account is made of it, as long as men judge according to their perceptions of what is outward. He does not indeed boast that he was free from it; but he so flattered himself, that he did not think that this sin was lurking in his heart. For though for a time he was deceived, and believed not that righteousness would be violated by coveting, he yet, at length, understood that he was a sinner, when he saw that coveting, from which no one is free, was prohibited by the law.

Augustine says, that Paul included in this expression the whole law; which, when rightly understood, is true: for when Moses had stated the things from which we must abstain, that we may not wrong our neighbour, he subjoined this prohibition as to coveting, which must be referred to all the things previously forbidden. There is no doubt but that

---

[1] It was the saying of *Ambrose,* "Lex index peccati est, non genitrix— the law is the discoverer, not the begetter of sin." "The law," says *Pareus,* "prohibits sin; it is not then the cause of it: sin is made known by the law; it is not then by the law produced."—*Ed.*

he had in the former precepts condemned all the evil desires which our hearts conceive; but there is much difference between a deliberate purpose, and the desires by which we are tempted. God then, in this last command, requires so much integrity from us, that no vicious lust is to move us to evil, even when no consent succeeds. Hence it was, that I have said, that Paul here ascends higher than where the understanding of men can carry them. But civil laws do indeed declare, that intentions and not issues are to be punished. Philosophers also, with greater refinement, place vices as well as virtues in the soul. But God, by this precept, goes deeper and notices coveting, which is more hidden than the will; and this is not deemed a vice. It was pardoned not only by philosophers, but at this day the Papists fiercely contend, that it is no sin in the regenerate.[1] But Paul says, that he had found out his guilt from this hidden disease: it hence follows, that all those who labour under it, are by no means free from guilt, except God pardons their sin. We ought, at the same time, to remember the difference between evil lustings or covetings which gain consent, and the lusting which tempts and moves our hearts, but stops in the midst of its course.

8. *But an occasion being taken,* &c. From sin, then, and the corruption of the flesh, proceeds every evil; the law is only the occasion. And though he may seem to speak only of that excitement, by which our lusting is instigated through the law, so that it boils out with greater fury; yet I refer this chiefly to the knowledge the law conveys; as though he had said, "It has discovered to me every lust or coveting which, being hid, seemed somehow to have no existence."

---

[1] As an instance of the frivolous and puerile mode of reasoning adopted by the Papists, the following may be adduced: quoting James i. 15, "When lust hath conceived, it bringeth forth sin; and sin, when it is finished, bringeth forth death," they reason thus:—"Lust is not simply a sin, for it brings it forth; and when it is sin, it is not mortal sin, for it afterwards brings forth death." Taking advantage of a metaphor, they apply it strictly and literally, without considering that the Apostle is only exhibiting the rise, progress, and termination—of what? of sin no doubt. The like produces its like. If lust were not sinful, it could not generate what is sinful. Such childish and profane reasoning is an outrage both on common sense and on religion.—*Ed.*

I do not yet deny, but that the flesh is more sharply stimulated to lusting by the law, and also by this means more clearly shows itself; which may have been also the case with Paul: but what I have said of the knowledge it brings, seems to harmonize better with the context;[1] for he immediately subjoins—

For without the law sin *was* dead.[2]	Sine Lege enim peccatum est mortuum:
9. For I was alive without the law once; but when the commandment came, sin revived, and I died.	9. Ego autem vivebam sine Lege aliquando;[3] adveniente autem mandato, peccatum revixit,
10. And the commandment, which *was ordained* to life, I found *to be* unto death.	10. Ego autem mortuus sum; et deprehensum est a me mandatum quod erat in vitam, cedere in mortem.
11. For sin, taking occasion by the commandment, deceived me, and by it slew *me*.	11. Peccatum enim, occasione sumpta per mandatum, abduxit me a via et per illud occidit:
12. Wherefore the law *is* holy, and the commandment holy, and just, and good.	12. Itaque Lex quidem sancta, et mandatum sanctum, et justum et bonum.

8. *For without the law,* &c. He expresses most clearly the meaning of his former words; for it is the same as though he had said, that the knowledge of sin without the law is buried. It is a general truth, which he presently applies to his own case. I hence wonder what could have come into the minds of interpreters to render the passage in the preterimperfect tense, as though Paul was speaking of himself; for it is easy to see that his purpose was to begin with a

---

[1] Most commentators take the opposite view,—that the irritation of sin occasioned by the law is more especially meant here. The two ideas, the knowledge and the excitement, or the increase of sin by the law, are no doubt referred to by the Apostle in these verses.—*Ed.*

[2] This clause is rightly separated from the former verse; for it clearly announces what is illustrated in the following verses. "Without the law," means without the knowledge of the law. The law is known and not known still.—*Ed.*

[3] " Aliquando;" ποτε—formerly, while he was a Pharisee, when he thought himself blameless. Critics often make difficulties when there are none. What is said here of being alive without the law, or when the law is not known, and of the commandment supposed to be for life being found to be unto death, is still exemplified in the character of men, and takes place in the experience of all who are brought out of darkness, as Paul was, unto marvellous light. Experience is often the best expositor.
To understand this passage, no more is necessary than to read what Paul says of himself in Phil. iii. 4-9; and also in Gal. ii. 19.—*Ed.*

general proposition, and then to explain the subject by his own example.

9. *For I was alive*, &c. He means to intimate that there had been a time when sin was dead to him or in him. But he is not to be understood as though he had been without law at any time, but this word *I was alive* has a peculiar import; for it was the absence of the law that was the reason why he was alive; that is, why he being inflated with a conceit as to his own righteousness, claimed life to himself while he was yet dead. That the sentence may be more clear, state it thus, "When I was formerly without the law, I was alive." But I have said that this expression is emphatic; for by imagining himself great, he also laid claim to life. The meaning then is this, "When I sinned, having not the knowledge of the law, the sin, which I did not observe, was so laid to sleep, that it seemed to be dead; on the other hand, as I seemed not to myself to be a sinner, I was satisfied with myself, thinking that I had a life of mine own." But the death of sin is the life of man, and again the life of sin is the death of man.

It may be here asked, what time was that when through his ignorance of the law, or as he himself says, through the absence of it, he confidently laid claim to life. It is indeed certain, that he had been taught the doctrine of the law from his childhood; but it was the theology of the letter, which does not humble its disciples, for as he says elsewhere, the veil interposed so that the Jews could not see the light of life in the law; so also he himself, while he had his eyes veiled, being destitute of the Spirit of Christ, was satisfied with the outward mask of righteousness. Hence he represents the law as absent, though before his eyes, while it did not really impress him with the consciousness of God's judgment. Thus the eyes of hypocrites are covered with a veil, that they see not how much that command requires, in which we are forbidden to lust or covet.

But when the commandment came, &c. So now, on the other hand, he sets forth the law as coming when it began to be really understood. It then raised sin as it were from the dead; for it discovered to Paul how great depravity abounded in the recesses of his heart, and at the same time it slew him. We must ever remember that he speaks of that inebriating confidence in which hypocrites settle, while they flatter themselves, because they overlook their sins.

10. *Was found by me,* &c. Two things are stated here—that the commandment shows to us a way of life in the righteousness of God, and that it was given in order that we by keeping the law of the Lord might obtain eternal life, except our corruption stood in the way. But as none of us obey the law, but, on the contrary, are carried headlong on our feet and hands into that kind of life from which it recalls us, it can bring us nothing but death. We must thus distinguish between the character of the law and our own wickedness. It hence follows, that it is incidental that the law inflicts on us a deadly wound, as when an incurable disease is more exasperated by a healing remedy. I indeed allow that it is an inseparable incident, and hence the law, as compared with the gospel, is called in another place the ministration of death; but still this remains unaltered, that it is not in its own nature hurtful to us, but it is so because our corruption provokes and draws upon us its curse.

11. *Led me out of the way,* &c. It is indeed true, that while the will of God is hid from us, and no truth shines on us, the life of men goes wholly astray and is full of errors; nay, we do nothing but wander from the right course, until the law shows to us the way of living rightly: but as we begin then only to perceive our erroneous course, when the Lord loudly reproves us, Paul says rightly, that we are led out of the way, when sin is made evident by the law. Hence the verb, ἐξαπατᾶν, must be understood, not of the thing itself, but of our knowledge; that is, that it is made manifest by the law how much we have departed from the right course. It must then be necessarily rendered, *led me out of the way;* for hence sinners, who before went on heedlessly, loathe and abominate themselves, when they perceive, through the light which the law throws on the turpitude of sin, that they had been hastening to death. But he again introduces the word *occasion,* and for this purpose—that we may know that the law of itself does not bring death, but

that this happens through something else, and that this is as it were adventitious.[1]

12. *So then the law is indeed holy,* &c. Some think that the words *law* and *commandment* is a repetition of the same thing; with whom I agree;[2] and I consider that there is a peculiar force in the words, when he says, that the law itself and whatever is commanded in the law, is *holy*, and therefore to be regarded with the highest reverence,—that it is *just*, and cannot therefore be charged with anything wrong,— that it is *good*, and hence pure and free from everything that can do harm. He thus defends the law against every charge of blame, that no one should ascribe to it what is contrary to goodness, justice, and holiness.

13. Was then that which is good made death unto me? God forbid. But sin, that it might appear sin, working death in me by that which is good; that sin by the commandment might become exceeding sinful.	13. Quod ergo bonum est, mihi in mortem cessit? Absit: imò peccatum, ut appareat peccatum, per bonum operatur mihi mortem: ut fiat super modum peccans peccatum per mandatum.

13. *Has then what is good,* &c. He had hitherto defended the law from calumnies, but in such a manner, that it

---

[1] This verse will be better understood if we consider it as in a manner a repetition, in another form, of what the former verse contains, and this is perfectly consistent with the usual manner of the Apostle. His object seems to have been to prevent a misapprehension of what he had said, that the commandment which was for life proved to be unto death. He hence says, that sin availed itself of the commandment, and by it deceived him, that is, promised him life, and then by it killed him, that is, proved fatal to him. There is a correspondence in meaning between the commandment unto life and deceiving, and between death and killing. In verse 8, sin, as a person, is said to take advantage of the commandment to work every kind of sinful desires; but it is said here to take this advantage to deceive by promising life, and then to destroy, to expose, and subject him to death and misery.—*Ed.*

[2] This is doubtless true; and it is an example of what the Apostle's manner of writing is, it being that of the ancient prophets. How various are the words used in the 119th Psalm to designate the law or the revealed will of God? and two different words are often used in the same verse.

Having spoken of the law in connection with sin, the Apostle may be supposed to have had the character of sin in view in characterizing the law. Sin works depraved desires and lusts; the law is *holy*: sin deceives and acts the traitor; the law is plain-dealing and *just*: sin leads to death and misery; the law is *good* and leads to happiness. The last contrast is evident from what follows in the next verse, " Was that which is good made death unto me?"—*Ed.*

still remained doubtful whether it was the cause of death; nay, the minds of men were on this point perplexed,—how could it be that nothing but death was gained from so singular a gift of God. To this objection then he now gives an answer; and he denies, that death proceeds from the law, though death through its means is brought on us by sin. And though this answer seems to militate in appearance against what he had said before—that he had found the commandment, which was given for life, to be unto death, there is yet no contrariety. He had indeed said before, that it is through our wickedness that the law is turned to our destruction, and that contrary to its own character; but here he denies, that it is in such a sense the cause of death, that death is to be imputed to it. In 2 Cor. iii. he treats more fully of the law. He there calls it the ministration of death; but he so calls it according to what is commonly done in a dispute, and represents, not the real character of the law, but the false opinion of his opponents.[1]

But sin, &c. With no intention to offend others, I must state it as my opinion, that this passage ought to be read as I have rendered it, and the meaning is this,—" Sin is in a manner regarded as just before it is discovered by the law; but when it is by the law made known, then it really obtains its own name of sin; and hence it appears the more wicked, and, so to speak, the more sinful, because it turns the goodness of the law, by perverting it, to our destruction; for that must be very pestiferous, which makes what is in its own nature salutary to be hurtful to us." The import of the whole is—that it was necessary for the atrocity of sin to be discovered by the law; for except sin had burst forth into outrageous, or, as they say, into enormous excess, it would not have been acknowledged as sin; and the more outrageous does its enormity appear, when it converts life into death; and thus every excuse is taken away from it.[2]

[1] This can hardly be admitted. The Apostle in Corinthians evidently states a fact, as he often does, without going into an explanation; and the fact was, that the law proved to be the ministration of death: but it proved to be so through the sin and wickedness of man.—*Ed.*

[2] *Erasmus, Beza, Pareus, Stuart,* and others, make up the ellipsis by putting in, " was made death to me," after " sin." But there is no need

14. For we know that the law is spiritual; but I am carnal, sold under sin.
15. For that which I do I allow not: for what I would, that do I not; but what I hate, that do I.
16. If then I do that which I would not, I consent unto the law that *it is* good.
17. Now then, it is no more I that do it, but sin that dwelleth in me.

14. Scimus enim quòd Lex spiritualis est: ego autem carnalis sum, venditus sub peccato.
15. Quod enim operor, non intelligo; siquidem non quod volo, hoc ago: sed quod odi, hoc facio.
16. Si verò quod nolo, hoc facio, consentio Legi Dei quòd sit bona.
17. Nunc verò non jam illud operor ego, sed quod habitat in me peccatum.

14. *For we know that the law,* &c. He now begins more closely to compare the law with what man is, that it may be more clearly understood whence the evil of death proceeds. He then sets before us an example in a regenerate man, in whom the remnants of the flesh are wholly contrary to the law of the Lord, while the spirit would gladly obey it. But first, as we have said, he makes only a comparison between nature and the law. Since in human things there is no greater discord than between spirit and flesh, the law being spiritual and man carnal, what agreement can there be between the natural man and the law? Even the same as between darkness and light. But by calling the law *spiritual,* he not only means, as some expound the passage, that it requires the inward affections of the heart; but that, by way of contrast, it has a contrary import to the word *carnal.*[1] These interpreters give this explanation, "The law is spiritual, that is, it binds not only the feet and hands as to external works, but regards the feelings of the heart, and requires the real fear of God."

But here a contrast is evidently set forth between the flesh and the spirit. And further, it is sufficiently clear from

of adding anything. The sentence throughout is thoroughly Hebraistic. What is partially announced in the words, "that it might appear sin," or, to be sin, &c., is more fully stated in the last clause; and the participle, "working"—*κατεργαζομένη,* is used instead of a verb, the auxiliary verb being understood. See similar instances in chap. xiv. 9-13. *Calvin's* version is no doubt the correct one. What follows the last *ἵνα* more fully explains what comes after the first.—*Ed.*

[1] This is evidently the case here. As *carnal* means what is sinful and corrupt, so *spiritual* imports what is holy, just, and good. As the works of the flesh are evil and depraved works, so the fruits of the Spirit are good and holy fruits. See Gal. v. 19, 22, and particularly John iii. 6.—*Ed.*

the context, and it has been in fact already shown, that under the term flesh is included whatever men bring from the womb; and flesh is what men are called, as they are born, and as long as they retain their natural character; for as they are corrupt, so they neither taste nor desire anything but what is gross and earthly. Spirit, on the contrary, is renewed nature, which God forms anew after his own image. And this mode of speaking is adopted on this account—because the newness which is wrought in us is the gift of the Spirit.

The perfection then of the doctrine of the law is opposed here to the corrupt nature of man: hence the meaning is as follows, " The law requires a celestial and an angelic righteousness, in which no spot is to appear, to whose clearness nothing is to be wanting: but I am a carnal man, who can do nothing but oppose it."[1] But the exposition of *Origen*, which indeed has been approved by many before our time, is not worthy of being refuted; he says, that the law is called spiritual by Paul, because the Scripture is not to be understood literally. What has this to do with the present subject?

Sold under sin. By this clause he shows what flesh is in

[1] " He is ' carnal' in exact proportion to the degree in which he falls short of *perfect* conformity to the law of God."—*Scott.*

It has been usual with a certain class of divines, such as *Hammond* and *Bull*, to hold that all the Fathers before *Augustine* viewed Paul here as not speaking of himself. But this is plainly contradicted by what *Augustine* declares himself in several parts of his writings. In his *Retractations*, B. i. chap. 23, he refers to some authors of divine discourses (*quibusdam divinorum tractatoribus eloquiorum*) by whose authority he was induced to change his opinion, and to regard Paul here as speaking of himself. He alludes again in his work against *Julian*, an advocate of Pelagianism, B. 6, chap. xi., to this very change in his view, and ascribes it to the reading of the works of those who were better and more intelligent than himself, (*melioribus et intelligentioribus cessi*.) Then he refers to them by name, and says, " Hence it was that I came to understand these things, as Hilary, Gregory, Ambrose, and other holy and known doctors of the Church, understood them, who thought that the Apostle himself strenuously struggled against carnal lusts, which he was unwilling to have, and yet had, and that he bore witness as to this conflict in these words," (referring to this very text,)—*Hinc factum est, ut sic ista intelligerem, quemadmodum intellexit* HILARIUS, GREGORIUS, AMBROSIUS, *et cæteri Ecclesiæ sancti notique doctores, qui et ipsum Apostolum adversus carnales concupiscentias, quas habere nolebat, et tamen habebat, strenue conflixisse, eundemque conflictum suum illis suis verbis contestatum fuisse senserunt.*—*Ed.*

itself; for man by nature is no less the slave of sin, than those bondmen, bought with money, whom their masters ill treat at their pleasure, as they do their oxen and their asses. We are so entirely controlled by the power of sin, that the whole mind, the whole heart, and all our actions are under its influence. Compulsion I always except, for we sin spontaneously, as it would be no sin, were it not voluntary. But we are so given up to sin, that we can do willingly nothing but sin; for the corruption which bears rule within us thus drives us onward. Hence this comparison does not import, as they say, a forced service, but a voluntary obedience, which an inbred bondage inclines us to render.

15. *For what I do I know not,* &c. He now comes to a more particular case, that of a man already regenerated;[1]

---

[1] It appears from this, that *Calvin* did not apply the foregoing words, "I am carnal, sold under sin," in the same way: but they are evidently connected together. They are indeed strong words, and some explain them in such a way as to be wholly unsuitable to a renewed man; but we ought to take the explanation as given by the Apostle himself in what follows, for he handles the subject to the end of the chapter.

Various fictions have been resorted to by critics on this point. The Apostle has been supposed by some to speak of himself as under the law, or as *Stuart* terms it, "in a law-state," and such is the scheme of *Hammond*. Others have imagined, that he personates a Jew living during the time between Abraham and the giving of the law; and this was *Locke's* idea. A third party have entertained the notion, that the Apostle, speaking in his own person, represents, by a sort of fiction, as *Vitringa* and some others have imagined, the effects of the law in Jews and proselytes, as opposed to the effects of the gospel, as delineated in the next chapter. And a fourth party maintain, that the Apostle describes a man in a transition-state, in whom God's Spirit works for his conversion, but who is as yet doubtful which way to turn, to sin or to God.

All these conjectures have arisen, because the language is not taken in its obvious meaning, and according to the Apostle's own explanation. As soon as we depart from the plain meaning of the text and the context, we open a door to endless conjectures and fictions. The Apostle says nothing here of himself, but what every real Christian finds to be true. Is not a Christian, yea, the best, in this world *carnal,* as well as spiritual? Is he not "sold under sin?" that is, subjected to a condition, in which he is continually annoyed, tempted, hindered, restrained, checked, and seduced by the depravity and corruption of his nature; and in which he is always kept far below what he aims at, seeks and longs for. It was the saying of a good man, lately gone to his rest, whose extended pilgrimage was ninety-three years, that he must have been often swallowed up by despair, had it not been for the seventh chapter of the Epistle to the Romans. The best interpreter of many things in Scripture is spiritual experience; without

in whom both the things which he had in view appear more clearly; and these were,—the great discord there is between the law of God and the natural man,—and how the law does not of itself produce death. For since the carnal man rushes into sin with the whole propensity of his mind, he seems to sin with such a free choice, as though it were in his power to govern himself; so that a most pernicious opinion has prevailed almost among all men—that man, by his own natural strength, without the aid of Divine grace, can choose what he pleases. But though the will of a faithful man is led to good by the Spirit of God, yet in him the corruption of nature appears conspicuously; for it obstinately resists and leads to what is contrary. Hence the case of a regenerated man is the most suitable; for by this you may know how much is the contrariety between our nature and the righteousness of the law. From this case, also, a proof as to the other clause may more fitly be sought, than from the mere consideration of human nature; for the law, as it produces only death in a man wholly carnal, is in him more easily impeached, for it is doubtful whence the evil proceeds. In a regenerate man it brings forth salutary fruits; and hence it appears, that it is the flesh only that prevents it from giving life: so far it is from producing death of itself.

That the whole, then, of this reasoning may be more fully and more distinctly understood, we must observe, that this conflict, of which the Apostle speaks, does not exist in man before he is renewed by the Spirit of God: for man, left to his own nature, is wholly borne along by his lusts without any resistance; for though the ungodly are tormented by the stings of conscience, and cannot take such delight in their vices, but that they have some taste of bitterness; yet you cannot hence conclude, either that evil is hated, or that good is loved by them; only the Lord permits them to be thus tormented, in order to show to them in a measure his judg-

it no right judgment can be formed. Hence it is that the learned often stumble at what is quite plain and obvious to the illiterate when spiritually enlightened. Critics sometimes find great difficulties in what is fully understood by a simpler minded Christian, taught from above. "Wayfaring men" are far better divines than any of the learned, who possess nothing more than natural talents and natural acquirements.—*Ed.*

ment; but not to imbue them either with the love of righteousness or with the hatred of sin.

There is then this difference between them and the faithful—that they are never so blinded and hardened, but that when they are reminded of their crimes, they condemn them in their own conscience; for knowledge is not so utterly extinguished in them, but that they still retain the difference between right and wrong; and sometimes they are shaken with such dread under a sense of their sin, that they bear a kind of condemnation even in this life: nevertheless they approve of sin with all their heart, and hence give themselves up to it without any feeling of genuine repugnance; for those stings of conscience, by which they are harassed, proceed from opposition in the judgment, rather than from any contrary inclination in the will. The godly, on the other hand, in whom the regeneration of God is begun, are so divided, that with the chief desire of the heart they aspire to God, seek celestial righteousness, hate sin, and yet they are drawn down to the earth by the relics of their flesh: and thus, while pulled in two ways, they fight against their own nature, and nature fights against them; and they condemn their sins, not only as being constrained by the judgment of reason, but because they really in their hearts abominate them, and on their account loathe themselves. This is the Christian conflict between the flesh and the spirit, of which Paul speaks in Gal. v. 17.

It has therefore been justly said, that the carnal man runs headlong into sin with the approbation and consent of the whole soul; but that a division then immediately begins for the first time, when he is called by the Lord and renewed by the Spirit. For regeneration only begins in this life; the relics of the flesh which remain, always follow their own corrupt propensities, and thus carry on a contest against the Spirit.

The inexperienced, who consider not the subject which the Apostle handles, nor the plan which he pursues, imagine, that the character of man by nature is here described; and indeed there is a similar description of human nature given to us by the Philosophers: but Scripture philosophizes much deeper; for it finds that nothing has remained in the heart of man but corruption, since the time in which Adam lost the image of God. So when the Sophisters wish to define free-will, or to form an estimate of what the power of nature can do, they fix on this passage. But Paul, as I have said already, does not here set before us simply the natural man, but in his own person describes what is the weakness of the faithful, and how great it is. *Augustine* was for a time involved in the common error; but after having more clearly examined the passage, he not only retracted what he had falsely taught, but in his first book to Boniface, he proves, by many strong reasons, that what is said cannot be applied to any but to the regenerate. And we shall now endeavour to make our readers clearly to see that such is the case.

I know not. He means that he acknowledges not as his own the works which he did through the weakness of the flesh, for he hated them. And so *Erasmus* has not unsuitably given this rendering, "I approve not," (*non probo.*)[1] We hence conclude, that the doctrine of the law is so consentaneous to right judgment, that the faithful repudiate the transgression of it as a thing wholly unreasonable. But as Paul seems to allow that he teaches otherwise than what the law prescribes, many interpreters have been led astray, and have thought that he had assumed the person of another; hence has arisen the common error, that the character of an unregenerate man is described throughout this portion of the chapter. But Paul, under the idea of transgressing the law, includes all the defects of the godly, which are not inconsistent with the fear of God or with the endeavour of acting uprightly. And he denies that he did what the law demanded, for this reason, because he did not perfectly fulfil it, but somewhat failed in his effort.

For not what I desire, &c. You must not understand that it was always the case with him, that he could not do good;

---

[1] "Pii quod perpetrant non agnoscunt, non approbant, non excusant, non palliant;"—"What the godly do [amiss,] they know not, approve not, excuse not, palliate not."—*Pareus.*

The verb γινώσκω is used here in the sense of the Hebrew verb ידע, which is often so rendered by the Septuagint. See Ps. i. 6; Hos. viii. 4; and Matt. vii. 23.—*Ed.*

but what he complains of is only this—that he could not perform what he wished, so that he pursued not what was good with that alacrity which was meet, because he was held in a manner bound, and that he also failed in what he wished to do, because he halted through the weakness of the flesh. Hence the pious mind performs not the good it desires to do, because it proceeds not with due activity, and doeth the evil which it would not; for while it desires to stand, it falls, or at least it staggers. But the expressions to will and not to will must be applied to the Spirit, which ought to hold the first place in all the faithful. The flesh indeed has also its own will, but Paul calls that the will which is the chief desire of the heart; and that which militates with it he represents as being contrary to his will.

We may hence learn the truth of what we have stated—that Paul speaks here of the faithful,[1] in whom the grace of the Spirit exists, which brings an agreement between the mind and the righteousness of the law; for no hatred of sin is to be found in the flesh.

16. *But if what I desire not, I do, I consent to the law,* &c.; that is, "When my heart acquiesces in the law, and is delighted with its righteousness, (which certainly is the case when it hates the transgression of it,) it then perceives and acknowledges the goodness of the law, so that we are fully convinced, experience itself being our teacher, that no evil ought to be imputed to the law; nay, that it would be salutary to men, were it to meet with upright and pure hearts." But this consent is not to be understood to be the same

---

[1] "As the Apostle was far more enlightened and humble than Christians in general are, doubtless this clog (indwelling sin) was more uneasy to him than it is to them, though most of us find our lives at times greatly embittered by it. So that this energetic language, which many imagine to describe an unestablished believer's experience, or even that of an unconverted man, seems to have resulted from the extraordinary degree of St. Paul's sanctification, and the depth of his self-abasement and hatred of sin; and the reason of our not readily understanding him seems to be, because we are far beneath him in holiness, humility, acquaintance with the spirituality of God's law, and the evil of our own hearts, and in our degree of abhorrence of moral evil."—*Scott.*

"What some mistake as the evidence of a spiritual decline on the part of the Apostle, was in fact the evidence of his growth. It is the effusion of a more quick and cultured sensibility than fell to the lot of ordinary men." —*Chalmers.*

with what we have heard exists in the ungodly, who have expressed words of this kind, "I see better things and approve of them; I follow the worse." Again, "What is hurtful I follow; I shun what I believe would be profitable." For these act under a constraint when they subscribe to the righteousness of God, as their will is wholly alienated from it, but the godly man consents to the law with the real and most cheerful desire of his heart; for he wishes nothing more than to mount up to heaven.[1]

17. *Now it is no more I who do it,* &c. This is not the pleading of one excusing himself, as though he was blameless, as the case is with many triflers who think that they have a sufficient defence to cover all their wickedness, when they cast the blame on the flesh; but it is a declaration, by which he shows how very far he dissented from his own flesh in his spiritual feeling; for the faithful are carried along in their obedience to God with such fervour of spirit that they deny the flesh.

This passage also clearly shows, that Paul speaks here of none but of the godly, who have been already born again; for as long as man remains like himself, whatsoever he may be, he is justly deemed corrupt; but Paul here denies that he is wholly possessed by sin; nay, he declares himself to be exempt from its bondage, as though he had said, that sin only dwelt in some part of his soul, while with an earnest feeling of heart he strove for and aspired after the righteousness of God, and clearly proved that he had the law of God engraven within him.[2]

18. For I know that in me (that is, in my flesh) dwelleth no good thing: for to will is present with me; but *how* to perform that which is good I find not.	18. Novi enim quòd non habitat[3] in me (hoc est, in carne mea) bonum: siquidem velle adest mihi, sed ut perficiam bonum non reperio.
19. For the good that I would I	19. Non enim quod volo facio

[1] "I consent—*consentio*—συμφημι, I say with, assent to, agree with, confirm."—*Ed.*

[2] The last clause of this verse is worthy of notice, as the expression "indwelling sin" seems to have arisen from the words ἡ οἰκοῦσα ἐν ἐμοὶ— "which dwells in me." Sin was in him as in a house or dwelling; it was an in-habiting sin, or that which is in-abiding or resident.—*Ed.*

[3] *Non habitat . . . . bonum*—οὐκ οἰκεῖ . . . . ἀγαθόν.—*Ed.*

do not: but the evil which I would not, that I do.	bonum; sed quod nolo malum, id ago.
20. Now, if I do that I would not, it is no more I that do it, but sin that dwelleth in me.	20. Si verò quod nolo ego id facio, non jam ego operor illud, sed quod habitat in me peccatum.

18. *For I know,* &c. He says that no good by nature dwelt in him. Then *in me,* means the same as though he had said, " So far as it regards myself." In the first part he indeed arraigns himself as being wholly depraved, for he confesses that no good dwelt in him; and then he subjoins a modification, lest he should slight the grace of God which also dwelt in him, but was no part of his flesh. And here again he confirms the fact, that he did not speak of men in general, but of the faithful, who are divided into two parts —the relics of the flesh, and grace. For why was the modification made, except some part was exempt from depravity, and therefore not flesh? Under the term *flesh,* he ever includes all that human nature is, everything in man, except the sanctification of the Spirit. In the same manner, by the term *spirit,* which is commonly opposed to the flesh, he means that part of the soul which the Spirit of God has so re-formed, and purified from corruption, that God's image shines forth in it. Then both terms, flesh as well as spirit, belong to the soul; but the latter to that part which is renewed, and the former to that which still retains its natural character.[1]

To will is present, &c. He does not mean that he had nothing but an ineffectual desire, but his meaning is, that the work really done did not correspond to his will; for the

---

[1] The Apostle here is his own interpreter; he explains who the *I* is that does what the other *I* disapproved, and who the *I* is that hates what the other *I* does. He tells us here that it is not the same *I*, though announced at first as though it were the same. The one *I*, he informs us here, was his flesh, his innate sin or corruption, and the other *I*, he tells us in verse 22, was " the inner man," his new nature. The " inner man," as *Calvin* will tell us presently, is not the soul as distinguished from the body, but the renewed man as distinguished from the flesh. It is the same as the " new man," as distinguished from " the old man." See Eph. iv. 22, 24; Rom. vi. 6; 2 Cor. v. 17. But " the inward man," and " the outward man," in 2 Cor. iv. 16, are the soul and the body; and " the inner man," in Eph. iii. 16, the same expression as in verse 22, means the soul, as it is evident from the context. The same is meant by " the hidden man of the heart," in 1 Peter iii. 4.—*Ed.*

flesh hindered him from doing perfectly what he did. So also understand what follows, *The evil I desire not, that I do:* for the flesh not only impedes the faithful, so that they cannot run swiftly, but it sets also before them many obstacles at which they stumble. Hence they do not, because they accomplish not, what they would, with the alacrity that is meet. This, *to will*, then, which he mentions, is the readiness of faith, when the Holy Spirit so prepares the godly that they are ready and strive to render obedience to God; but as their ability is not equal to what they wish, Paul says, that he found not what he desired, even the accomplishment of the good he aimed at.

19. The same view is to be taken of the expression which next follows,—that he *did not the good* which he *desired;* but, on the contrary, *the evil* which he *desired not:* for the faithful, however rightly they may be influenced, are yet so conscious of their own infirmity, that they can deem no work proceeding from them as blameless. For as Paul does not here treat of some of the faults of the godly, but delineates in general the whole course of their life, we conclude that their best works are always stained with some blots of sin, so that no reward can be hoped, unless God pardons them.

He at last repeats the sentiment,—that, as far as he was endued with celestial light, he was a true witness and subscriber to the righteousness of the law. It hence follows, that had the pure integrity of our nature remained, the law would not have brought death on us, and that it is not adverse to the man who is endued with a sound and right mind and abhors sin. But to restore health is the work of our heavenly Physician.

21. I find then a law, that, when I would do good, evil is present with me.	21. Reperio igitur Legem volenti mihi facere bonum quòd mihi malum insideat.[1]
22. For I delight in the law of God after the inward man:	22. Consentio enim Legi Dei secundum interiorem hominem.
23. But I see another law in my members warring against the law of	23. Video autem alterum Legem in membris meis, repugnantem[2] legi

[1] "Insideat,"—παράκειται; the same verb in verse 18, is rendered *adest* —is present. It means, to lie near, to be at hand.—*Ed.*

[2] "Repugnantem,"—ἀντιστρατευόμενον, placing itself in battle array, fight-

| my mind, and bringing me into captivity to the law of sin which is in my members. | mentis meæ, et captivum me redentem legi peccati, quæ est in membris meis. |

21. *I find then*, &c. Here Paul supposes a fourfold law. The first is the law of God, which alone is properly so called, which is the rule of righteousness, by which our life is rightly formed. To this he joins the law of the mind, and by this he means the prompt readiness of the faithful mind to render obedience to the divine law, it being a certain conformity on our part with the law of God. On the other hand, he sets in opposition to this the law of unrighteousness; and according to a certain kind of similarity, he gives this name to that dominion which iniquity exercises over a man not yet regenerated, as well as over the flesh of a regenerated man; for the laws even of tyrants, however iniquitous they may be, are called laws, though not properly. To correspond with this law of sin he makes the law of the members, that is, the lust which is in the members, on account of the concord it has with iniquity.

As to the first clause, many interpreters take the word *law* in its proper sense, and consider κατὰ or διὰ to be understood; and so *Erasmus* renders it, "by the law;" as though Paul had said, that he, by the law of God as his teacher and guide, had found out that his sin was innate. But without supplying anything, the sentence would run better thus, "While the faithful strive after what is good, they find in themselves a certain law which exercises a tyrannical power; for a vicious propensity, adverse to and resisting the law of God, is implanted in their very marrow and bones."

22. *For I consent[1] to the law of God*, &c. Here then you

---

ing or warring against, taking the field or marching against an enemy. Then follows "taking" an enemy "captive," αἰχμαλωτίζοντα. There are two sorts of captives, willing and unwilling. The latter is the case here; for the Apostle compares himself to captives of war, which are made so by force. The same is meant as by the expression, "sold under sin," verse 14,—the constrained condition of being subject during life, to the annoyances, to the tempting, seducing, and deadening power of innate corruption.—*Ed.*

[1] "Consentio," συνήδομαι: it is not the same verb as in ver. 16; this

see what sort of division there is in pious souls, from which arises that contest between the spirit and the flesh, which *Augustine* in some place calls the Christian struggle (*luctam Christianam.*) The law calls man to the rule of righteousness; iniquity, which is, as it were, the tyrannical law of Satan, instigates him to wickedness: the Spirit leads him to render obedience to the divine law; the flesh draws him back to what is of an opposite character. Man, thus impelled by contrary desires, is now in a manner a twofold being; but as the Spirit ought to possess the sovereignty, he deems and judges himself to be especially on that side. Paul says, that he was bound a captive by his flesh for this reason, because as he was still tempted and incited by evil lusts; he deemed this a coercion with respect to the spiritual desire, which was wholly opposed to them.[1]

signifies more than consent, for it includes gratification and delight. See Ps. i. 2. The verb is found only here. *Macknight's* version, " I am pleased with," is very feeble and inexpressive; *Stuart's* is better, " I take pleasure in;" but our common version is the best, " I delight in."

The γὰρ here would be better rendered "indeed;" the Apostle makes declaration as to his higher principle; and then in the next verse he states more fully what he had said in ver. 21. This exactly corresponds with his usual mode in treating subjects. He first states a thing generally, and afterwards more particularly, in more specific terms, and with something additional.—*Ed.*

[1] Some consider the conclusion of ver. 23, " to the law of sin which is in my members," as a paraphrase for " to itself;" as the Apostle describes it at the beginning as the law in his members: and the reason which may be assigned for the repetition is twofold,—to preserve the distinction between it and " the law of the mind" in the preceding clause,—and to give it a more distinctive character, by denominating it " the law of sin." We in fact find a gradation in the way in which it is set forth: in ver. 21, he calls it simply " a law;" in this verse he first calls it " another law in his members," and then, " the law of sin in his members."

The construction of ver. 21, is difficult. *Pareus* quotes *Chrysostom* as supposing συμφηναι from ver. 16, to be understood after " law," so as to give this rendering, " I find then that the law assents to me desiring to do good," &c., that is, that the law of God was on his side, " though evil was present with him." He then gives his own view, it being essentially that of *Augustine:* he supposes ὅτι καλὸς, from ver. 16, to be understood after " law," and that ὅτι, in the last clause, is to be construed " though:" the verse is then to be rendered thus,—" I find then the law, that it is good to me desiring to do good, though evil is present with me." The verse taken by itself may thus present a good meaning, but not one that harmonizes with the context, or that forms a part of the Apostle's argument. The only other construction that deserves notice is that of our own version, and of *Calvin,* and it is that alone which corresponds with the con-

But we ought to notice carefully the meaning of the *inner man* and of the *members;* which many have not rightly understood, and have therefore stumbled at this stone. The inner man then is not simply the soul, but that spiritual part which has been regenerated by God; and the members signify the other remaining part; for as the soul is the superior, and the body the inferior part of man, so the spirit is superior to the flesh. Then as the spirit takes the place of the soul in man, and the flesh, which is the corrupt and polluted soul, that of the body, the former has the name of the inner man, and the latter has the name of members. The inner man has indeed a different meaning in 2 Cor. iv. 16; but the circumstances of this passage require the interpretation which I have given: and it is called the inner by way of excellency; for it possesses the heart and the secret feelings, while the desires of the flesh are vagrant, and are, as it were, on the outside of man. Doubtless it is the same thing as though one compared heaven to earth; for Paul by way of contempt designates whatever appears to be in man by the term members, that he might clearly show that the hidden renovation is concealed from and escapes our observation, except it be apprehended by faith.

Now since the *law of the mind* undoubtedly means a principle rightly formed, it is evident that this passage is very

text. It has been adopted by *Beza, Grotius, Venema, Turrettin, Doddridge,* and others.

This verse, and the two which follow, conclude the subject, and also explain what he had been saying about willing and doing. He in fact accounts here for the paradoxical statements which he had made, by mentioning the operation and working of two laws, which were directly contrary to one another. It seems to be a mistake that he alludes to *four* laws; for the law of the mind and the law of God are the same, under different names; it is that of the mind, because it belongs to and resides in the mind: and it is the law of God, because it comes from him, and is implanted by his Spirit. To the other law he also gives two names, the " law in his members," and the " law of sin." This view is confirmed by the last verse in the chapter, which contains a summary of the whole.

The latter part of ver. 23 is in character with the Hebraistic style, when the noun is stated instead of the pronoun; see Gen. ix. 16; Ps. l. 23; and it is also agreeable to the same style to add the same sentiment with something more specific appended to it. This part then might be rendered thus,—" and making me captive *to itself, even* to the law of sin, which is in my members."—*Ed.*

absurdly applied to men not yet regenerated; for such, as Paul teaches us, are destitute of mind, inasmuch as their soul has become degenerated from reason.

| 24. O **wretched** man that I am! who shall deliver me from the body of this death? | 24. Miser ego homo! quis me eripiet à corpore mortis hoc? |
| 25. I thank God, through Jesus Christ our Lord. So then with the mind I myself serve the law of God, but with the flesh the law of sin. | 25. Gratias ago Deo per Iesum Christum Dominum nostrum: itaque idem ego mente servio Legi Dei, carne autem legi peccati. |

24. *Miserable*, &c. He closes his argument with a vehement exclamation, by which he teaches us that we are not only to struggle with our flesh, but also with continual groaning to bewail within ourselves and before God our unhappy condition. But he asks not by whom he was to be delivered, as one in doubt, like unbelievers, who understand not that there is but one real deliverer: but it is the voice of one panting and almost fainting, because he does not find immediate help,[1] as he longs for. And he mentions the word *rescue*,[2] in order that he might show, that for his liberation no ordinary exercise of divine power was necessary.

By the *body of death* he means the whole mass of sin, or those ingredients of which the whole man is composed; except that in him there remained only relics, by the captive bonds of which he was held. The pronoun τούτου, *this*, which I apply, as *Erasmus* does, to the body, may also be fitly referred to death, and almost in the same sense; for Paul meant to teach us, that the eyes of God's children are opened, so that through the law of God they wisely discern the corruption of their nature and the death which from it proceeds. But the word *body* means the same as the *external man* and *members;* for Paul points out this as the origin of evil, that man has departed from the law of his creation,

---

[1] Ταλαίπωρος, miser, ærumnosus; "it denotes," says *Schleusner*, "one who is broken down and wearied with the most grievous toils." It is used by the Septuagint for the word שדוד, wasted, spoiled, desolated. See Ps. cxxxvii. 8; Is. xxxiii. 1.—*Ed.*

[2] "Eripere"—pluck out, rescue, take away by force; ῥύσεται—shall draw, rescue or extricate; it means a forcible act, effected by power.—*Ed.*

and has become thus carnal and earthly. For though he still excels brute beasts, yet his true excellency has departed from him, and what remains in him is full of numberless corruptions, so that his soul, being degenerated, may be justly said to have passed into a body. So God says by Moses, " No more shall my Spirit contend with man, for he is even flesh," (Gen. vi. 3 :) thus stripping man of his spiritual excellency, he compares him, by way of reproach, to the brute creation.[1]

This passage is indeed remarkably fitted for the purpose of beating down all the glory of the flesh; for Paul teaches us, that the most perfect, as long as they dwell in the flesh, are exposed to misery, for they are subject to death; nay, when they thoroughly examine themselves, they find in their own nature nothing but misery. And further, lest they should indulge their torpor, Paul, by his own example, stimulates them to anxious groanings, and bids them, as long as they sojourn on earth, to desire death, as the only true remedy to their evils; and this is the right object in desiring death. Despair does indeed drive the profane often to such a wish; but they strangely desire death, because they are weary of the present life, and not because they loathe their iniquity. But it must be added, that though the faithful level at the true mark, they are not yet carried away by an unbridled desire in wishing for death, but submit themselves to the will of God, to whom it behoves us both to live and to die: hence they clamour not with displeasure against God, but humbly deposit their anxieties in his bosom; for they do not so dwell on the thoughts of their misery, but that being mindful of grace received, they blend their grief with joy, as we find in what follows.

25. *I thank God*, &c. He then immediately subjoined this thanksgiving, lest any should think that in his complaint he perversely murmured against God; for we know how easy

---

[1] " This body of death" is an evident Hebraism, meaning " this deadly or mortiferous body;" which is not the material body, but the body of " the old man," ver. 6; called the " body of sin," when its character is described, and the " body of death," when the issue to which it leads is intended: it conducts to death, condemnation, and misery.—*Ed.*

even in legitimate grief is the transition to discontent and impatience. Though Paul then bewailed his lot, and sighed for his departure, he yet confesses that he acquiesced in the good pleasure of God; for it does not become the saints, while examining their own defects, to forget what they have already received from God.[1]

But what is sufficient to bridle impatience and to cherish resignation, is the thought, that they have been received under the protection of God, that they may never perish, and that they have already been favoured with the first-fruits of the Spirit, which make certain their hope of the eternal inheritance. Though they enjoy not as yet the promised glory of heaven, at the same time, being content with the measure which they have obtained, they are never without reasons for joy.

So I myself, &c. A short epilogue, in which he teaches us, that the faithful never reach the goal of righteousness as long as they dwell in the flesh, but that they are running their course, until they put off the body. He again gives the name of *mind*, not to the rational part of the soul which philosophers extol, but to that which is illuminated by the Spirit of God, so that it understands and wills aright: for there is a mention made not of the understanding alone, but connected with it is the earnest desire of the heart. However, by the exception he makes, he confesses, that he was devoted to God in such a manner, that while creeping on the earth he was defiled with many corruptions. This is a suitable passage to disprove the most pernicious dogma of

---

[1] There is a different reading for the first clause of this verse, χάρις τῳ Θιῳ, "thanks to God," which, *Griesbach* says, is nearly equal to the received text; and there are a few copies which have ἡ χάρις κυρίου, "the grace of our Lord," &c.; which presents a direct answer to the foregoing question: but a considerable number more have ἡ χάρις τοῦ Θιου, "the grace of God," &c.; which also gives an answer to the preceding question. But the safest way, when there is no strong reason from the context, is to follow what is mostly sanctioned by MSS. Taking then the received text, we shall find a suitable answer to the foregoing question, if we consider the verb used in the question to be here understood, a thing not unusual; then the version would be, "I thank God, *who will deliver* me through Jesus Christ our Lord;" not as *Macknight* renders the verb, "who delivers me;" for the answer must be in the same tense with the question.—*Ed.*

the Purists, (*Catharorum,*) which some turbulent spirits attempt to revive at the present day.[1]

CHAPTER VIII.

1. *There is* therefore now no condemnation to them which are in Christ Jesus, who walk not after the flesh, but after the Spirit.[2]
2. For the law of the Spirit of life in Christ Jesus hath made me free from the law of sin and death.
3. For what the law could not do, in that it was weak through the flesh, God sending his own Son in the likeness of sinful flesh, and for sin condemned sin in the flesh;
4. That the righteousness of the law might be fulfilled in us, who walk not after the flesh, but after the Spirit.

1. Nulla igitur condemnatio est iis qui sunt in Christo Iesu, qui non secundum carnem ambulant, sed secundum Spiritum.
2. Lex enim Spiritus vitæ in Christo Iesu, liberum me reddidit à lege peccati et mortis.
3. Quod enim impossibile erat Legi, eò quòd infirmabatur per carnem, misso Deus Filio suo in similitudine carnis peccati, etiam de peccato damnavit peccatum in carne;
4. Ut justificatio Legis impleretur in nobis qui non secundum carnem ambulamus, sed secundum Spiritum.

1. *There is then,* &c. After having described the contest which the godly have perpetually with their own flesh, he returns to the consolation, which was very needful for them, and which he had before mentioned; and it was this,—That though they were still beset by sin, they were yet exempt from the power of death, and from every curse, provided they lived not in the flesh but in the Spirit: for he joins together these three things,—the imperfection under which the faithful always labour,—the mercy of God in pardoning and for-

---

[1] "Idem ego—the same I," or, "I the same;" αὐτὸς ἐγώ. *Beza* renders it the same—"idem ego," and makes this remark, "This was suitable to what follows, by which one man seems to have been divided into two." Others render it, "ipse ego—I myself," and say that Paul used this diction emphatically, that none might suspect that he spoke in the person of another. See ch. ix. 3; 2 Cor. x. 1, 12, 13. The phrase imports this, "It is I myself, and none else."

He terms his innate sin "the flesh." By the flesh, says *Pareus*, "is not meant physically the muscular substance, but theologically the depravity of nature,—not sensuality alone, but the unregenerated reason, will, and affections."—*Ed.*

[2] This clause, "who walk not," &c., is regarded as spurious by *Griesbach*: a vast preponderance of authority as to MSS. is against it; and its proper place seems to be at the end of the fourth verse. It being placed here does not, however, interfere with the meaning.—*Ed.*

giving it,—and the regeneration of the Spirit; and this indeed in the last place, that no one should flatter himself with a vain notion, as though he were freed from the curse, while securely indulging in the meantime his own flesh. As then the carnal man flatters himself in vain, when in no way solicitous to reform his life, he promises to himself impunity under the pretence of having this grace; so the trembling consciences of the godly have an invincible fortress, for they know that while they abide in Christ they are beyond every danger of condemnation. We shall now examine the words.

After the Spirit. Those who walk after the Spirit are not such as have wholly put off all the emotions of the flesh, so that their whole life is redolent with nothing but celestial perfection; but they are those who sedulously labour to subdue and mortify the flesh, so that the love of true religion seems to reign in them. He declares that such walk not after the flesh; for wherever the real fear of God is vigorous, it takes away from the flesh its sovereignty, though it does not abolish all its corruptions.

2. *For the law of the Spirit of life,* &c. This is a confirmation of the former sentence; and that it may be understood, the meaning of the words must be noticed. Using a language not strictly correct, by the *law of the Spirit* he designates the Spirit of God, who sprinkles our souls with the blood of Christ, not only to cleanse us from the stain of sin with respect to its guilt, but also to sanctify us that we may be really purified. He adds that it is life-giving, (for the genitive case, after the manner of the Hebrew, is to be taken as an adjective,) it hence follows, that they who detain man in the letter of the law, expose him to death. On the other hand, he gives the name of the *law of sin* and *death* to the dominion of the flesh and to the tyranny of death, which thence follows: the law of God is set as it were in the middle, which by teaching righteousness cannot confer it, but on the contrary binds us with the strongest chains in bondage to sin and to death.

The meaning then is,—that the law of God condemns men, and that this happens, because as long as they remain under the bond of the law, they are oppressed with the bondage of sin, and are thus exposed to death; but that the Spirit of Christ, while it abolishes the law of sin in us by destroying the prevailing desires of the flesh, does at the same time deliver us from the peril of death. If any one objects and says, that then pardon, by which our transgressions are buried, depends on regeneration; to this it may be easily answered, that the reason is not here assigned by Paul, but that the manner only is specified, in which we are delivered from guilt; and Paul denies that we obtain deliverance by the external teaching of the law, but intimates that when we are renewed by the Spirit of God, we are at the same time justified by a gratuitous pardon, that the curse of sin may no longer abide on us. The sentence then has the same meaning, as though Paul had said, that the grace of regeneration is never disjoined from the imputation of righteousness.

I dare not, with some, take *the law of sin and death* for the law of God, because it seems a harsh expression. For though by increasing sin it generates death, yet Paul before turned aside designedly from this invidious language. At the same time I no more agree in opinion with those who explain the law of sin as being the lust of the flesh, as though Paul had said, that he had become the conqueror of it. But it will appear very evident shortly, as I think, that he speaks of a gratuitous absolution, which brings to us tranquillizing peace with God. I prefer retaining the word *law*, rather than with *Erasmus* to render it *right* or *power:* for Paul did not without reason allude to the law of God.[1]

---

[1] *Calvin* has, in his exposition of this verse, followed *Chrysostom*, and the same view has been taken by *Beza, Grotius, Vitringa, Doddridge, Scott*, and *Chalmers*. But *Pareus*, following *Ambrose*, has taken another view, which *Haldane* has strongly advocated, and with considerable power of reasoning, though, as some may perhaps think, unsuccessfully. The exposition is this,—" The law of the spirit of life" is the law of faith, or the gospel, which is the ministration of the Spirit; and " the spirit of life" means either the life-giving spirit, or the spirit which conveys the life which is in Christ Jesus. Then " the law of sin and death" is the moral law, so called because it discloses sin and denounces death. It is said that this view corresponds with the " no condemnation " in the first verse, and with the word " law " in the verse which follows, which is no doubt the moral law, and with the truth which the verse exhibits. It is also added that freedom or deliverance from the law of sin, viewed as the power of

3. *For what was impossible for the law,* &c. Now follows the polishing or the adorning of his proof, that the Lord has by his gratuitous mercy justified us in Christ; the very thing which it was impossible for the law to do. But as this is a very remarkable sentence, let us examine every part of it.

That he treats here of free justification or of the pardon by which God reconciles us to himself, we may infer from the last clause, when he adds, *who walk not according to the flesh, but according to the Spirit.* For if Paul intended to teach us, that we are prepared by the spirit of regeneration to overcome sin, why was this addition made? But it was very proper for him, after having promised gratuitous remission to the faithful, to confine this doctrine to those who join penitence to faith, and turn not the mercy of God so as to promote the licentiousness of the flesh. And then the state of the case must be noticed; for the Apostle teaches us here how the grace of Christ absolves us from guilt.

Now as to the expression, τὸ ἀδύνατον, the impossibility of the law, it is no doubt to be taken for defect or impotency; as though it had been said, that a remedy had been found by God, by which that which was an impossibility to the law is removed. The particle, ἐν ᾧ, *Erasmus* has rendered "ea parte qua—in that part in which;" but as I think it to be causal, I prefer rendering it, " eo quod—because:" and though perhaps such a phrase does not occur among good authors in the Greek language, yet as the Apostles everywhere adopt Hebrew modes of expression, this interpretation ought not to be deemed improper.[1] No doubt intelligent readers will allow, that the cause of defect is what is

sin, is inconsistent with the latter part of the former chapter; and that the law of faith, which through the Spirit conveys life, makes us free from the moral law as the condition of life, is the uniform teaching of Paul. " This freedom," says *Pareus,* " is ascribed to God, to Christ, and to the Gospel,—to God as the author, chap. vii. 25,—to Christ as the mediator, —and to the Gospel as the instrument: and the manner of this deliverance is more clearly explained in the verse which follows."

[1] *Calvin* is not singular in this rendering. *Pareus* and *Grotius* give " quia *vel* quandoquidem—because *or* since;" and the latter says, that ἐν ᾧ is an Hebraism for ἐφ' ᾧ; see chap. v. 12. *Beza* refers to Mark ii. 19, and Luke v. 34, as instances where it means *when* or *while,* and says that it is used in Greek to designate not only a certain time, but also a certain state or condition. *Piscator's* rendering is " eo quod—because."—*Ed.*

here expressed, as we shall shortly prove again. Now though *Erasmus* supplies the principal verb, yet the text seems to me to flow better without it. The copulative καὶ, *and*, has led *Erasmus* astray, so as to insert the verb *præstitit*—hath performed; but I think that it is used for the sake of emphasis; except it may be, that some will approve of the conjecture of a Grecian scholiast, who connects the clause thus with the preceding words, " God sent his own Son in the likeness of the flesh of sin and on account of sin," &c. I have however followed what I have thought to be the real meaning of Paul. I come now to the subject itself.[1]

Paul clearly declares that our sins were expiated by the death of Christ, because it was impossible for the law to confer righteousness upon us. It hence follows, that more is required by the law than what we can perform; for if we were capable of fulfilling the law there would have been no

[1] The beginning of this verse, though the general import of it is evident, does yet present some difficulties as to its construction. The clause, as given by *Calvin*, is, " Quod enim impossibile erat legi,"—τὸ γὰρ ἀδύνατον τοῦ νόμου. *Pareus* supposes διὰ understood, " For on account of the impotency of the law," &c. *Stuart* agrees with *Erasmus* and *Luther*, and supplies the verb " did," or accomplish,—" For what the law could not accomplish...God...*accomplished*," &c. But the simpler construction is, " For this," (that is, freedom from the power of sin and death, mentioned in the former verse,) " *being* impossible for the law," &c. It is an instance of the nominative case absolute, which sometimes occurs in Hebrew. The possessive case, as *Grotius* says, has often the meaning of a dative after adjectives, as " malum hominis" is " *malum homini*—evil to man." The τὸ has sometimes the meaning of τοῦτο; it is separated by γὰρ from the adjective. Some say that it is for ὅτι γὰρ, " Because it was impossible for the law," &c. But changes of this kind are never satisfactory. The rendering of the whole verse may be made thus,—

3. For this *being* impossible for the law, because it was weak through the flesh, God having sent his own Son in the likeness of sinful flesh and on account of sin, has condemned sin in the flesh.

God sent his Son in that flesh which was polluted by sin, though his Son's flesh, *i.e.* human nature, was sinless; and he sent him on account of that sin which reigned in human nature or flesh; and for this end—to condemn, *i.e.*, to doom to ruin, to adjudge to destruction, the sin which ruled in the flesh, *i.e.*, in human nature as fallen and corrupted. This seems to be the meaning. Then in the following verse the design of this condemnation of sin is stated—that the righteousness of the law, or what the law requires, might be done by us. Without freedom from the power of sin, no service can be done to God. It is the destruction of the power of sin, and not the removal of guilt, that is contemplated here throughout; the text of the whole passage is walking after the flesh and walking after the Spirit.—*Ed.*

need to seek a remedy elsewhere. It is therefore absurd to measure human strength by the precepts of the law; as though God in requiring what is justly due, had regarded what and how much we are able to do.

Because it was weak, &c. That no one might think that the law was irreverently charged with weakness, or confine it to ceremonies, Paul has distinctly expressed that this defect was not owing to any fault in the law, but to the corruption of our flesh; for it must be allowed that if any one really satisfies the divine law, he will be deemed just before God. He does not then deny that the law is sufficient to justify us as to doctrine, inasmuch as it contains a perfect rule of righteousness: but as our flesh does not attain that righteousness, the whole power of the law fails and vanishes away. Thus condemned is the error or rather the delirious notion of those who imagine that the power of justifying is only taken away from ceremonies; for Paul, by laying the blame expressly on us, clearly shows that he found no fault with the doctrine of the law.

But further, understand the weakness of the law according to the sense in which the Apostle usually takes the word ασθενεια, weakness, not only as meaning a small imbecility but impotency; for he means that the law has no power whatever to justify.[1] You then see that we are wholly excluded from the righteousness of works, and must therefore flee to Christ for righteousness, for in us there can be none, and to know this is especially necessary; for we shall never be clothed with the righteousness of Christ except we first know assuredly that we have no righteousness of our own. The word *flesh* is to be taken still in the same sense, as meaning ourselves. The corruption then of our nature renders the law of God in this respect useless to us; for while it shows the way of life, it does not bring us back who are running headlong into death.

God having sent his own Son, &c. He now points out the way in which our heavenly Father has restored righteous-

---

[1] The adjective τὸ ἀσθενὲς is applied to the commandment in Heb. vii. 18. "Impotent, inefficacious," are the terms used by *Grotius;* "destitute of strength," by *Beza;* and "weak," by *Erasmus.—Ed.*

ness to us by his Son, even by condemning sin in the very flesh of Christ; who by cancelling as it were the handwriting, abolished sin, which held us bound before God; for the condemnation of sin made us free and brought us righteousness, for sin being blotted out we are absolved, so that God counts us as just. But he declares first that Christ was *sent*, in order to remind us that righteousness by no means dwells in us, for it is to be sought from him, and that men in vain confide in their own merits, who become not just but at the pleasure of another, or who borrow righteousness from that expiation which Christ accomplished in his own flesh. But he says, that he came in *the likeness of the flesh of sin;* for though the flesh of Christ was polluted by no stains, yet it seemed apparently to be sinful, inasmuch as it sustained the punishment due to our sins, and doubtless death exercised all its power over it as though it was subject to itself. And as it behoved our High-priest to learn by his own experience how to aid the weak, Christ underwent our infirmities, that he might be more inclined to sympathy, and in this respect also there appeared some resemblance of a sinful nature.

Even for sin, &c. I have already said that this is explained by some as the cause or the end for which God sent his own Son, that is, to give satisfaction for sin. *Chrysostom* and many after him understood it in a still harsher sense, even that sin was condemned for sin, and for this reason, because it assailed Christ unjustly and beyond what was right. I indeed allow that though he was just and innocent, he yet underwent punishment for sinners, and that the price of redemption was thus paid; but I cannot be brought to think that the word *sin* is put here in any other sense than that of an expiatory sacrifice, which is called אשם, *ashem*, in Hebrew,[1] and so the Greeks call a sacrifice to which a curse

---

[1] The reference had better been made to חטאת, a sin-offering, so called because חטא, sin, was imputed to what was offered, and it was accepted as an atonement. See Lev. i. 4; iv. 3, 4, 15; xvi. 21. See also Ex. xxx. 10. The *Septuagint* adopted the same manner, and rendered sin-offering in many instances by ἁμαρτία, sin; and Paul has done the same in 2 Cor. v. 21; Heb. ix. 28. That "sin" should have two different meanings in the same verse or in the same clause, is what is perfectly consonant to the Apostle's manner of writing; he seems to delight in this kind of contrast in meaning while using the same words, depending on the context as to the

is annexed καθαρμα, *catharma*. The same thing is declared by Paul in 2 Cor. v. 21, when he says, that "Christ, who knew no sin, was made sin for us, that we might become the righteousness of God in him." But the preposition περὶ, *peri*, is to be taken here in a causative sense, as though he had said, "On account of that sacrifice, or through the burden of sin being laid on Christ, sin was cast down from its power, so that it does not hold us now subject to itself." For using a metaphor, he says that it was *condemned*, like those who fail in their cause; for God no longer deals with those as guilty who have obtained absolution through the sacrifice of Christ. If we say that the kingdom of sin, in which it held us, was demolished, the meaning would be the same. And thus what was ours Christ took as his own, that he might transfer his own to us; for he took our curse, and has freely granted us his blessing.

Paul adds here, *In the flesh*, and for this end,—that by seeing sin conquered and abolished in our very nature, our

explanation. He uses the word *hope* both in this chapter and in chap. iv. 18, in this way. And this is not peculiar to Paul; it is what we observe in all parts of Scripture, both in the New and in the Old Testament. A striking instance of this, as to the word "life," ψυχή, is found in Matt. xvi. 25, 26, in the last verse it is rendered improperly "soul."

Fully admitting all this, I still think that "sin" here is to be taken in its common meaning, only personified. *Beza* connects περὶ ἁμαρτίας with the preceding clause, "God having sent his own Son in the likeness of sinful flesh, and that for or on account of sin, (idque pro peccato,)" &c., that is, as he explains, for expiating or taking away sin. "A sin-offering" may indeed be its meaning, for the same expression is often used in this sense in the *Septuagint*. See Lev. v. 7, 9, 11; Ps. xl. 6.

The sense of taking away strength, or depriving of power or authority, or of destroying, or of abolishing, does not belong, says *Schleusner*, to the verb κατακρίνειν, to condemn; he renders it here "punished—punivit," that is, God adjudged to sin the punishment due to it. The meaning is made to be the same as when it is said, that God "laid on him the iniquities of us all."

By taking a view of the whole passage, from chap. vii. 24 to chap. viii. 5, for the whole of this is connected, and by noticing the phraseology, we shall probably conclude that the *power* of sin and not its *guilt* is the subject treated of. "Law" here is used for a ruling power, for that which exercises authority and ensures obedience. "The law of sin," is the ruling power of sin; "the law of the Spirit of life," is the power of the Spirit the author of life; "the law of death," is the power which death exercises. Then "walking after the flesh" is to live in subjection to the flesh; as "walking after the Spirit" is to live in subjection to him. All these things have a reference to the *power* and not to the *guilt* of sin. The same subject is continued from chap. viii. 5 to the 15th verse.—*Ed.*

confidence might be more certain: for it thus follows, that our nature is really become a partaker of his victory; and this is what he presently declares.

4. *That the justification of the law might be fulfilled,* &c. They who understand that the renewed, by the Spirit of Christ, fulfil the law, introduce a gloss wholly alien to the meaning of Paul; for the faithful, while they sojourn in this world, never make such a proficiency, as that the justification of the law becomes in them full or complete. This then must be applied to forgiveness; for when the obedience of Christ is accepted for us, the law is satisfied, so that we are counted just. For the perfection which the law demands was exhibited in our flesh, and for this reason—that its rigour should no longer have the power to condemn us. But as Christ communicates his righteousness to none but to those whom he joins to himself by the bond of his Spirit, the work of renewal is again mentioned, lest Christ should be thought to be the minister of sin: for it is the inclination of many so to apply whatever is taught respecting the paternal kindness of God, as to encourage the lasciviousness of the flesh; and some malignantly slander this doctrine, as though it extinguished the desire to live uprightly.[1]

| 5. For they that are after the flesh do mind the things of the flesh; but they that are after the Spirit the things of the Spirit. | 5. Qui enim secundum carnem sunt, ea quæ carnis sunt cogitant; qui verò secundum Spiritum, ea quæ sunt Spiritus. |

[1] Commentators are divided as to the meaning of this verse. This and the second verse seem to bear a relation in sense to one another; so that if the second verse refers to justification, this also refers to it; but if freedom from the *power* of sin and death be what is taught in the former verse, the actual or personal fulfilment of the law must be what is intended here. Some, such as *Pareus* and *Venema,* consider justification to be the subject of both verses; and others, such as *Scott* and *Doddridge,* consider it to be sanctification. But *Beza, Chalmers,* as well as *Calvin,* somewhat inconsistently, regard the second verse as speaking of freedom from the power or dominion of sin, and not from its guilt or condemnation, and this verse as speaking of the imputed righteousness of Christ, and not of that righteousness which believers are enabled to perform by the Spirit's aid and influence. The verses seem so connected in the argument, that one of these two ideas must be held throughout.

There is nothing *decisive* in the wording of this verse, though the cast of the expressions seems more favourable to the idea entertained by *Doddridge* and *Scott,* and especially what follows in the context, where the work of the Spirit is exclusively spoken of. The word δικαίωμα, is better

6. For to be carnally minded *is* death; but to be spiritually minded *is* life and peace:

7. Because the carnal mind *is* enmity against God: for it is not subject to the law of God, neither indeed can be.

8. So then they that are in the flesh cannot please God.

6. Cogitatio certè carnis, mors est; cogitatio autem Spiritus, vita et pax:

7. Quandoquidem cogitatio carnis, inimicitia est adversus Deum; nam Legi Dei non subjicitur, nec enim potest.

8. Qui ergo in carne sunt, Deo placere non possunt.

5. *For they who are after the flesh,* &c. He introduces this difference between the flesh and the Spirit, not only to confirm, by an argument derived from what is of an opposite character, what he has before mentioned,—that the grace of Christ belongs to none but to those who, having been regenerated by the Spirit, strive after purity; but also to relieve the faithful with a seasonable consolation, lest being conscious of many infirmities, they should despair: for as he had exempted none from the curse, but those who lead a spiritual life, he might seem to cut off from all mortals the hope of salvation; for who in this world can be found adorned with so much angelic purity so as to be wholly freed from the flesh? It was therefore necessary to define what it is to *be in the flesh,* and to *walk after the flesh.* At first, indeed, Paul does not define the distinction so very precisely; but yet we shall see as we proceed, that his object is to afford good hope to the faithful, though they are bound to their flesh; only let them not give loose reins to its lusts, but give themselves up to be guided by the Holy Spirit.

rendered "righteousness" than "justification;" for "the righteousness of the law" means the righteousness which the law requires; and the words, "might be fulfilled in us," may, with equal propriety as to the *usus loquendi*, be rendered, "might be performed by us." The verb πληρόω has this meaning in chap. xiii. 8, and in other places.

Viewed in this light the verse contains the same truth with what is expressed by "serving the law of God," in chap. vii. 25, and the same with yielding our members as "instruments of righteousness unto God," in chap. vi. 13. That this is to establish a justification by the law, is obviated by the consideration, that this righteousness is performed through the efficacy of Christ's death, and through the reviving power of the Spirit, and not through the law, and that it is not a justifying righteousness before God, for it is imperfect, and the law can acknowledge nothing as righteousness but what is perfect. The sanctification now begun will be finally completed; but it is all through grace: and the completion of this work will be a complete conformity with the immutable law of God.—*Ed.*

By saying that *carnal* men care for, or think upon, the things of the flesh, he shows that he did not count those as carnal who aspire after celestial righteousness, but those who wholly devote themselves to the world. I have rendered φρονοῦσιν by a word of large meaning, *cogitant*—think, that readers may understand that those only are excluded from being the children of God who, being given to the allurements of the flesh, apply their minds and study to depraved lusts.[1] Now, in the second clause he encourages the faithful to entertain good hope, provided they find that they are raised up by the Spirit to the meditation of righteousness: for wherever the Spirit reigns, it is an evidence of the saving grace of God; as the grace of God does not exist where the Spirit being extinguished the reign of the flesh prevails. But I will briefly repeat here what I have reminded you of before,—That to be *in the flesh*, or, *after the flesh*, is the same thing as to be without the gift of regeneration:[2] and such are all they who continue, as they commonly say, in pure naturals, (*puris naturalibus.*)

6. *The minding of the flesh,* &c. *Erasmus* has rendered it "affection," (*affectum;*) the old translator, "prudence," (*prudentiam.*) But as it is certain that the τὸ φρόνημα of Paul is the same with what Moses calls the imagination (*figmentum*—devising) of the heart, (Gen. vi. 5;) and that under this word are included all the faculties of the soul—reason, understanding, and affections, it seems to me that minding (*cogitatio*—thinking, imagining, caring) is a more

---

[1] The verb φρονέω, as *Leigh* justly says, includes the action of the mind, will, and affections, but mostly in Scripture it expresses the action of the will and affections. It means to understand, to desire, and to relish or delight in a thing. It is rendered here by *Erasmus* and *Vatablus*, "curant—care for;" by *Beza*, *Pareus*, and the *Vulgate*, "sapiunt—relish or savour;" by *Doddridge* and *Macknight*, "mind," as in our version; and by *Stuart*, "concern themselves with." It evidently means attention, regard, pursuit and delight,—the act of the will and affections, rather than that of the mind.

"The verb," says *Turrettin*, "means not only to think of, to understand, to attend to a thing; but also to mind it, to value it, and to take great delight in it."—*Ed.*

[2] *Jerome* says, that to be *in the flesh* is to be in a married state! How superstition perverts the mind! and then the perverted mind perverts the word of God.—*Ed.*

suitable word.¹ And though Paul uses the particle γὰρ—for, yet I doubt not but that is only a simple confirmative: for there is here a kind of concession; for after having briefly defined what it is to be in the flesh, he now subjoins the end that awaits all who are slaves to the flesh. Thus by stating the contrary effect, he proves, that they cannot be partakers of the favour of Christ, who abide in the flesh, for through the whole course of their life they proceed and hasten unto death.

This passage deserves special notice; for we hence learn, that we, while following the course of nature, rush headlong into death; for we, of ourselves, contrive nothing but what ends in ruin. But he immediately adds another clause, to teach us, that if anything in us tends to life, it is what the Spirit produces; for no spark of life proceeds from our flesh.

The minding of the Spirit he calls *life*, for it is life-giving, or leads to life; and by *peace* he designates, after the manner of the Hebrews, every kind of happiness; for whatever the Spirit of God works in us tends to our felicity. There is, however, no reason why any one should on this account attribute salvation to works; for though God begins our salvation, and at length completes it by renewing us after his own image; yet the only cause is his good pleasure, whereby he makes us partakers of Christ.

7. *Because the minding of the flesh,*² &c. He subjoins a

¹ It is difficult to find a word to express the idea here intended. It is evident that τὸ φρόνημα τῆς σαρκὸς is the abstract of "minding the things of the flesh," in the preceding verse. The mindedness, rather than the minding of the flesh, would be most correct. But the phrase is no doubt Hebraistic, the adjective is put as a noun in the genitive case, so that its right version is, "The carnal mind;" and "mind" is to be taken in the wide sense of the verb, as including the whole soul, understanding, will, and affections. The phrase is thus given in the next verse in our version; and it is the most correct rendering. The mind of the flesh is its thoughts, desires, likings, and delight. This carnal mind is death, *i.e.*, spiritual death now, leading to that which is eternal; or death, as being under condemnation, and producing wretchedness and misery; it is also enmity towards God, including in its very spirit hatred and antipathy to God. On the other hand, "the spiritual mind" is "life," *i.e.*, a divine life, a living principle of holiness, accompanied with "peace," which is true happiness; or life by justification, and "peace" with God as the fruit of it.

The word φρόνημα is only found in one other place, in verse 27th of this chapter,—" the mind," wish, or desire " of the Spirit."—*Ed.*

² The *order* which the Apostle observes ought to be noticed. He be-

proof of what he had stated,—that nothing proceeds from the efforts of our flesh but death, because it contends as an enemy against the will of God. Now the will of God is the rule of righteousness ; it hence follows, that whatever is unjust is contrary to it ; and what is unjust at the same time brings death. But while God is adverse, and is offended, in vain does any one expect life ; for his wrath must be necessarily followed by death, which is the avenging of his wrath.

But let us observe here, that the will of man is in all things opposed to the divine will ; for, as much as what is crooked differs from what is straight, so much must be the difference between us and God.

For to the law of God, &c. This is an explanation of the former sentence ; and it shows how all the thinkings (*meditationes*) of the flesh carry on war against the will of God ; for his will cannot be assailed but where he has revealed it. In the law God shows what pleases him : hence they who wish really to find out how far they agree with God must test all their purposes and practices by this rule. For though nothing is done in this world, except by the secret governing providence of God ; yet to say, under this pretext, that nothing is done but what he approves, (*nihil nisi eo approbante fieri,*) is intolerable blasphemy ; and on this subject some fanatics are wrangling at this day. The law has set the difference between right and wrong plainly and distinctly before our eyes, and to seek it in a deep labyrinth, what sottishness is it ! The Lord has indeed, as I have said, his hidden counsel, by which he regulates all things as he pleases ; but as it is incomprehensible to us, let us know that we are to refrain from too curious an investigation of it. Let this in the mean time remain as a fixed principle,— that nothing pleases him but righteousness, and also, that no right estimate can be made of our works but by the law, in which he has faithfully testified what he approves and disapproves.

_{gins in ver. 5, or at the end of ver. 4, with two characters—the *carnal* and the *spiritual*. He takes the *carnal* first, because it is the first as to us in order of time. And here he does not reverse the order, as he sometimes does, when the case admits it, but goes on first with the carnal man, and then, in ver. 9 to 11, he describes the spiritual.—*Ed.*}

Nor can be. Behold the power of free-will! which the Sophists cannot carry high enough. Doubtless, Paul affirms here, in express words, what they openly detest,—that it is impossible for us to render our powers subject to the law. They boast that the heart can turn to either side, provided it be aided by the influence of the Spirit, and that a free choice of good or evil is in our power, when the Spirit only brings help; but it is ours to choose or refuse. They also imagine some good emotions, by which we become of ourselves prepared. Paul, on the contrary, declares, that the heart is full of hardness and indomitable contumacy, so that it is never moved naturally to undertake the yoke of God; nor does he speak of this or of that faculty, but speaking indefinitely, he throws into one bundle all the emotions which arise within us.[1] Far, then, from a Christian heart be this heathen philosophy respecting the liberty of the will. Let every one acknowledge himself to be the servant of sin, as he is in reality, that he may be made free, being set at liberty by the grace of Christ: to glory in any other liberty is the highest folly.

8. *They then who are in the flesh,* &c. It is not without reason that I have rendered the adversative δὲ as an illative: for the Apostle infers from what had been said, that those who give themselves up to be guided by the lusts of the

---

[1] *Stuart* attempts to evade this conclusion, but rather in an odd way. The whole amount, as he seems to say, of what the Apostle declares, is that this φρόνημα σαρκός *itself* is not subject, and cannot be, to the law of God; but whether the sinner who cherishes it "is actuated by other principles and motives," the expression, he says, does not seem satisfactorily to determine. Hence he stigmatizes with the name of "metaphysical reasoning" the doctrine of man's moral inability, without divine grace, to turn to God—a doctrine which *Luther, Calvin,* and our own Reformers equally maintained. The Apostle does not only speak abstractedly, but he applies what he advances to individuals, and concludes by saying, "So then they that are in the flesh cannot please God." Who and what can bring them out of this state? The influence of "other principles and motives," or the grace of God? This is no metaphysical question, and the answer to it determines the point. Our other American brother, *Barnes,* seems also to deprecate this doctrine of moral inability, and makes distinctions to no purpose, attempting to separate the carnal mind from him in whom it exists, as though man could be in a neutral state, neither in the flesh nor in the Spirit. "It is an expression," as our third American brother, *Hodge,* justly observes, "applied *to all* unrenewed persons, as those who are not in the flesh are in the Spirit."—*Ed.*

flesh, are all of them abominable before God; and he has thus far confirmed this truth,—that all who walk not after the Spirit are alienated from Christ, for they are without any spiritual life.

9. But ye are not in the flesh, but in the Spirit, if so be that the Spirit of God dwell in you. Now, if any man have not the Spirit of Christ, he is none of his.
10. And if Christ *be* in you, the body *is* dead because of sin; but the Spirit *is* life because of righteousness.
11. But if the Spirit of him that raised up Jesus from the dead dwell in you, he that raised up Christ from the dead shall also quicken your mortal bodies by his Spirit that dwelleth in you.

9. Vos autem non estis in carne, sed in Spiritu, siquidem Spiritus Dei habitat in vobis: si quis verò Spiritum Christi non habet, hic non est ejus.
10. Si verò Christus in vobis est, corpus quidem mortuum est propter peccatum, Spiritus autem vita est propter justitiam.
11. Si inquam Spiritus ejus qui suscitavit Iesum ex mortuis, habitat in vobis, qui suscitavit Christum ex mortuis, vivificabit et mortalia corpora propter Spiritum suum in vobis habitantem.

9. *But ye,* &c. He applies hypothetically a general truth to those to whom he was writing; not only that by directing his discourse to them particularly he might more powerfully affect them, but also that they might with certainty gather from the description already given, that they were of the number of those, from whom Christ had taken away the curse of the law. Yet, at the same time, by explaining what the Spirit of God works in the elect, and what fruit he brings forth, he encourages them to strive after newness of life.

If indeed the Spirit of God, &c. This qualifying sentence is fitly subjoined, by which they were stirred up to examine themselves more closely, lest they should profess the name of Christ in vain. And it is the surest mark by which the children of God are distinguished from the children of the world, when by the Spirit of God they are renewed unto purity and holiness. It seems at the same time to have been his purpose, not so much to detect hypocrisy, as to suggest reasons for glorying against the absurd zealots of the law, who esteem the dead letter of more importance than the inward power of the Spirit, who gives life to the law.

But this passage shows, that what Paul has hitherto meant by the Spirit, is not the mind or understanding (which is called the superior part of the soul by the advocates of free-will) but a celestial gift; for he shows that those are spiritual, not such as obey reason through their own will, but such as God rules by his Spirit. Nor are they yet said to be according to the Spirit, because they are filled with God's Spirit, (which is now the case with none,) but because they have the Spirit dwelling in them, though they find some remains of the flesh still remaining in them: at the same time it cannot dwell in them without having the superiority; for it must be observed that man's state is known by the power that bears rule in him.

But if any have not the Spirit of Christ, &c. He subjoins this to show how necessary in Christians is the denial of the flesh. The reign of the Spirit is the abolition of the flesh. Those in whom the Spirit reigns not, belong not to Christ; then they are not Christians who serve the flesh; for they who separate Christ from his own Spirit make him like a dead image or a carcase. And we must always bear in mind what the Apostle has intimated, that gratuitous remission of sins can never be separated from the Spirit of regeneration; for this would be as it were to rend Christ asunder.

If this be true, it is strange that we are accused of arrogance by the adversaries of the gospel, because we dare to avow that the Spirit of Christ dwells in us: for we must either deny Christ, or confess that we become Christians through his Spirit. It is indeed dreadful to hear that men have so departed from the word of the Lord, that they not only vaunt that they are Christians without God's Spirit, but also ridicule the faith of others: but such is the philosophy of the Papists.

But let readers observe here, that the Spirit is, without any distinction, called sometimes the Spirit of God the Father, and sometimes the Spirit of Christ; and thus called, not only because his whole fulness was poured on Christ as our Mediator and head, so that from him a portion might descend on each of us, but also because he is equally the Spirit of the Father and of the Son, who have one essence, and the same eternal divinity. As, however, we have no intercourse with God except through Christ, the Apostle wisely descends to Christ from the Father, who seems to be far off.

10. *But if Christ be in us,* &c. What he had before said of the Spirit he says now of Christ, in order that the mode of Christ's dwelling in us might be intimated; for as by the Spirit he consecrates us as temples to himself, so by the same he dwells in us. But what we have before referred to, he now explains more fully—that the children of God are counted spiritual, not on the ground of a full and complete perfection, but only on account of the newness of life that is begun in them. And he anticipates here an occasion of doubt, which might have otherwise disturbed us; for though the Spirit possesses a part of us, we yet see another part still under the power of death. He then gives this answer—that the power of quickening is in the Spirit of Christ, which will be effectual in swallowing up our mortality. He hence concludes that we must patiently wait until the relics of sin be entirely abolished.

Readers have been already reminded, that by the word Spirit they are not to understand the soul, but the Spirit of regeneration; and Paul calls the Spirit life, not only because he lives and reigns in us, but also because he quickens us by his power, until at length, having destroyed the mortal flesh, he perfectly renews us. So, on the other hand, the word *body* signifies that gross mass which is not yet purified by the Spirit of God from earthly dregs, which delight in nothing but what is gross; for it would be otherwise absurd to ascribe to the body the fault of sin: besides the soul is so far from being life that it does not of itself live. The meaning of Paul then is—that although sin adjudges us to death as far as the corruption of our first nature remains in us, yet that the Spirit of God is its conqueror: nor is it any hinderance, that we are only favoured with the first-fruits, for even one spark of the Spirit is the seed of life.[1]

---

[1] There are mainly two explanations of this verse and the following, with some shades of difference. The one is given here; according to which "the body," and "bodies," are taken figuratively for nature corrupted by sin; the "body," as it is flesh, or corrupted, is "dead," is crucified, or doomed to die "on account of sin;" and this "body," or these "bodies," which are mortal, and especially so as to their corruption, are to be quick-

11. *If the Spirit,* &c. This is a confirmation of the last verse, derived from the efficient cause, and according to this sense,—" Since by the power of God's Spirit Christ was raised, and since the Spirit possesses eternal power, he will also exert the same with regard to us." And he takes it as granted, that in the person of Christ was exhibited a specimen of the power which belongs to the whole body of the Church: and as he makes God the author of the resurrection, he assigns to him a life-giving Spirit.

Who raised, &c. By this periphrasis he describes God; which harmonizes better with his present object, than if he had called him simply by his own name. For the same reason he assigns to the Father the glory of raising Christ; for it more clearly proved what he had in view, than if he had ascribed the act to Christ himself. For it might have been objected, "That Christ was able by his own power to raise up himself, and this is what no man can do." But when he says, that God raised up Christ by his Spirit, and that he also communicated his Spirit to us, there is nothing that can be alleged to the contrary; so that he thus makes

ened, revived, and made subservient to the will of God. It appears that this is essentially the view taken by *Chrysostom,* and also by *Erasmus, Locke, Marckius,* and by *Stuart* and *Barnes.* It is said that νεκρόν and θνητά have the same meaning with " crucified " and " destroyed," in ch. vi. 6, and " dead," in ch. vi. 7, 8, and " dead," in ch. vi. 11, and " mortal," in ch. vi. 12. And as to the meaning of ζωοποιήσει, " shall quicken," reference is made to Col. ii. 12, 13; Eph. i. 19, 20; ii. 5, 6. It is also added, that the words " mortify the deeds of the body," in verse 13, confirm this view.

The other explanation, adopted by *Augustine,* and also by *Pareus, Vitringa, Turrettin, Doddridge, Scott, Chalmers, Haldane,* and *Hodge,* is the following,—The " body," and " bodies," are to be taken literally, and the spirit, in the 10th verse, is the renewed man, or the renewed soul, which has or possesses " life" through the righteousness of Christ, or is made to enjoy life through the righteousness implanted by the Spirit. The meaning then is this, " The body is dead through sin, is doomed to die because of sin; but the spirit is life through righteousness, the soul renewed has life through Christ's righteousness: but the dying body, now tabernacled by the Spirit, shall also be quickened and made immortal through the mighty power of the divine Spirit." Thus salvation shall be complete when the " redemption of the body " shall come. See verse 23.

While the two views are theologically correct, the latter is that which is the most consonant with the usual phraseology of Scripture, though the former seems the most suitable to the context. The subject evidently is the work of the Spirit in mortifying sin, and in bestowing and sustaining spiritual life. **The inference in the next verse seems favourable to this view.**—*Ed.*

sure to us the hope of resurrection. Nor is there anything here that derogates from that declaration in John, "I have power to lay down my life, and to take it up again." (John x. 18.) No doubt Christ arose through his own power; but as he is wont to attribute to the Father whatever Divine power he possesses, so the Apostle has not improperly transferred to the Father what was especially done by Christ, as the peculiar work of divinity.

By *mortal bodies* he understands all those things which still remain in us, that are subject to death; for his usual practice is to give this name to the grosser part of us. We hence conclude, that he speaks not of the last resurrection, which shall be in a moment, but of the continued working of the Spirit, by which he gradually mortifies the relics of the flesh and renews in us a celestial life.

12. Therefore, brethren, we are debtors, not to the flesh, to live after the flesh.
13. For if ye live after the flesh, ye shall die: but if ye through the Spirit do mortify the deeds of the body, ye shall live.
14. For as many as are led by the Spirit of God, they are the sons of God.

12. Itaque fratres, debitores sumus, non carni, ut secundum carnem vivamus.
13. Si enim secundum carnem vixeritis, moriemini: si vero Spiritu facta carnis[1] mortificaveritis, vivetis.
14. Quicunque enim Spiritu Dei aguntur, ii filii Dei sunt.

12. *So then, brethren,* &c. This is the conclusion of what has been previously said; for if we are to renounce the flesh, we ought not to consent to it; and if the Spirit ought to reign in us, it is inconsistent not to attend to his bidding. Paul's sentence is here defective, for he omits the other part of the contrast,—that we are debtors to the Spirit; but the meaning is in no way obscure.[2] This conclusion has the force of an exhortation; for he is ever wont to draw exhor-

---

[1] "Deeds of the *body*" is our version; and the preponderance of authority, according to *Griesbach*, is in its favour, though he admits that the other reading, τῆς σαρκὸς, is nearly equal to it, and deserves farther inquiry.—*Ed.*

[2] He did not mention the other part, says *Pareus*, "because it was so evident." Besides, what he had already stated, and what he proceeds to state, are so many evidences of our obligations to live after the Spirit, that it was unnecessary to make such an addition.—*Ed.*

tations from his doctrine. So in another place, Eph. iv. 30, he exhorts us " not to grieve the Spirit of God, by whom we have been sealed to the day of redemption:" he does the same in Gal. v. 25, "If we live in the Spirit, let us also walk in the Spirit." And this is the case, when we renounce carnal lusts, so as to devote ourselves, as those who are bound, to the righteousness of God. Thus indeed we ought to reason, not as some blasphemers are wont to do, who talk idly, and say,—that we must do nothing, because we have no power. But it is as it were to fight against God, when we extinguish the grace offered to us, by contempt and negligence.

13. *For if ye will live after the flesh*, &c. He adds a threatening, in order more effectually to shake off their torpor; by which also they are fully confuted who boast of justification by faith without the Spirit of Christ, though they are more than sufficiently convicted by their own conscience; for there is no confidence in God, where there is no love of righteousness. It is indeed true, that we are justified in Christ through the mercy of God alone; but it is equally true and certain, that all who are justified are called by the Lord, that they may live worthy of their vocation. Let then the faithful learn to embrace him, not only for justification, but also for sanctification, as he has been given to us for both these purposes, lest they rend him asunder by their mutilated faith.

But if ye by the Spirit, &c. He thus moderates his address, that he might not deject the minds of the godly, who are still conscious of much infirmity; for however we may as yet be exposed to sins, he nevertheless promises life to us, provided we strive to mortify the flesh: for he does not strictly require the destruction of the flesh, but only bids us to make every exertion to subdue its lusts.

14. *For whosoever are led by the Spirit of God,* &c. This is a confirmation of what has immediately preceded; for he teaches us, that those only are deemed the sons of God who are ruled by his Spirit; for by this mark God acknowledges them as his own people. Thus the empty boasting of hypocrites is taken away. who without any reason assume the

title; and the faithful are thus encouraged with unhesitating confidence to expect salvation. The import of the whole is this—"all those are the sons of God who are led[1] by God's Spirit; all the sons of God are heirs of eternal life: then all who are led by God's Spirit ought to feel assured of eternal life." But the middle term or assumption is omitted, for it was indubitable.

But it is right to observe, that the working of the Spirit is various: for there is that which is universal, by which all creatures are sustained and preserved; there is that also which is peculiar to men, and varying in its character: but what he means here is sanctification, with which the Lord favours none but his own elect, and by which he separates them for sons to himself.

15. For ye have not received the spirit of bondage again to fear; but ye have received the Spirit of adoption, whereby we cry, Abba, Father.
16. The Spirit itself beareth witness with our spirit, that we are the children of God:
17. And if children, then heirs; heirs of God, and joint-heirs with Christ: if so be that we suffer with *him*, that we may be also glorified together.
18. For I reckon that the sufferings of this present time *are* not worthy *to be compared* with the glory which shall be revealed in us.

15. Et enim non accepistis spiritum servitutis iterum in terrorem: sed accepistis Spiritum adoptionis, per quem clamamus, Abba, Pater.
16. Ipse enim Spiritus simul testificatur spiritui nostro quòd sumus filii Dei:
17. Si verò filii, etiam hæredes; hæredes quidem Dei, cohæredes autem Christi: siquidem compatimur, ut et unà glorificemur.
18. Existimo certè non esse pares afflictiones hujus temporis ad futuram gloriam quæ revelabitur erga nos.

He now confirms the certainty of that confidence, in which he has already bidden the faithful to rest secure; and he does this by mentioning the special effect produced by the Spirit; for he has not been given for the purpose of harassing us with trembling or of tormenting us with anxiety;

---

[1] Αγονται—are led or conducted: "A metaphor taken from the blind or those in darkness, who know not how to proceed without a conductor. So we have need to be led by the Spirit in the way of truth, for we are blind and see no light. Or it is a metaphor taken from infants, who can hardly walk without a guide; for the regenerated are like little children lately born. Thus we are reminded of our misery and weakness; and we ought not to ascribe to ourselves either knowledge or strength apart from the Spirit of God."—*Pareus.*

but on the contrary, for this end—that having calmed every perturbation, and restoring our minds to a tranquil state, he may stir us up to call on God with confidence and freedom. He does not then pursue only the argument which he had before stated, but dwells more on another clause, which he had connected with it, even the paternal mercy of God, by which he forgives his people the infirmities of the flesh and the sins which still remain in them. He teaches us that our confidence in this respect is made certain by the Spirit of adoption, who could not inspire us with confidence in prayer without sealing to us a gratuitous pardon: and that he might make this more evident, he mentions a twofold spirit; he calls one the spirit of bondage, which we receive from the law; and the other, the spirit of adoption, which proceeds from the gospel. The first, he says, was given formerly to produce fear; the other is given now to afford assurance. By such a comparison of contrary things the certainty of our salvation, which he intended to confirm, is, as you see, made more evident.[1] The same comparison is used by the author of the Epistle to the Hebrews, where he says, that we have not come to Mount Sinai, where all things were so terrible, that the people, being alarmed as it were by an immediate apprehension of death, implored that the word should be no more spoken to them, and Moses himself confessed that he was terrified; "but to Sion, the mount of the Lord, and to his city, the heavenly Jerusalem, where Jesus is, the Mediator of the New Testament," &c. (Heb. xii. 18.)

By the adverb *again*, we learn, that the law is here com-

---

[1] By the Spirit, πνεῦμα, (without the article,) some, as *Augustine*, *Beza*, and others, understand the Holy Spirit, and so *Calvin*, for the most part, seems to do. Then "the Spirit of bondage" means the Spirit the effect of whose administration was bondage; and "the Spirit of adoption" must signify the Spirit, the bestower of adoption. But we may take spirit here, in both instances, as it is often taken, in the sense of disposition or feeling; according to the expression, "the spirit of meekness"—πνεύματι πραότητος, 1 Cor. iv. 21, and "the spirit of fear"—πνεῦμα δειλίας, 2 Tim. i. 7. The word for adoption, υἱοθεσία, may be rendered sonship, or affiliation, or filiation, as *Luther* sometimes renders it: and as the spirit of meekness means a meek spirit, so we may translate the two clauses here, "a servile spirit," and "a filial spirit." At the same time it may be better to take the "spirit" throughout as the divine Spirit, as in several instances it must evidently be so taken.—*Ed.*

pared with the gospel: for the Son of God by his coming has brought to us this invaluable benefit,—that we are no longer bound by the servile condition of the law. You are not however to infer from this, either that no one before the coming of Christ was endued with the spirit of adoption, or that all who received the law were servants and not sons: for he compares the ministration of the law with the dispensation of the gospel rather than persons with persons. I indeed allow that the faithful are here reminded how much more bountifully God now deals with them than he did formerly with the fathers under the Old Testament; he yet regards the outward dispensation, in respect of which only we excel them: for though the faith of Abraham, of Moses, and of David, was superior to ours, yet as God kept them apparently under a schoolmaster, they had not advanced into that liberty which has been revealed to us.

But it must at the same time be noticed, that it was designedly, on account of false apostles, that a contrast was made between the literal disciples of the law, and the faithful whom Christ, the heavenly Teacher, not only addresses by words, but also teaches inwardly and effectually by his Spirit.

And though the covenant of grace is included under the law, it is yet far different from it; for in setting up the gospel in opposition to it, he regards nothing but what was peculiar to the law itself, as it commands and forbids, and restrains transgressors by the denunciation of death: and thus he gives the law its own character, in which it differs from the gospel; or this statement may be preferred by some,—" He sets forth the law only, as that by which God covenants with us on the ground of works." So then persons only must be regarded as to the Jewish people; for when the law was published, and also after it was published, the godly were illuminated by the same Spirit of faith; and thus the hope of eternal life, of which the Spirit is the earnest and seal, was sealed on their hearts. The only difference is, that the Spirit is more largely and abundantly poured forth in the kingdom of Christ. But if you regard only the dispensation of the law, it will then appear, that salvation was first clearly revealed at that time, when Christ was manifested in the flesh. All things under the Old Testament were involved in great obscurity, when compared with the clear light of the gospel.

And then, if the law be viewed in itself, it can do nothing but restrain those, devoted to its miserable bondage, by the horror of death; for it promises no good except under condition, and denounces death on all transgressors. Hence, as there is the spirit of bondage under the law, which oppresses the conscience with fear; so under the gospel there is the spirit of adoption, which exhilarates our souls by bearing a testimony as to our salvation. But observe, that *fear* is connected with bondage, as it cannot be otherwise, but that the law will harass and torment souls with miserable disquietness, as long as it exercises its dominion. There is then no other remedy for quieting them, except God forgives us our sin and deals kindly with us as a father with his children.

Through whom we cry, &c. He has changed the person, that he might describe the common privilege of all the saints; as though he had said,—" Ye have the spirit, through whom you and all we, the rest of the faithful, cry," &c. The imitation of their language is very significant; when he introduces the word Father, in the person of the faithful. The repetition of the name is for the sake of amplification; for Paul intimates, that God's mercy was so published through the whole world, that he was invoked, as *Augustine* observes, indiscriminately in all languages.[1] His object then was to express the consent which existed among all

---

[1] *Wolfius* gives a quotation from the Talmud, by which it appears that "servants" or slaves, and "maids" or bondmaids, were not allowed among the Jews to call their master *Abba* (אבא), nor their mistress *Aima* (אימא), these being names which children alone were permitted to use. And *Selden* says, that there is an evident allusion in this passage to that custom among the Jews. Under the law the people of God were servants, but under the gospel they are made children; and hence the privilege of calling God *Abba*. *Haldane,* quoting *Claude,* gives the same explanation. The repetition of the word is for the sake of emphasis, and is given as an expression of warm, ardent, and intense feeling. See an example of this in our Saviour's prayer in the garden, Mark xiv. 36, and in what he said on the cross, Matt. xxvii. 46. The idea mentioned by *Calvin,* derived from the Fathers, seems not to be well founded.—*Ed.*

nations. It hence follows, that there is now no difference between the Jew and the Greek, as they are united together. Isaiah speaks differently when he declares, that the language of Canaan would be common to all, (Is. xix. 18;) yet the meaning is the same; for he had no respect to the external idiom, but to the harmony of heart in serving God, and to the same undisguised zeal in professing his true and pure worship. The word *cry* is set down for the purpose of expressing confidence; as though he said, "We pray not doubtingly, but we confidently raise up a loud voice to heaven."

The faithful also under the law did indeed call God their Father, but not with such full confidence, as the vail kept them at a distance from the sanctuary: but now, since an entrance has been opened to us by the blood of Christ, we may rejoice fully and openly that we are the children of God; hence arises this crying. In short, thus is fulfilled the prophecy of Hosea, "I will say to them, My people are ye: they in their turn will answer, Thou art our God." (Hosea ii. 23.) For the more evident the promise is, the greater the freedom in prayer.

16. *The Spirit himself*, &c. He does not simply say, that God's Spirit is a witness to our spirit, but he adopts a compound verb, which might be rendered "contest," (*contestatur*,) were it not that contestation (*contestatio*) has a different meaning in Latin. But Paul means, that the Spirit of God gives us such a testimony, that when he is our guide and teacher, our spirit is made assured of the adoption of God: for our mind of its own self, without the preceding testimony of the Spirit, could not convey to us this assurance. There is also here an explanation of the former verse; for when the Spirit testifies to us, that we are the children of God, he at the same time pours into our hearts such confidence, that we venture to call God our Father. And doubtless, since the confidence of the heart alone opens our mouth, except the Spirit testifies to our heart respecting the paternal love of God, our tongues would be dumb, so that they could utter no prayers. For we must ever hold fast this principle,—that we do not rightly pray to God, unless we are surely persuaded in our hearts, that he is our Father, when we so

call him with our lips. To this there is a corresponding part,—that our faith has no true evidence, except we call upon God. It is not then without reason that Paul, bringing us to this test, shows that it then only appears how truly any one believes, when they who have embraced the promise of grace, exercise themselves in prayers.[1]

But there is here a striking refutation of the vain notions of the Sophists respecting moral conjecture, which is nothing else but uncertainty and anxiety of mind; nay, rather vacillation and delusion.[2] There is also an answer given here to

---

[1] The words αὐτὸ τὸ πνεῦμα, seem to mean the divine Spirit. The reference is to "the Spirit of God" in verse 14; "This self-same Spirit," or, "He the Spirit;" for so αὐτὸς, or αὐτο, may be rendered, especially when the article intervenes between it and its noun. See Luke xxiv. 15; John xvi. 27.

Beza renders συμμαρτυρεῖ τῷ πνεύματι ἡμῶν, "testifies together with our spirit—una cum nostro spiritu," and the *Vulgate* "testifies to our Spirit," as though the verb had not its compound; and it is said to have only the simpler meaning of testifying, though compounded, in chap. ix. 1; and in Rev. xxii. 18, where it has a dative case after it as here, "I testify to every man," &c. The soul appears to be here called "spirit," because the renewed soul is intended, or the soul having the spirit of adoption; or it may be an instance of the Apostle's mode of writing, who often puts the same word twice in a sentence, but in a different meaning. The Holy Spirit testifies to our spirit, say *Origen* and *Theodoret*, by producing obedience, love and imitation of God, which are evidences of our adoption; but *Chrysostom* and *Ambrose* say, by enabling us to cry Abba, Father, according to the former verse. The latter seems to be the meaning adopted by *Calvin*. It is said by *Estius*, according to *Poole*, that the compound verb is never used without the idea of a joint-testimony being implied. and that in Rev. xxii. 18, it is a testimony in conjunction with Christ. Then the import of this text would be, that the Holy Spirit testifies, together with the spirit of adoption, to our spirit, to our soul or renewed mind, that we are the children of God. Thus a direct influence of the Spirit, in addition to that which is sanctifying and filial, seems to have been intended. See 2 Cor. i. 22; Eph. i. 13, 14; 1 John ii. 20, 27.

Professor *Hodge* gives this paraphrase,—"Not only does our filial spirit towards God prove that we are his children, but the Holy Spirit itself conveys to our souls the assurance of this delightful fact." This seems to be the full and precise import of the passage.—*Ed.*

[2] "The [Roman] Catholic Church, with which all sects that proceed from Pelagian principles agree, deters from the certainty of the state of grace, and desires uncertainty towards God. Such uncertainty of *hearts* is then a convenient means to keep men in the leading-strings of the priesthood or ambitious founders of sects; for since they are not allowed to have any certainty themselves respecting their relation to God, they can only rest upon the judgments of their leaders about it, who thus rule souls with absolute dominion; the true evangelic doctrine makes free from such slavery to man."—*Olshausen.*

There is no doubt much truth in these remarks; but another reason

their objection, for they ask, "How can a man fully know the will of God?" This certainly is not within the reach of man, but it is the testimony of God's Spirit; and this subject he treats more at large in the First Epistle to the Corinthians, from which we may derive a fuller explanation of this passage. Let this truth then stand sure,—that no one can be called a son of God, who does not know himself to be such; and this is called knowledge by John, in order to set forth its certainty. (1 John v. 19, 20.)

17. *And if children,* &c. By an argument, taken from what is annexed or what follows, he proves that our salvation consists in having God as our Father. It is for children that inheritance is appointed: since God then has adopted us as his children, he has at the same time ordained an inheritance for us. He then intimates what sort of inheritance it is—that it is heavenly, and therefore incorruptible and eternal, such as Christ possesses; and his possession of it takes away all uncertainty: and it is a commendation of the excellency of this inheritance, that we shall partake of it in common with the only-begotten Son of God. It is however the design of Paul, as it will presently appear more fully, highly to extol this inheritance promised to us, that we may be contented with it, and manfully despise the allurements of the world, and patiently bear whatever troubles may press on us in this life.

If so be that we suffer together, &c. Various are the interpretations of this passage, but I approve of the following in preference to any other, "We are co-heirs with Christ, provided, in entering on our inheritance, we follow him in the same way in which he has gone before." And he thus made mention of Christ, because he designed to pass over by these steps to an encouraging strain,—"God's inheritance is ours, because we have by his grace been adopted as his children; and that it may not be doubtful, its possession has been already conferred on Christ, whose partners we are

may be added: Those who know not themselves what assurance is, cannot consistently teach the doctrine; and real, genuine assurance, is an elevated state, to which man, attached to merely natural principles, can never ascend.—*Ed.*

become: but Christ came to it by the cross; then we must come to it in the same manner."[1] Nor is that to be dreaded which some fear, that Paul thus ascribes the cause of our eternal glory to our labours; for this mode of speaking is not unusual in Scripture. He denotes the order, which the Lord follows in dispensing salvation to us, rather than the cause; for he has already sufficiently defended the gratuitous mercy of God against the merits of works. When now exhorting us to patience, he does not show whence salvation proceeds, but how God governs his people.

18. *I indeed judge*,[2] &c. Though they take not altogether an unsuitable view who understand this as a kind of modification; yet I prefer to regard it in the light of an encouragement, for the purpose of anticipating an objection, according to this import,—" It ought not indeed to be grievous to us, if we must pass through various afflictions into celestial glory, since these, when compared with the greatness of that glory, are of the least moment." He has mentioned *future* for eternal glory, intimating that the afflictions of the world are such as pass away quickly.

It is hence evident how ill understood has this passage been by the Schoolmen; for they have drawn from it their frivolous distinction between congruity and condignity. The

---

[1] The particle εἴπερ is rendered the same as here by *Ambrose* and *Beza*, "si modo—if in case that;" but by *Chrysostom* and Peter *Martyr*, in the sense of ἐπειδάν, "quandoquidem—since," " since we suffer together, in order that we may also be together glorified." The Vulgate has, " si tamen —if however." It may be suitably rendered " provided."—*Ed*.

[2] The particle γὰρ cannot be causal here. It has its primary meaning, *truly, indeed,* or *verily,* though it has commonly its secondary meaning, *for, because, therefore*. The context is our guide; when there is nothing previously said, for which a reason is given, then it has only an affirmative sense: or as some think, it is to be viewed as a particle of transition, or as signifying an addition, and may be rendered *besides, further, moreover*. Perhaps this latter meaning would be suitable here. In the preceding verse the Apostle says, for the encouragement of Christians, that their conformity to Christ in suffering would terminate in conformity to him in glory: and then, as an additional consideration, he states his full conviction, that present sufferings are as nothing to the glory which they would have to enjoy. The connection can hardly be otherwise seen, except indeed we consider something understood, as, " Not only so;" and then it may be rendered *for*, as giving a reason for the qualifying negative. An ellipsis of this kind is not without examples in Greek authors, as well as in the New Testament.—*Ed*.

19. For the earnest expectation of the creature waiteth for the manifestation of the sons of God.
20. For the creature was made subject to vanity, not willingly, but by reason of him who hath subjected *the same* in hope;
21. Because the creature itself also shall be delivered from the bondage of corruption into the glorious liberty of the children of God.
22. For we know that the whole creation groaneth and travaileth in pain together until now.

19. Siquidem intenta expectatio creaturæ, revelationem filiorum Dei expectat:
20. Vanitati enim creatura subjecta est non volens, sed propter eum qui subjecit ipsam in spe;
21. Quoniam ipsa quoque creatura asseretur à servitute corruptionis in libertatem gloriæ filiorum Dei.
22. Novimus enim quòd creatura universa congemiscit, et ad hunc diem parturit.

19. *For the intent expectation of the creation,* &c. He teaches us that there is an example of the patience, to which he had exhorted us, even in mute creatures. For, to omit various interpretations, I understand the passage to have this meaning—that there is no element and no part of the world which, being touched, as it were, with a sense of its present misery, does not intensely hope for a resurrection. He indeed lays down two things,—that all are creatures in distress,—and yet that they are sustained by hope. And it hence also appears how immense is the value of eternal glory, that it can excite and draw all things to desire it.

Further, the expression, *expectation expects,* or waits for, though somewhat unusual, yet has a most suitable meaning; for he meant to intimate, that all creatures, seized with great anxiety and held in suspense with great desire, look for that day which shall openly exhibit the glory of the children of God. *The revelation* of God's *children* shall be, when we shall be like God, according to what John says, "For though we know that we are now his sons, yet it appears not yet what we shall be." (1 John iii. 2.) But I have retained the words of Paul; for bolder than what is meet is the version of *Erasmus,* "Until the sons of God shall be manifest;" nor does it sufficiently express the meaning of the Apostle; for he means not, that the sons of God shall be manifested in the last day, but that it shall be then made known how desirable and blessed their condition will be, when they shall put off corruption and put on celestial glory. But he ascribes hope to creatures void of reason for this end,—that the faithful may open their eyes to behold the invisible life, though as yet it lies hid under a mean garb.

20. *For to vanity has the creation,* &c. He shows the object of expectation from what is of an opposite character; for as creatures, being now subject to corruption, cannot be restored until the sons of God shall be wholly restored; hence they, longing for their renewal, look forward to the manifestation of the celestial kingdom. He says, that they have been *subjected to vanity,* and for this reason, because they abide not in a constant and durable state, but being as it were evanescent and unstable, they pass away swiftly; for no doubt he sets vanity in opposition to a perfect state.

Not willingly, &c. Since there is no reason in such creatures, their will is to be taken no doubt for their natural inclination, according to which the whole nature of things tends to its own preservation and perfection: whatever then is detained under corruption suffers violence, nature being unwilling and repugnant. But he introduces all parts of the world, by a sort of personification, as being endued with reason; and he does this in order to shame our stupidity, when the uncertain fluctuation of this world, which we see, does not raise our minds to higher things.

But on account of him, &c. He sets before us an example of obedience in all created things, and adds, that it springs from hope; for hence comes the alacrity of the sun and moon, and of all the stars in their constant courses, hence is the sedulity of the earth's obedience in bringing forth fruits, hence is the unwearied motion of the air, hence is the prompt tendency to flow in water. God has given to everything its charge; and he has not only by a distinct order commanded what he would to be done, but also implanted inwardly the hope of renovation. For in the sad disorder which followed the fall of Adam, the whole machinery of the world would have instantly become deranged, and all its parts would have failed had not some hidden strength supported them. It would have been then wholly inconsistent that the earnest of the Spirit should be less efficacious in the children of God than hidden instinct in the lifeless parts of creation. How much soever then created things do naturally incline another way; yet as it has pleased God to bring them under vanity, they obey his order; and as he has given them a hope of a better condition, with this they sustain themselves, deferring their desire, until the incorruption promised to them shall be revealed. He now, by a kind of personification, ascribes *hope* to them, as he did *will* before.

21. *Because the creation itself,* &c. He shows how the creation has in hope been made subject to vanity; that is, inasmuch as it shall some time be made free, according to what Isaiah testifies, and what Peter confirms still more clearly.

It is then indeed meet for us to consider what a dreadful curse we have deserved, since all created things in themselves blameless, both on earth and in the visible heaven, undergo punishment for our sins; for it has not happened through their own fault, that they are liable to corruption. Thus the condemnation of mankind is imprinted on the heavens, and on the earth, and on all creatures. It hence also appears to what excelling glory the sons of God shall be exalted; for all creatures shall be renewed in order to amplify it, and to render it illustrious.

But he means not that all creatures shall be partakers of the same glory with the sons of God; but that they, according to their nature, shall be participators of a better condition; for God will restore to a perfect state the world, now fallen, together with mankind. But what that perfection will be, as to beasts as well as plants and metals, it is not meet nor right in us to inquire more curiously; for the chief effect of corruption is decay. Some subtle men, but hardly sober-minded, inquire whether all kinds of animals will be immortal; but if reins be given to speculations where will they at length lead us? Let us then be content with this simple doctrine,—that such will be the constitution and the complete order of things, that nothing will be deformed or fading.

22. *For we know,* &c. He repeats the same sentiment, that he might pass over to us, though what is now said has the effect and the form of a conclusion; for as creatures are subject to corruption, not through their natural desire, but through the appointment of God, and then, as they have a hope of being hereafter freed from corruption, it hence follows, that they groan like a woman in travail until they shall be delivered. But it is a most suitable similitude; it shows that the groaning of which he speaks will not be in vain and without effect; for it will at length bring forth a joyful and blessed fruit. The meaning is, that creatures are not content in their present state, and yet that they are not so distressed that they pine away without a prospect of a remedy, but that they are as it were in travail; for a restoration to a better state awaits them. By saying that they *groan together*, he does not mean that they are united together by mutual anxiety, but he joins them as companions to us. The particle *hitherto*, or, to this day, serves to alleviate the weariness of daily languor; for if creatures have continued for so many ages in their groaning, how inexcusable will our softness or sloth be if we faint during the short course of a shadowy life.[1]

---

[1] The various opinions which have been given on these verses are referred to at some length by *Stuart;* and he enumerates not less than *eleven*, but considers only *two* as entitled to special attention—the *material creation*, animate and inanimate, as held here by Calvin, and the *rational creation*, including mankind, with the exception of Christians, which he himself maintains. In favour of the first he names *Chrysostom, Theodoret, Theophylact, Œcumenius, Jerome, Ambrose, Luther, Koppe, Doddridge,* [this is not correct,] *Flatt*, and *Tholuck;* to whom may be added *Scott, Haldane,* and *Chalmers*, though *Scott*, rather inconsistently with the words of the text, if the material creation including animals be meant, regards as a reverie their resurrection; see verse 21.

After a minute discussion of various points, *Stuart* avows his preference to the opinion, that the "creature" means *mankind in general,* as being the least liable to objections; and he mentions as its advocates *Lightfoot, Locke, Turrettin, Semler, Rosenmüller,* and others. He might have added *Augustine.* Reference is made for the meaning of the word "creature" to Mark xvi. 15; Col. i. 23; and 1 Pet. ii. 13.

It appears from *Wolfius*, that the greater part of the Lutheran and Reformed Divines have entertained the first opinion, that the "creature" means the world, rational and animal; to which he himself mainly accedes; and what he considers next to this, as the most tenable, is the notion, that the "creature" means the faithful, that "the sons of God" are the blessed

23. And not only *they*, but ourselves also, which have the first-fruits of the Spirit, even we ourselves groan within ourselves, waiting for the adoption, *to wit*, the redemption of our body.
24. For we are saved by hope: but hope that is seen is not hope: for what a man seeth, why doth he yet hope for?
25. But if we hope for that we see not, *then* do we with patience wait for *it*.

23. Non solum autem, sed ipsi quoque qui primordia Spiritus habemus; nos inquam ipsi in nobis ipsis gemimus, adoptionem expectantes, redemptionem corporis nostri.
24. Spe enim salvi facti sumus; spes vero quæ conspicitur, non est spes; quod enim conspicit quis, quomodo etiam speret?
25. Si ergo non quod non conspicimus, speramus, per patientiam expectamus.

23. *And not only so*, &c. There are those who think that in heaven, and that the Apostles and apostolic men were those who enjoyed "the first-fruits of the Spirit."

This last opinion relieves us from difficulties which press on all other expositions; and it may be extricated from objections which have been made to it; only the last sentence needs not be introduced. The whole passage, from verse 18 to the end of verse 25, is in character with the usual style of the Apostle. He finishes the first part with verse 22; and then in the second part he announces the same thing in a different form, in more explicit terms, and with some additions. The "waiting" in verse 19, has a correspondent "waiting" in verse 23; and "the hope" in verse 20, has another "hope" to correspond with it in verse 24; and correspondent too is "the manifestation of the sons of God" in verse 19, and "the redemption of our body" in verse 23. To reiterate the same truth in a different way was to make a deeper impression, and accordant with the Apostle's manner of writing. He begins the second time, after verse 22, in which is stated the condition of the *whole world;* and it is in contrast with *that alone* that the 23d verse is to be viewed, which restates and explains what had been previously said; so that "the creature" are the "we ourselves;" and the Apostle proceeds with the subject to end of the 25th verse. Instances of the same sort of arrangement are to be found in chap. ii. 17-24; xi. 33-36.

The 21st verse may be considered as an explanation only of the "hope," at the end of the 20th; "For even it, the creature," though subjected to vanity, "shall be delivered from the bondage of corruption;" which means the same as "this body of death," in chap. vii. 24.

The word κτίσις, means, 1, creation, the world, Mark x. 6; xiii. 19; Rom. i. 20; 2 Peter iii. 4 :— 2, what is created—creature, what is formed—a building, what is instituted—an ordinance, Rom. i. 25; viii. 39; Heb. iv. 13; ix. 11; 1 Peter ii. 13:—3, mankind, the world of men, Mark xvi. 15; Col. i. 23 :—4, the renewed man, or renewed nature—Christians, 2 Cor. v. 17; Gal. vi. 15. There are only two other places where it is found, and is rendered in our version "creation," Col. i. 15, and Rev. iii. 14.

It is objected to its application here to Christians, because where it has this meaning, it is preceded by καινή, new. The same objection stands against applying it to mankind in general, for in these instances πάση precedes it. Its meaning must be gathered from the whole passage, and we must not stop at the end of verse 23, but include the two following verses. —*Ed.*

the Apostle intended here to exalt the dignity of our future blessedness, and by this proof, because all things look for it with ardent desire; not only the irrational parts of creation, but we also who have been regenerated by the Spirit of God. This view is indeed capable of being defended, but there seems to me to be a comparison here between the greater and the less; as though he said, "The excellency of our glory is of such importance even to the very elements, which are destitute of mind and reason, that they burn with a certain kind of desire for it; how much more it behoves us, who have been illuminated by the Spirit of God, to aspire and strive with firmness of hope and with ardour of desire, after the attainment of so great a benefit." And he requires that there should be a feeling of two kinds in the faithful: that being burdened with the sense of their present misery, they are to *groan;* and that notwithstanding they are to *wait* patiently for their deliverance; for he would have them to be raised up with the expectation of their future blessedness, and by an elevation of mind to overcome all their present miseries, while they consider not what they are now, but what they are to be.

Who have the beginnings, &c. Some render the word first-fruits, (*primitias,*) and as meaning a rare and uncommon excellency; but of this view I by no means approve. To avoid, therefore, any ambiguity, I have rendered the word *beginnings,* (*primordia,* the elements,) for I do not apply the expression, as they do, to the Apostles only, but to all the faithful who in this world are besprinkled only with a few drops by the Spirit; and indeed when they make the greatest proficiency, being endued with a considerable measure of it, they are still far off from perfection. These, then, in the view of the Apostle, are beginnings or first-fruits, to which is opposed the complete ingathering; for as we are not yet endued with fulness, it is no wonder that we feel disquietude. By repeating *ourselves* and adding *in ourselves,* he renders the sentence more emphatical, and expresses a more ardent desire, nor does he call it only a desire, but groaning: for in groaning there is a deep feeling of misery.

Waiting for the adoption, &c. Improperly indeed, but not without the best reason, is adoption employed here to designate the fruition of the inheritance to which we are adopted; for Paul means this, that the eternal decree of God, by which he has chosen us to himself as sons before the foundation of the world, of which he testifies to us in the gospel, the assurance of which he seals on our hearts by his Spirit, would be void, except the promised resurrection were certain, which is its consummation.[1] For to what end is God our Father, except he receives us after we have finished our earthly pilgrimage into his celestial inheritance? To the same purpose is what he immediately subjoins, *the redemption of the body*. For the price of our redemption was in such a way paid by Christ, that death should notwithstanding hold us tied by its chains, yea, that we should carry it within us; it hence follows, that the sacrifice of the death of Christ would be in vain and fruitless, except its fruit appeared in our heavenly renovation.

24. *For by hope*, &c. Paul strengthens his exhortation by another argument; for our salvation cannot be separated from some kind of death, and this he proves by the nature of hope. Since hope extends to things not yet obtained, and represents to our minds the form of things hidden and far remote, whatever is either openly seen or really possessed, is not an object of hope. But Paul takes it as granted, and what cannot be denied, that as long as we are in the world, salvation is what is hoped for; it hence follows, that it is laid up with God far beyond what we can see. By saying, that hope is not what is seen, he uses a concise expression, but the meaning is not obscure; for he means simply to teach us, that since hope regards some future and not present good, it can never be connected with what we have in possession. If then it be grievous to any to groan, they necessarily subvert the order laid down by God, who does not

---

[1] The impropriety, which *Calvin* notices, is according to the usual phraseology of Scripture. What commences in this world and is completed in the next is called by the same name. The word salvation is used in this way as designating its commencement and its progress as well as its completion. Besides, adoption here has a particular regard to the *body*, as it is explained by the words which follow.—*Ed.*

call his people to victory before he exercises them in the warfare of patience. But since it has pleased God to lay up our salvation, as it were, in his closed bosom, it is expedient for us to toil on earth, to be oppressed, to mourn, to be afflicted, yea, to lie down as half-dead and to be like the dead; for they who seek a visible salvation reject it, as they renounce hope which has been appointed by God as its guardian.[1]

25. *If then what we see not,* &c. This is an argument derived from what the antecedent implies; for patience necessarily follows hope. For when it is grievous to be without the good you may desire, unless you sustain and comfort yourselves with patience, you must necessarily faint through despair. Hope then ever draws patience with it. Thus it is a most apt conclusion—that whatever the gospel promises respecting the glory of the resurrection, vanishes away, except we spend our present life in patiently bearing the cross and tribulations. For if life be invisible, we must have death before our eyes: if glory be invisible, then our present state is that of degradation. And hence if you wish to include in a few words the meaning of the whole passage, arrange Paul's arguments in this way, "To all the godly there is salvation laid up in hope; it is the character of hope to look forward to future and absent benefits: then the salvation of the faithful is not visible. Now hope is not otherwise sustained than by patience; then the salvation of the faithful is not to be consummated except by patience."

It may be added, that we have here a remarkable passage, which shows, that patience is an inseparable companion of faith; and the reason of this is evident, for when we console ourselves with the hope of a better condition, the feeling of our present miseries is softened and mitigated, so that they are borne with less difficulty.[2]

---

[1] When we are said to be saved by hope, the meaning is that we are not fully or perfectly saved now, and that this is what we hope for. "Eternal salvation," says *Grotius*, "we have not yet, but we hope for it." There is present salvation, but that which is perfect is future. The Scripture speaks of salvation now, see Eph. ii. 8; Tit. iii. 4, 5; and of salvation as future, see Mark xiii. 13; x. 9.—*Ed.*

[2] "Patience," says *Pareus*, "is needful for three reasons,—the good expected is absent,—there is delay,—and many difficulties intervene."—*Ed.*

26. Likewise[1] the Spirit also helpeth our infirmities: for we know not what we should pray for as we ought; but the Spirit itself maketh intercession for us with groanings which cannot be uttered.
27. And he that searcheth the hearts knoweth what *is* the mind of the Spirit, because he maketh intercession for the saints according to *the will of* God.

26. Similiter[1] verò Spiritus etiam coopitulatur infirmitatibus nostris ; non enim quid oraturi sumus quemadmodum oportet, novimus ; verùm Spiritus ipse intercedit pro nobis gemitibus innarrabilibus.
27. Qui verò scrutatur corda, novit cogitationem Spiritus, quòd secundum Deum intercedit pro sanctis.

26. *And likewise the Spirit,* &c. That the faithful may not make this objection—that they are so weak as not to be able to bear so many and so heavy burdens, he brings before them the aid of the Spirit, which is abundantly sufficient to overcome all difficulties. There is then no reason for any one to complain, that the bearing of the cross is beyond their own strength, since we are sustained by a celestial power. And there is great force in the Greek word συναντιλαμβάνεται, which means that the Spirit takes on himself a part of the burden, by which our weakness is oppressed ; so that he not only helps and succours us, but lifts us up ; as though he went under the burden with us.[2] The word *infirmities,* being in the plural number, is expressive of extremity. For as experience shows, that except we are supported by God's hands, we are soon overwhelmed by innumerable evils, Paul reminds us, that though we are in every respect weak, and various infirmities threaten our fall, there is yet sufficient protection in God's Spirit to preserve us

---

[1] The connection here is not very evident 'Ωσαύτως—" similiter—in like manner," by *Calvin ;* " itidem—likewise," by *Pareus* and *Beza ;* " præterea—besides," by *Grotius ;* " moreover," by *Doddridge.* The word usually means, in the same, or, the like manner: but the two last seem to render it suitably to this place ; for what follows is mentioned in addition to what had been stated respecting hope and patience.—*Ed.*

[2] *Pareus* says, that this verb is taken metaphorically from assistance afforded to infants not able to support themselves, or to the sick, tottering and hardly able to walk.

" Coopitulatur" is *Calvin's* Latin—" co-assist;" *Beza's*, " una sublevat—lifts up together," that is, together with those who labour under infirmities. The *Vulgate* has " adjuvat—helps," like our version. *Schleusner* says, that it means to succour those whose strength is unequal to carry their burden alone. It is found in one other place, Luke x. 40. It is given by the *Septuagint* in Ps. lxxxix. 21, for אמץ—" to strengthen, to invigorate," and in Exod. xviii. 22, for נשא אתך—" to bear with," that is, " a burden with thee,"—the very idea that it seems to have here.—*Ed.*

from falling, and to keep us from being overwhelmed by any mass of evils. At the same time these supplies of the Spirit more clearly prove to us, that it is by God's appointment that we strive, by groanings and sighings, for our redemption.

For what we should pray for, &c. He had before spoken of the testimony of the Spirit, by which we know that God is our Father, and on which relying, we dare to call on him as our Father. He now again refers to the second part, invocation, and says, that we are taught by the same Spirit how to pray, and what to ask in our prayers. And appropriately has he annexed prayers to the anxious desires of the faithful; for God does not afflict them with miseries, that they may inwardly feed on hidden grief, but that they may disburden themselves by prayer, and thus exercise their faith.

At the same time I know, that there are various expositions of this passage;[1] but Paul seems to me to have simply meant this,—That we are blind in our addresses to God; for though we feel our evils, yet our minds are more disturbed and confused than that they can rightly choose what is meet and expedient. If any one makes this objection—that a rule is prescribed to us in God's word; to this I answer, that our thoughts nevertheless continue oppressed with darkness, until the Spirit guides them by his light.

But the Spirit himself intercedes,[2] &c. Though really or by the event it does not appear that our prayers have

---

[1] The opinions of *Chrysostom*, *Ambrose*, and *Origen*, are given by *Pareus*; and they are all different, and not much to the purpose. The view which *Augustine* gives is materially what is stated here. He gives a causative sense to the verb in the next clause, "Interpellare nos facit—he causes us to ask."—*Ed.*

[2] "Intercedit—ὑπερεντυγχάνει—abundantly intercedes," for so ὑπερ, prefixed to verbs, is commonly rendered. This is the proper action of an advocate, a name given to the Spirit by our Saviour, ἄλλον παράκλητον—"another advocate," not "comforter," as in our version; and Christ is called by the same name in 1 John ii. 1, and the same work, "interceding," is ascribed to him, Heb. vii. 25. But we learn in John xiv. 16, that the Spirit is an advocate *with us*—"that he may *abide with you* for ever;" and in 1 John ii. 1, that Christ is an advocate in heaven—"with the Father." The same name and a similar kind of work are ascribed to both. Some, as *Doddridge*, to avoid the blending the offices of the two, have rendered the verb here by a different term, but not wisely.—*Ed.*

been heard by God, yet Paul concludes, that the presence of the celestial favour does already shine forth in the desire for prayer; for no one can of himself give birth to devout and godly aspirations. The unbelieving do indeed blab out their prayers, but they only trifle with God; for there is in them nothing sincere, or serious, or rightly formed. Hence the manner of praying aright must be suggested by the Spirit: and he calls those groanings *unutterable*, into which we break forth by the impulse of the Spirit, for this reason—because they far exceed the capability of our own minds.[1] And the Spirit is said to *intercede*, not because he really humbles himself to pray or to groan, but because he stirs up in our hearts those desires which we ought to entertain; and he also affects our hearts in such a way that these desires by their fervency penetrate into heaven itself. And Paul has thus spoken, that he might more significantly ascribe the whole to the grace of the Spirit. We are indeed bidden to knock; but no one can of himself premeditate even one syllable, except God by the secret impulse of his Spirit knocks at our door, and thus opens for himself our hearts.

27. *But he who searches hearts*, &c. This is a remarkable reason for strengthening our confidence, that we are heard by God when we pray through his Spirit, for he thoroughly knows our desires, even as the thoughts of his own Spirit. And here must be noticed the suitableness of the word to *know;* for it intimates that God regards not these emotions of the Spirit as new and strange, or that he rejects them as unreasonable, but that he allows them, and at the same time kindly accepts them, as allowed and approved by him. As

---

[1] Or, " the comprehension of our mind—ingenii nostri captum." *Schleusner* says, that the word ἀλάλητος, has been improperly rendered ineffable or unutterable, and that the word to express such an idea is ἀνεκλάλητος, (1 Pet. i. 8,) and that from the analogy of the Greek language it must mean, " what is not uttered or spoken by the mouth ;" and he gives ἀκίνητον, " what is not moved," as an instance. *Bos* and *Grotius* give the same meaning, " sine voce—without voice ;" and the latter says, that this was expressly said, because the Jews entertained a notion that there could be no prayer except it was expressed by the lips. It is however considered by most to have the meaning given here, " inutterable," or ineffable, or inexpressible.—*Ed.*

then Paul had before testified, that God then aids us when he draws us as it were into his own bosom, so now he adds another consolation, that our prayers, of which he is the director, shall by no means be disappointed. The reason also is immediately added, because he thus conforms us to his own will. It hence follows, that in vain can never be what is agreeable to his will, by which all things are ruled. Let us also hence learn, that what holds the first place in prayer is consent with the will of the Lord, whom our wishes do by no means hold under obligation. If then we would have our prayers to be acceptable to God, we must pray that he may regulate them according to his will.

28. And we know that all things work together for good to them that love God, to them who are the called according to *his* purpose.	28. Novimus autem quòd iis qui diligunt Deum omnia cooperantur in bonum, iis scilicet qui secundum propositum vocati sunt sancti.
29. For whom he did foreknow, he also did predestinate *to be* conformed to the image of his Son, that he might be the firstborn among many brethren.	29. Quoniam quos præcognovit etiam præfinivit conformes imaginis Filii sui, ut sit ipse primogenitus inter multos fratres:
30. Moreover, whom he did predestinate, them he also called; and whom he called, them he also justified; and whom he justified, them he also glorified.	30. Quos vero præfinivit, eos et vocavit; et quos vocavit, eos etiam justificavit; et quos justificavit, eos etiam glorificavit.

28. *And we know,* &c. He now draws this conclusion from what had been said, that so far are the troubles of this life from hindering our salvation, that, on the contrary, they are helps to it. It is no objection that he sets down an illative particle, for it is no new thing with him to make somewhat an indiscriminate use of adverbs, and yet this conclusion includes what anticipates an objection. For the judgment of the flesh in this case exclaims, that it by no means appears that God hears our prayers, since our afflictions continue the same. Hence the Apostle anticipates this and says, that though God does not immediately succour his people, he yet does not forsake them, for by a wonderful contrivance he turns those things which seem to be evils in such a way as to promote their salvation. If any one prefers to read this verse by itself, as though Paul proceeded to a new argument in order to show that adversities which

assist our salvation, ought not to be borne as hard and grievous things, I do not object. At the same time, the design of Paul is not doubtful: "Though the elect and the reprobate are indiscriminately exposed to similar evils, there is yet a great difference; for God trains up the faithful by afflictions, and thereby promotes their salvation."

But we must remember that Paul speaks here only of adversities, as though he had said, "All things which happen to the saints are so overruled by God, that what the world regards as evil, the issue shows to be good." For though what *Augustine* says is true, that even the sins of the saints are, through the guiding providence of God, so far from doing harm to them, that, on the contrary, they serve to advance their salvation; yet this belongs not to this passage, the subject of which is the cross.

It must also be observed, that he includes the whole of true religion in the love of God, as on it depends the whole practice of righteousness.

Even to them who according to his purpose, &c. This clause seems to have been added as a modification, lest any one should think that the faithful, because they love God, obtain by their own merit the advantage of deriving such fruit from their adversities. We indeed know that when salvation is the subject, men are disposed to begin with themselves, and to imagine certain preparations by which they would anticipate the favour of God. Hence Paul teaches us, that those whom he had spoken of as loving God, had been previously chosen by him. For it is certain that the order is thus pointed out, that we may know that it proceeds from the gratuitous adoption of God, as from the first cause, that all things happen to the saints for their salvation. Nay, Paul shows that the faithful do not love God before they are called by him, as in another place he reminds us that the Galatians were known of God before they knew him. (Gal. iv. 9.) It is indeed true what Paul intimates, that afflictions avail not to advance the salvation of any but of those who love God; but that saying of John is equally true, that then only he is begun to be loved by us, when he anticipates us by his gratuitous love.

But the calling of which Paul speaks here, has a wide meaning, for it is not to be confined to the manifestation of election, of which mention is presently made, but is to be set simply in opposition to the course pursued by men; as though Paul had said,—"The faithful attain not religion by their own efforts, but are, on the contrary, led by the hand of God, inasmuch as he has chosen them to be a peculiar people to himself." The word *purpose* distinctly excludes whatever is imagined to be adduced mutually by men; as though Paul had denied, that the causes of our election are to be sought anywhere else, except in the secret good pleasure of God; which subject is more fully handled in the first chapter to the Ephesians, and in the first of the Second Epistle to Timothy; where also the contrast between this purpose and human righteousness is more distinctly set forth.[1] Paul, however, no doubt made here this express declaration,—that our salvation is based on the election of God, in order that he might make a transition to that which he immediately subjoined, namely, that by the same celestial decree, the afflictions, which conform us to Christ, have been appointed; and he did this for the purpose of connecting, as by a kind of necessary chain, our salvation with the bearing of the cross.

29. *For whom he has foreknown*, &c. He then shows, by the very order of election, that the afflictions of the faithful

---

[1] *Hammond* has a long note on the expression, κατὰ πρόθεσιν, and quotes *Cyril* of Jerusalem, *Clemens* of Alexandria, and *Theophylact*, as rendering the words, "according to *their* purpose," that is, those who love God,—a construction of itself strange, and wholly alien to the whole tenor of the passage, and to the use of the word in most other instances. Paul has never used the word, except in one instance, (2 Tim. iii. 10,) but with reference to God's purpose or decree,—see ch. ix. 11; Eph. i. 11; iii. 11; 2 Tim. i. 9. It seems that *Chrysostom*, *Origen*, *Theodoret*, and other Fathers, have given the same singularly strange explanation. But in opposition to these, *Poole* mentions *Ambrose*, *Augustine*, and even *Jerome*, as regarding "the purpose" here as that of God: in which opinion almost all modern Divines agree.

Grotius very justly observes, that κλητοί, the called, according to the language of Paul, mean those who obey the call, (*qui vocanti obediunt*,) and refers to ch. i. 6; 1 Cor. i. 24; Rev. xvii. 14. And *Stuart* says that the word has this meaning throughout the New Testament, except in two instances, Matt. xx. 16, and xxii. 14, where it means, invited. He therefore considers it as equivalent to ἐκλεκτοί, chosen, elected, or true Christians.—*Ed.*

are nothing else than the manner by which they are conformed to the image of Christ; and that this was necessary, he had before declared. There is therefore no reason for us to be grieved, or to think it hard and grievous, that we are afflicted, unless we disapprove of the Lord's election, by which we have been foreordained to life, and unless we are unwilling to bear the image of the Son of God, by which we are to be prepared for celestial glory.

But the foreknowledge of God, which Paul mentions, is not a bare prescience, as some unwise persons absurdly imagine, but the adoption by which he had always distinguished his children from the reprobate.[1] In the same sense Peter says, that the faithful had been elected to the sanctification of the Spirit according to the foreknowledge of God. Hence those, to whom I have alluded, foolishly draw this

[1] Much controversy has been about the meaning of the verb προέγνω, in this place. Many of the Fathers, such as *Jerome, Chrysostom,* and *Theodoret,* regarded it in the sense of simple prescience, as having reference to those who would believe and obey the gospel. The verb is found only in this place, and in the following passages, chap. xi. 2; Acts xxvi. 5; 1 Pet. i. 20; and 2 Pet. iii. 17. In the second, and in the last passage, it signifies merely a previous knowledge or acquaintance, and refers to men. In 1 Pet. i. 20, it is applied to Christ as having been " foreordained," according to our version, "before the foundation of the world." In this Epistle, chap. xi. 2, it refers to God,—" God hath not cast away his people whom he foreknew;" and according to the context, it means the same as elected; for the Apostle speaks of what God did " according to the election of grace," and not according to foreseen faith.

The noun derived from it is found in two places, Acts ii. 23, and 1 Pet. i. 2. In the first it evidently means decree, foreordination, and in the second, the same; where it is said, that those addressed by the Apostle were elected, " according to the foreknowledge of God, κατὰ πρόγνωσιν Θεοῦ, through the sanctification of the Spirit, *unto* obedience;" they were not then elected, according to God's foreknowledge or foreordination, *because* of their obedience. This entirely subverts the gloss put on the verb in this passage.

The usual meaning given to the verb here is fore-approved, or chosen. *Grotius, Turrettin,* and others, consider that γινώσκω has the same meaning with the verb ידע, in Hebrew, which is sometimes that of approving or favouring, or regarding with love and approbation. So the compound verb may be rendered here, "whom he fore-approved, or foreknew," as the objects of his choice: and this idea is what alone comports with the rest of the passage.

Stuart prefers another meaning, and that which it seems to have in 1 Pet. i. 20, " foreordained." He says that γινώσκω means sometimes to will, to determine, to ordain, to decree, and brings examples from *Josephus, Plutarch,* and *Polybius.* Then the compound verb would be here, " whom he foreordained," or foredetermined.—*Ed.*

inference,—That God has elected none but those whom he foresaw would be worthy of his grace. Peter does not indeed flatter the faithful, as though every one had been elected on account of his merit; but by reminding them of the eternal counsel of God, he wholly deprives them of all worthiness. So Paul does in this passage, who repeats by another word what he had said before of God's purpose. It hence follows, that this knowledge is connected with God's good pleasure; for he foreknew nothing out of himself, in adopting those whom he was pleased to adopt; but only marked out those whom he had purposed to elect.

The verb προορίζειν, which some translate, to *predestinate*, is to be understood according to what this passage requires; for Paul only meant, that God had so determined that all whom he has adopted should bear the image of Christ; nor has he simply said, that they were to be conformed to Christ, but to *the image of Christ*, that he might teach us that there is in Christ a living and conspicuous exemplar, which is exhibited to God's children for imitation. The meaning then is, that gratuitous adoption, in which our salvation consists, is inseparable from the other decree, which determines that we are to bear the cross; for no one can be an heir of heaven without being conformed to the image of the only-begotten Son of God.

That he may be, or, *that he might be, the first-born,* &c.; for the Greek infinitive, εἶναι, may be rendered in these two ways; but I prefer the first rendering. But in mentioning Christ's primogeniture, Paul meant only to express this,— that since Christ possesses a pre-eminence among the children of God, he is rightly given to us as a pattern, so that we ought to refuse nothing which he has been pleased to undergo. Hence, that the celestial Father may in every way bear testimony to the authority and honour which he has conferred on his own Son, he will have all those whom he adopts to be the heirs of his kingdom, to be conformed to his example. Though indeed the condition of the godly is apparently various, as there is a difference between the members of the same body, there is yet a connection between every one and his own head. As then the first-born sustains the name of the family, so Christ is placed in a state of preeminence, not only that he might excel in honour among the faithful, but also that he might include all under himself under the common name of brotherhood.

30. *And whom he has foredetermined,* (præfinivit,) *them has he also called,* &c. That he might now by a clearer proof show how true it is that a conformity with the humiliating state of Christ is for our good, he adopts a graduating process, by which he teaches us, that a participation of the cross is so connected with our vocation, justification, and, in short, with our future glory, that they can by no means be separated.

But that readers may better understand the Apostle's meaning, it may be well to repeat what I have already said, —that the word *foredetermine* does not refer to election, but to that purpose or decree of God by which he has ordained that the cross is to be borne by his people; and by declaring that they are now called, he intimates, that God had not kept concealed what he had determined respecting them, but had made it known, that they might resignedly and humbly submit to the condition allotted to them; for calling here is to be distinguished from secret election, as being posterior to it. That none then may make this objection—that it appears to no one what lot God has appointed for him, the Apostle says, that God by his calling bears an evident testimony respecting his hidden purpose. But this testimony is not only found in the outward preaching of the gospel, but it has also the power of the Spirit connected with it; for the elect are there spoken of, whom God not only addresses by the outward word, but whom he also inwardly draws.

Justification may fitly be extended to the unremitted continuance of God's favour, from the time of our calling to the hour of death; but as Paul uses this word throughout the Epistle, for gratuitous imputation of righteousness, there is no necessity for us to deviate from this meaning. What Paul indeed had in view was to show that a more precious compensation is offered to us, than what ought to allow us to shun afflictions; for what is more desirable than to be reconciled to God, so that our miseries may no longer be tokens of a curse, nor lead us to ruin?

He then immediately adds, that those who are now pressed down by the cross shall be *glorified;* so that their sorrows and reproaches shall bring them no loss. Though glorification is not yet exhibited except in our Head, yet as we in a manner behold in him our inheritance of eternal life, his glory brings to us such assurance respecting our own glory, that our hope may be justly compared to a present possession.

We may add, that Paul, imitating the style of the Hebrew language, adopts in these verbs the past instead of the present tense.[1] A continued act is no doubt what is meant, according to this import, " Those whom God now, consistently with his purpose, exercises under the cross, are called and justified, that they may have a hope of salvation, so that nothing of their glory decays during their humiliation; for though their present miseries deform it before the world, yet before God and angels it always shines forth as perfect." What Paul then means by this gradation is, That the afflictions of the faithful, by which they are now humbled, are intended for this end—that the faithful, having obtained the glory of the celestial kingdom, may reach the glory of Christ's resurrection, with whom they are now crucified.

31. What shall we then say to these things? If God *be* for us, who *can be* against us?	31. Quid ergo dicemus ad hæc?[2] Si Deus pro nobis, quis contra nos?
32. He that spared not his own Son, but delivered him up for us all, how shall he not with him also freely give us all things?	32. Qui proprio Filio non pepercit, sed pro nobis omnibus tradidit, quomodo non etiam cum eo donaret nobis omnia?
33. Who shall lay any thing to the charge of God's elect? *It is* God that justifieth.	33. Quis intentabit crimina[3] adversùs electos Dei? Deus est qui justificat.

[1] *Turrettin* gives somewhat a different reason: " Paul speaks of these things as past, because they are as already done in God's decree, and in order to show the certainty of their accomplishment."

[2] " Ad hæc,"—πρὸς ταῦτα. *Wolfius* says, that it should be " de his—of these things;" and Heb. iv. 13, is quoted as an instance, " πρὸς ὃν ἡμῖν ὁ λόγος—of whom we speak." —*Ed.*

[3] " Quis intentabit crimina—who shall charge crimes;" " τίς ἐγκαλέσει κατὰ ἐκλεκτῶν Θεοῦ—who shall implead, or bring a charge against the elect of God?" See Acts xix. 38.

Many, such as *Augustine, Grotius, Locke, Doddridge,* and *Griesbach,*

34. Who *is* he that condemneth? It *is* Christ that died, yea rather, that is risen again, who is even at the right hand of God, who also maketh intercession for us.	34. Quis ille qui condemnet? Christus est qui mortuus est, quin potius etiam suscitatus, qui et in dexterâ Patris est, qui et intercedit pro nobis.

31. *What then*, &c. The subject discussed having been sufficiently proved, he now breaks out into exclamations, by which he sets forth the magnanimity with which the faithful ought to be furnished when adversities urge them to despond. And he teaches us in these words that with the paternal favour of God is connected that invincible courage which overcomes all temptations. We indeed know, that judgment is usually formed of the love or of the hatred of God, in no other way than by a view of our present state; hence when things fall out untowardly, sorrow takes possession of our minds, and drives away all confidence and consolation. But Paul loudly exclaims, that a deeper principle ought to be inquired after, and that they reason absurdly who confine themselves to the sad spectacle of our present warfare. I indeed allow, that the scourges of God are in themselves justly deemed to be tokens of God's wrath; but as they are consecrated in Christ, Paul bids the saints to lay hold, above all things, on the paternal love of God, that relying on this shield they may boldly triumph over all evils; for this is a brazen wall to us, so that while God is propitious to us we shall be safe against all dangers. He does not, however, mean, that nothing shall oppose us; but he promises a victory over all kinds of enemies.

If God be for us, &c. This is the chief and the only support which can sustain us in every temptation. For except we have God propitious to us, though all things should smile on us, yet no sure confidence can be attained: but,

---

have made the next clause also a question; and also the clauses in the next verse. There is not much difference in the sense, but the passage will thus appear more striking,—
33. Who will lay a charge against God's elect? God the justifier?
34. Who is he who condemns? Christ who died, or rather who rose again, who is also at God's right hand, and who intercedes for us?
What favours this construction is, that the Apostle proceeds in the same strain.—*Ed.*

on the other hand, his favour alone is a sufficient solace in every sorrow, a protection sufficiently strong against all the storms of adversities. And on this subject there are many testimonies of Scripture, which show that when the saints rely on the power of God alone, they dare to despise whatever is opposed to them in the world. "When I walk in the midst of the shadow of death, I shall not fear evils, for thou art with me." (Ps. xxiii. 4.) "In the Lord I trust: what shall flesh do to me." (Ps. lvi. 11.) "I shall not fear the thousands of the people who beset me." (Ps. iii. 6.) For there is no power either under or above the heavens, which can resist the arm of God. Having him then as our defender, we need fear no harm whatever. Hence he alone shows real confidence in God, who being content with his protection, dreads nothing in such a way as to despond; the faithful are doubtless often shaken but are never utterly cast down. In short, the Apostle's object was to show, that the godly soul ought to rely on the inward testimony of the Holy Spirit, and not to depend on outward things.

32. *He who has not spared his own Son*, &c. As it greatly concerns us to be so thoroughly persuaded of the paternal love of God, as to be able to retain our rejoicing on its account, Paul brings forward the price of our redemption in order to prove that God favours us: and doubtless it is a remarkable and clear evidence of inappreciable love, that the Father refused not to bestow his Son for our salvation. And so Paul draws an argument from the greater to the less, that as he had nothing dearer, or more precious, or more excellent than his Son, he will neglect nothing of what he foresees will be profitable to us.[1]

This passage ought to remind us of what Christ brings to us, and to awaken us to contemplate his riches; for as he is a pledge of God's infinite love towards us, so he has not been

---

[1] *Calvin* renders χαρίσεται by "donaret;" *Capellus* more fully, "gratis donabit—will gratuitously give." Christ himself, and everything that comes with or through him, is a favour freely bestowed, and not what we merit. This shuts out, as *Pareus* observes, everything as meritorious on the part of man. All is grace. The "all things" include every thing necessary for salvation—every grace now and eternal glory hereafter.—*Ed.*

sent to us void of blessings or empty, but filled with all celestial treasures, so that they who possess him may not want anything necessary for their perfect felicity. To *deliver* up means here to expose to death.

33. *Who shall bring an accusation,* &c. The first and the chief consolation of the godly in adversities, is to be fully persuaded of the paternal kindness of God; for hence arises the certainty of their salvation, and that calm quietness of the soul through which it comes that adversities are sweetened, or at least the bitterness of sorrow mitigated. Hardly then a more suitable encouragement to patience could be adduced than this, a conviction that God is propitious to us; and hence Paul makes this confidence the main ground of that consolation, by which it behoves the faithful to be strengthened against all evils. And as the salvation of man is first assailed by accusation, and then subverted by condemnation, he in the first place averts the danger of accusation. There is indeed but one God, at whose tribunal we must stand; then there is no room for accusation when he justifies us. The antithetic clauses seem not indeed to be exactly arranged; for the two parts which ought rather to have been set in opposition to each other are these: " Who shall accuse ? Christ is he who intercedes :" and then these two might have been connected, " Who shall condemn ? God is he who justifies ;" for God's absolution answers to condemnation, and Christ's intercession to accusation. But Paul has not without reason made another arrangement, as he was anxious to arm the children of God, as they say, from head to foot, with that confidence which banishes all anxieties and fears. He then more emphatically concludes, that the children of God are not subject to an accusation, because God justifies, than if he had said that Christ is our advocate; for he more fully expresses that the way to a trial is more completely closed up when the judge himself pronounces him wholly exempt from guilt, whom the accuser would bring in as deserving of punishment. There is also a similar reason for the second clause; for he shows that the faithful are very far from being involved in the danger of condemnation, since Christ by expiating their sins has an-

ticipated the judgment of God, and by his intercession not only abolishes death, but also covers our sins in oblivion, so that they come not to an account.

The drift of the whole is, that we are not only freed from terror by present remedies, but that God comes to our aid beforehand, that he may better provide for our confidence.

But it must be here observed, as we have before reminded you, that to be justified, according to Paul, is to be absolved by the sentence of God, and to be counted just; and it is not difficult to prove this from the present passage, in which he reasons by affirming one thing which nullifies its opposite; for to absolve and to regard persons as guilty, are contrary things. Hence God will allow no accusation against us, because he has absolved us from all sins. The devil no doubt is an accuser of all the godly: the very law of God and their own conscience convict them; but all these prevail nothing with the judge, who justifies them. Therefore no adversary can shake or endanger our salvation.

Further, he so mentions the elect, as one who doubted not but that he was of their number; and he knew this, not by special revelation, (as some sophists falsely imagine,) but by a perception (*sensu*—feeling) common to all the godly. What then is here said of the elect, every one of the godly, according to the example of Paul, may apply to himself; for this doctrine would have been not only frigid, but wholly lifeless, had he buried election in the secret purpose of God. But when we know, that there is here designedly set before us what every one of the godly ought to appropriate to himself, there is no doubt but that we are all encouraged to examine our calling, so that we may become assured that we are the children of God.

34. *Who is he that condemns?* &c. As no one by accusing can prevail, when the judge absolves; so there remains no condemnation, when satisfaction is given to the laws, and the penalty is already paid. Now Christ is he, who, having once for all suffered the punishment due to us, thereby declared that he undertook our cause, in order to deliver us: he then who seeks hereafter to condemn us, must bring back Christ himself to death again. But he has not only died,

but also came forth, by a resurrection, as the conqueror of death, and triumphed over all its power.

He adds still more,—that he now *sits* at the right hand of the Father; by which is meant, that he possesses dominion over heaven and earth, and full power and rule over all things, according to what is said in Eph. i. 20. He teaches us also, that he thus sits, that he may be a perpetual advocate and intercessor in securing our salvation. It hence follows, that when any one seeks to condemn us, he not only seeks to render void the death of Christ, but also contends with that unequalled power with which the Father has honoured him, and who with that power conferred on him supreme authority. This so great an assurance, which dares to triumph over the devil, death, sin, and the gates of hell, ought to lodge deep in the hearts of all the godly; for our faith is nothing, except we feel assured that Christ is ours, and that the Father is in him propitious to us. Nothing then can be devised more pestilent and ruinous, than the scholastic dogma respecting the uncertainty of salvation.

Who intercedes, &c. It was necessary expressly to add this, lest the Divine majesty of Christ should terrify us. Though, then, from his elevated throne he holds all things in subjection under his feet, yet Paul represents him as a Mediator; whose presence it would be strange for us to dread, since he not only kindly invites us to himself, but also appears an intercessor for us before the Father. But we must not measure this intercession by our carnal judgment; for we must not suppose that he humbly supplicates the Father with bended knees and expanded hands; but as he appears continually, as one who died and rose again, and as his death and resurrection stand in the place of eternal intercession, and have the efficacy of a powerful prayer for reconciling and rendering the Father propitious to us, he is justly said to intercede for us.

35. Who shall separate us from the love of Christ? *shall* tribulation,

35. Quis nos dirimet[1] à dilectione Christi? tribulatio, an angustia, an

---

[1] "Dirimet—break us off," divide or part us; χωρίσει—set apart, sever, separate: τίς, "who," may be rendered, "what," as מי in Hebrew. It is not put, it may be, in the neuter gender, because of the gender of the nouns

or distress, or persecution, or famine, or nakedness, or peril, or sword?

36. As it is written, For thy sake we are killed all the day long; we are accounted as sheep for the slaughter.

37. Nay, in all these things we are more than conquerors, through him that loved us.

persequutio, an fames, an nuditas, an periculum, an gladius?

36. Quemadmodum scriptum est, Quòd propter te morimur quotidie, reputati sumus tanquam oves mactationi destinatæ:

37. Sed in iis omnibus supervincimus per eum qui dilexit nos.

35. *Who shall separate us,* &c. The conviction of safety is now more widely extended, even to lower things; for he who is persuaded of God's kindness towards him, is able to stand firm in the heaviest afflictions. These usually harass men in no small degree, and for various reasons,—because they interpret them as tokens of God's wrath, or think themselves to be forsaken by God, or see no end to them, or neglect to meditate on a better life, or for other similar reasons; but when the mind is purged from such mistakes, it becomes calm, and quietly rests. But the import of the words is,—That whatever happens, we ought to stand firm in this faith,—that God, who once in his love embraced us, never ceases to care for us. For he does not simply say that there is nothing which can tear God away from his love to us; but he means, that the knowledge and lively sense of the love which he testifies to us is so vigorous in our hearts, that it always shines in the darkness of afflictions: for as clouds, though they obscure the clear brightness of the sun, do not yet wholly deprive us of its light; so God, in adversities, sends forth through the darkness the rays of his favour, lest temptations should overwhelm us with despair; nay, our faith, supported by God's promises as by wings, makes its way upward to heaven through all the intervening obstacles. It is indeed true, that adversities are tokens of God's wrath, when viewed in themselves; but when pardon and reconciliation precede, we ought to be assured that God, though he chastises us, yet never forgets his mercy: he

which follow. As the Hebrews use often the future for the potential mood, so the case may be here—" What can separate us from the love of Christ? tribulation, or distress?" &c. It ought also to be added, that the verb " separate," is used to designate divorce or separation between man and his wife. See Matt. xix. 6; 1 Cor. vii. 20, 11, 15.—*Ed.*

indeed thus reminds us of what we have deserved; but he no less testifies, that our salvation is an object of his care, while he leads us to repentance.

But he calls it *the love of Christ,* and for this reason,— because the Father has in a manner opened his compassions to us in him. As then the love of God is not to be sought out of Christ, Paul rightly directs to him our attention, so that our faith may behold, in the rays of Christ's favour, the serene countenance of the Father. The meaning is,— that in no adversities ought our confidence to be shaken as to this truth—that when God is propitious, nothing can be adverse to us. Some take this love in a passive sense, for that by which he is loved by us, as though Paul would have us armed with invincible courage;[1] but this comment may be easily disproved by the whole tenor of Paul's reasoning; and Paul himself will presently remove all doubt by defining more clearly what this love is.

Tribulation, or distress, or persecution? &c. The pronoun masculine which he used at the beginning of the verse, contains a hidden power: for when he might have adopted the neuter gender and said—" What shall separate us?" &c., he preferred ascribing personality to things without life, and for this end,—that he might send forth with us into the contest as many champions as there are of temptations to try our faith.

---

[1] According to *Poole,* several of the Fathers entertained this opinion, such as *Origen, Chrysostom, Theodoret,* and *Ambrose:* but even *Hammond* and *Grotius,* great admirers of the Fathers, regard this love as that of God or of Christ to us. *Wolfius* says, that all the Lutheran divines give this exposition. It is indeed impossible rightly to view the whole passage without seeing that this explanation is the true one. In verse 32, it is incontestably evident that God's love to us is what is spoken of: then in verse 37, it is expressly said, "through him who loved us;" and the last verse seems sufficient to remove every possible doubt. The difficulty of *Barnes,* in thinking it " not conceivable how afflictions should have any tendency to alienate Christ's love *from us,*" arises from a misconception: for when we speak of not being separated from the love of Christ, the obvious meaning is, that nothing can separate us from participating in the effects of his love, that He, on account of his love, will sustain us under the greatest trials, and make " us more than conquerors." The substance of what is here said, is contained in the last clause of verse 32,—" How shall he not with him also freely give us all things?" It was the assurance of this truth that the Apostle obviously intended to convey.—*Ed.*

But these three things have this difference: *tribulation* includes every kind of trouble or evil; *distress* is an inward feeling, when difficulties reduce us to such an extremity, so that we know not what course to pursue. Such was the anxiety of Abraham and of Lot, when one was constrained to expose his wife to the danger of prostitution, and the other, his daughters; for being brought to straits and being perplexed, they found no way of escape. *Persecution* properly denotes the tyrannical violence by which the children of God were undeservedly harassed by the ungodly. Now though Paul denies in 2 Cor. iv. 8, that the children of God are reduced to straits, στενοχωρεῖσθαι, he does not yet disagree with himself; for he does not simply make them to be exempt from anxious solicitude, but he means that they are delivered from it, as also the examples of Abraham and Lot testify.

36. *As it is written*, &c. This testimony adds no small weight to the subject; for he intimates, that the dread of death is so far from being a reason to us for falling away, that it has been almost ever the lot of God's servants to have death as it were present before their eyes. It is indeed probable, that in that Psalm the miserable oppression of the people under the tyranny of Antiochus is described; for it is expressly said, that the worshippers of God were cruelly treated, for no other reason but through hatred to true religion. There is also added a remarkable protestation, that they had not departed from the covenant of God; which Paul, I think, had especially in view. It is no objection that the saints there complain of a calamity which then unusually pressed on them; for since they show, that they were oppressed with so many evils, having before testified their innocence, an argument is hence fitly drawn, that it is no new thing for the Lord to permit his saints to be undeservedly exposed to the cruelty of the ungodly. But this is not done except for their good; for the Scripture teaches us, that it is alien to the righteousness of God to destroy the just with the wicked, (Gen. xviii. 23); but that, on the contrary, it is meet for him to requite affliction to those who afflict, and rest to those who are afflicted. (2 Thess. i. 6, 9.)

And then they affirm that they suffer for the Lord; and Christ pronounces them blessed who suffer for the sake of righteousness. (Matt. v. 10.) By saying that they *died daily*, they intimated that death was so suspended over them, that their life differed but little from death.

37. *We do more than conquer,* &c.; that is, we always struggle and emerge. I have retained the word used by Paul,[1] though not commonly used by the Latins. It indeed sometimes happens that the faithful seem to succumb and to lie forlorn; and thus the Lord not only tries, but also humbles them. This issue is however given to them,—that they obtain the victory.

That they might at the same time remember whence this invincible power proceeds, he again repeats what he had said before: for he not only teaches us that God, because he loves us, supports us by his hand; but he also confirms the same truth by mentioning the love of Christ.[2] And this one sentence sufficiently proves, that the Apostle speaks not here of the fervency of that love which we have towards God, but of the paternal kindness of God and of Christ towards us, the assurance of which, being thoroughly fixed in our hearts, will always draw us from the gates of hell into the light of life, and will sufficiently avail for our support.

[1] " Supervincimus "—ὑπερνικῶμεν; *Beza's* version is, " amplius quam victores sumus;" *Macknight's*, " we do more than overcome;" *Schleusner* gives this as one of his explanations, " plenissime vincimus—we most fully overcome." Paul commonly uses ὑπὲρ in an enhansive sense; so the version may be, " we abundantly overcome," as though he said, " We have strength given us which far exceeds the power of evils." Some say that the faithful abundantly overcome, because they sustain no real loss, but like silver in the furnace, they lose only their dross; and not only so, but they also carry, as it were from the field of battle, rich spoils—the fruits of holiness and righteousness. Heb. xii. 10, 11. It is further said, that the victory will be this,—that Christ, who has loved them, will raise them from death and adorn them with that glory, with which all the evils of this life are not worthy to be compared.

Beza says, " Not only we are not broken down by so many evils nor despond, but we even glory in the cross."—*Ed.*

[2] " Per eum qui dilexit nos—διὰ τοῦ ἀγαπήσαντος ἡμᾶς—through him who has loved us." The aorist participle, says *Wolfius*, extends to every time, " who has loved and loves and will love us." From the fact that believers are overcome by no calamities, he draws the inference, that God's love is constant and most effectual, so that he is present with the distressed to give them courage, to strengthen their patience, and to moderate their calamities. See 1 Pet. v. 10.—*Ed.*

38. For I am persuaded, that neither death, nor life, nor angels, nor principalities, nor powers, nor things present, nor things to come,	38. Persuasus enim sum, quòd neque mors, neque vita,[1] neque angeli, neque principatus, neque virtutes, neque præsentia, neque futura,
39. Nor height, nor depth, nor any other creature, shall be able to separate us from the love of God, which is in Christ Jesus our Lord.	39. Neque altitudo, neque profunditas, neque ulla alia creatura, poterit nos dirimere à charitate Dei, quæ est in Christo Iesu.

38. He is now carried away into hyperbolic expressions, that he might confirm us more fully in those things which are to be experienced. Whatever, he says, there is in life or in death, which seems capable of tearing us away from God, shall effect nothing; nay, the very angels, were they to attempt to overturn this foundation, shall do us no harm. It is no objection, that angels are ministering spirits, appointed for the salvation of the elect, (Heb. i. 14:) for Paul reasons here on what is impossible, as he does in Gal. i. 8; and we may hence observe, that all things ought to be deemed of no worth, compared with the glory of God, since it is lawful to dishonour even angels in vindicating his truth.[2] Angels are also meant by *principalities* and *powers*,[3] and they are so called, because they are the primary instruments of the Divine power: and these two words were added, that if the word angels sounded too insignificant, something more might be expressed. But you would, perhaps, prefer this meaning, "Nor angels, and whatever powers there may be;" which is a mode of speaking that is used, when we refer to things unknown to us, and exceeding our capacities.

Nor present things, nor future things, &c. Though he

[1] Neither *death* threatened by persecutors, nor *life* promised on recantation.—*Ed.*

[2] Some of the Fathers, *Jerome, Chrysostom*, &c., have taken the same view, regarding the Apostle as speaking of good angels, as it were, hypothetically, as in Gal. i. 8. But *Grotius*, and many others, consider *evil* angels to be meant. Probably, angels, without any regard to what they are, are intended.—*Ed.*

[3] *Grotius* considers the words as being the abstract for the concrete, Princes and Potentates; being called ἀρχαὶ, as some think, as being the first, the chief in authority, and δυνάμεις, as having power. "By these words," says *Beza*, "Paul is wont to designate the character of spirits,— of the good in Eph. i. 21; Col. i. 16;—and of the bad in Eph. vi. 12; Col. ii. 15." Hence the probability is, that the words designate different ranks among angelic powers, without any reference to their character, whether good or evil.—*Ed.*

speaks hyperbolically, yet he declares, that by no length of time can it be effected, that we should be separated from the Lord's favour: and it was needful to add this; for we have not only to struggle with the sorrow which we feel from present evils, but also with the fear and the anxiety with which impending dangers may harass us.[1] The meaning then is,—that we ought not to fear, lest the continuance of evils, however long, should obliterate the faith of adoption.

This declaration is clearly against the schoolmen, who idly talk and say, that no one is certain of final perseverance, except through the gift of special revelation, which they make to be very rare. By such a dogma the whole faith is destroyed, which is certainly nothing, except it extends to death and beyond death. But we, on the contrary, ought to feel confident, that he who has begun in us a good work, will carry it on until the day of the Lord Jesus.[2]

---

[1] "Neither the evils we now feel, nor those which may await us,"—*Grotius*; rather, "Neither things which now exist, nor things which shall be."—*Ed.*

[2] The words, "neither height nor depth," are left unnoticed, $ὕψωμα$, $βάθος$. The first, says *Mede*, means prosperity, and the latter, adversity. *Grotius* regards what is meant as the *height* of honour, and the *depth* of disgrace. "Neither heaven nor hell," say others; "neither heaven nor earth," according to *Schleusner*. "Things in heaven and things on earth," is the explanation of *Chrysostom*. The first, $ὕψωμα$, is only found here and in 2 Cor. x. 5. Like מרום in Hebrew, it means what is high and elevated, and may, like that, sometimes signify heaven: and $βάθος$ is not earth, but what is deeper; it means a deep soil, Matt. xiii. 5,—the deep sea, Luke v. 4,—and in the plural, things deep and inscrutable, 1 Cor. ii. 10; it may therefore be very properly taken here for hell.

That the words are to be thus taken seems probable from the gradation evident in the passage. In the first catalogue in verse 35, he mentions the evils arising from this world, its trials and its persecutions, and those ending in death. In the second, after repeating the utmost length to which worldly persecutors can go, "death or life," he ascends the invisible world, and mentions angels, then their combined powers, then the powers which do and may exist, then both heaven and hell, and, that he might include everything, except the uncreated God himself, he finishes with the words, "nor any created thing."

The whole passage is sublime in an extraordinary degree. The contrast is the grandest that can be conceived. Here is the Christian, all weakness in himself, despised and trampled under foot by the world, triumphing over all existing, and all possible, and even impossible evils and opposition, having only this as his stay and support—that the God who has loved him, will never cease to love, keep, and defend him; yea, were everything created, everything except God himself, leagued against him and attempting his ruin.—*Ed.*

39. *Which is in Christ,* &c. That is, of which Christ is the bond; for he is the beloved Son, in whom the Father is well pleased. If, then, we are through him united to God, we may be assured of the immutable and unfailing kindness of God towards us. He now speaks here more distinctly than before, as he declares that the fountain of love is in the Father, and affirms that it flows to us from Christ.

CHAPTER IX.

1. I say the truth in Christ, I lie not, my conscience also bearing me witness in the Holy Ghost,
2. That I have great heaviness and continual sorrow in my heart.
3. For I could wish that myself were accursed from Christ for my brethren, my kinsmen according to the flesh:
4. Who are Israelites; to whom *pertaineth* the adoption, and the glory, and the covenants, and the giving of the law, and the service *of God,* and the promises;
5. Whose *are* the fathers, and of whom, as concerning the flesh, Christ *came,* who is over all, God blessed for ever. Amen.

1. Veritatem dico in Christo, non mentior, testimonium simul mihi reddente mea conscientia cum Spiritu sancto,
2. Quòd dolor sit mihi magnus, et assiduus cruciatus cordi meo:
3. Optarim enim ego ipse anathema esse à Christo pro fratribus meis, cognatis inquam meis secundum carnem;
4. Qui sunt Israelitæ, quorum est adoptio, et gloria, et testamenta, et legislatio, et cultus, et promissiones;
5. Quorum sunt Patres, et ex quibus est Christus secundum carnem, qui est super omnia Deus benedictus in secula. Amen.

In this chapter he begins to remove the offences which might have diverted the minds of men from Christ: for the Jews, for whom he was appointed according to the covenant of the law, not only rejected him, but regarded him with contempt, and for the most part hated him. Hence one of two things seemed to follow,—either that there was no truth in the Divine promise,—or that Jesus, whom Paul preached, was not the Lord's anointed, who had been especially promised to the Jews. This twofold knot Paul fully unties in what follows. He, however, so handles this subject, as to abstain from all bitterness against the Jews, that he might not exasperate their minds; and yet he concedes to them nothing to the injury of the gospel; for he allows to them their privileges in such a way, as not to detract anything from Christ. But he passes, as it were abruptly, to the mention of this subject, so that there appears to be no connection in the discourse.[1] He, however, so enters on this new subject, as though he had before referred to it. It so happened in this way,—Having finished the doctrine he discussed, he turned his attention to the Jews, and being astonished at their unbelief as at something monstrous, he burst forth into this sudden protestation, in the same way as though it was a subject which he had previously handled; for there was no one to whom this thought would not of itself immediately occur,—" If this be the doctrine of the law and the Prophets, how comes it that the Jews so pertinaciously reject it ?" And further, it was everywhere known, that all that he had hitherto spoken of the law of Moses, and of the grace of Christ, was more disliked by the Jews, than that the faith of the Gentiles should be assisted by their consent. It was therefore necessary to remove this obstacle, lest it should impede the course of the gospel.

1. *The truth I say in Christ*, &c. As it was an opinion entertained by most that Paul was, as it were, a sworn enemy to his own nation, and as it was suspected somewhat even by the household of faith, as though he had taught them to forsake Moses, he adopts a preface to prepare the minds of his readers, before he proceeds to his subject, and in this preface he frees himself from the false suspicion of evil will towards the Jews. And as the matter was not unworthy of an oath, and as he perceived that his affirmation would hardly be otherwise believed against a prejudice already entertained, he declares by an oath that he speaks the

[1] The connection seems to be this: he had been speaking of the impossibility of separating God's people from the protecting influence and preserving power of his love; he had clearly shown, that no divorce or separation can take place through any possible circumstances. Then the Jews might say, "If this be true, then we are safe, we are still God's people." Hence he proceeds to remove this objection, and in order to prepare their mind to receive what he is going to say and to prove, he speaks first of his deep concern for their welfare: and then he resumes the doctrine he touched upon in verses 28, 29, and 30 of the former chapter, and illustrates it by a reference to the past dealings of God with the Jews, and proves it by passages from the ancient Prophets. He shows that God's people are the called according to his purpose, and not all who wear the outward symbol of his covenant.—*Ed.*

truth. By this example and the like, (as I reminded you in the first chapter,) we ought to learn that oaths are lawful, that is, when they render that truth credible which is necessary to be known, and which would not be otherwise believed.

The expression, *In Christ,* means "according to Christ."[1] By adding *I lie not,* he signifies that he speaks without fiction or disguise. *My conscience testifying to me,* &c. By these words he calls his own conscience before the tribunal of God, for he brings in the Spirit as a witness to his feeling. He adduced the Spirit for this end, that he might more fully testify that he was free and pure from an evil disposition, and that he pleaded the cause of Christ under the guidance and direction of the Spirit of God. It often happens that a person, blinded by the passions of the flesh, (though not purposing to deceive,) knowingly and wilfully obscures the light of truth. But to swear by the name of God, in a proper sense of the word, is to call him as a witness for the purpose of confirming what is doubtful, and at the same time to bind ourselves over to his judgment, in case we say what is false.

2. *That I have great sorrow,* &c. He dexterously manages so to cut short his sentence as not yet to express what he was going to say; for it was not as yet seasonable openly to mention the destruction of the Jewish nation. It may be added, that he thus intimates a greater measure of sorrow, as imperfect sentences are for the most part full of pathos.

[1] "Idem valet ac secundum Christum,—it is the same with According to Christ;" "λέγω ἐν Χριστῷ—I speak in Christ," that is, as a Christian; to be in Christ and to be a Christian is the same. This idea bears on the import of the passage more than any other. It is as though he said, "Though I am in Christ or a Christian, yet I tell you this as the truth or the fact, and I have the testimony of conscience enlightened by the Spirit, that I have great grief and unceasing sorrow on your account." The Jews had the impression that the Apostle, having become the follower of Christ, must have necessarily entertained hatred towards them, and must have therefore felt no concern for them; for this is really the case with all *real* apostates, that is, with those who leave the truth for error, but not with them who leave error for the truth. To obviate this impression seems to have been the object here. How the idea of an oath comports with what follows it is difficult to see. It is no argument to say that ἐν here means the same as in Matt. v. 34, where it follows the verb "to swear." There is a passage similar to this in Eph. iv. 17; but ἐν κυρίῳ there clearly signifies "by the Lord's authority." We may add, that to swear by Christ would have had no influence on the Jews.—*Ed.*

But he will presently express the cause of his sorrow, after having more fully testified his sincerity.

But the perdition of the Jews caused very great anguish to Paul, though he knew that it happened through the will and providence of God. We hence learn that the obedience we render to God's providence does not prevent us from grieving at the destruction of lost men, though we know that they are thus doomed by the just judgment of God; for the same mind is capable of being influenced by these two feelings: that when it looks to God it can willingly bear the ruin of those whom he has decreed to destroy; and that when it turns its thoughts to men, it condoles with their evils. They are then much deceived, who say that godly men ought to have apathy and insensibility, (ἀπάθειαν καὶ ἀναλγησίαν,) lest they should resist the decree of God.

3. *For I could wish*, &c. He could not have expressed a greater ardour of love than by what he testifies here; for that is surely perfect love which refuses not to die for the salvation of a friend. But there is another word added, *anathema*, which proves that he speaks not only of temporal but of eternal death; and he explains its meaning when he says, *from Christ*, for it signifies a separation. And what is to be separated from Christ, but to be excluded from the hope of salvation? It was then a proof of the most ardent love, that Paul hesitated not to wish for himself that condemnation which he saw impending over the Jews, in order that he might deliver them. It is no objection that he knew that his salvation was based on the election of God, which could by no means fail; for as those ardent feelings hurry us on impetuously, so they see and regard nothing but the object in view. So Paul did not connect God's election with his wish, but the remembrance of that being passed by, he was wholly intent on the salvation of the Jews.

Many indeed doubt whether this was a lawful desire; but this doubt may be thus removed: the settled boundary of love is, that it proceeds as far as conscience permits;[1] if

---

[1] " Ut ad aras usque procedat." *Ainsworth* gives a similar phrase and explains its reason, " Usque ad aras amicus—As far as conscience permits," *Gell.*, because in swearing they held the horns of the altar.—*Ed.*

then we love in God and not without God's authority, our love can never be too much. And such was the love of Paul; for seeing his own nation endued with so many of God's benefits, he loved God's gifts in them, and them on account of God's gifts; and he deemed it a great evil that those gifts should perish, hence it was that his mind being overwhelmed, he burst forth into this extreme wish.[1]

[1] Most of those who take this view of the passage express the implied condition more distinctly than is done here. They have regarded the wish in this sense, "I could wish were it right or lawful." So thought *Chrysostom, Photius, Theophylact, Luther, Pareus, Beza, Estius, Lightfoot, Witsius, Mede, Whitby,* and others. The words of *Photius* are given by *Wolfius,* "He says not, I wish to be separated, but I could wish, that is, were it possible—ηὐχόμην ἄν, τουτ' ἐστιν, εἰ δυνατὸν ἦν." *Stuart* and *Hodge* adopt the same view. "It was a conditional wish," says *Pareus,* "like that of Christ in Matt. xxvi. 39. Christ knew and Paul knew that it could not be granted, and yet both expressed their strong desire." See Ex. xxxii. 32.

Almost all critics agree that the Vulgate is wrong in rendering the verb *optabam*—"I did wish," as though the Apostle referred to the time, as *Ambrose* supposed, when he was a Pharisee; but this is wholly inconsistent with the tenor of the passage. *Erasmus, Grotius, Beza,* and most others regard the verb as having an optative meaning; ἄν being understood after it, as the case is with ἐβουλόμην in Acts xxv. 22, and ἤθελον in Gal. iv. 20.

There are two other opinions which deserve notice. The first is, that "anathema" here means excommunication, and that "from Christ" signifies from his Church, Christ the head being taken for his body the Church, as in 1 Cor. xii. 12, and in Gal. iii. 27, according to the manner of the Hebrews, as *Grotius* says, who called the wife by the name of the husband. Is. iv. 1. This is the view taken by *Hammond, Grotius,* and some of the Lutheran divines. But the word "anathema" has not in Scripture this meaning, though in after-ages it had attained it both in the Church and among the Rabbins. In the New Testament it occurs only here and in Acts xxiii. 14; 1 Cor. xii. 3; xvi. 22; and Gal. i. 8, 9; and the verb ἀναθεματίζω is found in Mark xiv. 71; Acts xxiii. 12, 14, 21; and with κατὰ prefixed in Matt. xxvi. 74. The corresponding word in Hebrew, חרם, rendered "anathema" by the *Septuagint,* means two things: what is separated for a holy purpose and wholly devoted to God, incapable of being redeemed, Lev. xxvii. 28; and what is set apart and devoted to death or destruction, Josh. vi. 17; Ezra x. 8. It never means excommunication, but cutting off by death. Compare Ex. xxii. 20, and Deut. xiii. 1-11. It has hence been applied to designate a man that is execrable and accursed, deserving death. So the Apostle uses it in 1 Cor. xvi. 22, and Gal. i. 8, 9.

The other view is more in accordance with the meaning of the term. It is thought that "anathema" means an ignominious death, and that of one apparently separated from Christ; or that he wished to be made "an anathema" by Christ, or for the sake of Christ, or after Christ, that is, his example. The words ἀπὸ τοῦ Χριστοῦ create all the difficulty in this case. This is the explanation given by *Jerome, Locke, Limborch, Doddridge,*

Thus I consent not to the opinion of those who think that Paul spoke these words from regard to God only, and not to men; nor do I agree with others, who say, that without any thought of God, he was influenced only by love to men: but I connect the love of men with a zeal for God's glory.

I have not, however, as yet explained that which is the chief thing,—that the Jews are here regarded as they were adorned with those singular tokens, by which they were distinguished from the rest of mankind. For God had by his covenant so highly exalted them, that by their fall, the faithfulness and truth of God himself seemed also to fail in the world: for that covenant would have thus become void, the stability of which was promised to be perpetual, as long as the sun and moon should shine in heaven. (Ps. lxxii. 7.) So that the abolition of this would have been more strange, than the sad and ruinous confusion of the whole world. It was not therefore a simple and exclusive regard for men: for though it is better that one member should perish than the whole body; it was yet for this reason that Paul had such a high regard for the Jews, because he viewed them as bearing the character, and, as they commonly say, the quality of an elect people; and this will appear more evident, as we shall soon see, from what follows.

The words, *my kinsmen according to the flesh*, though they contain nothing new, do yet serve much for amplification. For first, lest any one should think that he willingly, or of his own accord, sought cause of quarrel with the Jews, he intimates, that he had not put off the feeling of kindred, so as not to be affected with the destruction of his own flesh. And secondly, since it was necessary that the gospel, of

and *Scott*. The first meaning, however, as materially given by *Calvin*, is the most obvious and natural.

Both *Haldane* and *Chalmers* follow the Vulgate, and put the clause in a parenthesis, as expressing the Apostle's wish when unconverted; but there is altogether an incongruity in the terms he employs to express this wish; he surely would not have said that he wished to be separated from Christ as an accursed thing, for that is the meaning of anathema; for while he was a Pharisee he deemed it a privilege and an honour even to persecute Christ. And we cannot suppose that the Apostle would now describe his former wish in terms unsuitable to what it really was, but as he now regarded it.—*Ed.*

which he was the preacher, should go forth from Sion, he does not in vain pronounce an eulogy in so many words on his own kindred. For the qualifying expression, *according to the flesh*, is not in my view added for the sake of extenuation, as in other places, but, on the contrary, for the sake of expressing his faith: for though the Jews had disowned Paul, he yet concealed not the fact, that he had sprung from that nation, the election of whom was still strong in the root, though the branches had withered. What *Budæus* says of the word *anathema*, is inconsistent with the opinion of *Chrysostom*, who makes ἀνάθεμα and ἀνάθημα, to be the same.

4. *Who are Israelites*, &c. Here the reason is now more plainly given, why the destruction of that people caused him so much anguish, that he was prepared to redeem them by his own death, namely, because they were Israelites; for the relative pronoun is put here instead of a causative adverb. In like manner this anxiety took hold on Moses, when he desired that he should be blotted out of the book of life, rather than that the holy and chosen race of Abraham should be reduced to nothing. (Ex. xxxii. 32.) Then in addition to his kind feeling, he mentions also other reasons, and those of a higher kind, which made him to favour the Jews, even because the Lord had, as it were, by a kind of privilege, so raised them, that they were separated from the common order of men: and these titles of dignity were testimonies of love; for we are not wont to speak thus favourably, but of those whom we love. And though by their ingratitude they rendered themselves unworthy to be esteemed on account of these gifts of God, yet Paul continued justly to respect them, that he might teach us that the ungodly cannot so contaminate the good endowments of God, but that they always deserve to be praised and admired: at the same time, those who abuse them acquire thereby nothing but a greater obloquy. But as we are not to act in such a manner as to contemn, through a detestation of the ungodly, the gifts of God in them; so, on the other hand, we must use prudence, lest by our kind esteem and regard for them we make them proud, and especially lest our praises bear the appearance of flattery. But let us imitate Paul, who con-

ceded to the Jews their privileges in such a manner, that he afterwards declared that they were all of no worth without Christ. But it was not in vain that he mentioned this as one of their praises,—that they were *Israelites;* for Jacob prayed for this as a great favour, that they should be called by his name. (Gen. xlviii. 16.)

Whose are the adoption, &c. The whole drift of Paul's discourse is to this purpose,—that though the Jews by their defection had produced an ungodly divorce between God and themselves, yet the light of God's favour was not wholly extinguished, according to what he had also said in ch. iii. 3. They had indeed become unbelievers and had broken his covenant; but still their perfidy had not rendered void the faithfulness of God; for he had not only reserved for himself some remnant seed from the whole multitude, but had as yet continued, according to their hereditary right, the name of a Church among them.

But though they had already stripped themselves of these ornaments, so that it availed them nothing to be called the children of Abraham, yet as there was a danger, lest through their fault the majesty of the gospel should be depreciated among the Gentiles, Paul does not regard what they deserved, but covers their baseness and disgraceful conduct by throwing vails over them, until the Gentiles were fully persuaded, that the gospel had flowed to them from the celestial fountain, from the sanctuary of God, from an elect nation. For the Lord, passing by other nations, had selected them as a people peculiar to himself, and had adopted them as his children, as he often testifies by Moses and the prophets; and not content simply to give them the name of children, he calls them sometimes his first-begotten, and sometimes his beloved. So the Lord says in Ex. iv. 22,—" My firstbegotten son is Israel; let my son go, that he may serve me." In Jer. xxxi. 9, it is said, " I am become a Father to Israel, and Ephraim is my first-begotten:" and again, " Is not my son Ephraim precious to me? Is he not a delightful child? Hence troubled for him are my bowels, and I will yet pity him." By these words he means, not only to set forth his kindness towards the people of Israel, but rather to exhibit the efficacy of adoption, through which the promise of the celestial inheritance is conveyed.

Glory means the excellency into which the Lord had raised up that people above all other nations, and that in many and various ways, and especially by dwelling in the midst of them; for besides many other tokens of his presence, he exhibited a singular proof of it in the ark, where he gave responses, and also heard his people, that he might show forth his power in helping them: and for this reason it was called " the glory of God." (1 Sam. iv. 22.)[1]

As he has distinguished here between *covenants*[2] and *promises*, we may observe this difference,—that a covenant is that which is expressed in distinct and accustomed words, and contains a mutual stipulation, as that which was made with Abraham; but promises are what we meet with everywhere in Scripture; for when God had once made a covenant with his ancient people, he continued to offer, often by new promises, his favour to them. It hence follows, that promises are to be traced up to the covenant as to their true source; in the same manner as the special helps of God, by which he testifies his love towards the faithful, may be said to flow from the true fountain of election. And as the law was nothing more than a renewal of the covenant, and more fully sanctioned the remembrance of it, *legislation*, or the giving of the law, seems to be here peculiarly applied to the things which the law decreed: for it was no common honour conferred on the Jewish people, that they had God as their lawgiver. For if some gloried in their Solons and Lycur-

---

[1] *Vitringa* thinks that " the glory" was the pillar of fire and the cloud in the wilderness: but *Beza, Grotius,* and *Hammond* agree with *Calvin,* that the ark is meant. See Ps. lxxviii. 61. It seems to refer to those manifestations made in the tabernacle, and afterwards in the temple, by peculiar brightness or splendour. See Ex. xl. 34; and 1 Kings viii. 11. This splendour or glory signified God's presence, a privilege peculiar to the Israelites.—*Ed.*

[2] Why he mentions " covenants," αἱ διαθῆκαι, in the plural number, has been variously accounted for,—" there were various things included—the land of Canaan, prosperity, and the priesthood,—there were three laws—the moral, ceremonial, and judicial,—there were several repetitions of the covenant made to the patriarchs:" but if we read Gal. iii. 17, we shall see the true reason, for the Apostle there makes a distinct difference between the Abrahamic and the Mosaic covenant; but both these belonged to the Jews. See also Eph. ii. 12.—*Ed.*

guses, how much more reason was there to glory in the Lord? of this you have an account in Deut. iv. 32. By *worship* he understands that part of the law in which the legitimate manner of worshipping God is prescribed, such as rites and ceremonies. These ought to have been deemed lawful on account of God's appointment; without which, whatever men devise is nothing but a profanation of religion.

5. *Whose are the fathers,* &c. It is indeed of some importance to be descended from saints and men beloved of God, since God promised to the godly fathers mercy with regard to their children, even to thousand generations, and especially in the words addressed to Abraham, Isaac, and Jacob, as we find in Gen. xvii. 4, and in other passages. It matters not, that this by itself, when separated from the fear of God and holiness of life, is vain and useless: for we find the same to have been the case as to *worship* and *glory,* as it is evident everywhere in the prophets, especially in Is. i. 11; lx. 1; and also in Jer. vii. 4. But as God dignified these things, when joined with attention to godliness, with some degree of honour, he justly enumerated them among the privileges of the Jews. They are indeed said to be the heirs of the promises for this very reason,—because they descended from the fathers. (Acts iii. 25.)

From whom is Christ, &c. They who apply this to the fathers, as though Paul meant only to say that Christ had descended from the fathers, have no reason to allege: for his object was to close his account of the pre-eminence of the Jews by this encomium,—that Christ proceeded from them; for it was not a thing to be lightly esteemed, to have been united by a natural relationship with the Redeemer of the world; for if he had honoured the whole human race, in joining himself to us by a community of nature, much more did he honour them, with whom he had a closer bond of union. It must at the same time be always maintained, that when this favour of being allied by kindred is unconnected with godliness, it is so far from being an advantage, that on the contrary it leads to a greater condemnation.

But we have here a remarkable passage,—that in Christ two natures are in such a manner distinguished, that they are at the same time united in the very person of Christ: for by saying that Christ had descended from the Jews, he declared his real humanity. The words *according to the flesh*, which are added, imply that he had something superior to flesh; and here seems to be an evident distinction made between humanity and divinity. But he at last connects both together, where he says, that the Christ, who had descended from the Jews according to the flesh, is God blessed for ever.

We must further observe, that this ascription of praise belongs to none but only to the true and eternal God; for he declares in another place, (1 Tim. i. 17,) that it is the true God alone to whom honour and glory are due. They who break off this clause from the previous context, that they may take away from Christ so clear a testimony to his divinity, most presumptuously attempt to introduce darkness in the midst of the clearest light; for the words most evidently mean this, —*Christ, who is from the Jews according to the flesh, is God blessed for ever.*[1] And I doubt not, but that Paul, who had

[1] *Stuart* has in a most convincing manner vindicated the true and obvious meaning of this clause. There is no reading of any authority, nor any early version, that affects the genuineness of the received text: and it is amazing what ingenuity has been exercised by various critics to evade the plain construction of the passage,—a remarkable instance of the debasing power of preconceived notions. It is somewhat singular too, that some who professed at least the doctrine of Christ's divinity, such as *Erasmus, Whitby*, and *Locke*, have attempted to make changes in the text, and those for the most part conjectural, by which the obvious meaning is wholly altered.

It is very clearly shown by *Stuart*, that the very position of the words, and their connection with the context, will admit of no other construction than that which our version contains.

It is well known, that in Hebrew the word "blessed" is *always* placed before "God," or Jehovah, when it is an ascription of praise; and it appears that the Septuagint has in more than *thirty* instances followed the same order, and, indeed, in every instance except one, (Ps. lxvii. 19,) and that evidently a typographical mistake. The same is the case with *all* the examples in the New Testament. So that if the phrase here was a doxology, it must have been written εὐλογητὸς ὁ Θεός. In the *Welsh* language, which in many of its idioms is identically the same with the Hebrew, the order of the words is the same: when it is a doxology, the word "blessed" invariably precedes the word "God;" and when otherwise it follows it.

The opinion of *Chrysostom* on this sentence, to which *Erasmus* attaches

to contend hard with a reproach urged against him, did designedly raise up his own mind to the contemplation of the eternal glory of Christ; nor did he do this so much for his own sake individually, as for the purpose of encouraging others by his example to raise up their thoughts.

6. Not as though the word of God hath taken none effect. For they *are* not all Israel which are of Israel:	6. Neque tamen, quasi exciderit verbum Dei: non enim omnes qui sunt ex Israele sunt Israelitæ:
7. Neither, because they are the seed of Abraham, *are they* all children: but, In Isaac shall thy seed be called;	7. Nec qui sunt semen Abrahæ, ideo omnes filii; sed in Isaac vocabitur tibi semen:
8. That is, They which are the children of the flesh, these *are* not the children of God: but the children of the promise are counted for the seed.	8. Hoc est, non qui sunt filii carnis, ii filii sunt Dei; sed qui sunt filii promissionis, censebuntur in semen:
9. For this *is* the word of promise, At this time will I come, and Sarah shall have a son.	9. Promissionis enim verbum hoc est, Secundum hoc tempus veniam, et erit Saræ filius.

6. *Not however,* &c. Paul had been carried away by the ardour of his wish, as it were, into an excess of feeling, (*in ecstasin,*) but now, returning to discharge his office as a teacher, he adds what may be viewed as somewhat qualifying what he had said, as though he would restrain immoderate grief. And inasmuch as by deploring the ruin of his own nation, this inconsistency seems to follow, that the covenant made by God with the seed of Abraham had failed, (for the favour of God could not have been wanting to the Israelites without the covenant being abolished,) he reasonably anticipates this inconsistency, and shows, that notwithstanding the great blindness of the Jews, the favour of God continued still to that people, so that the truth of the covenant remained firm.

some importance, is of no value whatever, as he did not understand Hebrew; and Paul, for the most part, wrote as a Hebraist.

The participle ὤν, being put for ἐστι, is what is common in Hebrew and in the New Testament. See a remarkable instance of two participles and a verb in the middle, in Rev. i. 4. It has been said, that "amen" unsuitably follows a declarative sentence; but see an instance in ch. i. 25.

It is justly observed by *Stuart,* that the context requires the application of this sentence to Christ, as otherwise there would be no antithesis to the words "according to the flesh."—*Ed.*

Some read, "But it is not possible," &c., as though it were in Greek οἷον τε;[1] but as I find this reading in no copy, I adopt the common reading, *Not however that it had failed,* &c., and according to this sense, "That I deplore the destruction of my nation is not because I think the promise, given formerly by God to Abraham, is now void or abolished."

For not all, &c. The statement is,—that the promise was so given to Abraham and to his seed, that the inheritance did not belong to every seed without distinction; it hence follows that the defection of some does not prove that the covenant does not remain firm and valid.

But that it may be more evident on what condition the Lord adopted the posterity of Abraham as a peculiar people to himself, two things are to be here considered. The first is, That the promise of salvation given to Abraham belongs to all who can trace their natural descent to him; for it is offered to all without exception, and for this reason they are rightly called the heirs of the covenant made with Abraham; and in this respect they are his successors, or, as Scripture calls them, the children of the promise. For since it was the Lord's will that his covenant should be sealed, no less in Ishmael and Esau, than in Isaac and Jacob, it appears that they were not wholly alienated from him; except, it may be, you make no account of the circumcision, which was conferred on them by God's command; but it cannot be so regarded without dishonour to God. But this belonged to them, according to what the Apostle had said before, "whose are the covenants," though they were unbelieving; and in Acts iii. 25, they are called by Peter, the children of the covenants, because they were the descendants of the Prophets. The second point to be considered is, That the children of the promise are strictly those in whom its power and effect are found. On this account Paul denies here that all the children of Abraham were the children of God, though a covenant had been made with them by the Lord,

---

[1] Were this the case, the verb which follows, as *Wolfius* says and proves by an example, must have been in the infinitive mood. *Piscator* says the same. But *Pareus* and *Beza* take this to be the meaning; and so does *Macknight,* "Now it is not possible that the promise of God hath fallen." —*Ed.*

for few continued in the faith of the covenant; and yet God himself testifies, in the sixth chapter of Ezekiel, that they were all regarded by him as children. In short, when a whole people are called the heritage and the peculiar people of God, what is meant is, that they have been chosen by the Lord, the promise of salvation having been offered them and confirmed by the symbol of circumcision; but as many by their ingratitude reject this adoption, and thus enjoy in no degree its benefits, there arises among them another difference with regard to the fulfilment of the promise. That it might not then appear strange to any one, that this fulfilment of the promise was not evident in many of the Jews, Paul denies that they were included in the true election of God.

Some may prefer such a statement as this,—" The general election of the people of Israel is no hinderance, that God should not from them choose by his hidden counsel those whom he pleases." It is indeed an illustrious example of gratuitous mercy, when God deigns to make a covenant of life with a nation: but his hidden favour appears more evident in that second election, which is confined to a part only.

But when he says, that *all who are of Israel are not Israelites*, and that *all who are of the seed of Abraham are not children*, it is a kind of change in the meaning of words, (παρονομασία); for in the first clause he includes the whole race, in the second he refers only to true sons, who were not become degenerated.

7. But, "*In Isaac shall thy seed be called.*" Paul mentions this, to show that the hidden election of God overrules the outward calling, and that it is yet by no means inconsistent with it, but, on the contrary, that it tends to its confirmation and completion. That he might then in due order prove both, he in the first place assumes, that the election of God is not tied to the natural descendants of Abraham, and that it is not a thing that is included in the conditions of the covenant: and this is what he now confirms by a most suitable example. For if there ought to have been any natural progeny, which fell not away from the covenant;

this ought to have been especially the case with those who obtained the privilege at first: but when we find, that of the first sons of Abraham, while he was yet alive, and the promise new, one of them was separated as the seed, how much more might the same thing have taken place in his distant posterity? Now this testimony is taken from Gen. xvii. 20, where the Lord gives an answer to Abraham, that he had heard his prayer for Ishmael, but that there would be another on whom the promised blessing would rest. It hence follows, that some men are by special privilege elected out of the chosen people, in whom the common adoption becomes efficacious and valid.

8. *That is, They are not,* &c. He now gathers from God's answer a proposition, which includes the whole of what he had in view. For if Isaac, and not Ishmael, was the seed, though the one as well as the other was Abraham's son, it must be that all natural sons are not to be regarded as the seed, but that the promise is specially fulfilled only in some, and that it does not belong commonly and equally to all. He calls those *the children of the flesh,* who have nothing superior to a natural descent; as they are the *children of the promise,* who are peculiarly selected by the Lord.

9. *For the word of promise is this,* &c. He adds another divine testimony; and we see, by the application made of it, with what care and skill he explains Scripture. When he says, the Lord said that he would come, and that a son would be born to Abraham of Sarah, he intimated that his blessing was not yet conferred, but that it was as yet suspended.[1] But Ishmael was already born when this was

[1] Gen. xviii. 10. The quotation is not from the Septuagint, but is much nearer a literal version of the Hebrew: the only material difference is in the words, " at this time," instead of " according to the time of life." The words in different forms occur *four* times,—Gen. xvii. 21; xviii. 10, 14; xxi. 2; we meet with the same words in 2 Kings iv. 16, 17. It appears that the Apostle here took this expression, " at this time," from Gen. xvii. 21, while he mainly followed the text in Gen. xviii. 10. The meaning of the phrase, " according to the time of life," as given in Genesis and in Kings, evidently is the time of child-bearing, what passes between conception and the birth. This was repeatedly mentioned in order to show that the usual course of nature would be followed, though the conception would be miraculous; the child to be born was to be nourished the usual time in the womb,—" according to the time of producing life," or of child-bearing.

said: then God's blessing had no regard to Ishmael. We may also observe, by the way, the great caution with which he proceeds here, lest he should exasperate the Jews. The cause being passed over, he first simply states the fact; he will hereafter open the fountain.

10. And not only *this;* but when Rebecca also had conceived by one, *even* by our father Isaac,	10. Non solum autem hic, sed et Rebecca, quæ ex uno conceperat, patre nostro Isaac:
11. (For *the children* being not yet born, neither having done any good or evil, that the purpose of God according to election might stand, not of works, but of him that calleth,)	11. Quum enim nondum nati essent pueri, nec quidpiam boni aut mali egissent, ut secundum electionem propositum Dei maneret,
12. It was said unto her, The elder shall serve the younger.	12. Non ex operibus, sed ex vocante, dictum est ei, Major serviet minori;
13. As it is written, Jacob have I loved, but Esau have I hated.	13. Quemadmodum scriptum est, Jacob dilexi, Esau autem odio habui.

10. *And not only,* &c. There are in this chapter some broken sentences, such as this is,—*But Rebecca also, who had conceived by one, our father Isaac;* for he leaves off in the middle, before he comes to the principal verb. The meaning, however, is, that the difference as to the possession of the promise may not only be seen in the children of Abraham, but that there is a much more evident example in Jacob and Esau: for in the former instance some might allege that their condition was unequal, the one being the son of an handmaid; but these were of the same mother, and were even twins: yet one was rejected, and the other was chosen by the Lord. It is hence clear, that the fulfilment of the promise does not take place in all the children of the flesh indiscriminately.

And as Paul refers to the persons to whom God made known his purpose, I prefer to regard a masculine pronoun to be understood, rather than a neuter, as *Erasmus* has done: for the meaning is, that God's special election had

---

The exposition of *Gesenius,* adopted by *Tholuck* and *Stuart,* " when the time shall be renewed," does not comport with the passage, as it introduces a tautology. *Hammond* says, that the Hebrews interpret the expression in Kings as meaning the time between the conception and the birth.—*Ed.*

not been revealed only to Abraham, but also to Rebecca, when she brought forth her twins.[1]

11. *For when the children,* &c. He now begins to ascend higher, even to show the cause of this difference, which he teaches us is nowhere else to be found except in the election of God. He had indeed before briefly noticed, that there was a difference between the natural children of Abraham, that though all were adopted by circumcision into a participation of the covenant, yet the grace of God was not effectual in them all; and hence that they, who enjoy the favour of God, are the children of the promise. But how it thus happened, he has been either silent or has obscurely hinted. Now indeed he openly ascribes the whole cause to the election of God, and that gratuitous, and in no way depending on men; so that in the salvation of the godly nothing higher (*nihil superius*) must be sought than the goodness of God,

---

[1] Here is a striking instance of a difficulty as to the construction, while the meaning of the whole passage is quite evident. The ellipsis has been variously supplied; " and not only *this,*" i.e., what I have stated; " and not only *he,*" i.e., Abraham to whom the first communication was made; " and not only *she,*" i.e., Sarah, mentioned in the preceding verse; " but Rebecca also is another instance." But it may be thus supplied,—" and not only *so,*" i.e., as to the word of promise; " but Rebecca also *had a word,*" or a message conveyed to her. That the verse has a distinct meaning in itself is evident, for the next begins with a γὰρ, " for;" and to include the 11th verse in a parenthesis, seems by no means satisfactory. The three verses may be thus rendered,—

10. And not only *so,* but Rebecca also *received a message,* when she conceived by the first, (*i.e.,* son or seed,) *even* our father Isaac:
11. for they being not yet born, and having not done any good or evil, that the purpose of God according to election might stand, not
12. through works, but through him who calls, it was said to her, " The elder shall serve the younger."

The words ἐξ ἑνὸς, rendered commonly " by one," have never been satisfactorily accounted for. It seems to be an instance of Hebraism; the word אחד, " one," means also " first." We have other instances of this in the New Testament; εἰς μίαν τῶν σαββάτων—" on the first (*i.e.,* day) of the week," Matt. xxviii. 1; see also Mark xvi. 2; John xx. 19. " The first day" in Gen. i. 5, is rendered by the Septuagint, ἡμέρα μία. Isaac was the *first* son or seed of promise: and a difference was made in the children of the very first seed. But this meaning of εἰς is said by *Schleusner* to be sanctioned by Greek writers, such as *Herodotus* and *Thucydides*. There is no necessity of introducing the word " children," at the beginning of verse 11; the antecedent in this case, as it sometimes happens, comes after the pronoun; and it is the " elder" and " younger" at the end of verse 12.—*Ed.*

and nothing higher in the perdition of the reprobate than his just severity.

Then the first proposition is,—" As the blessing of the covenant separates the Israelitic nation from all other people, so the election of God makes a distinction between men in that nation, while he predestinates some to salvation, and others to eternal condemnation." The second proposition is,—" There is no other basis for this election than the goodness of God alone, and also since the fall of Adam, his mercy; which embraces whom he pleases, without any regard whatever to their works." The third is,—" The Lord in his gratuitous election is free and exempt from the necessity of imparting equally the same grace to all; but, on the contrary, he passes by whom he wills, and whom he wills he chooses." All these things Paul briefly includes in one sentence: he then goes on to other things.

Moreover, by these words, *When the children had not yet been born, nor had done any good or evil,* he shows, that God in making a difference could not have had any regard to works, for they were not yet done. Now they who argue on the other side, and say, that this is no reason why the election of God should not make a difference between men according to the merits of works, for God foresees who those are who by future works would be worthy or unworthy of his grace, are not more clear-sighted than Paul, but stumble at a principle in theology, which ought to be well known to all Christians, namely, that God can see nothing in the corrupt nature of man, such as was in Esau and Jacob, to induce him to manifest his favour. When therefore he says, that neither of them had then done any good or evil, what he took as granted must also be added,—that they were both the children of Adam, by nature sinful, and endued with no particle of righteousness.

I do not dwell thus long on explaining these things, because the meaning of the Apostle is obscure; but as the Sophists, being not content with his plain sense, endeavour to evade it by frivolous distinctions, I wished to show, that Paul was by no means ignorant of those things which they allege.

It may further be said, that though that corruption alone, which is diffused through the whole race of man, is sufficient, before it breaks out, as they say, into action, for condemnation, and hence it follows, that Esau was justly rejected, for he was naturally a child of wrath, it was yet necessary, lest any doubt should remain, as though his condition became worse through any vice or fault, that sins no less than virtues should be excluded. It is indeed true, that the proximate cause of reprobation is the curse we all inherit from Adam; yet, that we may learn to acquiesce in the bare and simple good pleasure of God, Paul withdraws us from this view, until he has established this doctrine,—That God has a sufficiently just reason for electing and for reprobating, in his own will.[1]

That the purpose of God according to election, &c. He speaks of the gratuitous election of God almost in every instance. If works had any place, he ought to have said,— "That his reward might stand through works;" but he mentions the purpose of God, which is included, so to speak, in his own good pleasure alone. And that no ground of dispute might remain on the subject, he has removed all doubt by adding another clause, *according to election,* and then a third, *not through works, but through him who calls.* Let us now then apply our minds more closely to this passage: Since the purpose of God according to election is established

[1] Archbishop *Usher* asks this question, "Did God, before he made man, determine to save some and reject others?" To this he gives this answer,—"Yes, surely; before they had done either good or evil, God in his eternal counsel set them apart." It is the same sentiment that is announced here by *Calvin.* But to deduce it from what is said of Jacob and Esau, does not seem legitimate, inasmuch as they were in a fallen condition by nature, and the reference is evidently made to anything done personally by themselves. Election and reprobation most clearly presuppose man as fallen and lost: it is hence indeed, that the words derive their meaning. That it was God's eternal purpose to choose some of man's fallen race, and to leave others to perish, is clearly taught us: but this is a different question from the one touched upon here,—that this purpose was irrespective of man's fall,—a sentiment which, as far as I can see, is not recognised nor taught in Scripture. And not only *Calvin,* but many other divines, both before and after him, seem to have gone in this respect somewhat beyond the limits of revelation; it is true, by a process of reasoning apparently obvious; but when we begin to reason on this high and mysterious subject, we become soon bewildered and lost in mazes of difficulties.—*Ed.*

in this way,—that before the brothers were born, and had done either good or evil, one was rejected and the other chosen; it hence follows, that when any one ascribes the cause of the difference to their works, he thereby subverts the purpose of God. Now, by adding, *not through works, but through him who calls*, he means, not on account of works, but of the calling only; for he wishes to exclude works altogether. We have then the whole stability of our election inclosed in the purpose of God alone: here merits avail nothing, as they issue in nothing but death; no worthiness is regarded, for there is none; but the goodness of God reigns alone. False then is the dogma, and contrary to God's word,—that God elects or rejects, as he foresees each to be worthy or unworthy of his favour.[1]

12. *The elder shall serve the younger.* See how the Lord makes a difference between the sons of Isaac, while they were as yet in their mother's womb; for this was the hea-

---

[1] Nothing can be conceived more conclusive in argument than what is contained here. The idea of foreseen works, as the reason or the ground of election, is wholly excluded. The choice is expressly denied to be on account of any works, and is as expressly ascribed to the sovereign will of God.

"He does not oppose *works* to *faith*, but to him who calls, or to the calling, which precedes faith, that is, to that calling which is according to God's purpose. Paul means, that the difference between Jacob and Esau was made through the sole will and pleasure of God, not through their wills or works, existing or foreseen."—*Poli. Syn.*

Yet some of the Fathers, as *Chrysostom* and *Theodoret*, as well as some modern divines, ascribe election to foreseen works. How this is reconcilable with the argument of the Apostle, and with the instances he adduces, it is indeed a very hard matter to see. One way by which the Apostle's argument is evaded, is, that the election here is to temporal and outward privileges. Be it so: let this be granted; but it is adduced by the Apostle as an illustration—and of what? most clearly of spiritual and eternal election. He refers both to the same principle, to the free choice of God, and not to anything in man. " God foresaw the disposition of each."—*Theodoret* and *Chrysostom*. " His election corresponds with the foreseen disposition of men."—*Theodoret*. " It was done by the prescience of God, whereby he knew while yet unborn, what each would be."—*Augustine*. These are quotations made by a modern writer (*Bosanquet*) with approbation: but surely nothing could be suggested more *directly* contrary to the statements and the argument of the Apostle. There is a mistake, I apprehend, as to the last quotation; perhaps similar to that made in quoting *Augustine* on the latter part of the 7th chapter of this Epistle, where the writer quotes a sentiment of *Augustine*, which he afterwards retracted, a thing which has been often done by the advocates of Popery, but by no means becoming a Protestant.—*Ed.*

venly answer, by which it appeared that God designed to show to the younger peculiar favour, which he denied to the elder. Though this indeed had reference to the right of primogeniture, yet in this, as the symbol of something greater, was manifested the will of God : and that this was the case we may easily perceive, when we consider what little benefit, according to the flesh, Jacob derived from his primogeniture. For he was, on its account, exposed to great danger; and to avoid this danger, he was obliged to quit his home and his country, and was unkindly treated in his exile: when he returned, he tremblingly, and in doubt of his life, prostrated himself at the feet of his brother, humbly asked forgiveness for his offence, and lived through the indulgence shown to him. Where was his dominion over his brother, from whom he was constrained to seek by entreaty his life ? There was then something greater than the primogeniture promised in the answer given by the Lord.

13. *As it is written, Jacob I loved,* &c. He confirms, by a still stronger testimony, how much the heavenly answer, given to Rebecca, availed to his present purpose, that is, that the spiritual condition of both was intimated by the dominion of Jacob and servitude of Esau, and also that Jacob obtained this favour through the kindness of God, and not through his own merit. Then this testimony of the prophet shows the reason why the Lord conferred on Jacob the primogeniture : and it is taken from the first chapter of Malachi, where the Lord, reproaching the Jews for their ingratitude, mentions his former kindness to them,—" I have loved you," he says ; and then he refers to the origin of his love,—" Was not Esau the brother of Jacob ?" as though he said,—" What privilege had he, that I should prefer him to his brother ? None whatever. It was indeed an equal right, except that by the law of nature the younger ought to have served the elder; I yet chose the one, and rejected the other ; and I was thus led by my mercy alone, and by no worthiness as to works. I therefore chose you for my people, that I might show the same kindness to the seed of Jacob ; but I rejected the Edomites, the progeny of Esau. Ye are then so much the worse, inasmuch as the remembrance of so

great a favour cannot stimulate you to adore my majesty."[1] Now, though earthly blessings are there recorded, which God had conferred on the Israelites, it is not yet right to view them but as symbols of his benevolence: for where the wrath of God is, there death follows; but where his love is, there is life.

14. What shall we say then? *Is there* unrighteousness with God? God forbid.

15. For he saith to Moses, I will have mercy on whom I will have mercy, and I will have compassion on whom I will have compassion.

16. So then *it is* not of him that willeth, nor of him that runneth, but of God that sheweth mercy.

17. For the scripture saith unto Pharaoh, Even for this same purpose have I raised thee up, that I might shew my power in thee, and that my name might be declared throughout all the earth.

18. Therefore hath he mercy on whom he will *have mercy*, and whom he will he hardeneth.

14. Quid ergo dicemus? num injustitia est apud Deum? Absit:

15. Moses enim dicit, Miserebor cujus miserebor, et miserebor quem miseratus fuero.

16. Ergo non volentis neque currentis, sed miserentis est Dei.

17. Dicit enim Scriptura Pharaoni, In hoc ipsum excitavi te, ut ostendam in te potentiam meam, et ut prædicetur nomen meum in universa terra.

18. Ergo cujus vult miseretur, et quem vult indurat.

14. *What then shall we say?* &c. The flesh cannot hear of this wisdom of God without being instantly disturbed by numberless questions, and without attempting in a manner to call God to an account. We hence find that the Apostle, whenever he treats of some high mystery, obviates the many absurdities by which he knew the minds of men would be otherwise possessed; for when men hear anything of what Scripture teaches respecting predestination, they are especially entangled with very many impediments.

The predestination of God is indeed in reality a labyrinth, from which the mind of man can by no means extricate itself: but so unreasonable is the curiosity of man, that the more perilous the examination of a subject is, the more boldly he proceeds; so that when predestination is discussed, as he cannot restrain himself within due limits, he immedi-

---

[1] The meaning of the words " loving " and " hating " is here rightly explained. It is usual in Scripture to state a preference in terms like these. See Gen. xxix. 31; Luke xiv. 26; John xii. 25.—*Ed.*

ately, through his rashness, plunges himself, as it were, into the depth of the sea. What remedy then is there for the godly? Must they avoid every thought of predestination? By no means: for as the Holy Spirit has taught us nothing but what it behoves us to know, the knowledge of this would no doubt be useful, provided it be confined to the word of God. Let this then be our sacred rule, to seek to know nothing concerning it, except what Scripture teaches us: when the Lord closes his holy mouth, let us also stop the way, that we may not go farther. But as we are men, to whom foolish questions naturally occur, let us hear from Paul how they are to be met.

Is there unrighteousness with God? Monstrous surely is the madness of the human mind, that it is more disposed to charge God with unrighteousness than to blame itself for blindness. Paul indeed had no wish to go out of his way to find out things by which he might confound his readers; but he took up as it were from what was common the wicked suggestion, which immediately enters the minds of many, when they hear that God determines respecting every individual according to his own will. It is indeed, as the flesh imagines, a kind of injustice, that God should pass by one and show regard to another.

In order to remove this difficulty, Paul divides his subject into two parts; in the former of which he speaks of the elect, and in the latter of the reprobate; and in the one he would have us to contemplate the mercy of God, and in the other to acknowledge his righteous judgment. His first reply is, that the thought that there is injustice with God deserves to be abhorred, and then he shows that with regard to the two parties, there can be none.

But before we proceed further, we may observe that this very objection clearly proves, that inasmuch as God elects some and passes by others, the cause is not to be found in anything else but in his own purpose; for if the difference had been based on works, Paul would have to no purpose mentioned this question respecting the unrighteousness of God, no suspicion could have been entertained concerning it if God dealt with every one according to his merit. It may also, in the second place, be noticed, that though he saw that this doctrine could not be touched without exciting instant clamours and dreadful blasphemies, he yet freely and openly brought it forward; nay, he does not conceal how much occasion for murmuring and clamour is given to us, when we hear that before men are born their lot is assigned to each by the secret will of God; and yet, notwithstanding all this, he proceeds, and without any subterfuges, declares what he had learned from the Holy Spirit. It hence follows, that their fancies are by no means to be endured, who aim to appear wiser than the Holy Spirit, in removing and pacifying offences. That they may not criminate God, they ought honestly to confess that the salvation or the perdition of men depends on his free election. Were they to restrain their minds from unholy curiosity, and to bridle their tongues from immoderate liberty, their modesty and sobriety would be deserving of approbation; but to put a restraint on the Holy Spirit and on Paul, what audacity it is! Let then such magnanimity ever prevail in the Church of God, as that godly teachers may not be ashamed to make an honest profession of the true doctrine, however hated it may be, and also to refute whatever calumnies the ungodly may bring forward.

15. *For he saith to Moses,* &c.[1] With regard to the elect, God cannot be charged with any unrighteousness; for according to his good pleasure he favours them with mercy: and yet even in this case the flesh finds reasons for murmuring, for it cannot concede to God the right of showing favour to one and not to another, except the cause be made evident. As then it seems unreasonable that some should without merit be preferred to others, the petulancy of men quarrels with God, as though he deferred to persons more

---

[1] The quotation is from Ex. xxxiii. 19, and literally from the Septuagint. The verb ἐλεέω is to be taken here in the sense of showing favour rather than mercy, according to the meaning of the Hebrew word; for the idea of mercy is what the other verb, οἰκτείρω, conveys. *Schleusner* renders it here and in some other passages in this sense. The rendering then would be—" I will favour whom I favour," that is, whom I choose to favour; " and I will pity whom I pity," which means whom I choose to pity. The latter verb in both clauses is in Hebrew in the future tense, but rendered properly in Greek in the present, as it commonly expresses a present act.—*Ed.*

than what is right. Let us now see how Paul defends the righteousness of God.

In the first place, he does by no means conceal or hide what he saw would be disliked, but proceeds to maintain it with inflexible firmness. And in the second place, he labours not to seek out reasons to soften its asperity, but considers it enough to check vile barkings by the testimonies of Scripture.

It may indeed appear a frigid defence that God is not unjust, because he is merciful to whom he pleases; but as God regards his own authority alone as abundantly sufficient, so that he needs the defence of none, Paul thought it enough to appoint him the vindicator of his own right. Now Paul brings forward here the answer which Moses received from the Lord, when he prayed for the salvation of the whole people, "I will show mercy," was God's answer, "on whom I will show mercy, and I will have compassion on whom I will have compassion." By this oracle the Lord declared that he is a debtor to none of mankind, and that whatever he gives is a gratuitous benefit, and then that his kindness is free, so that he can confer it on whom he pleases; and lastly, that no cause higher than his own will can be thought of, why he does good and shows favour to some men but not to all. The words indeed mean as much as though he had said, "From him to whom I have once purposed to show mercy, I will never take it away; and with perpetual kindness will I follow him to whom I have determined to be kind." And thus he assigns the highest reason for imparting grace, even his own voluntary purpose, and also intimates that he has designed his mercy peculiarly for some; for it is a way of speaking which excludes all outward causes, as when we claim to ourselves the free power of acting, we say, "I will do what I mean to do." The relative pronoun also expressly intimates, that mercy is not to all indiscriminately. His freedom is taken away from God, when his election is bound to external causes.

The only true cause of salvation is expressed in the two words used by Moses. The first is חנן, *chenen*, which means to favour or to show kindness freely and bountifully; the other is רחם, *rechem*, which is to be treated with mercy. Thus is confirmed what Paul intended, that the mercy of God, being gratuitous, is under no restraint, but turns wherever it pleases.[1]

16. *It is not then of him who wills,* &c. From the testimony adduced he draws this inference, that beyond all controversy our election is not to be ascribed to our diligence, nor to our striving, nor to our efforts, but that it is wholly to be referred to the counsel of God. That none of you may think that they who are elected are elected because they are deserving, or because they had in any way procured for themselves the favour of God, or, in short, because they had in them a particle of worthiness by which God might be moved, take simply this view of the matter, that it is neither by our will nor efforts, (for he has put *running* for striving or endeavour,) that we are counted among the elect, but that it wholly depends on the divine goodness, which of itself chooses those who neither will, nor strive, nor even think of such a thing. And they who reason from this passage, that there is in us some power to strive, but that it effects nothing of itself unless assisted by God's mercy, maintain what is absurd; for the Apostle shows not what is in us, but excludes all our efforts. It is therefore a mere sophistry to say that we will and run, because Paul denies that it is of him who wills or runs, since he meant nothing else than that neither willing nor running can do anything.

They are, however, to be condemned who remain secure and idle on the pretence of giving place to the grace of God; for though nothing is done by their own striving, yet that effort which is influenced by God is not ineffectual. These

---

[1] These two words clearly show that election regards man as fallen; for favour is what is shown to the undeserving, and mercy to the wretched and miserable, so that the choice that is made is out of the corrupted mass of mankind, contemplated in that state, and not as in a state of innocence. *Augustine* says, "Deus alios facit vasa iræ secundum meritum; alios vasa misericordiæ secundum gratiam—God makes some vessels of wrath according to their merit; others vessels of mercy according to his grace." In another place he says, "Deus ex eadem massa damnata originaliter, tanquam figulus, fecit aliud vas ad honorem, aliud in contumeliam—God, as a potter, made of the same originally condemned mass, one vessel to honour, another to dishonour." "Two sorts of vessels God forms out of the great lump of fallen mankind."—*Henry.*

things, then, are not said that we may quench the Spirit of God, while kindling sparks within us, by our waywardness and sloth; but that we may understand that everything we have is from him, and that we may hence learn to ask all things of him, to hope for all things from him, and to ascribe all things to him, while we are prosecuting the work of our salvation with fear and trembling.

Pelagius has attempted by another sophistical and worthless cavil to evade this declaration of Paul, that it is not only of him who wills and runs, because the mercy of God assists. But *Augustine*, not less solidly than acutely, thus refuted him, "If the will of man is denied to be the cause of election, because it is not the sole cause, but only in part; so also we may say that it is not of mercy but of him who wills and runs, for where there is a mutual co-operation, there ought to be a reciprocal commendation: but unquestionably the latter sentiment falls through its own absurdity." Let us then feel assured that the salvation of those whom God is pleased to save, is thus ascribed to his mercy, that nothing may remain to the contrivance of man.[1]

---

[1] The terms "willing" and "running" are evidently derived from the circumstances connected with the history of Esau. "In vain," says *Turrettin*, "did Esau seek the blessing. In vain did Isaac hasten to grant it, and in vain did Esau run to procure venison for his father; neither the father's willingness nor the running of the son availed anything; God's favour overruled the whole." But the subject handled is God's sovereignty in the manifestation of his favour and grace. Esau was but a type of the unbelieving Jews, when the gospel was proclaimed, and of thousands of such as are in name Christians. There is some sort of "willing," and a great deal of "running," and yet the blessing is not attained. There was much of apparent willing and running in the strict formality and zeal of Pharisaism, and there is much of the same kind still in the austerities and mechanical worship of superstition, and also in the toils and devotions of self-righteousness. The word or the revealed will of God is in all these instances misunderstood and neglected.

Isaac's "willingness" to give the blessing to Esau, notwithstanding the announcement made at his birth, and Rebecca's conduct in securing it to Jacob, are singular instances of man's imperfections, and of the overruling power of God. Isaac acted as though he had forgotten what God had expressed as his will; and Rebecca acted as though God could not effect his purpose without her interference, and an interference, too, in a way highly improper and sinful. It was the trial of faith, and the faith of both halted exceedingly; yet the purpose of God was still fulfilled, but the improper manner in which it was fulfilled was afterwards visited with God's displeasure.—*Ed.*

Nor is there much more colour for what some advance, who think that these things are said in the person of the ungodly; for how can it be right to turn passages of Scripture in which the justice of God is asserted, for the purpose of reproaching him with tyranny? and then is it probable that Paul, when the refutation was at hand and easy, would have suffered the Scripture to be treated with gross mockery? But such subterfuges have they laid hold on, who absurdly measured this incomparable mystery of God by their own judgment. To their delicate and tender ears this doctrine was more grating than that they could think it worthy of an Apostle. But they ought rather to have bent their own stubbornness to the obedience of the Spirit, that they might not surrender themselves up to their gross inventions.

17. *For the Scripture saith,* &c. He comes now to the second part, the rejection of the ungodly, and as there seems to be something more unreasonable in this, he endeavours to make it more fully evident, how God, in rejecting whom he wills, is not only irreprehensible, but also wonderful in his wisdom and justice. He then takes his proof from Exodus ix. 16, where the Lord declares that it was he who raised up Pharaoh for this end, that while he obstinately strove to resist the power of God, he might, by being overcome and subdued, afford a proof how invincible the arm of God is; to bear which, much less to resist it, no human power is able. See then the example which the Lord designed to exhibit in Pharaoh![1]

There are here two things to be considered,—the predestination of Pharaoh to ruin, which is to be referred to the past and yet the hidden counsel of God,—and then, the design of this, which was to make known the name of God; and on this does Paul primarily dwell: for if this hardening was of such a kind, that on its account the name of God deserved to be made known, it is an impious thing, accord-

[1] "For," at the beginning of this verse, connects it with the 14th; it is the second reason given for what that verse contains: this is in accordance with Paul's manner of writing, and it may be rendered here, moreover, or besides, or farther. *Macknight* renders it "besides." Were γὰρ rendered thus in many instances, the meaning would be much more evident. —*Ed.*

ing to evidence derived from the contrary effect, to charge him with any unrighteousness.

But as many interpreters, striving to modify this passage, pervert it, we must first observe, that for the word, "I have raised," or stirred up, (*excitavi,*) the Hebrew is, "I have appointed," (*constitui,*) by which it appears, that God, designing to show, that the contumacy of Pharaoh would not prevent him to deliver his people, not only affirms, that his fury had been foreseen by him, and that he had prepared means for restraining it, but that he had also thus designedly ordained it, and indeed for this end,—that he might exhibit a more illustrious evidence of his own power.[1] Absurdly

---

[1] It is somewhat remarkable, that Paul, in quoting this passage, Exod. ix. 16, substitutes a clause for the first that is given by the *Septuagint:* instead of "ἕνεκεν τούτο διετηρήθης—on this account thou hast been preserved," he gives, "εἰς αὐτὸ τοῦτο ἐξήγειρά σε—for this very end have I raised thee." The Hebrew is, "And indeed for this end have I made thee to stand, העמדתיך." The verb used by Paul is found only in one other place in the New Testament, 1 Cor. vi. 14; where it refers to the resurrection. In the *Septuagint* it often occurs, but never, as *Stuart* tells us, in the sense of *creating*, or *bringing into existence*, but in that of *exciting, rousing* from sleep, or *rendering active.* References are made to Gen. xxviii. 16; Judges v. 12; Ps. vii. 7: Jer. l. 41; Joel iii. 9, &c. Hence it is by him rendered here, "I have roused thee up." But to make the Hebrew verb to bear this sense is by no means easy: the three places referred to, Neh. vi. 7, and Dan. xi. 11 and 13, do not seem to afford a satisfactory proof. Ps. cvii. 25, is more to the point. Its first meaning is, to *make to stand*, and then, to *present* persons, Numb. xiii. 6,—to *establish* or *make strong* a kingdom or a city, 1 Kings xv. 4,—to *fix* persons in office, 2 Chron. xxxv. 2,—to *set up* or build a house, Ezra ix. 9,—to *appoint* teachers, Neh. vi. 7,—and to *arrange* or *set in order* an army, Dan. xi. 13. Such are the ideas included in this verb. "I have made thee to stand," established, or made thee strong, may be its meaning in this passage. To establish or to make one strong, is more than to *preserve*, the word used by the *Septuagint:* and hence it was, it may be, that Paul adopted another word, which conveys the idea, that Pharaoh had been elevated into greater power than his predecessors, which the Hebrew verb seems to imply.

Venema, as well as *Stuart,* thought that the idea of *exciting, rousing* into action, or *stimulating,* is to be ascribed to the verbs here used, and that what is meant is, that God by his plagues awakened and excited all the evil that was in Pharaoh's heart for the purposes here described, and that by this process he "hardened" him; and the conclusion of verse 28 seems to favour this view, for the hardening mentioned there can have no reference to anything in the context except to what is said in this verse.

But the simpler view is that mentioned by *Wolfius*—that reference is made to the dangers which Pharaoh had already escaped. God says, "I have made thee to stand," *i.e.*, to remain alive in the midst of them. We hence see the reason why Paul changed the verb; for "preserve," used

then do some render this passage,—that Pharaoh was *preserved* for a time; for his beginning is what is spoken of here. For, seeing many things from various quarters happen to men, which retard their purposes and impede the course of their actions, God says, that Pharaoh proceeded from him, and that his condition was by himself assigned to him: and with this view agrees the verb, *I have raised up*. But that no one may imagine, that Pharaoh was moved from above by some kind of common and indiscriminate impulse, to rush headlong into that madness the special cause, or end, is mentioned; as though it had been said,—that God not only knew what Pharaoh would do, but also designedly ordained him for this purpose. It hence follows, that it is in vain to contend with him, as though he were bound to give a reason; for he of himself comes forth before us, and anticipates the objection, by declaring, that the reprobate, through whom he designs his name to be made known, proceed from the hidden fountain of his providence.

18. *To whom he wills then he showeth mercy,* &c. Here follows the conclusion of both parts; which can by no means be understood as being the language of any other but of the Apostle; for he immediately addresses an opponent, and adduces what might have been objected by an opposite party. There is therefore no doubt but that Paul, as we have already reminded you, speaks these things in his own person, namely, that God, according to his own will, favours with mercy them whom he pleases, and unsheathes the severity of his judgment against whomsoever it seemeth him good. That our mind may be satisfied with the difference which exists between the elect and the reprobate, and may not inquire for any cause higher than the divine will, his purpose was to convince us of this—that it seems good to God to illuminate some that they may be saved, and to blind others that they may perish: for we ought particularly to notice these words, *to whom he wills,* and, *whom he wills:* beyond this he allows us not to proceed.

by the *Septuagint,* did not fully express the meaning; but to "raise up," as it were from the jaws of death, conveys more fully what is meant by the original.—*Ed.*

But the word *hardens*, when applied to God in Scripture, means not only permission, (as some washy moderators would have it,) but also the operation of the wrath of God: for all those external things, which lead to the blinding of the reprobate, are the instruments of his wrath; and Satan himself, who works inwardly with great power, is so far his minister, that he acts not, but by his command.[1] Then that frivolous evasion, which the schoolmen have recourse to respecting foreknowledge, falls to the ground: for Paul teaches us, that the ruin of the wicked is not only foreseen by the Lord, but also ordained by his counsel and his will; and Solomon teaches us the same thing,—that not only the destruction of the wicked is foreknown, but that the wicked themselves have been created for this very end—that they may perish. (Prov. xvi. 4.)

[1] Much has been unnecessarily written on this subject of *hardening*. Pharaoh is several times said to have hardened his own heart, and God is said also several times to have hardened him too. The Scripture in many instances makes no minute distinctions, for these may be easily gathered from the general tenor of its teaching. God is in his nature holy, and therefore hardening as his act cannot be sinful: and as he is holy, he hates sin and punishes it; and for this purpose he employs wicked men, and even Satan himself, as in the case of Ahab. As a punishment, he affords occasions and opportunities to the obstinate even to increase their sins, and thus in an indirect way hardens them in their rebellion and resistance to his will; and this was exactly the case with Pharaoh. This, as *Calvin* says, was the operation or working of his wrath. The history of Pharaoh is a sufficient explanation of what is said here. He was a cruel tyrant and oppressor: and God in his first message to Moses said, " I am sure that the king of Egypt will not let you go, no, not by a mighty hand." God might indeed have softened his heart and disposed him to allow them to depart: but it pleased him to act otherwise, and to manifest his power and his greatness in another way: so that " whom he wills, he favours, and whom he wills, he hardens;" and for reasons known only to himself.

Reference is at the end of this section made to Prov. xvi. 4. The creation mentioned can be understood in no other sense than the continued exercise of divine power in bringing into existence human beings in their present fallen state. But " creation" is not the word used, nor is the passage correctly rendered. It is not ברא nor עשה, but פעל; and it is not a verb but a substantive. Literally rendered the passage is the following—

Every work of Jehovah *is* for its (or, his) purpose,
And even the wicked *is* for the day of calamity.

The Rev. *G. Holden* is very indignant that this text has been applied to support the doctrine of reprobation. Be it, that it has been misapplied; yet the doctrine does not thereby fall to the ground. If Paul does not maintain it in this chapter and in other passages, we must hold that

19. Thou wilt say then unto me, Why doth he yet find fault? For who hath resisted his will?
20. Nay but, O man, who art thou that repliest against God? Shall the thing formed say to him that formed it, Why hast thou made me thus?
21. Hath not the potter power over the clay, of the same lump to make one vessel unto honour, and another unto dishonour?

19. Dices itaque mihi, Quid adhuc conqueritur? voluntati ejus quis restitit?
20. Atqui, O homo, tu quis es qui contendis judicio cum Deo! num dicit fictile figulo, cur me sic fecisti?
21. An non habet potestatem figulus luti ex eadem massa, faciendi, aliud quidem vas in honorem, aliud in contumeliam?

19. *Thou wilt then say*, &c. Here indeed the flesh especially storms, that is, when it hears that they who perish have been destined by the will of God to destruction. Hence the Apostle adopts again the words of an opponent; for he saw that the mouths of the ungodly could not be restrained from boldly clamouring against the righteousness of God: and he very fitly expresses their mind; for being not content with defending themselves, they make God guilty instead of themselves; and then, after having devolved on him the blame of their own condemnation, they become indignant against his great power.[1] They are indeed constrained to yield; but they storm, because they cannot resist; and ascribing dominion to him, they in a manner charge him with tyranny. In the same manner the Sophists in their schools foolishly dispute on what they call his absolute justice, as though forgetful of his own righteousness, he would try the power of his authority by throwing all things into confusion. Thus then speak the ungodly in this passage,—" What cause has he to be angry with us? Since he has formed us such as we are, since he leads us at his will where he pleases, what else does he in destroying us but punish his own work in us? For it is not in our power to contend with him; how much soever we may resist, he will yet have the upper hand. Then unjust will be his judgment, if he condemns us; and unre-

words have no meaning. The history of God's providence is an obvious confirmation of the same awful truth.—*Ed.*

[1] The clause rendered by *Calvin*, " Quid adhuc conqueritur—why does he yet complain?" is rendered by *Beza*, " Quid adhuc succenset—why is he yet angry?" Our common version is the best, and is followed by *Doddridge, Macknight*, and *Stuart.* The γὰρ, in the next clause, is omitted by *Calvin*, but *Griesbach* says that it ought to be retained.—*Ed.*

strainable is the power which he now employs towards us." What does Paul say to these things?

20. *But, O man! who art thou?* &c.[1] As it is a participle in Greek, we may read what follows in the present tense, *who disputest*, or contendest, or strivest in opposition to God; for it is expressed in Greek according to this meaning,— "Who art thou who enterest into a dispute with God?" But there is not much difference in the sense.[2] In this first answer, he does nothing else but beat down impious blasphemy by an argument taken from the condition of man: he will presently subjoin another, by which he will clear the righteousness of God from all blame.

It is indeed evident that no cause is adduced higher than the will of God. Since there was a ready answer, that the difference depends on just reasons, why did not Paul adopt such a brief reply? But he placed the will of God in the highest rank for this reason,—that it alone may suffice us for all other causes. No doubt, if the objection had been false, that God according to his own will rejects those whom he honours not with his favour, and chooses those whom he gratuitously loves, a refutation would not have been neglected by Paul. The ungodly object and say, that men are exempted from blame, if the will of God holds the first place in their salvation, or in their perdition. Does Paul deny this? Nay, by his answer he confirms it, that is, that God determines concerning men, as it seems good to him, and that men in vain and madly rise up to contend with God; for he assigns, by his own right, whatever lot he pleases to what he forms.

But they who say that Paul, wanting reason, had recourse

---

[1] "But" is not sufficiently emphatical here; μενοῦνγε; "yes, verily," in ch. x. 18; "yea, rather," in Luke xi. 28; "doubtless," in Phil. iii. 8; it may be rendered here, "nay, rather."—*Ed.*

[2] "Quis es qui contendas judicio cum Deo;" τίς εἶ ὁ ἀνταποκρινόμενος, τῷ Θεῷ; "that repliest against God," is the rendering of *Macknight* and *Stuart;* "who enterest into a debate with God," is what *Doddridge* gives. The verb occurs once in another place, Luke xiv. 6, and "answer again" is our version. *Schleusner* says that ἀντὶ prefixed to verbs is often redundant. In Job xvi. 8, and xxxii. 12, this compound is used by the Septuagint simply in the sense of answering, for ענה. He renders it here, "cum Deo altercari—to quarrel, *or*, dispute with God."—*Ed.*

to reproof, cast a grievous calumny on the Holy Spirit: for the things calculated to vindicate God's justice, and ready at hand, he was at first unwilling to adduce, for they could not have been comprehended; yea, he so modifies his second reason, that he does not undertake a full defence, but in such a manner as to give a sufficient demonstration of God's justice, if it be considered by us with devout humility and reverence.

He reminds man of what is especially meet for him to remember, that is, of his own condition; as though he had said,—" Since thou art man, thou ownest thyself to be dust and ashes; why then doest thou contend with the Lord about that which thou art not able to understand?" In a word, the Apostle did not bring forward what might have been said, but what is suitable to our ignorance. Proud men clamour, because Paul, admitting that men are rejected or chosen by the secret counsel of God, alleges no cause; as though the Spirit of God were silent for want of reason, and not rather, that by his silence he reminds us, that a mystery which our minds cannot comprehend ought to be reverently adored, and that he thus checks the wantonness of human curiosity. Let us then know, that God does for no other reason refrain from speaking, but that he sees that we cannot contain his immense wisdom in our small measure; and thus regarding our weakness, he leads us to moderation and sobriety.

Does what is formed? &c. We see that Paul dwells continually on this,—that the will of God, though its reason is hid from us, is to be counted just; for he shows that he is deprived of his right, if he is not at liberty to determine what he sees meet concerning his creatures. This seems unpleasant to the ears of many. There are also those who pretend that God is exposed to great reproach were such a power ascribed to him, as though they in their fastidiousness were better divines than Paul, who has laid down this as the rule of humility to the faithful, that they are to admire the sovereignty of God, and not to estimate it by their own judgment.

But he represses this arrogance of contending with God

by a most apt similitude, in which he seems to have alluded to Is. xlv. 9, rather than to Jer. xviii. 6; for nothing else is taught us by Jeremiah, than that Israel was in the hand of the Lord, so that he could for his sins wholly break him in pieces, as a potter the earthen vessel. But Isaiah ascends higher, "Woe to him," he says, "who speaks against his maker;" that is, the pot that contends with the former of the clay; "shall the clay say to its former, what doest thou?" &c. And surely there is no reason for a mortal man to think himself better than earthen vessel, when he compares himself with God. We are not however to be over-particular in applying this testimony to our present subject, since Paul only meant to allude to the words of the Prophet, in order that the similitude might have more weight.[1]

21. *Has not the worker of the clay?* &c. The reason why what is formed ought not to contend with its former, is, that the former does nothing but what he has a right to do. By the word *power*, he means not that the maker has strength to do according to his will, but that this privilege rightly and justly belongs to him. For he intends not to claim for God any arbitrary power but what ought to be justly ascribed to him.

And further, bear this in mind,—that as the potter takes away nothing from the clay, whatever form he may give it; so God takes away nothing from man, in whatever condition he may create him. Only this is to be remembered, that God is deprived of a portion of his honour, except such an authority over men be conceded to him as to constitute him the arbitrator of life and death.[2]

---

[1] The words in the 20th verse are taken almost literally from Is. xxix. 16, only the latter clause is somewhat different; the sentence is, "μὴ ἐρεῖ τὸ πλάσμα τῷ πλάσαντι αὐτό, οὐ σύ με ἔπλασας—shall what is formed say to its former, Thou hast not formed me?" This is a faithful rendering of the Hebrew.

Then the words in the 21st verse are not verbally taken from either of the two places referred to above; but the simile is adopted.—*Ed.*

[2] The metaphor in these verses is doubtless to be interpreted according to the context. Not only *Calvin*, but many others, have deduced from it what is not consistent with what the next verse contains, which gives the necessary explanation. By the " mass " or the lump of clay, is not meant mankind, contemplated as creatures, but as fallen creatures; or, as *Augustine* and *Pareus* call them, " massa damnata—the condemned mass;" for

22. *What* if God, willing to show his wrath, and to make his power known, endured with much long-suffering the vessels of wrath fitted to destruction:

23. And that he might make known the riches of his glory on the vessels of mercy, which he had afore prepared unto glory,

22. Quid autem si Deus volens demonstrare iram, et notam facere potentiam suam, sustinuit in multa patientia vasa iræ, in interitum apparata;

23. Ut notas quoque faceret divitias gloriæ suæ in vasa misericordiæ, quæ preparavit in gloriam?

22. *And what,* &c. A second answer, by which he briefly shows, that though the counsel of God is in fact incomprehensible, yet his unblamable justice shines forth no less in the perdition of the reprobate than in the salvation of the elect. He does not indeed give a reason for divine election, so as to assign a cause why this man is chosen and that man rejected; for it was not meet that the things contained in the secret counsel of God should be subjected to the judgment of men; and, besides, this mystery is inexplicable. He therefore keeps us from curiously examining those things which exceed human comprehension. He yet shows, that as far as God's predestination manifests itself, it appears perfectly just.

The particles, εἰ δὲ, used by Paul, I take to mean, *And what if?* so that the whole sentence is a question; and thus the sense will be more evident: and there is here an ellipsis, when we are to consider this as being understood,—" Who then can charge him with unrighteousness, or arraign him?" for here appears nothing but the most perfect course of justice.[1]

they are called in the next verse *vessels of wrath,* that is, the objects of wrath; and such are all by nature, according to what Paul says in Eph. ii. 3; " we were," he says, " by nature the children of wrath, even as others."

" The words, 'I will have mercy on whom I will have mercy,' imply that all deserved wrath; so that the lump of clay in the hands of the potter must refer to men already existing in God's foreknowledge as fallen creatures."—*Scott.*

In all the instances in which this metaphor is used by Isaiah and Jeremiah, it is applied to the Jews in *their state of degeneracy,* and very pointedly in Isaiah lxiv. 8: where it is preceded, in the 6th verse, by that remarkable passage, " We are all as an unclean thing," &c. The clay then, or the mass, is the mass of mankind as corrupted and depraved.—*Ed.*

[1] Critics have in various ways attempted to supply the ellipsis, but what is here proposed is most approved. *Beza* considered the corresponding

But if we wish fully to understand Paul, almost every word must be examined. He then argues thus,—There are vessels prepared for destruction, that is, given up and appointed to destruction: they are also vessels of wrath, that is, made and formed for this end, that they may be examples of God's vengeance and displeasure. If the Lord bears patiently for a time with these, not destroying them at the first moment, but deferring the judgment prepared for them, and this in order to set forth the decisions of his severity, that others may be terrified by so dreadful examples, and also to make known his power, to exhibit which he makes them in various ways to serve ; and, further, that the amplitude of his mercy towards the elect may hence be more fully known and more brightly shine forth ;—what is there worthy of being reprehended in this dispensation? But that he is silent as to the reason, why they are vessels appointed to destruction, is no matter of wonder. He indeed takes it as granted, according to what has been already said, that the

clause to be at verse 30, and viewed the intervening verses as parenthetic, " And if God," &c.,—" What then shall we say?" *Grotius* subjoined, " Does God do any wrong?" *Elsner*, " Has he not the power?" and *Wolfius*, " What canst thou say against God?" *Stuart* proposes to repeat the question in verse 20, " Who art thou?" &c. Some connect this verse with the question in verse 20, and include the latter part of it and verse 21 in a parenthesis. Whatever way may be adopted, the sense is materially the same. It has also been suggested that εἰ δὲ is for εἴπερ, *since, seeing*, 2 Thess. i. 6; 1 Pet. ii. 3. In this case no apodosis is necessary. But we may take εἰ, as meaning *since*, and δὲ as an illative, and render the three verses thus,—

22. " Since then God willed (or, it was God's will) to show his wrath and to make known his power, he endured with much forbearance the vessels
23. of wrath, fitted for destruction ; so *he willed* to make known the riches of his glory towards the vessels of mercy, whom he has fore-prepared
24. for glory, even us, whom he has called not only from the Jews but also from the Gentiles."

The verb ἐστι, or ἦν, is often understood after participles, especially in Hebrew; and καὶ has the meaning of *so* in some instances, Matt. vi. 10; Acts vii. 51; Gal. i. 9; and in some cases, as *Schleusner* says, without being preceded by any particle of comparison, such as Matt. xii. 26, and 1 John ii. 27, 28; but εἰ here stands somewhat in that character.

The beginning of verse 23 presents an anomaly, if, with *Stuart* and others, we consider " willing " or wills to be understood, as it is followed in the preceding verse by an infinitive, and here by a subjunctive mood. But *Beza, Grotius,* and *Hammond*, seem to regard the verb " endured," to be here, as it were, repeated, which gives the same meaning to the passage as that which is given to it by *Calvin.—Ed.*

reason is hid in the secret and inexplorable counsel of God; whose justice it behoves us rather to adore than to scrutinize.

And he has mentioned *vessels,* as commonly signifying instruments; for whatever is done by all creatures, is, as it were, the ministration of divine power. For the best reason then are we, the faithful, called the vessels of mercy, whom the Lord uses as instruments for the manifestation of his mercy; and the reprobate are the vessels of wrath, because they serve to show forth the judgments of God.

22. *That he might also make known the riches of his glory,* &c. I doubt not but the two particles καὶ ἵνα, is an instance of a construction, where the first word is put last; (ὕστερον πρότερον;) and that this clause may better unite with the former, I have rendered it, *That he might also make known,* &c. (*Ut notas quoque faceret,* &c.) It is the second reason which manifests the glory of God in the destruction of the reprobate, because the greatness of divine mercy towards the elect is hereby more clearly made known; for how do they differ from them except that they are delivered by the Lord from the same gulf of destruction? and this by no merit of their own, but through his gratuitous kindness. It cannot then be but that the infinite mercy of God towards the elect must appear increasingly worthy of praise, when we see how miserable are all they who escape not his wrath.

The word *glory,* which is here twice mentioned, I consider to have been used for God's mercy, a metonymy of effect for the cause; for his chief praise or glory is in acts of kindness. So in Eph. i. 13, after having taught us, that we have been adopted to the praise of the glory of his grace, he adds, that we are sealed by the Spirit of promise unto the praise of his glory, the word grace being left out. He wished then to show, that the elect are instruments or vessels through whom God exercises his mercy, that through them he may glorify his name.

Though in the second clause he asserts more expressly, that it is God who prepares the elect for glory, as he had simply said before that the reprobate are vessels prepared for destruction; there is yet no doubt but that the preparation of both is connected with the secret counsel of God. Paul might have otherwise said, that the reprobate give up or cast themselves into destruction; but he intimates here, that before they are born they are destined to their lot.

24. Even us, whom he hath called, not of the Jews only, but also of the Gentiles?	24. Quos etiam vocavit, nimirum nos, non solum ex Iudæis, sed etiam ex Gentibus:
25. As he saith also in Osee, I will call them my people, which were not my people; and her beloved, which was not beloved.	25. Quemadmodum et in Osee dicit, Vocabo populum meum eum qui non est populus, et dilectam eam quæ non est dilecta:
26. And it shall come to pass, *that* in the place where it was said unto them, Ye *are* not my people; there shall they be called the children of the living God.	26. Et erit in loco ubi dictum est eis, Non populus meus vos, illic vocabuntur filii Dei viventis.
27. Esaias also crieth concerning Israel, Though the number of the children of Israel be as the sand of the sea, a remnant shall be saved:	27. Iesaias autem clamat super Israel, Si fuerit numerus filiorum Israel ut arena maris, reliquiæ servabuntur:
28. For he will finish the work, and cut *it* short in righteousness; because a short work will the Lord make upon the earth.	28. Sermonem enim consummans et abbrevians,[1] quoniam sermonem abbreviatum faciet Dominus in terra:
29. And as Esaias said before, Except the Lord of Sabaoth had left us a seed, we had been as Sodoma, and been made like unto Gomorrha.	29. Et quemadmodum prius dixerat Iesaias, Nisi Dominus Sabbaoth reliquisset nobis semen, instar Sodomæ facti essemus, et Gomorrhæ essemus assimilati.

24. *Whom he also called,* &c. From the reasoning which he has been hitherto carrying on respecting the freedom of divine election, two things follow,—that the grace of God is not so confined to the Jewish people that it does not also flow to other nations, and diffuse itself through the whole world,—and then, that it is not even so tied to the Jews that it comes without exception to all the children of Abraham according to the flesh; for if God's election is based on his own good pleasure alone, wherever his will turns itself, there his election exists. Election being then established, the way is now in a manner prepared for him to proceed to those things which he designed to say respecting the calling of the Gentiles, and also respecting the rejection of the Jews;

---

[1] "In righteousness," left out. The word rendered "matter" is "sermo," but it is explained in this sense in the comment.—*Ed.*

the first of which seemed strange for its novelty, and the other wholly unbecoming. As, however, the last had more in it to offend, he speaks in the first place of that which was less disliked. He says then, that the vessels of God's mercy, whom he selects for the glory of his name, are taken from every people, from the Gentiles no less than from the Jews.

But though in the relative *whom* the rule of grammar is not fully observed by Paul,[1] yet his object was, by making as it were a transition, to subjoin that we are the vessels of God's glory, who have been taken in part from the Jews and in part from the Gentiles; and he proves from the calling of God, that there is no difference between nations made in election. For if to be descended from the Gentiles was no hinderance that God should not call us, it is evident that the Gentiles are by no means to be excluded from the kingdom of God and the covenant of eternal salvation.

25. *As he says in Hosea,*[2] &c. He proves now that the calling of the Gentiles ought not to have been deemed a new thing, as it had long before been testified by the prediction of the prophet. The meaning is evident; but there is some difficulty in the application of this testimony; for no one can deny but that the prophet in that passage speaks of the Israelites. For the Lord, having been offended with their wickedness, declared that they should be no longer his people: he afterwards subjoined a consolation, and said, that of those who were not beloved he would make some beloved, and from those who were not a people he would make a people. But Paul applies to the Gentiles what was expressly spoken to the Israelites.

They who have hitherto been most successful in untying this knot have supposed that Paul meant to adopt this kind of reasoning,—" What may seem to be an hinderance to the Gentiles to become partakers of salvation did also exist as to the Jewish nation: as then God did formerly receive into favour the Jews, whom he had cast away and exterminated, so also now he exercises the same kindness towards the

---

[1] It is an instance of Hebraism, the use of a double pronoun—*whom* and *us*, governed by the same verb.—*Ed*.
[2] Hos. ii. 23. See 1 Pet. ii. 10.

Gentiles." But as this interpretation, though it may be supported, yet seems to me to be somewhat strained, let the readers consider this,—Whether it would not be a more suitable view to regard the consolation given by the prophet, as intended, not only for the Jews, but also for the Gentiles: for it was not a new or an unusual thing with the prophets, after having pronounced on the Jews God's vengeance on account of their sins, to turn themselves to the kingdom of Christ, which was to be propagated through the whole world. And this they did, not without reason; for since the Jews so provoked God's wrath by their sins, that they deserved to be rejected by him, no hope of salvation remained, except they turned to Christ, through whom the covenant of grace was to be restored: and as it was based on him, so it was then renewed, when he interposed. And doubtless, as Christ was the only refuge in great extremities, no solid comfort could have been brought to miserable sinners, and such as saw God's wrath impending over them, except by setting Christ before their eyes. Yes, it was usual with the prophets, as we have reminded you, after having humbled the people by pronouncing on them divine vengeance, to call their attention to Christ, as the only true asylum of those in despair. And where the kingdom of Christ is erected there also is raised up that celestial Jerusalem, into which citizens from all parts of the world assemble. And this is what is chiefly included in the present prophecy: for when the Jews were banished from God's family, they were thus reduced to a common class, and put on a level with the Gentiles. The difference being taken away, God's mercy is now indiscriminately extended to all the Gentiles. We hence see that the prophet's prediction is fitly applied to the present subject; in which God declares, that after having equalized the Jews and the Gentiles, he would gather a Church for himself from aliens, so that they who were not a people would begin to be so.

I will call them my people which are not a people. This is said with respect to the divorce, which God had already made with the people, by depriving them of all honour, so that they did not excel other nations. Though they indeed, whom God in his eternal counsel has destined as sons to himself, are perpetually his sons, yet Scripture in many parts counts none to be God's children but those, the election of whom has been proved by their calling: and hence he teaches us not to judge, much less to decide, respecting God's election, except as far as it manifests itself by its own evidences. Thus Paul, after having shown to the Ephesians that their election and adoption had been determined by God before the creation of the world, shortly after declares, that they were once alienated from God, (Eph. ii. 12,) that is, during that time when the Lord had not manifested his love towards them; though he had embraced them in his eternal mercy. Hence, in this passage, they are said not to be beloved, to whom God declares wrath rather than love: for until adoption reconciles men to God, we know that his wrath abides on them.

The feminine gender of the participle depends on the context of the prophet; for he had said, that a daughter had been born to him, to whom he gave this name, *Not beloved*, in order that the people might know that they were hated by God. Now as rejection was the reason for hatred, so the beginning of love, as the prophet teaches, is, when God adopts those who had been for a time strangers.[1]

27. *And Isaiah exclaims*, &c. He proceeds now to the second part, with which he was unwilling to begin, lest he should too much exasperate their minds. And it is not without a wise contrivance, that he adduces Isaiah as exclaiming, not speaking, in order that he might excite more attention. But the words of the Prophet were evidently intended to keep the Jews from glorying too much in the flesh: for it was a thing dreadful to be heard, that of so large a multitude, a small number only would obtain salvation. For though the Prophet, after having described the

---

[1] The quotation is from Hosea ii. 23, and is not literal either from the Hebrew or from the *Septuagint*. The order of the verse is reversed; and the word "beloved" is taken from the *Septuagint*. "Not beloved," in Hebrew, is *lo-ruhamah*, i.e., one not pitied, or one who has not received mercy: which is the same in meaning.

In the next verse, 26, the words are taken from Hos. i. 10, and are not *verbatim* either from the Hebrew or the *Septuagint*, but the difference is very trifling.—*Ed.*

devastation of the people, lest the faithful should think that the covenant of God was wholly abolished, gave some remaining hope of favour; yet he confined it to a few. But as the Prophet predicted of his own time, let us see how could Paul rightly apply this to his purpose. It must be in this sense,—When the Lord resolved to deliver his people from the Babylonian captivity, his purpose was, that this benefit of deliverance should come only to a very few of that vast multitude; which might have been said to be the remnant of that destruction, when compared with the great number which he suffered to perish in exile. Now that temporal restoration was typical of the real renovation of the Church of God; yea, it was only its commencement. What therefore happened then, is to be now much more completely fulfilled as the very progress and completion of that deliverance.

28. *For I will finish and shorten the matter,* &c.[1] Omitting various interpretations, I will state what appears to me to be the real meaning: The Lord will so cut short, and cut off his people, that the residue may seem as it were a consumption, that is, may have the appearance and the vestige of a very great ruin. However, the few who shall remain from the consumption shall be a proof of the work of God's righteousness, or, what I prefer, shall serve to testify the righteousness of God throughout the world. As *word* often in Scripture means a thing, the consummated word is put for consumption. Many interpreters have here been grossly mistaken, who have attempted to philosophize with too

---

[1] Sermonem enim consummans et abbrevians," &c.; Λόγον γὰρ, &c. It is literally the *Septuagint* except in two instances: Paul puts in γὰρ, and substitutes ἐπὶ τῆς γῆς for ἐν τῇ οἰκουμένῃ ὅλῃ. It is a difficult passage in Hebrew: but the following rendering will make it materially consistent with the words of the Apostle, who evidently did not intend to give the words literally,

> A destruction, soon executed,
> *Shall* overflow in righteousness;
> For completed and soon executed shall it be;
> The Lord, Jehovah of hosts, shall do *it*,
> In the midst of the whole land.

The word rendered above "soon executed," means literally, abbreviated or cut short, signifying the quick execution of a thing or work. "*Shall* overflow in righteousness," imports, "*shall* justly or deservedly overflow."—*Ed.*

much refinement; for they have imagined, that the doctrine of the gospel is thus called, because it is, when the ceremonies are cut off, a brief compendium of the law; though the word means on the contrary a consumption.[1] And not only here is an error committed by the translator, but also in Isaiah x. 22, 23; xxviii. 22; and in Ezek. xi. 13; where it is said, "Ah! ah! Lord God! wilt thou make a completion of the remnant of Israel?" But the Prophets meant to say, " Wilt thou destroy the very remnant with utter destruction?" And this has happened through the ambiguity of the Hebrew word. For as the word, כלה, *cale*, means to finish and to perfect, as well as to consume, this difference has not been sufficiently observed according to the passages in which it occurs.

But Isaiah has not in this instance adopted one word only, but has put down two words, *consumption* and *termination*, or cutting off; so that the affectation of Hebraism in the Greek translator was singularly unseasonable; for to what purpose was it to involve a sentence, in itself clear, in an obscure and figurative language? It may be further added, that Isaiah speaks here hyperbolically; for by consumption he means diminution, such as is wont to be after a remarkable slaughter.

29. *And as Isaiah had before said*, &c.[2] He brings another

---

[1] There are many venerable names in favour of this opinion, such as *Ambrose, Chrysostom, Augustine*, &c. Not knowing the Hebrew language, they attached a classical meaning to the expression, λόγον συντιτμημίνον, wholly at variance with what the Hebrew means, as *Calvin* justly observes. The word, συντιτμημίνον, in this passage, as *Schleusner* says, bears a meaning different from what it has in the classics; it imports what is cut short, that is, quickly executed.—*Ed.*

[2] Isaiah i. 9. The words of the Septuagint are given literally, and differ only in one instance from the Hebrew; " seed" is put for " remnant;" but as " seed" in this case evidently means a small portion reserved for sowing, the idea of the original is conveyed. *Schleusner* refers to examples both in *Josephus* and *Plato*, in which the word " seed," is used in the sense of a small reserved portion. Its most common meaning in Scripture is posterity.

Paul has given " Sabaoth" from the Septuagint, which is the Hebrew untranslated. This word, in connection with God, is variously rendered by the Septuagint: for the most part in Isaiah, and in some other places, it is found untranslated as here; but in the Psalms and in other books, it is often rendered τῶν δυναμίων, that is, Jehovah or Lord " of the powers," and often παντοκράτωρ, " omnipotent;" and sometimes ὁ ἅγιος, " the holy

testimony from the first chapter, where the Prophet deplores the devastation of Israel in his time: and as this had happened once, it was no new thing. The people of Israel had indeed no pre-eminence, except what they had derived from their ancestors; who had yet been in such a manner treated, that the Prophet complained that they had been so afflicted, that they were not far from having been destroyed, as Sodom and Gomorrah had been. There was, however, this difference, that a few were preserved for a seed, to raise up the name, that they might not wholly perish, and be consigned to eternal oblivion. For it behoved God to be ever mindful of his promise, so as to manifest his mercy in the midst of the severest judgments.

30. What shall we say then? That the Gentiles, which followed not after righteousness, have attained to righteousness, even the righteousness which is of faith:
31. But Israel, which followed after the law of righteousness, hath not attained to the law of righteousness.
32. Wherefore? Because *they sought it* not by faith, but as it were by the works of the law. For they stumbled at that stumblingstone:
33. As it is written, Behold, I lay in Sion a stumblingstone and rock of offence: and whosoever believeth on him shall not be ashamed.

30. Quid ergo dicemus? Quòd gentes quæ non sectabantur justitiam, adeptæ sunt justitiam, justitiam autem ex fide:
31. Israel autem sectando legem justitiæ, ad legem justitiæ non pervenit.
32. Quare? Quia non ex fide, sed quasi ex operibus; offenderunt enim ad lapidem offensionis:
33. Quemadmodum scriptum est, Ecce pono in Sion lapidem offensionis et petram offendiculi: et omnis qui crediderit in eum non pudefiet.

30. *What then,* &c. That he might cut off from the Jews every occasion of murmuring against God, he now begins to show those causes, which may be comprehended by human minds, why the Jewish nation had been rejected. But they do what is absurd and invert all order, who strive to assign and set up causes above the secret predestination of God, which he has previously taught us is to be counted as the first cause. But as this is superior to all other causes, so the corruption and wickedness of the ungodly afford a reason and an occasion for the judgments of God: and as he was

one." But our version, "Jehovah" or "Lord of hosts," is the proper rendering. It means the hosts of animate and inanimate creatures; in fact, the whole universe, all created things; but, according to the context, it often specifically refers to material things, or to things immaterial.—*Ed.*

engaged on a difficult point, he introduced a question, and, as though he were in doubt, asked what might be said on the subject.

That the Gentiles who did not pursue, &c. Nothing appeared more unreasonable, or less befitting, than that the Gentiles, who, having no concern for righteousness, rolled themselves in the lasciviousness of their flesh, should be called to partake of salvation, and to obtain righteousness; and that, on the other hand, the Jews, who assiduously laboured in the works of the law, should be excluded from the reward of righteousness. Paul brings forward this, which was so singular a paradox, in such a manner, that by adding a reason he softens whatever asperity there might be in it; for he says, that the righteousness which the Gentiles attained was by faith; and that it hence depends on the Lord's mercy, and not on man's own worthiness; and that a zeal for the law, by which the Jews were actuated, was absurd; for they sought to be justified by works, and thus laboured for what no man could attain to; and still further, they stumbled at Christ, through whom alone a way is open to the attainment of righteousness.

But in the first clause it was the Apostle's object to exalt the grace of God alone, that no other reason might be sought for in the calling of the Gentiles but this,—that he deigned to embrace them when unworthy of his favour.

He speaks expressly of righteousness, without which there can be no salvation: but by saying that the righteousness of the Gentiles proceeded from faith, he intimates, that it was based on a gratuitous reconciliation; for if any one imagines that they were justified, because they had by faith obtained the Spirit of regeneration, he departs far from the meaning of Paul; it would not indeed have been true, that they had attained what they sought not, except God had freely embraced them while they were straying and wandering, and had offered them righteousness, for which, being unknown, they could have had no desire. It must also be observed, that the Gentiles could not have obtained righteousness by faith, except God had anticipated their faith by his grace; for they followed it when they first by faith aspired to righteousness; and so faith itself is a portion of his favour.

31. *But Israel, by pursuing,* &c. Paul openly states what seemed incredible,—that it was no wonder that the Jews gained nothing by sedulously following after righteousness; for by running out of the way, they wearied themselves in vain. But in the first place it seems to me that the law of righteousness is here an instance of transposition, and means the righteousness of the law;[1] and then, that when repeated in the second clause, it is to be taken in another sense, as signifying the model or the rule of righteousness.

The meaning then is,—"That Israel, depending on the righteousness of the law, even that which is prescribed in the law, did not understand the true method of justification." But there is a striking contrast in the expression, when he teaches us that the legal righteousness was the cause, that they had fallen away from the law of righteousness.

32. *Not by faith, but as it were by works,* &c. As false zeal seems commonly to be justly excused, Paul shows that

---

[1] There seems to be no necessity for this transposition. "A law (not the law) of righteousness" means a law which prescribes righteousness, and which, if done, would have conferred righteousness. But the Jews following this did not attain to a law of righteousness, such a law as secured righteousness. The Apostle often uses the same words in the same verse in a different sense, and leaves the meaning to be made out by the context. *Grotius* takes "law" as meaning way, "They followed the way of righteousness, but did not attain to a way of righteousness."

What follows the question in the next verse stands more connected with ver. 30 than with ver. 31; and we must consider that the word righteousness, and not law, is referred to by "it" after the verb "pursue," which is evidently to be understood before the words, "not by faith," &c., as the sentence is clearly elliptical.

The verb διώκω, rendered "sector" by *Calvin*, means strictly to pursue what flees away from us, whether a wild beast or an enemy; it signifies also to follow a leader, and to *run* a race, and further, to desire, to attend to, or earnestly to seek a thing: and in this latter sense Paul often uses it. See ch. xii. 13; xiv. 19; 1 Cor. xiv. 1. Similar is the application of the corresponding verb, רדף, in Hebrew. See Deut. xvi. 20; Ps. xxxiv. 14. "Quæro—to seek," is the word adopted by *Grotius*.

But *Pareus* and *Hammond* consider that there are here three agonistic terms, διώκων, κατίλαβι, and ἔφθασι. The first signifies the running; the third, the reaching of the goal; and the second, the laying hold on the prize: and with this corresponds the stumbling afterwards mentioned. The Gentiles did not run at all, but the Jews did, and in running, they stumbled; while the Gentiles reached the goal, not by running, or by their own efforts, but by faith, and laid hold on the prize of righteousness.—*Ed.*

they are deservedly rejected, who attempt to attain salvation by trusting in their own works ; for they, as far as they can, abolish faith, without which no salvation can be expected. Hence, were they to gain their object, such a success would be the annihilation of true righteousness. You farther see how faith and the merits of works are contrasted, as things altogether contrary to each other. As then trust in works is the chief hinderance, by which our way to obtain righteousness is closed up, it is necessary that we should wholly renounce it, in order that we may depend on God's goodness alone. This example of the Jews ought indeed justly to terrify all those who strive to obtain the kingdom of God by works. Nor does he understand by the works of the law, ceremonial observances, as it has been before shown, but the merits of those works to which faith is opposed, which looks, as I may say, with both eyes on the mercy of God alone, without casting one glance on any worthiness of its own.

For they have stumbled at the stone, &c. He confirms by a strong reason the preceding sentence. There is indeed nothing more inconsistent than that they should obtain righteousness who strive to destroy it. Christ has been given to us for righteousness, whosoever obtrudes on God the righteousness of works, attempts to rob him of his own office. And hence it appears that whenever men, under the empty pretence of being zealous for righteousness, put confidence in their works, they do in their furious madness carry on war with God himself.

But how they stumble at Christ, who trust in their works, it is not difficult to understand ; for except we own ourselves to be sinners, void and destitute of any righteousness of our own, we obscure the dignity of Christ, which consists in this, that to us all he is light, life, resurrection, righteousness, and healing. But how is he all these things, except that he illuminates the blind, restores the lost, quickens the dead, raises up those who are reduced to nothing, cleanses those who are full of filth, cures and heals those infected with diseases ? Nay, when we claim for ourselves any righteousness, we in a manner contend with the power of Christ ; for his office is no less to beat down all the pride of the flesh, than to relieve and comfort those who labour and are wearied under their burden.

The quotation is rightly made; for God in that passage declares that he would be to the people of Judah and of Israel for a rock of offence, at which they should stumble and fall. Since Christ is that God who spoke by the Prophets, it is no wonder that this also should be fulfilled in him. And by calling Christ the *stone of stumbling*, he reminds us that it is not to be wondered at if they made no progress in the way of righteousness, who through their wilful stubbornness stumbled at the rock of offence, when God had showed to them the way so plainly.[1] But we must observe, that this stumbling does not properly belong to Christ viewed in himself; but, on the contrary, it is what happens through the wickedness of men, according to what immediately follows.

33. *And every one who believes in him shall not be ashamed.* He subjoins this testimony from another part for the consolation of the godly; as though he had said, "Because Christ is called the stone of stumbling, there is no reason that we should dread him, or entertain fear instead of confidence; for he is appointed for ruin to the unbelieving, but for life and resurrection to the godly." As then the former prophecy, concerning the stumbling and offence, is fulfilled in the rebellious and unbelieving, so there is another which is intended for the godly, and that is, that he is a firm stone, precious, a corner-stone, most firmly fixed, and whosoever builds on it shall never fall. By putting *shall not be ashamed* instead of *shall not hasten* or fall, he has followed the Greek Translator. It is indeed certain that the Lord in that passage intended to strengthen the hope of his people: and when the Lord bids us to entertain good hope, it hence follows that we cannot be ashamed.[2] See a passage like this in 1 Peter ii. 10.

---

[1] "Error is often a greater obstacle to the salvation of men than carelessness or vice. . . . Let no man think error in doctrine a slight practical evil. No road to perdition has ever been more thronged than that of false doctrine. Error is a shield over the conscience and a bandage over the eyes."—*Professor Hodge.*

[2] The citation in this verse is made in a remarkable manner. The first

CHAPTER X.

1. Brethren, my heart's desire and prayer to God for Israel is, that they might be saved.
2. For I bear them record, that they have a zeal of God, but not according to knowledge.
3. For they, being ignorant of God's righteousness, and going about to establish their own righteousness, have not submitted themselves unto the righteousness of God.
4. For Christ *is* the end of the law for righteousness to every one that believeth.

1. Fratres, benevolentia certè cordis mei, et deprecatio ad Deum super Israel, est in salutem.
2. Testimonium enim reddo illis, quòd zelum Dei habent, sed non secundum scientiam:
3. Ignorantes enim Dei justitiam, et propriam justitiam quærentes statuere, justitiæ Dei subjecti non fuerunt;
4. Finis enim Legis Christus in justitiam omni credenti.[1]

We here see with what solicitude the holy man obviated offences; for in order to soften whatever sharpness there may have been in his manner of explaining the rejection of the Jews, he still testifies, as before, his goodwill towards them, and proves it by the effect; for their salvation was an object of concern to him before the Lord, and such a feeling arises only from genuine love. It may be at the same time that he was also induced by another reason to testify his love towards the nation from which he had sprung; for his doctrine would have never been received by the Jews had they thought that he was avowedly inimical to them; and his defection would have been also suspected by the Gentiles, for they would have thought, as we have said in the last chapter, that he became an apostate from the law through his hatred of men.[2]

part, "Behold I lay in Zion," is taken from Is. xxviii. 16; what follows, "a stone of stumbling and rock of offence," is taken from Is. viii. 14: and then the last words, "and whosoever believes in him shall not be ashamed," are given from the preceding passage in Is. xxviii. 16. The subject is the same.

With respect to the last clause Paul has followed the *Septuagint*, "shall not be ashamed." But the Hebrew word, rendered in our version "shall not make haste," will bear a similar meaning, and may be translated, shall not hurry or be confounded.—*Ed.*

[1] The γὰρ, "for," at the beginning of this verse, connects it with the latter part of the preceding, as the γὰρ, "for," in the preceding connects it with the latter part of verse 2; and γὰρ also in verse 5 expresses a reason for what verse 4 contains. So that we have a regular chain; the following sentence gives a reason for the one immediately preceding in four instances. —*Ed.*

[2] *Calvin's* Latin for this verse is: "Fratres, benevolentia certè cordis

2. *For I bear to them a testimony,* &c. This was intended to secure credit to his love. There was indeed a just cause why he should regard them with compassion rather than hatred, since he perceived that they had fallen only through ignorance, and not through malignancy of mind, and especially as he saw that they were not led except by some regard for God to persecute the kingdom of Christ. Let us hence learn where our good intentions may guide us, if we yield to them. It is commonly thought a good and a very fit excuse, when he who is reproved pretends that he meant no harm. And this pretext is held good by many at this day, so that they apply not their minds to find out the truth of God, because they think that whatever they do amiss through ignorance, without any designed maliciousness, but with good intention, is excusable. But no one of us would excuse the Jews for having crucified Christ, for having cruelly raged against the Apostles, and for having attempted to destroy and extinguish the gospel; and yet they had the same defence as that in which we confidently glory. Away then with these vain evasions as to good intention; if we seek God sincerely, let us follow the way by which alone we can come to him. For it is better, as *Augustine* says, even to go limping in the right way than to run with all our might out of the way. If we would be really religious, let us remember that what *Lactantius* teaches is true, that true religion is alone that which is connected with the word of God.[1]

mei et deprecatio ad Deum super Israel est in salutem—Brethren, the goodwill indeed of my heart and prayer to God for Israel is for *their* salvation." The word for "goodwill," εὐδοκία, means a kind disposition towards another, it means here a benevolent or a sincere desire, or, according to *Theophylact*, an earnest desire. *Doddridge* renders it "affectionate desire;" *Beza*, "propensa voluntas—propense wish;" and *Stuart*, "kind desire."

At the beginning of the last chapter the Apostle expressed his great *grief* for his brethren the Jews, he now expresses his great *love* towards them, and his strong desire for their highest good—their salvation.—*Ed.*

[1] "A zeal of God," ζῆλον Θεοῦ, is a zeal *for* God, a genitive case of the object. Some regard "God" here as meaning something great, as it is sometimes used in Hebrew, and render the phrase, as *Macknight* does, "a great zeal;" but this is not required by the context. The Jews had professedly "a zeal for God," but not accompanied with knowledge. The necessity of knowledge as the guide of zeal is noted by *Turrettin* in four particulars: 1. That we may distinguish truth from falsehood, as there

And further, since we see that they perish, who with good intention wander in darkness, let us bear in mind, that we are worthy of thousand deaths, if after having been illuminated by God, we wander knowingly and wilfully from the right way.

3. *For being ignorant of the righteousness of God*, &c. See how they went astray through inconsiderate zeal! for they sought to set up a righteousness of their own; and this foolish confidence proceeded from their ignorance of God's righteousness. Notice the contrast between the righteousness of God and that of men. We first see, that they are opposed to one another, as things wholly contrary, and cannot stand together. It hence follows, that God's righteousness is subverted, as soon as men set up their own. And again, as there is a correspondence between the things contrasted, the righteousness of God is no doubt his gift; and in like manner, the righteousness of men is that which they derive from themselves, or believe that they bring before God. Then he who seeks to be justified through himself, submits not to God's righteousness; for the first step towards obtaining the righteousness of God is to renounce our own righteousness: for why is it, that we seek righteousness from another, except that necessity constrains us?

We have already stated, in another place, how men put on the righteousness of God by faith, that is, when the righteousness of Christ is imputed to them. But Paul grievously dishonours the pride by which hypocrites are inflated, when they cover it with the specious mask of zeal; for he says, that all such, by shaking off as it were the yoke, are adverse to and rebel against the righteousness of God.

4. *For the end of the law is Christ*, &c. The word *completion*,[1] seems not to me unsuitable in this place; and *Eras-*

may be zeal for error and false doctrine as well as for that which is true; 2. That we may understand the comparative *importance* of things, so as not to make much of what is little, and make little account of what is great; 3. That we may prosecute and defend the truth in the *right way*, with prudence, firmness, fidelity, and meekness; 4. That our zeal may have the *right object*, not our own interest and reputation, but the glory of God and the salvation of men.—*Ed.*

[1] " Complementum—the complement," the filling up, the completion. The word τέλος, " end," is used in various ways, as signifying—1. The

mus has rendered it *perfection :* but as the other reading is almost universally approved, and is not inappropriate, readers, for my part, may retain it.

The Apostle obviates here an objection which might have been made against him ; for the Jews might have appeared to have kept the right way by depending on the righteousness of the law. It was necessary for him to disprove this false opinion; and this is what he does here. He shows that he is a false interpreter of the law, who seeks to be justified by his own works; because the law had been given for this end,—to lead us as by the hand to another righteousness: nay, whatever the law teaches, whatever it commands, whatever it promises, has always a reference to Christ as its main object; and hence all its parts ought to be applied to him. But this cannot be done, except we, being stripped of all righteousness, and confounded with the knowledge of our sin, seek gratuitous righteousness from him alone.

It hence follows, that the wicked abuse of the law was justly reprehended in the Jews, who absurdly made an obstacle of that which was to be their help : nay, it appears that they had shamefully mutilated the law of God ; for they

---

termination of any thing, either of evils, or of life, &c., Matt. x. 22; John xiii. 1 ;—2. Completion or fulfilment, Luke xxii. 37 ; 1 Tim. i. 9 ;—3. The *issue*, the effect, the consequence, the result, chap. vi. 21 ; 1 Pet. i. 9 ; 2 Cor. xi. 15 ;—4. *Tribute* or custom, chap. xiii. 7 ;—5. The *chief thing*, summary or substance, 1 Pet. iii. 8.

The meaning of the word depends on what is connected with it. The end of *evils*, or of life, is their termination; the end of a *promise* is its fulfilment; the end of a *command*, its performance or obedience; the end of *faith* is salvation. In such instances, the general idea is the result, or the effect, or the consequence. Now the law may be viewed as an economy, comprising the whole Jewish law, not perfect, but introductory ; in this view Christ may be said to be its end—its perfection or " its landing place." But we may also regard the law in its moral character, as the rule and condition of life ; then the end of the law is its fulfilment, the performance of what it requires in order to attain life : and Christ in this respect is its end, having rendered to it perfect obedience. This last meaning is most consistent with the words which follow, and with the Apostle's argument. The first view is taken by *Chrysostom, Beza, Turrettin,* as well as *Calvin ;* the second, by *Mede, Stuart,* and *Chalmers*. There is really not much difference in the two views ; only the sequel of the verse, " for righteousness to every one who believes," and the opposite sentiment in the next verse, " the man who doeth these shall live in (or through) them," seem to favour the latter view.—*Ed.*

rejected its soul, and seized on the dead body of the letter. For though the law promises reward to those who observe its righteousness, it yet substitutes, after having proved all guilty, another righteousness in Christ, which is not attained by works, but is received by faith as a free gift. Thus the righteousness of faith, (as we have seen in the first chapter,) receives a testimony from the law. We have then here a remarkable passage, which proves that the law in all its parts had a reference to Christ; and hence no one can rightly understand it, who does not continually level at this mark.

5. For Moses describeth the righteousness which is of the law, That the man which doeth those things shall live by them.
6. But the righteousness which is of faith speaketh on this wise, Say not in thine heart, Who shall ascend into heaven? (that is, to bring Christ down *from above*:)
7. Or, Who shall descend into the deep? (that is, to bring up Christ again from the dead.)
8. But what saith it? The word is nigh thee, *even* in thy mouth, and in thy heart: that is, the word of faith which we preach;
9. That if thou shalt confess with thy mouth the Lord Jesus, and shalt believe in thine heart that God hath raised him from the dead, thou shalt be saved.
10. For with the heart man believeth unto righteousness; and with the mouth confession is made unto salvation.

5. Moses enim describit justitiam quæ est ex Lege, Quòd qui fecerit ea homo vivet in ipsis.
6. Quæ vero est ex fide justitia sic dicit, Ne dixeris in corde tuo, Quis ascendet in cœlum? hoc est Christum deducere:
7. Aut, Quis descendet in abyssum? hoc est Christum ex mortuis reducere:
8. Sed quid dicit? Propè est verbum, in ore tuo et in corde tuo; hoc est verbum fidei quod prædicamus,
9. Quod si confessus fueris in ore tuo Dominum Iesum, et credideris in corde tuo quòd Deus suscitavit illum ex mortuis, salvus eris:
10. Corde enim creditur in justitiam, ore fit confessio in salutem.

5. *For Moses,* &c. To render it evident how much at variance is the righteousness of faith and that of works, he now compares them; for by comparison the opposition between contrary things appears more clear. But he refers not now to the oracles of the Prophets, but to the testimony of Moses, and for this reason,—that the Jews might understand that the law was not given by Moses in order to detain them in a dependence on works, but, on the contrary, to

lead them to Christ. He might have indeed referred to the Prophets as witnesses; but still this doubt must have remained, "How was it that the law prescribed another rule of righteousness?" He then removes this, and in the best manner, when by the teaching of the law itself he confirms the righteousness of faith.

But we ought to understand the reason why Paul harmonizes the law with faith, and yet sets the righteousness of one in opposition to that of the other:—The law has a twofold meaning; it sometimes includes the whole of what has been taught by Moses, and sometimes that part only which was peculiar to his ministration, which consisted of precepts, rewards, and punishments. But Moses had this common office—to teach the people the true rule of religion. Since it was so, it behoved him to preach repentance and faith; but faith is not taught, except by propounding promises of divine mercy, and those gratuitous: and thus it behoved him to be a preacher of the gospel; which office he faithfully performed, as it appears from many passages. In order to instruct the people in the doctrine of repentance, it was necessary for him to teach what manner of life was acceptable to God; and this he included in the precepts of the law. That he might also instil into the minds of the people the love of righteousness, and implant in them the hatred of iniquity, promises and threatenings were added; which proposed rewards to the just, and denounced dreadful punishments on sinners. It was now the duty of the people to consider in how many ways they drew curses on themselves, and how far they were from deserving anything at God's hands by their works, that being thus led to despair as to their own righteousness, they might flee to the haven of divine goodness, and so to Christ himself. This was the end or design of the Mosaic dispensation.

But as evangelic promises are only found scattered in the writings of Moses, and these also somewhat obscure, and as the precepts and rewards, allotted to the observers of the law, frequently occur, it rightly appertained to Moses as his own and peculiar office, to teach what is the real righteousness of works, and then to show what remuneration awaits the observance of it, and what punishment awaits those who come short of it. For this reason Moses is by John compared with Christ, when it is said, " That the law was given by Moses, but that grace and truth came by Christ." (John i. 17.) And whenever the word law is thus strictly taken, Moses is by implication opposed to Christ: and then we must consider what the law contains, as separate from the gospel. Hence what is said here of the *righteousness* of the law, must be applied, not to the whole office of Moses, but to that part which was in a manner peculiarly committed to him. I come now to the words.

For Moses describes, &c. Paul has γράφει, *writes;* which is used for a verb which means to describe, by taking away a part of it [ἐπιγράφει.] The passage is taken from Lev. xviii. 5, where the Lord promises eternal life to those who would keep his law ; for in this sense, as you see, Paul has taken the passage, and not only of temporal life, as some think. Paul indeed thus reasons,—" Since no man can attain the righteousness prescribed in the law, except he fulfils strictly every part of it, and since of this perfection all men have always come far short, it is in vain for any one to strive in this way for salvation : Israel then were very foolish, who expected to attain the righteousness of the law, from which we are all excluded." See how from the promise itself he proves, that it can avail us nothing, and for this reason, because the condition is impossible. What a futile device it is then to allege legal promises, in order to establish the righteousness of the law! For with these an unavoidable curse comes to us ; so far is it, that salvation should thence proceed. The more detestable on this account is the stupidity of the Papists, who think it enough to prove merits by adducing bare promises. "It is not in vain," they say, " that God has promised life to his servants." But at the same time they see not that it has been promised, in order that a consciousness of their own transgressions may strike all with the fear of death, and that being thus constrained by their own deficiency, they may learn to flee to Christ.

6. *But the righteousness*[1] *which is by faith,* &c. This passage is such as may not a little disturb the reader, and for two reasons—for it seems to be improperly applied by Paul—and the words are also turned to a different meaning. Of the words we shall hereafter see what may be said: we shall first notice the application. It is a passage taken from Deut. xxx. 12, where, as in the former passage, Moses speaks of the doctrine of the law, and Paul applies it to evangelic promises. This knot may be thus untied:—Moses shows, that the way to life was made plain: for the will of God was not now hid from the Jews, nor set far off from them, but placed before their eyes. If he had spoken of the law only, his reasoning would have been frivolous, since the law of God being set before their eyes, it was not easier to do it, than if it was afar off. He then means not the law only, but generally the whole of God's truth, which includes in it the gospel: for the word of the law by itself is never in our heart, no, not the least syllable of it, until it is implanted in us by the faith of the gospel. And then, even after regeneration, the word of the law cannot properly be said to be in our heart; for it demands perfection, from which even the faithful are far distant: but the word of the gospel has a seat in the heart, though it does not fill the heart; for it offers pardon for imperfection and defect. And Moses throughout that chapter, as also in the fourth, endeavours to commend to the people the remarkable kindness of God, because he had taken them under his own tuition and government, which commendation could not have belonged to the law only. It is no objection that Moses there speaks of forming the life according to the rule of the law; for the spirit of regeneration is connected with the gratuitous righteousness of faith. Nor is there a doubt but that this verse depends on that main truth, "The Lord shall circumcise thine heart," which he had recorded shortly before in the same chapter. They may therefore be easily disproved, who say that Moses speaks only in that passage of good works. That he speaks of works I indeed allow; but I

---

[1] Righteousness is here personified, according to the usual manner of the Apostle: law and sin had before been represented in the same way.—*Ed.*

deny it to be unreasonable, that the keeping of the law should be traced from its own fountain, even from the righteousness of faith. The explanation of the words must now follow.[1]

Say not in thine heart, Who shall ascend? &c. Moses mentions *heaven* and the *sea*, as places remote and difficult of access to men. But Paul, as though there was some spiritual mystery concealed under these words, applies them to the death and resurrection of Christ. If any one thinks that this interpretation is too strained and too refined, let him understand that it was not the object of the Apostle strictly to explain this passage, but to apply it to the explanation of his present subject. He does not, therefore, repeat verbally what Moses has said, but makes alterations, by which he accommodates more suitably to his own purpose the testimony of Moses. He spoke of inaccessible places; Paul refers to those, which are indeed hid from the sight of us all, and may yet be seen by our faith. If then you take these things as spoken for illustration, or by way of improvement, you cannot say that Paul has violently or inaptly changed the words of Moses; but you will, on the contrary, allow, that without loss of meaning, he has, in a striking manner, alluded to the words *heaven* and the *sea*.

Let us now then simply explain the words of Paul:—As the assurance of our salvation lies on two foundations, that is, when we understand, that life has been obtained for us, and death has been conquered for us, he teaches us that faith through the word of the gospel is sustained by both these; for Christ, by dying, destroyed death, and by rising again he

---

[1] It seems not necessary to have recourse to the distinctions made in the foregoing section. The character of the quotation given is correctly described in the words of *Chrysostom*, as quoted by *Poole*, " Paulus ea transtulit et aptavit ad justitiam fidei—Paul transferred and accommodated these things to the righteousness of faith." He evidently borrowed the words of Moses, not literally, but substantially, for the purpose of setting forth the truth he was handling. The speaker is not Moses, but " the righteousness of faith," represented as a person. *Luther*, as quoted by *Wolfius*, says, that " Paul, under the influence of the Spirit, took from Moses the occasion to form, as it were, a new and a suitable text against the justiciaries." It appears to be an application, by way of analogy, of the words of Moses to the gospel, and not a confirmatory testimony. *Chalmers* hesitates on the subject; but *Pareus, Wolfius, Turrettin*, and *Doddridge*, consider the words as applied by way of accommodation.—*Ed.*

obtained life in his own power. The benefit of Christ's death and resurrection is now communicated to us by the gospel: there is then no reason for us to seek anything farther. That it may thus appear, that the righteousness of faith is abundantly sufficient for salvation, he teaches us, that included in it are these two things, which are alone necessary for salvation. The import then of the words, *Who shall ascend into heaven?* is the same, as though you should say, "Who knows whether the inheritance of eternal and celestial life remains for us?" And the words, *Who shall descend into the deep?* mean the same, as though you should say, "Who knows whether the everlasting destruction of the soul follows the death of the body?" He teaches us, that doubt on those two points is removed by the righteousness of faith; for the one would draw down Christ from heaven, and the other would bring him up again from death. Christ's ascension into heaven ought indeed fully to confirm our faith as to eternal life; for he in a manner removes Christ himself from the possession of heaven, who doubts whether the inheritance of heaven is prepared for the faithful, in whose name, and on whose account he has entered thither. Since in like manner he underwent the horrors of hell to deliver us from them, to doubt whether the faithful are still exposed to this misery, is to render void, and, as it were, to deny his death.

8. *What does it say?*[1] For the purpose of removing the impediments of faith, he has hitherto spoken negatively: but now in order to show the way of obtaining righteousness, he adopts an affirmative mode of speaking. Though the whole might have been announced in one continuous sentence, yet a question is interposed for the sake of exciting attention: and his object at the same time was to show how great is the difference between the righteousness of the law and that of the gospel; for the one, showing itself at a distance, restrains all men from coming nigh; but the other, offering itself at hand, kindly invites us to a fruition of itself, *Nigh thee is the word.*

---

[1] "The righteousness of faith" is evidently the "it" in this question: See ver. 6.—*Ed.*

It must be further observed, that lest the minds of men, being led away by crafts, should wander from the way of salvation, the limits of the word are prescribed to them, within which they are to keep themselves: for it is the same as though he had bidden them to be satisfied with the word only, and reminded them, that in this mirror those secrets of heaven are to be seen, which would otherwise by their brightness dazzle their eyes, and would also stun their ears and overpower the mind itself.

Hence the faithful derive from this passage remarkable consolation with regard to the certainty of the word; for they may no less safely rest on it, than on what is actually present. It must also be noticed, that the word, by which we have a firm and calm trust as to our salvation, had been set forth even by Moses:

This is the word of faith. Rightly does Paul take this as granted; for the doctrine of the law does by no means render the conscience quiet and calm, nor supply it with what ought to satisfy it. He does not, however, exclude other parts of the word, no, not even the precepts of the law; but his design is, to show that remission of sins stands for righteousness, even apart from that strict obedience which the law demands. Sufficient then for pacifying minds, and for rendering certain our salvation, is the word of the gospel; in which we are not commanded to earn righteousness by works, but to embrace it, when offered gratuitously, by faith.

The *word of faith* is to be taken for the word of promise, that is, for the gospel itself, because it bears a relation to faith.[1] The contrast, by which the difference between the law and the gospel appears, is indeed to be understood: and from this distinction we learn,—that as the law demands works, so the gospel requires nothing else, but that men bring faith to receive the grace of God. The words, *which we preach*, are added, that no one might have the suspicion that Paul differed from Moses; for he testifies, that in the ministration of the gospel there was complete consent be-

---

[1] It is "the word" which requires "faith," and is received by faith; or it is the word entitled to faith, worthy of being believed; or it is the word which generates and supports faith.—*Ed.*

tween him and Moses; inasmuch as even Moses placed our felicity in nothing else but in the gratuitous promise of divine favour.

9. *That if thou wilt confess*, &c. Here is also an allusion, rather than a proper and strict quotation: for it is very probable that Moses used the word *mouth*, by taking a part for the whole, instead of the word *face*, or sight. But it was not unsuitable for the Apostle to allude to the word mouth, in this manner:—"Since the Lord sets his word before our face, no doubt he calls upon us to confess it." For wherever the word of the Lord is, it ought to bring forth fruit; and the fruit is the confession of the mouth.

By putting *confession* before *faith*, he changes the order, which is often the case in Scripture: for the order would have been more regular if the faith of the heart had preceded, and the confession of the mouth, which arises from it, had followed.[1] But he rightly confesses the Lord Jesus, who adorns him with his own power, acknowledging him to be such an one as he is given by the Father, and described in the gospel.

Express mention is made only of Christ's resurrection; which must not be so taken, as though his death was of no moment, but because Christ, by rising again, completed the whole work of our salvation: for though redemption and satisfaction were effected by his death, through which we are reconciled to God; yet the victory over sin, death, and

---

[1] "He puts 'mouth' before 'heart,'" says *Pareus*, "for he follows the order in which they are given by Moses, and for this reason, because we know not faith otherwise than by profession."

This is one of the many instances both in the New and Old Testament, in which the most apparent act is mentioned first, and then the most hidden, or in which the deed is stated first, and then the principle from which it proceeds. See ch. xiii. 13; xv. 13. And we have here another instance of the Apostle's style; he reverses the order in the 10th verse, mentioning faith first, and confession last. The two verses may be thus rendered,—

9. That if thou wilt confess with thy mouth the Lord Jesus,
  And believe in thine heart that God raised him from the dead,
  Thou shalt be saved:
10. For with the heart we believe unto righteousness,
  And with the mouth we confess unto salvation.

He begins and ends with confession, and in the middle clauses he mentions faith.—*Ed.*

Satan was attained by his resurrection; and hence also came righteousness, newness of life, and the hope of a blessed immortality. And thus is resurrection alone often set before us as the assurance of our salvation, not to draw away our attention from his death, but because it bears witness to the efficacy and fruit of his death: in short, his resurrection includes his death. On this subject we have briefly touched in the sixth chapter.

It may be added, that Paul requires not merely an historical faith, but he makes the resurrection itself its end. For we must remember the purpose for which Christ rose again;—it was the Father's design in raising him, to restore us all to life: for though Christ had power of himself to reassume his soul, yet this work is for the most part ascribed in Scripture to God the Father.

10. *For with the heart we believe*[1] *unto righteousness,* &c. This passage may help us to understand what justification by faith is; for it shows that righteousness then comes to us, when we embrace God's goodness offered to us in the gospel. We are then for this reason just, because we believe that God is propitious to us in Christ. But let us observe this,—that the seat of faith is not in the head, (*in cerebro*—in the brain,) but in the heart. Yet I would not contend about the part of the body in which faith is located: but as the word *heart* is often taken for a serious and sincere feeling, I would say that faith is a firm and effectual confidence, (*fiducia*—trust, dependence,) and not a bare notion only.

[1] "Creditur;" πιστεύεται, "it is believed." It is an impersonal verb, and so is the verb in the next clause. The introduction of a person is necessary in a version, and we may say, "We believe;" or, as "thou" is used in the preceding verse, it may be adopted here,—"For by the heart thou believest unto righteousness," *i.e.*, in order to attain righteousness; "and with the mouth thou confessest unto salvation," *i.e.*, in order to attain salvation. "God knows our faith," as *Pareus* observes, "but it is made known to man by confession." *Turrettin's* remarks on this verse are much to the purpose. He says, that Paul loved antitheses, and that we are not to understand faith and confession as separated and applied only to the two things here mentioned, but ought to be viewed as connected, and that a similar instance is found in ch. iv. 25, where Christ is said to have been delivered for our offences, and to have risen again for our justification; which means, that by his death and resurrection our offences are blotted out, and justification is obtained. In the same manner the import of what is here said is, that by sincere faith and open confession we obtain justification and salvation.—*Ed.*

With the mouth confession is made unto salvation. It may seem strange, that he ascribes no part of our salvation to faith, as he had before so often testified, that we are saved by faith alone. But we ought not on this account to conclude that confession is the cause of our salvation. His design was only to show how God completes our salvation, even when he makes faith, which he implants in our hearts, to show itself by confession: nay, his simple object was, to mark out true faith, as that from which this fruit proceeds, lest any one should otherwise lay claim to the empty name of faith alone: for it ought so to kindle the heart with zeal for God's glory, as to force out its own flame. And surely, he who is justified has already obtained salvation: hence he no less believes with the heart unto salvation, than with the mouth makes a confession. You see that he has made this distinction,—that he refers the cause of justification to faith,—and that he then shows what is necessary to complete salvation; for no one can believe with the heart without confessing with the mouth: it is indeed a necessary consequence, but not that which assigns salvation to confession.

But let them see what answer they can give to Paul, who at this day proudly boast of some sort of imaginary faith, which, being content with the secrecy of the heart, neglect the confession of the mouth, as a matter superfluous and vain; for it is extremely puerile to say, that there is fire, when there is neither flame nor heat.

11. For the scripture saith, Whosoever believeth on him shall not be ashamed.	11. Dicit enim scriptura, omnis qui credit in eum non pudefiet:
12. For there is no difference between the Jew and the Greek: for the same Lord over all is rich unto all that call upon him.	12. Non enim est distinctio Iudæi et Græci; unus enim Dominus omnium, dives in omnes qui invocant eum;
13. For whosoever shall call upon the name of the Lord shall be saved.	13. Quisquis enim invocaverit nomen Domini salvus erit.

11. *For the Scripture saith,* &c. Having stated the reasons why God had justly repudiated the Jews, he returns to prove the calling of the Gentiles, which is the other part of the question which he is discussing. As then he had explained the way by which men obtain salvation, and one that is common and opened to the Gentiles no less than to

the Jews, he now, having first hoisted an universal banner, extends it expressly to the Gentiles, and then invites the Gentiles by name to it : and he repeats the testimony which he had before adduced from Isaiah, that what he said might have more authority, and that it might also be evident, how well the prophecies concerning Christ harmonize with the law.¹

12. *For there is no distinction,* &c. Since faith alone is required, wherever it is found, there the goodness of God manifests itself unto salvation : there is then in this case no difference between one people or nation and another. And he adds the strongest of reasons ; for since he who is the Creator and Maker of the whole world is the God of all men, he will show himself kind to all who will acknowledge and call on him as their God : for as his mercy is infinite, it cannot be but that it will extend itself to all by whom it shall be sought.

Rich is to be taken here in an active sense, as meaning kind and bountiful.² And we may observe, that the wealth of our Father is not diminished by his liberality ; and that therefore it is not made less for us, with whatever multiplied affluence of his grace he may enrich others. There is then no reason why some should envy the blessings of others, as though anything were thereby lost by them.

But though this reason is sufficiently strong, he yet strengthens it by the testimony of the Prophet Joel ; which, according to the general term that is used, includes all alike. But readers can see much better by the context, that what Joel declares harmonizes with the present subject ; for he prophesies in that passage of the kingdom of Christ : and further, after having said, that the wrath of God would burn in a dreadful manner, in the midst of his ardour, he promises

---

[1] As in chap. ix. 33, the Apostle quotes from the *Septuagint;* for to " make haste," as the Hebrew is, conveys the same idea as " to be ashamed :" for he who hastens, acts for the most part foolishly and brings himself to shame, as Saul did, when he did not wait for Samuel, but hastened to sacrifice, and thereby brought shame on himself.—*Ed.*

[2] " Pro benigno et benefico :" the word " rich," is rather to be taken as meaning one who possesses abundance, or an exuberance of things, and here, of gifts and blessings, of mercy and grace to pardon, to cleanse, and to endow with spiritual privileges.—*Ed.*

salvation to all who would call on the name of the Lord. It hence follows, that the grace of God penetrates into the abyss of death, if only it be sought there; so that it is not by any means to be withheld from the Gentiles.[1]

14. How then shall they call on him in whom they have not believed? and how shall they believe in him of whom they have not heard? and how shall they hear without a preacher?	14. Quomodo ergo invocabunt eum in quem non crediderint? quomodo vero in eum credent de quo non audiverint? quomodo autem audient absque prædicante?
15. And how shall they preach, except they be sent? as it is written, How beautiful are the feet of them that preach the gospel of peace, and bring glad tidings of good things!	15. Quomodo autem prædicabunt nisi mittantur? quemadmodum scriptum est, Quàm pulchri pedes annuntiantium pacem, annuntiantium bona!
16. But they have not all obeyed the gospel: for Esaias saith, Lord, who hath believed our report?	16. Sed non omnes obedierunt evangelio; Iesaias enim dicit, Domine, quis credidit sermoni nostro?
17. So then faith *cometh* by hearing, and hearing by the word of God?	17. Ergo fides ex auditu, auditus autem per verbum Dei.

I shall not engage the reader long in reciting and disproving the opinions of others. Let every one have his own view; and let me be allowed to bring forward what I think. That you may then understand the design of this gradation, bear in mind first, that there was a mutual connection between the calling of the Gentiles and the ministry of Paul, which he exercised among them; so that on the evidence for the one depended the evidence for the other. It was now necessary for Paul to prove, beyond a doubt, the calling of the Gentiles, and, at the same time, to give a reason for his own ministry, lest he should seem to extend the favour of God without authority, to withhold from the children the bread intended for them by God, and to bestow it on dogs. But these things he therefore clears up at the same time. But how he connects the thread of his discourse, will not be fully understood, until every part be in order explained.

The import of what he advances is the same as though

---

[1] The passage referred to is in Joel ii. 32. It is taken *verbatim* from the *Septuagint;* and it is literally according to the Hebrew, except that the last verb מלט, in that language, means to be set free, rescued, or delivered, rather than to be saved; but the idea is nearly the same.—*Ed.*

he had said, "Both Jews and Gentiles, by calling on the name of God, do thereby declare that they believe on him; for a true calling on God's name cannot be except a right knowledge of him were first had. Moreover, faith is produced by the word of God, but the word of God is nowhere preached, except through God's special providence and appointment. Where then there is a calling on God, there is faith; and where faith is, the seed of the word has preceded; where there is preaching there is the calling of God. Now where his calling is thus efficacious and fruitful, there is there a clear and indubitable proof of the divine goodness. It will hence at last appear, that the Gentiles are not to be excluded from the kingdom of God, for God has admitted them into a participation of his salvation. For as the cause of faith among them is the preaching of the gospel, so the cause of preaching is the mission of God, by which it had pleased him in this manner to provide for their salvation." We shall now consider each portion by itself.

14. *How shall they call?* &c. Paul intends here to connect prayer with faith, as they are indeed things most closely connected, for he who calls on God betakes himself, as it were, to the only true haven of salvation, and to a most secure refuge; he acts like the son, who commits himself into the bosom of the best and the most loving of fathers, that he may be protected by his care, cherished by his kindness and love, relieved by his bounty, and supported by his power. This is what no man can do who has not previously entertained in his mind such a persuasion of God's paternal kindness towards him, that he dares to expect everything from him.

He then who calls on God necessarily feels assured that there is protection laid up for him; for Paul speaks here of that calling which is approved by God. Hypocrites also pray, but not unto salvation; for it is with no conviction of faith. It hence appears how completely ignorant are all the schoolmen, who doubtingly present themselves before God, being sustained by no confidence. Paul thought far otherwise; for he assumes this as an acknowledged axiom, that we cannot rightly pray unless we are surely persuaded of success. For he does not refer here to hesitating faith, but to that certainty which our minds entertain respecting his paternal kindness, when by the gospel he reconciles us to himself, and adopts us for his children. By this confidence only we have access to him, as we are also taught in Eph. iii. 12.

But, on the other hand, learn that true faith is only that which brings forth prayer to God; for it cannot be but that he who has tasted the goodness of God will ever by prayer seek the enjoyment of it.

How shall they believe on him? &c. The meaning is, that we are in a manner mute until God's promise opens our mouth to pray, and this is the order which he points out by the Prophet, when he says, "I will say to them, my people are ye;" and they shall say to me, "Thou art our God." (Zech. xiii. 9.) It belongs not indeed to us to imagine a God according to what we may fancy; we ought to possess a right knowledge of him, such as is set forth in his word. And when any one forms an idea of God as good, according to his own understanding, it is not a sure nor a solid faith which he has, but an uncertain and evanescent imagination; it is therefore necessary to have the word, that we may have a right knowledge of God. No other word has he mentioned here but that which is preached, because it is the ordinary mode which the Lord has appointed for conveying his word. But were any on this account to contend that God cannot transfer to men the knowledge of himself, except by the instrumentality of preaching, we deny that to teach this was the Apostle's intention; for he had only in view the ordinary dispensation of God, and did not intend to prescribe a law for the distribution of his grace.

15. *How shall they preach except they be sent?* &c. He intimates that it is a proof and a pledge of divine love when any nation is favoured with the preaching of the gospel; and that no one is a preacher of it, but he whom God has raised up in his special providence, and that hence there is no doubt but that he visits that nation to whom the gospel is proclaimed. But as Paul does not treat here of the lawful call of any one, it would be superfluous to speak at large on

the subject. It is enough for us to bear this only in mind, that the gospel does not fall like rain from the clouds, but is brought by the hands of men wherever it is sent from above.

As it is written, How beautiful, &c. We are to apply this testimony to our present subject in this manner, The Lord, when he gave hope of deliverance to his people, commended the advent of those who brought the glad tidings of peace, by a remarkable eulogy; by this very circumstance he has made it evident that the apostolic ministry was to be held in no less esteem, by which the message of eternal life is brought to us. And it hence follows, that it is from God, since there is nothing in the world that is an object of desire and worthy of praise, which does not proceed from his hand.[1]

But hence we also learn how much ought all good men to desire, and how much they ought to value the preaching of the gospel, which is thus commended to us by the mouth of the Lord himself. Nor is there indeed a doubt, but that God has thus highly spoken of the incomparable value of this treasure, for the purpose of awakening the minds of all, so that they may anxiously desire it. Take *feet,* by metonymy, for *coming.*[2]

16. *But all have not obeyed the gospel,* &c. This belongs

---

[1] "This prophecy," says *Gomarus,* " has not two meanings—the proper and the allegorical, as the Papists foolishly assert, but two fulfilments; the first when heralds announced the return of the people from Babylon to their own country; and the second, (shadowed forth by the first as its destined type,) when the heralds of the gospel announced and proclaimed its tidings to the world."—*Ed.*

[2] This passage is taken from Isaiah lii. 7. This is a striking instance that the Apostle quotes not from the *Septuagint,* when that version materially departs from the Hebrew, as is the case here. Though it appears to be a version of his own, he yet gives not the original literally, but accommodates it to his own purpose: he leaves out " on the mountains," and adopts the plural number instead of the singular, both as to the participle " announcing " or evangelizing, and as to the word " good." The words peace, good, and salvation, in Hebrew, seem to refer to the same thing, according to the usual style of the Prophets.

The words of Paul, as rendered by *Calvin,* coincide more with the Hebrew, than as they are rendered in our common version. The verb εὐαγγελίζω, is often used simply in the sense of announcing, publishing, declaring or preaching, as in Luke iii. 18 ; iv. 43 ; Acts v. 42, &c. ; and in this sense it exactly corresponds with בשר, which means the same, though the other idea of the Greek verb, that of evangelizing, has been wrongly given to it; for it is applied to the *announcing* of bad as well as of good news.—*Ed.*

not to the argument, which Paul designed to follow in the gradation he lays down; nor does he refer to it in the conclusion which immediately follows. It was yet expedient for Paul to introduce the sentence here, in order to anticipate an objection, lest any one should build an argument on what he had said,—that the word in order always precedes faith, as the seed the corn,—and draw this inference, that faith everywhere follows the word: for Israel, who had never been without the word, might have made a boast of this kind. It was therefore necessary, that, in passing, he should give them this intimation,—that many are called, who are yet not chosen.

He also quotes a passage from Isaiah liii. 1; where the Prophet, before he proceeds to announce a remarkable prediction respecting the death and the kingdom of Christ, speaks with astonishment of the few number of believers, who appeared to him in the Spirit to be so few, that he was constrained to exclaim, "O Lord, who has believed our report?" that is, the word which we preach. For though in Hebrew the term שמועה, *shimuoe*, means passively a word,[1] yet the Greeks have rendered it, ἀκοὴν—*hearing*, and the Latins, *auditum—hearing;* incorrectly indeed, but with no ambiguity in the meaning.

We now see why this exception was by the way introduced; it was, that no one might suppose that faith necessarily follows where there is preaching. He however does afterwards point out the reason, by saying, "To whom has the arm of the Lord been revealed?" by which he intimates that there is no benefit from the word, except when God shines in us by the light of his Spirit; and thus the inward

---

[1] Or, what is heard; it being a noun from שמע, to hear, in its passive sense, it signifies a report, a message, or any tidings conveyed to the hearing of men. The Greek word ἀκοή is used in various senses, as signifying the *act* of hearing, Matt. xiii. 14,—the *faculty* of hearing, 1 Cor. xii. 17,—the *organ* of hearing, the ear, Mark. vii. 35,—and *what is heard*, a word, a report, as here and in John xii. 38. *Schleusner* refers to instances in the classics in which the word is used in all these meanings. It is not necessary, nor is it in accordance with the usual manner of the Apostle, to give the word the same meaning in the next verse as in this. It is the practice of the Apostle to use the same words in different senses in the same passage. See chap. iv. 18; viii. 24. Here it means what is heard, report; and in the following verse, the act, that is, hearing.—*Ed.*

calling, which alone is efficacious and peculiar to the elect, is distinguished from the outward voice of men. It is hence evident, how foolishly some maintain, that all are indiscriminately the elect, because the doctrine of salvation is universal, and because God invites all indiscriminately to himself. But the generality of the promises does not alone and by itself make salvation common to all: on the contrary, the peculiar revelation, mentioned by the Prophet, confines it to the elect.

17. *Faith then is by hearing,* &c. We see by this conclusion what Paul had in view by the gradation which he formed; it was to show, that wherever faith is, God has there already given an evidence of his election; and then, that he, by pouring his blessing on the ministration of the gospel, to illuminate the minds of men by faith, and thereby to lead them to call on his name, had thus testified, that the Gentiles were admitted by him into a participation of the eternal inheritance.

And this is a remarkable passage with regard to the efficacy of preaching; for he testifies, that by it faith is produced. He had indeed before declared, that of itself it is of no avail; but that when it pleases the Lord to work, it becomes the instrument of his power. And indeed the voice of man can by no means penetrate into the soul; and mortal man would be too much exalted, were he said to have the power to regenerate us; the light also of faith is something sublimer than what can be conveyed by man: but all these things are no hindrances, that God should not work effectually through the voice of man, so as to create faith in us through his ministry.

It must be further noticed, that faith is grounded on nothing else but the truth of God; for Paul does not teach us that faith springs from any other kind of doctrine, but he expressly restricts it to the word of God; and this restriction would have been improper if faith could rest on the decrees of men. Away then with all the devices of men when we speak of the certainty of faith. Hence also the Papal conceit respecting implicit faith falls to the ground, because it tears away faith from the word; and more detestable still is that blasphemy, that the truth of the word remains suspended until the authority of the Church establishes it.

18. But I say, Have they not heard? Yes verily, their sound went into all the earth, and their words unto the ends of the world.	18. Sed dico, Nunquid non audierunt? Quinimo, In omnem terram exivit sonus eorum, et in fines orbis verba eorum.
19. But I say, Did not Israel know? First, Moses saith, I will provoke you to jealousy by *them that are* no people, *and* by a foolish nation I will anger you.	19. Sed dico, Nunquid non cognovit Israel? Primus Moses dicit, Ego ad æmulationem provocabo vos in eo qui non est populus, et in gente stulta irritabo vos.
20. But Esaias is very bold, and saith, I was found of them that sought me not; I was made manifest unto them that asked not after me.	20. Iesaias autem audet et dicit, Inventus sum à non quærentibus me, conspicuus factus sum iis qui me non interrogabant.
21. But to Israel he saith, All day long I have stretched forth my hands unto a disobedient and gainsaying people.	21. De Israele autem dicit, Quotidie expandi manus meas ad populum contumacem et contradicentem (*vel,* non credentem.)

18. *But I say, have they not heard?* &c. Since the minds of men are imbued, by preaching, with the knowledge of God, which leads them to call on God, it remained a question whether the truth of God had been proclaimed to the Gentiles; for that Paul had suddenly betaken himself to the Gentiles, there was by that novelty no small offence given. He then asks, whether God had ever before directed his voice to the Gentiles, and performed the office of a teacher towards the whole world. But in order that he might show that the school, into which God collects scholars to himself from any part, is open in common to all, he brings forward a Prophet's testimony from Ps. xix. 4; which yet seems to bear apparently but little on the subject: for the Prophet does not speak there of Apostles but of the material works of God; in which he says the glory of God shines forth so evidently, that they may be said to have a sort of tongue of their own to declare the perfections of God.

This passage of Paul gave occasion to the ancients to explain the whole Psalm allegorically, and posterity have followed them: so that, without doubt, the sun going forth as a bridegroom from his chamber, was Christ, and the heavens were the Apostles. They who had most piety, and showed a greater modesty in interpreting Scripture, thought that what was properly said of the celestial architecture, has been transferred by Paul to the Apostles by way of allusion. But as I find that the Lord's servants have everywhere with great reverence explained Scripture, and have not turned them at pleasure in all directions, I cannot be persuaded, that Paul has in this manner misconstrued this passage. I then take his quotation according to the proper and genuine meaning of the Prophet; so that the argument will be something of this kind,—God has already from the beginning manifested his divinity to the Gentiles, though not by the preaching of men, yet by the testimony of his creatures; for though the gospel was then silent among them, yet the whole workmanship of heaven and earth did speak and make known its author by its preaching. It hence appears, that the Lord, even during the time in which he confined the favour of his covenant to Israel, did not yet so withdraw from the Gentiles the knowledge of himself, but that he ever kept alive some sparks of it among them. He indeed manifested himself then more particularly to his chosen people, so that the Jews might be justly compared to domestic hearers, whom he familiarly taught as it were by his own mouth; yet as he spoke to the Gentiles at a distance by the voice of the heavens, he showed by this prelude that he designed to make himself known at length to them also.

But I know not why the Greek interpreter rendered the word קום, *kum*, φθόγγον αὐτῶν, *their sound;* for it means a line, sometimes in building, and sometimes in writing.[1] As

[1] Interpreters have been very much at a loss to account for this difference. The Apostle adopts the rendering of the *Septuagint*, as though the Hebrew word had been קולם. Though there is no copy, yet consulted, that favours this reading, it is yet the probable one; not only because the Apostle sanctions it, but it is what the context demands, and especially the parallelism which prevails in Hebrew poetry. In the next line "words" are mentioned, and "voice" here would be the most suitable corresponding term. But we may go back to the preceding distich, and find not only a confirmation of this, but also an instance of terms being used in the same passage in different senses, while yet the meaning is obvious to a common reader, and at the same time intricate and puzzling to a critic. The two distichs may be thus rendered,—

    4. Without speech, and without words!
       Not heard is their voice!—
    5. Through all the earth goes forth their voice,
       And through the extremity of the world their words.

it is certain that the same thing is mentioned twice in this passage, it seems to me probable, that the heavens are introduced as declaring by what is written as it were on them, as well as by voice, the power of God; for by the word *going forth* the Prophet reminds us, that the doctrine, of which the heavens are the preachers, is not included within the narrow limits of one land, but is proclaimed to the utmost regions of the world.

19. *But I say, has not Israel known?* This objection of an opponent is taken from the comparison of the less with the greater. Paul had argued, that the Gentiles were not to be excluded from the knowledge of God, since he had from the beginning manifested himself to them, though only obscurely and through shadows, or had at least given them some knowledge of his truth. What then is to be said of Israel, who had been illuminated by a far different light of truth? for how comes it that aliens and the profane should run to the light manifested to them afar off, and that the holy race of Abraham should reject it when familiarly seen by them? For this distinction must be ever borne in mind, "What nation is so renowned, that it has gods coming nigh to it, as thy God at this day descends to thee?" It was not then without reason asked, why knowledge had not followed the doctrine of the law, with which Israel was favoured.

First, Moses saith, &c. He proves by the testimony of Moses, that there was nothing inconsistent in God in preferring the Gentiles to the Jews. The passage is taken from that celebrated song, in which God, upbraiding the Jews with their perfidiousness, declares, that he would execute vengeance on them, and provoke them to jealousy by taking the Gentiles into covenant with himself, because they had

---

They have no words, and yet they have words; they have no voice, and yet they have a voice. Here the first and the last line correspond, and the second and the third. There is indeed a different term used for "words" in the last line from that which is adopted in the first, but in the first there are two, "speech," אמר, and "words," דברים, which are expressed by one, מלים, in the last. It seems then most probable, that the true reading has been retained by the *Septuagint*.

The "sound," or voice, as applied in this passage, means the report, the news, respecting the gospel; and the "words," the actual preaching of it. —*Ed.*

departed to fictitious gods. "Ye have," he says, "by despising and rejecting me, transferred my right and honour to idols: to avenge this wrong, I will also substitute the Gentiles in your place, and I will transfer to them what I have hitherto given to you." Now this could not have been without repudiating the Jewish nation: for the emulation, which Moses mentions, arose from this,—that God formed for himself a nation from that which was not a nation, and raised up from nothing a new people, who were to occupy the place from which the Jews had been driven away, inasmuch as they had forsaken the true God and prostituted themselves to idols. For though, at the coming of Christ, the Jews were not gone astray to gross and external idolatry, they had yet no excuse, since they had profaned the whole worship of God by their inventions; yea, they at length denied God the Father, as revealed in Christ, his only-begotten Son, which was an extreme kind of impiety.

Observe, that a *foolish nation,* and *no nation,* are the same; for without the hope of eternal life men have properly no existence. Besides, the beginning or origin of life is from the light of faith: hence spiritual existence flows from the new creation; and in this sense Paul calls the faithful the work of God, as they are regenerated by his Spirit, and renewed after his image. Now from the word *foolish,* we learn that all the wisdom of men, apart from the word of God, is mere vanity.[1]

20. *But Isaiah is bold, and says,* &c. As this prophecy is somewhat clearer, that he might excite greater attention he says that it was expressed with great confidence; as though he had said,—"The Prophet did not speak in a figurative language, or with hesitation, but had in plain and clear words declared the calling of the Gentiles." But the things which Paul has here separated, by interposing a few words,

---

[1] The quotation is from Deut. xxxii. 21, and it is literally the Hebrew as well as the *Septuagint,* except that "you" is put for "them." The contrast in Hebrew is very striking; the whole verse is this,—
  21. They have made me jealous by a no-God,
     They have provoked me by their foolish idols:
     And I will make them jealous by a no-people,
     By a foolish nation will I provoke them.—*Ed.*

are found connected together in the Prophet, ch. lxv. 1, where the Lord declares, that the time would come when he should turn his favour to the Gentiles; and he immediately subjoins this reason,—that he was wearied with the perverseness of Israel, which, through very long continuance, had become intolerable to him. He then speaks thus,—" They who inquired not of me before, and neglected my name, have now sought me, (the perfect tense for the future to denote the certainty of the prophecy;) they who sought me not have beyond hope and desire found me."[1]

I know that this whole passage is changed by some Rabbins, as though God promised that he would cause that the Jews should repent of their defection: but nothing is more clear than that he speaks of aliens; for it follows in the same context,—" I have said, Behold I come to a people, on whom my name is not called." Without doubt, then, the Prophet declares it as what would take place, that those who were before aliens would be received by a new adoption unto the family of God. It is then the calling of the Gentiles; and in which appears a general representation of the calling of all the faithful; for there is no one who anticipates the Lord; but we are all, without exception, delivered by his free mercy from the deepest abyss of death, when there is no knowledge of him, no desire of serving him, in a word, no conviction of his truth.

21. *But of Israel,* &c. A reason is subjoined why God passed over to the Gentiles; it was because he saw that his favour was become a mockery to the Jews. But that readers may more fully understand that the blindness of the people is pointed out in the second clause, Paul expressly reminds us that the elect people were charged with their own wickedness. Literally it is, "He says to Israel;" but Paul has imitated the Hebrew idiom; for ל, *lamed,* is often put for מן, *men.* And he says, that to Israel he stretched forth his hands, whom he continually by his word invited to himself,

---

[1] Is. lxv. 1. The two sentences are reversed; the *Septuagint* and the Hebrew are the same. The reason for changing the order does not appear; but it may be observed, that it is an instance common in Hebrew, where essentially the same idea is expressed in two successive lines, so that it is immaterial which of them is put first.—*Ed.*

and ceased not to allure by every sort of kindness; for these are the two ways which he adopts to call men, as he thus proves his good-will towards them. However, he chiefly complains of the contempt shown to his truth; which is the more abominable, as the more remarkable is the manner by which God manifests his paternal solicitude in inviting men by his word to himself.

And very emphatical is the expression, that he *stretches out his hands;* for by seeking our salvation through the ministers of his word, he stretches forth to us his hands no otherwise than as a father who stretches forth his arms, ready to receive his son kindly into his bosom. And he says *daily,* that it might not seem strange to any one if he was wearied in showing kindness to them, inasmuch as he succeeded not by his assiduity. A similar representation we have in Jer. vii. 13; and xi. 7, where he says that he rose up early to warn them.

Their unfaithfulness is also set forth by two most suitable words. I have thought it right to render the participle ἀπειθοῦντα, *refractory,* or rebellious, and yet the rendering of *Erasmus* and of the Old Translator, which I have placed in the margin, is not to be wholly disapproved. But since the Prophet accuses the people of perverseness, and then adds that they wandered through ways which were not good, I doubt not but that the Greek Translator meant to express the Hebrew word סורר, *surer,* by two words, calling them first disobedient or rebellious, and then gainsaying; for their contumacy showed itself in this, because the people, with untamable pride and bitterness, obstinately rejected the holy admonitions of the Prophets.[1]

---

[1] The passage is taken from Is. lxv. 2. The *Septuagint* is followed, except that the order of the words in the first part of the sentence is changed, though the *Septuagint* has preserved the order of the original. The version is according to the Hebrew, with the exception of the last word, which from its form, the last radical letter being doubled, can hardly be expressed in another language by a single term, and so the *Septuagint* has employed two. It means " revolting again and again," or wilfully revolting. The simple verb סר, signifies to turn aside, to revolt, to apostatize; and in a reduplicate form, as here, it means either a repeated or an obstinate revolt. Indeed the revolt or the apostasy of the Jews was both reiterated and perverse, as their history abundantly testifies.—*Ed.*

CHAPTER XI.

1. I say then, Hath God cast away his people? God forbid. For I also am an Israelite, of the seed of Abraham, *of* the tribe of Benjamin.

2. God hath not cast away his people which he foreknew. Wot ye not what the scripture saith of Elias? how he maketh intercession to God against Israel, saying,

3. Lord, they have killed thy prophets, and digged down thine altars; and I am left alone, and they seek my life.

4. But what saith the answer of God unto him? I have reserved to myself seven thousand men, who have not bowed the knee to *the image of* Baal.

5. Even so then at this present time also there is a remnant according to the election of grace.

6. And if by grace, then *is it* no more of works; otherwise grace is no more grace. But if *it be* of works, then is it no more grace; otherwise work is no more work.

1. Dico igitur, Num abjecit Deus populum suum? absit: etenim ego Israelita sum, ex genere Abrahæ, tribu Beniamin.

2. Non abjecit Deus populum suum quem præcognovit. An nescitis in Elia quid scriptura dicat? quomodo appellet Deum adversus Israel, dicens,

3. Domine, Prophetas tuas occiderunt, et altaria tua diruerunt, et ego relictus sum solus, et quærunt animam meam.

4. Sed quid dicit ei oraculum?[1] Reservavi mihi ipsi septem millia virorum, qui non flexerunt genu *imagini* Baal.

5. Sic ergo et hoc tempore, reliquiæ secundum electionem gratiæ supersunt:

6. Quòd si per gratiam, jam non ex operibus; alioqui gratia, jam non est gratia: si verò ex operibus, jam non est gratia; alioqui opus, jam non est opus.

1. *I say then,* &c. What he has hitherto said of the blindness and obstinacy of the Jews, might seem to import that Christ at his coming had transferred elsewhere the promises of God, and deprived the Jews of every hope of salvation. This objection is what he anticipates in this passage, and he so modifies what he had previously said respecting the repudiation of the Jews, that no one might think that the covenant formerly made with Abraham is now abrogated, or that God had so forgotten it that the Jews were now so entirely alienated from his kingdom, as the Gentiles were before the coming of Christ. All this he denies, and he will presently show that it is altogether false. But the question is not whether God had justly or unjustly rejected the people; for

---

[1] "Oraculum," ὁ χρηματισμός, the oracle, the divine response. The answer is put for him who gave the answer, for it is "Jehovah" in the passage that is quoted; as "Scripture" in verse 2, and in other places, means him who speaks in the Scripture.—*Ed.*

it was proved in the last chapter that when the people, through false zeal, had rejected the righteousness of God, they suffered a just punishment for their presumption, were deservedly blinded, and were at last cut off from the covenant.

The reason then for their rejection is not now under consideration; but the dispute is concerning another thing, which is this, That though they deserved such a punishment from God, whether yet the covenant which God made formerly with the fathers was abolished. That it should fail through any perfidiousness of men, was wholly unreasonable; for Paul holds this as a fixed principle, that since adoption is gratuitous and based on God alone and not on men, it stands firm and inviolable, howsoever great the unfaithfulness of men may be, which may tend to abolish it. It was necessary that this knot should be untied, lest the truth and election of God should be thought to be dependent on the worthiness of men.

For I am also an Israelite, &c. Before he proceeds to the subject, he proves, in passing, by his own example, how unreasonable it was to think that the nation was utterly forsaken by God; for he himself was in his origin an Israelite, not a proselyte, or one lately introduced into the commonwealth of Israel. As then he was justly deemed to be one of God's special servants, it was an evidence that God's favour rested on Israel. He then assumes the conclusion as proved, which yet he will hereafter explain in a satisfactory manner.

That in addition to the title of an Israelite, he called himself the seed of Abraham, and mentioned also his own tribe; this he did that he might be counted a genuine Israelite, and he did the same in his Epistle to the Philippians, ch. iii. 4. But what some think, that it was done to commend God's mercy, inasmuch as Paul sprung from that tribe which had been almost destroyed, seems forced and far-fetched.

2. *God has not cast away*, &c. This is a negative answer, accompanied with a qualifying clause; for had the Apostle unreservedly denied that the people were rejected, he would

have been inconsistent with himself; but by adding a modification, he shows it to be such a rejection, as that God's promise is not thereby made void. So the answer may be divided into two parts,—that God has by no means cast away the whole race of Abraham, contrary to the tenor of his own covenant,—and that yet the fruit of adoption does not exist in all the children of the flesh, for secret election precedes. Thus general rejection could not have caused that no seed should be saved; for the visible body of the people was in such a manner rejected, that no member of the spiritual body of Christ was cut off.

If any one asks, " Was not circumcision a common symbol of God's favour to all the Jews, so that they ought to have been all counted his people?" To this the obvious answer is,—That as outward calling is of itself ineffectual without faith, the honour which the unbelieving refuse when offered, is justly taken from them. Thus a special people remain, in whom God exhibits an evidence of his faithfulness; and Paul derives the origin of constancy from secret election. For it is not said here that God regards faith, but that he stands to his own purpose, so as not to reject the people whom he has foreknown.

And here again must be noticed what I have before reminded you of,—that by the verb *foreknow*, is not to be understood a foresight, I know not what, by which God foresees what sort of being any one will be, but that good pleasure, according to which he has chosen those as sons to himself, who, being not yet born, could not have procured for themselves his favour.[1] So he says to the Galatians, that

---

[1] That foreknowledge here includes election or predestination, as *Augustine* maintains, is evident from what follows in verse 5, where " the remnant" is said to be reserved " according to the election of grace," or gratuitous election. If it be gratuitous, then it cannot be according to any foreseen works: and works are expressly excluded in verse 6. Were it otherwise, were foreseen works the ground of election, there would be no suitableness nor congruity in such terms as foreknowledge and election on the subject. It would have been much more appropriate in this case for the Apostle to say, " God will receive every Jew who will render himself worthy by his works." On this supposition there was no necessity for him to go back to election to remove the objection which he had stated: he had only to refer to the terms of the gospel, which regard Jews and Gentiles without any difference. But instead of doing this, which *seems* ade-

they had been known by God, (Gal. iv. 9); for he had anticipated them with his favour, so as to call them to the knowledge of Christ. We now perceive, that though universal calling may not bring forth fruit, yet the faithfulness of God does not fail, inasmuch as he always preserves a Church, as long as there are elect remaining; for though God invites all people indiscriminately to himself, yet he does not inwardly draw any but those whom he knows to be his people, and whom he has given to his Son, and of whom also he will be the faithful keeper to the end.

Know ye not, &c. As there were so few of the Jews who had believed in Christ, hardly another conclusion could have been drawn from this small number, but that the whole race of Abraham had been rejected; and creep in might this thought,—that in so vast a ruin no sign of God's favour appeared: for since adoption was the sacred bond by which the children of Abraham were kept collected under the protection of God, it was by no means probable, unless that had ceased, that the people should be miserably and wretchedly dispersed. To remove this offence, Paul adopts a most suitable example; for he relates, that in the time of Elias there was such a desolation, that there remained no appearance of a Church, and yet, that when no vestige of God's favour appeared, the Church of God was, as it were, hid in the grave, and was thus wonderfully preserved.

It hence follows, that they egregiously mistake who form an opinion of the Church according to their own perceptions. And surely if that celebrated Prophet, who was endued with so enlightened a mind, was so deceived, when he attempted by his own judgment to form an estimate of God's people, what shall be the case with us, whose highest perspicuity, when compared with his, is mere dulness? Let us not then determine any thing rashly on this point; but rather let this truth remain fixed in our hearts—that the Church, though it may not appear to our eyes, is sustained by the

---

quate to the purpose, he gives an answer by referring to the foreknowledge and free election of God. There is no way to account for this, except by admitting, that election is an efficacious purpose which secures the salvation of those who are its objects, who have been chosen in Christ before the foundation of the world.—*Ed.*

secret providence of God. Let it also be remembered by us, that they are foolish and presumptuous who calculate the number of the elect according to the extent of their own perception: for God has a way, easy to himself, hidden from us, by which he wonderfully preserves his elect, even when all things seem to us past all remedy.

And let readers observe this,—that Paul distinctly compares here, and elsewhere, the state of things in his time with the ancient condition of the Church, and that it serves in no small degree to confirm our faith, when we bear in mind, that nothing happens to us, at this day, which the holy Fathers had not formerly experienced: for novelty, we know, is a grievous engine to torment weak minds.

As to the words, *In Elias,* I have retained the expression of Paul; for it may mean either in the history or in the business of Elias; though it seems to me more probable, that Paul has followed the Hebrew mode of speaking; for ב, *beth,* which is rendered in the Greek by ἐν, *in,* is often taken in Hebrew for *of.*

How he appeals to God, &c.[1] It was certainly a proof how much Elias honoured the Lord, that for the glory of his name he hesitated not to make himself an enemy to his own nation, and to pray for their utter ruin, because he thought that the religion and worship of God had perished among them: but he was mistaken in charging the whole nation, himself alone excepted, with that impiety, for which he wished them to be severely visited. There is however in this passage, which Paul quotes, no imprecation, but a com-

---

[1] "Quomodo appellet Deum adversus Israel—how he appeals to or calls on God against Israel;" ὡς ἐντυγχάνει τῷ Θεῷ κατὰ τοῦ Ἰσραήλ; "how he solicits (interpellet) God against Israel," *Beza;* "when he pleadeth with God against Israel," *Doddridge;* "when he complaineth to God against Israel," *Macknight.* To "complain to God against, or, with respect to, Israel," would probably be the most suitable rendering. See Acts xxv. 24.

The quotation in the following verse is from 1 Kings xix. 10, and is not taken literally, either from the Hebrew, or from the *Septuagint.* The order of the two first clauses is changed; "prophets," and not "altars," are mentioned first: in these he has adopted the words of the *Septuagint,* but in the clause which follows he has changed the terms; instead of καὶ ὑπολέλειμμαι ἐγὼ μονώτατος, the Apostle has κἀγὼ ὑπελείφθην μόνος; and he has left out the words, "to take it away" after life. The case is similar with the quotation in ver. 4, from 1 Kings xix. 18. The sense is given, but not exactly the words, either from the Hebrew or the *Septuagint.*—*Ed.*

plaint only: but as he complains in such a way as to despair of the whole people, there is no doubt but that he gave them up to destruction. Let us then especially notice what is said of Elias, which was this,—that when impiety had everywhere prevailed, and overspread almost the whole land, he thought, that he was left alone.

I have reserved for myself seven thousand, &c. Though you may take this finite for an indefinite number, it was yet the Lord's design to specify a large multitude. Since then the grace of God prevails so much in an extreme state of things, let us not lightly give over to the devil all those whose piety does not openly appear to us. It also ought to be fully imprinted on our minds,—that however impiety may everywhere prevail, and dreadful confusion spread on every side, yet the salvation of many remains secured under the seal of God.[1] But that no one may under this error indulge his own sloth, as many seek hiding-places for their vices in the hidden providences of God, it is right to observe again,—that they only are said to be saved who continue sound and unpolluted in the faith of God. This circumstance in the case ought also to be noticed,—that those only remained safe who did not prostitute their body, no, not even by an external act of dissimulation, to the worship of idols; for he not only ascribes to them a purity of mind, but that they had also kept their body from being polluted by any filthiness of superstition.[2]

So then also at this time, &c. He applies the example to his own age; and to make all things alike, he calls God's people a remnant, that is, in comparison with the vast number in whom impiety prevailed: and alluding at the same time to the prophecy he had quoted from Isaiah, he shows,

---

[1] *Pareus* observes, that these seven thousand had no public ministry, for that was idolatrous; and that yet they were preserved by such instruction as they derived from the written word.—*Ed.*

[2] *Calvin,* as some others, has supplied "image" before "Baal," as the feminine article τῇ is by Paul prefixed to it. In the *Septuagint* it is τῷ, and a masculine pronoun is found at the end of the verse in 1 Kings xix. 18, so that it could not have been a female deity, as some have supposed. It is indeed evident, especially from a passage in Tobit, ch. i. 5, that there was a female deity of this name; but the text in Kings will not allow us to regard this goddess to be intended.—*Ed.*

that in the midst of a miserable and confused desolation the faithfulness of God yet shone forth, for there was still some remnant: and in order more fully to confirm this, he expressly calls them a remnant that survived through the grace of God: and thus he bore witness that God's election is unchangeable, according to what the Lord said to Elias, —that where the whole people had fallen away to idolatry, he had reserved for himself seven thousand: and hence we conclude, that through his kindness they were delivered from destruction. Nor does he simply speak of grace; but he now calls our attention also to election, that we may learn reverently to rely on the hidden purpose of God.

One thing then that is laid down is,—that few are saved in comparison with the vast number of those who assume the name of being God's people; the other is,—that those are saved by God's power whom he has chosen with no regard to any merit. The *election of grace* is a Hebrew idiom for gratuitous election.

6. *If through grace, it is no more by works,* &c. This amplification is derived from a comparison between things of an opposite character; for such is the case between God's grace and the merit of works, that he who establishes the one overturns the other.

But if no regard to works can be admitted in election, without obscuring the gratuitous goodness of God, which he designed thereby to be so much commended to us, what answer can be given to Paul by those infatuated persons, (*phrenetici*—insane,) who make the cause of election to be that worthiness in us which God has foreseen? For whether you introduce works future or past, this declaration of Paul opposes you; for he says, that grace leaves nothing to works. Paul speaks not here of our reconciliation with God, nor of the means, nor of the proximate causes of our salvation; but he ascends higher, even to this,—why God, before the foundation of the world, chose only some and passed by others: and he declares, that God was led to make this difference by nothing else, but by his own good pleasure; for if any place is given to works, so much, he maintains, is taken away from grace.

It hence follows, that it is absurb to blend foreknowledge of works with election. For if God chooses some and rejects others, as he has foreseen them to be worthy or unworthy of salvation, then the grace of God, the reward of works being established, cannot reign alone, but must be only in part the cause of our election. For as Paul has reasoned before concerning the justification of Abraham, that where reward is paid, there grace is not freely bestowed; so now he draws his argument from the same fountain,—that if works come to the account, when God adopts a certain number of men unto salvation, reward is a matter of debt, and that therefore it is not a free gift.[1]

Now, though he speaks here of election, yet as it is a general reasoning which Paul adopts, it ought to be applied to the whole of our salvation; so that we may understand, that whenever it is declared that there are no merits of works, our salvation is ascribed to the grace of God, or rather, that we may believe that the righteousness of works is annihilated, whenever grace is mentioned.

7. What then? Israel hath not obtained that which he seeketh for; but the election hath obtained it, and the rest were blinded

8. (According as it is written, God hath given them the spirit of slumber, eyes that they should not see, and ears that they should not hear) unto this day.

7. Quid ergo? Quod quærit Israel, non est assequutus;[2] electio autem assequuta est, reliqui verò excæcati fuerunt;

8. Quemadmodum scriptum est, Dedit illis Deus spiritum compunctionis, oculos ut non videant, et aures ut non audiant, usque ad hodiernum diem.

---

[1] The last half of this verse is considered spurious by *Griesbach*, being not found in the greatest number of MSS., nor in the *Vulgate*, nor in the Latin Fathers; but it is found in some of the Greek Fathers, *Theodoret*, *Œcumenius*, *Photius*, and in the text, though not in the comment of *Chrysostom*, and in *Theophylact*, with the exception of the last clause, "Otherwise work," &c. The *Syriac* and *Arabic* versions also contain the whole verse. The argument is complete without the last portion, which is, in fact, a repetition of the first in another form. But this kind of statement is wholly in unison with the character of the Apostle's mode of writing. He often states a thing positively and negatively, or in two different ways. See chap. iv. 4, 5; ix. 1; Eph. ii. 8, 9. Then an *omission* is more probable than an *addition*. *Beza, Pareus, Wolfius*, &c., regard it as genuine, and *Doddridge* and *Macknight* have retained it in their versions. Every reason, except the number of MSS., is in favour of its genuineness.—*Ed.*

[2] Literally it is, "what Israel seeks, this he has not obtained." The pronoun for "this," τούτου *Griesbach* has displaced, and introduced τοῦτο in its stead, as the most approved reading.—*Ed.*

9. And David saith, Let their table be made a snare, and a trap, and a stumblingblock, and a recompense unto them:

10. Let their eyes be darkened, that they may not see, and bow down their back alway.

9. Et David dicit, Fiat mensa eorum in laqueum et in captionem et in offendiculum et in retributionem ipsis:

10. Obscurentur oculi eorum ne videant, et dorsum eorum semper incurva.

7. *What then? What Israel seeks*, &c. As he is here engaged on a difficult subject, he asks a question, as though he was in doubt. He intended, however, by expressing this doubt, to render the answer, which immediately follows, more evident; for he intimates, that no other can be given; and the answer is,—that Israel in vain laboured to seek salvation, because his attempt was absurd. Though he mentions here no cause, yet as he had expressed it before, he certainly meant it to be understood in this place. For his words are the same, as though he had said,—that it ought not to seem strange, that Israel gained nothing in striving after righteousness. And hence is proved what he presently subjoins concerning election,—For if Israel has obtained nothing by merit, what have others obtained whose case or condition was not better? Whence has come so much difference between equals? Who does not here see that it is election alone which makes the difference?

Now the meaning of the word *election* here is doubtful; for to some it seems that it ought to be taken in a collective sense, for the elect themselves, that there may be a correspondence between the two clauses. Of this opinion I do not disapprove, provided it be allowed that there is something more in the word than if he had said, the elect, even this,— that he intimates that there was no other reason for obtaining their election, as though he said,—"They are not those who strive by relying on merits, but those whose salvation depends on the gratuitous election of God." For he distinctly compares with the whole of Israel, or body of the people, the remnant which was to be saved by God's grace. It hence follows, that the cause of salvation exists not in men, but depends on the good pleasure of God alone.

And the rest have been blinded.[1] As the elect alone are

---

[1] "Excæcati fuerunt," ἐπωρώθησαν; it means hardened, stupified, rendered callous or obdurate. *Occalluerunt*—" were hardened," *Beza;* both *Mac-*

delivered by God's grace from destruction, so all who are not elected must necessarily remain blinded. For what Paul means with regard to the reprobate is,—that the beginning of their ruin and condemnation is from this—that they are forsaken by God.

The quotations which he adduces, collected from various parts of Scripture, and not taken from one passage, do seem, all of them, to be foreign to his purpose, when you closely examine them according to their contexts; for you will find that in every passage, blindness and hardening are mentioned as scourges, by which God punished crimes already committed by the ungodly; but Paul labours to prove here, that not those were blinded, who so deserved by their wickedness, but who were rejected by God before the foundation of the world.

You may thus briefly untie this knot,—that the origin of the impiety which provokes God's displeasure, is the perversity of nature when forsaken by God. Paul therefore, while speaking of eternal reprobation, has not without reason referred to those things which proceed from it, as fruit from the tree or river from the fountain. The ungodly are indeed, for their sins, visited by God's judgment with blindness; but if we seek for the source of their ruin, we must come to this,—that being accursed by God, they cannot by all their deeds, sayings, and purposes, get and obtain any thing but a curse. Yet the cause of eternal reprobation is so hidden from us, that nothing remains for us but to wonder at the incomprehensible purpose of God, as we shall at length see by the conclusion. But they reason absurdly who, whenever a word is said of the proximate causes, strive, by bringing forward these, to cover the first, which is hid from our view; as though God had not, before the fall of Adam, freely determined to do what seemed good to him with respect to the whole human race on this account,—because he condemns his corrupt and depraved seed, and also, because he repays to individuals the reward which their sins have deserved.[1]

knight and *Doddridge* render it, "blinded." It is applied to the heart in Mark vi. 52; viii. 17; John xii. 40,—to the mind in 2 Cor. iii. 14.—*Ed.*

The foregoing reasoning is not satisfactory: it goes beyond the evident meaning of the Apostle. He no doubt quoted the texts according to

8. *Given them has God,* &c. There is no doubt, I think, but that the passage quoted here from Isaiah is that which Luke refers to in Acts, as quoted from him, only the words are somewhat altered. Nor does he record here what we find in the Prophet, but only collects from him this sentiment,—that they were imbued from above with the spirit of maliciousness, so that they continued dull in seeing and hearing. The Prophet was indeed bidden to harden the heart of the people: but Paul penetrates to the very fountain,—that brutal stupor seizes on all the senses of men, after they are given up to this madness, so that they excite themselves by virulent stimulants against the truth. For he does not call it the spirit of giddiness, but of compunction, when the bitterness of gall shows itself; yea, when there is also a fury in rejecting the truth. And he declares, that by the secret judgment of God the reprobate are so demented, that being stupified, they are incapable of forming a judgment; for when it is said, that by seeing they see nothing, the dulness of their senses is thereby intimated.[1]

Then Paul himself adds, *to this very day,* lest any one should object and say, that this prophecy had been formerly fulfilled, and that it was therefore absurd to apply it to the

their original design, and to say he did not is to assert what is incapable of being proved, and what is even contrary to the Apostle's reasoning throughout. The hardening or blinding spoken of by the Prophets, is stated uniformly as a punishment for previous unbelief and impenitence, as admitted by our author himself, and the obvious fact as to the Jews in the Apostle's days, was an evidence of the same, and though he states not this fact here, he states it in the sequel of this Epistle. But why some were hardened and others were softened, is what must be resolved altogether to the will of God. This, and no more than this, is what the Apostle evidently teaches here: and it is neither wise nor right to go beyond what is expressly taught, especially on a subject of a nature so mysterious and incomprehensible.—*Ed.*

[1] The quotation in this verse is taken from two passages: the first clause is from Is. xxix. 10, and the rest from Is. vi. 9, or Deut. xxix. 4. The first clause is not exactly according to the Hebrew or the *Septuagint:* instead of "God gave them," &c., it is in the *Septuagint,* "the Lord hath made you drink," &c., and in Hebrew, "Jehovah has poured upon you," &c. It is the "spirit of slumber" in both, or rather, "of deep sleep"— תרדמה, a dead or an overwhelming sleep; and κατανυξις, though not as to its primary sense the same, is yet used according to this meaning. The verb means to puncture, to prick, either with grief or remorse, and also to affect with stupor. The latter idea the noun must have in this place, for the Hebrew does not admit of the other. The latter part is found in substance, though not in the same form of words in the two places referred to.—*Ed.*

time of the gospel: this objection he anticipates, by subjoining, that it was not only a blindness of one day, which is described, but that it had continued, together with the unhealable obstinacy of the people, to the coming of Christ.[1]

9. *And David says,* &c. In this testimony of David there is also made some change in the words, but it is not what changes the meaning. For he thus speaks, "Let their table before them become a snare, and their peaceful things a trap;" there is no mention of retribution. As to the main point there is sufficient agreement. The Prophet prays, that whatever is desirable and happy in life might turn out to the ruin and destruction of the ungodly; and this is what he means by *table* and *peaceful things*.[2] He then gives them up to blindness of spirit and weakening of strength; the one of which he expresses by the darkening of the eyes, and

---

[1] Some consider this passage as taken from Deut. xxix. 4, and regard the last words as part of the quotation.—*Ed.*

[2] *Grotius* understands by "table" guests, or friends, who partake of the provisions spread on the table. The wish is, that these should be a snare, &c. "Table," according to *Pareus,* means luxury or festivity: and he adds, that there are here three metaphors,—the ensnaring of birds—the entrapping of wild beasts—and the stumbling in the dark, or that of blind men. Then the recompense or retaliation implies, that this evil of being ensnared and entrapped, and of stumbling, are only just retaliations for similar acts on their part: as they had ensnared, entrapped, and caused others to stumble, it was but just that they should be treated in the same way. And if we take "table" as a metonymy for friends or guests, the meaning would be very striking. And we know that the very friends and confederates of the Jews became their enemies and effected their ruin. See Jer. xxxviii. 22.

The subject of imprecations is attended with some difficulty. To imprecate, or to pronounce a curse on others, or to wish others accursed, was forbidden even under the law, and it is expressly forbidden under the gospel, Matt. v. 45; Rom. xii. 14; we have the example of our Saviour praying for his enemies even on the cross; and yet we find that God pronounced a curse on all the transgressors of the law, Deut. xxvii. 26,—that Christ pronounced a curse on Chorazin and Bethsaida,—that the Psalmist often imprecated vengeance on his enemies, Ps. v. 10; cix. 7-15,—that the Apostle cursed Alexander the coppersmith, 2 Tim. iv. 14,—and that John bids us not to pray for him who sins the sin unto death, 1 John v. 16.

The truth is, that circumstances make the difference; what is forbidden in one respect is allowed in another. The rule to man is, not to curse, but to bless, except to pronounce on God's enemies as such the judgment which God has already denounced on them. But to curse individuals is what no one is allowed to do, except he be inspired so as to know who those are who are given up by God to final judgment; which may be supposed to have been the case with the Psalmist and with St. Paul.—*Ed.*

the other by the incurvation of the back. But that this should be extended almost to the whole nation, is not to be wondered at; for we know, that not only the chief men were incensed against David, but that the common people were also opposed to him. It appears plain, that what is read in that passage was not applied to a few, but to a large number; yea, when we consider of whom David was a type, there appears to be a spiritual import in the opposite clause.[1]

Seeing then that this imprecation remains for all the adversaries of Christ,—that their meat shall be converted into poison, (as we see that the gospel is to be the savour of death unto death,) let us embrace with humility and trembling the grace of God. We may add, that since David speaks of the Israelites, who descended according to the flesh from Abraham, Paul fitly applies his testimony to the subject in hand, that the blindness of the majority of the people might not appear new or unusual.

11. I say then, Have they stumbled that they should fall? God forbid: but *rather* through their fall salvation *is come* unto the Gentiles, for to provoke them to jealousy.

12. Now, if the fall of them *be* the riches of the world, and the diminishing of them the riches of the Gentiles; how much more their fulness?

13. For I speak to you Gentiles, inasmuch as I am the apostle of the Gentiles, I magnify mine office:

14. If by any means I may provoke to emulation *them which are* my flesh, and might save some of them.

15. For if the casting away of them

11. Dico igitur, Num impegerunt ut corruerent? Absit: sed eorum lapsu salus *contigit* gentibus in hoc, ut ipsi ad æmulationem provocarentur.

12. Si verò eorum lapsus divitiæ sunt mundi, et imminutio eorum divitiæ gentium, quanto magis complementum ipsorum?

13. Vobis enim dico gentibus, quatenus certè ego gentium sum Apostolus, ministerium meum illustror,

14. Si quomodo ad æmulationem provocavero carnem meam, et aliquos ex ea salvos fecero:

15. Si enim rejectio eorum, recon-

---

[1] Ps. lxix. 22, 23. The passage is given as in the *Septuagint*, except that καὶ εἰς θήραν is added, and the two following words are transposed, with αὐτοῖς put after them, and ἀνταπόδομα is put for ἀνταπόδοσιν. The 10th verse is given without any variation from the *Septuagint*. The Hebrew is in words considerably different, and more so in our version than it really is. The word, שלומים, is improperly rendered "welfare," while it ought to be "recompenses," or, according to *Tremelius* and Bp. *Horseley*, "retributions," or "retribution." See Is. xxxiv. 8. The last clause of the 10th verse, though in meaning the same, is yet wholly different in words from the Hebrew, which is thus correctly rendered in our version, "and make their loins continually to shake." The idea in both instances is the taking away of vigour and strength.—*Ed.*

be the reconciling of the world, what *shall* the receiving *of them be*, but life from the dead?	ciliatio est mundi, quid assumptio nisi vita ex mortuis?

11. *Have they stumbled*, &c. You will be greatly hindered in understanding this argument, except you take notice, that the Apostle speaks sometimes of the whole nation of the Jews, and sometimes of single individuals; for hence arises the diversity, that onewhile he speaks of the Jews as being banished from the kingdom of God, cut off from the tree and precipitated by God's judgment into destruction, and that at another he denies that they had fallen from grace, but that on the contrary they continued in the possession of the covenant, and had a place in the Church of God.

It is then in conformity with this difference that he now speaks; for since the Jews for the most part rejected Christ, so that perverseness had taken hold almost on the whole nation, and few among them seemed to be of a sane mind, he asks the question, whether the Jewish nation had so stumbled at Christ, that it was all over with them universally, and that no hope of repentance remained. Here he justly denies that the salvation of the Jews was to be despaired of, or that they were so rejected by God, that there was to be no future restoration, or that the covenant of grace, which he had once made with them, was entirely abolished, since there had ever remained in that nation the seed of blessing. That we are so to understand his meaning is evident from this,—that having before connected a sure ruin with blindness, he now gives a hope of rising again; which two things are wholly different. They then, who perversely stumbled at Christ, fell and fell into destruction; yet the nation itself had not fallen, so that he who is a Jew must necessarily perish or be alienated from God.

But by their fall salvation has come *to the Gentiles*, &c. The Apostle asserts two things in this place,—that the fall of the Jews had turned out for salvation to the Gentiles; but to this end—that they might be kindled by a sort of jealousy, and be thus led to repentance. He no doubt had an eye to the testimony of Moses, which he had already quoted, where the Lord threatened Israel,—that as he had been provoked by them to emulation through their false gods; so he also, according to the law of retaliation, would provoke them by a foolish nation.

The word here used denotes the feeling of emulation or jealousy with which we are excited, when we see another preferred before us. Since then it was the Lord's purpose that Israel should be provoked to emulation, they were not so fallen as to be precipitated into eternal ruin; but that God's blessing, despised by them, might come to the Gentiles, in order that they might at length be also stirred up to seek the Lord, from whom they had fallen away.

But there is no reason for readers to weary themselves much as to the application of this testimony: for Paul does not dwell on the strict meaning of the word, but alludes only to a common and well-known practice. For as emulation stimulates a wife, who for her fault has been rejected by her husband, so that she strives to be reconciled again; so it may be now, he says, that the Jews, seeing the Gentiles introduced into their place, will be touched with grief for their divorce, and seek reconciliation.

12. *And if their fall,* &c. As he had taught us that after the Jews were repudiated, the Gentiles were introduced in their place, that he might not make the salvation of the Jews to be disliked by the Gentiles, as though their salvation depended on the ruin of the Jews, he anticipates this false notion, and lays down a sentiment of an opposite kind, that nothing would conduce more to advance the salvation of the Gentiles, than that the grace of God should flourish and abound among the Jews. To prove this, he derives an argument from the less,—" If their fall had raised the Gentiles, and their diminution had enriched them, how much more their fulness?" for the first was done contrary to nature, and the last will be done according to a natural order of things. And it is no objection to this reasoning, that the word of God had flowed to the Gentiles, after the Jews had rejected, and, as it were, cast it from them; for if they had received it, their faith would have brought forth much more fruit than their unbelief had occasioned; for the truth of

God would have been thereby confirmed by being accomplished in them, and they also themselves would have led many by their teaching, whom they, on the contrary, by their perverseness, had turned aside.

Now he would have spoken more strictly correct, if, to the *fall*, he had opposed *rising :*[1] of this I remind you, that no one may expect here an adorned language, and may not be offended with this simple mode of speaking; for these things were written to mould the heart and not the tongue.

13. *For to you Gentiles I speak*, &c. He confirms by a strong reason, that nothing shall be lost by the Gentiles, were the Jews to return again to favour with God; for he shows, that the salvation of both is so connected, that it can by the same means be promoted. For he thus addresses the Gentiles,—"Though I am peculiarly destined to be your Apostle, and ought therefore with special care to seek your salvation, with which I am charged, and to omit as it were all other things, and to labour for that only, I shall yet be faithfully discharging my office, by gaining to Christ any of my own nation; and this will be for the glory of my ministry, and so for your good."[2] For whatever served to render

---

[1] This is not quite correct: the first part is a mere announcement of a fact—the fall of the Jews; and then in what follows, according to the usual style of Scripture, the same thing is stated in other words, and a corresponding clause is added; and the antithesis is found to be suitable—the diminution and the completion. The reason for the restatement of the first clause seems to be this,—that the fall might not be deemed as total, but in part; it was ἥττημα, a less part, a diminution, a lessening of their number in God's kingdom. A contrast to this is the πλήρωμα, the full or complete portion, that is, their complete restoration, as it is said in verse 26. To preserve the antithesis, the first word must have its literal meaning, a diminution or lessening, that is, as to the number saved. *Hammond* renders the phrase, "their paucity."—*Ed.*

[2] The meaning attached here to the words τὴν διακονίαν μου δοξάζω, is somewhat different from what is commonly understood. Its classical sense, "highly to estimate," is what is generally given here to the verb: but *Calvin* takes it in a sense in which it is mostly taken in Scripture, as meaning, "to render illustrious," or eminent, "to render glorious." The construction of the two verses, 13 and 14, is somewhat difficult, and the meaning is not very clear. To include the words, "as I am indeed the Apostle of the Gentiles," in a parenthesis, as it is done by some, would render the sense more evident, and to add "this" after "say," and "that" before "I render." The version then would be as follows,—

13. For I say *this* to you Gentiles (as I am indeed the Apostle of the
14. Gentiles,) *that* I render my ministry glorious, if I shall by any

Paul's ministry illustrious, was advantageous to the Gentiles, whose salvation was its object.

And here also he uses the verb παραζηλῶσαι, *to provoke to emulation*, and for this purpose, that the Gentiles might seek the accomplishment of Moses' prophecy, such as he describes, when they understood that it would be for their benefit.

14. *And save*, &c. Observe here that the minister of the word is said in some way to save those whom he leads to the obedience of faith. So conducted indeed ought to be the ministry of our salvation, as that we may feel that the whole power and efficacy of it depends on God, and that we may give him his due praise: we ought at the same time to understand that preaching is an instrument for effecting the salvation of the faithful, and though it can do nothing without the Spirit of God, yet through his inward operation it produces the most powerful effects.

15. *For if their rejection*, &c. This passage, which many deem obscure, and some awfully pervert, ought, in my view, to be understood as another argument, derived from a comparison of the less with the greater, according to this import, "Since the rejection of the Jews has availed so much as to occasion the reconciling of the Gentiles, how much more effectual will be their resumption? Will it not be to raise them even from the dead?" For Paul ever insists on this, that the Gentiles have no cause for envy, as though the restoration of the Jews to favour were to render their condition worse. Since then God has wonderfully drawn forth life from death and light from darkness, how much more ought we to hope, he reasons, that the resurrection of a people, as

---

means excite to emulation my own flesh and save some of them.

The sentiment in the last clause is the same as that at the end of verse 11. The *Vulgate*, and some of the Latin Fathers, and also *Luther*, read δοξάσω in the future tense; which would make the passage read better,—"*that* I shall render," &c. These two verses are not necessarily connected with the Apostle's argument; for in the following verse he resumes the subject of verse 12, or rather, as his usual manner is, he states the same thing in other words and in more explicit and stronger terms. So that the γὰρ in the next verse may very properly be rendered "yea," or as an illative, "then."—*Ed.*

it were, wholly dead, will bring life to the Gentiles.[1] It is no objection what some allege, that reconciliation differs not from resurrection, as we do indeed understand resurrection in the present instance, that is, to be that by which we are translated from the kingdom of death to the kingdom of life, for though the thing is the same, yet there is more force in the expression, and this a sufficient answer.

16. For if the first-fruit *be* holy, the lump *is* also *holy;* and if the root *be* holy, so *are* the branches.

17. And if some of the branches be broken off, and thou, being a wild olive-tree, wert graffed in among them, and with them partakest of the root and fatness of the olive-tree;

18. Boast not against the branches: but if thou boast, thou bearest not the root, but the root thee.

19. Thou wilt say then, The branches were broken off, that I might be graffed in.

20. Well; because of unbelief they were broken off, and thou standest by faith. Be not high-minded, but fear:

21. For if God spared not the natural branches, *take heed* lest he also spare not thee.

16. Quòd si primitiæ sanctæ, etiam conspersio; et si radix sancta etiam rami:

17. Si verò ex ramis quidam defracti sunt, tu verò oleaster quum esses, insitus es pro ipsis, et particeps factus es radicis et pinguedinis oleæ;

18. Ne contra ramos glorieris: quòd si gloriaris, non tu radicem portas; sed radix te.

19. Dices ergo, Defracti sunt rami, ut ego insererer.

20. Bene; propter incredulitatem defracti sunt, tu verò fide stabilitus es; Ne animo efferaris, sed timeas.

21. Si enim Deus naturalibus ramis non perpercit, *vide* ne qua fit, *ut* et tibi non parcat.

16. *For if the first-fruits,* &c. By comparing the worthiness of the Jews and of the Gentiles, he now takes away

[1] Some view the last words, "life from the dead," as understood of the Jews and not of the Gentiles. But the antithesis seems to require the latter meaning. The rejection or casting away, ἀποβολὴ, of the Jews was the occasion of reconciliation to the world, that is, the Gentiles; then the reception, πρόσληψις, of the Jews will be "life from the dead" to the Gentiles or to the world. He expresses by stronger terms the sentiment in verse 12, " the riches of the world," only intimating, as it appears, the decayed state of religion among the Gentiles; for to be dead sometimes means a religious declension, Rev. iii. 1, 2; or a state of oppression and wretchedness, as the case was with the Israelites when in captivity, Ezek. xxxvii. 1-14; Is. xxvi. 19. The phrase is evidently figurative, and signifies a wonderful revival, such as the coming to life of those in a condition resembling that of death. The restoration of the Jews unto God's favour will occasion the revival and spread of true religion through the whole Gentile world. This is clearly the meaning.

Some of the fathers, such as *Chrysostom* and *Theodoret*, regarded the words as referring to the last resurrection: but this is wholly at variance with the context.—*Ed.*

pride from the one and pacifies the other, as far as he could; for he shows that the Gentiles, if they pretended any prerogative of honour of their own, did in no respect excel the Jews, nay, that if they came to a contest, they should be left far behind. Let us remember that in this comparison man is not compared with man, but nation with nation. If then a comparison be made between them, they shall be found equal in this respect, that they are both equally the children of Adam; the only difference is that the Jews had been separated from the Gentiles, that they might be a peculiar people to the Lord.[1]

They were then sanctified by the holy covenant, and adorned with peculiar honour, with which God had not at that time favoured the Gentiles; but as the efficacy of the covenant appeared then but small, he bids us to look back to Abraham and the patriarchs, in whom the blessing of God was not indeed either empty or void. He hence concludes, that from them an hereditary holiness had passed to all their posterity. But this conclusion would not have been right had he spoken of persons, or rather had he not regarded the promise; for when the father is just, he cannot yet transmit his own uprightness to his son: but as the Lord had sanctified Abraham for himself for this end, that his seed might also be holy, and as he thus conferred holiness not only on his person but also on his whole race, the Apostle does not unsuitably draw this conclusion, that all the Jews were sanctified in their father Abraham.[2]

---

[1] There were two kinds of first-fruits: the sheaf, being the first ripe fruit, Lev. xxiii. 10; and the dough, the first kneaded cake, Num. xv. 20. It is to the last that the reference is here made.

The first-fruits are considered by some, such as *Mede* and *Chalmers*, to have been the first Jewish converts to Christianity—the apostles and disciples; but this is not consistent with the usual manner of the Apostle, which is to express the same thing in two ways, or by two metaphors. Besides, the whole context refers to the first adoption of the Jewish nation, or to the covenant made with Abraham and confirmed to the patriarchs. —*Ed.*

[2] That the holiness here mentioned is external and relative, and not personal and inward, is evident from the whole context. The children of Israel were denominated holy in all their wickedness and disobedience, because they had been consecrated to God, adopted as his people, and set apart for his service, and they enjoyed all the external privileges of the covenant which God had made with their fathers.

Then to confirm this view, he adduces two similitudes: the one taken from the ceremonies of the law, and the other borrowed from nature. The first-fruits which were offered sanctified the whole lump, in like manner the goodness of the juice diffuses itself from the root to the branches; and posterity hold the same connection with their parents from whom they proceed as the lump has with the first-fruits, and the branches with the tree. It is not then a strange thing that the Jews were sanctified in their father.

There is here no difficulty if you understand by holiness the spiritual nobility of the nation, and that indeed not belonging to nature, but what proceeded from the covenant. It may be truly said, I allow, that the Jews were naturally holy, for their adoption was hereditary; but I now speak of our first nature, according to which we are all, as we know, accursed in Adam. Therefore the dignity of an elect people, to speak correctly, is a supernatural privilege.

17. *And if some of the branches*, &c. He now refers to the present dignity of the Gentiles, which is no other than to be of the branches; which, being taken from another, are set in some noble tree: for the origin of the Gentiles was as it were from some wild and unfruitful olive, as nothing but a curse was to be found in their whole race. Whatever glory

Pareus makes a distinction between what passes from progenitors to their offspring and what does not pass. In the present case the rights and privileges of the covenant were transmitted, but not faith and inward holiness. "Often," he says, "the worst descend from the best, and the best from the worst; from wicked Ahaz sprang good Hezekiah, from Hezekiah descended impious Manasse, from Manasse again came good Josiah, and from Josiah sprang wicked sons, Shallum and Jehoiakim." But all were alike holy in the sense intended here by the Apostle, as they were circumcised, and inherited the transmissible rights and privileges of the covenant.

"The holiness," says *Turrettin*, "of the first-fruits and of the root was no other than an external, federal, and national consecration, such as could be transferred from parents to their children."

"The attentive reader," says *Scott*, "will readily perceive that *relative* holiness, or consecration to God, is here exclusively meant. . . . Abraham was as it were the root of the visible Church. Ishmael was broken off, and the tree grew up in Isaac; and when Esau was broken off, it grew up in Jacob and his sons. . . . When the nation rejected the Messiah, their relation to Abraham and to God was as it were suspended. They no longer retained even the outward seal of the covenant; for circumcision lost its validity and baptism became the sign of regeneration: they were thenceforth deprived of the ordinances of God."—*Ed.*

then they had was from their new insition, not from their old stock. There was then no reason for the Gentiles to glory in their own dignity in comparison with the Jews. We may also add, that Paul wisely mitigates the severity of the case, by not saying that the whole top of the tree was cut off, but that some of the branches were broken, and also that God took some here and there from among the Gentiles, whom he set in the holy and blessed trunk.[1]

18. *But if thou gloriest, thou bearest not the root,* &c. The Gentiles could not contend with the Jews respecting the excellency of their race without contending with Abraham himself; which would have been extremely unbecoming, since he was like a root by which they were borne and nourished. As unreasonable as it would be for the branches to boast against the root, so unreasonable would it have been for the Gentiles to glory against the Jews, that is, with respect to the excellency of their race; for Paul would have them ever to consider whence was the origin of their salvation. And we know that after Christ by his coming has pulled down the partition-wall, the whole world partook of the favour which God had previously conferred on the chosen people. It hence follows, that the calling of the Gentiles was like an ingrafting, and that they did not otherwise grow up as God's people than as they were grafted in the stock of Abraham.

19. *Thou wilt then say,* &c. In the person of the Gentiles

---

[1] There is a difference of opinion as to the precise meaning of the words ἐνεκεντρίσθης ἐν αὐτοῖς; *Calvin's* version is, "insitus es pro ipsis—thou hast been ingrafted for them," or in their stead; that of *Beza* and *Pareus* is the same, and also that of *Macknight;* but *Grotius* has "inter illos—between them," that is, the remaining branches; and *Doddridge* renders the words "among them," according to our version. What is most consonant with the first part of the verse, is the rendering of *Calvin;* what is stated is the cutting off of some of the branches, and the most obvious meaning is, that others were put in for them, or in their stead. It has been said, that it was not the practice to graft a wild olive in a good olive, except when the latter was decaying. Such may have been the case; but the Apostle's object was not so much to refer to what was usual, as to form a comparison suitable to his purpose; and this is what our Saviour in his parables had sometimes done. Contrary to what the case is in nature, the Apostle makes the stock good and the graft bad, and makes the stock to communicate its goodness to the graft and to improve the quality of its fruit. But his main object is to show the fact of incision, without any regard to the character of the stock and of the graft in natural things; for both *his* stock and *his* graft are of a different character.—*Ed.*

he brings forward what they might have pleaded for themselves; but that was of such a nature as ought not to have filled them with pride, but, on the contrary, to have made them humble. For if the cutting off of the Jews was through unbelief, and if the ingrafting of the Gentiles was by faith, what was their duty but to acknowledge the favour of God, and also to cherish modesty and humbleness of mind? For it is the nature of faith, and what properly belongs to it, to generate humility and fear.[1] But by fear understand that which is in no way inconsistent with the assurance of faith; for Paul would not have our faith to vacillate or to alternate with doubt, much less would he have us to be frightened or to quake with fear.[2]

Of what kind then is this fear? As the Lord bids us to take into our consideration two things, so two kinds of feeling must thereby be produced. For he would have us ever to bear in mind the miserable condition of our nature; and this can produce nothing but dread, weariness, anxiety, and despair; and it is indeed expedient that we should thus be thoroughly laid prostrate and broken down, that we may at length groan to him; but this dread, derived from the knowledge of ourselves, keeps not our minds while relying on his goodness, from continuing calm; this weariness hinders us not from enjoying full consolation in him; this

---

[1] "Be not elated in mind—ne animo efferaris;" μὴ ὑψηλοφρόνει; "be not high-minded," as in our version, is the literal rendering.—*Ed.*

[2] Some have deduced from what Paul says here the uncertainty of faith, and its possible failure. This has been done through an entire misapprehension of the subject handled by the Apostle. He speaks not of individuals, but of the Gentile world, not of living faith but of professed faith, not the inward change, but of outward privileges, not of the union of the soul to Christ, but of union with his Church. The two things are wholly different; and to draw an argument from the one to the other is altogether illegitimate; that is to say, that as professed faith may be lost, therefore living faith may be lost.

Augustine, in commenting on Jer. xxxii. 40, says, "God promised perseverance when he said, 'I will put fear in their heart, that they may not depart from me.' What else does it mean but this, 'Such and so great will my fear be, which I shall put in their heart, that they shall perseveringly cleave to me.'"

"As those," says *Pareus,* "who believe for a time never had true faith, though they seem to have had it, and hence fall away and do not persevere: so they who possess true faith never fail, but continue steadfast, for God infallibly sustains them and secures their perseverance."—*Ed.*

anxiety, this despair, does not prevent us from obtaining in him real joy and hope. Hence the fear, of which he speaks, is set up as an antidote to proud contempt; for as every one claims for himself more than what is right, and becomes too secure and at length insolent towards others, we ought then so far to fear, that our heart may not swell with pride and elate itself.

But it seems that he throws in a doubt as to salvation, since he reminds them to beware lest they also should not be spared. To this I answer,—that as this exhortation refers to the subduing of the flesh, which is ever insolent even in the children of God, he derogates nothing from the certainty of faith. And we must especially notice and remember what I have before said,—that Paul's address is not so much to individuals as to the whole body of the Gentiles, among whom there might have been many, who were vainly inflated, professing rather than having faith. On account of these Paul threatens the Gentiles, not without reason, with excision, as we shall hereafter find again.

21. *For if God has not spared the natural branches*, &c. This is a most powerful reason to beat down all self-confidence: for the rejection of the Jews should never come across our minds without striking and shaking us with dread. For what ruined them, but that through supine dependence on the dignity which they had obtained, they despised what God had appointed? They were not spared, though they were natural branches; what then shall be done to us, who are the wild olive and aliens, if we become beyond measure arrogant? But this thought, as it leads us to distrust ourselves, so it tends to make us to cleave more firmly and steadfastly to the goodness of God.

And here again it appears more evident, that the discourse is addressed generally to the body of the Gentiles, for the excision, of which he speaks, could not apply to individuals, whose election is unchangeable, based on the eternal purpose of God. Paul therefore declares to the Gentiles, that if they exulted over the Jews, a reward for their pride would be prepared for them; for God will again reconcile to himself the first people whom he has divorced.

22. Behold therefore the goodness and severity of God: on them which fell, severity; but toward thee, goodness, if thou continue in *his* goodness; otherwise thou also shalt be cut off.

23. And they also, if they abide not still in unbelief, shall be graffed in: for God is able to graff them in again.

24. For if thou were cut out of the olive-tree, which is wild by nature, and wert graffed contrary to nature into a good olive-tree; how much more shall these, which be the natural *branches*, be graffed into their own olive-tree?

22. Vide igitur lenitatem[1] et severitatem Dei; in eos quidem qui ceciderunt, severitatem;[2] in te vero lenitatem, si permanseris in lenitate; alioqui tu quoque excideris:

23. Et illi, si non perstiterint in incredulitate, inserentur; potens enim est Deus rursum inserere ipsos.

24. Si enim tu ex oleastro, quæ tibi nativa erat, exectus es, et præter naturam insitus es in veram oleam; multo magis hi secundum naturam propriæ oleæ inserentur.

22. *See then,* &c. By laying the case before their eyes he more clearly and fully confirms the fact,—that the Gentiles had no reason to be proud. They saw in the Jews an example of God's severity, which ought to have terrified them; while in themselves they had an evidence of his grace and goodness, by which they ought to have been stimulated to thankfulness only, and to exalt the Lord and not themselves. The words import the same, as though he had said, —" If thou exultest over their calamity, think first what thou hast been; for the same severity of God would have impended over thee, hadst thou not been delivered by his gratuitous favour: then consider what thou art even now; for salvation shall not continue to thee, except thou humbly

---

[1] "Lenitatem;" χρηστότητα; "indulgentiam—indulgence," *Jerome;* "benignitatem—benignity," *Beza.* Its most literal meaning is "beneficence," as χρηστὸς is useful or beneficial: but "goodness," as in our version, expresses its sense here perhaps better than any other word. It is rendered "kindness" in 2 Cor. vi. 6; Eph. ii. 7; Col. iii. 12; Tit. iii. 4, —"gentleness" in Gal. v. 22,—and "good" in Rom. iii. 12. It is nowhere else found and has a similar meaning in the *Septuagint,* and stands often for טוב, which signifies good, goodness, benevolence.—*Ed.*

[2] "Severitatem;" ἀποτομίαν; "rigorem—rigour," *Erasmus;* "præcisam severitatem—a cut-off severity," *Beza.* It means literally excision, cutting off, amputation, and metaphorically, rigour, severity; and it is taken, says *Schleusner,* not from the amputation of infected limbs, but from the cutting off of barren and useless branches of trees. It occurs here only, and is not found in the *Septuagint.* Ἀποτμία τῶν νόμων—rigour of the laws, *Diod. Sic.* It is used adverbially in two places, 2 Cor. xiii. 10, and Tit. i. 13; where it means rigidly, sharply, severely. The adjective, ἀπότομος, is found in Wisdom of Sol. v. 20, and vi. 6, connected with "wrath" and "judgment," and means rigid or severe.—*Ed.*

recognisest the mercy of God ; for if thou forgettest thyself and arrogantly exultest, the ruin, into which they have fallen, awaits thee: it is not indeed enough for thee to have once embraced the favour of God, except thou followest his call through the whole course of thy life." They indeed who have been illuminated by the Lord ought always to think of perseverance ; for they continue not in the goodness of God, who having for a time responded to the call of God, do at length begin to loathe the kingdom of heaven, and thus by their ingratitude justly deserve to be blinded again.

But he addresses not each of the godly apart, as we have already said, but he makes a comparison between the Gentiles and the Jews. It is indeed true that each individual among the Jews received the reward due to his own unbelief, when they were banished from the kingdom of God, and that all who from among the Gentiles were called, were vessels of God's mercy; but yet the particular design of Paul must be borne in mind. For he would have the Gentiles to depend on the eternal covenant of God, so as to connect their own with the salvation of the elect people, and then, lest the rejection of the Jews should produce offence, as though their ancient adoption were void, he would have them to be terrified by this example of punishment, so as reverently to regard the judgment of God. For whence comes so great licentiousness on curious questions, except that we almost neglect to consider those things which ought to have duly taught us humility ?

But as he speaks not of the elect individually, but of the whole body, a condition is added, *If they continued in his kindness.* I indeed allow, that as soon as any one abuses God's goodness, he deserves to be deprived of the offered favour ; but it would be improper to say of any one of the godly particularly, that God had mercy on him, when he chose him, provided he would continue in his mercy ; for the perseverance of faith, which completes in us the effect of God's grace, flows from election itself. Paul then teaches us, that the Gentiles were admitted into the hope of eternal life on the condition, that they by their gratitude retained possession of it. And dreadful indeed was the defection of the whole world, which afterwards happened; and this clearly proves, that this exhortation was not superfluous; for when God had almost in a moment watered it with his grace, so that religion flourished everywhere, soon after the truth of the gospel vanished, and the treasure of salvation was taken away. And whence came so sudden a change, except that the Gentiles had fallen away from their calling?

Otherwise thou also shalt be cut off, &c. We now understand in what sense Paul threatens them with excision, whom he has already allowed to have been grafted into the hope of life through God's election. For, first, though this cannot happen to the elect, they have yet need of such warning, in order to subdue the pride of the flesh; which being really opposed to their salvation, ought justly to be terrified with the dread of perdition. As far then as Christians are illuminated by faith, they hear, for their assurance, that the calling of God is without repentance; but as far as they carry about them the flesh, which wantonly resists the grace of God, they are taught humility by this warning, "Take heed lest thou be cut off." Secondly, we must bear in mind the solution which I have before mentioned,—that Paul speaks not here of the special election of individuals, but sets the Gentiles and Jews in opposition the one to the other; and that therefore the elect are not so much addressed in these words, as those who falsely gloried that they had obtained the place of the Jews: nay, he speaks to the Gentiles generally, and addresses the whole body in common, among whom there were many who were faithful, and those who were members of Christ in name only.

But if it be asked respecting individuals, "How any one could be cut off from the grafting, and how, after excision, he could be grafted again,"—bear in mind, that there are three modes of insition, and two modes of excision. For instance, the children of the faithful are ingrafted, to whom the promise belongs according to the covenant made with the fathers; ingrafted are also they who indeed receive the seed of the gospel, but it strikes no root, or it is choked before it brings any fruit; and thirdly, the elect are ingrafted, who are illuminated unto eternal life according to the immutable purpose of God. The first are cut off, when they refuse the promise given to their fathers, or do not receive it on account of their ingratitude; the second are cut off, when the seed is withered and destroyed; and as the danger of this impends over all, with regard to their own nature, it must be allowed that this warning which Paul gives belongs in a certain way to the faithful, lest they indulge themselves in the sloth of the flesh. But with regard to the present passage, it is enough for us to know, that the vengeance which God had executed on the Jews, is pronounced on the Gentiles, in case they become like them.

23. *For God is able*, &c. Frigid would this argument be to the profane; for however they may concede power to God, yet as they view it at a distance, shut up as it were in heaven, they do for the most part rob it of its effect. But as the faithful, whenever they hear God's power named, look on it as in present operation, he thought that this reason was sufficient to strike their minds. We may add, that he assumes this as an acknowledged axiom,—that God had so punished the unbelief of his people as not to forget his mercy; according to what he had done before, having often restored the Jews, after he had apparently banished them from his kingdom. And he shows at the same time by the comparison, how much more easy it would be to reverse the present state of things than to have introduced it; that is, how much easier it would be for the natural branches, if they were again put in the place from which they had been cut off, to draw substance from their own root, than for the wild and the unfruitful, from a foreign stock: for such is the comparison made between the Jews and the Gentiles.

25. For I would not, brethren, that ye should be ignorant of this mystery, lest ye should be wise in your own conceits, that blindness in part is happened to Israel, until the fulness of the Gentiles be come in.

26. And so all Israel shall be saved: as it is written, There shall come out of Sion the Deliverer, and shall turn away ungodliness from Jacob:

25. Nolo enim vos ignorare, fratres, mysterium hoc, ut ne apud vosmetipsos superbiatis, quòd cæcitas ex parte Isræli contigit, donec plenitudo gentium ingrediatur:

26. Atque ita universus Isræl salvus fiet; quemadmodum scriptum est, Veniet ex Sion is qui liberat, et avertet impietates a Iacob:

| 27. For this *is* my covenant unto them, when I shall take away their sins. | 27. Et hoc illis à me testamentum, quum abstulero peccata eorum. |

25. *I would not*, &c. Here he rouses his hearers to a greater attention, while he avows that he is going to declare something that was secret. Nor did he do this without reason; for he wished to conclude, by a brief or plain sentence, a very perplexed question; and yet he declares what no one could have expected. But the words, *Lest ye should be proud in yourselves*,[1] show what was his designed object; and that was, to check the arrogance of the Gentiles, lest they should exult over the Jews. This admonition was also necessary, lest the defection of that people should immoderately disturb the minds of the weak, as though the salvation of them all was to be for ever despaired of. The same is still not less useful to us at this day, so that we may know, that the salvation of the remnant, whom the Lord will at length gather to himself, is hid, sealed as it were by his signet. And whenever a long delay tempts us to despair, let us remember this word *mystery;* by which Paul clearly reminds us, that the mode of their conversion will neither be common nor usual; and hence they act absurdly who attempt to measure it by their own judgment; for what can be more unreasonable than to regard that as incredible which is far removed from our view? It is called a mystery, because it will be incomprehensible until the time of its revelation.[2] It is, however, made known to us, as it was to the

---

[1] "Ne apud vos superbiatis;" ἵνα μὴ ἦτε παρ' ἑαυτοῖς φρόνιμοι; "ut ne sitis apud vosmetipsos sapientes—lest ye should be wise in yourselves,"—*Beza* and *Piscator*. The meaning, as given by *Grotius*, is, "Lest ye think yourselves so wise as to suppose that ye can by your own understanding know what is to come." But the object of the Apostle seems to have been, to keep down self-elevation on account of the privileges they had attained. The phrase seems to have been taken from Prov. iii. 7; where the *Septuagint* render, "in thine own eyes," בְּעֵינֶיךָ, παρὰ σεαυτῷ, "in thyself," that is, in thine own esteem. And it appears to be its meaning here, "Lest ye should be wise in your own esteem," which signifies, "Lest ye should be proud," or elated, that is, on account of your now superior privileges and advantages. *Doddridge's* version expresses the idea, "Lest you should have too high an opinion of yourselves."—*Ed.*

[2] The mystery is accounted for in rather a singular way. The most obvious meaning is, that the mystery was the fact of the restoration, and not the manner of it. No doubt the word sometimes means what is ob-

Romans, that our faith may be content with the word, and support us with hope, until the event itself come to light.

That blindness in part, &c. " In part," I think, refers not simply to time, nor to the number, but means, in a manner, or in a measure; by which expression he intended, as it seems to me, only to qualify a declaration which in itself was severe. *Until* does not specify the progress or order of time, but signifies the same thing, as though he had said, " That the fulness of the Gentiles," &c. The meaning then is,—That God had in a manner so blinded Israel, that while they refused the light of the gospel, it might be transferred to the Gentiles, and that these might occupy, as it were, the vacated possession. And so this blindness served the providence of God in furthering the salvation of the Gentiles, which he had designed. And the *fulness* of the Gentiles is to be taken for a great number: for it was not to be, as before, when a few proselytes connected themselves with the Jews; but such was to be the change, that the Gentiles would form almost the entire body of the Church.[1]

scure, sublime, or profound, as "great is the mystery of godliness," 1 Tim. iii. 16: but here the mystery is made known, in the same manner as Paul mentions a fact respecting the resurrection, 1 Cor. xv. 51, and also the call of the Gentiles, Rom. xvi. 25.—*Ed.*

[1] The explanation of this verse is by no means satisfactory. It does not correspond at all with what the Apostle has already declared in verses 11, 12, and 15; where the restoration of the Jews to the faith is most clearly set forth. Besides, by making Israel, in the next verse, to mean generally the people of God, the contrast, observable through the whole argument, is completely destroyed.

The word for " blindness " is πώρωσις, hardness, callousness, and hence contumacy. " In part," is generally regarded as having reference both to extent and duration: the hardness did not extend to all the Jews, and it was not to endure, but to continue for a time; and the time is mentioned, "until the fulness of the Gentiles come in." This is obviously the meaning, and confirmed by the whole context. The attempt of *Grotius* and *Hammond*, and of some of the Fathers, to confine what is said to the Apostolic times, is wholly irreconcilable with the drift of the whole passage and with facts.

Much has been written on the words, ἄχρις οὗ τὸ πλήρωμα τῶν ἐθνῶν εἰσέλθῃ. That the event was future in the Apostle's time (and future still as history proves) is evident, especially from the following verse, " and so all Israel shall be saved." The plain construction of the passage is, " until the fulness of the Gentiles shall come." What this " fulness " is to be has been much controverted. But by taking a view of the whole context, without regard to any hypothesis, we shall, with no great difficulty, ascertain its meaning. The " fulness" of the Jews in verse 12, is determined

26. *And so all Israel,* &c. Many understand this of the Jewish people, as though Paul had said, that religion would again be restored among them as before: but I extend the word *Israel* to all the people of God, according to this meaning,—" When the Gentiles shall come in, the Jews also shall return from their defection to the obedience of faith; and thus shall be completed the salvation of the whole Israel of God, which must be gathered from both; and yet in such a way that the Jews shall obtain the first place, being as it were the first-born in God's family." This interpretation seems to me the most suitable, because Paul intended here to set forth the completion of the kingdom of Christ, which is by no means to be confined to the Jews, but is to include the whole world. The same manner of speaking we find in Gal. vi. 16. The Israel of God is what he calls the Church, gathered alike from Jews and Gentiles; and he sets the people, thus collected from their dispersion, in opposition to the carnal children of Abraham, who had departed from his faith.

As it is written, &c. He does not confirm the whole passage by this testimony of Isaiah, (Is. lix. 20,) but only one clause,—that the children of Abraham shall be partakers of redemption. But if one takes this view,—that Christ had

by verse 26; it includes the whole nation. Then the "fulness of the Gentiles" must mean the same thing, the introduction of all nations into the Church. The grafting more particularly signifies profession. It then follows that all nations shall be brought publicly to profess the gospel prior to the removal of the hardness from the whole nation of the Jews. There may be isolated cases of conversion before this event, for "in part" as to extent the hardness is to be: but all shall not be brought to the faith, until the faith spread through the whole world: and the effect of their restoration will be a great revival of vital religion among the professing Gentiles, according to what is said in verse 15. This is clearly the view presented to us in this extraordinary passage, when all its parts are compared with each other.

Hammond tells us, that many of the Fathers wholly denied the future restoration of the Jews; and we are told by *Pareus,* who mentions some of the same Fathers, that they maintained it. But it appears from the quotations made by the first, that the restoration disallowed was that to their own land, and that the restoration referred to by the latter was restoration to the faith; two things wholly distinct. That "Israel" means exclusively the Jewish nation, was almost the unanimous opinion of the Fathers, according to *Estius;* and that their future restoration to the faith is here foretold was the sentiment held by *Beza, Pareus, Willet, Mede,* and others, and is generally held by modern divines.—*Ed.*

been promised and offered to them, but that as they rejected him, they were deprived of his grace; yet the Prophet's words express more, even this,—that there will be some remnant, who, having repented, shall enjoy the favour of deliverance.

Paul, however, does not quote what we read in Isaiah, word for word; "come," he says, "shall a Redeemer to Sion, and to those who shall repent of iniquity in Jacob, saith the Lord." (Is. lix. 20.) But on this point we need not be very curious; only this is to be regarded, that the Apostles suitably apply to their purpose whatever proofs they adduce from the Old Testament; for their object was to point out passages, as it were by the finger, that readers might be directed to the fountain itself.

But though in this prophecy deliverance to the spiritual people of God is promised, among whom even Gentiles are included; yet as the Jews are the first-born, what the Prophet declares must be fulfilled, especially in them: for that Scripture calls all the people of God Israelites, is to be ascribed to the pre-eminence of that nation, whom God had preferred to all other nations. And then, from a regard to the ancient covenant, he says expressly, that a Redeemer shall come to Sion; and he adds, that he will redeem those in Jacob who shall return from their transgression.[1] By these words God distinctly claims for himself a certain seed, so that his redemption may be effectual in his elect and peculiar nation. And though fitter for his purpose would

---

[1] There is more discrepancy in this reference than any we have met with. The Apostle follows not literally either the Hebrew or the Septuagint, though the latter more than the former. In the Hebrew, it is, "to Sion," לציון, and in the Septuagint, "for the sake of Sion," ἕνεκεν Σιών. Then the following clause is given verbatim from the *Septuagint*, and differs materially from the Hebrew, at least as translated in our version. The Syriac and Chaldee give the verb a causative meaning, so as to make the sense the same as here. But it may be regarded as an infinitive with a paragogic ו, and in a transitive sense, which it sometimes has. See 1 Kings ii. 16; Ps. cxxxii. 10. If so, the verse will agree with the Apostle's words, and may be thus rendered,—

   Come to Sion shall a deliverer,
   And to turn away the ungodliness *that is* in Jacob.

He shall come to Sion, and shall come "to turn away," &c.; or the ו may be rendered even, "Even to turn away," &c. This rendering corresponds more than that of our version with the substance of the verse which follows.—*Ed.*

have been the expression used by the Prophet, "shall come to Sion;" yet Paul made no scruple to follow the commonly received translation, which reads, "The Redeemer shall come forth from Mount Sion." And similar is the case as to the second part, "He shall turn away iniquities from Jacob:" for Paul thought it enough to regard this point only,—that as it is Christ's peculiar office to reconcile to God an apostate and faithless people, some change was surely to be looked for, lest they should all perish together.

27. *And, This is my covenant with them,* &c. Though Paul, by the last prophecy of Isaiah, briefly touched on the office of the Messiah, in order to remind the Jews what was to be expected especially from him, he further adds these few words from Jeremiah, expressly for the same purpose; for what is added is not found in the former passage.[1] This also tends to confirm the subject in hand; for what he said of the conversion of a people who were so stubborn and obstinate, might have appeared incredible: he therefore removes this stumblingblock, by declaring that the covenant included a gratuitous remission of sins. For we may gather from the words of the Prophet,—that God would have no more to do with his apostate people, until he should remit the crime of perfidy, as well as their other sins.

28. As concerning the gospel, *they are* enemies for your sakes: but as touching the election, *they are* beloved for the fathers' sakes.

29. For the gifts and calling of God *are* without repentance.

30. For as ye in times past have not believed God, yet have now obtained mercy through their unbelief;

31. Even so have these also now not believed, that through your

28. Secundum Evangelium quidem inimici propter vos; secundum electionem verò dilecti propter Patres:

29. Sine pœnitentia enim sunt dona et vocatio Dei.

30. Quemadmodum enim vos quoque[2] increduli fuistis Deo, nunc autem misericordiam estis consequuti istorum incredulitate:

31. Sic et ii nunc increduli facti sunt, eò quòd adepti estis misericor-

---

[1] The former part of it is, "This is my covenant," but not the latter, "When I shall take away their sins." Some suppose that this is taken from Is. xxvii. 9, where we find this phrase in the *Septuagint*, "When I shall take away his sin," τὴν ἁμαρτίαν αὐτοῦ: but the Hebrew is somewhat different and farther from the form of the sentence here. We must therefore consider it as an abridgment of what is contained in Jer. xxxi. 33, and quoted in Heb. viii. 10.—*Ed.*

[2] Ποτὲ—formerly, left out.

mercy they also may obtain mercy.	diam, ut ipsi quoque misericordiam consequantur.¹
32. For God hath concluded them all in unbelief, that he might have mercy upon all.	32. Concludit enim Deus omnes sub incredulitate, ut omnium misereatur.

28. *With regard indeed to the gospel,* &c. He shows that the worst thing in the Jews ought not to subject them to the contempt of the Gentiles. Their chief crime was unbelief: but Paul teaches us, that they were thus blinded for a time by God's providence, that a way to the gospel might be made for the Gentiles;² and that still they were not for ever excluded from the favour of God. He then admits, that they were for the present alienated from God on account of the gospel, that thus the salvation, which at first was deposited with them, might come to the Gentiles; and yet that God was not unmindful of the covenant which he had made with their fathers, and by which he testified that according to his eternal purpose he loved that nation: and this he confirms by this remarkable declaration,—that the grace of the divine calling cannot be made void; for this is the import of the words,—

29. *The gifts and calling of God are without repentance.* He has mentioned gifts and calling; which are to be understood, according to a figure in grammar,³ as meaning the gift of calling: and this is not to be taken for any sort of calling but of that, by which God had adopted the posterity of Abraham into covenant; since this is especially the subject here, as he has previously, by the word, election, designated

---

[1] Our common version departs here from the original by connecting "your mercy" with the last clause. *Calvin* keeps the proper order of the words, though he paraphrases them, τῷ ὑμετέρῳ ἐλέει, "eo quòd adepti estis misericordiam." They might have been rendered, "through your mercy," that is, the mercy shown to you, or the mercy of which you are the objects. —*Ed.*

[2] They were "enemies" to Paul and the Church, say *Grotius* and *Luther*,—to the gospel, says *Pareus*,—to God, say *Mede* and *Stuart.* The parallel in the next clause, "beloved," favours the last sentiment. They were become God's enemies, and alienated through their rejection of the gospel; but they were still regarded as descendants of the Fathers and in some sense on their account "beloved," as those for whom God entertained love, inasmuch as his "gifts and calling" made in their behalf, were still in force and never to be changed.—*Ed.*

[3] *Hypallage*—transposition, a change in the arrangement of a sentence.

the secret purpose of God, by which he had formerly made a distinction between the Jews and the Gentiles.[1] For we must bear this in mind,—that he speaks not now of the election of individuals, but of the common adoption of the whole nation, which might seem for a time, according to the outward appearance, to have failed, but had not been cut up by the roots. As the Jews had fallen from their privilege and the salvation promised them, that some hope might remain to the remnant, Paul maintains that the purpose of God stands firm and immovable, by which he had once deigned to choose them for himself as a peculiar nation. Since then it cannot possibly be, that the Lord will depart from that covenant which he made with Abraham, " I will be the God of thy seed," (Gen. xvii. 7,) it is evident that he has not wholly turned away his kindness from the Jewish nation.

He does not oppose the gospel to election, as though they were contrary the one to the other, for whom God has chosen

---

[1] It is not desirable to amalgamate words in this manner; nor is it necessary. The Apostle ascends; he mentions first the "gifts," the free promises which God made to the Jews; and then he refers to the origin of them, the calling or the election of God, and says that both are irreversible, or, as *Castellio* well explains the word ἀμεταμέλητα, *irrevocable*. See a similar instance in chap. xiii. 13.

Calvin seems to regard " the gifts and calling" as having reference to the adoption of the Jewish nation, and their adoption to certain privileges included in the Abrahamic covenant, probably those mentioned in chap. ix. 4. But *Pareus, Mede,* and others, extend the meaning farther, and consider " the gifts" as including those of " faith, remission of sins, sanctification, perseverance and salvation;" and they understand by " calling," not the external, which often fails, but the internal, made by the Spirit, and ever efficacious, of which the Apostle had spoken, when he said, " Those whom he has predestinated, he has called, justified, and glorified." According to this view the Apostle must be considered to mean, that according to what is said in verse 5, the gifts and calling of God shall be effectual towards *some* of the Jews throughout all ages, and towards the whole nation, when the fulness of the Gentiles shall come in; or, that though they may be suspended, they shall yet be made evident at the appointed time; so that what secures and renders certain the restoration of the Jews is the covenant of free grace which God made with their fathers.

Some, as *Pareus* informs us, have concluded from what is here said, that no Gentile nation, once favoured with " the gifts and calling of God," shall be wholly forsaken; and that though religion may for a long season be in a degenerated state, God will yet, in his own appointed time, renew his gifts and his calling, and restore true religion. The ground of hope is the irrevocability of his gifts and calling.—*Ed.*

he calls; but inasmuch as the gospel had been proclaimed to the Gentiles beyond the expectation of the world, he justly compares this favour with the ancient election of the Jews, which had been manifested so many ages before: and so election derives its name from antiquity; for God had in past ages of the world chosen one people for himself.

On account of the Fathers, he says not, because they gave any cause for love, but because God's favour had descended from them to their posterity, according to the tenor of the covenant, " Thy God and the God of thy seed." How the Gentiles had obtained mercy through the unbelief of the Jews, has been before stated, namely, that God, being angry with the Jews for their unbelief, turned his kindness to them. What immediately follows, that they became unbelievers through the mercy manifested to the Gentiles, seems rather strange; and yet there is in it nothing unreasonable; for Paul assigns not the cause of blindness, but only declares, that what God transferred to the Gentiles had been taken away from the Jews. But lest what they had lost through unbelief, should be thought by the Gentiles to have been gained by them through the merit of faith, mention is made only of mercy. What is substantially said then is,— that as God purposed to show mercy to the Gentiles, the Jews were on this account deprived of the light of faith.

32. *For God has shut up*, &c. A remarkable conclusion, by which he shows that there is no reason why they who have a hope of salvation should despair of others; for whatever they may now be, they have been like all the rest. If they have emerged from unbelief through God's mercy alone, they ought to leave place for it as to others also. For he makes the Jews equal in guilt with the Gentiles, that both might understand that the avenue to salvation is no less open to others than to them. For it is the mercy of God alone which saves; and this offers itself to both. This sentence then corresponds with the testimony of Hosea, which he had before quoted, " I will call those my people who were not my people." But he does not mean, that God so blinds all men that their unbelief is to be imputed to him; but that he hath so arranged by his providence, that all

should be guilty of unbelief, in order that he might have them subject to his judgment, and for this end,—that all merits being buried, salvation might proceed from his goodness alone.[1]

Paul then intends here to teach two things—that there is nothing in any man why he should be preferred to others, apart from the mere favour of God; and that God in the dispensation of his grace, is under no restraint that he should not grant it to whom he pleases. There is an emphasis in the word *mercy;* for it intimates that God is bound to none, and that he therefore saves all freely, for they are all equally lost. But extremely gross is their folly who hence conclude that all shall be saved; for Paul simply means that both Jews and Gentiles do not otherwise obtain salvation than through the mercy of God, and thus he leaves to none any reason for complaint. It is indeed true that this mercy is without any difference offered to all, but every one must seek it by faith.

33. O the depth of the riches both of the wisdom and knowledge of God! how unsearchable *are* his judgments, and his ways past finding out!
34. For who hath known the mind of the Lord? or who hath been his counsellor?
35. Or who hath first given to him, and it shall be recompensed unto him again?

33. O profunditatem divitiarum et sapientiæ et cognitionis Dei! quàm incomprehensibilia[2] sunt judicia ejus et impervestigabiles[3] viæ ipsius!
34. Quis enim cognovit mentem Domini? aut quis illi à consiliis fuit?
35. Aut quis prior dedit ei et retribuetur illi?

---

[1] The verb which *Calvin* renders *conclusit*, συνέκλεισε, means to shut up together. The paraphrase of *Chrysostom* is, that " God has proved (ἤλεγξεν) all to be unbelieving." *Wolfius* considers the meaning the same with verse 9 of chap. iii., and with Gal. iii. 22. God has in his providence, as well as in his word, proved and demonstrated, that all mankind are by nature in a state of unbelief and of sin and of condemnation.

God has shut up together, &c., " how ?" asks *Pareus:* then he answers, " by manifesting, accusing, and condemning unbelief, but not by effecting or approving it."—*Ed.*

[2] "Incomprehensibilia," so the *Vulgate;* " ἀνεξερεύνητα—inscrutabilia—inscrutable," *Beza.* It means what cannot be found out by searching. Our version conveys the correct idea—" unsearchable."—*Ed.*

[3] "Impervestigabiles," so *Beza;* " ἀνεξιχνίαστοι—investigabiles—uninvestigable," *Vulgate;* what cannot be investigated, and of which there are no footsteps—untraceable; " cannot be traced out" is the version of *Doddridge.*—*Ed.*

36. For of him, and through him, and to him, *are* all things : to whom *be* glory for ever. Amen.	36. Quoniam ex illo et per illum et in illum sunt omnia : Ipsi gloria in secula. Amen.

33. *Oh!* the depth, &c. Here first the Apostle bursts into an exclamation, which arose spontaneously from a devout consideration of God's dealings with the faithful; then in passing he checks the boldness of impiety, which is wont to clamour against the judgments of God. When therefore we hear, *Oh! the depth,* this expression of wonder ought greatly to avail to the beating down of the presumption of our flesh; for after having spoken from the word and by the Spirit of the Lord, being at length overcome by the sublimity of so great a mystery, he could not do otherwise than wonder and exclaim, that the riches of God's wisdom are deeper than our reason can penetrate to. Whenever then we enter on a discourse respecting the eternal counsels of God, let a bridle be always set on our thoughts and tongue, so that after having spoken soberly and within the limits of God's word, our reasoning may at last end in admiration. Nor ought we to be ashamed, that if we are not wiser than he, who, having been taken into the third heaven, saw mysteries to man ineffable, and who yet could find in this instance no other end designed but that he should thus humble himself.

Some render the words of Paul thus, "Oh! the deep riches, and wisdom, and knowledge of God!" as though the word βάθος was an adjective; and they take *riches* for abundance, but this seems to me strained, and I have therefore no doubt but that he extols God's deep riches of wisdom and knowledge.[1]

---

[1] It has indeed been thought by many that πλούτου, riches, is a noun belonging to wisdom and knowledge, used, after the Hebrew manner, instead of an adjective. It means abundance or exuberance. The sentence, according to our idiom, would then be, "O the profundity of the abounding wisdom and knowledge of God!" The Apostle, as in the words "the gifts and calling of God," adopts an ascending scale, and mentions wisdom first, and then knowledge, which in point of order precedes it. Then in the following clause, according to his usual practice, he retrogrades, and states first what belongs to knowledge—"judgments," decisions, divine decrees, such as knowledge determines; and then "ways," actual proceedings, for the guiding of which wisdom is necessary. Thus we see that his style is thoroughly Hebraistic.

It appears from Poole's Syn., that *Origen, Chrysostom,* and *Theodoret,*

How incomprehensible, &c. By different words, according to a practice common in Hebrew, he expresses the same thing. For he speaks of *judgments*, then he subjoins *ways*, which mean appointments or the mode of acting, or the manner of ruling. But he still continues his exclamation, and thus the more he elevates the height of the divine mystery, the more he deters us from the curiosity of investigating it. Let us then learn to make no searchings respecting the Lord, except as far as he has revealed himself in the Scriptures; for otherwise we shall enter a labyrinth, from which the retreat is not easy. It must however be noticed, that he speaks not here of all God's mysteries, but of those which are hid with God himself, and ought to be only admired and adored by us.

connected " riches" with " depth," " O the abounding depth," &c. ; but that *Ambrose* and *Augustine* connected it with " wisdom," &c. The use of the term in Eph. i. 7, favours the last; for "the riches of his grace" mean clearly " his abounding grace."

But some, with *Stuart*, suppose that by "riches" here is meant God's goodness or mercy, according to verse 12, and Eph. iii. 8. And *Stuart* gives this version, " O the boundless goodness, and wisdom, and knowledge of God!" But this destroys the evident correspondence that is to be found in the latter clause of the verse, except we take in the remaining portion of the chapter, and this perhaps is what ought to be done. But if we do this, then πλούτου means "treasures," or blessings," or " copia beneficiorum," as *Schleusner* expresses it. " Riches of Christ" mean the abounding blessings laid up in him, Eph. iii. 8. God may be viewed as set forth here as the source of all things, and as infinite in wisdom and knowledge ; and these *three* things are the subjects to the end of the chapter, the two last verses referring to the first, and the end of the thirty-third and the thirty-fourth to the two others, and in an inverted order. The depth or vastness of his wealth or bounty is such, that he has nothing but his own, no one having given him anything, (verse 35,) and from him, and through him, and to him are all things, (verse 36.) Then as to the vastness of his wisdom and of his knowledge ; what his knowledge has decided cannot be searched out, and what his wisdom has devised, as to the manner of executing his purposes, cannot be investigated ; and no one can measure the extent of his knowledge, and no one has been his counsellor, so as to add to the stores of his wisdom, (verse 34.) That we may see the connection of the different parts, it is necessary to present the whole passage in lines.—

33. Oh the depth of God's bounty and wisdom and knowledge!
    How inscrutable his judgments
    And untraceable his ways!
34. Who indeed hath known the Lord's mind,
    Or who has become his counsellor?
35. Or who has first given to him?
    And it shall be repayed to him:
36. For from him and through him and to him *are* all things:
    To him the glory for ever.—Amen.—*Ed*.

34. *Who has known the mind of the Lord?* He begins here to extend as it were his hand to restrain the audacity of men, lest they should clamour against God's judgments, and this he does by stating two reasons: the first is, that all mortals are too blind to take a view of God's predestination by their own understanding, and to reason on a thing unknown is presumptuous and absurd; the other is, that we can have no cause of complaint against God, since no mortal can boast that God is a debtor to him; but that, on the contrary, all are under obligations to him for his bounty.[1]

Within this limit then let every one remember to keep his own mind, lest he be carried beyond God's oracles in investigating predestination, since we hear that man can distinguish nothing in this case, any more than a blind man in darkness. This caution, however, is not to be so applied as to weaken the certainty of faith, which proceeds not from the acumen of the human mind, but solely from the illumination of the Spirit; for Paul himself in another place, after having testified that all the mysteries of God far exceed the comprehension of our minds, immediately subjoins that the faithful understand the mind of the Lord, because they have not received the spirit of this world, but the Spirit which has been given them by God, by whom they are instructed as to his goodness, which otherwise would be incomprehensible to them.

As then we cannot by our own faculties examine the secrets of God, so we are admitted into a certain and clear knowledge of them by the grace of the Holy Spirit: and if we ought to follow the guidance of the Spirit, where he leaves us, there we ought to stop and as it were to fix our

---

[1] The words of this verse seem to have been taken literally from Is. xl. 13, as given in the *Septuagint*. The Hebrew is in some measure different, but the words will admit of a rendering approaching nearer to the meaning here than what is presented in our version, as follows—
    Who has weighed the spirit of Jehovah,
    And, *being* a man of his counsel, has taught him?
To "weigh the spirit" is to know it thoroughly: the same verb, תכן, is used in this sense in Prov. xvi. 2; xxiv. 12. It indeed means to compute by measure or by weight; so that it may be rendered "measure" as well as "weigh," and if we adopt "measure," it will then appear that to "know the mind of the Lord," is to know the *extent* of his understanding or knowledge; an idea which remarkably corresponds with the passage.—*Ed.*

standing. If any one will seek to know more than what God has revealed, he shall be overwhelmed with the immeasurable brightness of inaccessible light. But we must bear in mind the distinction, which I have before mentioned, between the secret counsel of God, and his will made known in Scripture; for though the whole doctrine of Scripture surpasses in its height the mind of man, yet an access to it is not closed against the faithful, who reverently and soberly follow the Spirit as their guide; but the case is different with regard to his hidden counsel, the depth and height of which cannot by any investigation be reached.

35. *Who has first given to him*, &c. Another reason, by which God's righteousness is most effectually defended against all the accusations of the ungodly: for if no one retains him bound to himself by his own merits, no one can justly expostulate with him for not having received his reward; as he, who would constrain another to do him good, must necessarily adduce those deeds by which he has deserved a reward. The import then of Paul's words is this— " God cannot be charged with unrighteousness, except it can be proved, that he renders not to every one his due: but it is evident, that no one is deprived by him of his right, since he is under obligation to none; for who can boast of any thing of his own, by which he has deserved his favour?"[1]

Now this is a remarkable passage; for we are here taught, that it is not in our power to constrain God by our good works to bestow salvation on us, but that he anticipates the undeserving by his gratuitous goodness. But if we desire to make an honest examination, we shall not only find, that God is in no way a debtor to us, but that we are all subject to his judgment,—that we not only deserve no favour, but that we are worthy of eternal death. And Paul not only

---

[1] There is a passage in Job xli. 11, (2, in the Hebrew Bible,) of which this verse seems to be a translation, made by the Apostle himself, as totally another meaning is given in the *Septuagint*. The person is alone changed. The Hebrew is literally this,
   Who has anticipated me,
   And I will repay?
To " anticipate" means here with favour or gift; for the remainder of the verse is the following,—
   Everything under the whole heaven, mine it *is.—Ed.*

concludes, that God owes us nothing, on account of our corrupt and sinful nature; but he denies, that if man were perfect, he could bring anything before God, by which he could gain his favour; for as soon as he begins to exist, he is already by the right of creation so much indebted to his Maker, that he has nothing of his own. In vain then shall we try to take from him his own right, that he should not, as he pleases, freely determine respecting his own creatures, as though there was mutual debt and credit.

36. *For from him and through him,* &c. A confirmation of the last verse. He shows, that it is very far from being the case, that we can glory in any good thing of our own against God, since we have been created by him from nothing, and now exist through him. He hence infers, that our being should be employed for his glory: for how unreasonable would it be for creatures, whom he has formed and whom he sustains, to live for any other purpose than for making his glory known? It has not escaped my notice, that the phrase, εἰς αὐτὸν, *to him,* is sometimes taken for ἐν αὐτῷ, *in* or *by him,* but improperly: and as its proper meaning is more suitable to the present subject, it is better to retain it, than to adopt that which is improper. The import of what is said is,—That the whole order of nature would be strangely subverted, were not God, who is the beginning of all things, the end also.

To him be glory, &c. The proposition being as it were proved, he now confidently assumes it as indubitable,—That the Lord's own glory ought everywhere to continue to him unchangeably: for the sentence would be frigid were it taken generally; but its emphasis depends on the context, that God justly claims for himself absolute supremacy, and that in the condition of mankind and of the whole world nothing is to be sought beyond his own glory. It hence follows, that absurd and contrary to reason, and even insane, are all those sentiments which tend to diminish his glory.

CHAPTER XII.

1. I beseech you therefore, brethren, by the mercies of God, that ye present your bodies a living sacrifice, holy, acceptable unto God, *which is* your reasonable service.
2. And be not conformed to this world; but be ye transformed by the renewing of your mind, that ye may prove what *is* that good, and acceptable, and perfect will of God.

1. Obsecro itaque vos fratres, per miserationes Dei, ut sistatis corpora vestra hostiam vivam, sanctam, acceptam Deo, rationabilem cultum vestrum.
2. Et ne conformetis vos huic mundo, sed transfiguremini renovatione mentis vestræ, ut probetis quæ sit voluntas Dei bona et placita et perfecta.

After having handled those things necessary for the erection of the kingdom of God,—that righteousness is to be sought from God alone, that salvation is to come to us alone from his mercy, that all blessings are laid up and daily offered to us in Christ only,—Paul now passes on, according to the best order, to show how the life is to be formed. If it be, that through the saving knowledge of God and of Christ, the soul is, as it were, regenerated into a celestial life, and that the life is in a manner formed and regulated by holy exhortations and precepts; it is then in vain that you show a desire to form the life aright, except you prove first, that the origin of all righteousness in men is in God and Christ; for this is to raise them from the dead.

And this is the main difference between the gospel and philosophy: for though the philosophers speak excellently and with great judgment on the subject of morals, yet whatever excellency shines forth in their precepts, it is, as it were, a beautiful superstructure without a foundation; for by omitting principles, they offer a mutilated doctrine, like a body without a head. Not very unlike this is the mode of teaching under the Papacy: for though they mention, by the way, faith in Christ and the grace of the Holy Spirit, it yet appears quite evident, that they approach heathen philosophers far nearer than Christ and his Apostles.

But as philosophers, before they lay down laws respecting morals, discourse first of the end of what is good, and inquire into the sources of virtues, from which afterwards they draw and derive all duties; so Paul lays down here the principle from which all the duties of holiness flow, even this,—that we are redeemed by the Lord for this end—that we may consecrate to him ourselves and all our members. But it may be useful to examine every part.

1. *I therefore beseech you by the mercies* (miserationes—*compassions*) *of God,* &c. We know that unholy men, in order to gratify the flesh, anxiously lay hold on whatever is set forth in Scripture respecting the infinite goodness of God; and hypocrites also, as far as they can, maliciously darken the knowledge of it, as though the grace of God extinguished the desire for a godly life, and opened to audacity the door of sin. But this exhortation teaches us, that until men really apprehend how much they owe to the mercy of God, they will never with a right feeling worship him, nor be effectually stimulated to fear and obey him. It is enough for the Papists, if they can extort by terror some sort of forced obedience, I know not what. But Paul, that he might bind us to God, not by servile fear, but by the voluntary and cheerful love of righteousness, allures us by the sweetness of that favour, by which our salvation is effected; and at the same time he reproaches us with ingratitude, except we, after having found a Father so kind and bountiful, do strive in our turn to dedicate ourselves wholly to him.[1]

And what Paul says, in thus exhorting us, ought to have more power over us, inasmuch as he excels all others in setting forth the grace of God. Iron indeed must be the heart which is not kindled by the doctrine which has been laid down into love towards God, whose kindness towards itself it finds to have been so abounding. Where then are

---

[1] By "mercies," the Apostle refers, as some think, to the various acts of God's mercy, such as election, vocation, justification, and final salvation. *Grotius* considers that God's attributes are referred to, such as are described in Exod. xxxiv. 6, 7. *Erasmus,* quoting *Origen,* says, that the plural is used for amplification, in order to show the greatness of God's mercy, as though the Apostle had said, " by God's great mercy." *Schleusner* renders the clause, " per summam Dei benignitatem—by God's great kindness," that is, in bringing you to the knowledge of the gospel. So " Father of mercies," in 2 Cor. i. 3, may mean " most merciful Father," or the meaning may be, "the Father of all blessings," as mercy signifies sometimes what mercy bestows, (Phil. ii. 1,) as grace or favour often means the gift which flows from it. According to this view, " mercies" here are the blessings which God bestows, even the blessings of redemption.—*Ed.*

they who think that all exhortations to a holy life are nullified, if the salvation of men depends on the grace of God alone, since by no precepts, by no sanctions, is a pious mind so framed to render obedience to God, as by a serious meditation on the Divine goodness towards it?

We may also observe here the benevolence of the Apostle's spirit,—that he preferred to deal with the faithful by admonitions and friendly exhortations rather than by strict commands; for he knew that he could prevail more with the teachable in this way than in any other.

That ye present your bodies, &c. It is then the beginning of a right course in good works, when we understand that we are consecrated to the Lord; for it hence follows, that we must cease to live to ourselves, in order that we may devote all the actions of our life to his service.

There are then two things to be considered here,—the first, that we are the Lord's,—and secondly, that we ought on this account to be holy, for it is an indignity to God's holiness, that anything, not first consecrated, should be offered to him. These two things being admitted, it then follows that holiness is to be practised through life, and that we are guilty of a kind of sacrilege when we relapse into uncleanness, as it is nothing else than to profane what is consecrated.

But there is throughout a great suitableness in the expressions. He says first, that our *body* ought to be offered a sacrifice to God; by which he implies that we are not our own, but have entirely passed over so as to become the property of God; which cannot be, except we renounce ourselves and thus deny ourselves. Then, secondly, by adding two adjectives, he shows what sort of sacrifice this ought to be. By calling it *living*, he intimates, that we are sacrificed to the Lord for this end,—that our former life being destroyed in us, we may be raised up to a new life. By the term *holy*, he points out that which necessarily belongs to a sacrifice, already noticed; for a victim is then only approved, when it had been previously made holy. By the third word, *acceptable*, he reminds us, that our life is framed aright, when this sacrifice is so made as to be pleasing to God: he brings to us at the same time no common consolation; for he teaches us, that our work is pleasing and acceptable to God when we devote ourselves to purity and holiness.

By *bodies* he means not only our bones and skin, but the whole mass of which we are composed; and he adopted this word, that he might more fully designate all that we are: for the members of the body are the instruments by which we execute our purposes.[1] He indeed requires from us holiness, not only as to the body, but also as to the soul and spirit, as in 1 Thess. v. 23. In bidding us to *present* our bodies, he alludes to the Mosaic sacrifices, which were presented at the altar, as it were in the presence of God. But he shows, at the same time, in a striking manner, how prompt we ought to be to receive the commands of God, that we may without delay obey them.

Hence we learn, that all mortals, whose object is not to worship God, do nothing but miserably wander and go astray. We now also find what sacrifices Paul recommends to the Christian Church: for being reconciled to God through the one only true sacrifice of Christ, we are all through his grace made priests, in order that we may dedicate ourselves and all we have to the glory of God. No sacrifice of expiation is wanted; and no one can be set up, without casting a manifest reproach on the cross of Christ.

Your reasonable service. This sentence, I think, was added, that he might more clearly apply and confirm the preceding

---

[1] The word σώματα, "bodies," he seems to have used, because of the similitude he adopts respecting sacrifices; for the bodies of beasts we are to consecrate our own bodies. As he meant before by "members," ch. vi. 13, the whole man, so he means here by "bodies," that is, themselves.

They were to be *living* sacrifices, not killed as the legal sacrifices. They were to be *holy*, not maimed or defective, but whole and perfect as to all the members, and free from diseases. See Lev. xxii. 19-22. They were to be *acceptable*, ιὐάρεστον; "placentem—pleasing," *Beza;* "well-pleasing," *Doddridge.* It was not sufficient under the law for the sacrifices themselves to be holy, blameless, such as God required; but a right motive and a right feeling on the part of the offerer were necessary, in order that they might be accepted or approved by God. Without faith and repentance, and a reformed life, they were not accepted, but regarded as abominations. See Ps. li. 19; Is. i. 11-19.

It is said by *Wolfius,* that all the terms here are derived from the sacrificial rites of the law, and that Christians are represented both as the priests who offered, and as the sacrifices which were offered by them.—*Ed.*

exhortation, as though he had said,—"Offer yourselves a sacrifice to God, if ye have it in your heart to serve God: for this is the right way of serving God; from which, if any depart, they are but false worshippers." If then only God is rightly worshipped, when we observe all things according to what he has prescribed, away then with all those devised modes of worship, which he justly abominates, since he values obedience more than sacrifice. Men are indeed pleased with their own inventions, which have an empty show of wisdom, as Paul says in another place; but we learn here what the celestial Judge declares in opposition to this by the mouth of Paul; for by calling that a reasonable service which he commands, he repudiates as foolish, insipid, and presumptuous, whatever we attempt beyond the rule of his word.[1]

2. *And conform ye not to this world,* &c. The term *world* has several significations, but here it means the sentiments and the morals of men; to which, not without cause, he forbids us to conform. For since the whole world lies in wickedness, it behoves us to put off whatever we have of the old man, if we would really put on Christ: and to remove all doubt, he explains what he means, by stating what is of a contrary nature; for he bids us to be transformed into a newness of mind. These kinds of contrast are common in Scripture; and thus a subject is more clearly set forth.

[1] The word λογικὴν, "reasonable," was considered by *Origen,* and by many after him, as designating Christian service consonant with reason, in opposition to the sacrifices under the law, which were not agreeable to reason. But *Chrysostom,* whom also many have followed, viewed the word as meaning what is *spiritual,* or what belongs to the mind, in contradistinction to the ritual and external service of the law: but there is no example of the word having such a meaning, except it be 1 Pet. ii. 2, which is by no means decisive. Rational, or reasonable, is its meaning, or, what agrees with the word, as *Phavorinus* explains it. There is no need here to suppose any contrast: the expression only designates the act or the service which the Apostle prescribes; as though he said, "What I exhort you to do is nothing but a reasonable service, consistent with the dictates of reason. God has done great things for you, and it is nothing but right and just that you should dedicate yourselves wholly to him." This seems to be the obvious meaning. To draw this expression to another subject, in order to set up reason as an umpire in matters of faith, is wholly a perversion: and to say, that as it seems to refer to the word in 1 Pet. ii. 2, it must be so considered here, is what does not necessarily follow; for as λόγος sometimes means "word," and sometimes "reason," so its derivative may have a similar variety.—*Ed.*

Now attend here, and see what kind of renovation is required from us: It is not that of the flesh only, or of the inferior part of the soul, as the Sorbonists explain this word; but of the mind, which is the most excellent part of us, and to which philosophers ascribe the supremacy; for they call it ἡγεμονικὸν, the leading power; and reason is imagined to be a most wise queen. But Paul pulls her down from her throne, and so reduces her to nothing by teaching us that we must be renewed in mind. For how much soever we may flatter ourselves, that declaration of Christ is still true, —that every man must be born again, who would enter into the kingdom of God; for in mind and heart we are altogether alienated from the righteousness of God.

That ye may prove,[1] &c. Here you have the purpose for which we must put on a new mind,—that bidding adieu to our own counsels and desires, and those of all men, we may be attentive to the only will of God, the knowledge of which is true wisdom. But if the renovation of our mind is necessary, in order that we may prove what is the will of God, it is hence evident how opposed it is to God.

The epithets which are added are intended for the pur-

---

[1] *Ut probetis*, εἰς τὸ δοκιμάζειν ὑμᾶς; "ut noscatis—that ye may know," *Theophylact;* "ut diligenter scrutemini—that ye may carefully search," *Jerome;* "that ye may experimentally know," *Doddridge;* "that ye may learn," *Stuart*. The verb means chiefly three things,—to *test*, *i.e.*, metals by fire, to *try*, to *prove*, to *examine*, 1 Pet. i. 7; Luke xiv. 19; 2 Cor. xiii. 5,—to *approve* what is proved, Rom. xiv. 22; 1 Cor. xvi. 3,—and also to *prove* a thing so as to make a proper distinction, to *discern*, to *understand*, to *distinguish*, Luke xii. 56; Rom. ii. 18. The last idea is the most suitable here, " in order that ye may understand what the will of God is, even that which is good and acceptable and perfect."

What *Stuart* says on the last clause seems just, that it is to be taken by itself, and that the words do not agree with "will," but stand by themselves, being in the neuter gender. Otherwise we cannot affix any idea to "acceptable;" for it would be unsuitable to say that God's will is "acceptable" to him, that being self-evident.

"Good," ἀγαθὸν, is useful, advantageous, beneficial; "acceptable," εὐάρεστον, is what is pleasing to and accepted by God; and "perfect," τέλειον, is complete, entire, without any defect, or just and right.

It ought to be borne in mind, as *Pareus* observes, that in order to discern, and rightly to understand God's will, the Apostle teaches us, that "the renewing of the mind" is necessary; otherwise, as he adds, "our corrupt nature will fascinate our eyes that they may not see, or if they see, will turn our hearts and wills, that they may not approve, or if they approve, will hinder us to follow what is approved."—*Ed.*

pose of recommending God's will, that we may seek to know it with greater alacrity: and in order to constrain our perverseness, it is indeed necessary that the true glory of justice and perfection should be ascribed to the will of God. The world persuades itself that those works which it has devised are good; Paul exclaims, that what is good and right must be ascertained from God's commandments. The world praises itself, and takes delight in its own inventions; but Paul affirms, that nothing pleases God except what he has commanded. The world, in order to find perfection, slides from the word of God into its own devices; Paul, by fixing perfection in the will of God, shows, that if any one passes over that mark he is deluded by a false imagination.

3. For I say, through the grace given unto me, to every man that is among you, not to think *of himself* more highly than he ought to think; but to think soberly, according as God hath dealt to every man the measure of faith.

3. Dico enim per gratiam, quæ data est mihi, cuilibet vestrum, ne supra modum sapiat præter id quod oportet sapere, sed sapiat ad sobrietatem, sicuti unicuique distribuit Deus mensuram fidei.

3. *For I say, through the grace,* &c. If you think not the causal particle superfluous, this verse will not be unsuitably connected with the former; for since he wished that our whole study should be employed in investigating the will of God, the next thing to this was, to draw us away from vain curiosity. As however the causal particle is often used redundantly by Paul, you may take the verse as containing a simple affirmation; for thus the sense would also be very appropriate.

But before he specifies his command, he reminds them of the authority which had been given to him, so that they might not otherwise attend to his voice than if it was the voice of God himself; for his words are the same, as though he had said, "I speak not of myself; but, as God's ambassador, I bring to you the commands which he has entrusted to me." By "*grace*" (as before) he means the Apostleship, with respect to which he exalts God's kindness, and at the same time intimates, that he had not crept in through his own presumption, but that he was chosen by the calling of God. Having then by this preface secured authority to himself, he laid the Romans under the necessity of obeying, unless they were prepared to despise God in the person of his minister.

Then the command follows, by which he draws us away from the investigation of those things which can bring nothing but harassment to the mind, and no edification; and he forbids every one to assume more than what his capacity and calling will allow; and at the same time he exhorts us to think and meditate on those things which may render us sober-minded and modest. For so I understand the words, rather than in the sense given by *Erasmus*, who thus renders them, " Let no one think proudly of himself;" for this sense is somewhat remote from the words, and the other is more accordant with the context. The clause, *Beyond what it behoves him to be wise,* shows what he meant by the former verb ὑπερφρόνειν, to be above measure wise; that is, that we exceed the measure of wisdom, if we engage in those things concerning which it is not meet that we should be anxious.[1] To be *wise unto sobriety* is to attend to the study of those things by which you may find that you learn and gain moderation.

To every one as God has distributed, &c. (*Unicuique ut divisit Deus.*) There is here an inversion of words, instead of—*As to every one God has distributed.*[2] And here a reason is given for that sober-minded wisdom which he had mentioned; for as distribution of graces is various, so every one preserves himself within the due boundaries of wisdom, who

---

[1] " Ne supra modum sapiat," so the *Vulgate* and *Beza*; μὴ ὑπερφρόνειν, " ne supra modum de se sentiat—let him not think immoderately of himself," *Mede;* " not to arrogate to himself," *Doddridge;* " not to overestimate himself," *Stuart*. This and the following clause may be thus rendered, " not to think highly above what it behoves him to think," that is, of himself. Then what follows may admit of this rendering, " but to think so as to think rightly," or modestly, (εἰς τὸ σωφρονεῖν.) The last verb occurs elsewhere five times; thrice it means " to be of a sane mind," Mark vii. 15; Luke viii. 35; 2 Cor. v. 13; and twice it means " to act prudently," Titus ii. 6; 1 Peter iv. 7; or, it may be, in the last passage, " to live temperately." As it refers here to the mind, it must mean such an estimate of one's self as is sound, just, and right, such as becomes one who is sound and sane in his mind. Pride is a species of insanity; but humility betokens a return to a sane mind: and an humble estimate of ourselves, as Professor *Hodge* observes, is the only sound, sane, and right estimate.—*Ed.*

[2] We find a similar transposition in 1 Cor. iii. 5.—*Ed.*

keeps within the limits of that grace of faith bestowed on him by the Lord. Hence there is an immoderate affectation of wisdom, not only in empty things and in things useless to be known, but also in the knowledge of those things which are otherwise useful, when we regard not what has been given to us, but through rashness and presumption go beyond the measure of our knowledge; and such outrage God will not suffer to go unpunished. It is often to be seen, with what insane trifles they are led away, who, by foolish ambition, proceed beyond those bounds which are set for them.[1]

The meaning is, that it is a part of our reasonable sacrifice to surrender ourselves, in a meek and teachable spirit, to be ruled and guided by God. And further, by setting up faith in opposition to human judgment, he restrains us from our own opinions, and at the same time specifies the due measure of it, that is, when the faithful humbly keep themselves within the limits allotted to them.[2]

4. For as we have many members in one body, and all members have not the same office;

5. So we, *being* many, are one body in Christ, and every one members one of another.

6. Having then gifts, differing according to the grace that is given to us, whether prophecy, *let us prophesy* according to the proportion of faith;

7. Or ministry, *let us wait* on *our* ministering; or he that teacheth, on teaching;

4. Quemadmodum enim in uno corpore membra multa habemus, membra verò omnia non eandem habent actionem;

5. Sic multi unum sumus corpus in Christo membra mutuò alter alterius.

6. Habentes autem dona secundum gratiam nobis datam differentia; sive prophetiam, secundum analogiam fidei;

7. Sive ministerium, in ministerio; sive qui docet, in doctrina;

---

[1] "It is better," says *Augustine*, "to doubt respecting hidden things, than to contend about things uncertain."—*Ed.*

[2] The expression "the measure of faith," μέτρον πίστεως, is differently explained. Some, as *Beza* and *Pareus*, consider "faith" here as including religion or Christian truth, because faith is the main principle, "as God has divided to each the measure of Christian truth or knowledge." Others suppose with *Mede*, that "faith" here is to be taken for those various gifts and endowments which God bestowed on those who believed or professed the faith of the gospel; "as God has divided to each the measure of those gifts which come by faith, or which are given to those who believe." The last view is most suitable to the context. We may, however, take "faith" here for grace, and consider the meaning the same as in Eph. iv. 7. The subject there is the same as here, for the Apostle proceeds there to mention the different offices which Christ had appointed in his Church.—*Ed.*

8. Or he that exhorteth, on exhortation: he that giveth, *let him do it* with simplicity; he that ruleth, with diligence; he that sheweth mercy, with cheerfulness.

8. Sive qui exhortatur, in exhortatione; sive qui largitur, in simplicitate; sive qui præest, in studio; sive qui miseretur, in hilaritate.

4. *For as in one body,* &c. The very thing which he had previously said of limiting the wisdom of each according to the measure of faith, he now confirms by a reference to the vocation of the faithful; for we are called for this end, that we may unite together in one body, since Christ has ordained a fellowship and connection between the faithful similar to that which exists between the members of the human body; and as men could not of themselves come together into such an union, he himself becomes the bond of this connection. As then the case is with the human body, so it ought to be with the society of the faithful. By applying this similitude he proves how necessary it is for each to consider what is suitable to his own nature, capacity, and vocation. But though this similitude has various parts, it is yet to be chiefly thus applied to our present subject,—that as the members of the same body have distinct offices, and all of them are distinct, for no member possesses all powers, nor does it appropriate to itself the offices of others; so God has distributed various gifts to us, by which diversity he has determined the order which he would have to be observed among us, so that every one is to conduct himself according to the measure of his capacity, and not to thrust himself into what peculiarly belongs to others; nor is any one to seek to have all things himself, but to be content with his lot, and willingly to abstain from usurping the offices of others. When, however, he points out in express words the communion which is between us, he at the same time intimates, how much diligence there ought to be in all, so that they may contribute to the common good of the body according to the faculties they possess.[1]

[1] The Apostle pursues this likeness of the human body much more at large in 1 Cor. xii. 12-31. There are two bonds of union; one, which is between the believer and Christ by true faith; and the other, which is between the individual member of a church or a congregation and the rest of the members by a professed faith. It is the latter that is handled by the Apostle, both here and in the Epistle to the Corinthians.—*Ed.*

6. *Having gifts,* &c. Paul speaks not now simply of cherishing among ourselves brotherly love, but commends humility, which is the best moderator of our whole life. Every one desires to have so much himself, so as not to need any help from others; but the bond of mutual communication is this, that no one has sufficient for himself, but is constrained to borrow from others. I admit then that the society of the godly cannot exist, except when each one is content with his own measure, and imparts to others the gifts which he has received, and allows himself by turns to be assisted by the gifts of others.

But Paul especially intended to beat down the pride which he knew to be innate in men; and that no one might be dissatisfied that all things have not been bestowed on him, he reminds us that according to the wise counsel of God every one has his own portion given to him; for it is necessary to the common benefit of the body that no one should be furnished with fulness of gifts, lest he should heedlessly despise his brethren. Here then we have the main design which the Apostle had in view, that all things do not meet in all, but that the gifts of God are so distributed that each has a limited portion, and that each ought to be so attentive in imparting his own gifts to the edification of the Church, that no one, by leaving his own function, may trespass on that of another. By this most beautiful order, and as it were symmetry, is the safety of the Church indeed preserved; that is, when every one imparts to all in common what he has received from the Lord, in such a way as not to impede others. He who inverts this order fights with God, by whose ordinance it is appointed; for the difference of gifts proceeds not from the will of man, but because it has pleased the Lord to distribute his grace in this manner.

Whether prophecy, &c. By now bringing forward some examples, he shows how every one in his place, or as it were in occupying his station, ought to be engaged. For all gifts have their own defined limits, and to depart from them is to mar the gifts themselves. But the passage appears somewhat confused; we may yet arrange it in this manner, "Let him who has prophecy, test it by the analogy of faith;

let him in the ministry discharge it in teaching,"¹ &c. They who will keep this end in view, will rightly preserve themselves within their own limits.

But this passage is variously understood. There are those who consider that by *prophecy* is meant the gift of predicting, which prevailed at the commencement of the gospel in the Church; as the Lord then designed in every way to commend the dignity and excellency of his Church; and they think that what is added, *according to the analogy of faith*, is to be applied to all the clauses. But I prefer to follow those who extend this word wider, even to the peculiar gift of revelation, by which any one skilfully and wisely performed the office of an interpreter in explaining the will of God. Hence prophecy at this day in the Christian Church is hardly anything else than the right understanding of the Scripture, and the peculiar faculty of explaining it, inasmuch as all the ancient prophecies and all the oracles of God have been completed in Christ and in his gospel. For in this sense it is taken by Paul when he says, "I wish that you spoke in tongues, but rather that ye prophesy," (1 Cor. xiv. 5;) "In part we know and in part we prophesy," (1 Cor. xiii. 9.) And it does not appear that Paul intended here to mention those miraculous graces by which Christ at first rendered illustrious his gospel; but, on the contrary, we find that he refers only to ordinary gifts, such as were to continue perpetually in the Church.²

---

¹ The ellipsis to be supplied here is commonly done as in our version, adopted from *Beza*. The supplement proposed by *Pareus* is perhaps more in unison with the passage; he repeats after "prophecy" the words in verse 3, changing the person, "let us think soberly," or "let us be modestly wise."—*Ed.*

² It is somewhat difficult exactly to ascertain what this "prophecy" was. The word "prophet," נביא, means evidently two things in the Old Testament and also in the New—a foreteller and a teacher, or rather an interpreter of the word. Prophecy in the New Testament sometimes signifies prediction, its primary meaning, Acts xii. 27; 2 Pet. i. 21; Rev. i. 3; but most commonly, as it is generally thought, the interpretation of prophecy, that is, of prophecies contained in the Old Testament, and for this work there were some in the primitive Church, as it is supposed, who were inspired, and thus peculiarly qualified. It is probable that this kind of prophecy is what is meant here. See 1 Cor. xii. 10; xiii. 2, 8; xiv. 3, 6, 22; 1 Thess. v. 20.

That it was a distinct function from that of apostles, evangelists, pastors,

Nor does it seem to me a solid objection, that the Apostle to no purpose laid this injunction on those who, having the Spirit of God, could not call Christ an anathema; for he testifies in another place that the spirit of the Prophets is subject to the Prophets; and he bids the first speaker to be silent, if anything were revealed to him who was sitting down, (1 Cor. xiv. 32;) and it was for the same reason it may be that he gave this admonition to those who prophesied in the Church, that is, that they were to conform their prophecies to the rule of faith, lest in anything they should deviate from the right line. By *faith* he means the first principles of religion, and whatever doctrine is not found to correspond with these is here condemned as false.[1]

As to the other clauses there is less difficulty. Let him who is ordained a minister, he says, execute his office in ministering; nor let him think, that he has been admitted into that degree for himself, but for others; as though he had said, "Let him fulfil his office by ministering faithfully, that he may answer to his name." So also he immediately adds with regard to teachers; for by the word teaching, he

and teachers, is evident from Eph. iv. 11; and from the interpretation of tongues, as it appears from 1 Cor. xii. 10; and from revelation, knowledge, and doctrine, as we find from 1 Cor. xiv. 6. It also appears that it was more useful than other extraordinary gifts, as it tended more to promote edification and comfort, 1 Cor. xiv. 1, 3. It is hence most probable that it was the gift already stated, that of interpreting the Scriptures, especially the prophecies of the Old Testament, and applying them for the edification of the Church. "Prophets" are put next to "apostles" in Eph. iv. 11.—*Ed.*

[1] "Secundum analogiam fidei," so *Pareus*; κατὰ τὴν ἀναλογίαν τῆς πίστεως; "pro proportione fidei—according to the proportion of faith," *Beza, Piscator;* that is, as the former explains the phrase, "according to the measure or extent of the individual's faith;" he was not to go beyond what he knew or what had been communicated to him by the Spirit. But the view which *Calvin* takes is the most obvious and consistent with the passage; and this is the view which *Hammond* gives, "according to that form of faith or wholesome doctrine by which every one who is sent out to preach the gospel is appointed to regulate his preaching, according to those heads or principles of faith and good life which are known among you." The word ἀναλογία means properly congruity, conformity, or proportion, not in the sense of measure or extent, but of equality, as when one thing is equal or conformable to another; hence the analogy of faith must mean what is conformable to the faith. And faith here evidently signifies divine truth, the object of faith, or what faith receives. See chap. x. 8; Gal. iii. 23; Tit. i. 4; Jude verse 3.—*Ed.*

recommends sound edification, according to this import,— " Let him who excels in teaching know that the end is, that the Church may be really instructed ; and let him study this one thing, that he may render the Church more informed by his teaching :" for a teacher is he who forms and builds the Church by the word of truth. Let him also who excels in the gift of exhorting, have this in view, to render his exhortation effectual.

But these offices have much affinity and even connection ; not however that they were not different. No one indeed could exhort, except by doctrine : yet he who teaches is not therefore endued with the qualification to exhort. But no one prophesies or teaches or exhorts, without at the same time ministering. But it is enough if we preserve that distinction which we find to be in God's gifts, and which we know to be adapted to produce order in the Church.[1]

8. *Or he who gives,* let him do so *in simplicity,* &c. From the former clauses we have clearly seen, that he teaches us here the legitimate use of God's gifts. By the μεταδιδοῦντοις, *the givers,* of whom he speaks here, he did not understand

[1] Critics have found it difficult to distinguish between these offices. The word διακονία, ministry, is taken sometimes in a restricted sense, as meaning deaconship, an office appointed to manage the temporal affairs of the Church, Acts vi. 1-3 ; 1 Tim. iii. 8-13 ; and sometimes in a general sense, as signifying the ministerial office, 2 Cor. vi. 3 ; Eph. iii. 7 ; Col. i. 23. As the " teacher " and " exhorter " are mentioned, some think that the deaconship is to be understood here, and that the Apostle first mentioned the highest office, next to the apostleship—prophecy, and the lowest—the deaconship, and afterwards named the intervening offices—those of teachers and exhorters.

But what are we to think of those mentioned in the following clauses ? *Stuart* thinks that they were not public officers, but private individuals, and he has sustained this opinion by some very cogent reasons. The form of the sentence is here changed ; and the Apostle, having mentioned the deaconship, cannot be supposed to have referred to the same again. The word that seems to stand in the way of this view is what is commonly rendered " ruler," or, " he who rules :" but ὁ προϊστάμενος, as our author shows, means a helper, an assistant, (see chap. xvi. 2,) as well as a ruler ; it means to stand over, either for the purpose of taking care of, assisting, protecting others, or of presiding over, ruling, guiding them. Then ἐν σπουδῇ, with promptness or diligence, will better agree with the former than with the latter idea. The other two clauses correspond also more with this view than with the other. It has been said, that if a distributor of alms had been intended, the word would have been διαδιδοὺς and not μεταδιδοὺς. See Eph. iv. 28. The expression, ἐν ἁπλότητι, means " with liberality, or liberally." See 2 Cor. viii. 2 ; ix. 11, 13 ; James i. 5.—*Ed.*

those who gave of their own property, but the deacons, who presided in dispensing the public charities of the Church; and by the ἐλεοῦντοις, *those who showed mercy,* he meant the widows, and other ministers, who were appointed to take care of the sick, according to the custom of the ancient Church: for there were two different offices,—to provide necessaries for the poor, and to attend to their condition. But to the first he recommends *simplicity,* so that without fraud or respect of persons they were faithfully to administer what was entrusted to them. He required the services of the other party to be rendered with *cheerfulness,* lest by their peevishness (which often happens) they marred the favour conferred by them. For as nothing gives more solace to the sick or to any one otherwise distressed, than to see men cheerful and prompt in assisting them; so to observe sadness in the countenance of those by whom assistance is given, makes them to feel themselves despised.

Though he rightly calls those προϊστάμενους, *presidents,* to whom was committed the government of the Church, (and they were the elders, who presided over and ruled others and exercised discipline;) yet what he says of these may be extended universally to all kinds of governors: for no small solicitude is required from those who provide for the safety of all, and no small diligence is needful for them who ought to watch day and night for the wellbeing of the whole community. Yet the state of things at that time proves that Paul does not speak of all kinds of rulers, for there were then no pious magistrates; but of the elders who were the correctors of morals.

9. *Let* love be without dissimulation. Abhor that which is evil, cleave to that which is good.	9. Dilectio sit non simulata; sitis aversantes malum, adherentes bono;
10. *Be* kindly affectioned one to another with brotherly love; in honour preferring one another;	10. Fraterna charitate ad vos mutuò amandos propensi, alii alios honore prævenientes;
11. Not slothful in business; fervent in spirit; serving the Lord;	11. Studio non pigri, spiritu ferventes, tempori servientes;
12. Rejoicing in hope; patient in tribulation; continuing instant in prayer;	12. Spe gaudientes, in tribulatione patientes, in oratione perseverantes;
13. Distributing to the necessity of saints; given to hospitality.	13. Necessitatibus sanctorum communicantes, hospitalitatem sectantes.

9. *Let love be,* &c. Proceeding now to speak of particular duties, he fitly begins with love, which is the bond of perfection. And respecting this he enjoins what is especially necessary, that all disguises are to be cast aside, and that love is to arise from pure sincerity of mind. It is indeed difficult to express how ingenious almost all men are to pretend a love which they really have not, for they not only deceive others, but impose also on themselves, while they persuade themselves that those are not loved amiss by them, whom they not only neglect, but really slight. Hence Paul declares here, that love is no other but that which is free from all dissimulation: and any one may easily be a witness to himself, whether he has anything in the recesses of his heart which is opposed to love.[1] The words *good* and *evil*, which immediately follow in the context, have not here a general meaning; but *evil* is to be taken for that malicious wickedness by which an injury is done to men; and *good* for that kindness, by which help is rendered to them; and there is here an antithesis usual in Scripture, when vices are first forbidden and then virtues enjoined.

As to the participle, ἀποστυγοῦντες, I have followed neither *Erasmus* nor the old translators, who have rendered it " hating," (*odio habentes;*) for in my judgment Paul intended to express something more; and the meaning of the term " turning away," corresponds better with the opposite clause; for he not only bids us to exercise kindness, but even to cleave to it.

10. *With brotherly love,* &c. By no words could he satisfy himself in setting forth the ardour of that love, with which we ought to embrace one another: for he calls it *brotherly*, and its emotion στοργὴν, affection, which, among the Latins, is the mutual affection which exists between relatives; and truly such ought to be that which we should have towards the children of God.[2] That this may be the case, he subjoins

---

[1] " Love," says an old author, " is the sum and substance of all virtues. Philosophers make justice the queen of virtues; but love is the mother of justice, for it renders to God and to our neighbour what is justly due to them."—*Ed*

[2] It is difficult to render this clause: *Calvin's* words are, " Fraterna charitate ad vos mutuò amandos propensi;" so *Beza*. The Apostle joins two

a precept very necessary for the preservation of benevolence, —that every one is to give honour to his brethren and not to himself; for there is no poison more effectual in alienating the minds of men than the thought, that one is despised. But if by honour you are disposed to understand every act of friendly kindness, I do not much object: I however approve more of the former interpretation. For as there is nothing more opposed to brotherly concord than contempt, arising from haughtiness, when each one, neglecting others, advances himself; so the best fomenter of love is humility, when every one honours others.

11. *Not slothful in business,* &c. This precept is given to us, not only because a Christian life ought to be an active life; but because it often becomes us to overlook our own benefit, and to spend our labours in behalf of our brethren. In a word, we ought in many things to forget ourselves; for except we be in earnest, and diligently strive to shake off all sloth, we shall never be rightly prepared for the service of Christ.[1]

By adding *fervent in spirit,* he shows how we are to attain the former; for our flesh, like the ass, is always torpid, and has therefore need of goads; and it is only the fervency of the Spirit that can correct our slothfulness. Hence diligence in doing good requires that zeal which the Spirit of God kindles in our hearts. Why then, some one may say, does Paul exhort us to cultivate this fervency? To this I

---

things—mutual love of brethren, with the natural love of parents and children, as though he said, " Let your brotherly love have in it the affectionate feeling which exists between parents and children." " In brotherly love, be mutually full of tender affection," *Doddridge.* " In brotherly love, be kindly disposed toward each other," *Macknight.* It may be thus rendered, " In brotherly love, be tenderly affectionate to one another."

Calvin's version of the next clause is, " Alii alios honore prævenientes;" so *Erasmus;* τῇ τιμῇ ἀλλήλους προηγούμενοι; " honore alii aliis præuntes— in honour (that is, in conceding honour) going before one another," *Beza, Piscator, Macknight.* It is thus explained by *Mede,* " Wait not for honour from others, but be the first to concede it." The particle means to take the lead, to outrun, to go before, to anticipate; " in bestowing honour, taking the lead of, or outrunning, one another." See Phil. ii. 3.—*Ed.*

[1] " Studio non pigri," τῇ σπουδῇ μὴ ὀκνηροί; " Be not slothful in haste," that is, in a matter requiring haste. " We must strive," says *Theophylact,* " to assist with promptness those whose circumstances require immediate help and relief."—*Ed.*

answer,—that though it be the gift of God, it is yet a duty enjoined the faithful to shake off sloth, and to cherish the flame kindled by heaven, as it for the most part happens, that the Spirit is suppressed and extinguished through our fault.

To the same purpose is the third particular, *serving the time:* for as the course of our life is short, the opportunity of doing good soon passes away; it hence becomes us to show more alacrity in the performance of our duty. So Paul bids us in another place to redeem the time, because the days are evil. The meaning may also be, that we ought to know how to accommodate ourselves to the time, which is a matter of great importance. But Paul seems to me to set in opposition to idleness what he commands as to the serving of time. But as κυρίῳ, *the Lord*, is read in many old copies, though it may seem at first sight foreign to this passage, I yet dare not wholly to reject this reading. And if it be approved, Paul, I have no doubt, meant to refer the duties to be performed towards brethren, and whatever served to cherish love, to a service done to God, that he might add greater encouragement to the faithful.[1]

12. *Rejoicing in hope*, &c. Three things are here connected together, and seem in a manner to belong to the clause " serving the time;" for the person who accommodates himself best to the time, and avails himself of the opportunity of actively renewing his course, is he who derives his joy from the hope of future life, and patiently bears tribulations. However this may be, (for it matters not much whether you regard them as connected or separated,) he first forbids us to acquiesce in present blessings, and to ground our joy on earth and on earthly things, as though our happiness were based on them; and he bids us to raise our minds up to heaven, that we may possess solid and full joy. If our joy is derived from the hope of future life, then patience will grow up in adversities; for no kind of sorrow will be able to

---

[1] The balance of evidence, according to *Griesbach*, is in favour of τῷ καιρῷ, "time," though there is much, too, which countenances the other reading. *Luther, Erasmus*, and *Hammond* prefer the former, while *Beza, Piscator, Pareus*, and most of the moderns, the latter. The most suitable to the context is the former.—*Ed.*

overwhelm this joy. Hence these two things are closely connected together, that is, joy derived from hope, and patience in adversities. No man will indeed calmly and quietly submit to bear the cross, but he who has learnt to seek his happiness beyond this world, so as to mitigate and allay the bitterness of the cross with the consolation of hope.

But as both these things are far above our strength, we must be instant in prayer, and continually call on God, that he may not suffer our hearts to faint and to be pressed down, or to be broken by adverse events. But Paul not only stimulates us to prayer, but expressly requires perseverance; for we have a continual warfare, and new conflicts daily arise, to sustain which, even the strongest are not equal, unless they frequently gather new vigour. That we may not then be wearied, the best remedy is diligence in prayer.

13. *Communicating to the necessities,*[1] &c. He returns to the duties of love; the chief of which is to do good to those from whom we expect the least recompense. As then it commonly happens, that they are especially despised who are more than others pressed down with want and stand in need of help, (for the benefits conferred on them are regarded as lost,) God recommends them to us in an especial manner. It is indeed then only that we prove our love to be genuine, when we relieve needy brethren, for no other reason but that of exercising our benevolence. Now *hospitality* is not one of the least acts of love; that is, that kindness and liberality which are shown towards strangers, for they are for the most part destitute of all things, being far away from their friends: he therefore distinctly recommends this to us. We hence see, that the more neglected any one commonly is by men, the more attentive we ought to be to his wants.

[1] There is here an instance of the depravation of the text by some of the fathers, such as *Ambrose*, *Hilary*, *Pelagius*, *Optatus*, &c., who substituted μνίας, monuments, for χρείας, necessities, or wants: but though there are a few copies which have this reading, yet it has been discarded by most; it is not found in the *Vulgate*, nor approved by *Erasmus* nor *Grotius*. The word was introduced evidently, as *Whitby* intimates, to countenance the superstition of the early Church respecting the monuments or sepulchres of martyrs and confessors. The *fact*, that there were no monuments of martyrs at *this* time at Rome, was wholly overlooked.—*Ed.*

Observe also the suitableness of the expression, when he says, that we are to *communicate* to the necessities of the saints; by which he implies, that we ought so to relieve the wants of the brethren, as though we were relieving our own selves. And he commands us to assist especially the *saints:* for though our love ought to extend itself to the whole race of man, yet it ought with peculiar feeling to embrace the household of faith, who are by a closer bond united to us.

14. Bless them which persecute you: bless, and curse not.	14. Benedicite iis qui vos persequuntur; benedicite et ne malum imprecemini.
15. Rejoice with them that do rejoice, and weep with them that weep.	15. Gaudete cum gaudentibus, flete cum flentibus;
16. *Be* of the same mind one toward another. Mind not high things, but condescend to men of low estate. Be not wise in your own conceits.	16. Mutuò alii in alios sensu affecti, non arroganter de vobis sentientes, sed humilibus vos accommodantes: ne sitis apud vos ipsos prudentes.

14. *Bless them,* &c. I wish, once for all, to remind the reader, that he is not scrupulously to seek a precise order as to the precepts here laid down, but must be content to have short precepts, unconnected, though suited to the formation of a holy life, and such as are deduced from the principle the Apostle laid down at the beginning of the chapter.

He will presently give direction respecting the retaliation of the injuries which we may suffer: but here he requires something even more difficult,—that we are not to imprecate evils on our enemies, but to wish and to pray God to render all things prosperous to them, how much soever they may harass and cruelly treat us: and this kindness, the more difficult it is to be practised, so with the more intense desire we ought to strive for it; for the Lord commands nothing, with respect to which he does not require our obedience; nor is any excuse to be allowed, if we are destitute of that disposition, by which the Lord would have his people to differ from the ungodly and the children of this world.

Arduous is this, I admit, and wholly opposed to the nature of man; but there is nothing too arduous to be overcome by the power of God, which shall never be wanting to us, provided we neglect not to seek for it. And though you can hardly find one who has made such advances in the law of the Lord that he fulfils this precept, yet no one can claim to be the child of God or glory in the name of a Christian, who has not in part attained this mind, and who does not daily resist the opposite disposition.

I have said that this is more difficult than to let go revenge when any one is injured: for though some restrain their hands and are not led away by the passion of doing harm, they yet wish that some calamity or loss would in some way happen to their enemies; and even when they are so pacified that they wish no evil, there is yet hardly one in a hundred who wishes well to him from whom he has received an injury; nay, most men daringly burst forth into imprecations. But God by his word not only restrains our hands from doing evil, but also subdues the bitter feelings within; and not only so, but he would have us to be solicitous for the wellbeing of those who unjustly trouble us and seek our destruction.

Erasmus was mistaken in the meaning of the verb εὐλογεῖν, to bless; for he did not perceive that it stands opposed to curses and maledictions: for Paul would have God in both instances to be a witness of our patience, and to see that we not only bridle in our prayers the violence of our wrath, but also show by praying for pardon that we grieve at the lot of our enemies when they wilfully ruin themselves.

15. *Rejoice with those who rejoice,* &c. A general truth is in the third place laid down,—that the faithful, regarding each other with mutual affection, are to consider the condition of others as their own. He first specifies two particular things,—That they were to "rejoice with the joyful, and to weep with the weeping." For such is the nature of true love, that one prefers to weep with his brother, rather than to look at a distance on his grief, and to live in pleasure or ease. What is meant then is,—that we, as much as possible, ought to sympathize with one another, and that, whatever our lot may be, each should transfer to himself the feeling of another, whether of grief in adversity, or of joy in prosperity. And, doubtless, not to regard with joy the happiness of a brother is envy; and not to grieve for his misfor-

tunes is inhumanity. Let there be such a sympathy among us as may at the same time adapt us to all kinds of feelings.

16. *Not thinking arrogantly of yourselves*,[1] &c. The Apostle employs words in Greek more significant, and more suitable to the antithesis, "Not thinking," he says, "of high things:" by which he means, that it is not the part of a Christian ambitiously to aspire to those things by which he may excel others, nor to assume a lofty appearance, but on the contrary to exercise humility and meekness: for by these we excel before the Lord, and not by pride and contempt of the brethren. A precept is fitly added to the preceding; for nothing tends more to break that unity which has been mentioned, than when we elevate ourselves, and aspire to something higher, so that we may rise to a higher situation. I take the term *humble* in the neuter gender, to complete the antithesis.

Here then is condemned all ambition and that elation of mind which insinuates itself under the name of magnanimity; for the chief virtue of the faithful is moderation, or

---

[1] The first clause is omitted. The text of *Calvin* is, " Mutuo alii in alios sensu affecti;" τὸ αὐτὸ εἰς ἀλλήλους φρονοῦντες; " Itidem alii in alios affecti—Feel alike towards one another," *Beza;* " Be entirely united in your regards for each other," *Doddridge;* " Be of the same disposition towards one another," *Macknight.* The verb means to think, or to feel, or to mind, in the sense of attending to, or aspiring after a thing. It is used also in the next clause, evidently in the last sense, *minding.* There is no reason why its meaning should be different here: it would then be, " Mind the same thing towards one another," that is, Do to others what you expect others to do to you. It is to reduce to an axiom what is contained in the former verse. We may indeed give this version, " Feel the same, or alike towards one another," that is, sympathize with one another: and this would still be coincident in meaning with the former verse; and it would be in accordance with the Apostle's mode of writing.

But another construction has been given, " Think the same of one another," that is, Regard one another alike in dignity and privilege as Christians, without elevating yourselves, and viewing yourselves better than others. This would well agree with the sentence which follows.

The two following clauses are thus given by *Doddridge,* " Affect not high things, but condescend to men of low rank,"—and by *Macknight,* " Do not care for high things; but associate with lowly men." The word ταπεινοῖς, is not found in the New Testament to be applied to things, but to persons. "Associate" is perhaps the best rendering of συναπαγόμενοι, which literally means to withdraw from one party in order to walk with another: they were to withdraw from those who minded high things, and walk or associate with the humble and lowly. " And cleave to the humble," is the Syriac version.—*Ed.*

rather lowliness of mind, which ever prefers to give honour to others, rather than to take it away from them.

Closely allied to this is what is subjoined: for nothing swells the minds of men so much as a high notion of their own wisdom. His desire then was, that we should lay this aside, hear others, and regard their counsels. *Erasmus* has rendered φρονίμους, *arrogantes*—arrogant; but the rendering is strained and frigid; for Paul would in this case repeat the same word without any meaning. However, the most appropriate remedy for curing arrogance is, that man should not be over-wise in his own esteem.

17. Recompense to no man evil for evil. Provide things honest in the sight of all men.
18. If it be possible, as much as lieth in you, live peaceably with all men.
19. Dearly beloved, avenge not yourselves, but *rather* give place unto wrath: for it is written, Vengeance *is* mine; I will repay, saith the Lord.

17. Nemini malum pro malo rependentes, providentes bona coram omnibus hominibus.
18. Si fieri potest, quantum est in vobis, cum omnibus hominibus pacem habentes;
19. Non vosmetipsos ulciscentes, dilecti; sed date locum iræ; scriptum est enim, Mihi vindictam, et ego rependam, dicit Dominus.

17. *Repaying to no one*, &c. This differs but little from what shortly after follows, except that revenge is more than the kind of repaying of which he speaks here; for we render evil for evil sometimes, even when we exact not the requiting of an injury, as when we treat unkindly those who do us no good. We are indeed wont to form an estimate of the deserts of each, or of what they merit at our hands, so that we may confer our benefits on those, by whom we have been already obliged, or from whom we expect something: and again, when any one denies help to us when we need it, we, by returning like for like, as they say, do not help him in time of need, any more than he assisted us. There are also other instances of the same kind, in which evil is rendered for evil, when there is no open revenge.

Providing good things, &c. I no not disapprove of the rendering of *Erasmus*, "Providently preparing," (*Providè parantes;*) but I prefer a literal rendering. As every one is more than justly devoted to his own advantage, and provident in avoiding losses, Paul seems to require a care and an attention of another kind. What is meant is, that we ought diligently to labour, that all may be edified by our honest dealings. For as purity of conscience is necessary for us before God, so uprightness of character before men is not to be neglected: for since it is meet that God should be glorified by our good deeds, even so much is wanting to his glory, as there is a deficiency of what is praiseworthy in us; and not only the glory of God is thus obscured, but he is branded with reproach; for whatever sin we commit, the ignorant employ it for the purpose of calumniating the gospel.

But when we are bidden to prepare good things before men,[1] we must at the same time notice for what purpose: it is not indeed that men may admire and praise us, as this is a desire which Christ carefully forbids us to indulge, since he bids us to admit God alone as the witness of our good deeds, to the exclusion of all men; but that their minds being elevated to God, they may give praise to him, that by our example they may be stirred up to the practice of righteousness, that they may, in a word, perceive the good and the sweet odour of our life, by which they may be allured to the love of God. But if we are evil spoken of for the name of Christ, we are by no means to neglect to provide good things before men: for fulfilled then shall be that saying, that we are counted as false, and are yet true. (2 Cor. vi. 8.)

18. *If it be possible*, &c. Peaceableness and a life so ordered as to render us beloved by all, is no common gift in a Christian. If we desire to attain this, we must not only be endued with perfect uprightness, but also with very courteous and kind manners, which may not only conciliate the just and the good, but produce also a favourable impression on the hearts of the ungodly.

But here two cautions must be stated: We are not to seek to be in such esteem as to refuse to undergo the hatred

---

[1] "Providentes bona;" προνοούμενοι καλά; "procurantes honesta—providing honest things," *Beza;* "providing things reputable," *Doddridge;* "premeditating things comely," *Macknight*. The participle means to mind beforehand, to prepare, to provide, and also to take care of or to attend to a thing. "Attending to things honourable" may be the rendering here. The adjective καλὸς, means fair, good; and good in conduct as here is not "comely," but just, right, or reputable, as *Doddridge* renders it. The word "honest" does not now retain its original idea of honourable.—*Ed.*

of any for Christ, whenever it may be necessary. And indeed we see that there are some who, though they render themselves amicable to all by the sweetness of their manners and peaceableness of their minds, are yet hated even by their nearest connections on account of the gospel. The second caution is,—that courteousness should not degenerate into compliance, so as to lead us to flatter the vices of men for the sake of preserving peace. Since then it cannot always be, that we can have peace with all men, he has annexed two particulars by way of exception, *If it be possible*, and, *as far as you can*. But we are to conclude from what piety and love require, that we are not to violate peace, except when constrained by either of these two things. For we ought, for the sake of cherishing peace, to bear many things, to pardon offences, and kindly to remit the full rigour of the law; and yet in such a way, that we may be prepared, whenever necessity requires, to fight courageously: for it is impossible that the soldiers of Christ should have perpetual peace with the world, whose prince is Satan.

19. *Avenge not yourselves*, &c. The evil which he corrects here, as we have reminded you, is more grievous than the preceding, which he has just stated; and yet both of them arise from the same fountain, even from an inordinate love of self and innate pride, which makes us very indulgent to our own faults and inexorable to those of others. As then this disease begets almost in all men a furious passion for revenge, whenever they are in the least degree touched, he commands here, that however grievously we may be injured, we are not to seek revenge, but to commit it to the Lord. And inasmuch as they do not easily admit the bridle, who are once seized with this wild passion, he lays, as it were, his hand upon us to restrain us, by kindly addressing us as *beloved*.

The precept then is,—that we are not to revenge nor seek to revenge injuries done to us. The manner is added, a *place* is to be *given to wrath*. To give place to wrath, is to commit to the Lord the right of judging, which they take away from him who attempt revenge. Hence, as it is not lawful to usurp the office of God, it is not lawful to revenge;

for we thus anticipate the judgment of God, who will have this office reserved for himself. He at the same time intimates, that they shall have God as their defender, who patiently wait for his help; but that those who anticipate him leave no place for the help of God.[1]

But he prohibits here, not only that we are not to execute revenge with our own hands, but that our hearts also are not to be influenced by a desire of this kind: it is therefore superfluous to make a distinction here between public and private revenge; for he who, with a malevolent mind and desirous of revenge, seeks the help of a magistrate, has no more excuse than when he devises means for self-revenge. Nay, revenge, as we shall presently see, is not indeed at all times to be sought from God: for if our petitions arise from a private feeling, and not from pure zeal produced by the Spirit, we do not make God so much our judge as the executioner of our depraved passion.

Hence, we do not otherwise give place to wrath, than when with quiet minds we wait for the seasonable time of deliverance, praying at the same time, that they who are now our adversaries, may by repentance become our friends.

For it is written, &c. He brings proof, taken from the song of Moses, Deut. xxxii. 35, where the Lord declares that he will be the avenger of his enemies; and God's enemies are all who without cause oppress his servants. "He who touches you," he says, "touches the pupil of mine eye." With this consolation then we ought to be content,—that they shall not escape unpunished who undeservedly oppress us,—and that we, by enduring, shall not make ourselves

---

[1] Many have been the advocates of this exposition, *Chrysostom, Theophylact, Luther, Beza, Hammond, Macknight, Stuart,* &c. But there is no instance of the expression, "to give place," having this meaning. In the two places where it occurs, it means to give way, to yield. See Luke xiv. 9; Eph. iv. 27. Then to give place to wrath, is to yield to and patiently to endure the wrath of the man who does the wrong. Some have maintained that the meaning is, that the injured man is to give place to his own wrath, that is, allow it time to cool: but this view comports not with the passage. The subject is, that a Christian is not to retaliate, or to return wrath for wrath, but to endure the wrath of his enemy, and to leave the matter in the hand of God. With this sense the quotation accords as much as with that given by *Calvin.* Not a few have taken this view, *Basil, Ambrose, Drusius, Mede, Doddridge, Scott,* &c.—*Ed.*

more subject or open to the injuries of the wicked, but, on the contrary, shall give place to the Lord, who is our only judge and deliverer, to bring us help.

Though it be not indeed lawful for us to pray to God for vengeance on our enemies, but to pray for their conversion, that they may become friends; yet if they procced in their impiety, what is to happen to the despisers of God will happen to them. But Paul quoted not this testimony to show that it is right for us to be as it were on fire as soon as we are injured, and according to the impulse of our flesh, to ask in our prayers that God may become the avenger of our injuries; but he first teaches us that it belongs not to us to revenge, except we would assume to ourselves the office of God; and secondly, he intimates, that we are not to fear that the wicked will more furiously rage when they see us bearing patiently; for God does not in vain take upon himself the office of executing vengeance.

20. Therefore if thine enemy hunger, feed him; if he thirst, give him drink: for in so doing thou shalt heap coals of fire on his head.
21. Be not overcome of evil, but overcome evil with good.

20. Itaque si esurit inimicus tuus, pasce illum; si sitit, potum da illi: hoc enim faciens carbones ignis congeres in caput ipsius.
21. Ne vincaris à malo, sed vincas bono malum.

20. *If therefore*, &c. He now shows how we may really fulfil the precepts of not revenging and of not repaying evil, even when we not only abstain from doing injury but when we also do good to those who have done wrong to us; for it is a kind of an indirect retaliation when we turn aside our kindness from those by whom we have been injured. Understand as included under the words *meat* and *drink*, all acts of kindness. Whatsoever then may be thine ability, in whatever business thy enemy may want either thy wealth, or thy counsel, or thy efforts, thou oughtest to help him. But he calls him our enemy, not whom we regard with hatred, but him who entertains enmity towards us. And if they are to be helped according to the flesh, much less is their salvation to be opposed by imprecating vengeance on them.

Thou shalt heap coals of fire, &c. As we are not willing

to lose our toil and labour, he shows what fruit will follow, when we treat our enemies with acts of kindness. But some by *coals* understand the destruction which returns on the head of our enemy, when we show kindness to one unworthy, and deal with him otherwise than he deserves; for in this manner his guilt is doubled. Others prefer to take this view, that when he sees himself so kindly treated, his mind is allured to love us in return. I take a simpler view, that his mind shall be turned to one side or another; for doubtless our enemy shall either be softened by our benefits, or if he be so savage that nothing can tame him, he shall yet be burnt and tormented by the testimony of his own conscience, on finding himself overwhelmed with our kindness.[1]

21. *Be not overcome by evil,* &c. This sentence is laid down as a confirmation; for in this case our contest is altogether with perverseness, if we try to retaliate it, we confess that we are overcome by it; if, on the contrary, we return good for evil, by that very deed we show the invincible firmness of our mind. This is truly a most glorious kind of victory, the fruit of which is not only apprehended by the mind, but really perceived, while the Lord is giving success to their patience, than which they can wish nothing

[1] *Calvin* has in this exposition followed *Chrysostom* and *Theodoret*. The former part no doubt contains the right view; the following verse proves it, "Overcome evil with good." The idea of "heaping coals of fire" is said to have been derived from the practice of heaping coals on the fire to melt hard metals; but as "the coals of fire" must mean "burning coals," as indeed the word in Prov. xxv. 22, whence the passage is taken, clearly means, this notion cannot be entertained. It seems to be a sort of a proverbial saying, signifying something intolerable, which cannot be borne without producing strong effects. Such is represented to be kindness to an enemy, to feed him when hungry and to give him drink when thirsty, has commonly such a power over him that he cannot resist its influence, no more than he can withstand the scorching heat of burning coals. Of course the natural tendency of such a conduct is all that is intended, and not that it invariably produces such an effect; for in Scripture things are often stated in this way; but human nature is such a strange thing, that it often resists what is right, just, and reasonable, and reverses, as it were, the very nature of things.

It is not true what *Whitby* and others have held, that "coals of fire" always mean judgments or punishment. The word indeed in certain connections, as in Ps. xviii. 13; cxl. 11, has this meaning, but in Prov. xxv. 22, it cannot be taken in this sense, as the preceding verse most clearly proves. There is no canon of interpretation more erroneous than to make words or phrases to bear the same meaning in every place.—*Ed.*

better. On the other hand, he who attempts to overcome evil with evil, may perhaps surpass his enemy in doing injury, but it is to his own ruin; for by acting thus he carries on war for the devil.

CHAPTER XIII.

1. Let every soul be subject unto the higher powers. For there is no power but of God: the powers that be are ordained of God.

2. Whosoever therefore resisteth the power, resisteth the ordinance of God; and they that resist shall receive to themselves damnation.

1. Omnis anima potestatibus supereminentibus subdita sit: non enim est potestas, nisi à Deo; quæ vero sunt potestates à Deo sunt ordinatæ.

2. Itaque qui resistit potestati, Dei ordinationi resistit; qui verò restiterint judicium sibi accersent.

1. *Let every soul,*[1] &c. Inasmuch as he so carefully handles this subject, in connection with what forms the Christian life, it appears that he was constrained to do so by some great necessity which existed especially in that age, though the preaching of the gospel at all times renders this necessary. There are indeed always some tumultuous spirits who believe that the kingdom of Christ cannot be sufficiently elevated, unless all earthly powers be abolished, and that they cannot enjoy the liberty given by him, except they shake off every yoke of human subjection. This error, however, possessed the minds of the Jews above all others; for it seemed to them disgraceful that the offspring of Abraham, whose kingdom flourished before the Redeemer's coming, should now, after his appearance, continue in submission to another power. There was also another thing which alienated the Jews no less than the Gentiles from their rulers, because they all not only hated piety, but also persecuted religion with the most hostile feelings. Hence

---

[1] "Anima," ψυχὴ, not only the Hebrews, (see Gen xiv. 21; xlvi. 27,) but the Greeks also designate man by this word. Man is sometimes designated by his immaterial part, *soul,* and sometimes by his material part, *flesh,* or body, as in ch. xii. 1. One author says that the word soul is used here in order to show that the obedience enforced should be from the soul, not feigned, but sincere and genuine. *Let every soul,* that is " every one," says *Grotius,* " even apostles, prophets, and bishops."—*Ed.*

it seemed unreasonable to acknowledge them for legitimate princes and rulers, who were attempting to take away the kingdom from Christ, the only Lord of heaven and earth.

By these reasons, as it is probable, Paul was induced to establish, with greater care than usual, the authority of magistrates, and first he lays down a general precept, which briefly includes what he afterwards says: secondly, he subjoins an exposition and a proof of his precept.

He calls them the *higher powers*,[1] not the supreme, who possess the chief authority, but such as excel other men. Magistrates are then thus called with regard to their subjects, and not as compared with each other. And it seems indeed to me, that the Apostle intended by this word to take away the frivolous curiosity of men, who are wont often to inquire by what right they who rule have obtained their authority; but it ought to be enough for us, that they *do rule;* for they have not ascended by their own power into this high station, but have been placed there by the Lord's hand. And by mentioning *every soul*, he removes every exception, lest any one should claim an immunity from the common duty of obedience.[2]

For there is no power, &c. The reason why we ought to be subject to magistrates is, because they are constituted by God's ordination. For since it pleases God thus to govern the world, he who attempts to invert the order of God, and thus to resist God himself, despises his power; since to

---

[1] " Potestates supereminentes—pre-eminent powers." *Hammond* renders the words ἐξουσίαις ὑπερεχούσαις, supreme powers, meaning kings, and refers to ἄρχοντες in ver. 3, as a proof: but this word means magistrates as well as kings. See Acts xvii. 98. The ruling power as exercised by those in authority is evidently what is meant here, without any reference to any form of government. Of course obedience to kings, or to emperors, or to any exercising a ruling power, whatever name they may bear, is included.—*Ed.*

[2] *Grotius* qualifies this obedience by saying, that it should not extend to what is contrary to the will of God. But it is remarkable, that often in Scripture things are stated broadly and without any qualifying terms, and yet they have limits, as it is clear from other portions. This peculiarity is worthy of notice. Power is from God, the abuse of power is from what is evil in men. The Apostle throughout refers only to power justly exercised. He does not enter into the subject of tyranny and oppression. And this is probably the reason why he does not set limits to the obedience required: he contemplated no other than the proper and legitimate use of power.—*Ed.*

despise the providence of him who is the founder of civil power, is to carry on war with him. Understand further, that powers are from God, not as pestilence, and famine, and wars, and other visitations for sin, are said to be from him; but because he has appointed them for the legitimate and just government of the world. For though tyrannies and unjust exercise of power, as they are full of disorder, (ἀταξίας,) are not an ordained government; yet the right of government is ordained by God for the wellbeing of mankind. As it is lawful to repel wars and to seek remedies for other evils, hence the Apostle commands us willingly and cheerfully to respect and honour the right and authority of magistrates, as useful to men : for the punishment which God inflicts on men for their sins, we cannot properly call ordinations, but they are the means which he designedly appoints for the preservation of legitimate order.

2. *And they who resist,* &c. As no one can resist God but to his own ruin, he threatens, that they shall not be unpunished who in this respect oppose the providence of God. Let us then beware, lest we incur this denunciation. And by *judgment*,[1] I understand not only the punishment which is inflicted by the magistrate, as though he had only said, that they would be justly punished who resisted authority; but also the vengeance of God, however it may at length be executed: for he teaches us in general what end awaits those who contend with God.

3. For rulers are not a terror to good works, but to the evil. Wilt thou then not be afraid of the power? Do that which is good, and thou shalt have praise of the same:

4. For he is the minister of God to thee for good. But if thou do that which is evil, be afraid; for he beareth not the sword in vain: for he is the minister of God, a revenger to *execute* wrath upon him that doeth evil.

3. Principes enim non sunt terrori bonis operibus sed malis; vis ergo non timere potestatem? bene fac, et habebis laudem ab ea;

4. Dei enim minister est tibi in bonum : si verò quid mali feceris, time; non enim frustra gladium gerit; Dei enim minister est, vindex in iram adversus eos qui malè agunt.[2]

[1] " Judicium," κρίμα ; some render it " punishment;" *Beza,* " condemnation." The word is used in both senses: but according to the tenor of the former part of the verse, it seems that the Apostle means that which is inflicted by God.—*Ed.*

[2] The words, " Vindex in iram adversus eos qui malè agunt," can

3. *For princes,* &c. He now commends to us obedience to princes on the ground of utility; for the causative γὰρ, *for,* is to be referred to the first proposition, and not to the last verse. Now, the utility is this,—that the Lord has designed in this way to provide for the tranquillity of the good, and to restrain the waywardness of the wicked; by which two things the safety of mankind is secured: for except the fury of the wicked be resisted, and the innocent be protected from their violence, all things would come to an entire confusion. Since then this is the only remedy by which mankind can be preserved from destruction, it ought to be carefully observed by us, unless we wish to avow ourselves as the public enemies of the human race.

And he adds, *Wilt not thou then fear the power? Do good.* By this he intimates, that there is no reason why we should dislike the magistrate, if indeed we are good; nay, that it is an implied proof of an evil conscience, and of one that is devising some mischief, when any one wishes to shake off or to remove from himself this yoke. But he speaks here of the true, and, as it were, of the native duty of the magistrate, from which however they who hold power often degenerate; yet the obedience due to princes ought to be rendered to them. For since a wicked prince is the Lord's scourge to punish the sins of the people, let us remember, that it happens through our fault that this excellent blessing of God is turned into a curse.

Let us then continue to honour the good appointment of God, which may be easily done, provided we impute to ourselves whatever evil may accompany it. Hence he teaches us here the end for which magistrates are instituted by the Lord; the happy effects of which would always appear, were not so noble and salutary an institution marred through our fault. At the same time, princes do never so far abuse their power, by harassing the good and innocent, that they do not retain in their tyranny some kind of just government: there can then be no tyranny which does not in some respects assist in consolidating the society of men.

hardly be translated; and the latter part is improperly put in the plural. —*Ed.*

He has here noticed two things, which even philosophers have considered as making a part of a well-ordered administration of a commonwealth, that is, rewards for the good, and punishment for the wicked. The word *praise* has here, after the Hebrew manner, a wide meaning.

4. *For he is God's minister for good,* &c. Magistrates may hence learn what their vocation is, for they are not to rule for their own interest, but for the public good; nor are they endued with unbridled power, but what is restricted to the wellbeing of their subjects; in short, they are responsible to God and to men in the exercise of their power. For as they are deputed by God and do his business, they must give an account to him: and then the ministration which God has committed to them has a regard to the subjects, they are therefore debtors also to them. And private men are reminded, that it is through the divine goodness that they are defended by the sword of princes against injuries done by the wicked.

For they bear not the sword in vain, &c. It is another part of the office of magistrates, that they ought forcibly to repress the waywardness of evil men, who do not willingly suffer themselves to be governed by laws, and to inflict such punishment on their offences as God's judgment requires; for he expressly declares, that they are armed with the sword, not for an empty show, but that they may smite evil-doers.

And then he says, *An avenger,* to execute *wrath,*[1] &c. This is the same as if it had been said, that he is an executioner of God's wrath; and this he shows himself to be by having the sword, which the Lord has delivered into his hand. This is a remarkable passage for the purpose of proving the right of the sword; for if the Lord, by arming the magistrate, has also committed to him the use of the sword, whenever he visits the guilty with death, by executing God's

---

[1] *Vindex in iram,* ἔκδικος εἰς ὀργὴν; "a revenger to *execute* wrath," Com. Ver., *Doddridge;* "a revenger for wrath," *Hammond.* Wrath is here taken to mean punishment, by *Luther, Beza, Grotius, Mede,* &c. See chap. ii. 5; iii. 5; iv. 15. The phrase then might be rendered, "condemning to punishment the doer of evil." There is a contrast between "for wrath" and "for good" at the beginning of the verse.—*Ed.*

vengeance, he obeys his commands. Contend then do they with God who think it unlawful to shed the blood of wicked men.

5. Wherefore *ye* must needs be subject, not only for wrath, but also for conscience sake.	5. Itaque necesse est subjici, non modò propter iram, sed etiam propter conscientiam.
6. For, for this cause pay ye tribute also: for they are God's ministers, attending continually upon this very thing.	6. Propterea enim tributa quoque solutis; ministri[1] enim Dei sunt, in hoc incumbentes.
7. Render therefore to all their dues: tribute to whom tribute *is due;* custom to whom custom; fear to whom fear; honour to whom honour.	7. Reddite ergo omnibus quod debetur; cui tributum, tributum; cui vectigal, vectigal; cui timorem, timorem; cui honorem, honorem.

5. *It is therefore necessary,* &c. What he had at first commanded as to the rendering of obedience to magistrates, he now briefly repeats, but with some addition, and that is, —that we ought to obey them, not only on the ground of necessity arising from man, but that we thereby obey God; for by *wrath* he means the punishment which the magistrates inflict for the contempt of their dignity; as though he had said, "We must not only obey, because we cannot with impunity resist the powerful and those armed with authority, as injuries are wont to be borne with which cannot be repelled; but we ought to obey willingly, as conscience through God's word thus binds us." Though then the magistrate were disarmed, so that we could with impunity provoke and despise him, yet such a thing ought to be no more attempted than if we were to see punishment suspended over us; for it belongs not to a private individual to take away authority from him whom the Lord has in power set over us. This whole discourse is concerning civil government; it is therefore to no purpose that they who would exercise dominion over consciences do hence attempt to establish their sacrilegious tyranny.

[1] "Ministri," λιιτουργοὶ, administrators, functionaries, the performers of public services, or public ministers, according to *Macknight*. Rulers were called before, in verse 4, διάκονοι, servants, deacons, ministers. The same titles are given to them as to the Apostles and ministers of the gospel, and even to Christ himself: and they are said to be the ministers and functionaries of *God*, being so in civil matters, as those are in spiritual things who preach the gospel.—*Ed.*

6. *For this reason also,* &c. He takes occasion to introduce the subject of tributes, the reason for which he deduces from the office of magistrates; for if it be their duty to defend and safely preserve the peace of the good, and to resist the mischievous attempts of the wicked, this they cannot do unless they are aided by sufficient force. Tributes then are justly paid to support such necessary expenses.[1] But respecting the proportion of taxes or tributes, this is not the place to discuss the subject; nor does it belong to us either to prescribe to princes how much they ought to expend in every affair, or to call them to an account. It yet behoves them to remember, that whatever they receive from the people, is as it were public property, and not to be spent in the gratification of private indulgence. For we see the use for which Paul appoints these tributes which are to be paid—even that kings may be furnished with means to defend their subjects.

7. *Render then to all what is due,* &c. The Apostle seems here summarily to include the particulars in which the duties of subjects towards magistrates consist,—that they are to hold them in esteem and honour,—that they are to obey their edicts, laws, and judgments,—that they are to pay tributes and customs. By the word *fear,* he means obedience; by *customs* and *tributes,* not only imposts and taxes, but also other revenues.[2]

Now this passage confirms what I have already said,— that we ought to obey kings and governors, whoever they may be, not because we are constrained, but because it is a service acceptable to God; for he will have them not only to be feared, but also honoured by a voluntary respect.

---

[1] The words "to this very thing," εἰς αὐτὸ τοῦτο, seem to be an instance of Hebraism, as זאת, "this," in that language is both singular and plural, and means "this," or "those," according to the context. "To these very things," before mentioned, as to the works and duties of magistrates, appears to be the meaning here: and so the words are rendered in the Syriac and Ethiopic versions. A singular instance is found at the begining of verse 9, "For this," τὸ γὰρ, and then several commandments are mentioned; "for this" is the law, says *Stuart;* but the word for "law" is of a different gender. What we would say in English is, "for these," &c. It is a Hebrew idiom transferred into Greek.—*Ed.*

[2] The distinction commonly made between the two words is this,— φόρος, "tribute," is a tax on the person or on lands, and τίλος, "custom," is what is levied on merchandise.—*Ed.*

8. Owe no man any thing, but to love one another: for he that loveth another hath fulfilled the law.
9. For this, Thou shalt not commit adultery, Thou shalt not kill, Thou shalt not steal, Thou shalt not bear false witness, Thou shalt not covet; and if *there be* any other commandment, it is briefly comprehended in this saying, namely, Thou shalt love thy neighbour as thyself.
10. Love worketh no ill to his neighbour: therefore love *is* the fulfilling of the law.

8. Nemini quicquam debeatis, nisi ut invicem diligatis; qui enim diligit alterum Legem implevit.
9. Illud enim, Non mœchaberis, Non occides, Non falsum testimonium dices, Non concupisces, et si quod est aliud præceptum, in hoc sermone comprehenditur, Diliges proximum sicut teipsum.
10. Dilectio proximo malum non infert: plenitudo ergo legis est dilectio.

8. *To no one owe ye,* &c. There are those who think that this was not said without a taunt, as though Paul was answering the objection of those who contended that Christians were burdened in having other precepts than that of love enjoined them. And indeed I do not deny, but that it may be taken ironically, as though he conceded to those who allowed no other law but that of love, what they required, but in another sense. And yet I prefer to take the words simply as they are; for I think that Paul meant to refer the precept respecting the power of magistrates to the law of love, lest it should seem to any one too feeble; as though he had said,—"When I require you to obey princes, I require nothing more than what all the faithful ought to do, as demanded by the law of love: for if ye wish well to the good, (and not to wish this is inhuman,) ye ought to strive, that the laws and judgments may prevail, that the administrators of the laws may have an obedient people, so that through them peace may be secured to all." He then who introduces anarchy, violates love; for what immediately follows anarchy, is the confusion of all things.[1]

For he who loves another, &c. Paul's design is to reduce all the precepts of the law to love, so that we may know that we then rightly obey the commandments, when we observe the law of love, and when we refuse to undergo no burden in order to keep it. He thus fully confirms what he has

[1] The debt of love is to be always paid, and is always due: for love is ever to be exercised. We are to pay other debts, and we may pay them fully and finally; but the debt of love ever continues, and is to be daily discharged.—*Ed.*

commanded respecting obedience to magistrates, in which consists no small portion of love.

But some are here impeded, and they cannot well extricate themselves from this difficulty,—that Paul teaches us that the law is fulfilled when we love our neighbour, for no mention is here made of what is due to God, which ought not by any means to have been omitted. But Paul refers not to the whole law, but speaks only of what the law requires from us as to our neighbour. And it is doubtless true, that the whole law is fulfilled when we love our neighbours; for true love towards man does not flow except from the love of God, and it is its evidence, and as it were its effects. But Paul records here only the precepts of the second table, and of these only he speaks, as though he had said,—" He who loves his neighbour as himself, performs his duty towards the whole world." Puerile then is the gloss of the Sophists, who attempt to elicit from this passage what may favour justification by works: for Paul declares not what men do or do not, but he speaks hypothetically of that which you will find nowhere accomplished. And when we say, that men are not justified by works, we deny not that the keeping of the law is true righteousness: but as no one performs it, and never has performed it, we say, that all are excluded from it, and that hence the only refuge is in the grace of Christ.

9. *For this, Thou shalt not commit adultery,* &c. It cannot be from this passage concluded what precepts are contained in the second table, for he subjoins at the end, *and if there be any other precept.* He indeed omits the command respecting the honouring of parents; and it may seem strange, that what especially belonged to his subject should have been passed by. But what if he had left it out, lest he should obscure his argument? Though I dare not to affirm this, yet I see here nothing wanting to answer the purpose he had in view, which was to show,—that since God intended nothing else by all his commandments than to teach us the duty of love, we ought by all means to strive to perform it. And yet the uncontentious reader will readily acknowledge, that Paul intended to prove, by things of a like

nature, that the import of the whole law is, that love towards one another ought to be exercised by us, and that what he left to be implied is to be understood, and that is,—that obedience to magistrates is not the least thing which tends to nourish peace, to preserve brotherly love.

10. *Love doeth no evil to a neighbour,* &c. He demonstrates by the effect, that under the word love are contained those things which are taught us in all the commandments; for he who is endued with true love will never entertain the thought of injuring others. What else does the whole law forbid, but that we do no harm to our neighbour? This, however, ought to be applied to the present subject; for since magistrates are the guardians of peace and justice, he who desires that his own right should be secured to every one, and that all may live free from wrong, ought to defend, as far as he can, the power of magistrates. But the enemies of government show a disposition to do harm. And when he repeats that the fulfilling of the law is love, understand this, as before, of that part of the law which refers to mankind; for the first table of the law, which contains what we owe to God, is not here referred to at all.

11. And that, knowing the time, that now *it is* high time to awake out of sleep: for now *is* our salvation nearer than when we believed.	11. Hoc enim, quum noverimus tempus, quia hora est qua jam è somno expergiscamur (nunc enim propior est salus nostra quàm quum credidimus,)
12. The night is far spent, the day is at hand: let us therefore cast off the works of darkness, and let us put on the armour of light.	12. Nox progressa est, dies verò appropinquavit: abjiciamus ergo opera tenebrarum, et induamus arma lucis.
13. Let us walk honestly, as in the day; not in rioting and drunkenness, not in chambering and wantonness, not in strife and envying:	13 Sicut in die decenter ambulemus; non comessationibus neque ebrietatibus, neque cubilibus neque lasciviis, neque contentione neque æmulatione:
14. But put ye on the Lord Jesus Christ, and make not provision for the flesh, to *fulfil* the lusts *thereof.*	14. Sed induamini Dominum Iesum Christum, et carnis curam ne agatis ad concupiscentias.

11. *Moreover,* &c. He enters now on another subject of exhortation, that as the rays of celestial life had begun to shine on us as it were at the dawn, we ought to do what they are wont to do who are in public life and in the sight of men, who take diligent care lest they should commit any-

thing that is base or unbecoming; for if they do anything amiss, they see that they are exposed to the view of many witnesses. But we, who always stand in the sight of God and of angels, and whom Christ, the true sun of righteousness, invites to his presence, we indeed ought to be much more careful to beware of every kind of pollution.

The import then of the words is this, "Since we know that the seasonable time has already come, in which we should awake from sleep, let us cast aside whatever belongs to the night, let us shake off all the works of darkness, since the darkness itself has been dissipated, and let us attend to the works of light, and walk as it becomes those who are enjoying the day." The intervening words are to be read as in a parenthesis.

As, however, the words are metaphorical, it may be useful to consider their meaning: Ignorance of God is what he calls *night;* for all who are thus ignorant go astray and sleep as people do in the night. The unbelieving do indeed labour under these two evils, they are blind and they are insensible; but this insensibility he shortly after designated by sleep, which is, as one says, an image of death. By *light* he means the revelation of divine truth, by which Christ the sun of righteousness arises on us.[1] He mentions *awake,* by which he intimates that we are to be equipped and prepared to undertake the services which the Lord requires from us. The *works of darkness* are shameful and wicked works; for night, as some one says, is shameless. The

---

[1] The preceding explanation of *night* and *day,* as here to be understood, does not comport with what is afterwards said on verse 12. The distinction between night and day, when ignorance and knowledge are intended, and the night and day of a Christian, ought to be clearly kept in view. The first is what is here described, but the latter is what the passage refers to. And the *sleep* mentioned here is not the sleep of ignorance and unbelief, but the sleep, the torpor, or inactivity of Christians.

That the present state of believers, their condition in this world, is meant here by "night," and their state of future glory is meant by "day," appears evident from the words which follow, "for nearer now is our salvation than when we believed." Salvation here, as in chap. viii. 24, and in 1 Pet. i. 9, means salvation made complete and perfect, the full enjoyment of all its blessings. Indeed in no other sense can what is said here of night and day be appropriate. The night of heathen ignorance as to Christians had already passed, and the day of gospel light was not approaching, but had appeared.—*Ed.*

armour of light represents good, and temperate, and holy actions, such as are suitable to the day; and armour is mentioned rather than works, because we are to carry on a warfare for the Lord.

But the particles at the beginning, *And this*, are to be read by themselves, for they are connected with what is gone before; as we say in Latin *Adhæc*—besides, or *præterea*—moreover. The *time*, he says, was known to the faithful, for the calling of God and the day of visitation required a new life and new morals, and he immediately adds an explanation, and says, that it was the *hour* to awake: for it is not χρόνος but καιρὸς, which means a fit occasion or a seasonable time.[1]

For nearer is now our salvation, &c. This passage is in various ways perverted by interpreters. Many refer the word *believed* to the time of the law, as though Paul had said, that the Jews believed before Christ came; which view I reject as unnatural and strained; and surely to confine a general truth to a small part of the Church, would have been wholly inconsistent. Of that whole assembly to which he wrote, how few were Jews? Then this declaration could not have been suitable to the Romans. Besides, the comparison between the night and the day does in my judgment dissipate every doubt on the point. The declaration then seems to me to be of the most simple kind,—" Nearer

---

[1] The words καὶ τοῦτο, according to *Beza, Grotius, Mede*, &c., connect what follows with the preceding exhortation to love, " And this do, or let us do, as we know," &c. But the whole tenor of what follows by no means favours this view. The subject is wholly different. It is evidently a new subject of exhortation, as *Calvin* says, and the words must be rendered as he proposes, or be viewed as elliptical; the word " I say," or " I command," according to *Macknight*, being understood, " This also *I say*, since we know the time," &c. If we adopt " I command," or " moreover," as *Calvin* does, it would be better to regard the participle εἰδότες as having the meaning of an imperative, ἐστί being understood, several instances of which we have in the preceding chapter, verses 9, 16, 17. The whole passage would then read better in this manner,—

11. Moreover, know the time, that it is even now the very time for us to awake from sleep; for nearer now is our salvation than when we
12. believed: the night has advanced, and the day has approached; let us then cast away the works of darkness, and let us put on the
13. armour of light; let us, as in the day, walk in a becoming manner, &c.—*Ed*.

is salvation now to us than at that time when we began to believe:" so that a reference is made to the time which had preceded as to their faith. For as the adverb here used is in its import indefinite, this meaning is much the most suitable, as it is evident from what follows.

12. *The night has advanced, and the day,* &c. This is the season which he had just mentioned; for as the faithful are not as yet received into full light, he very fitly compares to the dawn the knowledge of future life, which shines on us through the gospel: for *day* is not put here, as in other places, for the light of faith, (otherwise he could not have said that it was only approaching, but that it was present, for it now shines as it were in the middle of its progress,) but for that glorious brightness of the celestial life, the beginnings of which are now seen through the gospel.

The sum of what he says is,—that as soon as God begins to call us, we ought to do the same, as when we conclude from the first dawn of the day that the full sun is at hand; we ought to look forward to the coming of Christ.

He says that the *night had advanced,* because we are not so overwhelmed with thick darkness as the unbelieving are, to whom no spark of life appears; but the hope of resurrection is placed by the gospel before our eyes; yea, the light of faith, by which we discover that the full brightness of celestial glory is nigh at hand, ought to stimulate us, so that we may not grow torpid on the earth. But afterwards, when he bids us to walk in the light, as it were during the day time, he does not continue the same metaphor; for he compares to the day our present state, while Christ shines on us. His purpose was in various ways to exhort us,—at one time to meditate on our future life; at another, to contemplate the present favour of God.

13. *Not in revellings,* &c. He mentions here three kinds of vices, and to each he has given two names,—intemperance and excess in living,—carnal lust and uncleanness, which is connected with it,—and envy and contention. If these have in them so much filthiness, that even carnal men are ashamed to commit them before the eyes of men, it behoves us, who are in the light of God, at all times to abstain

from them; yea, even when we are withdrawn from the presence of men. As to the third vice, though contention is put before envying, there is yet no doubt but that Paul intended to remind us, that strifes and contests arise from this fountain; for when any one seeks to excel, there is envying of one another; but ambition is the source of both evils.[1]

14. *But put ye on the Lord Jesus Christ,* &c. This metaphor is commonly used in Scripture with respect to what tends to adorn or to deform man; both of which may be seen in his clothing: for a filthy and torn garment dishonours a man; but what is becoming and clean recommends him. Now to *put on* Christ, means here to be on every side fortified by the power of his Spirit, and be thereby prepared to discharge all the duties of holiness; for thus is the image of God renewed in us, which is the only true ornament of the soul. For Paul had in view the end of our calling; inasmuch as God, by adopting us, unites us to the body of his only-begotten Son, and for this purpose,—that we, renouncing our former life, may become new men in him.[2] On this account he says also in another place, that we put on Christ in baptism. (Gal. iii. 27.)

And have no care, &c. As long as we carry about us our flesh, we cannot cast away every care for it; for though our conversation is in heaven, we yet sojourn on earth. The things then which belong to the body must be taken care of,

---

[1] The case is the same with the two preceding instances; the vice which seems to follow is placed first. Revelling is first mentioned, though drunkenness goes before it; and " chambering," or concubinage, or indulgence in unlawful lusts is first stated, though lasciviousness or wantonness is the source from which it proceeds. It is an example of the Apostle's mode of writing similar to what we find in chap. xi. 29, as to " the gifts and calling of God," and in verse 33, as to " the wisdom and knowledge of God."—*Ed.*

[2] Many have explained " the putting on " here in a manner wholly inconsistent with the passage, as though the putting on of Christ's righteousness was intended. *Calvin* keeps to what accords with the context, the putting on of Christ as to his holy image. Sanctification, and not justification, is the subject of the passage. To put on Christ, then, is to put on his virtues and graces, to put on or be endued with his spirit, to imitate his conduct and to copy his example. This is in addition to the putting him on as our righteousness, and not as a substitute for it. Both are necessary: for Christ is our sanctification, the author, worker, and example of it, as well as our righteousness.—*Ed.*

but not otherwise than as they are helps to us in our pilgrimage, and not that they may make us to forget our country. Even heathens have said, that a few things suffice nature, but that the appetites of men are insatiable. Every one then who wishes to satisfy the desires of the flesh, must necessarily not only fall into, but be immerged in a vast and deep gulf.

Paul, setting a bridle on our desires, reminds us, that the cause of all intemperance is, that no one is content with a moderate or lawful use of things: he has therefore laid down this rule,—that we are to provide for the wants of our flesh, but not to indulge its lusts. It is in this way that we shall use this world without abusing it.

CHAPTER XIV.

1. Him that is weak in the faith receive ye, *but* not to doubtful disputations.
2. For one believeth that he may eat all things: another, who is weak, eateth herbs.
3. Let not him that eateth despise him that eateth not; and let not him which eateth not judge him that eateth: for God hath received him.
4. Who art thou that judgest another man's servant? to his own master he standeth or falleth; yea, he shall be holden up: for God is able to make him stand.

1. Eum verò qui fide est imbecilla, suscipite, non ad disceptationes quæstionum.
2. Qui credit, vescatur quibusvis: qui autem infirmus est, olera edit.
3. Qui edit, non contemnat eum qui abstinet; et qui abstinet, eum non condemnet qui edit: Dominus enim illum suscepit.
4. Tu quis es qui judicas alienum servum? proprio Domino stat vel cadit. Stabit verò: potens est enim Deus efficere ut stet.

1. *Him indeed,* &c. He passes on now to lay down a precept especially necessary for the instruction of the Church,—that they who have made the most progress in Christian doctrine should accommodate themselves to the more ignorant, and employ their own strength to sustain their weakness; for among the people of God there are some weaker than others, and who, except they are treated with great tenderness and kindness, will be discouraged, and become at length alienated from religion. And it is very probable that this happened especially at that time; for the Churches were formed of both Jews and Gentiles; some of whom,

having been long accustomed to the rites of the Mosaic law, having been brought up in them from childhood, were not easily drawn away from them; and there were others who, having never learnt such things, refused a yoke to which they had not been accustomed.[1]

Now, as man's disposition is to slide from a difference in opinion to quarrels and contentions, the Apostle shows how they who thus vary in their opinions may live together without any discord; and he prescribes this as the best mode,— that they who are strong should spend their labour in assisting the weak, and that they who have made the greatest advances should bear with the more ignorant. For God, by making us stronger than others, does not bestow strength that we may oppress the weak; nor is it the part of Christian wisdom to be above measure insolent, and to despise others. The import then of what he addresses to the more intelligent and the already confirmed, is this,—that the ampler the grace which they had received from the Lord, the more bound they were to help their neighbours.

Not for the debatings of questions.[2] This is a defective sentence, as the word which is necessary to complete the sense is wanting. It appears, however, evident, that he meant nothing else than that the weak should not be wearied with

---

[1] Some, as *Haldane*, have found fault with this classification, as there is nothing in the chapter which countenances it. But as the Apostle's object throughout the epistle was to reconcile the Jews and Gentiles, there is reason sufficient to regard them as the two parties here intended: and, as *Chalmers* justly observes, it is more probable that the Gentiles were the despisers, inasmuch as the Jews, who, like Paul, had got over their prejudices, were no doubt disposed to sympathize with their brethren, who were still held fast by them.—*Ed.*

[2] *Non ad disceptationes quæstionum,* μὴ εἰς διακρίσεις διαλογισμῶν; "non ad altercationes disceptationum—not for the altercations of disputings" or debatings, *Beza;* "not to debates about matters in doubt," *Doddridge;* "not in order to the strifes of disputations," *Macknight.* Both words are in the plural number; therefore to give the first the sense of "judging," as *Hodge* does, cannot be right; for in that case it would have been in the singular number. The words may be rendered, "not for the solutions of doubts." One of the meanings of the first word, according to *Hesychius,* is διάλυσις—untying, loosening, dissolving; and for the latter, see Luke xxiv. 38, and 1 Tim. ii. 8. According to the frequent import of the preposition εἰς, the sentence may be thus paraphrased, "Him who is weak in the faith receive, *but* not that ye may solve his doubts," or, "debate his reasonings," or, "contend in disputations."—*Ed.*

fruitless disputes. But we must remember the subject he now handles: for as many of the Jews still clave to the shadows of the law, he indeed admits, that this was a fault in them; he yet requires that they should be for a time excused; for to press the matter urgently on them might have shaken their faith.[1]

He then calls those contentious questions which disturb a mind not yet sufficiently established, or which involve it in doubts. It may at the same time be proper to extend this farther, even to any thorny and difficult questions, by which weak consciences, without any edification, may be disquieted and disturbed. We ought then to consider what questions any one is able to bear, and to accommodate our teaching to the capacity of individuals.

2. *Let him who believes*, &c. What *Erasmus* has followed among the various readings I know not; but he has mutilated this sentence, which, in Paul's words, is complete; and instead of the relative article he has improperly introduced *alius*—one, "One indeed believes," &c. That I take the infinitive for an imperative, ought not to appear unnatural nor strained, for it is a mode of speaking very usual with Paul.[2] He then calls those believers who were endued with

---

[1] *Scott's* remarks on this verse are striking and appropriate,—"Notwithstanding," he says, "the authority vested by Christ in his Apostles, and their infallibility in delivering his doctrine to mankind, differences of opinion prevailed even among real Christians; nor did St. Paul, by an express decision and command, attempt to put a final termination to them. A proposition indeed may be certain and important truth; yet a man cannot profitably receive it without due preparation of mind and heart;—so that a compelled assent to any doctrine, or conformity to any outward observances, without conviction, would in general be hypocrisy, and entirely unavailing. So essential are the rights and existence of private judgment, in all possible cases, to the exercise of true religion! and so useless an encumbrance would an infallible judge be, for deciding controversies, and producing unanimity among Christians!"

[2] This is true, but the passage here seems not to require such a construction. Both sentences are declarative, announcing a fact respecting two parties: the one believed he might eat everything; the other did eat only herbs. The relative ὅς, when repeated, often means "one," as in ver. 5, and in 1 Cor. xi. 21: and the article ὁ stands here for that repetition; an example of which *Raphelius* adduces from the Greek classics.

Some think that this abstinence from meat was not peculiar to the Jews; but that some Gentiles also had scruples on the subject. It is true that heathens, who held the transmigration of souls, did not eat flesh: but it is not likely that abstinence, arising from such an absurd notion, would

a conscience fully satisfied; to these he allowed the use of all things without any difference. In the mean time the weak did eat herbs, and abstained from those things, the use of which he thought was not lawful. If the common version be more approved, the meaning then will be,—that it is not right that he who freely eats all things, as he believes them to be lawful, should require those, who are yet tender and weak in faith, to walk by the same rule. But to render the word *sick*, as some have done, is absurd.

3. *Let not him who eats*, &c. He wisely and suitably meets the faults of both parties. They who were strong had this fault,—that they despised those as superstitious who were scrupulous about insignificant things, and also derided them: these, on the other hand, were hardly able to refrain from rash judgments, so as not to condemn what they did not follow; for whatever they perceived to be contrary to their own sentiments, they thought was evil. Hence he exhorts the former to refrain from contempt, and the latter from excessive moroseness. And the reason which he adds, as it belongs to both parties, ought to be applied to the two clauses,—"When you see," he says, "a man illuminated with the knowledge of God, you have evidence enough that he is received by the Lord; if you either despise or condemn him, you reject him whom God has embraced."[1]

4. *Who art thou who judgest*, &c. " As you would act uncourteously, yea, and presumptuously among men, were you to bring another man's servant under your own rules,

have been thus treated by the Apostle. It indeed appears evident, that the abstinence here referred to did arise from what was regarded to be the will of God: and though abstinence from all animal food was not enjoined on the Jews, yet it appears from history that Jews, living among heathens, wholly abstained, owing to the fear they had of being in any way contaminated. This was the case with Daniel and his companions, Dan. i. 8-16.

Professor *Hodge* says, in a note on this passage, " Josephus states in his life (ch. xxiii.) that certain Jewish priests, while at Rome, lived entirely upon fruit, from the dread of eating anything unclean." We may also suppose that some of the *Essenes*, who abstained both from meat and from wine, were among the early converts.—*Ed.*

[1] The last clause is by *Haldane* confined to the strong, and he objects to this extension of it; and certainly the following verse is in favour of his view, for the weak, the condemner, is the person reproved, and therefore the strong is he who to his own master stands or falls. The condemner throughout is the weak, and the despiser is the strong.—*Ed.*

and try all his acts by the rule of your own will; so you assume too much, if you condemn anything in God's servant, because it does not please you; for it belongs not to you to prescribe to him what to do and what not to do, nor is it necessary for him to live according to your law."

Now, though the power of judging as to the person, and also as to the deed, is taken from us, there is yet much difference between the two; for we ought to leave the man, whatever he may be, to the judgment of God; but as to his deeds we may indeed form a decisive opinion, though not according to our own views, but according to the word of God; and the judgment, derived from his word, is neither human, nor another man's judgment. Paul then intended here to restrain us from presumption in judging; into which they fall, who dare to pronounce anything respecting the actions of men without the warrant of God's word.

To his own Lord he stands or falls, &c. As though he said,—"It belongs rightly to the Lord, either to disapprove, or to accept what his servant doeth: hence he robs the Lord, who attempts to take to himself this authority." And he adds, *he shall indeed stand:* and by so saying, he not only bids us to abstain from condemning, but also exhorts us to mercy and kindness, so as ever to hope well of him, in whom we perceive anything of God; inasmuch as the Lord has given us a hope, that he will fully confirm, and lead to perfection, those in whom he has begun the work of grace.

But by referring to the power of God, he means not simply, as though he had said, that God can do this if he will; but, after the usual manner of Scripture, he connects God's will with his power: and yet he speaks not here of perpetuity, as though they must stand to the end whom God has once raised up; but he only reminds us, that we are to entertain a good hope, and that our judgments should lean this way; as he also teaches us in another place, "He who began in you a good work, will perform it to the end." (Phil. i. 6.) In short, Paul shows to what side their judgments incline, in whom love abounds.

5. One man esteemeth one day above another; another esteemeth	5. Hic quidem diem præ die æstimat; ille autem peræquè æstimat

every day *alike.* Let every man be fully persuaded in his own mind.

6. He that regardeth the day, regardeth *it* unto the Lord; and he that regardeth not the day, to the Lord he doth not regard *it.* He that eateth, eateth to the Lord, for he giveth God thanks; and he that eateth not, to the Lord he eateth not, and giveth God thanks.

omnem diem. Unusquisque sententiæ suæ certus sit.

6. Qui curat diem, Domino curat; qui non curat diem, Domino non curat. Qui vescitur, Domino vescitur, gratias enim agit Deo; et qui abstinet, Domino abstinet, et gratias agit Deo.

5. *One indeed,* &c. He had spoken before of scruples in the choice of meats; he now adds another example of difference, that is, as to days; and both these arose from Judaism. For as the Lord in his law made a difference between meats and pronounced some to be unclean, the use of which he prohibited, and as he had also appointed festal and solemn days and commanded them to be observed, the Jews, who had been brought up from their childhood in the doctrine of the law, would not lay aside that reverence for days which they had entertained from the beginning, and to which through life they had been accustomed; nor could they have dared to touch these meats from which they had so long abstained. That they were imbued with these notions, was an evidence of their weakness; they would have thought otherwise, had they possessed a certain and a clear knowledge of Christian liberty. But in abstaining from what they thought to be unlawful, they evidenced piety, as it would have been a proof of presumption and contempt, had they done anything contrary to the dictates of conscience.

Here then the Apostle applies the best rule, when he bids every one to be fully assured as to his own mind; by which he intimates that there ought to be in Christians such a care for obedience, that they do nothing, except what they think, or rather feel assured, is pleasing to God.[1] And this

---

[1] " Unusquisque sententiæ suæ certus sit;" *ἕκαστος ἐν τῷ ἰδίῳ νοὶ πληροφορείσθω*; "unusquisque in animo suo plenè certus esto—let every one be fully sure in his own mind," *Beza, Pareus;* " let every one be convinced in his mind," *Macknight;* " let every one freely enjoy his own sentiment," *Doddridge.* This last is by no means the sense: Our own version is the best and the most literal, " let every man be fully persuaded in his own mind;" and with which *Calvin's* exposition perfectly agrees. For the meaning of the verb here see ch. iv. 21. " The Greek word is a metaphor borrowed from ships, which are carried with full sail, and signifieth a most certain persuasion of the truth."—*Leigh.* The certain persuasion

ought to be thoroughly borne in mind, that it is the first principle of a right conduct, that men should be dependent on the will of God, and never allow themselves to move even a finger, while the mind is doubtful and vacillating; for it cannot be otherwise, but that rashness will soon pass over into obstinacy when we dare to proceed further than what we are persuaded is lawful for us. If any object and say, that infirmity is ever perplexing, and that hence such certainty as Paul requires cannot exist in the weak: to this the plain answer is,—That such are to be pardoned, if they keep themselves within their own limits. For Paul's purpose was none other than to restrain undue liberty, by which it happens, that many thrust themselves, as it were, at random, into matters which are doubtful and undetermined. Hence Paul requires this to be adopted,—that the will of God is to preside over all our actions.

6. *He who regards a day,* &c. Since Paul well knew that a respect for days proceeded from ignorance of Christ, it is not probable that such a corruption was altogether defended by him; and yet his words seem to imply, that he who regarded days committed no sin; for nothing but good can be accepted by God. Hence, that you may understand his purpose, it is necessary to distinguish between the notion, which any one may have entertained as to the observance of days, and the observance itself to which he felt himself bound. The notion was indeed superstitious, nor does Paul deny this; for he has already condemned it by calling it infirmity, and he will again condemn it still more plainly. Now, that he who was held fast by this superstition, dared not to violate the solemnity of a particular day; this was approved by God, because he dared not to do any thing with a doubtful conscience. What indeed could the Jew do, who had not yet made such progress, as to be delivered from scruples about days? He had the word of God, in which the keeping of days was commended; there was a necessity laid on him by the law; and its abrogation was not clearly seen by him. Nothing then remained, but that

here refers to both parties—the eater and the abstainer: both were to do what they were fully convinced was agreeable to the will of God.—*Ed.*

he, waiting for a fuller revelation, should keep himself within the limits of his own knowledge, and not to avail himself of the benefit of liberty, before he embraced it by faith.[1]

The same also must be thought of him who refrained from unclean meats: for if he ate in a doubtful state of mind, it would not have been to receive any benefit from God's hand, but to lay his own hand on forbidden things. Let him then use other things, which he thinks is allowed to him, and follow the measure of his knowledge: he will thus give thanks to God; which he could not do, except he was persuaded that he is fed by God's kindness. He is not then to be despised, as though he offended the Lord by this his temperance and pious timidity: and there is nothing unreasonable in the matter, if we say, that the modesty of the weak is approved by God, not on the ground of merit, but through indulgence.

But as he had before required an assurance of mind, so that no one ought rashly of his own will to do this or that, we ought to consider whether he is here exhorting rather than affirming; for the text would better flow in this strain, —"Let a reason for what he does be clear to every one; as an account must be given before the celestial tribunal; for whether one eats meat or abstains, he ought in both instances to have regard to God." And doubtless there is nothing more fitted to restrain licentiousness in judging and to correct superstitions, than to be summoned before the tribunal of God: and hence Paul wisely sets the judge before all, to whose will they are to refer whatever they do. It is no objection that the sentence is affirmative; for he immediately subjoins, that no one lives or dies for himself; where he declares, not what men do, but commands what they ought to do.

Observe also what he says,—that we then eat to the Lord, or abstain, when we give thanks. Hence, eating is impure, and abstinence is impure, without thanksgiving. It is only

---

[1] It has been suggested as a question by some, whether the Christian Sabbath is included here? The very subject in hand proves that it is not. The subject discussed is the observance of *Jewish* days, as in Gal. iv. 10, and Col. ii. 16, and not what belonged to Christians in common.—*Ed.*

the name of God, when invoked, that sanctifies us and all we have.

7. For none of us liveth to himself, and no man dieth to himself.
8. For whether we live, we live unto the Lord; and whether we die, we die unto the Lord: whether we live therefore, or die, we are the Lord's.
9. For to this end Christ both died, and rose, and revived,[1] that he might be Lord both of the dead and living.

7. Nemo enim nostrum sibi ipsi vivit, et nemo sibi moritur.
8. Sive enim vivimus, Domino vivimus; sive morimur, Domino morimur: sive vivimus sive morimur, Domini sumus.
9. In hoc enim et mortuus est Christus, et resurrexit, et revixit,[1] ut vivis dominetur et mortuis.

7. *For no one of us*, &c. He now confirms the former verse by an argument derived from the whole to a part,—that it is no matter of wonder that particular acts of our life should be referred to the Lord's will, since life itself ought to be wholly spent to his glory; for then only is the life of a Christian rightly formed, when it has for its object the will of God. But if thou oughtest to refer whatever thou doest to his good pleasure, it is then an act of impiety to undertake anything whatever, which thou thinkest will displease him; nay, which thou art not persuaded will please him.

8. *To the Lord we live*, &c. This does not mean the same as when it is said in chap. vi. 11, that we are made *alive unto God* by his Spirit, but that we conform to his will and pleasure, and design all things to his glory. Nor are we only to live to the Lord, but also to die; that is, our death as well as our life is to be referred to his will. He adds the best of reasons, for *whether we live or die, we are his:* and it hence follows, that he has full authority over our life and our death.

The application of this doctrine opens into a wide field. God thus claims authority over life and death, that his own condition might be borne by every one as a yoke laid on him; for it is but just that he should assign to every one his station and his course of life. And thus we are not only

---

[1] The words, και ανέστη, are dismissed by *Griesbach* as spurious, and he substitutes έζησεν for ανέζησιν. The difference in meaning is none; only it comports with the style of the Apostle to add words of similar import for the sake of greater emphasis, as the case often is in the Prophets.—*Ed.*

forbidden rashly to attempt this or that without God's command, but we are also commanded to be patient under all troubles and losses. If at any time the flesh draws back in adversities, let it come to our minds, that he who is not free nor has authority over himself, perverts right and order if he depends not on the will of his lord. Thus also is taught us the rule by which we are to live and to die, so that if he extends our life in continual sorrows and miseries, we are not yet to seek to depart before our time; but if he should suddenly call us hence in the flower of our age, we ought ever to be ready for our departure.

9. *For to this end Christ also died*, &c. This is a confirmation of the reason which has been last mentioned; for in order to prove that we ought to live and to die to the Lord, he had said, that whether we live or die we are under the power of Christ. He now shows how rightly Christ claims this power over us, since he has obtained it by so great a price; for by undergoing death for our salvation, he has acquired authority over us which cannot be destroyed by death, and by rising again, he has received our whole life as his peculiar property. He has then by his death and resurrection deserved that we should, in death as well as in life, advance the glory of his name. The words *arose and lived again* mean, that by resurrection he attained a new state of life; and that as the life which he now possesses is subject to no change, his dominion over us is to be eternal.

10. But why dost thou judge thy brother?[1] or why dost thou set at nought thy brother? for we shall all stand before the judgment-seat of Christ:

11. For it is written, *As* I live, saith the Lord, every knee shall bow to me, and every tongue shall confess to God.

12. So then every one of us shall give account of himself to God.

13. Let us not therefore judge one

10. Tu verò quid judicas fratrem tuum? aut etiam tu, quid contemnis fratrem tuum? Omnes enim sistemur ad tribunal Christi:

11. Scriptum est enim, Vivo ego, dicit Dominus, mihi flectetur omne genu, et omnis lingua confitebitur Deo.

12. Unusquisque igitur de se rationem reddet Deo.

13. Quare ne ampliùs judicemus

---

[1] It appears from the order of the words σὺ δὲ, τί—, and ἢ καὶ σὺ, τί—, that the address was made to two parties, "But thou, *the weak*, why condemnest thou thy brother? and thou also, *the strong*, why dost thou despise thy brother?"—*Ed.*

another any more: but judge this rather, that no man put a stumblingblock, or an occasion to fall, in *his* brother's way.

alius alium: sed hoc judicate potiùs, ne lapsus occasio detur fratri aut offendiculum.

10. *But thou, why dost thou,* &c. As he had made the life and death of us all subject to Christ, he now proceeds to mention the authority to judge, which the Father has conferred on him, together with the dominion over heaven and earth. He hence concludes, that it is an unreasonable boldness in any one to assume the power to judge his brother, since by taking such a liberty he robs Christ the Lord of the power which he alone has received from the Father.

But first, by the term *brother*, he checks this lust for judging; for since the Lord has established among us the right of a fraternal alliance, an equality ought to be preserved; every one then who assumes the character of a judge acts unreasonably. Secondly, he calls us before the only true judge, from whom no one can take away his power, and whose tribunal none can escape. As then it would be absurd among men for a criminal, who ought to occupy a humble place in the court, to ascend the tribunal of the judge; so it is absurd for a Christian to take to himself the liberty of judging the conscience of his brother. A similar argument is mentioned by James, when he says, that "he who judges his brother, judges the law," and that "he who judges the law, is not an observer of the law but a president;" and, on the other hand, he says, that "there is but one lawgiver, who can save and destroy." (James iv. 12.) He has ascribed *tribunal* to Christ, which means his power to judge, as the voice of the archangel, by which we shall be summoned, is called, in another place, a trumpet; for it will pierce, as it were with its sound, into the minds and ears of all.[1]

11. *As I live,* &c. He seems to me to have quoted this testimony of the Prophet, not so much to prove what he had said of the judgment-seat of Christ, which was not doubted

---

[1] The words "We shall all stand," &c., may be rendered, "We must all stand," &c. It is indeed the future tense, but this is according to what is often the case in Hebrew, for in that language the future has frequently this meaning. The 12th verse may be rendered in the same manner, "So then every one of us must give account of himself to God." —*Ed.*

among Christians, as to show that judgment ought to be looked for by all with the greatest humility and lowliness of mind; and this is what the words import. He had first then testified by his own words, that the power to judge all men is vested in Christ alone; he now demonstrates by the words of the Prophet, that all flesh ought to be humbled while expecting that judgment; and this is expressed by the bending of the knee. But though in this passage of the Prophet the Lord in general foreshows that his glory should be known among all nations, and that his majesty should everywhere shine forth, which was then hid among very few, and as it were in an obscure corner of the world; yet if we examine it more closely, it will be evident that its complete fulfilment is not now taking place, nor has it ever taken place, nor is it to be hoped for in future ages. God does not now rule otherwise in the world than by his gospel; nor is his majesty otherwise rightly honoured but when it is adored as known from his word. But the word of God has ever had its enemies, who have been perversely resisting it, and its despisers, who have ever treated it with ridicule, as though it were absurd and fabulous. Even at this day there are many such, and ever will be. It hence appears, that this prophecy is indeed begun to be fulfilled in this life, but is far from being completed, and will not be so until the day of the last resurrection shall shine forth, when Christ's enemies shall be laid prostrate, that they may become his footstool. But this cannot be except the Lord shall ascend his tribunal: he has therefore suitably applied this testimony to the judgment-seat of Christ.

This is also a remarkable passage for the purpose of confirming our faith in the eternal divinity of Christ: for it is God who speaks here, and the God who has once for all declared, that he will not give his glory to another. (Is. xlii. 8.) Now if what he claims here to himself alone is accomplished in Christ, then doubtless he in Christ manifests himself. And unquestionably the truth of this prophecy then openly appeared, when Christ gathered a people to himself from the whole world, and restored them to the worship of his majesty and to the obedience of his gospel. To this purpose are the words of Paul, when he says that God gave a name to his Christ, at which every knee should bow, (Phil. ii. 10:) and it shall then still more fully appear, when he shall ascend his tribunal to judge the living and the dead; for all judgment in heaven and on earth has been given to him by the Father.

The words of the Prophet are, "Every tongue shall swear to me:" but as an oath is a kind of divine worship, the word which Paul uses, *shall confess*, does not vary in sense:[1] for the Lord intended simply to declare, that all men should not only acknowledge his majesty, but also make a confession of obedience, both by the mouth and by the external gesture of the body, which he has designated by the bowing of the knee.

12. *Every one of us*, &c. This conclusion invites us to humility and lowliness of mind: and hence he immediately draws this inference,—that *we are not to judge one another;* for it is not lawful for us to usurp the office of judging, who must ourselves submit to be judged and to give an account.

From the various significations of the word to *judge*, he has aptly drawn two different meanings. In the first place he forbids us to judge, that is, to condemn; in the second place he bids us to judge, that is, to exercise judgment, so as not to give offence. He indeed indirectly reproves those malignant censors, who employ all their acuteness in finding out something faulty in the life of their brethren: he therefore bids them to exercise wariness themselves; for by their neglect they often precipitate, or drive their brethren against some stumblingblock or another.[2]

---

[1] The passage is from Isaiah xlv. 23. In two instances the Apostle gives the sense, and not the words. Instead of "by myself have I sworn," he gives the form of the oath, "*As* I live." This is the manner in which God swears by himself, it is by his life—his eternal existence. Then the conclusion of the verse in Hebrew is, "every tongue shall swear," that is, "unto me." To swear to God or by his name is to avow allegiance to him, to profess or to confess his name. See Ps. xliii. 11; Is. lxviii. 1; Zeph. i. 5. The Apostle therefore does no more than interpret the Hebrew idiom when he says, "every tongue shall confess to God."—*Ed.*

[2] The two words, πρόσκομμα and σκάνδαλον, mean nearly the same thing, but with this difference, that the first seems to be an hinderance or an obstacle which occasions stumbling or falling, and the other is an obstacle which stops or impedes progress in the way. See Matt. xvi. 23. The

14. I know, and am persuaded by the Lord Jesus,[1] that *there is* nothing unclean of itself: but to him that esteemeth any thing to be unclean, to him *it is* unclean.	14. Novi et persuasus sum in Domino Iesu, nihil commune per se esse; nisi qui existimat aliquid esse commune, ei commune est.
15. But if thy brother be grieved with *thy* meat, now walkest thou not charitably. Destroy not him with thy meat for whom Christ died.	15. Verùm si propter cibum frater tuus contristatur, jam non secundum charitatem ambulas; ne cibo tuo illum perdas, pro quo Christus mortuus est.
16. Let not then your good be evil spoken of:	16. Ne vestrum igitur bonum hominum maledicentiæ sit obnoxium:
17. For the kingdom of God is not meat and drink; but righteousness, and peace, and joy in the Holy Ghost.	17. Non enim est regnum Dei esca et potus; sed justitia, et pax, et gaudium in Spiritu sancto.
18. For he that in these things serveth Christ *is* acceptable to God, and approved of men.	18. Qui enim servit per hæc Christo, acceptus est Deo, et probatus hominibus.

14. *I know*, &c. To anticipate their objection, who made such progress in the gospel of Christ as to make no distinction between meats, he first shows what must be thought of meats when viewed in themselves; and then he subjoins how sin is committed in the use of them. He then declares, that no meat is impure to a right and pure conscience, and that there is no hinderance to a pure use of meats, except ignorance and infirmity; for when any imagines an impurity in them, he is not at liberty to use them. But he afterwards adds, that we are not only to regard meats themselves, but also the brethren before whom we eat: for we ought not to view the use of God's bounty with so much indifference as to disregard love. His words then have the same meaning as though he had said,—" I know that all

two parties, the strong and the weak, are here evidently addressed; the former was not, by eating, to put a stumblingblock in the way of the weak brother; nor was the weak, by condemning, to be a hinderance or impediment in the way of the strong so as to prevent him to advance in his course. Thus we see that forbearance is enjoined on both parties, though the Apostle afterwards dwells more on what the strong was to do.

The clause might be thus rendered,—

" But rather judge it right to do this,—not to lay before a brother a stumbling-stone, or an impediment."—*Ed.*

[1] " At the very time of giving forth the sentence, and on the highest of all authority, that there is nothing unclean of itself, he yet leaves others at liberty to esteem anything unclean. We are not sure if anywhere else in Scripture, the divine authority of toleration is so clearly manifested."— *Chalmers.*

meats are clean, and therefore I leave to thee the free use of them ; I allow thy conscience to be freed from all scruples: in short, I do not simply restrain thee from meats; but laying aside all regard for them, I still wish thee not to neglect thy neighbour."

By the word *common*, in this place, he means unclean, and what is taken indiscriminately by the ungodly ; and it is opposed to those things which had been especially set apart for the use of the faithful people. He says that he knew, and was fully convinced, that all meats are pure, in order to remove all doubts. He adds, *in the Lord Jesus;* for by his favour and grace it is, that all the creatures which were accursed in Adam, are blessed to us by the Lord.[1] He intended, however, at the same time, to set the liberty given by Christ in opposition to the bondage of the law, lest they thought that they were bound to observe those rites from which Christ had made them free. By the exception which he has laid down, we learn that there is nothing so pure but what may be contaminated by a corrupt conscience : for it is faith alone and godliness which sanctify all things to us. The unbelieving, being polluted within, defile all things by their very touch. (Tit. i. 15.)

15. *But if through meat thy brother is grieved*, &c. He now explains how the offending of our brethren may vitiate the use of good things. And the first thing is,—that love is violated, when our brother is made to grieve by what is so trifling ; for it is contrary to love to occasion grief to any one. The next thing is,—that when the weak conscience is wounded, the price of Christ's blood is wasted ; for the most abject brother has been redeemed by the blood of Christ : it is then a heinous crime to destroy him by gratifying the stomach ; and we must be basely given up to our own lusts, if we prefer meat, a worthless thing, to Christ.[2] The third

[1] To elicit this meaning, which is in itself true, *Calvin* must have construed the sentence thus, " I know, and I am persuaded, that through the Lord Jesus nothing is of itself unclean:" but this is not the meaning. What the Apostle says is, that he knew, and was fully assured by the Lord Jesus, that is, by the teaching of his word and Spirit, that nothing was in itself unclean, all ceremonial distinctions having been now removed and abolished.—*Ed.*

[2] From the words " destroy not," &c., some have deduced the senti-

reason is,—that since the liberty attained for us by Christ is a blessing, we ought to take care, lest it should be evil spoken of by men and justly blamed, which is the case, when we unseasonably use God's gifts. These reasons then ought to influence us, lest by using our liberty, we thoughtlessly cause offences.[1]

17. *For the kingdom of God*, &c. He now, on the other hand, teaches us, that we can without loss abstain from the use of our liberty, because the kingdom of God does not consist in such things. Those things indeed, which are necessary either to build up or preserve the kingdom of God, are by no means to be neglected, whatever offences may hence follow: but if for love's sake it be lawful to abstain from meat, while God's honour is uninjured, while Christ's kingdom suffers no harm, while religion is not hindered, then they are not to be borne with, who for meat's sake disturb the Church. He uses similar arguments in his first Epistle to the Corinthians: "Meat," he says, "for the stomach, and the stomach for meat; but God will destroy both," (1 Cor. vi. 13:) again, "If we eat, we shall not abound," (1 Cor. viii. 8.) By these words he meant briefly to show, that meat and drink were things too worthless,

ment, that those for whom Christ died may perish for ever. It is neither wise nor just to draw a conclusion of this kind; for it is one that is negatived by many positive declarations of Scripture. Man's inference, when contrary to God's word, cannot be right. Besides, the Apostle's object in this passage is clearly this,—to exhibit the *sin* of those who disregarded the good of their brother, and to show what that sin was *calculated* to do, without saying that it actually effected that evil. Some have very unwisely attempted to obviate the inference above mentioned, by suggesting, that the destruction meant was that of comfort and edification. But no doubt the Apostle meant the ruin of the soul; hence the urgency of his exhortation,—" Do not act in such a way as tends to endanger the safety of a soul for whom Christ has shed his blood ;" or, " Destroy not," that is, as far as you can do so. Apostles and ministers are said to " save" men; some are exhorted here not to "destroy" them. Neither of these effects can follow, except in the first instance, God grants his blessing, and in the second his permission; and his permission as to his people he will never grant, as he has expressly told us. See John x. 27-29.—*Ed.*

[1] " Vestrum bonum," ὑμῶν τὸ ἀγαθόν. Some, such as *Grotius* and *Hammond*, *Scott*, *Chalmers*, &c., agree with *Calvin*, and view this "good," or privilege, to be Christian liberty, or freedom from ceremonial observances, (see 1 Cor. x. 29:) but *Origen*, *Ambrose*, *Theodoret*, *Mede*, &c., consider that the gospel is meant. The first opinion is the most suitable to the passage.—*Ed.*

that on their account the course of the gospel should be impeded.

But righteousness and peace, &c. He, in passing, has set these in opposition to meat and drink; not for the purpose of enumerating all the things which constitute the kingdom of Christ, but of showing, that it consists of spiritual things. He has at the same time no doubt included in few words a summary of what it is ; namely, that we, being well assured, have peace with God, and possess real joy of heart through the Holy Spirit dwelling in us. But as I have said, these few things he has accommodated to his present subject. He indeed who is become partaker of true righteousness, enjoys a great and an invaluable good, even a calm joy of conscience ; and he who has peace with God, what can he desire more?[1]

By connecting *peace* and *joy* together, he seems to me to express the character of this joy ; for however torpid the reprobate may be, or however they may elevate themselves, yet the conscience is not rendered calm and joyful, except when it feels God to be pacified and propitious to it ; and there is no solid joy but what proceeds from this peace. And though it was necessary, when mention was made of these things, that the Spirit should have been declared as the author ; yet he meant in this place indirectly to oppose the Spirit to external things, that we might know, that the things which belong to the kingdom of God continue complete to us without the use of meats.

[1] What is here said is no doubt true of the kingdom of God; but by considering what is afterwards said in the two following verses, we cannot well accede to this exposition. Righteousness, peace, and joy, mentioned here, are things acceptable to God and *approved by men*: they must then be things apparent and visible, which men see and observe; and to follow " the things of peace," refers to the conduct. " Righteousness" then must mean here the doing of what is right and just towards one another; "peace," concord and unanimity, as opposed to discord and contentions; "joy," the fruit of this peaceable state, a cheering delight, a mutual rejoicing, instead of the sorrow and grief occasioned by discord; and these come " through the Holy Spirit" and are produced by him; and they are not the semblances of such virtues and graces, presented in some instances by false religions. See Gal. v. 22, 23. *Doddridge, Stuart,* and *Chalmers* have viewed the passage in this light, though the latter, as well as *Scott,* seemed inclined to combine the two views: but this is to mix up things together unnecessarily, and to destroy the harmony of the context.—*Ed.*

18. *For he who in these things,* &c. An argument drawn from the effect : for it is impossible, but that when any one is acceptable to God and approved by men, the kingdom of God fully prevails and flourishes in him : he, who with a quiet and peaceful conscience serves Christ in righteousness, renders himself approved by men as well as by God. Wherever then there is righteousness and peace and spiritual joy, there the kingdom of God is complete in all its parts : it does not then consist of material things. But he says, that man is acceptable to God, because he obeys his will; he testifies that he is approved by men, because they cannot do otherwise than bear testimony to that excellency which they see with their eyes : not that the ungodly always favour the children of God ; nay, when there is no cause, they often pour forth against them many reproaches, and with forged calumnies defame the innocent, and in a word, turn into vices things rightly done, by putting on them a malignant construction. But Paul speaks here of honest judgment, blended with no moroseness, no hatred, no superstition.

19. Let us therefore follow after the things which make for peace, and things wherewith one may edify another.	19 Proinde quæ pacis sunt, et ædificationis mutuæ, sectemur.
20. For meat destroy not the work of God. All things indeed *are* pure; but *it is* evil for that man who eateth with offence.	20. Ne propter cibum destruas opus Dei. Omnia quidem pura, sed malum est homini qui per offensionem vescitur.
21. *It is* good neither to eat flesh, nor to drink wine, nor *any thing* whereby thy brother stumbleth, or is offended, or is made weak.	21. Bonum est non edere carnem, nec vinum bibere,[1] nec *aliud facere* in quo frater tuus concidat, vel offendatur, vel infirmetur.

19. *Let us then follow,* &c. He recalls us, as much as possible, from a mere regard to meats, to consider those greater things which ought to have the first place in all our actions, and so to have the precedence. We must indeed eat, that we may live ; we ought to live, that we may serve the Lord; and he serves the Lord, who by benevolence and kindness edifies his neighbour ; for in order to promote these two

[1] *Jerome* often employed the former part of this verse for the purpose of encouraging monasticism ; and by thus disconnecting it from the context, he got a passage quite suitable to his purpose. Even *Erasmus* condemned this shameful perversion.—*Ed.*

things, concord and edification, all the duties of love ought to be exercised. Lest this should be thought of little moment, he repeats the sentence he had before announced,—that corruptible meat is not of such consequence that for its sake the Lord's building should be destroyed. For wherever there is even a spark of godliness, there the work of God is to be seen; which they demolish, who by their unfeeling conduct disturb the conscience of the weak.

But it must be noticed, that edification is joined to peace; because some, not unfrequently, too freely indulge one another, so that they do much harm by their compliances. Hence in endeavouring to serve one another, discretion ought to be exercised, and utility regarded, so that we may willingly grant to our brother whatever may be useful to further his salvation. So Paul reminds us in another place: "All things," he says, "are lawful to me; but all things are not expedient;" and immediately he adds the reason, "Because all things do not edify." (1 Cor. x. 23.)

Nor is it also in vain that he repeats again, *For meat destroy not*,[1] &c., intimating, that he required no abstinence, by which there would be, according to what he had said before, any loss to piety: though we eat not anything we please, but abstain from the use of meats for the sake of our brethren; yet the kingdom of God continues entire and complete.

20. *All things are indeed pure*, &c. By saying, that all things are pure, he makes a general declaration; and by adding, that it is evil for man to eat with offence, he makes an exception; as though he had said,—"Meat is indeed good, but to give offence is bad." Now meat has been given to us, that we may eat it, provided love be observed: he then pollutes the use of pure meat, who by it violates love. Hence he concludes, that it is good to abstain from all things which tend to give offence to our brethren.

[1] This is a similar, but not the same sentence as in verse 15. The verb is different, καταλυι; which means to undo, to loosen, to pull down: and as "work" follows, which, as *Calvin* and others think, is to be understood of God's building, the work of edifying or building up his people, the verb may in this sense be rendered here, "Pull not down the work of God." But here, as in verse 15, it is the *tendency* of the deed that is to be considered, and the effect as far as man's doing was concerned. The Apostle says nothing of what God would do.—*Ed.*

He mentions three things in order, *to fall, to stumble, to be weakened:* the meaning seems to be this,—" Let no cause of falling, no, nor of stumbling, no, nor of weakening, be given to the brethren." For to be weakened is less than to stumble, and to stumble is less than to fall. He may be said to be weakened whose conscience wavers with doubt,—to stumble when the conscience is disturbed by some greater perplexity, and to fall when the individual is in a manner alienated from his attention to religion.[1]

22. Hast thou faith? have *it* to thyself before God. Happy *is* he that condemneth not himself in that thing which he alloweth.
23. And he that doubteth is damned if he eat, because *he eateth* not of faith: for whatsoever *is* not of faith is sin.

22. Tu fidem habes? apud teipsum habe coram Deo. Beatus qui non judicat seipsum in eo quod examinat.
13. Qui verò dijudicat si comederit condemnatus est; quia non ex fide: quicquid verò non est ex fide, peccatum est.

22. *Hast thou faith?* In order to conclude, he shows in what consists the advantage of Christian liberty: it hence appears, that they boast falsely of liberty who know not how to make a right use of it. He then says, that liberty really understood, as it is that of faith, has properly a regard to God; so that he who is endued with a conviction of this kind, ought to be satisfied with peace of conscience before God; nor is it needful for him to show before men that he possesses it. It hence follows, that if we offend our weak brethren by eating meats, it is through a perverse opinion; for there is no necessity to constrain us.

It is also plainly evident how strangely perverted is this passage by some, who hence conclude, that it is not material how devoted any one may be to the observance of foolish and superstitious ceremonies, provided the conscience remains pure before God. Paul indeed intended nothing less,

---

[1] What is said here proves what is stated in a note on verse 13; that is, that σκάνδαλον is a less evil than πρόσκομμα, only that the idea of stumbling, instead of hinderance or impediment, is given here to the former word. The Apostle still adopts, as it were, the ascending scale. He first mentions the most obvious effect, the actual fall, the extreme evil, and then the next to it, the obstacle in the way; and, in the third place, the weakening of the faith of the individual. The real order of the process is the reverse,—the weakening, then the impediment, and, lastly, the stumblingblock which occasions the fall.—*Ed.*

as the context clearly shows; for ceremonies are appointed for the worship of God, and they are also a part of our confession: they then who tear off faith from confession, take away from the sun its own heat. But Paul handles nothing of this kind in this place, but only speaks of our liberty in the use of meat and drink.

Happy is he who condemns not himself, &c. Here he means to teach us, first, how we may lawfully use the gifts of God; and, secondly, how great an impediment ignorance is; and he thus teaches us, lest we should urge the uninstructed beyond the limits of their infirmity. But he lays down a general truth, which extends to all actions,— "Happy," he says, "is he who is not conscious of doing wrong, when he rightly examines his own deeds." For it happens, that many commit the worst of crimes without any scruple of conscience; but this happens, because they rashly abandon themselves, with closed eyes, to any course to which the blind and violent intemperance of the flesh may lead them; for there is much difference between insensibility and a right judgment. He then who examines things is happy, provided he is not bitten by an accusing conscience, after having honestly considered and weighed matters; for this assurance alone can render our works pleasing to God. Thus is removed that vain excuse which many allege on the ground of ignorance; inasmuch as their error is connected with insensibility and sloth: for if what they call good intention is sufficient, their examination, according to which the Spirit of God estimates the deeds of men, is superfluous.[1]

23. *But he who is undecided,* &c. He very fitly expresses

[1] The version of *Calvin* is, " Beatus qui non judicat seipsum in eo quod examinat," μακάριος ὁ μὴ κρίνων ἑαυτὸν ἐν ᾧ δοκιμάζει; the latter part is rendered by *Beza* and *Piscator,* " in eo quod approbat—in that which he approves;" by *Doddridge,* " in the thing which he alloweth;" by *Macknight,* " by what he approveth." The reference is no doubt to the strong, who had " faith," who believed all meats lawful. The verb means to try, to examine, as well as to approve; but the latter seems to be its meaning here. To approve and to have faith appears in this case to be the same: then to have faith and not to abuse it by giving offence to a brother was to be a happy man, who did not condemn himself. The meaning then most suitable to the passage is this, " Happy the man! who condemns not himself by what he approves," that is, by eating meat to the annoyance and stumbling of the weak.—*Ed.*

in one word the character of that mind which vacillates and is uncertain as to what ought to be done; for he who is undecided undergoes alternate changes, and in the midst of his various deliberations is held suspended by uncertainty. As then the main thing in a good work is the persuasion of a mind conscious of being right before God, and as it were a calm assurance, nothing is more opposed to the acceptance of our works than vacillation.[1] And, oh! that this truth were fixed in the minds of men, that nothing ought to be attempted except what the mind feels assured is acceptable to God, men would not then make such an uproar, as they often do now, nor waver, nor blindly hurry onward wherever their own imagination may lead them. For if our way of living is to be confined to this moderation, that no one is to touch a morsel of meat with a doubting conscience, how much greater caution is to be exercised in the greatest things?

And whatever is not from faith, &c. The reason for this condemnation is, that every work, however splendid and excellent in appearance, is counted as sin, except it be founded on a right conscience; for God regards not the outward display, but the inward obedience of the heart, by this alone is an estimate made of our works. Besides, how can that be obedience, when any one undertakes what he is not persuaded is approved by God? Where then such a doubt exists, the individual is justly charged with prevarication; for he proceeds in opposition to the testimony of his own conscience.

---

[1] The Greek is ὁ διακρινόμενος, "he who discerns," that is, a difference as to meats; so *Doddridge*, *Macknight*, and *Chalmers* regard its meaning. *Beza* has "qui dubitat—who doubts," and so our version. The word used by *Calvin* is *dijudicat*, which properly means to judge between things, to discern, but according to his explanation it means to judge in two ways, to be undecided.

The verb no doubt admits of these two meanings; it is used evidently in the sense of making or putting a difference, but only, as some say, in the active voice. There are indeed two places where it seems to have this meaning in its passive or middle form, James ii. 4, and Jude verse 22. But as Paul has before used it in this Epistle, chap. iv. 20, in the sense of hesitating, staggering, or doubting, we may reasonably suppose that it has this meaning here, and especially as in every place where he expresses the other idea, he has employed the active form. See 1 Cor. iv. 7; xi. 29, 31; &c. —*Ed.*

The word *faith* is to be taken here for a fixed persuasion of the mind, or, so to speak, for a firm assurance, and not that of any kind, but what is derived from the truth of God. Hence doubt or uncertainty vitiates all our actions, however specious they may otherwise be. Now, since a pious mind can never acquiesce with certainty in anything but the word of God, all fictitious modes of worship do in this case vanish away, and whatever works there may be which originate in the brains of men; for while everything which is not from faith is condemned, rejected is whatever is not supported and approved by God's word. It is at the same time by no means sufficient that what we do is approved by the word of God, except the mind, relying on this persuasion, prepares itself cheerfully to do its work. Hence the first thing in a right conduct, in order that our minds may at no time fluctuate, is this, that we, depending on God's word, confidently proceed wherever it may call us.

CHAPTER XV.[1]

1. We then that are strong ought to bear the infirmities of the weak, and not to please ourselves.

2. Let every one of us please *his* neighbour for *his* good to edification.

3. For even Christ pleased not himself; but, as it is written, The reproaches of them that reproached thee fell on me.

1. Debemus autem nos qui potentes sumus, infirmitates impotentium portare, et non placere nobis ipsis:

2. Unusquisque enim nostrum proximo placeat in bonum, ad ædificationem.

3. Etenim Christus non placuit sibi ipsi; sed quemadmodum scriptum est, Opprobria exprobrantium tibi, ceciderunt super me.

1. *We then who are strong*, &c. Lest they who had made more advances than others in the knowledge of God should

---

[1] Introduced here, as the conclusion of the last chapter, by *Griesbach* and other collators of MSS., are the three last verses of the Epistle, 25-27. It appears that the largest number of copies is in favour of this arrangement, countenanced by the Greek fathers, and the Syriac and Arabic versions. In favour of the present order, as in our version, there are some good MSS., the Latin fathers, and the Vulgate, &c. What strongly favours and decidedly confirms the order which we have, is the evident connection as to matter between this and the last chapter, which shows the impropriety of having those verses intervening between them.—*Ed.*

think it unreasonable, that more burden was to be laid on them than on others, he shows for what purpose this strength, by which they excelled others, was bestowed on them, even that they might so sustain the weak as to prevent them to fall. For as God has destined those to whom he has granted superior knowledge to convey instruction to the ignorant, so to those whom he makes strong he commits the duty of supporting the weak by their strength; thus ought all gifts to be communicated among all the members of Christ. The stronger then any one is in Christ, the more bound he is to bear with the weak.[1]

By saying that a Christian ought not to *please* himself, he intimates, that he ought not to be bent on satisfying himself, as they are wont to be, who are content with their own judgment, and heedlessly neglect others: and this is indeed an admonition most suitable on the present subject; for nothing impedes and checks acts of kindness more than when any one is too much swallowed up with himself, so that he has no care for others, and follows only his own counsels and feelings.

2. *Let indeed*[2] *every one of us*, &c. He teaches us here, that we are under obligations to others, and that it is therefore our duty to please and to serve them, and that there is no exception in which we ought not to accommodate ourselves to our brethren when we can do so, according to God's word, to their edification.

There are here two things laid down,—that we are not to be content with our own judgment, nor acquiesce in our own desires, but ought to strive and labour at all times to please our brethren,—and then, that in endeavouring to accommodate

---

[1] The word for "strong" is δυνατοὶ, "able," which *Calvin* renders *potentes*, powerful, or able. They were the more advanced in knowledge and in piety. They were to "bear," βαστάζειν, in the sense of carrying or sustaining the infirmities of the weak, *impotentium*, "the unable," ἀδυνάτων, such as were unable to carry their own burdens. The duty is not merely to bear with or tolerate weaknesses, (for this is not the meaning of the verb,) but to help and assist the weak and the feeble to carry them. The most literal rendering is—

"We then who are able ought to bear (or carry) the infirmities of the unable."—*Ed.*

[2] The γὰρ in this verse is considered by *Griesbach* as wholly spurious; and *Beza* has left it out.—*Ed.*

ourselves to our brethren, we ought to have regard to God, so that our object may be their edification; for the greater part cannot be pleased except you indulge their humour; so that if you wish to be in favour with most men, their salvation must not be so much regarded, but their folly must be flattered; nor must you look to what is expedient, but to what they seek to their own ruin. You must not then strive to please those to whom nothing is pleasing but evil.

3. *For even Christ pleased not himself,* &c. Since it is not right that a servant should refuse what his lord has himself undertaken, it would be very strange in us to wish an exemption from the duty of bearing the infirmities of others, to which Christ, in whom we glory as our Lord and King, submitted himself; for he having no regard for himself, gave up himself wholly to this service. For in him was really verified what the Prophet declares in Ps. lxix. 10: and among other things he mentions this, that "zeal for God's house had eaten him up," and that "the reproaches of those who reproached God fell on him." By these words it is intimated, that he burned with so much fervour for God's glory that he was possessed by such a desire to promote his kingdom, that he forgot himself, and was, as it were, absorbed with this one thought, and that he so devoted himself to the Lord that he was grieved in his soul whenever he perceived his holy name exposed to the slandering of the ungodly.[1]

The second part, "the reproaches of God," may indeed be understood in two ways,—either that he was not less affected by the contumelies which were heaped on God, than if he himself had endured them,—or, that he grieved not otherwise to see the wrong done to God, than if he himself had been the cause. But if Christ reigns in us, as he must necessarily reign in his people, this feeling is also vigorous in our hearts, so that whatever derogates from the glory of God

---

[1] The intention of producing Christ's example here is to enjoin disinterestedness. He denied himself for the sake of glorifying God in the salvation of men: so his followers ought to show the same spirit; they ought to inconvenience themselves, and undergo toil, trouble, suffering, and reproaches, if necessary, in order to help and assist their fellow-Christians.—*Ed.*

does not otherwise grieve us than if it was done to ourselves. Away then with those whose highest wish is to gain honours from them who treat God's name with all kinds of reproaches, tread Christ under foot, contumeliously rend, and with the sword and the flame persecute his gospel. It is not indeed safe to be so much honoured by those by whom Christ is not only despised but also reproachfully treated.

4. For whatsoever things were written aforetime were written for our learning; that we, through patience and comfort of the scriptures, might have hope.	4. Quæcunque enim antè scripta sunt, in nostram doctrinam sunt scripta, ut per patientiam et consolationem Scripturarum spem habeamus.
5. Now the God of patience and consolation grant you to be like minded one toward another, according to Christ Jesus;	5. Deus autem patientiæ et consolationis det vobis idem mutuò cogitare secundum Christum Iesum;
6. That ye may with one mind *and* one mouth glorify God, even the Father of our Lord Jesus Christ.	6. Ut uno animo, uno ore, glorificetis Deum et Patrem Domini nostri Iesu Christi.

4. *For whatsoever things*, &c. This is an application of the example, lest any one should think, that to exhort us to imitate Christ was foreign to his purpose ; "Nay," he says, "there is nothing in Scripture which is not useful for your instruction, and for the direction of your life."[1]

This is an interesting passage, by which we understand that there is nothing vain and unprofitable contained in the oracles of God ; and we are at the same time taught that it is by the reading of the Scripture that we make progress in piety and holiness of life. Whatever then is delivered in Scripture we ought to strive to learn ; for it were a reproach offered to the Holy Spirit to think, that he has taught anything which it does not concern us to know; let us also know, that whatever is taught us conduces to the advancement of religion. And though he speaks of the Old Testament, the same thing is also true of the writings of the Apostles ; for since the Spirit of Christ is everywhere like itself, there is no doubt but that he has adapted his teaching

---

[1] "The object of this verse is not so much to show the propriety of applying the passage quoted from the Psalms to Christ, as to show that the facts recorded in the Scriptures are designed for our instruction."— *Hodge.*

by the Apostles, as formerly by the Prophets, to the edification of his people. Moreover, we find here a most striking condemnation of those fanatics who vaunt that the Old Testament is abolished, and that it belongs not in any degree to Christians; for with what front can they turn away Christians from those things which, as Paul testifies, have been appointed by God for their salvation?

But when he adds, *that through the patience and the consolation of the Scriptures we might have hope*,[1] he does not include the whole of that benefit which is to be derived from God's word; but he briefly points out the main end; for the Scriptures are especially serviceable for this purpose—to raise up those who are prepared by patience, and strengthened by consolations, to the hope of eternal life, and to keep them in the contemplation of it.[2] The word *consolation* some render exhortation; and of this I do not disapprove, only that consolation is more suitable to patience, for this arises from it; because then only we are prepared to bear adversities with patience, when God blends them with consolation. The patience of the faithful is not indeed that hardihood which philosophers recommend, but that meekness, by which we willingly submit to God, while a taste of his goodness and paternal love renders all things sweet to us: this nourishes and sustains hope in us, so that it fails not.

5. *And the God of patience*, &c. God is so called from what he produces; the same thing has been before very fitly ascribed to the Scriptures, but in a different sense: God alone is doubtless the author of patience and of consolation; for he conveys both to our hearts by his Spirit: yet he em-

---

[1] Or, That we might possess, enjoy, or retain hope. He does not describe this hope, it being sufficiently evident—the hope of the gospel.—*Ed.*

[2] Some take "patience" apart from "consolation,"—"through patience, and the consolation of the Scriptures;" but what is evidently meant is the patience and consolation which the Scriptures teach and administer, or are the means of supplying; for it is the special object of the passage to show the benefits derived from the Scriptures. Then it is no doubt "consolation," and not exhortation, though the word has also that meaning; for in the next verse it clearly means consolation. It is thus rendered, and in connection with "patience," by *Beza, Pareus, Doddridge, Macknight*, &c.

In our version it is "comfort" in ver. 4, and "consolation" in ver. 5; but it would have been better to have retained the same word.—*Ed.*

ploys his word as the instrument; for he first teaches us what is true consolation, and what is true patience; and then he instils and plants this doctrine in our hearts.

But after having admonished and exhorted the Romans as to what they were to do, he turns to pray for them: for he fully understood, that to speak of duty was to no purpose, except God inwardly effected by his Spirit what he spoke by the mouth of man. The sum of his prayer is,—that he would bring their minds to real unanimity, and make them united among themselves: he also shows at the same time what is the bond of unity, for he wished them to agree together *according to Christ Jesus.* Miserable indeed is the union which is unconnected with God, and that is unconnected with him, which alienates us from his truth.[1]

And that he might recommend to us an agreement in Christ, he teaches us how necessary it is: for God is not truly glorified by us, unless the hearts of all agree in giving him praise, and their tongues also join in harmony. There is then no reason for any to boast that he will give glory to God after his own manner; for the unity of his servants is

[1] There is a difference of opinion as to the unity contemplated here, whether it be that of sentiment or of feeling. The phrase, τὸ αὐτὸ φρονεῖν, occurs in the following places, Rom. xii. 16; xv. 5; 2 Cor. xiii. 11; Phil. ii. 2; iii. 16; iv. 2. *Leigh* says, that the phrase signifies to be of *one mind,* of *one judgment,* of *one affection,* towards one another. But though the verb φρονεῖν may admit of these three significations, yet the Apostle no doubt had in view a specific idea; and when we consider that he had been inculcating the principle of toleration as to unity of sentiment with regard to the eating of meats and of observing of days, and that he has been enforcing the duty of forbearance, and of sympathy, and of love towards each other, it appears probable that unity of feeling and of concern for each other's welfare is what is intended here. *Beza, Scott,* and *Chalmers* take this view, while *Pareus, Mede,* and *Stuart* take the other, that is, that unity of sentiment is what is meant.

What confirms the former, in addition to the general import of the context, is the clause which follows, "according to Christ Jesus," which evidently means, "according to his example," as mentioned in ver. 3.

Then in the next verse, the word ὁμοθυμαδὸν refers to the unity of feeling and of action, rather than to that of sentiment. It occurs, besides here, in these places, Acts i. 14; ii. 1, 46; iv. 24; v. 12; vii. 57; viii. 6; xii. 20; xv. 25; xviii. 12; xix. 29. It is used by the *Septuagint* for יַחַד, which means "together." It is rendered "unanimiter—unanimously," or, with one mind, by *Erasmus;* "concorditer—with one accord," by *Beza;* "with one mind," by *Doddridge;* and "unanimously," by *Macknight.* It is thus paraphrased by *Grotius,* "with a mind full of mutual love, free from contempt, free from hatred."—*Ed.*

so much esteemed by God, that he will not have his glory sounded forth amidst discords and contentions. This one thought ought to be sufficient to check the wanton rage for contention and quarrelling, which at this day too much possesses the minds of many.

7. Wherefore receive ye one another, as Christ also received us to the glory of God.
8. Now I say, that Jesus Christ was a minister of the circumcision for the truth of God, to confirm the promises *made* unto the fathers:
9. And that the Gentiles might glorify God for *his* mercy; as it is written, For this cause I will confess to thee among the Gentiles, and sing unto thy name.
10. And again he saith, Rejoice, ye Gentiles, with his people.
11. And again, Praise the Lord, all ye Gentiles; and laud him, all ye people.
12. And again, Esaias saith, There shall be a root of Jesse, and he that shall rise to reign over the Gentiles; in him shall the Gentiles trust.

7. Itaque suscipite vos mutuò, quemadmodum Christus vos suscepit, in gloriam Dei.
8. Dico autem Iesum Christum ministerium fuisse circumcisionis super veritate Dei ad promissiones Patrum confirmandas:
9. Gentes autem pro misericordia glorificare debent Deum; quemadmodum scriptum est, Propter hoc confitebor tibi inter Gentes et nomini tuo psallam:
10. Et rursum dicit, Exultate Gentes cum populo ejus;
11. Et rursum, Laudate Dominum omnes Gentes, et collaudate eum omnes populi.
12. Et rursum Iesaias dicit, Erit radix Jesse, et qui exurget ad imperandum Gentibus; in ipso Gentes sperabunt.

7. *Receive ye then*, &c. He returns to exhortation; and to strengthen this he still retains the example of Christ. For he, having received, not one or two of us, but all together, has thus connected us, so that we ought to cherish one another, if we would indeed continue in his bosom. Only thus then shall we confirm our calling, that is, if we separate not ourselves from those whom the Lord has bound together.

The words, *to the glory of God*, may be applied to us only, or to Christ, or to him and us together: of the last I mostly approve, and according to this import,—" As Christ has made known the glory of the Father in receiving us into favour, when we stood in need of mercy; so it behoves us, in order to make known also the glory of the same God, to establish and confirm this union which we have in Christ."[1]

[1] *In gloriam Dei*, εἰς δόξαν Θεοῦ, *i.e.*, in order to set forth the glory of God, or, in other words, that God might be glorified. So *Erasmus*, *Chalmers*, and *Stuart*. Others regard this "glory" as that which God bestows, even eternal happiness, according to this meaning,—" Receive ye

8. *Now I say, that Jesus Christ,* &c. He now shows that Christ has embraced us all, so that he leaves no difference between the Jews and the Gentiles, except that in the first place he was promised to the Jewish nation, and was in a manner peculiarly destined for them, before he was revealed to the Gentiles. But he shows, that with respect to that which was the seed of all contentions, there was no difference between them ; for he had gathered them both from a miserable dispersion, and brought them, when gathered, into the Father's kingdom, that they might be one flock, in one sheepfold, under one shepherd. It is hence right, he declares, that they should continue united together, and not despise one another; for Christ despised neither of them.[1]

He then speaks first of the Jews, and says, that Christ was sent to them, in order to accomplish the truth of God by performing the promises given to the Fathers: and it was no common honour, that Christ, the Lord of heaven and earth, put on flesh, that he might procure salvation for them ; for the more he humbled himself for their sake, the greater was the honour he conferred on them. But this point he evidently assumes as a thing indubitable. The more strange it is, that there is such effrontery in some fanatical heads, that they hesitate not to regard the promises of the Old Testament as temporal, and to confine them to the present world. And lest the Gentiles should claim any excellency above the Jews, Paul expressly declares, that the salvation which Christ has brought, belonged by

one another into communion and fellowship, as Christ has received you into the glory of God," that is, into that glorious state which God has provided and promised. See John xvii. 24. For "you," our version has "us;" but *Griesbach* considers "you" as the true reading.—*Ed.*

[1] The beginning of this verse, "Now I say," *Dico autem,* Λίγω δὶ, is read by *Beza* and *Grotius,* Λίγω γὰρ, "For I say," and *Griesbach* regards it of nearly equal authority. If we retain δὶ, it may be rendered "moreover," or " further ;" and to render the clause more distinct, the word " this," as proposed by *Beza* and *Pagninus,* may be added,—" I further say *this,*" &c. The two verses may be thus rendered,—

  8. I further say *this,* that Christ became a minister of the circumcision for the truth of God, that he might confirm the promises *made* to
  9. the fathers, and that the Gentiles might glorify God for *his* mercy, as it is written, " I will therefore confess thee among the nations, and to thy name will I sing."

The reasons for this rendering are given in the next note.—*Ed.*

covenant to the Jews; for by his coming he fulfilled what the Father had formerly promised to Abraham, and thus he became the minister of that people. It hence follows that the old covenant was in reality spiritual, though it was annexed to earthly types; for the fulfilment, of which Paul now speaks, must necessarily relate to eternal salvation. And further, lest any one should cavil, and say, that so great a salvation was promised to posterity, when the covenant was deposited in the hand of Abraham, he expressly declares that the promises were made to the Fathers. Either then the benefits of Christ must be confined to temporal things, or the covenant made with Abraham must be extended beyond the things of this world.

9. *The Gentiles also*,[1] &c. This is the second point, on proving which he dwells longer, because it was not so evident. The first testimony he quotes is taken from Ps. xviii.; which psalm is recorded also in 2 Sam. xxii., where no doubt a prophecy is mentioned concerning the kingdom of Christ; and from it Paul proves the calling of the Gentiles, because it is there promised, that a confession to the glory of God should be made among the Gentiles; for we cannot really

---

[1] The construction of this first sentence is differently viewed. *Grotius* and *Stuart* connect it with "I say" at the beginning of the former verse; but *Beza* and *Pareus* connect it with the last clause, and consider εἰς τὸ as being here understood: and this seems to be the best construction. Christ became the minister of the circumcision, a minister under the Abrahamic economy, for two objects,—that he might confirm the promises made to the Fathers,—and that the Gentiles might glorify God for his mercy. Mercy was destined to come to the Gentiles through the covenant made with Abraham, of which circumcision was the sign and seal. The promise, "In thee shall the nations of the earth be blessed," was made to Abraham, and not to the Gentiles. Hence it is called "mercy" to them, there being no previous promise made distinctly *to them*, while the same mercy as to the Jews is called "truth," because it was the fulfilment of a promise. A remarkable instance of this difference, noticed by *Haldane*, is found in Micah vii. 20. What is said to be "mercy" to Abraham, to whom the promise was first made, is said to be "truth" to Jacob, to whom it was confirmed. It may also, by the way, be observed, that this verse in Micah affords an example of what we often find in Paul's style; for in mentioning two or more things, he often reverses the regular order. What Micah mentions first is "truth" to Jacob, and then he goes back to God's "mercy" to Abraham.

The quotation from Psalm xviii. 49, is verbatim from the Septuagint. The Hebrew verb with its postfix, אוֹדְךָ, in our version, "I will give thanks to thee," may more properly be rendered, "I will confess thee."—*Ed.*

make God known, except among those who hear his praises while they are sung by us. Hence that God's name may be known among the Gentiles, they must be favoured with the knowledge of him, and come into communion with his people: for you may observe this everywhere in Scripture, that God's praises cannot be declared, except in the assembly of the faithful, who have ears capable of hearing his praise.

10. *Exult, ye Gentiles, with his people.* This verse is commonly considered as if it was taken from the song of Moses; but with this I cannot agree; for Moses' design there was to terrify the adversaries of Israel by setting forth his greatness, rather than to invite them to a common joy. I hence think that this is quoted from Ps. xlvii. 5, where it is written, " Exult and rejoice let the Gentiles, because thou judgest the nations in equity, and the Gentiles on the earth thou guidest." And Paul adds, *with his people,* and he did this by way of explanation; for the Prophet in that psalm no doubt connects the Gentiles with Israel, and invites both alike to rejoice; and there is no joy without the knowledge of God.[1]

11. *Praise God, all ye Gentiles,* &c. This passage is not inaptly applied; for how can they, who know not God's greatness, praise him? They could no more do this than to call on his name, when unknown. It is then a prophecy most suitable to prove the calling of the Gentiles; and this appears still more evident from the reason which is there added; for he bids them to give thanks for God's truth and mercy. (Ps. cxvii. 1.)

12. *And again, Isaiah,* &c. This prophecy is the most illustrious of them all: for in that passage, the Prophet, when things were almost past hope, comforted the small

---

[1] This passage is evidently taken from Deut. xxxii. 43, given literally as it is found in the Septuagint, and literally too from the Hebrew, if the reading of two copies, referred to by *Kennicalt,* be adopted, in which את, " with," is placed before עמו, " his people." It is no objection that " adversaries" are mentioned in the context. There have ever been adversaries to God's people; and God even now denounces his judgments on his adversaries, though the Gentiles as a people, as a separate class from the Jews, have been long ago admitted to the privilege of rejoicing with his people.—*Ed.*

remnant of the faithful, even by this,—that there would arise a shoot from the dry and the dying trunk of David's family, and that a branch would flourish from his despised root, which would restore to God's people their pristine glory. It is clear from the account there given, that this shoot was Christ, the Redeemer of the world. And then, he added, that he would be raised for a sign to the Gentiles, that might be to them for salvation. The words do indeed differ a little from the Hebrew text; for we read here, *arise*, while in Hebrew it is *stand for a sign*, which is the same; for he was to appear conspicuous like a sign. What is here *hope*, is in Hebrew *seek;* but according to the most common usage of Scripture, to seek God is nothing else but to hope in him.[1]

But twice in this prophecy is the calling of the Gentiles confirmed,—by the expression, that Christ was to be raised up as a sign, and he reigns among the faithful alone,—and by the declaration, that they shall hope in Christ, which cannot take place without the preaching of the word and illumination of the Spirit. With these things corresponds the song of Simeon. It may be further added, that hope in Christ is an evidence of his divinity.

13. Now the God of hope fill you with all joy and peace in believing, that ye may abound in hope, through the power of the Holy Ghost.

14. And I myself also am persuaded of you, my brethren, that ye also are full of goodness, filled with all knowledge, able also to admonish one another.

13. Deus autem spei impleat vos omni gaudio et pace in credendo, quò abundetis in spe per potentiam Spiritus sancti.

14. Persuasus autem sum, fratres mei, ipse quoque de vobis, quòd et ipsi pleni sitis bonitate, referti omni cognitione, idonei ad vos mutuò admonendos.

[1] Isaiah xi. 10. The whole of this quotation is given as it is found in the Septuagint. The difference, as noticed by *Calvin*, between the words as given in Hebrew, is considerable. The language of the Prophet is metaphorical, the Septuagint interpreted it, and this interpretation the Apostle approved and adopted. The Messiah is represented by the Prophet as a general or leader of an army, raising his banner for the nations, (עַמִּים, not " people," as in our version;) and the Gentiles repair or resort to this banner for protection; and so *Lowth* renders the verb יִדְרֹשׁוּ, only he does not preserve the metaphor, by rendering אֵלָיו, " unto him," instead of " to it," as in our version. It hence appears evident, that the passage is substantially the same; and indeed the verb ἄρχειν, retains in some measure the idea of the original, for it strictly means to be a leader, to rule as a chief.—*Ed.*

15. Nevertheless, brethren, I have written the more boldly unto you in some sort, as putting you in mind, because of the grace that is given to me of God,

16. That I should be the minister of Jesus Christ to the Gentiles, ministering the gospel of God, that the offering up of the Gentiles might be acceptable, being sanctified by the Holy Ghost.

15. Audaciùs autem scripsi vobis, fratres, ex parte, veluti commonefaciens vos, propter gratiam mihi datam à Deo;

16. Ut sim minister Christi erga Gentes, consecrans evangelium Christi, ut sit oblatio Gentium acceptabilis, sanctificata per Spiritum sanctum.

13. *And may the God,* &c. He now concludes the passage, as before, with prayer; in which he desires the Lord to give them whatever he had commanded. It hence appears, that the Lord does in no degree measure his precepts according to our strength or the power of free-will; and that he does not command what we ought to do, that we, relying on our own power, may gird up ourselves to render obedience; but that he commands those things which require the aid of his grace, that he may stimulate us in our attention to prayer.

In saying *the God of hope,* he had in view the last verse; as though he said,—" May then the God in whom we all hope fill you with joy, that is, with cheerfulness of heart, and also with unity and concord, and this by believing:"[1] for in order that our peace may be approved by God, we must be bound together by real and genuine faith. If any one prefers taking *in believing,* for, in order to believe,[2] the sense will be,—that they were to cultivate peace for the purpose of believing; for then only are we rightly prepared to believe, when we, being peaceable and unanimous, do willingly embrace what is taught us. It is however preferable, that faith should be connected with peace and joy; for it is the bond of holy and legitimate concord, and the support of godly joy. And though the peace which one has within with

---

[1] The God of hope may mean one of two things,—the giver or author of hope, as in 1 Pet. i. 3,—or the object of hope, he in whom hope is placed, as in 1 Tim. vi. 17.

Why does he mention joy before peace? It is in accordance with his usual manner,—the most visible, the stream first, then the most hidden, the spring.—*Ed.*

[2] That is, *εἰς τὸ*, instead of *ἐν τῷ*.—*Ed.*

God may also be understood, yet the context leads us rather to the former explanation.[1]

He further adds, *that ye may abound in hope;* for in this way also is hope confirmed and increased in us. The words, *through the power of the Holy Spirit,* intimate that all things are the gifts of the divine bounty: and the word *power* is intended emphatically to set forth that wonderful energy, by which the Spirit works in us faith, hope, joy, and peace.

14. *But even I myself am persuaded,* &c. This was said to anticipate an objection, or it may be deemed a kind of concession, made with the view of pacifying the Romans, in case they thought themselves reproved by so many and so urgent admonitions, and thus unjustly treated. He then makes an excuse for having ventured to assume towards them the character of a teacher and of an exhorter; and he says, that he had done so, not because he had any doubt as to their wisdom, or kindness, or perseverance; but because he was constrained by his office. Thus he removed every suspicion of presumption, which especially shows itself when any one thrusts himself into an office which does not belong to him, or speaks of those things which are unsuitable to him. We see in this instance the singular modesty of this holy man, to whom nothing was more acceptable than to be thought of no account, provided the doctrine he preached retained its authority.

There was much pride in the Romans; the name even of their city made the lowest of the people proud; so that they

---

[1] This is the view approved by *Theophylact, Beza, Grotius, Mede,* and *Hammond:* but *Doddridge, Scott, Stuart,* and *Chalmers* consider "peace" here to be that with God, and "joy" as its accompaniment; while *Pareus* and *Hodge* view both as included, especially the latter. If we consider the subject in hand, that the Apostle was attempting to produce union and concord between the Jews and the Gentiles, we shall see reason to accede to *Calvin's* explanation. This joy and peace seem to be the same as in ch. xiv. 17. Concord, union, and mutual enjoyment, are graces which come by believing, or by faith, as well as concord or peace with God, and its accompanying joy; and these graces have no doubt an influence on hope, so as to make it brighter and stronger, when they are produced by the Holy Spirit. There are three things which distinguish these graces from such as are fictitious,—they proceed from faith,—they increase hope,— they are produced by the Spirit.—*Ed.*

could hardly bear a teacher of another nation, much less a barbarian and a Jew. With this haughtiness Paul would not contend in his own private name: he however subdued it, as it were, by soothing means; for he testified that he undertook to address them on account of his Apostolic office.

Ye are full of goodness, being filled with knowledge, &c. Two qualifications are especially necessary for him who gives admonitions : the first is kindness, which disposes his mind to aid his brethren by his advice, and also tempers his countenance and his words with courtesy,—and the second is skill in advice or prudence, which secures authority to him, inasmuch as he is able to benefit the hearers whom he addresses. There is indeed nothing more opposed to brotherly admonitions than malignity and arrogance, which make us disdainfully to despise the erring, and to treat them with ridicule, rather than to set them right. Asperity also, whether it appears in words or in the countenance, deprives our admonitions of their fruit. But however you may excel in the feeling of kindness, as well as in courtesy, you are not yet fit to advise, except you possess wisdom and experience. Hence he ascribes both these qualifications to the Romans, bearing them a testimony,—that they were themselves sufficiently competent, without the help of another, to administer mutual exhortations : for he admits, that they abounded both in kindness and wisdom. It hence follows, that they were able to exhort.

15. *The more boldly, however, have I written to you,* &c. The excuse follows, and in adducing this, that he might more fully show his modesty, he says, by way of concession, that he acted boldly in interposing in a matter which they themselves were able to do ; but he adds that he was led to be thus bold on account of his office, because he was the minister of the gospel to the Gentiles, and could not therefore pass by them who were also Gentiles. He however thus humbles himself, that he might exalt the excellency of his office ; for by mentioning the favour of God, by which he was elevated to that high honour, he shows that he could not suffer what he did according to his apostolic office to be despised. Besides, he denies that he had assumed the part

of a teacher, but that of an admonisher, whose office it is to bring to remembrance what is not otherwise unknown.[1]

16. *Consecrating the gospel,* &c. This rendering I prefer to that which *Erasmus* in the first place adopts, that is, "Administering;" for nothing is more certain than that Paul here alludes to the holy mysteries which were performed by the priest. He then makes himself a chief priest or a priest in the ministration of the gospel, to offer up as a sacrifice the people whom he gained for God, and in this manner he laboured in the holy mysteries of the gospel. And doubtless this is the priesthood of the Christian pastor, that is, to sacrifice men, as it were, to God, by bringing them to obey the gospel, and not, as the Papists have hitherto haughtily vaunted, by offering up Christ to reconcile men to God. He does not, however, give here the name of priests to the pastors of the Church simply as a perpetual title, but intending to commend the honour and power of the ministry, Paul availed himself of the opportunity of using this metaphor. Let then the preachers of the gospel have this end in view while discharging their office, even to offer up to God souls purified by faith.

What *Erasmus* afterwards puts down as being more correct, "sacrificing the gospel," is not only improper but obscures also the meaning; for the gospel is, on the contrary, like a sword, by which the minister sacrifices men as victims to God.[2]

---

[1] It does not clearly appear what meaning *Calvin* attached to the words ἀπὸ μέρους, which he renders *ex parte*. Some, like *Origen*, connect the expression with the verb, "I have written to you in part," that is, not fully, which seems to have no meaning consistently with the evident tenor of the passage. Others, as *Chrysostom, Erasmus,* and *Pareus,* connect the words with the adjective, "I have in part (or somewhat) more boldly (or more freely, or more confidently) written to you." *Macknight* connects them with the following clause, "partly as calling things to your remembrance." *Doddridge* and *Stuart* render them "in *this* part *of the Epistle.*" The most suitable view is to consider them as qualifying the adjective.—*Ed.*

[2] "Consecrans evangelium," so *Augustine;* ἱερουργοῦντα τὸ εὐαγγέλιον, "operans evangelio—being employed in the gospel," *Beza* and *Pareus;* "docens sacrum evangelium—teaching the holy gospel," *Vatablus.* The verb means to "perform sacred rites," or to officiate in holy things. It has no connection, as some think, with a sacrificing priest; indeed ἱερεὺς itself, that is a priest, is a holy person, who did sacrifice no doubt among

He adds that such sacrifices are *acceptable* to God; which is not only a commendation of the ministry, but also a singular consolation to those who surrender themselves to be thus consecrated. Now as the ancient victims were dedicated to God, having been externally sanctified and washed, so these victims are consecrated to the Lord by the Spirit of holiness, through whose power, inwardly working in them, they are separated from this world. For though the purity of the soul proceeds from faith in the word, yet as the voice of man is in itself inefficacious and lifeless, the work of cleansing really and properly belongs to the Spirit.

17. I have therefore whereof I may glory through Jesus Christ in those things which pertain to God.
18. For I will not dare to speak of any of those things which Christ hath not wrought by me, to make the Gentiles obedient, by word and deed,
19. Through mighty signs and wonders, by the power of the Spirit of God; so that from Jerusalem, and round about unto Illyricum, I have fully preached the gospel of Christ.
20. Yea, so have I strived to preach the gospel, not where Christ was named, lest I should build upon another man's foundation :
21. But, as it is written, To whom he was not spoken of, they shall see : and they that have not heard shall understand.

17. Habeo igitur quòd glorier per Iesum Christum in iis quæ ad Deum pertinent.
18. Non enim ausim loqui quicquam de iis quæ non effecit Christus per me, in obedientiam Gentium, sermone et opere ;
19. In potentia signorum et prodigiorum, in potentia Spiritus Dei, ut ab Ierusalem et in circuitu usque in Illyricum impleverim evangelium Christi :
20. Ita annitens prædicare evangelium, non ubi nominatus erat Christus, ne super alienum fundamentum ædificarem ;
21. Sed quemadmodum scriptum est, Ii quibus non annuntiatum est de eo, videbunt, et qui non audierunt, intelligent.

17. *I have then*, &c. After having in general commended his own calling, that the Romans might know that he was a true and undoubted apostle of Christ, he now adds testi-

other things, but the word does not import a sacrificer any more than כהן in Hebrew. The word here does not mean to consecrate, or to sanctify, or to sacrifice, but to discharge a holy function. Perhaps the most literal rendering would be " performing a holy office as to the gospel," but dispensing, administering, or preaching the gospel would be the best version. The Apostle had previously called himself λιιτουργὸν, a public functionary, a public minister of Jesus Christ ; he now designates his work as such, being a sacred administrator of the gospel, and then he states the object, that the offering of the Gentiles, that is, that the Gentiles being offered, might be an acceptable sacrifice to God, sanctified by the Spirit. See chap. xii. 1.—*Ed.*

monies, by which he proved that he had not only taken upon him the apostolic office conferred on him by God's appointment, but that he had also eminently adorned it. He at the same time records the fidelity which he had exhibited in discharging his office. It is indeed to little purpose that we are appointed, except we act agreeably to our calling and fulfil our office. He did not make this declaration from a desire to attain glory, but because nothing was to be omitted which might procure favour and authority to his doctrine among the Romans. In God then, not in himself, did he glory; for he had nothing else in view but that the whole praise should redound to God.

And that he speaks only negatively, it is indeed an evidence of his modesty, but it availed also to gain credit to what he was proceeding to announce, as though he said, " The truth itself affords me such cause for glorying, that I have no need to seek false praises, or those of another, I am content with such as are true." It may be also that he intended to obviate the unfavourable reports which he knew were everywhere scattered by the malevolent, he therefore mentioned beforehand that he would not speak but of things well known.

18. *In order to make the Gentiles obedient,* &c. These words prove what his object was, even to render his ministry approved by the Romans, that his doctrine might not be without fruit. He proves then by evidences that God by the presence of his power had given a testimony to his preaching, and in a manner sealed his apostleship, so that no one ought to have doubted, but that he was appointed and sent by the Lord. The evidences were *word, work,* and *miracles.* It hence appears that the term *work* includes more than *miracles.* He at last concludes with this expression, *through the power of the Spirit;* by which he intimates that these things could not have been done without the Spirit being the author. In short, he declares that with regard to his teaching as well as his doing, he had such strength and energy in preaching Christ, that it was evidently the wonderful power of God, and that miracles were also added, which were seals to render the evidence more certain.

He mentions *word* and *work* in the first place, and then he states one kind of work, even the power of performing miracles. The same order is observed by Luke, when he says that Christ was mighty in word and work, (Luke xxiv. 19;) and John says that Christ referred the Jews to his own works for a testimony of his divinity. (John v. 36.) Nor does he simply mention miracles, but gives them two designations. But instead of what he says here, *the power of signs and of wonders*, Peter has " miracles and signs and wonders." (Acts ii. 22.) And doubtless they were testimonies of divine power to awaken men, that being struck with God's power, they might admire and at the same time adore him; nor are they without an especial meaning, but intended to stimulate us, that we may understand what God is.

This is a striking passage respecting the benefit of miracles: they are designed to prepare men to reverence and to obey God. So you read in Mark, that the Lord confirmed the truth by the signs which followed. (Mark xvi. 20.) Luke declares in the Acts, that the Lord by miracles gave testimony to the word of his grace. (Acts xiv. 3.) It is then evident that those miracles which bring glory to creatures and not to God, which secure credit to lies and not to God's word, are from the devil. *The power of the Spirit*, which he mentions in the third place, I apply to both the preceding clauses.[1]

---

[1] Some, as *Beza* and *Grotius*, understand by the last clause, "through the power of the Spirit of God," the internal power of speaking with tongues, &c., and by " signs and wonders," the external work of healing the sick, &c. But this passage is evidently an instance of the Apostle's usual mode of stating things. " Word" means preaching; and "work," the doing of miracles. He first specifies the last, the work was that of " signs and wonders;" and then he mentions what belongs to the first, and shows how it became effectual, that is, through the power of the Spirit. See a similar arrangement in 1 Cor. vi. 11; where he mentions washed, sanctified and justified; and then he mentions first what belongs to the last, " in the name of the Lord Jesus," and afterwards what appertains to the first words, " and by the Spirit of our God." " Signs and wonders" are often mentioned together: they designate the same things by different names: miracles were called " signs," because they were evidences of divine power, and they were called " wonders," or prodigies, because they were not according to the course of nature, but were extraordinary things. By these words their design and character are set forth.— *Ed.*

19. *So that from Jerusalem,* &c. He joins also a testimony from the effect; for the success which followed his preaching exceeded all the thoughts of men. For who could have gathered so many churches for Christ, without being aided by the power of God? " From Jerusalem," he says, " I have propagated the gospel as far as Illyricum, and not by hastening to the end of my course by a straight way, but by going all around, and through the intervening countries." But the verb πεπληρωκέναι, which after others I have rendered *filled up* or completed, means both to perfect and to supply what is wanting. Hence πλήρωμα in Greek means perfection as well as a supplement. I am disposed to explain it thus,—that he diffused, as it were by filling up, the preaching of the gospel; for others had before begun, but he spread it wider.[1]

20. *Thus striving to preach the gospel,* &c. As it was necessary for Paul not only to prove himself to be the servant of Christ and a pastor of the Christian Church, but also to show his title to the character and office of an Apostle, that he might gain the attention of the Romans, he mentions here the proper and peculiar distinction of the apostleship; for the work of an Apostle is to propagate the gospel where it had not been preached, according to that command, " Go ye, preach the gospel to every creature." (Mark xvi. 15.) And this is what we ought carefully to notice, lest we make a general rule of what specially belongs to the Apostolic order: nor ought we to consider it a fault, that a successor was substituted who built up the Church. The Apostles

---

[1] The clause is rendered by B*eza* and *Grotius,* " Impleverim prædicandi evangelii Christi munus—I have fulfilled the office of preaching the gospel of Christ." The gospel is put for preaching the gospel. See Acts xii. 25; Col. i. 25. *Vatablus* renders the verb " plenè annunciaverim—I have fully announced;" and *Mede,* " propagaverim—I have propagated." Some, as *Wolfius* and *Vitringa,* think the verb is used in a sense borrowed from Hebrew: the verb גמר, which in its common meaning is to *fill* or to finish, is used in the sense of teaching, not indeed in the Hebrew bible, but in the Talmud. That the idea of teaching, or propagating, or preaching, belongs to it here, and in Col. i. 25, is evident. The notion of filling up, which *Calvin* gives to it, is hardly consistent with what the Apostle says in verse 20. The *full* preaching is referred by *Erasmus,* not to its extent, but to its fidelity, " omitting nothing which a faithful evangelist ought to have proclaimed."—*Ed.*

then were the founders as it were of the Church; the pastors who succeeded them, had to strengthen and amplify the building raised up by them.¹ He calls that *another's foundation*, which had been laid by the hand of another: otherwise Christ is the only stone on which the Church is founded. See 1 Cor. iii. 11; and Eph. ii. 20.

21. *But as it is written*, &c. He confirms by the testimony of Isaiah what he had said of the evidence of his apostleship; for in chap. lii. 15, speaking of the kingdom of Messiah, among other things he predicts, that the knowledge of Christ would be spread among the Gentiles throughout the whole world, that his name would be declared to those by whom it had not been heard of before. It was meet that this should be done by the Apostles, to whom the command was specifically given. Hence the apostleship of Paul was made evident from this circumstance,—that this prophecy was fulfilled in him.²

It is absurd for any one to attempt to apply what is here said to the pastoral office; for we know that in Churches rightly formed, where the truth of the gospel has been already received, Christ's name must be constantly preached. Paul then was a preacher of Christ, yet unknown to foreign nations, for this end,—that after his departure the same doctrine should be daily proclaimed in every place by the mouth of the pastors; for it is certain that the Prophet speaks of the commencement of the kingdom of Christ.

¹ The participle, "striving," rendered *annitens* by *Calvin* and by *Erasmus*, is φιλοτιμούμενος, which means to strive honourably: it is to seek a thing as an object of honour or ambition. It may be rendered here, " honourably striving;" *Doddridge* has, " It hath been the object of my ambition;" *Stuart*, " I was strongly desirous;" and *Wolfius*, " honori mihi ducentem —esteeming it an honour to me." It is used to express both an honourable and an earnest or diligent pursuit. It is found in two other places, 2 Cor. v. 9; 1 Thess. iv. 11. Perhaps the best rendering would be, " Esteeming it an honour," or, " Being ambitious."—*Ed.*

² Isaiah lii. 15. The quotation is literally from the Septuagint, and is nearly according to the Hebrew, only the tense is altered, it being the past in that language, as prophecies are often found to be, in order to show their certainty. The Hebrew is as follows,—

For what had not been told them, have they seen,
And what they had not heard, have they understood.

To render the last verb " consider," as in our version, is not proper; it means to distinguish between things, to discern, to understand. It bears strictly the same meaning with the Greek verb here used.—*Ed.*

22. For which cause also I have been much hindered from coming to you.
23. But now having no more place in these parts, and having a great desire these many years to come unto you;
24. Whensoever I take my journey into Spain, I will come to you: for I trust to see you in my journey, and to be brought on my way thitherward by you, if first I be somewhat filled with your *company*.

22. Itaque impeditus etiam sæpiùs fui quominus venirem ad vos:
23. Nunc verò nullum ampliùs locum habens in his regionibus, desiderium autem habens à multis annis veniendi ad vos;
24. Si quando in Hispaniam proficiscar, veniam ad vos:[1] spero enim fore ut istac iter faciens videam vos, et illuc à vobis deducar, si tamen priùs ex parte vestra consuetudine fuero expletus.

22. *And on this account*, &c. What he had said of his apostleship he applies now to another point, even for the purpose of excusing himself for not having come to them, though he was destined for them as well as for others. He, in passing, then intimates, that in propagating the gospel from Judea as far as to Illyricum, he performed, as it were, a certain course enjoined him by the Lord; which being accomplished, he purposed not to neglect them. And lest they should yet think that they had been neglected, he removes this suspicion by testifying, that there had been for a long time no want of desire. Hence, that he had not done this sooner was owing to a just impediment: he now gives them a hope, as soon as his calling allowed him.

From this passage is drawn a weak argument respecting his going to Spain. It does not indeed immediately follow that he performed this journey, because he intended it: for he speaks only of hope, in which he, as other faithful men, might have been sometimes frustrated.[2]

[1] This clause, and γὰρ in the next, *Griesbach* dismisses as being spurious: then the verse would be,—
24. "Whenever I go into Spain, I hope, in passing through, to see you, and to be by you sent there, when I shall first be in a measure refreshed by you;" or, literally, "filled with you;" or it may be rendered, "satisfied with you."
The *Vulgate* renders the words, "Si vobis primum ex parte fruitus fuero—when I shall first in part enjoy you, *i.e.*, your society. *Stuart's* version is, "When I am in part first satisfied with your company." The expression, "in part," seems to imply that his stay would not be long.—*Ed.*

[2] On this subject *Wolfius* says, "Paul's journey to Spain was unknown to *Origen* and *Eusebius;* nor does it comport with the records connected with him. The Apostle, when freed from the chains of Nero, did not go to Spain, but to Asia; and there is no vestige of a Church founded by Paul in Spain. *Basnage* has carefully examined this subject as well as W. *Wall* in his critical Notes in English on the New Testament." As

24. *For I hope,* &c. He refers to the reason why he had for a long time wished to come to them, and now intended to do so,—even that he might see them, enjoy an interview and an intercourse with them, and make himself known to them in his official character; for by the coming of the Apostles the gospel also came.

By saying, *to be brought on my way thither by you,* he intimates how much he expected from their kindness; and this, as we have already observed, is the best way for conciliating favour; for the more confidence any one hears is reposed in him, the stronger are the obligations under which he feels himself; inasmuch as we deem it base and discourteous to disappoint the good opinion formed of us. And by adding, *When I shall first be in part filled,* &c., he bears witness to the benevolence of his mind towards them; and to convince them of this was very necessary for the interest of the gospel.

25. But now I go unto Jerusalem to minister unto the saints.

26. For it hath pleased them of Macedonia and Achaia to make a certain contribution for the poor saints which are at Jerusalem.

27. It hath pleased them verily; and their debtors they are. For if the Gentiles have been made partakers of their spiritual things, their duty is also to minister unto them in carnal things.

25. Nunc verò proficiscor Ierosolymam ad ministrandum sanctis.

26. Placuit enim Macedoniæ et Achaiæ communicationem facere in pauperes sanctos qui sunt Ierosolymis:

27. Placuit, inquam, et debitores sunt ipsorum; si enim spiritualibus ipsorum communicarunt Gentes, debent et in carnalibus[1] ministrare ipsis.

is common in many things connected with antiquity, fathers later than *Origen* and *Eusebius* came to know of this journey, but how, it is not easy to know: and in process of time various particulars were discovered, or rather invented, in connection with this journey. It is something similar to the story of Peter being the founder of the Church of Rome.—*Ed.*

[1] "In carnalibus;" ἐν τοῖς σαρκικοῖς. The word "carnal" in our language does not convey the meaning. The Apostle uses it here in opposition to what is "spiritual," and therefore "temporal" expresses its meaning. See 1 Cor. ix. 11. It sometimes means "human," as in 2 Cor. i. 12, where man's wisdom is set in contrast with God's wisdom. In 2 Cor. x. 4, it means "weak," or feeble, or powerless, being opposed to the "mighty" weapons of God. It has its own proper meaning in Rom. vii. 14, and in 1 Pet. ii. 11, "carnal," that is, wicked, sinful, corrupt, depraved. In 1 Cor. iii. 1, it signifies weak, ignorant, imperfect in knowledge, as opposed to spiritual and enlightened persons. And in Heb. vii. 16, it expresses what is fleeting and transitory. In no language is there one word which can convey all the meanings of a similar word in another: hence the necessity of changing a word sometimes in a translation.— *Ed.*

28. When therefore I have performed this, and have sealed to them this fruit, I will come by you into Spain.

29. And I am sure that, when I come unto you, I shall come in the fulness of the blessing of the gospel of Christ.

28. Hoc igitur quum perfecero, et obsignavero illis fructum hunc, proficiscar per vos in Hispaniam.

29. Scio autem quòd quum venero ad vos, in plenitudine benedictionis evangelii Christi venturus sum.

25. *But I am going now,* &c. Lest they should expect his immediate coming, and think themselves deceived, if he had not come according to their expectation, he declares to them what business he had then in hand, which prevented him from going soon to them, and that was,—that he was going to Jerusalem to bear the alms which had been gathered in Macedonia and Achaia. Availing himself at the same time of this opportunity, he proceeds to commend that contribution; by which, as by a kind of intimation, he stirs them up to follow this example: for though he does not openly ask them, yet, by saying that Macedonia and Achaia had done what they ought to have done, he intimates, that it was also the duty of the Romans, as they were under the same obligation; and that he had this view, he openly confesses to the Corinthians,—" I boast," he says, " of your promptitude to all the Churches, that they may be stirred up by your example." (2 Cor. ix. 2.)

It was indeed a rare instance of kindness, that the Grecians, having heard that their brethren at Jerusalem were labouring under want, considered not the distance at which they were separated from them; but esteeming those sufficiently nigh, to whom they were united by the bond of faith, they relieved their necessities from their own abundance. The word *communication*, which is here employed, ought to be noticed; for it well expresses the feeling, by which it behoves us to succour the wants of our brethren, even because there is to be a common and mutual regard on account of the unity of the body. I have not rendered the pronoun τινὰ, because it is often redundant in Greek, and seems to lessen the emphasis of this passage.[1] What we have ren-

---

[1] The words are, κοινωνίαν τινὰ ποιήσασθαι, " to make a certain contribution," or, " some contribution," or, as *Doddridge* has it, " a certain collection." There seems to be no necessity for leaving out the word τινὰ.—*Ed.*

dered *to minister*, is in Greek a participle, *ministering;* but the former seems more fitted to convey the meaning of Paul: for he excuses himself, that by a lawful occupation he was prevented from going immediately to Rome.

27. *And their debtors they are,* &c. Every one perceives, that what is said here of obligation, is said not so much for the sake of the Corinthians as for the Romans themselves; for the Corinthians or the Macedonians were not more indebted to the Jews than the Romans. And he adds the ground of this obligation,—that they had received the gospel from them: and he takes his argument from the comparison of the less with the greater. He employs also the same in another place, that is, that it ought not to have appeared to them an unjust or a grievous compensation to exchange carnal things, which are immensely of less value, for things spiritual. (2 Cor. ix. 11.) And it shows the value of the gospel, when he declares, that they were indebted not only to its ministers, but also to the whole nation, from whom they had come forth.

And mark the verb λειτουργῆσαι, *to minister;* which means to discharge one's office in the commonwealth, and to undergo the burden of one's calling: it is also sometimes applied to sacred things. Nor do I doubt but that Paul meant that it is a kind of sacrifice, when the faithful gave of their own to relieve the wants of their brethren; for they thus perform that duty of love which they owe, and offer to God a sacrifice of an acceptable odour. But in this place what he had peculiarly in view was the mutual right of compensation.

28. *And sealed to them this fruit,* &c. I disapprove not of what some think, that there is here an allusion to a practice among the ancients, who closed up with their seals what they intended to lay up in safety. Thus Paul commends his own faithfulness and integrity; as though he had said, that he was an honest keeper of the money deposited in his hands, no otherwise than if he carried it sealed up.[1]—

[1] More satisfactory is the explanation of *Stuart:* he says, that the word " sealed " means that the instrument to which a seal is applied is *authenticated, made valid, i.e.,* " sure to answer the purpose intended. So here the Apostle would not stop short in the performance of his duty,

The word *fruit* seems to designate the produce, which he had before said returned to the Jews from the propagation of the gospel, in a way similar to the land, which by bringing forth fruit supports its cultivator.

29. *And I know, that when I come,* &c. These words may be explained in two ways: the first meaning is,—that he should find a plentiful fruit from the gospel at Rome; for the blessing of the gospel is, when it fructifies by good works: but to confine this to alms, as some do, is not what I approve. The second is, that in order to render his coming to them more an object of desire, he says, that he hopes that it would not be unfruitful, but that it would make a great accession to the gospel; and this he calls *fulness of blessing*, which signifies a full blessing; by which expression he means great success and increase. But this blessing depended partly on his ministry and partly on their faith. Hence he promises, that his coming to them would not be in vain, as he would not disappoint them of the grace given to him, but would bestow it with the same alacrity with which their minds were prepared to receive the gospel.

The former exposition has been most commonly received, and seems also to me the best; that is, that he hoped that at his coming he would find what he especially wished, even that the gospel flourished among them and prevailed with evident success,—that they were excelling in holiness and in all other virtues. For the reason he gives for his desire is, that he hoped for no common joy in seeing them, as he expected to see them abounding in all the spiritual riches of the gospel.[1]

as the almoner of the Churches, until he had seen the actual distribution of their charity." It seems then that "sealed" here means "secured," or safely conveyed. "Delivered to them safely," is the paraphrase of *Hammond.—Ed.*

[1] This explanation is that of *Chrysostom;* but how to make the words to give such a meaning is a matter of some difficulty. The obvious import of the passage corresponds with ch. i. 11. All the authors quoted by *Poole*, except *Estius*, take the other view, such as *Grotius, Beza, Mede*, &c. The last gives the following as the sentiments of *Origen* and *Anselm*—" My preaching and conversation shall impart to you an abundant knowledge of the gospel mysteries, love, comfort, grace, and spiritual fruit." The word "blessing," εὐλογία, is said by *Grotius* to mean everything that is freely bestowed on us. See Gal. iii. 14; Eph. i. 3.

30. Now I beseech you, brethren, for the Lord Jesus Christ's sake, and for the love of the Spirit, that ye strive together with me in *your* prayers to God for me;

31. That I may be delivered from them that do not believe in Judea; and that my service which *I have* for Jerusalem may be accepted of the saints;

32. That I may come unto you with joy by the will of God, and may with you be refreshed.

33. Now the God of peace *be* with you all. Amen.

30. Obsecro autem vos fratres, per Dominum nostrum Iesum Christum et per dilectionem Spiritus, ut concertetis mihi in precibus vestris pro me ad Deum;

31. Ut liberer ab incredulis in Iudea, et ut ministerium meum quod suscipio erga Ierusalem acceptum sit sanctis;

32. Ut cum gaudio veniam ad vos per voluntatem Dei, unàque vobiscum refociller. Deus autem pacis sit cum omnibus vobis. Amen.[1]

30. *Now I beseech you*, &c. It is well known from many passages how much ill-will prevailed against Paul in his own nation on account of false reports, as though he taught a departure from Moses. He knew how much calumnies might avail to oppress the innocent, especially among those who are carried away by inconsiderate zeal. Added also to this, was the testimony of the Spirit, recorded in Acts xx. 23; by which he was forewarned, that bonds and afflictions awaited him at Jerusalem. The more danger then he perceived, the more he was moved: hence it was, that he was so solicitous to commend his safety to the Churches; nor let us wonder, that he was anxious about his life, in which he knew so much danger to the Church was involved.

He then shows how grieved his godly mind was, by the earnest protestation he makes, in which he adds to the name of the *Lord*, the *love of the Spirit*, by which the saints ought to embrace one another. But though in so great a fear, he yet continued to proceed; nor did he so dread danger, but that he was prepared willingly to meet it. At the same time he had recourse to the remedies given him by God; for he solicited the aid of the Church, so that

---

The words τοῦ εὐαγγελίου τοῦ, are not considered genuine by *Griesbach* and by most critics. This makes no difference in the meaning: the clause then would be,—"With the fulness of the blessings of Christ," or, with the abounding blessing of Christ; or, as *Beza* renders it, "with the full blessing of Christ."—*Ed.*

[1] The word "Amen," is regarded as spurious: *Griesbach* and others have left it out.—*Ed.*

being helped by its prayers, he might find comfort, according to the Lord's promise,—" Where two or three shall assemble in my name, there in the midst of them am I," (Matt. xviii. 20 ;) and, " Whatsoever they agree in on earth, they shall obtain in heaven," (Matt. xviii. 19.) And lest no one should think it an unmeaning commendation, he besought them both by Christ and by the love of the Spirit. The love of the Spirit is that by which Christ joins us together; for it is not that of the flesh, nor of the world, but is from his Spirit, who is the bond of our unity.

Since then it is so great a favour from God to be helped by the prayers of the faithful, that even Paul, a most choice instrument of God, did not think it right to neglect this privilege, how great must be our stupidity, if we, who are abject and worthless creatures, disregard it? But to take a handle from such passages for the purpose of maintaining the intercessions of dead saints, is an instance of extreme effrontery.[1]

That ye strive together with me,[2] &c. *Erasmus* has not given an unsuitable rendering, " That ye help me labouring :" but as the Greek word, used by Paul, has more force, I have preferred to give a literal rendering: for by the word *strive*, or contend, he alludes to the difficulties by which he was oppressed, and by bidding them to assist in this contest, he shows how the godly ought to pray for their brethren, that they are to assume their person, as though

---

[1] *Scott* quotes the following from *Whitby*,—" If Paul, saith *Estius*, might desire the prayers of the Romans, why might not the Romans desire the prayers of Paul? I answer, they might desire his prayers, *as* he did theirs, by a letter directed to him to pray for them. He adds, If they might desire his prayers for them when living, why not when dead and reigning with Christ? I answer, Because they could direct no epistle to him, or in any other way acquaint him with their mind."—*Ed.*

[2] " Ut concertetis mihi," συναγωνίσασθαί μοι; " ut mecum certetis—that ye strive with me,"—*Beza ;* " ut mecum laboretis—that ye labour with me,"—*Tremelius*, from the Syriac. Literally it is, " that ye agonize with me." It is an allusion, says *Grotius*, to Jacob's wrestling with the angel. Gen. xxxii. 24. A strenuous and earnest supplication is intended. *Pareus* says, that it is a metaphor taken from warfare, when a soldier comes to the help of another: but rather from the games, when there is a striving for the prize. He would have the Romans to make a similar strenuous effort for him in prayer to God. The word ἀγών, is an agonistic and not a military term.—*Ed.*

they were placed in the same difficulties; and he also intimates the effect which they have; for he who commends his brother to the Lord, by taking to himself a part of his distress, do so far relieve him. And indeed if our strength is derived from prayer to God, we can in no better way confirm our brethren, than by praying to God for them.

31. *That my ministration,* &c. Slanderers had so prevailed by their accusations, that he even feared that the present would hardly be acceptable, as coming from his hands, which otherwise, under such a distress, would have been very seasonable. And hence appears his wonderful meekness, for he ceased not to labour for those to whom he doubted whether he would be acceptable. This disposition of mind we ought to imitate, so that we may not cease to do good to those of whose gratitude we are by no means certain. We must also notice that he honours with the name of *saints* even those by whom he feared he would be suspected, and deemed unwelcome. He also knew that saints may sometimes be led away by false slanders into unfavourable opinions, and though he knew that they wronged him, he yet ceased not to speak honourably of them.

By adding *that I may come to you*, he intimates that this prayer would be profitable also to them, and that it concerned them that he should not be killed in Judea. To the same purpose is the expression *with joy;* for it would be advantageous to the Romans for him to come to them in a cheerful state of mind and free from all grief, that he might in a more lively and strenuous manner labour among them. And by the word *refreshed*,[1] or satisfied, he again shows how fully persuaded he was of their brotherly love. The words *by the will of God* remind us how necessary it is to be diligent in prayer, for God alone directs all our ways by his providence.

And the God of peace,[2] &c. From the universal word *all,*

---

[1] It was a mutual refreshment, according to chap. i. 12. The verb here used, says *Grotius*, means to *give* and to *receive* comfort. The verb without its compound σὺν, is found in 1 Cor. xvi. 18; 2 Cor. vii. 13; Phil. verse 7, &c.—*Ed.*

[2] Lover, author, or bestower of peace. This intimates that there were strifes and contentions among them. Paul often speaks of God as the

I conclude that he did not simply pray that God would be present with and favour the Romans in a general sense, but that he would rule and guide every one of them. But the word *peace* refers, I think, to their circumstances at the time, that God, the author of peace, would keep them all united together.

CHAPTER XVI.

1. I commend unto you Phebe our sister, which is a servant of the church which is at Cenchrea;
2. That ye receive her in the Lord, as becometh saints, and that ye assist her in whatsoever business she hath need of you: for she hath been a succourer of many, and of myself also.
3. Greet Priscilla and Aquila my helpers in Christ Jesus;
4. (Who have for my life laid down their own necks: unto whom not only I give thanks, but also all the churches of the Gentiles:)
5. Likewise *greet* the church that is in their house. Salute my wellbeloved Epenetus, who is the firstfruits of Achaia unto Christ.
6. Greet Mary, who bestowed much labour on us.
7. Salute Andronicus and Junia, my kinsmen, and my fellow-prisoners, who are of note among the apostles, who also were in Christ before me.
8. Greet Amplias, my beloved in the Lord.
9. Salute Urbane, our helper in Christ, and Stachys my beloved.

10. Salute Apelles, approved in Christ. Salute them which are of Aristobulus' *household*.
11. Salute Herodion my kinsman. Greet them that be of the

1. Commendo autem vobis Phœben sororem nostram, quæ est ministra ecclesiæ Cenchreensis;
2. Ut eam suscipiatis in Domino, ut dignum est sanctis, et adsitis ei in quocunque vobis eguerit negotio; etenim ipsa cum multis affuit, tum etiam mihi ipsi.
3. Salutate Priscam et Acylam, cooperarios meos in Christo Iesu;
4. Qui pro anima mea suam ipsorum cervicem posuerunt, quibus non ego solus gratias ago, sed etiam omnes ecclesiæ Gentium;
5. Et domesticam eorum ecclesiam. Salutate Epænetum mihi dilectum qui est primitiæ Achaiæ in Domino.
6. Salutate Mariam, quæ multùm laboravit erga vos.
7. Salutate Andronicum et Juniam, cognatos meos et cocaptivos meos, qui sunt insignes inter Apostolos, qui etiam ante me fuerunt in Christo.
8. Salutate Ampliam, dilectum meum in Domino.
9. Salutate Urbanum, adjutorem nostrum in Christo et Stachyn dilectum meum.
10. Salutate Apellen, probatum in Christo. Salutate eos qui sunt ex Aristobuli familiaribus.
11. Salutate Herodionem, cognatum meum. Salutate eos qui sunt

God of peace, especially when referring to the discords which prevailed among Christians. See 1 Cor. xiv. 33; 2 Cor. xiii. 11; Phil. iv. 9; 1 Thess. v. 23; 2 Thess. iii. 16; Heb. xiii. 20.—*Ed.*

household of Narcissus, which are in the Lord.

12. Salute Tryphena and Tryphosa, who labour in the Lord. Salute the beloved Persis, which laboured much in the Lord.

13. Salute Rufus, chosen in the Lord, and his mother and mine.

14. Salute Asyncritus, Phlegon, Hermas, Patrobas, Hermes, and the brethren which are with them.

15. Salute Philologus, and Julia, Nereus, and his sister, and Olympas, and all the saints which are with them.

16. Salute one another with an holy kiss. The churches of Christ salute you.

ex Narcissi familiaribus, hos qui sunt in Domino.

12. Salutate Tryphænam et Tryphosam, quæ laborant in Domino. Salutate Persidem dilectam, quæ multùm laboravit in Domino.

13. Salutate Rufum electum in Domino et matrem illius ac meam.

14. Salutate Asynchritum, Phlegontem, Hermam, Patrobam, Mercurium, et qui cum his sunt fratres.

15. Salutate Philologum et Iuliam, Nereum et sororem ejus, et Olympam, et qui cum his sunt omnes sanctos.

16. Salutate vos invicem in osculo sancto. Salutant vos ecclesiæ Christi.

1. *I commend to you,* &c. The greater part of this chapter is taken up with salutations; and as they contain no difficulties, it would be useless to dwell long on them. I shall only touch on those things which require some light by an explanation.

He first commends to them Phœbe, to whom he gave this Epistle to be brought to them; and, in the first place, he commends her on account of her office, for she performed a most honourable and a most holy function in the Church; and then he adduces another reason why they ought to receive her and to show her every kindness, for she had always been a helper to all the godly. As then she was an assistant[1] of the Cenchrean Church, he bids that on that

---

[1] "Ministra," διάκονος—minister, or servant, or deaconess, one who ministers. *Origen* and *Chrysostom* considered her to be a deaconess, but the word does not necessarily prove this; for it is used often to designate generally one who does service and contributes to the help and assistance of others. She was evidently a person of wealth and influence, and was no doubt a great support and help to the Cenchrean Church. Those spoken of by Paul in 1 Tim. v. 10, and Tit. ii. 3, were *widows* and *aged*, and they are not called αἱ διάκονοι, deaconesses. There arose, as it appears, an order of this kind in the early Church, and *Grotius* says that they were ordained by imposition of hands before the Laodicean Council, which forbade the practice. Their office was, according to *Bingham* and *Suicer*, referred to by *Schleusner*, to baptize women, to teach female catechumens, to visit the sick, and to perform other inferior offices in the Church. But this was a state of things after the apostolic times, and there is no reason to believe that Phœbe was of this order. She was evidently a great helper of the Christian cause, as some other women also are mentioned in this

account she should be received in the Lord ; and by adding *as it is meet for saints,* he intimates that it would be unbecoming the servants of Christ not to show her honour and kindness. And since it behoves us to embrace in love all the members of Christ, we ought surely to regard and especially to love and honour those who perform a public office in the Church. And besides, as she had always been full of kindness to all, so he bids that help and assistance should now be given to her in all her concerns ; for it is what courtesy requires, that he who is naturally disposed to kindness should not be forsaken when in need of aid, and to incline their minds the more, he numbers himself among those whom she had assisted.

But this service, of which he speaks as to what it was, he teaches us in another place, in 1 Tim. v. 9, for as the poor were supported from the public treasury of the Church, so they were taken care of by those in public offices, and for this charge widows were chosen, who being free from domestic concerns, and cumbered by no children, wished to consecrate themselves wholly to God by religious duties, they were therefore received into this office as those who had wholly given up themselves, and became bound to their charge in a manner like him, who having hired out his own labours, ceases to be free and to be his own master. Hence the Apostle accuses them of having violated their faith, who renounced the office which they had once undertaken, and as it behoved them to live in widowhood, he forbade them to be chosen under sixty years of age, (1 Tim. v. 9, 11,) because he foresaw that under that age the vow of perpetual celibacy was dangerous, yea, liable to prove ruinous. This most sacred function, and very useful to the Church, when the state of things had become worse, degenerated into the idle order of Nuns ; which, though corrupt at its beginning, and contrary to the word of God, has yet so fallen away from what it was at its commencement, that there is no difference

---

chapter, and she had been the helper of many, (verse 2,) and not of one Church, and also of Paul himself; and from what is said in verse 2, it appears probable that she was a woman carrying on some business or traffic, and that she went to Rome partly at least on this account.—*Ed.*

between some of the sanctuaries of chastity and a common brothel.

3. *Salute Prisca[1] and Aquila.* The testimonies which he brings here in favour of some individuals, were partly intended for this end, that by honouring those who were faithful and worthy, faithfulness itself might be honoured, and that they who could and would do more good than others, might have authority; and partly that they themselves might study to act in a manner corresponding to their past life, and not fail in their religious course, nor ever grow languid in their pious ardour.

It is a singular honour which he ascribes here to Prisca and Aquila, especially with regard to a woman. The modesty of the holy man does on this account more clearly shine forth; for he disdained not to have a woman as his associate in the work of the Lord; nor was he ashamed to confess this. She was the wife of Aquila, and Luke calls her Priscilla. (Acts xviii. 2.)[2]

4. *To whom not only I,* &c. As Prisca and Aquila had not spared their life for preserving the life of Paul, he testifies that he himself was individually thankful to them: he however adds, that thanks were given them by all the Churches of Christ; and he added this that he might, by such an example, influence the Romans. And deservedly dear and precious to all the Gentiles was the life of such a man, as it was an incomparable treasure: it was therefore no wonder that all the Churches of the Gentiles thought themselves to be under obligations to his preservers.[3]

What he adds respecting the Church in their house is worthy of being observed; for he could not have more splendidly adorned their household than by giving it the

---

[1] So reads *Griesbach;* it is the same with Priscilla. See Acts xviii. 2, 26, and 2 Tim. iv. 19, where she is also called Prisca. Names in former times, as well as now, were sometimes used in an abbreviated form.—*Ed.*

[2] Whether Aquila was a layman or not, the Apostle connects his wife with him in the work of co-operation with him in his ministerial work; and we see by Acts xviii. 26, that they both taught Apollos. It is somewhat singular, that the wife, not only here but in several other instances, though not in all, is mentioned before the husband.—*Ed.*

The occasion is not mentioned. It was probably at Corinth, according to the account given in 18th of Acts.

title of a Church. The word *congregation*, which *Erasmus* has adopted, I do not approve; for it is plainly evident, that Paul, by way of honour, had used the sacred name of Church.¹

5. *Who is the first-fruit*, &c. This is an allusion to the rites of the law; for as men are sanctified to God by faith, they who first offer themselves are fitly called the first-fruit. Whosoever then is called first in time to the faith, Paul allows him the prerogative of honour: yet he retains this eminence only when the end corresponds with the beginning. And doubtless it is no common honour when God chooses some for first-fruits: and there is in addition a greater and an ampler trial of faith, through a longer space of time, provided they who have first begun are not wearied in their course.²

6. He again testifies his gratitude, in recording the kindness of Mary to him. Nor is there any doubt but that he commemorates these praises, in order to recommend those whom he praised to the Romans.³

7. *Salute Andronicus.* Though Paul is not wont to make much of kindred, and of other things belonging to the flesh, yet as the relationship which Junia and Andronicus bore to him, might avail somewhat to make them more fully known, he neglected not this commendation. There is more weight in the second eulogy, when he calls them his *fellow-prison-*

---

¹ Some of the Fathers considered that the family, being all religious, was the Church; but this is wholly inconsistent with the mode of expression that is used, and with the state of things at that time. They had no churches or temples to meet in; private houses were their churches. Superstitious ideas as to places of worship no doubt led men to seek such an explanation. Would the Apostle have used such a phraseology as the following, if he meant only the family,—" Aquila and Priscilla salute you much in the Lord, with (σύν—together with) the Church that is in their house," 1 Cor. xvi. 19.—*Ed.*

² Epenetus, who is here called the first-fruit of Achaia, may have been of the family of Stephanas, who is said to have been the first-fruit in 1 Cor. xvi. 15. But the majority of copies has Asia, 'Ασίας, here, instead of Achaia, 'Αχαίας. By Asia is often meant Asia Minor, and so here, no doubt, if it be the right reading.—*Ed.*

³ It is said of Mary, that she " laboured much," εἰς ἡμᾶς, towards us, or among us; " inter nos—among us," *Beza;* " pro nobis—for us," *Grotius.* The reading εἰς ὑμᾶς, towards you, has many MSS. in its favour, and also ἐν ὑμῖν, among you.—*Ed.*

ers;[1] for among the honours belonging to the warfare of Christ, bonds are not to be counted the least. In the third place, he calls them *Apostles:* he uses not this word in its proper and common meaning, but extends it wider, even to all those who not only teach in one Church, but also spend their labour in promulgating the gospel everywhere. He then, in a general way, calls those in this place Apostles, who planted Churches by carrying here and there the doctrine of salvation; for elsewhere he confines this title to that first order which Christ at the beginning established, when he appointed the twelve disciples. It would have been otherwise strange, that this dignity should be only ascribed to them, and to a few others. But as they had embraced the gospel by faith before Paul, he hesitates not to set them on this account before himself.[2]

11. *Who are of the family of Narcissus.* It would have been unbeseeming to have passed by Peter in so long a catalogue, if he was then at Rome: yet he must have been there, if we believe the Romanists. But since in doubtful things nothing is better than to follow probable conjecture, no one, who judges impartially, will be persuaded that what they affirm is true; for he could not surely have been omitted by Paul.

It is further to be noticed, that we hear nothing here of splendid and magnificent titles, by which we might conclude that men high in rank were Christians; for all those whom Paul mentions were the obscure and the ignoble at Rome. *Narcissus*, whom he here names, was, I think, the freeman

---

[1] It is not certain to what the Apostle refers; for we have no particular account of him hitherto as a prisoner, except for a short time at Philippi, Acts xvi. 23-40; and it is probable, that it was on that occasion that they had been his fellow-prisoners; for it appears from the narrative, that there were more prisoners than Paul and Silas, as it is said that the "prisoners" heard them singing, verse 25; and Paul's saying to the jailor, in verse 28, "we are *all* here," clearly implies that he had some with him besides Silas.—*Ed.*

[2] The words ἐπίσημοι ἐν τοῖς ἀποστόλοις, noted among the Apostles, can hardly admit of a meaning different from what is here given, though some have explained the sense to be, that they were much esteemed by the Apostles, or that they were "distinguished in the Apostles' judgment," or that they were well known to the Apostles. But as "Apostles" in some other instances mean teachers, as Barnabas was, (Acts xiv. 14,) the explanation here given is most to be approved.—*Ed.*

of Claudius, a man notorious for many crimes and vices. The more wonderful was the goodness of God, which penetrated into that impure house, abounding in all kinds of wickedness; not that Narcissus himself had been converted to Christ, but it was a great thing that a house, which was like hell, should be visited by the grace of Christ. And as they, who lived under a foul pander, the most voracious robber, and the most corrupt of men, worshipped Christ in purity, there is no reason that servants should wait for their masters, but every one ought to follow Christ for himself. Yea, the exception added by Paul shows that the family was divided, so that the faithful were only a few.

16. *Salute one another with a holy kiss.* It is clear from many parts of Scripture, that a kiss was a usual and common symbol of friendship among the Jews; it was perhaps less used by the Romans, though not unfrequent, only it was not lawful to kiss women, except those only who were relatives. It became however a custom among the ancients for Christians to kiss one another before partaking of the Supper, to testify by that sign their friendship; and then they bestowed their alms, that they might in reality and by the effect confirm what they had represented by the kiss: all this appears evident from one of the homilies of *Chrysostom*.[1] Hence has arisen that practice among the Papists at this day, of kissing the paten, and of bestowing an offering: the former of which is nothing but superstition without any benefit, the other serves no other purpose but to satisfy the avariciousness of the priests, if indeed it can be satisfied.

Paul however seems not here positively to have enjoined

[1] It appears from *Justin Martyr* and *Tertullian*, that the early Christians kissed one another always after prayers, or at the end of the service. They did so, says *Grotius*, to " show that they were all equal; for the Persians and the orientals kissed the mouth of those only of the same rank, and gave their hands to be kissed by their inferiors." It was evidently a custom among the Jews. See 2 Sam. xx. 9; Luke vii. 45; Matt. xxvi. 49. This " holy kiss " is mentioned in 1 Cor. xvi. 20; 2 Cor. xiii. 12; 1 Thess. v. 26. It is called the kiss of love, or charity, by Peter, 1 Peter v. 14. It was one of those things which arose from peculiar habits, and is not to be considered as binding on all nations, any more than the washing of feet. The Apostle's object seems to have been, not to enjoin a rite, but to regulate a practice, already existing, and to preserve it from abuse: it was to be a *holy* kiss.—*Ed.*

a ceremony, but only exhorts them to cherish brotherly love; and he distinguishes it from the profane friendships of the world, which, for the most part, are either disguised or attained by vices, or retained by wicked arts, and never tend to any good. By sending salutations from the Churches,[1] he was endeavouring, as much as he could, to bind all the members of Christ by the mutual bond of love.

17. Now, I beseech you, brethren, mark them which cause divisions and offences contrary to the doctrine which ye have learned; and avoid them.

18. For they that are such serve not our Lord Jesus Christ, but their own belly; and by good words and fair speeches deceive the hearts of the simple.

19. For your obedience is come abroad unto all *men*. I am glad therefore on your behalf: but yet I would have you wise unto that which is good, and simple concerning evil.

20. And the God of peace shall bruise Satan under your feet shortly. The grace of our Lord Jesus Christ *be* with you. Amen.

17. Obsecro autem vos fratres, ut observetis eos qui dissidia et offensiones contra doctrinam, quam vos didicistis, excitant; et ut declinetis ab illis.

18. Qui enim tales sunt, Christo Domino non serviunt, sed suo ventri; ac per blandiloquentiam et assentationem decipiunt corda simplicium.

19. Vestra quidem obedientia ad omnes permanavit: gaudeo igitur de vobis; sed volo vos sapientes esse ad bonum, simplices verò ad malum.

20. Deus autem pacis conteret brevi Satanam sub pedibus vestris. Gratia Domini nostri Iesu Christi sit vobiscum. Amen.

17. *And I beseech you*, &c. He now adds an exhortation, by which all Churches have often need of being stirred up; for the ministers of Satan are ever ready to take occasion to disturb the kingdom of Christ: and they attempt to make disturbances in two ways; for they either sow discord, by which the minds of men are drawn away from the unity of truth, or they occasion offences, by which men are alienated from the love of the gospel.[2] The former evil is done when

---

[1] *Griesbach* approves of πάσαι, "all," after Churches; then it would be "all the Churches;" that is, of Greece, says *Grotius*, but of Corinth, says *Wolfius*, even those which assembled at different private houses: and this is a more likely supposition, than that Paul, according to *Origen* and others, took it as granted that all the Churches which he had founded wished well to the Church of Rome. That they wished well to it there can be no doubt; but it is not probable that Paul acted on such a supposition.—*Ed.*

[2] The two words are διχοστασίαι and σκάνδαλα, divisions and offences, or hinderances. He had, no doubt, in view, what he noticed in chapter 14, about eating and observing of days; and according to his usual manner he

the truth of God is mixed with new dogmas devised by men; and the latter takes place, when by various arts it is made odious and contemptible. He therefore bids all, who did either of these two things, to be observed, lest they should deceive and catch the unwary; and also to be shunned, for they were injurious. Nor was it without reason that he required this attention from the faithful; for it often happens through our neglect or want of care, that such wicked men do great harm to the Church, before they are opposed; and they also creep in, with astonishing subtlety, for the purpose of doing mischief, except they be carefully watched.

But observe, that he speaks of those who had been taught the pure truth of God. It is indeed an impious and sacrilegious attempt to divide those who agree in the truth of Christ: but yet it is a shameful sophistry to defend, under the pretext of peace and unity, a union in lies and impious doctrines. There is therefore no ground for the Papists to seek countenance from this passage, in order to raise ill-will against us; for we do not impugn and tear asunder the gospel of Christ, but the falsehoods of the devil, by which it has been hitherto obscured: nay, Paul clearly shows, that he did not condemn all kinds of discords, but those which destroyed consent in the orthodox faith; for the force of the passage is in the words, *which ye have learnt;* for it was the duty of the Romans, before they were rightly taught, to depart from the habits of their fathers and the institutions of their ancestors.

18. *For they who are such,* &c. He mentions an unvarying mark, by which false prophets are to be distinguished from the servants of Christ; for they have no care for the

---

mentions first the effect—" divisions," and then the cause—" offences." The Gentile Christians, by eating, gave offence to the believing Jews, and this offence led to a division or separation. The evils which he had previously attempted to correct were doubtless those referred to here. " Serving their own belly," in the next verse, has in this respect an emphatic meaning. Instead of denying themselves in the use of meats for the sake of Christ, and for the peace of his Church, they preferred to gratify their own appetites. And being led away by their lust, they covered their real motive by kindly or plausibly addressing (χρηστολογία) and eulogizing (εὐλογία) those who joined them, imitating in this respect the arts of all false professors and zealots, whatever be the false principle by which they may be guided.—*Ed.*

glory of Christ, but seek the benefit of their stomach. As, however, they deceitfully crept in, and by assuming another character, concealed their own wickedness, he at the same time pointed out, in order that no one might be deceived, the arts which they adopted—that they ingratiated themselves by a bland address. The preachers of the gospel have also their courtesy and their pleasing manner, but joined with honesty, so that they neither soothe men with vain praises, nor flatter their vices: but impostors allure men by flattery, and spare and indulge their vices, that they may keep them attached to themselves. He calls those *simple* who are not cautious enough to avoid deceptions.

19. *Your obedience,*[1] &c. This is said to anticipate an objection; for he shows that he did not warn them, as though he thought unfavourably of them, but because a fall in their case was such as might have easily happened; as if he had said,—" Your obedience is indeed commended everywhere, and for this reason I rejoice on your account: yet since it often happens, that a fall occurs through simplicity, I would have you to be harmless and simple as to the doing of evil; but in doing good, to be most prudent, whenever it may be necessary, so that you may preserve your integrity."

We here see what that simplicity is which is commended in Christians; so that they have no reason to claim this distinction, who at this day count as a high virtue their stupid ignorance of the word of God. For though he approves in the Romans, that they were obedient and teachable, yet he would have them to exercise wisdom and judgment, lest their readiness to believe exposed them to impositions. So then he congratulates them, because they were free from a wicked disposition; he yet wished them to be wise, so as to exercise caution.[2]

[1] This he calls "faith" in chap. i. 8: so that obedience to the gospel is faith in what it declares. To believe is the special command of the gospel: hence to believe is the special act of obedience that is required; and he who believes is he who shall be saved. But this faith is that of the heart, and not of the lips; and a faith which works by love and overcomes the world, the mighty power of which we learn from Heb. xi.—*Ed.*

[2] "Good" and "evil" in this clause, is beneficence and mischief. To be wise as to good, is to be wise in acts of kindness, in promoting good, as *Beza* seems to take it; and to be harmless or guileless, or simple as to

20. What follows, *God shall bruise Satan*, &c., is a promise to confirm them, rather than a prayer. He indeed exhorts them to fight manfully against Satan, and promises that they should shortly be victorious. He was indeed once conquered by Christ, but not in such a way but that he renews the war continually. He then promises ultimate defeat, which does not appear in the midst of the contest. At the same time he does not speak only of the last day, when Satan shall be completely bruised; but as Satan was then confounding all things, raging, as it were, with loose or broken reins, he promises that the Lord would shortly subdue him, and cause him to be trodden, as it were, under foot. Immediately a prayer follows,—that the grace of Christ would be with them, that is, that they might enjoy all the blessings which had been procured for them by Christ.

21. Timotheus my work-fellow, and Lucius, and Jason, and Sosipater, my kinsmen, salute you.
22. I Tertius, who wrote *this* epistle, salute you in the Lord.
23. Gaius mine host, and of the whole church, saluteth you. Erastus, the chamberlain of the city, saluteth you, and Quartus a brother.
24. The grace of our Lord Jesus Christ *be* with you all. Amen.
25. Now to him that is of power to stablish you according to my gospel, and the preaching of Jesus Christ, (according to the revelation of the mystery, which was kept secret since the world began,
26. But now is made manifest, and by the scriptures of the prophets, according to the commandment of the

21. Salutant vos Timotheus, cooperarius meus, et Lucius et Iason et Sosipater, cognati mei.
22. Saluto ego vos Tertius, qui scripsi epistolam, in Domino.
23. Salutat vos Gaius, hospes meus et Ecclesiæ totius. Salutat vos Erastus, quæstor ærarius urbis, et Quartus fråter.
24. Gratia Domini nostri Iesu Christi sit cum omnibus vobis. Amen.
25. Ei verò qui potens est vos confirmare secundum evangelium meum, et præconium scilicet Iesu Christi, secundum revelationem mysterii, quod temporibus secularibus tacitum,
26. Manifestatum nunc fuit, et per scripturas propheticas, secundum æterni Dei ordinationem, in obedien-

evil, is to exercise no arts, by plausible speeches and flatteries, as was done by those referred to in verse 17, in order to do mischief, to create divisions. The Apostle's object throughout seems to have been to produce unanimity between the Jews and Gentiles. Hence in the next verse he speaks of God as "the God of peace," the author of peace among his people; and he says that this God of peace would soon tread down Satan, the author of discord, the promoter of divisions and offences; or, as most consider the passage, he prays that God would do this; for the future, after the manner of the Hebrew, is sometimes used by the Apostle as an optative. And indeed the verb is found in some copies in this mood (*συντρίψαι*) and in the Syriac, Ethiopic, and Vulgate versions.—*Ed.*

everlasting God, made known to all nations for the obedience of faith :)
27. To God only wise, *be* glory through Jesus Christ for ever. Amen.

¶ Written to the Romans from Corinthus, *and sent* by Phebe, servant of the church at Cenchrea.

tiam fidei ad omnes gentes promulgatum,—
27. Soli sapienti Deo per Iesum Christum gloria in secula. Amen.

Ad Romanos missa fuit à Corintho per Phœben, ministram Cenchreensis ecclesiæ.

21. *Timothy,* &c. The salutations which he records, served in part to foster union between those who were far asunder, and in part to make the Romans know that their brethren subscribed to the Epistle; not that Paul had need of the testimony of others, but because the consent of the godly is not of small importance.

The Epistle closes, as we see, with praise and thanksgiving to God. It indeed records the remarkable kindness of God in favouring the Gentiles with the light of the gospel, by which his infinite and unspeakable goodness has been made evident. The conclusion has, at the same time, this to recommend it,—that it serves to raise up and strengthen the confidence of the godly, so that with hearts lifted up to God they may fully expect all those things which are here ascribed to him, and may also confirm their hope as to what is to come by considering his former benefits.[1] But as he has made a long period, by collecting many things into one passage, the different clauses, implicated by being transposed, must be considered apart.

He ascribes first all the glory to God alone ; and then, in order to show that it is rightly due to him, he by the way mentions some of his attributes ; whence it appears that he alone is worthy of all praise. He says that he *only is wise;* which praise, being claimed for him alone, is taken away from all creatures. Paul, at the same time, after having spoken of the secret counsel of God, seems to have designedly annexed this eulogy, in order that he might draw all men to

[1] This conclusion bears an evident reference to the point the Apostle had especially in view—the reconciling of the Jews and Gentiles. He connects the gospel with the ancient Scriptures, and mentions the gospel as being in unison with them. Then the Jews had no reason to complain. As in verses 17 to 20 inclusive, he reproved the Gentiles who caused divisions; so in these verses his special object is to put an end to the objections of the Jews.—*Ed.*

reverence and adore the wisdom of God : for we know how inclined men are to raise a clamour, when they can find out no reason for the works of God.

By adding, that God was *able* to confirm the Romans, he made them more certain of their final perseverance. And that they might acquiesce more fully in his power, he adds, that a testimony is borne to it in the gospel. Here you see, that the gospel not only promises to us present grace, but also brings to us an assurance of that grace which is to endure for ever ; for God declares in it that he is our Father, not only at present, but that he will be so to the end : nay, his adoption extends beyond death, for it will conduct us to an eternal inheritance.

The other things are mentioned to commend the power and dignity of the gospel. He calls the gospel *the preaching of Jesus Christ;* inasmuch as the whole sum and substance of it is no doubt included in the knowledge of Christ. Its doctrine is *the revelation of the mystery ;* and this its character ought not only to make us more attentive to hear it, but also to impress on our minds the highest veneration for it : and he intimates how sublime a secret it is, by adding that it was hid for many ages, from the beginning of the world.[1]

It does not indeed contain a turgid and proud wisdom, such as the children of this world seek ; and by whom it is held on this account in contempt : but it unfolds the ineffable treasures of celestial wisdom, much higher than all human learning ; and since the very angels regard them with wonder, surely none of us can sufficiently admire them. But this wisdom ought not to be less esteemed, because it is con-

---

[1] The words are χρόνοις αἰωνίοις, rendered improperly by *Hammond* and others, from the eternal ages, or eternity. We find them preceded by πρὸ, before, in 2 Tim. i. 9, and in Tit. i. 2 : " before the eternal ages," could not be right rendering ; nor is " before the world began," as in our version, correct; for a reference in Titus is made to God's promise. " In the times of the ages " is the rendering of *Beza* and of *Macknight;* and, in " ancient times," is that of *Doddridge* and *Stuart.* The same subject is handled in two other places, Eph. iii. 5, and Col. i. 26 : and the words used by him are " in other ages," ἐν ἑτέραις γενεαῖς, and, " from ages and generations," ἀπὸ τῶν αἰώνων καὶ ἀπὸ τῶν γενεῶν. *Theodoret* explained the terms by ἄνωθεν —in past times; and *Theophylact* by πάλαι—formerly; and *Schleusner* by a similar word, *olim.—Ed.*

veyed in an humble, plain, and simple style; for thus it has pleased the Lord to bring down the arrogance of the flesh.

And as it might have created some doubt how this mystery, concealed for so many ages, could have so suddenly emerged, he teaches us, that this has not happened through the hasty doings of men, or through chance, but through the eternal ordination of God. Here, also, he closes up the door against all those curious questions which the waywardness of the human mind is wont to raise; for whatever happens suddenly and unexpectedly, they think, happens at random; and hence they absurdly conclude, that the works of God are unreasonable; or at least they entangle themselves in many perplexing doubts. Paul therefore reminds us, that what appeared then suddenly had been decreed by God before the foundation of the world.

But that no one might raise a dispute on the subject, and charge the gospel with being a new thing, and thus defame it, he refers to the prophetic Scriptures, in which we now see, that what is fulfilled had been foretold; for all the Prophets have rendered to the gospel so clear a testimony, that it can in no other way be so fully confirmed. And God thus duly prepared the minds of his people, lest the novelty of what they were not accustomed to should too much astonish them.[1]

---

[1] This clause is differently construed: some connect "prophetic Scriptures" with "manifested," or made manifest. So *Doddridge* and *Stuart;* but *Beza, Pareus,* and *Macknight* agree with *Calvin,* and connect the words with "made known" or proclaimed. The conjunctive τι after διὰ favours this construction; and διὰ means here "by the means," or by the aid and sanction, "of the prophetic Scriptures." Then the meaning is—"that the mystery, hid for ages, is now manifest, that is, by the gospel, and by means of the prophetic Scriptures, and consistently with the decree (ἐπιταγὴν) or ordination of the eternal God, is made known to all nations for the obedience of faith." According to this view is the exposition of *Calvin,* which is no doubt correct.

But it is more consistent with the tenor of the latter part of this epistle, and with the other passages, such as Eph. iii. 4-6, and Col. i. 26, 27, where he mentions the same mystery, to consider the reference here to be exclusively to the union of Jews and Gentiles, and not generally to the gospel, as *Calvin* and others have thought.

There is a grammatical difficulty in the last verse: the relative ᾧ is found before "glory." *Beza* and others considered it redundant. The verse is literally as follows,—

27. To the only wise God, through Jesus Christ, to whom *be* the glory for ever. Amen.

It is omitted in a few copies; several copies have αὐτῷ, which would read

If any one objects and says, that there is an inconsistency in the words of Paul, because he says that the mystery, of which God had testified by his Prophets, was hid throughout all the ages;—the solution of this knot is plainly given by Peter,—that the Prophets, when they sedulously inquired of the salvation made known to us, ministered, not to themselves, but to us. (1 Pet. i. 12.) God then was at that time silent, though he spoke; for he held in suspense the revelation of those things concerning which he designed that his servants should prophesy.

Though it is not agreed among the learned in what sense he calls the gospel a hidden mystery in this place, and in Eph. iii. 9, and in Col. i. 26; yet their opinion has most in its favour, who apply it to the calling of the Gentiles, to which Paul himself expressly refers in his Epistle to the Colossians. Now, though I allow this to be one reason, I yet cannot be brought to believe that it is the only reason. It seems to me more probable that Paul had also a regard to some other differences between the Old and the New Testament. For though the Prophets formerly taught all those things which have been explained by Christ and his Apostles, yet they taught them with so much obscurity, that in comparison with the clear brightness of gospel light, it is no wonder that those things are said to have been hidden which are now made manifest. Nor was it indeed to no purpose that Malachi declared that the Sun of righteousness would arise, (Mal. iv. 2;) or that Isaiah had beforehand so highly eulogized the embassy of the Messiah. And lastly, it is not without reason that the gospel is called the kingdom of God: but we may conclude from the event itself,

better: but its genuineness is rejected by *Griesbach* and others. The ascription of praise is evidently given to God, as one who has contrived and arranged his dispensation of grace and mercy: and his wisdom here refers to the same thing, as in ch. xi. 33. However mysterious may his dispensation appear to us with regard to the Jews and Gentiles, in leaving the latter for so long a time in ignorance, in favouring the former only in the first instance with a revelation of himself, and then in showing favour to the Gentiles, and in rejecting the Jews for a time, and afterwards restoring them—however mysterious all these things may appear, the Apostle assures us that they are the arrangements of the only wise God. —*Ed.*

that then only were opened the treasures of celestial wisdom, when God appeared to his ancient people through his only-begotten Son, as it were face to face, all shadows having been done away. He again refers to the end, mentioned at the beginning of the first chapter, for which the gospel is to be preached,—that God may lead all nations to the obedience of faith.

PRAISE FOR EVER TO

THE ONLY WISE GOD:

AMEN.

A TRANSLATION

OF

CALVIN'S VERSION

OF

THE EPISTLE TO THE ROMANS.

CHAPTER I.

1 PAUL, a servant of Jesus Christ, a called Apostle, chosen for
2 the gospel of God, which he had before promised by his Pro-
3 phets in the holy Scriptures, concerning his Son, who came
4 from the seed of David according to the flesh; declared the Son
of God in power, through the Spirit of holiness, by the resur-
5 rection from the dead, *even* Jesus Christ our Lord; through
whom we have received grace and apostleship for the obedi-
6 ence of faith among all nations, for his name's sake; among
7 whom ye are also the called of Jesus Christ; To all of you who
are at Rome, beloved by God, called saints : grace to you, and
peace from God the Father, and the Lord Jesus Christ.
8 First indeed I give thanks to my God, through Jesus Christ,
for you all, because your faith is proclaimed through the whole
9 world. For my witness is God, whom I serve with my spirit
in the gospel of his Son, that I continually make mention of
10 you, in all my prayers, requesting that by some means a prosperous journey may some time be given me, through God's
11 will, to come to you: for I desire to see you, that I may impart
12 to you some spiritual gift to confirm you; that is, that we may
mutually partake of encouragement through mutual faith, even
yours and mine.
13 And I would not that you should not know, brethren, that I
have often proposed to come to you, (and have been hitherto
hindered,) that I might have some fruit among you as also
14 among other nations. Both to the Greeks and to the barba-
15 rians, both to the wise and to the foolish, am I a debtor; so

16 that, as far as I can, I am ready to preach the gospel to you also who are at Rome; for I am not ashamed of the gospel of Christ, since it is the power of God for salvation to every one
17 who believes, to the Jew first, then to the Greek; for the righteousness of God is in it revealed from faith to faith, as it is written, " The just by his faith shall live."
18 Revealed also is the wrath of God from heaven, against all the impiety and injustice of men, who unjustly suppress the truth
19 of God; because what may be known of God, is manifest in
20 them, for God has manifested it to them; since his invisible things are seen from the creation of the world, being understood by his works, *even* his eternal power and divinity, so that they are
21 inexcusable; inasmuch as when they knew God, they glorified him not as God, nor were thankful; but became vain in their
22 thoughts, and darkened was their foolish heart: when they
23 thought themselves wise, they became fools, and changed the glory of the incorruptible God into the likeness of an image, *into that* of a corruptible man and of birds and of quadrupeds and of reptiles.
24 Therefore God gave them up to the lusts of their own hearts for uncleanness, that they might degrade their bodies among
25 themselves, who had transformed the truth respecting God into falsehood, and worshipped and adored the creature above
26 the Creator; who is blessed for ever; Amen:—Therefore, I say, God gave them up to disgraceful passions; for their women turned the natural habit into that which is contrary to
27 nature; and in like manner the men also, having left off the natural use of the woman, burned with mutual lust, one towards another, males working filthiness with males, and receiving in themselves the reward due to them for their going astray.
28 And as they chose not to retain the knowledge of God, God gave them up to a reprobate mind, to do things not becoming;
29 that they might be full of all unrighteousness, wickedness, lust, avarice, malignity, being filled with envy, murder, strife, guile,
30 perversity, *being* whisperers, calumniators, haters of God, villanous, disdainful, haughty, inventors of evils, disobedient to
31 parents, without understanding, insociable, void of natural
32 affections, truce-breakers, merciless; Who, when they knew the judgment of God, that they who do such things are worthy of death, not only do them, but approve of those who do them.

CHAPTER II.

1 Therefore inexcusable art thou, O man, who judgest; for in what thou judgest another, thou condemnest thyself, for
2 the same things doest thou who judgest. Now we know that God's judgment is according to truth on those who do such things.

3 And thinkest thou, O man, who judgest those who do such things and doest the same, that thou shalt escape the judgment
4 of God? Or despisest thou the riches of his goodness and forbearance and gentleness, not knowing that the goodness of God
5 leads thee to repentance? but according to thy hardness and a heart that cannot repent, thou treasurest for thyself wrath for the day of wrath and of the revelation of the righteous judg-
6 ment of God; who will render to every one according to his
7 works,—to those indeed, who by perseverance in doing good,
8 seek glory and honour and immortality, eternal life; but to those who are contentious and disobedient to the truth and obey
9 unrighteousness, *there shall be* indignation and wrath: tribulation and anguish *shall be* on every soul of man who doeth evil,
10 the Jew first, then the Greek; but glory and honour and peace *shall be* to every one who works good, to the Jew first, then
11 to the Greek; since there is no respect of persons with God.
12 For whosoever have without the law sinned, shall also without the law perish; but whosoever have under the law sinned,
13 shall by the law be judged: for not the hearers of the law are just before God; but they who do the law shall be justified.
14 When indeed the Gentiles, who have not the law, do by nature the things of the law, they, having not the law, are a law to
15 themselves; who show the work of the law written on their hearts, their conscience at the same time attesting, and their
16 thoughts accusing or excusing each other, in the day in which God will judge the secrets of men, according to my gospel, through Jesus Christ.
17 Behold, thou art named a Jew, and restest in the law and
18 gloriest in God, and knowest his will and approvest of things
19 excellent, being instructed from the law, and art confident that thou thyself art a leader to the blind, a light to those who are
20 in darkness, an instructor to the foolish, a teacher to the ignorant, because thou hast the form of knowledge and of the truth
21 according to the law: Yet thou who teachest another, dost not teach thyself; thou who preachest " steal not," stealest; thou
22 who sayest, " commit no adultery," committest adultery; thou
23 who hatest idols, committest sacrilege; thou who gloriest in the
24 law, by transgressing the law dishonourest God; for the name of God, as it is written, is reproached on your account among the nations.
25 For circumcision indeed profits, if thou keep the law; but if thou be a transgressor of the law, thy circumcision is turned
26 into uncircumcision. If then the uncircumcision keep the righteousness of the law, shall not his uncircumcision be count-
27 ed for circumcision? and shall not he who is by nature uncircumcision judge thee, (if he keep the law,) who by the letter and
28 circumcision art a transgressor of the law? For not he who is a *Jew* openly, is a Jew; nor is that circumcision which is openly
29 in the flesh: but he who is one in secret is a Jew; and circum-

cision is *that* of the heart, in the spirit, not in the letter; the praise of whom is not from men, but from God.

CHAPTER III.

1 What then is the privilege of the Jew, or what is the benefit
2 of circumcision? Much in every way; and first indeed, because to them have been intrusted the oracles of God.
3 What indeed if some have not believed? Shall their unbe-
4 lief render void the faithfulness of God? By no means; but let God be true, and every man false, as it is written, " That thou mightest be justified in thy words, and overcome when
5 thou art judged." But if our unrighteousness commend the righteousness of God, what shall we say? Is God unjust who
6 executes wrath? (according to man I speak:) by no means;
7 for how then shall God judge the world? If indeed the truth of God has through my falsehood redounded to his glory, why
8 still am even I judged as a sinner,—and *why* not (as we are reproached, and as some declare that we say) " Let us do evils, that good things may come?" the judgment of whom is just.
9 What then? do we excel? Not at all; for we have before brought a charge against both Jews and Greeks, that they are
10 all under sin; as it is written, " There is none righteous, not
11 indeed one; there is none who understands, there is none who
12 seeks God; all have turned aside; they have become together unprofitable; there is none who doeth kindness, no, not even
13 one: An open grave is their throat; with *their* tongues have
14 they dealt deceitfully: The poison of asps is under their lips:
15 Whose mouth is full of cursing and bitterness: Swift are their
16 feet to shed blood; ruin and misery are in their ways; and
17 the way of peace have they not known: There is no fear of
18 God before their eyes."
19 Now we know that whatever the law says, it speaks to those who are under the law, that every mouth may be stopped, and
20 the whole world may become guilty before God: because no flesh shall by the works of the law be justified before him, since by the law is the knowledge of sin.
21 But now the righteousness of God without the law is mani-
22 fested, being approved by the law and the Prophets,—even the righteousness of God through faith in Jesus Christ, *which is* to all and upon all who believe: there is indeed no difference; for
23 all have sinned, and are become destitute of the glory of God;
24 *and* they are justified gratuitously by his grace through the re-
25 demption which is in Christ Jesus; whom God has set forth *as* a propitiatory through faith in his blood, for a demonstration of
26 his righteousness on account of the remission of sins, which before existed through the forbearance of God,—for a demonstra-

tion of his righteousness, at this time, that he might be just and the justifier of him who believes in Jesus.
27 Where then is glorying? It is excluded: by what law? of
28 works? no; but by the law of faith. We then conclude, that
29 by faith is man justified without the works of the law. Is he the God of the Jews only? and not also of the Gentiles? Yes,
30 of the Gentiles also; since one is God, who will justify the circumcision by faith and the uncircumcision through faith.
31 Do we then make void the law by faith? By no means; but we confirm the law.

CHAPTER IV.

1 What shall we then say, that Abraham, our father according
2 to the flesh, had obtained? For if Abraham was by works justified, he has what he may glory in, but not before God.
3 But what saith the Scripture? "Abraham believed God, and
4 it was imputed to him for righteousness." To him indeed who works the reward is not imputed as a grace, but as a debt:
5 but to him who works not, but believes on him who justifies the ungodly, imputed is his faith for righteousness.
6 As David also describes the blessedness of the man, to
7 whom God imputes righteousness without works, "Blessed are they whose iniquities are forgiven, and whose sins are
8 covered; blessed is the man to whom God has not imputed sin."
9 Was then this blessedness on the circumcision *only*, or also on the uncircumcision? for we say, that imputed to Abraham
10 was faith for righteousness: how then was it imputed? when he was in circumcision, or in uncircumcision? not in circum-
11 cision, but in uncircumcision; and he received the sign of circumcision *as* a seal of the righteousness of the faith which he had in uncircumcision, that he might be the father of all who believe while in uncircumcision, in order that to them also
12 righteousness might be imputed,—and the father of the circumcision, not to those who are in circumcision only, but who walk in the footsteps of that faith which our father Abraham had in uncircumcision.
13 It was not indeed by the law that the promise was to Abraham and to his seed, that he should be the heir of the world,
14 but through the righteousness of faith. For if they who are of the law are heirs, *then* made void is faith, and abolished
15 is the promise. For the law causeth wrath: but where no law
16 is, there is also no transgression. It is therefore by faith, that *it might be* through grace, in order that the promise might be sure to all the seed, not to that only which is of the law, but
17 which also is of the faith of Abraham, who is the father of us all, (as it is written, "The father of many nations have I made

thee,") before God whom he believed, who quickens the dead,
18 and calls things which are not, as though they were: Who against hope believed through hope, that he would be the father of many nations, according to what had been said, "So
19 shall thy seed be." And being not in faith weak, he considered not his own body, now dead, when he was nearly an
20 hundred years old, nor the dead womb of Sarah; nor did he indeed search into the promise of God through unbelief, but
21 was strengthened by faith, giving glory to God; and being assuredly persuaded, that what he had promised he was also
22 able to perform: and it was therefore imputed to him for righteousness.
23 Now it was not written on his account only, that it was im-
24 puted to him: but also on our account, to whom it shall be imputed, *even to us* who believe on him, who raised Jesus our
25 Lord from the dead; who was delivered for our offences and raised for our justification.

CHAPTER V.

1 Being then justified, we have peace with God through our
2 Lord Jesus Christ; through whom we have had access by faith to this grace in which we stand, and glory in the hope
3 of the glory of God: and not only so, but we glory also in
4 tribulations; knowing that tribulation produces patience;
5 and patience, experience; and experience, hope: moreover, hope makes *us* not ashamed, because the love of God is diffused in our hearts by the Holy Spirit, who has been given to us.
6 For Christ, when we were as yet as to time weak, died for
7 the ungodly. Hardly indeed for the just will any one die; but for the good perhaps some one may even venture to die:
8 but God confirms his love towards us, because when we were
9 yet sinners, Christ died for us. Much more then, having been now justified by his blood, shall we be saved by him from wrath.
10 If indeed when we were enemies we were reconciled to God by
11 the death of his Son, much more, having been reconciled, shall we be saved through his life: and not only so, but we also glory in God through our Lord Jesus Christ, through whom we have now received reconciliation.
12 Wherefore as by one man sin entered into the world, and through sin death; and so over all men has death spread, since
13 all have sinned; (for until the law sin was in the world; but
14 sin is not imputed when there is no law. Yet reign did sin from Adam to Moses, even over them who had not sinned after the likeness of the transgression of Adam, who is the
15 figure of him that was to come. But not as the offence, so also the gift: for if through the offence of one many died,

much more has the grace of God, and the gift of God through
16 grace, abounded unto many. And not as through one who
had sinned, so the gift; for judgment was from one *offence* to
condemnation, but the gift is from many offences unto justi-
17 fication. For if by the offence of one death reigned through
one, much more shall they who have received abundance of
grace, and the gift of righteousness, reign in life through one,
18 Jesus Christ.) Therefore as through the offence of one *judgment came* on all men to condemnation, so also through the
justification of one, *the gift comes* to all men to the justification
19 of life: for as through the disobedience of one man many were
made sinners, so also through the obedience of one many shall
be made righteous.
20 But the law intervened, that the offence might abound: but
where sin abounded, grace has superabounded; that as sin has
reigned through death, so grace also might reign through
righteousness unto eternal life through Jesus Christ our Lord.

CHAPTER VI.

1 What then shall we say? Shall we continue in sin that
2 grace may abound? By no means: we who have died to sin,
3 how shall we still live in it? Know ye not, that we all, who
have been baptized into Jesus Christ, have been baptized into
4 his death? Buried then have we been with him through baptism unto death, that as Christ was raised from the dead by
the glory of the Father, so we also should walk in newness of
5 life: for if we have been ingrafted in the likeness of his death,
6 doubtless we shall also be partakers of *his* resurrection; knowing this, that our old man was crucified together with him,
that abolished might be the body of sin, so that we may no
7 longer serve sin: for he who has died, has been freed from sin.
8 Now if we have died with Christ, we believe that we shall
9 also live with him; knowing that Christ, having been raised
10 from the dead, dies no more, death no more reigns over him:
for that he died, he once for sin died; and that he lives, he
lives to God.
11 So also regard ye yourselves to be dead indeed to sin, but
12 alive to God in Christ Jesus our Lord. Let not sin then
13 reign in your mortal body, so as to obey it in its lusts. Neither present your members, as weapons of unrighteousness, to
sin; but present yourselves to God, as alive from the dead,
14 and your members, as weapons of righteousness, to God: for
sin shall not rule over you, since ye are not under the law,
but under grace.
15 What then? Shall we sin, because we are not under the
16 law, but under grace? By no means: know ye not that to
whom ye present yourselves servants for obedience, ye are the
17 servants of him whom ye obey, whether of sin for death, or

of obedience for righteousness? But thanks to God; for ye have been the servants of sin, but ye have obeyed from the
18 heart the form of doctrine into which you were delivered; and having been freed from sin, ye became the servants of righteousness.
19 I speak what is human on account of the infirmity of your flesh: As ye have presented your members to uncleanness and to iniquity for iniquity, so also now present your members ser-
20 vants to righteousness for holiness: for when ye were the servants of sin, ye were free from righteousness.
21 What fruit therefore had you then in those things, of which
22 ye are now ashamed? for their end is death; but now, having been freed from sin and made servants to God, ye have your
23 fruit, holiness, and *your* end, eternal life: for the wages of sin is death; but the gift of God is eternal life in Christ Jesus our Lord.

CHAPTER VII.

1 Know ye not, brethren, (for to those who know the law I
2 speak,) that the law rules over a man as long as he lives. For a woman, subject to a husband, is bound by the law to a living husband: but if the husband die, she is loosed from the law of
3 *her* husband. While then the husband is living, she shall be called an adulteress, if she be united to another man: but if the husband be dead, she is freed from *his* law, so that she is not an adulteress by marrying another man.
4 And thus, my brethren, are ye also dead to the law through the body of Christ, that hereafter ye should be united to another, *even* to him who has been raised from the dead, that ye
5 might bring forth fruit to God. For when ye were in the flesh, the emotions of sin which are through the law wrought in
6 your members to bring forth fruit to death: but now ye are loosed from the law, having died to that by which we were held, that we might serve in newness of spirit, and not in the oldness of the letter.
7 What then shall we say? Is the law sin? By no means: yet sin I knew not except through the law; for concupiscence I
8 had not known, had not the law said, "Thou shalt not lust." And the occasion being taken, sin through the commandment
9 wrought in me every concupiscence. Sin indeed without the law is dead: and I lived some time without the law; but when
10 the commandment came, sin revived, and I died; and the commandment, which was for life, was found by me to be
11 unto death: for sin, taking occasion through the commandment,
12 led me astray, and through it slew me. So then the law indeed is holy, and the commandment holy and just and good.
13 Did then what is good become death to me? By no means: but sin, that it might appear to be sin, wrought death in me

through that which is good, in order that sin through the commandment might become above measure sinful.

14 We indeed know that the law is spiritual; but I am carnal,
15 sold under sin: for what I work I know not; since what I
16 would, this I do not, but what I hate, this I do. If then, what I would not, this I do, I consent to the law of God, that it is
17 good: and now, it is no longer I who do it, but sin which
18 dwells in me.[1] I indeed know that no good dwells in me, that is,
19 in my flesh; for to will is present with me, but to perform what is good I find not; since the good I would I do not; but the evil
20 I would not, that I do. But if what I would not, that I do, it is
21 no longer I who do it, but sin which dwells in me. I find then a law that while I am willing to do good, evil lies in wait for me.
22 I consent then to the law of God according to the inner
23 man: but I see another law in my members, resisting the law of my mind and making me captive to the law of sin which is
24 in my members. Miserable man am I! who shall rescue me
25 from this body of death?—I give thanks to God through Jesus Christ our Lord: so then with the mind I serve myself the law of God, but with the flesh the law of sin.

CHAPTER VIII.

1 There is now then no condemnation to those who are in
2 Christ Jesus, who walk not after the flesh, but after the Spirit. For the law of the Spirit of life in Christ Jesus has made me
3 free from the law of sin and of death: for it being impossible for the law, because it was weak through the flesh, God, having sent his own Son in the likeness of sinful flesh, even by a
4 sin-offering condemned sin in the flesh; that the justification of the law might be fulfilled in us, who walk not after the flesh, but after the Spirit.
5 For they who are after the flesh, think of the things of the flesh; but they who are after the Spirit, of the things of the
6 Spirit. Doubtless the thinking of the flesh is death; but the
7 thinking of the Spirit is life and peace: because the thinking of the flesh is enmity against God; for to the law of God it is
8 not subject, nor can it be; they therefore who are in the flesh, cannot please God.
9 But ye are not in the flesh, but in the Spirit, if indeed the Spirit of God dwells in you; but if any one has not the Spirit
10 of Christ, he is not his. But if Christ is in you, the body indeed is dead with respect to sin, but the spirit is life with regard
11 to righteousness. If then the Spirit of him, who raised Jesus from the dead, dwells in you, he who raised Christ from the dead will quicken your mortal bodies through his Spirit who dwells in you.

[1] Here is repeated in a different way what had been before stated, only the reference before was to the weakness of good, but here to the power of evil.

12   So then, brethren, debtors we are, not to the flesh, that we
13 may live after the flesh; for if ye live after the flesh, ye shall
   die; but if by the Spirit ye mortify the deeds of the flesh, ye
14 shall live: for as many as are led by the Spirit of God, these
   are the sons of God.
15   Ye have not indeed received the spirit of bondage again to
   fear; but ye have received the spirit of adoption, through
16 whom we cry, Abba, Father: the very Spirit itself testifies
17 together with our spirit, that we are the sons of God: and if
   sons, then heirs; the heirs of God, and co-heirs with Christ;
   if indeed we suffer with him, that we may also be glorified to-
18 gether. I indeed judge, that the afflictions of this time are not
   to be compared to the future glory which shall be revealed
   to us.
19   For the intent expectation of the creation waits for the reve-
20 lation of the sons of God; for to vanity has the creation been
   subjected, not willingly, but on account of him who has sub-
21 jected it in hope; because the creation itself shall also be reclaimed from the bondage of corruption into the glorious liberty
22 of the sons of God; for we know that the whole creation
23 groans and labours in pain to this day: and not only so, but
   we ourselves also, who have the beginnings of the Spirit, even
   we ourselves do groan in ourselves, waiting for *our* adoption,
24 the redemption of our body; for by hope are we saved: but
   hope that is seen is not hope; for what one sees, how can he
25 hope for *it?* If then for what we see not we hope, we wait for
   it in patience.[1]

[1] To exhibit the meaning of this passage according to what is advanced in a note in pp. 306, 307, it shall be presented here in lines,—
   19. Truly the intent expectation of the creature
        Waits for the revelation of the sons of God;
   20. For to vanity has the creature been subjected, not willingly,
        But on his account who has subjected it in hope;
   21. For even the creature itself shall be freed from the bondage of corruption,
        Into the glorious liberty of the sons of God;
   22. For we know that every creature groans together,
        And together travails in pain to this day:—
   23. And not only *they*, but we also ourselves,
        Who possess the first-fruit of the Spirit,
        Even we ourselves groan within ourselves,
        Anxiously waiting for *our* adoption,
        The redemption of our body;
   24. For in hope are we saved,
        But hope seen is not hope;
        For what one sees, why does he yet hope for it?
   25. But if what we see not, we hope for,
        We wait for *it* in patience.

We *may* indeed consider " every creature" in verse 22 as referring to every renewed creature then living, (except the Apostles and those endowed with the extraordinary gifts of the Spirit,) and all such from the beginning of the world. In this case, " to this day" has a striking import. All God's servants from the beginning had been groaning under the body of sin, and not only they, but even those who had enjoyed the first outpouring of the Spirit, and had been

26 And in like manner the Spirit also assists our infirmities; for what to pray for as we ought we know not; but the Spirit
27 himself intercedes for us with groanings unutterable: and he who searches the hearts knows the mind of the Spirit; because he intercedes according to God's *will* for the saints.
28 We further know, that to those who love God all things co-operate for good, even to those who are called according to
29 *his* purpose: for whom he has foreknown, he has also predetermined to be conformed to the image of his Son, that he might
30 be the first-born among many brethren; and whom he has predetermined, them has he also called; and whom he has called, them has he also justified; and whom he has justified, them has he also glorified.
31 What then shall we say to these things? If God be for us,
32 who can be against us? He who spared not his own Son, but delivered him up for us all, how shall he not with him also freely give us all things?
33 Who shall bring an accusation against the elect of God? God
34 is he who justifies. Who is he who condemns? Christ is he who died; nay, rather who has been raised, who also is at the right hand of the Father, and who intercedes for us.
35 Who shall separate us from the love of Christ? tribulation, or distress, or persecution, or famine, or nakedness, or danger,
36 or sword? As it is written, "For thee we die daily, we are
37 counted as sheep destined for the slaughter:" but in all these things we do more than overcome through him who has loved
38 us. For I am persuaded, that neither death nor life, neither angels nor principalities nor powers, neither things present
39 nor things future, neither height nor depth, nor any other created thing, shall be able to separate us from the love of God, which is in Christ Jesus.

CHAPTER IX.

1 The truth I say in Christ, I lie not, my conscience bearing me
2 a testimony together with the Holy Spirit, that I have a great
3 grief and a continual sorrow in my heart; for I myself could wish to be an anathema from Christ for my brethren, my
4 kindred according to the flesh; who are Israelites, whose are the adoption and the glory and the covenants and the lawgiv-
5 ing and the worship and the promises; whose are the fathers, and from whom is Christ according to the flesh, who is above all, God blessed for ever. Amen.

endued with extraordinary gifts. The gifts of the Spirit, however abundant, did not free any from the bondage of corruption, from the body of sin; but this was an object of hope, for which they were to wait. The context, before and after, clearly shows that the present condition of God's people is the subject. —*Ed*.

6   Not however as though God's word has failed; for not all
7 who are from Israel are Israelites; nor are they who are the
    seed of Abraham, on this account all sons; but, "In Isaac
8 shall thy seed be called;" that is, They who are the sons of
    the flesh, are not the sons of God; but they who are the sons
9 of the promise shall be counted for a seed. For the word of
    promise is this, " According to this time shall I come, and
10 there shall be a son to Sarah." And not only *he*, but Rebecca
11 also, who had conceived by one, our father Isaac; for when
    the *children* were not yet born, and had done neither good nor
    evil, that the purpose of God according to election might stand,
12 not by works, but through him who calls, it was said to her,
13 " The elder shall serve the younger;" according to what is
    written, " Jacob have I loved, but Esau have I hated."
14   What then shall we say? Is there unrighteousness with
15 God? By no means: for he says to Moses, " I will have
    mercy on whom I will have mercy, and I will have compas-
16 sion on whom I will have compassion." It is not then of him
    who wills, nor of him who runs; but of God who shows
17 mercy. For the Scripture saith to Pharaoh, " For this have
    I raised thee, that I might show in thee my power, and that
18 my name might be proclaimed through the whole earth." So
    then on whom he wills he has mercy, and whom he wills he
    hardens.
19   Thou wilt then say to me, Why does he still blame? His will,
20 who has resisted *it?* But, O man, who art thou who contend-
    est in judgment with God? Does the earthen vessel say to
21 the potter, Why hast thou thus made me? Has not the former
    of the clay power, from the same mass, to make one vessel to
22 honour, another to dishonour? And what if God, willing to
    show *his* wrath and to make known his power, has endured
23 with much patience the vessels of wrath, prepared for destruc-
    tion; that he might also make known the riches of his grace
    towards the vessels of mercy, which he has foreprepared for
24 glory? Whom he has also called, even us, not only from the
25 Jews, but also from the Gentiles; as he says in Hosea, " I will
    call them my people, who is not a people, and her beloved,
26 who is not beloved: and it shall be in the place where it was
    said to them, ' Not my people are ye;' there shall they be
27 called the sons of the living God:" and Isaiah exclaims re-
    specting Israel, " Though the number of the sons of Israel
28 should be as the sand of the sea, *yet only* a remnant shall be
    saved; for the work *he will* finish and shorten, because a short-
29 ened work will the Lord do on the earth;" as Isaiah had also
    said before, " Except the Lord of hosts had left us a seed, we
    should have been as Sodom and made like to Gomorrha."
30   What then shall we say? That the Gentiles, who did not
    follow after righteousness, have obtained righteousness, even
31 the righteousness which is by faith: but Israel, by following
    after the law of righteousness, has not attained to the law of

32 righteousness. Why? Because [they followed after it] not by faith, but as it were by works; for they have stumbled at the
33 stone of stumbling, according to what is written, " Behold, I lay in Sion a stone of stumbling and a rock of offence:" and, " Every one who believes in him shall not be ashamed."

CHAPTER X.

1 Brethren, the kind desire of my heart, and prayer to God
2 for Israel, is for *their* salvation. For I bear to them a testimony, that they have a zeal for God; but not according to
3 knowledge: for being ignorant of the righteousness of God, and seeking to establish their own righteousness, they have not
4 submitted to the righteousness of God; for the end of the law is Christ for righteousness to every one who believes.
5 For Moses describes the righteousness which is by the law,
6 " The man who shall do these things shall live by them:" but the righteousness, which is by faith, saith thus, " Say not in thine heart, ' Who shall ascend into heaven?' this is to bring
7 down Christ; or, ' Who shall descend into the deep?' that is to bring up Christ again from the dead:" but what does it say?
8 " Nigh thee is the word, in thy mouth and in thy heart:" this
9 is the word of faith which we preach,—That if thou wilt confess with thy mouth the Lord Jesus, and believe in thy heart that
10 God has raised him from the dead, thou shalt be saved; for with the heart we believe to righteousness, and with the mouth
11 confession is made to salvation; for the Scripture says, " Every
12 one who believes in him shall not be ashamed:" for there is no difference between the Jew and the Greek; for the same is the
13 Lord of all, being rich to all who call on him; for, " whosoever shall call on the name of the Lord shall be saved."
14 How then shall they call on him in whom they have not believed? and how shall they believe in him of whom they have not heard? and how shall they hear without a preacher? and
15 how shall they preach except they be sent? As it is written, " How beautiful are the feet of those who proclaim peace,
16 who proclaim good things!" But all have not obeyed the gospel; for Isaiah says, " Who has believed our report?"
17 Faith then is by hearing, and hearing through the word of
18 God. But I say, Have they not heard? Yes, verily, " Into all the earth has gone forth their sound, and into the ends of
19 the world their words." But I say, Has not Israel known? First, Moses says, " I will provoke them to jealousy by them who are not a people, and by a foolish nation will I irritate
20 them:" then Isaiah is bold and says, " I have been found by those who sought me not, I have been made manifest to those
21 who inquired not for me;" but of Israel he says, " Daily have I stretched forth my hands to a people disobedient and gainsaying."

CHAPTER XI.

1 I say then, Hath God cast away his people? By no means; for I also am an Israelite, from the seed of Abraham, *from* the
2 tribe of Benjamin. God has not cast away his people whom he has foreknown. Know ye not what the Scripture saith as
3 to Elias? how he appeals to God against Israel, saying, "Lord, thy prophets have they killed, and thy altars have they pulled
4 down, and I am left alone, and they seek my life?" But what says the answer of God to him? "I have reserved for myself seven thousand men, who have not bowed the knee to the
5 image of Baal." So now, even at this time, there is a remnant
6 according to the election of grace : and if through grace, then no longer by works, otherwise grace is no longer grace; but if by works, then no longer by grace, otherwise work is no longer work.
7 What then? That which Israel seeks, he has not obtained; but election has obtained it, and the rest have been blinded,
8 as it is written, " God has given them the spirit of compunction, eyes so as not to see, and ears so as not to hear," even to
9 this day; and David says, " Be their table for a snare and for a trap, and for a stumbling, and for a recompense to them;
10 darkened be their eyes so as not to see, and their back ever bow thou down."
11 I say then, Have they stumbled so as wholly to fall? By no means; but by their fall salvation *is come* to the Gentiles
12 in order to provoke them to jealousy. But if their fall be the riches of the world, and their diminution the riches of the
13 Gentiles, how much more their fulness? Even to you Gentiles do I speak,—As far, doubtless, as I am the Apostle of the Gen-
14 tiles, I make illustrious my office, if by any means I shall pro-
15 voke to emulation my flesh, and shall save some of them. If indeed their rejection be the reconciliation of the world, what *will be their* resumption but life from the dead?
16 Now if the first-fruits be holy, even so the lump; and if the
17 root be holy, so also the branches. If indeed some of the branches have been broken off, and thou, a wild olive, hast been ingrafted instead of them, and hast become a partaker of the
18 root and fatness of the olive, glory not against the branches;
19 but if thou gloriest, it is not thou who bearest the root, but the root thee. Thou wilt then say, " Broken off have been the
20 branches, that I might be ingrafted." Be it so: for unbelief have they been broken off, and thou by faith standest; be not
21 high-minded, but fear: for if God spared not the natural branches, *beware* lest he should not spare thee.
22 See then the kindness and the severity of God; towards those indeed who have fallen, severity; but towards thee kindness, if thou continuest in *his* kindness; otherwise thou also shalt be
23 cut off : and they, if they remain not in unbelief, shall be in-

24 grafted; for God is able to ingraft them again. For if thou hast been cut off from the wild olive, which is so by nature, and hast contrary to nature been ingrafted in the true olive, much more shall they, according to nature, be ingrafted in their own olive.
25 I would not indeed, brethren, that you should be ignorant of this mystery, lest you should be proud among yourselves, that blindness has in part happened to Israel, until the fulness of
26 the Gentiles shall come in: and so all Israel shall be saved, as it is written, " Come from Sion shall the Deliverer, and shall
27 turn away impieties from Jacob; and this *shall be* my covenant
28 with them, when I shall take away their sins." As to the gospel they are indeed enemies on your account; but as to
29 election they are beloved on account of the fathers; for with-
30 out repentance are the gifts and the calling of God. As indeed ye also formerly believed not God, but have now obtained
31 mercy through their unbelief; so also they have not now believed, because ye have obtained mercy, that they may also
32 obtain mercy: for God has shut up all under unbelief, that he might show mercy to all.
33 O the depth of the riches both of the wisdom and of the knowledge of God! how incomprehensible are his judgments
34 and unsearchable his ways! Who indeed has known the mind
35 of the Lord? or who has been to him a counsellor? or, who
36 has first given to him, and it shall be rendered to him again? for from him and through him and for him are all things: to him be glory for ever. Amen.

CHAPTER XII.

1 I beseech you then, brethren, by the mercies of God, to present your bodies a living sacrifice, holy, acceptable to God,
2 *as* your rational service. And conform not yourselves to this world, but be ye transformed by the renovation of your mind, that ye may prove what is the good and acceptable and perfect will of God.
3 I indeed say, through the grace which has been given to me, to every one of you, that he be not above measure wise, beyond what he ought to be wise; but that he be wise unto sobriety, as God has to each distributed the measure of faith.
4 For as in one body we have many members, but all the members have not the same office; so we, being many, are one
5 body in Christ, and severally members of one another. Now
6 having gifts differing according to the grace given to us, whether
7 prophecy, *let us use it* according to the analogy of faith; or
8 ministry, in ministering; or the teacher, in teaching; or the exhorter, in exhortation; or the giver, in simplicity; or the president, with care; or he who shows mercy, with cheerfulness.
9 Let love be undissembled: turn away from evil, cleave to

10 what is good. Be ready with brotherly love to love one an-
11 other, anticipating each other with honour. In business be not
12 slothful, in spirit fervent, serving the time; Rejoicing in hope,
13 patient in tribulation, persevering in prayer, distributing to the
14 necessities of the saints, following hospitality. Bless those who
15 persecute you; bless and pray for no evil. Rejoice with those
16 who rejoice, and weep with those who weep, having the same feeling towards one another, not thinking arrogantly of yourselves, but accommodating yourselves to humble things: be
17 not wise in your own esteem. To no man render evil for evil,
18 providing honest things before all men. If it be possible, as far as you can, cultivate peace with all men.
19 Avenge not yourselves, beloved; but give place to wrath; for it is written, "Mine is vengeance, and I will repay, saith
20 the Lord." If then thine enemy hungers, feed him; if he thirsts, give him drink: for by so doing, thou shalt heap coals of fire on his head. Be not overcome by evil, but overcome evil by good.

CHAPTER XIII.

1 Let every soul be subject to the supreme powers; for there is no power but from God; and the powers that be have been
2 ordained by God. He therefore who resists the power, resists the ordination of God; and they who resist, shall for themselves receive judgment.
3 For princes are not for terror to good but to evil works: wouldest thou then not fear the power? Do good, and from it
4 thou shalt have praise; for he is God's minister to thee for good: but if thou doest any evil, fear; for not in vain does he bear the sword, since he is God's minister, an avenger for wrath
5 against those who do evil. It is therefore necessary to be subject, not only on account of wrath, but also on account of conscience.
6 For this reason also pay tributes, since they are God's minis-
7 ters, constantly attending to this very thing. Render then to all what is due; to whom tribute *is due*, tribute; to whom custom, custom; to whom fear, fear; to whom honour, honour.
8 To no one owe ye anything, except to love one another; for he
9 who loves another, has fulfilled the law; for this, " Thou shalt not commit adultery, Thou shalt not kill, Thou shalt not bear false testimony, Thou shalt not covet, and if there be any other
10 precept, it is comprehended in this saying, Thou shalt love thy neighbour as thyself." Love works no evil to a neighbour; the fulfilling then of the law is love.
11 Moreover, as ye know the time, that the hour is, when we ought to have awakened already from sleep, (for nearer is now
12 our salvation than when we believed,) the night is far advanced,

and the day has approached; let us then cast away the works
13 of darkness, and let us put on the armour of light: let us walk
decently as in the day, not in revellings and drunkenness, not
in chamberings and lasciviousness, not in contention and envy;
14 but put ye on the Lord Jesus Christ, and have no care for the
flesh for the sake of *its* lusts.

CHAPTER XIV.

1 Now him who is weak in faith receive, not for the debatings of questions.
2 Let him indeed who believes eat everything; but he who is
3 weak, eats herbs. Let not him who eats, despise him who abstains; and let not him who abstains, condemn him who eats,
4 since God has received him. Who art thou who judgest the servant of another? to his own Lord he stands or falls: he shall indeed stand, for God is able to make him stand.
5 One indeed esteems a day above a day; but another esteems every day alike: let every one be fully persuaded in his own mind.
6 He who regards a day, regards it for the Lord; and he who regards not a day, regards it not for the Lord: he who eats, eats for the Lord, for he gives thanks to God; and he who ab-
7 stains, abstains for the Lord, and gives thanks to God: for no
8 one of us lives to himself, and no one dies to himself; for whether we live, we live to the Lord, and whether we die, we die to the Lord; whether then we live or die, we are the Lord's.
9 For to this end Christ both died, and rose and lived again, that he might be the Lord both of the dead and of the living.
10 But thou,[1] why dost thou judge thy brother? or also thou,[2] why dost thou despise thy brother? for we must all stand be-
11 fore the tribunal of Christ; for it is written, "Live do I, saith the Lord; to me shall bow every knee, and every tongue shall
12 confess to God." Every one of us then shall give an account
13 of himself to God. Let us therefore no more judge one another; but rather judge this, that no occasion of falling or an offence be given to a brother.
14 I know and am persuaded, that in the Lord Jesus nothing is in itself unclean: but he who regards anything unclean, to him
15 it is unclean. But if on account of meat thy brother is grieved, thou no longer walkest consistently with love: by thy meat
16 destroy not him for whom Christ died. Let not then your
17 good be subject to the evil-speaking of men: for the kingdom of God is not meat and drink, but righteousness and peace and
18 joy through the Holy Spirit. For he who in these things serves Christ, is acceptable to God and approved by men.

[1] The Jewish convert.   [2] The Gentile believer.

19 Let us then follow the things of peace and of mutual edifica-
20 tion : on account of meat destroy not the work of God.
  All things are indeed pure ; but evil *it is* for man to eat with
21 offence. It is good not to eat flesh, nor to drink wine, nor to do anything, by which thy brother may fall, or be offended, or be weakened.
22 Hast thou faith ? Have it for thyself before God : happy is he who condemns not himself in that which he examines : but he who is undecided, if he eat, is condemned ; for *he eats* not in faith : and whatsoever is not from faith is sin.

CHAPTER XV.

1 Now we who are able ought to bear the infirmities of the
2 unable, and not to please ourselves : let indeed each of us
3 please *his* neighbour for good, to *his* edification. For even Christ did not please himself ; but, as it is written, "The re-
4 proaches of those who reproached thee, fell upon me." For whatsoever things have been before written, have been written for our instruction, that through the patience and consolation
5 of the Scriptures we might have hope : and may the God of patience and of consolation grant you to have the same mind
6 towards one another, according to Christ Jesus, that ye may unanimously, with one mouth, glorify the God and Father of our Lord Jesus Christ.
7 Receive ye then one another, as Christ has received us, to the
8 glory of God. Now I say, that Jesus Christ became the minister of the circumcision for the truth of God, to confirm the
9 promises *made* to the fathers : the Gentiles also ought to glorify God for his mercy, as it is written, " On this account will I confess to thee among the Gentiles, and to thy name will I
10 sing :" and again he says, " Exult, ye Gentiles, with his people ;"
11 and further, " Praise the Lord, all ye Gentiles, and praise him
12 together, all ye nations :" and again Isaiah says, " There shall be the root of Jesse, and he who shall rise up to reign over the
13 Gentiles ; in him shall the Gentiles hope." And may the God of hope fill you with all joy and peace in believing, that ye may abound in hope through the power of the Holy Spirit.
14 But I am persuaded, my brethren, even I myself, concerning you, that ye are also yourselves full of goodness, having been filled with all knowledge, being able to admonish one an-
15 other. The more boldly, however, have I written to you, my brethren, in part, as putting you in mind, on account of the
16 grace given to me by God, that I should be the minister of Christ to the Gentiles, consecrating the gospel of Christ, that the offering up of the Gentiles might be acceptable, being sanctified by the Holy Spirit.

17 I have therefore reason for glorying, through Jesus Christ,
18 in the things of God. I will not indeed dare to speak anything of those things which Christ has not done through me, as to
19 the obedience of the Gentiles, by word and work, through the power of signs and of wonders, through the power of the Holy Spirit; so that from Jerusalem, and round about to Illyricum,
20 I have spread more fully[1] the gospel of Christ; thus endeavouring to preach the gospel, not where Christ was named, that I
21 might not build on another's foundation; but, as it is written, "They to whom it has not been declared concerning him, shall see; and they who have not heard, shall understand."
22 I have on this account also been often hindered from coming
23 to you: but now, having a place no longer in these regions,
24 and having a desire for many years to come to you, when I go to Spain, I shall come to you. For I hope that when I go there I shall see you, and that I shall be brought on my way thither by you, if however I shall first be in part filled by a converse with you.
25 But I am now going to Jerusalem to minister to the saints:
26 for it has pleased Macedonia and Achaia to make a contribu-
27 tion to the saints who are at Jerusalem: it has pleased them, I say, and their debtors they are; for if the Gentiles have partaken of their spiritual things, they ought also to minister
28 to them in temporal things. When therefore I shall have performed this, and have sealed to them this fruit, I shall go by
29 you to Spain: and I know that when I come to you, I shall come in the fulness of the blessing of the gospel of Christ.
30 Now I beseech you, brethren, by our Lord Jesus Christ and by the love of the Spirit, that ye strive with me in your prayers
31 for me to God, that I may be delivered from the unbelieving in Judea, and that my service, undertaken for Jerusalem, may
32 be acceptable to the saints; that with joy I may come to you by the will of God, and may, together with you, be refreshed. And the God of peace be with you all. Amen.

CHAPTER XVI.

1 Now I commend to you Phœbe, our sister, who is a deacon-
2 ess of the Cenchrean Church; that ye receive her in the Lord, as it becomes saints, and that ye assist her in whatsoever matter she may have need of you; for she has been a helper to many, and to me also.
3 Salute Prisca and Aquila, [my fellow-workers in Christ
4 Jesus, who for my life laid down their own necks, to whom

---

[1] "I have supplemented," is what *Calvin* approves: the gospel had already been partially preached, but Paul had filled up or supplied what was deficient.

not I alone give thanks, but also all the Churches of the
5 Gentiles,] and the Church in their house.
  Salute Epenetus, my beloved, who is the first-fruit of Achaia
6 in the Lord. Salute Mary, who has laboured much with us.
7 Salute Andronicus and Junia, my kinsmen and my fellow-captives, who are celebrated among the Apostles, and who were
8 before me in Christ. Salute Amplias, my beloved in the
9 Lord. Salute Urban, our helper in Christ, and Stachys, my
10 beloved. Salute Apelles, approved in Christ. Salute those
11 who are of the family of Aristobulus. Salute Herodion, my kinsman. Salute those of the family of Narcissus, who are in
12 the Lord. Salute Tryphena and Tryphosa, who have laboured much in the Lord. Salute the beloved Persis, who has
13 laboured much in the Lord. Salute Rufus, chosen in the Lord,
14 and his mother and mine. Salute Asyncritus, Phlegon, Hermas, Patrobas, Hermes, and the brethren who are with them.
15 Salute Philologus and Julia, Nereus and his sister, and Olym-
16 pas, and all the saints who are with them. Salute one another with an holy kiss. The Churches of Christ salute you.
17 But I beseech you, brethren, to observe those who stir up divisions and offences, contrary to the doctrine which ye have
18 learnt, and to avoid them: for they, who are such, serve not our Lord Jesus Christ, but their own belly; and by courteous
19 language and flattery deceive the hearts of the simple. Your obedience indeed has been published to all: I am therefore glad on your account; but I wish you to be wise for good, and
20 simple for evil. And the God of peace shall shortly bruise Satan under your feet. The grace of our Lord Jesus Christ be with you. Amen.
21 Salute you do Timothy, my fellow-worker, and Lucius and
22 Jason and Sosipater, my kinsmen. Salute you do I Tertius,
23 who have written this Epistle, in the Lord. Salute you does Gaius, my host and of the whole Church. Salute you does
24 Erastus, the treasurer of the city, and Quartus a brother. The grace of our Lord Jesus Christ be with you all. Amen.
25 Now to him who is able to confirm you according to my gospel, even the preaching of Jesus Christ according to the
26 revelation of the mystery, which was hid in former ages, but has been now made known, and through the prophetic Scriptures proclaimed, according to the appointment of the eternal God, for the obedience of faith among all nations;—to the only wise God, through Jesus Christ, be glory for ever. Amen.

Sent to the Romans, from Corinth, by Phœbe, a deaconess of the Cenchrean Church.

END OF THE NEW TRANSLATION.

INDICES

TO THE

COMMENTARIES

ON

ST. PAUL'S EPISTLE TO THE ROMANS.

INDEX

OF GREEK WORDS EXPLAINED.

	Page		Page
αἰτιάσθαι	124	καταργεῖν	115
ἀμάρτυρον	71	κρίνεσθαι	117
ἀλλα	233	κυρίῳ	466
ἀναθεμα	388	λειτουργῆσαι	536
ἀναθημα	388	μεταδιδουντοις	462
ἀναλγησίαν	335	μόρφωσιν	104
ἀνθρωποφάγους	126	οἷον τε	344
ἀνταξίας	479	ὁμοιώματι	223
ἀντίλυτρον	227	οὗ	172
ἀπάθειαν	335	παντοτε	56
ἀποστυγουντες	464	παραζηλῶσαι	424
ἀσθενεία	280	πάρεργον	130
βαθος	444	περὶ	282
γὰρ	195, 286	πεπληρωκέναι	531
γραφει	387	πλήρωμα	531
δὲ	288	προϊσταμενους	463
διὰ	166	πονηρίαν	81
δικαιοσύνη	211	πορνείαν	81
δικαίωμα	211	προληψεις	96
δραστίκον κακου	81	προτίθεναι	142
εἰ δὲ	101, 367	στενοχωρεισθαι	328
εἶναι	318	στοργὴν	464
εἰς αὐτὸν	448	συναντιλαμβάνεται	311
ελεουντοις	463	τέλος	242
ἐν	412	τινὰ	535
ἐν ᾧ	278	τὸ ἀδύνατον	278
ἐξαπατάν	256	τὸ γνωστὸν	69
εὐλογεῖν	469	τὸ φρονημα	285
εὑρηκέναι	153	τούτου	272
ἡγεμονικὸν	454	τύπον	104
θεοστυγεῖς	81	ὑβριστας	82
θυμὸς	92	ὑπερηφάνους	82
ἱλαστήριον	142	ὑπερφρόνειν	456
και ἵνα	369	φρονοῦσιν	285
καιρὸς	488	χρόνος	488
κακοηθείαν	81		

INDEX

OF HEBREW WORDS EXPLAINED.

	Page		Page
אשם	281	כלה	375
ב	69, 412	רחם	357
חנן	356	שמועה	400

INDEX

OF PASSAGES REFERRED TO, QUOTED, OR EXPLAINED.

GENESIS.			1 SAMUEL.			Chap.	Ver.	Page	Chap.	Ver.	Page
						li.	4	117	liii.	5	185
Chap.	Ver.	Page	Chap.	Ver.	Page	lvi.	11	322	lix.	7, 8	127
iii.	15	137	iv.	22	340	lxix.	10	515		20	437
vi.	3	273					22	419	lx.	1	341
	5	235					23	419	lxi.	1	215
	16	437	2 SAMUEL.			lxxii.	7	337	lxv.	1	406
xv.	6	155				cvi.	30	161			
xvii.	4	341	xxii.	50	521	cxvi.	11	116			
	7	165				cxvii.	1	522	JEREMIAH.		
		441				cxxviii.	1	162			
	20	346	1 KINGS.						vii.	4	341
xviii.	23	328								13	407
	25	120	xix.	10	412	PROVERBS.			ix.	24	71
xlviii.	16	339		18	413						102
						ii.	14	83	xi.	7	407
EXODUS.						x.	7	183	xviii.	6	366
			JOB.			xvi.	4	362	xxx.	22	52
iv.	22	339									150
ix.	16	359	xxxiv.	17	120				xxxi.	9	339
xxxii.	32	338	xl.	4	130	ISAIAH.				33	112
											439
						i.	9	375			
LEVITICUS.			PSALMS.				11	341	EZEKIEL.		
						vi.	9	418			
xviii.	5	387	i.	2	162	viii.	14	380	xi.	13	375
			ii.	7	45	x.	22, 23	374	xvi.	25	83
DEUTERONOMY.			iii.	6	322	xi.	10	522	xxxvi.	20	107
			v.	9	126	xix.	18	299			
iv.	1	95	x.	7	127	xxviii.	16	379			
		161	xiv.	1	126		22	375	DANIEL.		
	32	341			128	xxix.	10	418			
x.	16	165	xviii.	49	521	xxxvii.	4	53	vi.	20	53
xxvii.	26	95	xix.	4	402	xlii.	8	502			
xxix.	4	98		5	403	xlv.	9	366	HOSEA.		
xxx.	6	165	xxiii.	4	322	lii.	5	107			
	12	388	xxxvi.	1	127		7	399	i.	10	373
xxxii.	21	404	xlvii.	5	522		15	532	ii.	23	299
	32	474	l.	16	105	liii.	1	400			

INDEX OF SCRIPTURE PASSAGES.

Chap.	Ver.	Page
ii.	23	371
		372
		442
xiii.	9	77

JOEL.

Chap.	Ver.	Page
ii.	2	89
	32	395

AMOS.

Chap.	Ver.	Page
v.	18	89

HABAKKUK.

Chap.	Ver.	Page
ii.	4	65

ZEPHANIAH.

Chap.	Ver.	Page
i.	15	89

ZECHARIAH.

Chap.	Ver.	Page
xiii.	9	398

MALACHI.

Chap.	Ver.	Page
i.	2, 3	352
iv.	2	555

MATTHEW.

Chap.	Ver.	Page
v.	10	329
	17	151
xii.	42	110
xviii.	19	539
	20	539

MARK.

Chap.	Ver.	Page
xvi.	15	531
	20	530

LUKE.

Chap.	Ver.	Page
vii.	37	196

Chap.	Ver.	Page
xi.	32	110
xxiv.	19	530
	25	98

JOHN.

Chap.	Ver.	Page
i.	14	44
	17	387
ii.	19	46
iii.	16	142
	23	47
v.	36	530
viii.	36	238
ix.	31	196
x.	18	46
		293
xii.	43	140
xiv.	17	46
xv.	16	59
xvii.	3	71

ACTS.

Chap.	Ver.	Page
ii.	22	530
iii.	25	341
		344
vi.	7	48
ix.	15	47
xiv.	3	530
	17	71
xviii.	2	544
xx.	23	538
xxviii.	26	418

1 CORINTHIANS.

Chap.	Ver.	Page
iii.	11	532
iv.	5	100
vi.	13	506
viii.	8	506
x.	23	509
xii.	11	57
	22	195
xiii.	9	460
xiv.	5	460
	32	461

2 CORINTHIANS.

Chap.	Ver.	Page
i.	23	54
iii.	6	112
iv.	8	191

Chap.	Ver.	Page
iv.	8	328
	16	271
v.	20	47
	21	282
vi.	8	472
ix.	2	535
	11	536
x.	10	195

GALATIANS.

Chap.	Ver.	Page
i.	8	330
	15	42
iii.	11	158
	12	135
	27	221
		490
iv.	9	315
		411
v.	17	263
	25	294

EPHESIANS.

Chap.	Ver.	Page
i.	20	325
ii.	12	273
	20	532
iii.	9	555
iv.	13	57
	30	294

PHILIPPIANS.

Chap.	Ver.	Page
i.	6	495
ii.	10	503
iii.	3	54
	4	409

COLOSSIANS.

Chap.	Ver.	Page
i.	26	555

1 THESSALONIANS.

Chap.	Ver.	Page
iv.	7	50
		239
v.	3	65
	23	452

2 THESSALONIANS.

Chap.	Ver.	Page
i.	6, 9	328

1 TIMOTHY.

Chap.	Ver.	Page
i.	17	342
v.	9, 11	543

TITUS.

Chap.	Ver.	Page
i.	15	505

HEBREWS.

Chap.	Ver.	Page
i.	2	169
	14	330
ix.	15	144
xi.	3	71
xii.	18	296
xiii.	15	52

JAMES.

Chap.	Ver.	Page
i.	3	191
ii.	20	149
iv.	12	501

1 PETER.

Chap.	Ver.	Page
i.	2	317
	12	555
ii.	10	380

2 PETER.

Chap.	Ver.	Page
i.	4	189

1 JOHN.

Chap.	Ver.	Page
iii.	2	189
		303
	16	196
iv.	10	315
v.	19, 20	301

GENERAL INDEX.

A

ABBA, Father, 298, 299.
Abound, to, in hope, 525.
Abraham justified by faith through life, after his regeneration, 134, 136; a pattern of the righteousness by faith, 153, &c.; a descent from, an honour, 154; his faith described, 156; how the heir of the world, 161; circumcised after he believed, 165; the father of the faithful, 174; his strong faith, 177, 178; his laughter, blameless, 180; and Lot, examples of distress, 328; all his children not God's children, 344.
Acceptable, sacrifices, to God, 451.
Access to God through Christ, 188.
Achaia, Epenetus the first-fruit of, 545; sent contributions to Jerusalem, 535, 536.
Adam, when he became a sinner, shunned God's presence, 140; and Christ, compared, 199-213; death reigned from, to Moses, 204; a type of Christ, 204, 205; and Christ, how they differ, 210; disobedience of, 212, 213.
Admonitions, two things necessary for administering, 526.
Adoption, the spirit of, 295-299; the, of our body, to be waited for, 309; belonged to Israel, 339; based on God's mercy alone, 409.
Adversaries, the, of the truth, ever slanderous, 122, 123.
Adversities turned into blessings, 327.
Afflictions, promote the glory of the faithful, 190-192; are only momentary, 302; ought to be patiently borne, 316-319.
Alive, to be, without the law, 255.
Ambition, the cause of discord, 470.
Ambrose, his view of "name" in ch. i. 5, 47.
Ammonius, quoted, 81.
Anabaptists denied oaths to be lawful 53, 54.
Analogy, the, of faith, 459.

Anathema, the meaning of, 335.
Antiquity often fabulous, 43.
Apostles, pretended successors of, 42; their special office, 49; how they quoted Scripture, 117, 438.
Apostleship, the, a favour, 47; its peculiar work, 531, 532.
Approbation, the, of vices, a heinous sin, 82, 83.
Approval, a twofold, 103.
Arts and sciences, worthless, compared with the knowledge of God, 126.
Ashamed, the believer shall not be, 380.
Aquila saluted, 544.
Assurance, given by the Spirit, 299; the, of God's love, a sufficient support, 323; the, of salvation, rests on two foundations, 389.
Assured, to be fully, in one's own mind, 496, 497.
Asylum, the, of the sinner, faith, 155.
Avenge, to, forbidden, 473.
Avenger, the, assumes God's office, 475.
Augustine, his notion as to the word, Paul, 40; referred to on image-worship, 75; his saying respecting mercy, 82; his false view of "the righteousness of God," 134; what he says of Abraham disapproved, 178; mistaken in his view of "the love of God," 193; what he says of the "law," wrong, 214; his opinion of the tenth commandment, 252; retracted his opinion on chap. vii. 264; how he calls the Christian conflict, 270; quoted on chap. viii., 15, 298; his view of "all things" in chap. viii. 28, disapproved, 315; his answer to Pelagius, 358; a saying of, 382.
Authority belongs only to God's word, 125; not given to truth by the Church, 401, 402; the civil, to resist, is to resist God, 478, 479.

B

BABYLON, restoration from, a type of spiritual restoration, 374.

Banner, an universal, hoisted by Paul, 395.
Baptism, without holiness, an empty sign, 109; alone does not justify, 109; substituted for circumcision, 165, 166; sins after, as well as before, forgiven, 208, 209; what it signifies, 220; sometimes taken as connected with what it typifies, 221.
Barrenness of Sarah, 177.
Beginnings, the, of the Spirit, 308.
Benefits, earthly, pledges to the godly of eternal life, 169.
Benevolence, the, of God, its design, 87.
Blasphemers, how they excuse themselves, 294.
Blasphemy, the, of fanatics, 287; of the Papists, in making truth dependent on the Church, 401, 402.
Bless, to, persecutors, 468.
Blessing, the fulness of, what, 537.
Blessings, earthly, given for different purposes, 88.
Blindness, a judgment on the Jews, 418, 419; in part, what it means, 436.
Bodies, mortal, what they mean, 293; to be presented as living sacrifices, 451, 452.
Body, the, of sin, how crucified, 224; the, of death, 272; taken for the corrupt nature of man, 291.
Bondage, the spirit of, 295-298; the, of corruption, 305.
Bond of unity, Christ the, 518.
Branches, natural, the Jews were, 430.
Brother, a, to judge, is to assume God's office, 501.
Brotherly love, how to be exercised, 464.
Bucer, quoted, 51, 58.
Building on another's foundation, 532.
Budæus, quoted, 338.
Business, not to be slothful in, 465.

C

CALLING, distinguished from election, 319; and works, opposed to each other, 351; an evidence of election, 373; on God, a proof of faith, 397; effectual, 401.
Calumny, that grace favours sin, 236; that God is unjust in election, 354.
Care for the flesh, what it ought to be, 490, 491.
Cenchrea, the Church at, 542.
Ceremonies, the works of the law not confined to, 159; not meant by the law which cannot justify, 280, 379; lawful, when appointed by God, 341.

Cheerfulness, mercy to be shown with, 463.
Chosen, the, of the Father, committed to Christ's care, 49.
Christ, the manifestation of, twofold, 137; a propitiatory, 141, 142; restores the inheritance lost in Adam, 169; was delivered for our offences, 184; was raised for our justification, 185; is our peace, 187, 188; died for the ungodly, 194, 195; reconciled sinners, 197, 198; and Adam, compared, 199-213; how they differ, 210; died once to sin, 227; how he dwells in his people, 291; is an example in suffering, 328; is the brother of all the faithful, 318; is filled with all blessings, 322, 323; is our mediator and intercessor, 325; descended from the Jews, 341; his two natures, 342; and Moses, contrasted, 387; died and arose, that he might be the Lord of all, 500; his eternal divinity, 502, 503; pleased not himself, 515; became a minister of the circumcision for two ends, 520-522.
Christian philosophy, what, 241; the, priesthood, 527.
Christians die to sin, 218, 219; rise to a new life, 228, 229.
Church, the truth's authority not derived from, 402; to judge of, by appearances, not right, 411, 412; the sacrifices of, 452; its true unity, 549.
Chrysostom, his mistake as to the works of the law, 131; his opinion of "likeness," 223; quoted on chap. viii. 3, 281; his homilies referred to, 547.
Cicero, quoted, 92, 124.
Circumcision a symbol of God's covenant, 108; its true character, 108; required perfection, 109; what it really signifies, 111; why gloried in by the Jews, 132, 163; a seal of the righteousness of faith, 164, 165; why administered to infants, 165; why discontinued, 166.
Civil powers. See Magistrates.
Clay, the, the former of, 366.
Coals of fire, to heap, what, 475, 476.
Commandment, the, found to be to death, 256; is holy, just, and good, 257, 258.
Communication, mutual, required of the faithful, 459.
Compunction, the spirit of, 418.
Condemnation, doubly merited, 84; the, of the impenitent increased by

GENERAL INDEX. 583

God's bounty, 88; none to those in Christ, 275, 276.
Confession, necessary, 392.
Confidence, the ground of, 326; increases obligation, 534.
Conflict, the, of the faithful, 179; different in the natural and in the spiritual man, 262, 263; how it exists in the Christian, 270.
Conform, to, we ought not, to this world, 453, 454.
Congruity and condignity, 147.
Conjecture, the moral, of the Schoolmen, 173, 189, 300.
Conquer. See Overcome.
Conscience, ascribed to the heathens, 98; appealed to by Paul, 334.
Consciences, quieted only by faith, 135, 168, 170, 187.
Consolation and patience, given by the Scriptures, 517; the author of, God, 517, 518.
Contention, the effect of envy, 490.
Contentious, the, threatened with wrath, 91.
Corruption, the, of the heathens, 78, 79; the, of all mankind, 125-130, 199-205.
Counsel, God's, hidden, not to be curiously searched, 287, 446, 447.
Counsellor, a strange one, 105; none to God, 446.
Courteousness, to be limited, 473.
Covenant, the old, was spiritual, 521.
Covenants, the, belonged to the Jews, 340.
Coveting, made known by the law, 251, 252.
Creation, the, ought to lead us to the Creator, 70; waits for renovation, 303-306.
Creature, the, subject to vanity, 304.
Creatures, rational and irrational, the renovation of, 305, 306.
Crucified, the old man is to be, 226, 227.
Curiosity, not to be indulged on intricate questions, 353.
Custom, due to rulers, 483.

D

DARKNESS, the works of, 487, 488.
David, Christ's descent from, 44; was justified by faith after a long life of holiness, 136; his imprecation on his enemies, 419.
Day, the, of Judgment, a day of wrath to the wicked, 89; what it means, 489.

Days, a difference made in, by the Jews, 496; the observance of, an infirmity, 497.
Death, its reign from Adam to Moses, 204, 205; derives its power from sin, 215; the, of sin, the life of man, 255; the body of, 272; how to be wished, 273, 274; the law of, 277; the punishment of, given to the magistrate, 481, 482.
Debatings, the, of questions, 492, 493.
Debtor, a, Paul, to all, 60.
Debtors, none to the flesh, 293, 294; the Gentiles to the Jews, 336.
Deity, a, the idea of, implanted in all, 71.
Depth, the, of God's wisdom and knowledge, 444, 445.
Despair makes men to seek death, 273.
Destroy, to, a brother, by meat, 505, 506.
Devil, the, accuser of the faithful, 324.
Die, to, to the Lord, what, 499.
Difference, none in justification, 139; between the Jews and the Gentiles, from God's favour, 150; between Jacob and Esau, 351, 352; between the law and the gospel, 388; none between the Jew and the Greek, 395; between the gospel and philosophy, 449; a, in opinion, leads to discord, 492; in days among the Jews, 496.
Diminution, the, of the Jews, 422, 423.
Discord, occasioned by ambition, 470.
Disobedience, the, of Adam, 212, 213.
Dispensation, the, of the law and of the gospel, 297; the Mosaic, the design of, 386, 387.
Distinction. See Difference.
Distress, defined, 328.
Diversity, the, of gifts, 458, 459.
Divinity, the, and the humanity of Christ, 44; the, of God, proved by his works, 70; the, of Christ, attested, 502, 503.
Dominion, not allowed to sin, 230-233; the, of sin, when it ceases, 236; the, of Christ, over the living and the dead, 500.
Domitian, as described by Pliny, 127.
Drunkenness, leads to revelling, 489.

E

EDIFICATION, what promotes it, to be followed, 508, 509; to, to please one another, 514, 515.
Elder, the, serving the younger, 351, 352.
Elect, the, cannot be condemned,

584 GENERAL INDEX.

323, 324; a remnant, 401, 402, 413, 414.
Election, general and particular, 343-353, 440, 441; not confined to Abraham's children, 345; not based on works, 350, 351; is to be referred to God's counsel, 357; a great mystery, 367; dependent only on God's good pleasure, 370; not confined to nations, 371; manifested by calling, 373; the, the grace of, 414; what it means in chap. xi. 7, 416.
Elections, two, as to Israel, 345.
Elias, his complaint against Israel, 411-413; 7000 reserved by God in his time, 413.
Emotions, the, of sin, 249.
Emulation, the Jews provoked to, by the Gentiles, 424.
End, the, of the law, Christ is, 383, 384.
Enemy, an, ought to be fed, 475.
Enemies, no evil to be imprecated on, 468; to wish evil to, natural to man, 469.
Envy, and pride, prevent improvement, 58; no ground for, 395; produces contention, 490.
Equality among Christians, 501.
Epenetus, the first-fruits of Achaia, 545.
Erasmus, quoted, 60, 92, 179, 181, 205, 229, 236, 264, 277-279, 285, 303, 464, 469, 471, 527, 545.
Esau, why rejected, 349-352.
Eternal life, to whom promised, 90; the gift of God, 242.
Eusebius referred to, 75.
Evil, to turn away from, 464; to be overcome by good, 476; not done by love, 487.
Example, the, of Christ, in not pleasing himself, 515.
Examples, the, of Scripture, for our instruction, 182, 183.
Excellencies, those of a neutral kind, 104, 105.
Excision, the, of the Gentiles, threatened, 433; two modes of, 433, 434.
Exhortations are to follow doctrines, 229, 293, 294.
Exhorting, the office of, 462.
Experience, produced by patience, 191.
Expressions, paraphrastic, the design of, 184.

F

FAITH, the, obedience of, 48; the, of the Romans, 52; the peculiar gift of God, 52; from, to faith, 65; the righteous live by, 65, 66; receives all from God, 148; and works, blended by the self-righteous, 148; the, of Abraham, 155, 156; brings nothing but a confession of need and misery, 155; how counted righteousness, 158, 159; and sacraments, to be distinguished, 167; borrows nothing from the law, 167; different from regeneration, 173; mounts on celestial wings, 176; its weakness, twofold, 179; regards not human weakness but God's power, 181; and the word, connected, 182; the true defined, 189; sustained by promises, 326; and works, incompatible, 379; its seat, the heart, 393; produced by the word, 397; comes by hearing, 401; based on God's truth, 401; implicit, of the Papists, vain, 401, 402; generates humility and fear, 429; perseverance in, flows from God's election, 432; the weak in, how to be treated, 491-503; to act without, a sin, 512.
Faithful, the, ought, like Abraham, to believe against hope, 180; groan and wait, 306; are one body in Christ, 458.
Falsehoods, the duty of exposing, 123.
Fanatics, their blasphemy, 287.
Fathers, the, were saved through Christ, 195; how they differed from us, 297.
Fear, the, of God, takes from the flesh its sovereignty, 276; alone quelled by forgiveness, 298; compatible with the assurance of faith, 429; due to those in power, 482, 483.
Feeding an enemy, what, 475.
Feelings, of two kinds, in the faithful, 308; of two kinds, entertained by Paul, 335.
Fervent, to be, in the Spirit, 465.
First-born, the Jews were, in God's family, 437.
First-fruit, the, and the lump, in what sense holy, 425-427.
Flesh, what it means, 133; the, murmurs against God's mysteries, 234, 253; to be in, what, 249; means corrupt nature, 267; the, to walk after, what, 284, 285; the, the thinking of, 285, 286.
Forbearance, the, of God, 145.
Foreknowledge, its meaning, 316-318; not a simple prescience, 410; the, of works, to blend with election, absurd, 415.

Foundation, another's, Paul built not on, 532.
Freedom, from the law, only through Christ, 247, 248; from sin and the law, cotemporaneous, 248, 249; from sin, gained only by Christ, 288.
Free-will, proved false, 262; carried high by Sophists, 288.
Fruit, Paul wished to gather, among the Romans, 59; the, of charity, to seal, what, 536, 537.
Fulness, the, of the Jews, 422; of the Gentiles, 436; of blessings, what, 537.

G

Garrulity, the, of hypocrites, 105.
Gentiles, the, a law to themselves, 96-98; had some knowledge of the law, 98; ascribed majesty to idols, 106; called the uncircumcision, 110; all under sin, 123, 124; justified in the same way with the Jews, 134-139, 149, 150; obtained righteousness without seeking it, 377, 378; had the preaching of God's works, 402-404; received mercy in order to provoke the Jews to jealousy, 404, 405; their calling foretold by Isaiah, 405, 406; will be benefited by the restoration of the Jews, 422, 423; the Jews provoked to emulation by the, 424; compared to a wild olive, 427-430; warned not to glory, 428; the calling of, foretold in various passages, 521-523; their offering up to God, the object of Paul's ministry, 528; how made obedient, 529; the gospel preached to them according to God's command, 553-556. See Heathens.
Gift, the, of Prophecy, 459, 460.
Gifts, God's object in granting, 57; the, of God, ought to be valued, 336, 337; the, and calling of God, without repentance, 440, 441; various, in the Church, 457-463.
Glory, the, of God, to come short of, 140; given to God by faith, 180; the, of the Father, its meaning, 222; the, what it means in ch. ix. 4, 340; the riches of, 369.
Glorying excluded, 147; not allowed to Abraham, 154, 155.
God, his greatness incomprehensible, 69; his power and divinity made evident by his works, 70, 71; gave up the heathens to vile lusts, 76, 77; gave them up to a perverted mind, 79, 80; is an impartial judge, 85;
is necessarily a righteous judge, 120, 121; works good by evil, 122; his power not easily believed, 181; his love diffused in the heart by the Spirit, 192; confirms his love, 196, 197; is pleased with nothing but righteousness, 287; is the searcher of hearts, 313, 314; turns evils into benefits, 314; his favour all-sufficient, 322; spared not his own Son, 322; his gifts, wherever found, to be valued, 336-341; is debtor to none, 356, 447, 448; shows mercy to whom he wills, 361; hardens whom he wills, 362; is silent on some things, because we cannot understand them, 365; preached to the Gentiles by his works, 402, 403; ever preserves a Church for himself, 411; his gifts and calling irrevocable, 440, 441; the depth of his wisdom and knowledge, 444, 445; ordains the powers that be, 477, 478; claims authority over life and death, 499; the, of hope, 524; the, of peace, 540; is the only wise, 552.
Godly, the, enjoy lawfully what they have, 169; are divided and pulled two ways, 263; wish death, why, 273; check impatience, how, 274.
Good, the, man, described, 196; no, dwells in us, 267; intentions, often deceptive, 382, 511; and evil, what they mean, 464.
Goodness, the, of God, leads to repentance, 87, 88; the, of God, to the Gentiles, 431, 432; the, of God, abused by hypocrites, 450; the, of God, its constraining power, 450; the Romans full of, 526.
Gospel, the, included in Christ, 43; offered to the wise and the unwise, 60; contemptible in the eyes of the world, 61; the power of God, 62; how it becomes the savour of death, 62; an extraordinary knowledge of, claimed by vain talkers, 105; came to the Gentiles from the Jews, 339; conveys certainty, 391; requires nothing but faith, 391; preached in every place through God's special providence, 397; believed by few, 400; the preaching of, a sacred work, 527; formerly hid, now revealed, 553, 554; preached among all nations consistently with the prophetic writings, 554.
Government, God's ordination, 477-480; a bad, better than none, 480.

Grace, salvation wholly by, 50; men are made partakers of, by faith only, 150; opposed to offence, 207; absurdly defined by Schoolmen, 208; its superabounding, 215; calumniated by the ungodly, 218; destroys sin, 218, 219; to be under, what, 235; and merit, incompatible, 414.
Grafting into Christ, 222, 223.
Greeks, the, and Barbarians, Paul a debtor to, 60; put for all nations, 63.
Grief for the reprobate, how allowable, 334, 335.
Groaning and waiting, the case with the faithful, 308.
Groanings, unutterable, 313.

H

Hands, the extention of, what, 407.
Haters, the, of God, 81.
Haughty, who they are, 82.
Hearers, the, of the law, 95.
Heart, means the understanding, 37, 38.
Heathens, their ignorance, wilful, 71; their idolatry, 73-75; being wise, became fools, 73; their vices, evidences of God's wrath, 76.
Heavens, the, preached to the heathens, 402-404.
Herbs, the weak lived on, 494.
Hinderances, the, of the godly and of the ungodly, different, 59; the chief, in attaining righteousness, 379.
History, a teacher, 182, 183.
Holy, the Law is, 257.
Honour, to be conceded to others, 465; due to those in power, 483.
Honours, to seek, from God's enemies a disgrace, 516.
Hope, Abraham believed against, 176, 177; increased by experience, 190-192; ascribed to creatures void of reason, 304; saved by, 309; sustained by patience, 310; to rejoice in, 466; and patience, connected, 467; the God of, 524; to abound in, 525.
Hosea, a quotation from, in what sense applicable to the Gentiles, 371, 372.
Hospitality, enjoined, 467, 468.
Humility, commended, 459; and meekness, the highest excellencies, 470.
Hypocrisy, the best mode of dealing with, 86.
Hypocrites, are influenced by sinister motives, 55; make great display of sanctity, 83; summoned to God's tribunal, 85; take prosperity a proof of God's favour, 87; their garrulity, 105; glory in outward rites, 109, 132; their inebriating confidence, 256; their specious zeal, 383; pray without faith, 397.

I

Idolatry, a sacrilege, 78, 106.
Ignorance, the, of the heathens, wilful, 71; the, of God, the cause of inhumanity, 85; the sins of, less culpable than those of knowledge, 171, 172; a vain excuse, 511.
Illyricum, Paul preached as far as to, 531.
Image, an, the heathens made, of God, 74.
Impatience, how restrained, 274.
Impenitent, the, their condemnation increased by God's bounty, 88.
Impiety and unrighteousness, what they mean, 68.
Implicit faith, the, of the Papists, vain, 401, 402.
Impossibility, the, of the Law, 278.
Inconsistency, an apparent, reconciled, 198.
Incomprehensible, God's judgments are, 445.
Indignation and wrath, the lot of the disobedient, 92.
Inexcusable, the heathens were, for their idolatry, 71-74; the guilty, who judges another, 83, 84.
Infants, why circumcised, 165; included in Adam's sin, 204.
Inheritance, belongs to children, 301; attained by the cross, 301, 302; belongs only to the children of the promise, 344.
Injuries, not to be repayed, 473.
Inner man, the, and the members, how to be distinguished, 271.
Insition, three modes of, 433, 434.
Insolent, the, described, 82.
Intentions, good, often deceptive, 382, 511.
Intercession, the, of the Spirit, 312, 313; the, of Christ, how to be understood, 325.
Interpreters, pervert what is said of Pharaoh, 360; misrepresent the meaning of Isaiah x. 22, 23, 374, 375; make the second to be the first cause of perdition, 376.
Intricate questions, curiosity not to be indulged on, 353.
Invisible things, the, of God, 71.

GENERAL INDEX.

Isaac, the seed of promise, 345.
Ishmael, not the heir of promise, 346.
Israel, what it means, 437.
Israelite, an, Paul was, 409.

J

JACOB chosen, and Esau rejected, 347; loved, and Esau hated, 352.
James, consistent on justification with Paul, 149.
Jealousy, the Jews excited to, by the Gentiles, 421, 422.
Jerome, his mistake as to " the works of the law," 131.
Jerusalem, Paul preached from, to Illyricum, 531; visited by Paul, 535.
Jesse, the root of, 523.
Jew, a, who is, 111, 112.
Jews, the, called the Messiah the son of David, 44; were allowed their prerogatives by Paul, 63; when and why called Jews, 101, 102; rested in the law and boasted of their privileges, 102-105 ; their superiority was owing to God's mercy, 113, 124; were peculiarly guilty, 129, 130; their privileges enumerated, 332-341; were first-born in God's family, 339; their fall rendered not void God's truth, 343; sought righteousness without finding it, 377, 378; turned the law to a wrong purpose, 384, 385; were excluded for their sins, 405; stumbled, but fall not finally, 421 ; were moved to jealousy by the Gentiles, 421, 422 ; the first-born in God's family, 437; and Gentiles, were peculiarly tempted to disobey heathen rulers, 477 ; made a difference between meats, and also between days, 496.
Joel, his testimony as to the calling of the Gentiles, 395.
Josephus, quoted, 101.
Joy, the godly have ever reasons for, 274 ; and peace, by believing, 524, 525.
Judge, to, of the Church, by outward appearances, is wrong, 411, 412; to, a brother, is to assume Christ's office, 501 ; to, has two meanings, 503.
Judges, how they became unjust, 120.
Judging, the power of, taken from man, 495.
Judgment, the, of the world, worthless, 53; the, of God, according to truth, 85; the day of, the day of wrath to the wicked, 89; the, of those who calumniate the truth, just, 123.
Judgment-seat, the, of Christ, all must appear before, 502.
Judgments, the, of God, incomprehensible, 445.
Just, the, described, 195, 196 ; sinners counted, by God, 281-283.
Justified, to be, what it means, 324.
Justification, not by the law, 95, 96; 130-133; through grace only without any merits, 134-137, 140, 141, 414; by faith only, 156, 138, 157-159; by imputation, 144; and sanctification, united, 217, 219, 277; extends to the whole of life, 319.
Justify, baptism alone does not, 109.

K

KINDNESS, paternal, the, of God, 323, 329.
Kingdom, the, of God is not meat and drink, 506; what it consists of, 507.
Kiss, a holy, to salute with, 547.
Knot, a twofold, untied by Paul, 332, 333.
Knowledge, the, of Christ, what, 43; the form of, 103, 104; the, of God, the highest, 126; the, of God, the bond of society, 126; the, of sin by the law, 133; the, of God, alone from his word, 398 ; the, of God, the depth of, 444, 445 ; the Romans filled with, 526.

L

LASCIVIOUSNESS, condemned, 489.
Lactantius, referred to, 75 ; a saying of, 382.
Law, the, requires perfection, 95; the knowledge of, different from the power to fulfil, 97 ; the works of, what, 130-132; promises reward to good works, 131 ; discovers sin, 133; delivers us over to death, 147 ; its design, 152; not made void by faith, 151, 152; brings condemnation, 171; to be under, to be subject to the curse, 173; increases sin, 213, 214 ; to be under, what it imports, 232, 233; in what sense abolished, 234, 243, 248 ; absent, in what sense, 255; demands perfect obedience, 246, 260, 387 ; called the hand-writing, 247; freedom from, only through Christ, 247, 248; excites sin, 249; is holy, 257; is good, 265; the, of the mind, 271, 272 ; the, of sin and death, 277;

the, the impossibility of, 278 ; weak through the flesh, 280; cannot justify, 280 ; the, an expression of God's will, 287 ; its end, Christ, 383, 384 ; leads to Christ, 384 ; and the gospel, their respective demands, 391 ; its precepts reduced to love, 484; made a difference in meats and in days, 496.

Lawgiving, one of the privileges of the Jews, 340.

Letter, the, what it means, 111, 112; the oldness of, 251.

Liberty. See Freedom.

Life, eternal, God's gift, 242 ; the right object of, 499; and death, in the power of God, 499.

Live, to, to God, what, 499.

Love, evidences of, 53, 56 ; the, of God, diffused in the heart, 192; the, of God, the shield of the saints, 321 ; the, of God, separation from, impossible, 326-332 ; an evidence of, a concern for others, 381; ought to be undissembled, 464; brotherly, enjoined, 464, 465 ; comprehends the whole law, 484; to a neighbour, a fulfilling of the law, 485 ; works no evil, 487.

Lycurgus, deemed sacrilegious, 106.

M

Macedonia and Achaia, relieved the poor at Jerusalem, 535, 536.

Magistrate, the punishment of death given to the, 481, 482.

Magistrates, obedience to, required, 478-480; are ordained by God for the public good, 481; obedience to, enforced on two grounds, 482.

Maliciousness, defined, 81.

Man, naturally without a spark of good, 175; the old, why so called, 224 ; the old, to be crucified, 226, 227 ; is become earthly, 230, 273 ; when renewed, a twofold being, 270 ; the inner, and his members, 271; audacious, disputing with God, 364.

Marriage, the bond of, 245, 246.

Measure, the, of one's knowledge, 498.

Meats, a difference in, made by the Jews, 496; not to destroy a brother by, 505, 506.

Members, what they mean, 231; termed weapons, 231 ; Christians are, of one another, 458.

Men, more disposed to blame God than themselves, 354 ; think themselves wiser than God's Spirit, 355; their evasions as to election, 359; their cavils with regard to election and reprobation, 363.

Mercies, by the, of God, 450.

Mercy, shown to whom God wills, 361 ; the vessels of, 369 ; to show, with cheerfulness, 463.

Merit, not proved by reward, 90, 302, 303; excluded, 147, 148, 317, 318 ; not the cause of election, 355-366 ; human, disproved, 379.

Message, the, of the Gospel, glad tidings, 399.

Minding, the, of the flesh and spirit, 285-289.

Ministers, an encouragement to, 55.

Ministry, the, the office of, 461.

Miracles, the design of, 530.

Mortal bodies, what they mean, 293.

Mouth, the, stopped, what, 130.

Mysteries, the, of God, objected to, by the flesh, 234; not to be searched farther than the Scripture warrants, 444, 445.

Mystery, the rejection of the Jews, 435 ; the, the revelation of, 553.

N

Nature, the, of Christ, resembled sinful nature, 281.

Necessities, the, of the saints, to be relieved, 467.

Night, what it means, 487, 489.

Novatus, his error, 145.

Novelty, suspicious, 43.

Nuns, a degenerated order, 543.

O

Oath, when necessary, 53, 54 ; declared to be unlawful by the Anabaptists, 53, 54.

Obedience, the, of faith, 48 ; the, of the Romans, universally known, 52, 53, 550 ; the, of Christ, called his righteousness, 213 ; proves who our master is, 234, 235 ; to rulers, enforced on two grounds, 482 ; the, of the Gentiles, how produced, 529.

Offence, not to be given, 503, 510.

Offences, how to be avoided, 218 ; removed by Paul, 332 ; taken by the ungodly, 353, 354.

Old man to be crucified, 226, 227.

Olive-tree, an, the Jews compared to, 427-430.

Olive, a wild, the Gentiles compared to, 427-430.

Oracles, the, of God, entrusted to the Jews, 113, 114.

Origen, his idea as to the name Paul, 40; his mistake as to the works of the law, 131; his error on original sin, 205.
Original sin, the error of Pelagius as to, 201.
Overcome, the faithful more than, 329; to, evil by good, 476.
Ovid, quoted, 106.

P

PAPACY, the, the teaching of, more heathen than Christian, 449.
Papists, deny sin to be in the regenerate, 253; their philosophy, 290; absurdly support merit by adducing promises, 387; extort obedience by terror, 450.
Paradox, a, as to the Gentiles and the Jews, 377.
Paradoxes, God's mysteries are, to the flesh, 119.
Paraphrastic expressions, the meaning of, 184.
Pardon, only for sins committed, 145.
Passions, disgraceful, the heathens given up to, 79.
Past tense implies certainty, 174.
Paternal kindness of God, 323, 329.
Patience, produced by tribulation, 190, 191; necessary for hope, 310; and consolation, given by the Scriptures, 517; the God of, 517.
Paul, why so called, 40; a chosen Apostle, 41; calls God *his* God, 52, 53; his prayers for the Romans, 56; his modesty, 57, 58; a debtor to all, 60; adopts Hebrew phrases, 69; how he speaks of signs, 109; declares his own case as to the spiritual conflict, 261-273; expresses his concern for the Jews, 333-336; had sorrow and resignation, 335; his wish as to his own nation, 335, 336; owns the Jews as his kinsmen, 337; expresses his goodwill towards them, 381; reminds the Romans of his apostleship, 455, 526; proves his apostleship by the effects, 529; ascribes his success to the Spirit, 529; intended to go to Spain, 533; acknowledged his obligations to Prisca and Aquila, 544.
Peace, with God, through Christ, 187; to be cultivated with all, 472, 473; and joy, united, 507; the God of, 540.
Pelagius, his error as to original sin, 201; his evasion as to grace, 358.
Perseverance, final, denied by Sophists,

189; implied by the fact of glorying, 189.
Persons, the respect of, what, 93, 94.
Perversity, what it means, 81.
Pharaoh, predestinated to ruin, 359; interpreters pervert what is said of him, 360; hardened, 362.
Pharisee, the, and the thoughtless sinner, 187.
Pharisees, their character, 110.
Philosophers, did not originate but adopt the superstitions of the people, 73, 74; their view of virtues and vices, 253.
Philosophy, what is Christian, 261.
Phœbe, recommended to the Romans, 542.
Plato, involved in idolatry, 74.
Please, to, one another for edification, 514, 515.
Pliny, his character of Domitian, 127.
Powers, the higher, obedience due to, 477-482.
Pray, to, we know not how, 312.
Prayer, when right, 299; must be according to God's will, 314; and faith, connected, 397; perseverance in, 467; the Romans besought to strive in, for Paul, 539.
Preacher, the true, sent by God, 398, 399.
Preaching, the contempt of, a contempt of God's authority, 48; made the means of salvation, 62; when blessed, produces faith, 401; the means of saving through the Spirit, 424.
Precepts, the, of the law, included in love, 484.
Predestination, what it means, 318; a labyrinth, 353; our views of, to be limited to Scripture, 354, 446; the second made by some the first cause of, 376.
Preparations, a vain figment, 188.
Presidents, how they were to rule, 263, 264.
Pride, innate in man, 459; breaks unity, 470; much, in the Romans, 525, 526.
Priesthood, the, of Christian pastors, 527.
Priests, Christians are made, 452.
Princes, obedience due to, 480.
Prisca and Aquila saluted, 544.
Promise, the, of salvation, how to be viewed as made to Israel, 345.
Promises, the, and the gospel, not to be confounded, 43; in order to be sure, are made to faith, 170, 171; the, of the Old Testament, deemed only temporal by fanatics, 520.

Prophecy, the gift of, 459, 460.
Prophets, the, the spirit of, subject to, 461; false, their unvarying mark, 549.
Propitiatory, a, Christ was made, 141-143.
Provide, to, good things, 471.
Punishment, the, of death, given to the civil power, 481, 482.
Pure, all things are, 509.
Purists, their dogma, 275.
Purpose, God's, explained, 315, 316.
Put on, to, Christ, what, 490.

Q

QUESTIONS, intricate, curiosity not to be indulged in, 353; the debatings of, 492, 493; difficult, harass weak consciences, 493.

R

RABBINS, their gloss on Is. lxv. 1, 406.
Reason, human, rebels against God's wisdom, 119; the highest, for imparting grace, 356; deemed a queen by heathens, dethroned by Paul, 454.
Reasonable, a, service, 452, 453.
Rebecca, the mother of twins, 347.
Redemption through Christ, 141; the, of the body, 309.
Regeneration, and justification, united, 217, 219, 277; progressive, 226, 262, 291.
Reign, the, of sin, what, 231.
Rejection of Esau, 349-352.
Rejoice, to, in hope, 466; to, with those who rejoice, 469.
Relics, the, of sin in the godly, 263.
Remission, the, of sins past, 143; and merit, incompatible, 144, 159, 160; connected with regeneration, 290.
Remnant, a, the elect are, 413, 414.
Renewal, and justification, united, 283, 284; an evidence of true religion, 289.
Repay, to, evil for evil, forbidden, 471.
Repentance, God's gifts and calling without, 440, 441.
Reprobate, the, demented by God's judgment, 418.
Reprobation, its proximate and its primary cause, 350, 417; cavils as to, 363.
Resignation, how to be cherished, 274.
Respect of persons, what, 93, 94.
Resurrection, the, of Christ, why ascribed to the Father, 292; manifested the efficacy of his atonement, 390, 392, 393.

Revelation, the, of God's sons, what, 303; the, of the mystery hidden for ages, 553.
Revellings, condemned, 489.
Revenge, forbidden, 471.
Reward, allotted to good works by the law, 131.
Rich, God is, to all, 395.
Riches, the, of God's goodness, 87; the, of God's wisdom and knowledge, 444, 445.
Right and wrong, somewhat understood by the light of nature, 263.
Righteous, the, alone loved by God, 63; none, by nature, 126; sinners counted, by God, 281.
Righteousness, the, of God revealed in the gospel, 63, 64; the, of God, by faith in Christ, 134; the, of God proved by the law and the Prophets, 137, 138; partial, confuted, 140; the, of faith consists of two parts, 146; the, of faith, imputative, 155; the, of faith, a gift, 158; by works, what it imports, 161, 162; the, of Christ, called obedience, 213; the servants of, freed from sin, 237, 238; and salvation, united, 377; the, of God and of man, opposed to one another, 383; the, of faith and of the law, compared, 385-394; forms a part of God's kingdom, 507.
Romance, the, of initial righteousness, 161; the, of the advocates of ceremonies, 167, 168.
Root, the, of Jesse, 523.
Rulers, custom due to, 483.

S

SACRAMENTS, how they are seals, 164, 165; the, of the Old and New Testament, the same, 167.
Saints, the, their purposes sometimes upset by God, 59; retain the relics of sin, 128; glory in tribulations, 190, 191; relying on God, superior to all trials, 322; ever subject to persecutions, 328; more than conquerors, 329; descent from, an advantage, 431; their necessities, to be relieved, 467.
Saintlings, hypocrites so called, 84, 89.
Salvation, the work of a human and divine person, 44; the gospel the power of God unto, 61, 62; alone by grace, 155; the certainty of, 197; based on election, 316; the promise of, how made to Israel, 345; the true cause of, 356; the assurance of, lies on two foundations, 389; drawing near, 488.

GENERAL INDEX.

Sarah, her barrenness, 177; received the promise of a son, 346.
Satan, a minister of God's wrath, 362; his ministers disturb the Church in two ways, 548; shall be bruised, 551.
Satisfactions, contrary to Paul's doctrine, 160.
School, the, of God, common to all, 402.
Schoolmen, their maxim as to rewards, 131; their fiction of half remission, 160; their faith, a moral conjecture, 173; absurdly define grace, 208; pervert chap. viii. 17, 300, 301; deny final perseverance, 331; advocate hesitating faith, 397.
Scourges, God's, tokens of his wrath, 321.
Scriptures, the, were written for our instruction, 516; administer patience and consolation, 517.
Scruples, the Jews had, about meats and days, 497.
Seal, to, the fruit of charity, 596.
Secrets, the, of men, shall come to judgment, 99.
Seed of promise, Isaac the, 345.
Separation, from God's love, impossible, 326-332.
Servant, the, of another, we are not to judge, 494, 495.
Servants, the, of sin, 235, 236; the, of righteousness, 237, 238.
Service, a reasonable, 452, 453.
Seven thousand reserved by God in the time of Elias, 413.
Severity, the, of God, towards the Jews, 431, 432.
Shame, when felt for sin, 241.
Signs and wonders, accompanying Paul's preaching, 530.
Simple, the, liable to be deceived, 550.
Simplicity, to give with, 462, 463.
Sin, the cause of, not from God, 77; to be under, what, 125; the, original, 200; the body of, 224, 225; to die to, what, 218; the reign of, 231; its two effects, 242; excited by the law, 250; made known by the law, 251, 252; works death by the law, 256; above measure sinful, 258; the law of, 277; put for a sin-offering, 281, 282; a, to act without faith, 512.
Sincerity, the proof of, 55.
Sion, the Redeemer from, 438.
Slanderers differ from whisperers, 81, 82.
Slothful, not to be, in business, 465.
Sober-minded, to be, what, 456, 457.

Sodom, destroyed for sin against the law of nature, 202.
Sold under sin, what, 260, 261.
Sons, the, of God, are guided by his Spirit, 294; know themselves to be his sons, 301; the revelation of, what, 303.
Sonship, a proof of heirship, 295.
Sophists, their pestilential dogmas, 189; defend free-will, 264-288; deny assurance, 324; make love meritorious, 485. See Schoolmen.
Sorbonists, the, their view of the mind, 454.
Sorrow and resignation, combined in Paul, 335.
Spain, Paul intended to go to, 533.
Spirit, the, of holiness, 46; in the, what it means, 111, 112; the love of God diffused by, 191-193; the, to walk after, 276; his work, 276, 277; called the Spirit of God and the Spirit of Christ, 290; why called life, 291; dwells in the justified, 294; the, of bondage and of adoption, 295-299; his direct testimony, 299; aids our infirmities, 311, 312; needed in prayer, 312; intercedes for the saints, 312, 313; the power of, 529; the love of, 538.
Spiritual, the, who they are, 290; why God's children so called, 291.
Spiritual things, the Jews communicated, to the Gentiles, 536.
State, the, of man, known by what rules him, 290.
Stone, the, of stumbling, 379.
Strong, the, who he is, 491, 513; his duty towards the weak, 492, 513, 514; the, the fault of, 494.
Stumblingblock, not to be set before a brother, 503, 510.
Sufferings, present, not to be compared to future glory, 302, 303.
Superiority, the, of the Jews, not from merit, but from mercy, 113, 124.
Superstitious. See Philosophers.
Sword, the, given to magistrates, 481.
Sympathy, required among Christians, 469.

T

Teachers, ought to accommodate themselves to all, 61; ecclesiastical, their duty, 125.
Teaching, the office of, 462; the, of the Prophets, obscure, compared with that of the Gospel, 555.
Tense, the past, implies certainty, 174.
Testimony, the direct, of the Spirit, 299.

Thanksgiving, for faith, proves it is from God, 52 ; is an acknowledgment of grace, 236.
Theology, the, of the letter, 255.
Thousand, seven, reserved by God in the time of Elias, 413.
Time, to serve, what, 466.
Transformed, we ought to be, 453.
Transgressor, every, dishonours God, 106.
Tribulation, produces patience, 190, 191; not able to separate the saints from the love of God, 327; and distress, how they differ, 328.
Tribulations, to glory in, 191.
Tribute, due to rulers, 483.
Trifles, men are led away by, 457.
Truth, the, of God, what it means, 69 ; signifies integrity, 85; means the revealed will of God, 92 ; none, unnecessarily taught by the Spirit in the Scriptures, 354.
Type, a, of Christ, Adam was, 204, 205.

U

Unanimity, necessary in worship, 518.
Unbelief, the, of the Jews, did not nullify God's faithfulness, 115, 116 ; the Jews fell through, 430.
Uncircumcision, the Gentiles, 110.
Unclean, nothing in itself, 504, 505.
Uncleanness, a sacrilege, 451.
Undecided, the, forbidden to eat, 511, 512.
Understanding, "the heart" used for the, 37, 38.
Ungodly, the, have no right to earthly blessings, 169.
Union, not in false doctrines, but in the truth, 549.
Unity, the bond of, Christ, 518.
Unrighteousness, the heathens filled with, 81; the, of man, made to display God's glory, 118-123.
Unsearchable, the ways of God, 445.
Unsociable, the, who they are, 82.

V

Vanity, the creation subjected to, 304.
Vessels, the, of wrath, 368 ; the, of mercy, 369.
Vices, the, of the heathens, evidences of God's wrath, 75, 76.
Villainous, the, described, 82.

W

Wages, the, of sin, 242.

Ways, the, of God, unsearchable, 445.
Weak, the law is, through the flesh, 280; the, in faith, how to be treated, 491-503; ought not to be troubled by fruitless questions, 492, 493 ; lived on herbs, 494; the fault of, 494.
Weakness, the, of faith, twofold, 179.
Weapons, our members so called, 231.
Whisperers, differ from slanderers, 81, 82.
Wickedness, what it means, 81.
Wise, to be, unto sobriety, 456 ; not to be, in our own esteem, 471 ; to be, for good, 550.
Wisdom, the, of God, 444, 445; true, the knowledge of God's will, 454.
Will, to, what, 268 ; the, of God, the highest cause of election, 364 ; the, of God, holy, 454 ; the, of God, paramount in all things, 497.
Wonders, signs and, accompanying Paul's preaching, 530.
Word, the, of God, our boundary, 391 ; the, of faith, what, 391 ; the, of God, generates faith, 397 ; the, alone gives a right knowledge of God, 398 ; effectual only through God's Spirit, 400, 401.
Worker, a, defined, 157, 158.
Works, good, how rewarded, 90, 139 ; the, of the law, what, 130-132 ; the, of the regenerate, excluded in justification, 135 ; alone accepted through Christ, 161, 162 ; and faith, incompatible, 170, 171, 379 ; and calling, opposed to one another, 351; trust in, the chief hinderance in attaining righteousness, 379 ; the, of darkness, 487, 488.
Works of the law not confined to ceremonies, 159.
Worship, unanimity necessary in, 318.
Worthiness, foreseen, the cause of election, an insane notion, 414.
Wrath, the, of God, what it imports, 68, 171 ; the day of, 89, 120; the vessels of, 368 ; to give place to, 473, 474 ; executed by magistrates, 481.
Wrong and right, somewhat understood by the light of nature, 263.

Z

Zeal, a, the Jews had for God, 382 ; inconsiderate, leads astray, 383 ; the specious, of hypocrites, 383.

www.ingramcontent.com/pod-product-compliance
Lightning Source LLC
Chambersburg PA
CBHW052042290426
44111CB00011B/1593